Interdisciplinary Assessment
of Infants

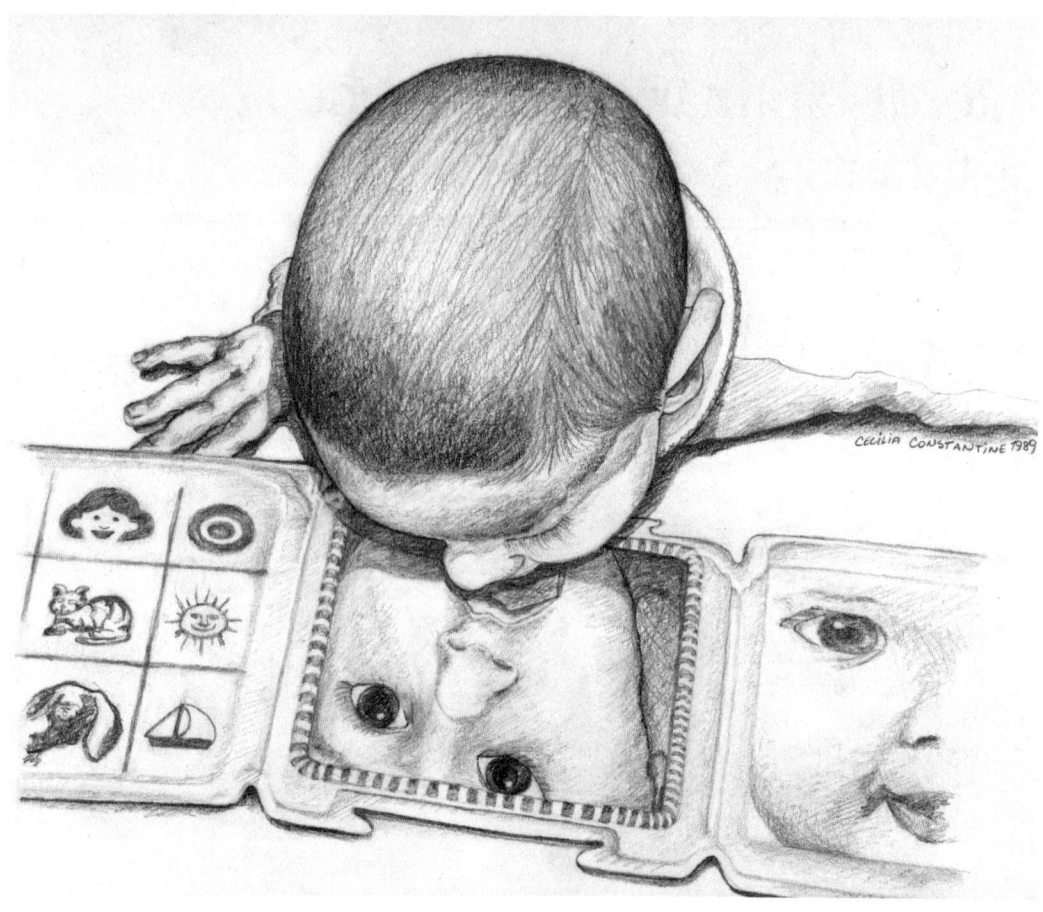

Interdisciplinary Assessment of Infants
A Guide for Early Intervention Professionals

edited by

Elizabeth D. Gibbs, Ph.D.
Clinical Genetics and Child Development Center
Department of Maternal and Child Health
Dartmouth Medical School
Hanover, New Hampshire

and

Douglas M. Teti, Ph.D.
Department of Psychology
University of Maryland–Baltimore County
Catonsville, Maryland

Illustrations by Cecilia A. Constantine

Baltimore • London • Toronto • Sydney

Paul H. Brookes Publishing Co.
P.O. Box 10624
Baltimore, Maryland 21285-0624

Copyright © 1990 by Paul H. Brookes Publishing Co., Inc.
All rights reserved.

Typeset by Brushwood Graphics, Inc., Baltimore, Maryland.
Manufactured in the United States of America by
The Maple Press Company, York, Pennsylvania.

Library of Congress Cataloging-in-Publication Data

Interdisciplinary assessment of infants : a guide for early intervention
  professionals / edited by Elizabeth D. Gibbs and Douglas M. Teti ;
  illustrations by Cecilia Constantine.
      p.   cm.
  Includes bibliographical references.
  ISBN 1-55766-030-1
  1. Infants—Development—Testing.   2. Behavioral assessment of infants.
  I. Gibbs, Elizabeth D., 1955–   II. Teti, Douglas M., 1951–
  [DNLM: 1. Child Development.   2. Child Psychology.   3. Infant.
4. Psychological Tests—in infancy and childhood.   WS 105.5.E8 I61]
RJ134.I57   1990
618.92′0075—dc20
DNLM/DLC
for Library of Congress   89-71223
                                                                   CIP

Contents

	Contributors	vii
	Preface	ix
	Acknowledgments	xi

I FOUNDATIONS

1. Infant Assessment: Historical Antecedents and Contemporary Issues
   Douglas M. Teti and Elizabeth D. Gibbs 3
2. Questions of Measurement in Early Childhood
   Jeffrey K. Smith 15

II ASSESSING NEUROMOTOR INTEGRITY

3. Newborn Assessment and Support for Parenting:
   The Neonatal Behavioral Assessment Scale
   John Worobey and T. Berry Brazelton 33
4. Neuromotor Assessment
   Lynette S. Chandler 45
5. Oral-Motor and Respiratory-Phonatory Assessment
   Rona Alexander 63

III COGNITIVE, LANGUAGE, AND DEVELOPMENTAL ASSESSMENT

6. Assessment of Infant Mental Ability:
   Conventional Tests and Issues of Prediction
   Elizabeth D. Gibbs 77
7. Strategies for Assessing Infant Sensorimotor Interactive Competencies
   Carl J. Dunst, Karen A. Holbert, and Linda L. Wilson 91
8. Play Assessment: Reflecting and Promoting Cognitive Competence
   Lynne A. Bond, Gary L. Creasey, and Craig L. Abrams 113
9. Infant Information Processing: An Alternative Approach
   Philip R. Zelazo and Michael J. Weiss 129
10. Early Language Assessment
    Froma P. Roth 145
11. Curriculum-Based Developmental Assessment for Infants with Special
    Needs: Synchronizing the Pediatric Early Intervention Team
    Stephen J. Bagnato and Dena Hofkosh 161
12. Assessment of the Infant with Multiple Handicaps
    Steven A. Rosenberg and Cordelia C. Robinson 177

IV ASSESSING SOCIAL BEHAVIOR AND CHARACTERISTICS OF THE SOCIAL ENVIRONMENT

13. Assessing Attachment in Infancy: The Strange Situation and Alternate Systems
    Douglas M. Teti and Miyuki Nakagawa 191
14. Assessment of Coping and Temperament: Contributions to Adaptive Functioning
    G. Gordon Williamson and Shirley Zeitlin 215

15	Measures of Parent-Child Interaction *Dale C. Farran, Kathryn S. Clark, and Adele R. Ray*	227
16	Use of Family Assessment in Early Intervention *Barbara M. Ostfeld and Elizabeth D. Gibbs*	249
V	**THE ASSESSMENT PROCESS**	
17	Portrait of the Arena Evaluation: Assessment in the Transdisciplinary Approach *Gilbert M. Foley*	271
18	Family-Staff Collaboration for Tailored Infant Assessment *Linda Kjerland and JoAnne Kovach*	287
19	Communicating Assessment Findings to Parents: Toward More Effective Informing *Ann Murphy*	299
VI	**CONCLUSION**	
20	Issues and Future Directions in Infant and Family Assessment *Elizabeth D. Gibbs and Douglas M. Teti*	311
VII	**APPENDIX**	
	Bibliography of Assessments	321
Index		337

Contributors

Craig L. Abrams, B.A.
Department of Psychology
University of Vermont
Burlington, Vermont 05405

Rona Alexander, Ph.D., CCC-SP
P.O. Box 26734
Wauwatosa, Wisconsin 53226

Stephen J. Bagnato, Ed.D.
Coordinator, Toddler/Preschool Program
Child Development Unit
Department of Pediatrics
Children's Hospital of Pittsburgh
University of Pittsburgh School of Medicine
Pittsburgh, Pennsylvania 15213

Lynne A. Bond, Ph.D.
Department of Psychology
University of Vermont
Burlington, Vermont 05405

T. Berry Brazelton, M.D.
Harvard Medical School
Boston, Massachusetts 02115

Lynette S. Chandler, Ph.D.
School of Occupational and Physical Therapy
University of Puget Sound
Tacoma, Washington 98416

Kathryn S. Clark, M.S.
Department of Child Development and Family
  Relations
University of North Carolina–Greensboro
Greensboro, North Carolina 27412

Gary L. Creasey, Ph.D.
Department of Psychology
Illinois State University
Normal, Illinois 61761

Carl J. Dunst, Ph.D.
Family, Infant and Preschool Program
Western Carolina Center
Morganton, North Carolina 28655

Dale C. Farran, Ph.D.
Department of Child Development and Family
  Relations
University of North Carolina–Greensboro
Greensboro, North Carolina 27412

Gilbert M. Foley, Ed.D.
Visiting Clinical Instructor of Pediatrics
Medical College of Pennsylvania
Philadelphia, Pennsylvania
Director, Psychological Services Center
Albright College
Reading, Pennsylvania 19612-5234

Elizabeth D. Gibbs, Ph.D.
Clinical Genetics and Child Development Center
Department of Maternal and Child Health
Dartmouth Medical School
Hanover, New Hampshire 03756

Dena Hofkosh, M.D.
Coordinator, Infant Development Program
Child Development Unit
Department of Pediatrics
Children's Hospital of Pittsburgh
University of Pittsburgh School of Medicine
Pittsburgh, Pennsylvania 15213

Karen A. Holbert, Ed.M.
Family, Infant and Preschool Program
Western Carolina Center
Morganton, North Carolina 28655

Linda Kjerland, M.A.Ed.
Project Dakota
Dakota, Inc.
680 O'Neill Drive
Eagan, Minnesota 55121

JoAnne Kovach, M.A.
American Guidance Services, Inc.
Circle Pines, Minnesota 55014-1796

Ann Murphy, L.I.C.S.W.
Developmental Evaluation Clinic
The Children's Hospital
Boston, Massachusetts 02115

Miyuki Nakagawa, M.S.
Department of Psychology
University of Maryland–Baltimore County
Baltimore, Maryland 21228

Barbara M. Ostfeld, Ph.D.
Division of Neonatology and Department of
  Pediatrics
St. Peter's Medical Center
New Brunswick, New Jersey 08903-0591

Contributors

Adele R. Ray, M.Ed.
Department of Child Development and Family
  Relations
University of North Carolina–Greensboro
Greensboro, North Carolina 27412

Cordelia C. Robinson, Ph.D., R.N.
Human Development Center
School of Education
Winthrop College
Rock Hill, South Carolina 29733

Steven A. Rosenberg, Ph.D.
Senior Psychologist
Kaiser Permanente Medical Care
5950 Fairview Rd., Fleet 117
Charlotte, North Carolina 28210

Froma P. Roth, Ph.D.
Department of Hearing and Speech Sciences
University of Maryland
College Park, Maryland 20742

Jeffrey K. Smith, Ph.D.
Department of Educational Psychology
Rutgers–The State University
New Brunswick, New Jersey 08903

Douglas M. Teti, Ph.D.
Department of Psychology
University of Maryland–Baltimore County
Baltimore, Maryland 21228

Michael J. Weiss, Ph.D.
Department of Psychology
Montreal Children's Hospital
and
Department of Psychiatry
Mortimer B. Davis Jewish General Hospital
McGill University School of Medicine
Montreal, Quebec
Canada

G. Gordon Williamson, Ph.D., OTR
Director, Pediatric Rehabilitation Department
John F. Kennedy Medical Center
2050 Oak Tree Road
Edison, New Jersey 08820

Linda L. Wilson, B.S.
Family, Infant and Preschool Program
Western Carolina Center
Morganton, North Carolina 28655

John Worobey, Ph.D.
Department of Nutritional Sciences
Rutgers–The State University
New Brunswick, New Jersey 08903

Shirley Zeitlin, Ed.D.
Director, COPING Project
John F. Kennedy Medical Center
Edison, New Jersey 08820

Philip R. Zelazo, Ph.D.
Department of Psychology
Montreal Children's Hospital/McGill University
Montreal, Quebec H3H 1P3
Canada

Preface

We began work on this volume with two interrelated goals. The first was to create a broad, comprehensive compendium on infant assessments, with an emphasis on interdisciplinary approaches and on the issues faced by practitioners in the delivery of services to infants and their families. The second was to foster a conceptualization of infant assessment that integrates theory, basic and applied research, and individual practice. Thus, Betsy Gibbs, a developmental psychologist with substantial expertise in assessment and intervention with at-risk and handicapped infants, and Douglas Teti, a developmental psychologist and director of several basic and applied research projects, teamed up to shape what we hope is a volume that will appeal to practitioners and researchers alike.

Our interests in this topic date back to the late 1970s, when we collaborated on a basic, longitudinal research project examining the social correlates of infant intellectual and linguistic development. As part of this project we became involved in assessing various aspects of infant psychological functioning (cognitive, linguistic, social) as well as assessing parent-infant and sibling-infant interaction. At the same time, Dr. Gibbs began an internship consulting to a therapeutic day care center for abused and neglected children. She began looking for ways of assessing early sensorimotor capabilities of infants and of assessing parent-child interactions, methods that would assist the teachers and therapists in developing the most appropriate interventions. Locating information about infant assessments proved difficult. Dr. Gibbs's clinical training had provided her with methods of assessing school-age children but had overlooked the need to assess infants and young children. Our developmental training had provided us with excellent information on infant capabilities, but the translation from research to practice was uncharted territory. How helpful it would have been to have a book such as this to use as a resource.

Over the years, we have continued to search for meaningful assessment methods to assist in our clinical and research work. Dr. Gibbs's experience working with interdisciplinary and transdisciplinary teams led to an awareness that assessment of infants must be conducted from interdisciplinary perspectives. This point was poignantly demonstrated during her first assessment of a child with cerebral palsy. The physical therapist drew attention to the child's tightly fisted hands and restricted movement pattern, aspects of the child's behavior to which Dr. Gibbs had not been trained to attend. From this and other experiences it became obvious that without the input of multiple disciplines, it is frighteningly easy to make inaccurate and inappropriate diagnoses.

Dr. Teti's applied developmental research on interventions with families of low-birth-weight infants and infants of clinically depressed mothers, and his basic research on the developing relationships among infants, parents, and siblings, have collectively focused on the importance of social contributions to infant behavior and development. Intervention providers have only recently begun to shift their focus from the infant to the broader family system and can turn to the newly emerging research on social development for ideas about how to improve their interventions. Since 1986, Dr. Teti has been a faculty and research advisor to a variety of graduate students in a Ph.D. program in applied developmental psychology, all of whom have strong interests in how developmental theory and research can be used to facilitate the delivery of services to high-risk infants and children. Like Dr. Gibbs, Dr. Teti strongly advocates a reciprocal relationship between research and practice. That is, what roles can basic and applied research play in the individual assessment of normal and handicapped infants? Furthermore, how can the rich data of the practitioner contribute to the development of important and meaningful research questions about infant capabilities? As we argue here and elsewhere in this volume, such a reciprocal relationship is critical for the advancement of the field of the infant assessment.

Hopefully, having an editorial team composed of a clinical infant specialist and an applied developmental researcher has yielded a volume that is useful to individuals from a wide variety of professional orientations. To the newcomer, we hope the book will offer a broad overview of the field. To the seasoned infant specialist, we hope it will provide up-to-date information on assessment methods and the resources necessary to pursue additional training. Finally, we hope this book will provide professors with a useful set of readings for students learning about infant assessment.

Acknowledgments

I would like to acknowledge the many people who have helped along the way, too many to name directly. Let me highlight some of the people whose encouragement has made this book a reality. Lynne Bond and Joe Hasazi and others at the University of Vermont helped me pursue my interest in children with special needs. Teresa Martin and all the staff at the Family Resource Center provided a supportive training ground. Debra Lobato and the staff of the Rhode Island Child Development Center allowed the opportunity to learn about young handicapped children and provided a first taste of transdisciplinary assessment. Colleagues at Rutgers University offered me the opportunity to teach in the Infant Specialist Interdisciplinary Studies program and thereby consolidate my thoughts on infant assessment. The staff and families involved with the Jerry Davis Early Childhood Program have contributed to my knowledge of parent-child assessment, language development in children with Down syndrome, and contributed photographs from which some of the illustrations in this book were drawn.

Elizabeth D. Gibbs, Ph.D.

I owe much to Lynne Bond of the University of Vermont for fostering my initial interest in infancy, prevention, and applied developmental issues, and for her continued support and friendship. Jon Rolf, then of the University of Vermont, offered encouragement during my tenure with the Vermont Child Development Project. My skills with both basic and applied research were developed further with the help of Virginia Rauh and Barry Nurcombe, who made it possible for me to spend 2 years with the Vermont Infant Studies Project, a large intervention study of low-birth-weight infants. Also acknowledged are Donna Gelfand and Michael Lamb, whose expertise, guidance, and friendship have been major influences on my career. I also credit my graduate students, whose intelligence and enthusiasm help make teaching and research even more exciting. Finally, I would like to thank Cecilia and Adrian, whose undying patience helped make this book possible.

Douglas M. Teti, Ph.D.

*In loving memory of
Robert H. Gibbs, Jr.
and
JoAnn Teti*

Interdisciplinary Assessment
of Infants

I
FOUNDATIONS

1

Infant Assessment
Historical Antecedents and Contemporary Issues

Douglas M. Teti and Elizabeth D. Gibbs

The past 25 years have witnessed a veritable explosion of interest in infancy, as evidenced by a confluence of developments in sociopolitical, scientific, medical, and technological arenas. Never before have infants been scrutinized so closely and systematically by researchers, practitioners, and parents. The period of infancy has proven to be a unique period of life for studying the nature-nurture controversy, describing core developmental processes, and examining how developmental trajectories are affected by variations in early experience.

This intense interest has led to dramatic advances in the ability to diagnose and treat handicaps in their earliest stages of development. Further, it has resulted in a greater appreciation of the kinds of environments that foster or impede development and the degree to which the development of specific competencies are robust to variations in environmental experience. Language development in children without organic handicaps, for example, appears to be relatively robust to variations in maternal linguistic input within the "normal" range (Bates, Bretherton, Beeghly-Smith, & McNew, 1982). By contrast, certain facets of social development (e.g., the affective quality of children's behavior with mothers, siblings, and nonfamilial persons) seem to be more sensitive to differences in maternal behavior (Main & Weston, 1981; Pastor, 1981; see Teti & Nakagawa, this volume). Finally, the exclusive emphasis on the infant-mother dyad has given way to an appreciation that infant development occurs within a family system. This has furthered efforts to examine how mothers, fathers, and siblings interact with and influence infant development (Lamb, 1981; Teti, Gibbs, & Bond, 1989; Zukow, 1989). Moreover, it has focused attention on the impact of specific handicapping conditions and developmental anomalies on families and how families struggle to cope (Gallagher & Vietze, 1986; Ostfeld & Gibbs, this volume).

The growing recognition that handicapped children are best served when interventive services are provided early in life (Shonkoff & Hauser-Cram, 1987) has spurred the development of a variety of infant assessment procedures that can be used to diagnose and develop treatment strategies. The present volume attempts to provide the reader with "state-of-the-art" information about diagnostic and prescriptive infant assessment procedures. Given the extensive interplay in infancy between different developmental systems and the salience of social-environmental influences on infant development, it is essential that infant assessment be both multidimensional and interdisciplinary. Thus, this volume draws from traditionally separate and distinct disciplines such as psychology, physical and occupational therapy, neurology, speech and language pathology, social work, psychiatry, and education.

In the present chapter, we discuss the roots of infant assessment and detail the more recent developments underlying the infant assessment movement. We then discuss some of the special issues encountered in the study of infants and the basic characteristics of infant assessments. Finally, we close with an overview of the organization of the present volume and a brief description of each chapter.

HISTORICAL ANTECEDENTS OF INFANT ASSESSMENT

The Child Study Movement

Although the first published infant assessments, designed to measure intelligence, did not appear until the 1920s (Brooks & Weinraub, 1976), the infant assessment movement was perhaps an inevitable outgrowth of the Child Study Movement that commenced around the late 1800s. Of course, developmental psychology as a discipline was emerging at this same time, spurred by the evolutionist Charles Darwin (1968), whose writings on natural selection, the survival value of specific behaviors as well as physical traits, and the development of such behaviors and traits in individuals helped focus attention on the need to understand childhood in order to understand the human condition. Indeed, Darwin's publication of a "baby biography" in 1877, detailing his son's early development, paved the way for a variety of systematically recorded biographical accounts of infant development that were published in the late 19th and early 20th centuries (Zigler & Finn-Stevenson, 1987). Although these accounts suffered from subjectivity and emotional overinvestment (Frank, 1943), they nevertheless reflected a general new-found appreciation of infancy and early childhood as important developmental periods of life.

The Child Study Movement gained much momentum through the efforts of G. Stanley Hall, a profoundly influential psychologist in the early 20th century who argued that studying child development provided insights into the evolutionary development of the human species (ontogeny recapitulates phylogeny; Hall, 1904). Although these notions are not seriously considered today, Hall nevertheless is credited with beginning the *normative* study of child development. The normative approach, which forms the basis for norm-referenced assessment (discussed later in this chapter) involves assessing a particular behavior or attribute among members of particular age groups, computing group means, and then using these group means to establish normative developmental curves against which individual development can be compared. Hall distributed questionnaires to thousands of schoolchildren asking for information about a wide variety of topics (e.g., play, friends, interests). As Sears (1975) noted, Hall's lack of a theoretical framework in the development of these questionnaires and his unsystematic methods rendered much of his data unusable. However, through Hall's efforts the normative study of child development had begun and continues to this day.

At about the same time that Hall was spearheading the Child Study Movement in the United States, Alfred Binet, an experimental psychologist, and his colleague Theodore Simon were working in Paris to develop a test to identify children in the Paris school system who were mentally retarded and in need of specialized education. Unlike his predecessors (e.g., Galton, Cattell, and Jastrow), who viewed intelligence as a collection of sensory and motor abilities, Binet defined intelligence in terms of higher order mental functions such as memory, comprehension, attention, language, imagination, suggestibility, and judgment (Brooks & Weinraub, 1976; Cairns, 1983). Today it is clear that Binet's focus on complex rather than elemental mental processes as the components of intelligence had a profound impact on conceptualizations of intelligence and the intelligence testing movement. In 1905, Binet and Simon published a 30-item intelligence scale that was to be the precursor to standardized tests as we know them today. All items were pass/fail and were administered in the order of least to most difficult. In addition, the Binet-Simon test established the notion of global test scores, standardization procedures, and mental age levels (Brooks & Weinraub, 1976).

Although the Binet scale underwent several revisions by Binet and others, it was Terman's U.S. revision at Stanford University that culminated in the widely popular Stanford-Binet Intelligence Scale. Terman was the first to conduct a large-scale standardization of the scale on over 1,000 schoolchildren and the first to employ the *intelligence quotient* (IQ) as an index of test performance (Cairns, 1983). The Stanford-Binet instrument has become a staple of the intelligence testing movement, and virtually all standardized intelligence tests subsequently constructed for infants and young children are, on some level, patterned after Binet's and Terman's work.

As Brooks and Weinraub (1976) noted, initial interest in infant testing was evident in the 1920s with the advent of Trable's "Mentimeter"; Kuhlmann's second revision of the Binet scale, which included items for infants; and Linfert and Hierholzer's infant intelligence scale. Although none of these assessments gained any noteworthy attention, their appearance reflected a developing concern for infant mental abilities, and by the 1920s several infant tests emerged that achieved widespread use. These include the Gesell Developmental Schedules, developed by Arnold Gesell at the Yale Clinic of Child Development; Buhler's Baby Tests, developed by Charlotte Buhler in Vienna; the infant tests of Mary Shirley in Minnesota; and the California First Year Mental Scale, developed by Nancy Bayley, who later revised it into the Bayley Scales of Infant Development (Bayley, 1969).

Psychodynamic and Piagetian Contributions

It should also be noted that, although Jean Piaget and Sigmund Freud are not typically associated with the development of formal assessments of infants and young children, both created sweeping movements that ultimately culminated in a variety of tests of infant functioning. Freud's psychodynamic theorizing (Freud, 1940) and the revisions of his theory by such notables as Erik Erikson (1963) and John Bowlby (1951, 1969/1982) led to new and exciting ways of conceptualizing and assessing infants' early attachment to their parents. Ainsworth and her colleagues (Ainsworth, Blehar, Waters, & Wall, 1978; Ainsworth & Wittig, 1969) developed the Strange Situation Procedure to assess the quality of an infant's attachment to the parent. This procedure, perhaps the most well-known assessment of infant-parent relations, is predicated on the notion that infant attachment to an attachment figure could be examined in terms of the infant's ability to use the attachment figure as a secure base to explore the environment (see Teti & Nakagawa, this volume). Piaget's (1926a, 1926b, 1952) structuralist notions about cognitive development, his view of the child as an active constructor of her or his development, and his emphasis on how children think rather than what they know led to a critical appraisal of what intelligence tests did and did not reveal about children's cognitive functioning. Piaget's views gained much popularity among American developmental psychologists, and much scrutiny was given to Piagetian methods for testing children's knowledge of such concepts as conservation, classification, ordinal relations, and number. Further, Piaget's careful descriptions of infant intelligence led to new insights into infant functioning and led Ina Uzgiris and J. McVicker Hunt (1975) to develop the Ordinal Scales of Psychological Development, an assessment of infant sensorimotor intelligence that was conceptually distinct from traditional measures of infant intelligence (see Dunst, Holbert, & Wilson, this volume).

INFANCY: THE MODERN ERA

The study of infants has become almost a discipline in its own right during the last three decades. There are a variety of reasons for this. To begin, technological breakthroughs and innovative research techniques in the 1960s and 1970s led to the realization that infants were "capable" creatures, and more competent with regard to perceptual and learning abilities and more responsive to environmental stimulation than was previously believed (Lamb & Bornstein, 1987; Rosenblith & Sims-Knight, 1985). Further, the sensitivity infants manifested to environmental events prompted closer looks at the mother-infant dyad and the relationship between the quality of mother-infant interaction and early social and cognitive development (e.g., Ainsworth et al., 1978; Clarke-Stewart, 1973). The intense scrutiny given to infants also fostered a growing awareness of individual differences in infant behavioral capacities almost from birth, and this led to seminal efforts to characterize individual differences in infant "temperament," how these differences affected the quality of infants' relationships with their caregivers, and how predictive temperamental differences were of later personality (e.g., Thomas, Chess, & Birch, 1968). In short, the new-found appreciation of infant capabilities led researchers to examine more closely the developmental significance of infantile experience and the ways infants had an impact on their environment. Indeed, developmental psychologists have come to view development as a *transactional* process, conceptualizing the infant and environment to be in dynamic interplay as they continuously influence each other over time (Sameroff, 1975). In addition, infancy research has contributed to the growing belief among social scientists and legislators in the concept of *primary prevention,* the notion that a great deal of physical and mental illness can be prevented or minimized in a society that stresses the quality of the early environment (Albee & Joffe, 1977).

Also contributing to the modern infancy era were several widespread sociopolitical movements. The 1960s witnessed the beginnings of the Civil Rights Movement, one impact of which was to focus attention on the effects of discriminatory practices on families and children. Concern for the environmentally disadvantaged was exemplified by the Head Start educational enrichment programs targeting preschool children. As Lamb and Bornstein (1987) noted, the inconsistent effects of these programs prompted efforts to intervene at earlier ages, loosing an avalanche of literature designed to help parents provide intellectually stimulating environments for their infants. This resulted in a mushrooming market for complex infant toys such as busy boxes, mobiles, and other paraphernalia designed to foster infants' mastery of their environment.

The Civil Rights Movement also led to greater awareness of the plight of handicapped children, who, along with racial minorities, were frequent targets of discrimination. In response to parents' difficulties in finding an appropriate education for their handicapped children, a series of federal laws have been passed during the last three decades that have had a direct impact on the welfare of handicapped children. These laws were initially stimulated in the late 1950s by the Joint Commission on Mental Illness and Health and in the early 1960s by John F. Kennedy's call to Congress to enact laws to combat mental retardation and mental illness. Of the variety of laws passed since that time (see Bricker, 1986), several deserve special mention. In 1967, PL 90-248 established the Early and Periodic Screening, Diagnostic, and Treatment Program, designed to provide support for early detection and treatment of children with developmental problems. PL 90-538, the Handicapped Children's Early Education Assistance Act, was passed in 1968, providing federal funds to serve handicapped children through the establishment of model demonstration programs.

Perhaps the most significant piece of legislation to affect handicapped children to date, however, is PL 94-142, the Education for All Handicapped Children Act, enacted in 1975. This law made a free and appropriate public education the right of every handicapped child. In addition, the law mandates the right of all handicapped children to have created for them an individualized education program (IEP), to be educated in the least restrictive environment, and to due process. In addition, the law mandates the right of parents to participate in the planning and implementation of special education programs for their children. PL 94-142 did not mandate these rights for children below school age, however, and in response PL 99-457, an amendment to PL 94-142, was enacted in 1986 to extend all the rights and privileges of PL 94-142 to 3–5-year-old handicapped children and, in addition, establish a grant program to eligible states to plan for the creation of early intervention services to handicapped children from birth to 2 years.

A second sociopolitical development that heightened societal concern for infants was the Women's Liberation Movement, which prompted a reevaluation of traditional family roles and created new educational and vocational opportunities for women. This movement, along with a significant decrease in buying power for a growing number of families, rendered more acceptable the notion that women could be mothers and have a career, and be successful at both. As more and more women entered the workforce, the need grew to find acceptable substitute care for infants and young children, and the 1970s and 1980s witnessed a dramatic increase in day care centers and family day care. These developments, in turn, raised questions about the "impact" of maternal employment and children's day care experience on child development. Indeed, the impact of out-of-home care on infant socioemotional development has very recently become one of the hottest issues in developmental psychology, with some arguing that full-time infant day care disrupts the development of secure infant-mother attachments (Belsky, 1986) and others contending that such assertions are baseless without a consideration of the quality of day care and its relationship to infant development (Phillips, McCartney, Scarr, & Howes, 1987). Although this controversy is far from being resolved, the vast attention it has received from psychologists, pediatricians, politicians, and the media is indicative of just how immensely important the period of infancy has become in the 1980s.

SPECIAL CONSIDERATIONS IN INFANT ASSESSMENT

Infancy can be one of the most fascinating and frustrating periods to study. Perhaps there is no other phase of the life cycle in which reliable assessment can be compromised by virtue of limited behavioral and verbal repertoire, volatile states of arousal, and very rapid development. Nevertheless, as the present volume attests, infant assessment has yielded useful information about the early diagnosis of developmental anomalies and the responsivity of these conditions to specific early experiences. In addition, improvements in infant assessment have allowed researchers to identify more precisely the types of environments that foster or prevent developmental deviation, although much remains to be discovered.

The Issue of Developmental Continuity

One of the assumptions behind infant assessment is that there is potential continuity between functioning in infancy and in later childhood. This assumption has received support in some instances but not in others. In cases in which organic dysfunction is detected in infancy (e.g., Down syndrome), continuity of impairment from infancy onward is more reliable, although in many cases the severity of handicap can be affected by environmental quality (Shonkoff & Hauser-Cram, 1987; White, 1985–86). In cases without organic impairment, continuity of functioning may depend in part on the nature of the construct or attribute under investigation and the degree to which environmental circumstances endure over time. For example, infants judged to be insecurely attached to their mothers seem to have a higher likelihood of manifesting socioemotional difficulties if the unfavorable environmental circumstances that fostered early insecurity persist over time (Lamb, Thompson, Gardner, & Charnov, 1985). The predictability of infant intelligence in non–organically impaired infants appears to depend in part on the method by which it is assessed. Gibbs (this volume) notes that infant intelligence as assessed by traditional tests predicts poorly to later intelligence, although predictability improves under conditions of substantial developmental delay. By contrast, the predictive validity of the new wave of infant intelligence tests, based on information processing techniques, is markedly higher than that of the more traditional procedures (see Zelazo & Weiss, this volume).

The ability to predict from infancy to later childhood is, of course, compromised by the qualitative differences that exist between infant functioning, which is largely sensorimotor, and the more verbal and representational functioning of later childhood. Indeed, the poor predictability of traditional measures of infant intelligence relative to information processing tests is likely related to the fact that, unlike measures of intelligence in later childhood, traditional measures of infant intelligence are strongly influenced by fine motor coordination and sociability (Bornstein & Sigman, 1986; Stevenson & Lamb, 1979). Further, the dynamic, transactional nature of development suggests that environmental events over which the infant has little control may alter previously established developmental trajectories, which in turn would mitigate against the ability to predict from a single "snapshot" of functioning taken in infancy. It is thus very noteworthy that, despite these obstacles, prediction from infancy to later childhood has been achieved in certain circumstances (Carew, 1980; Clarke-Stewart, 1973; Cohen & Beckwith, 1979; LaFreniere & Sroufe, 1985; Pastor, 1981). At the same time, however, the fact that prediction of later functioning from infancy is imperfect indicates that early development is also plastic and malleable and thus receptive to early intervention.

The Need for Interdisciplinary Assessment

More characteristic of infancy than any other period of life is the remarkably close interdependence of developmental systems. For example, sensorimotor intelligence as indexed by the Bayley Scales of Infant Development is closely intertwined with motor development. Thus, obtaining accurate assessment of sensorimotor intelligence would be particularly problematic if the infant had a neuromotor disability such as cerebral palsy. A multidimensional, interdisciplinary assessment of this infant is necessary to ascertain how the motor disability might be affecting other developmental systems such as cognition, language, attachment, and sociability. Further, as Teti and Nakagawa (this volume) point out, infants' development and expression of attachment to parents depends upon the achievement of a rudimentary sense of person permanence, the ability to locomote, and the ability to be aware of the presence and absence of the attachment figure. Thus, the assessment of infants' quality of attachment to parents becomes particulary problematic when cognitive, motor, visual, and/or auditory systems are compromised in some way. A complete understanding of infant functioning is, quite simply, impossible without attending to the multidimensional aspects of infant development and their interdependent influences.

It is now widely acknowledged that an interdisciplinary approach to infant assessment must be used if a comprehensive understanding of infant and family needs is to be obtained (Foley, this volume). Furthermore, Haynes and her colleagues (1976) and others in the field argue that a *transdisciplinary* approach is especially appropriate for achieving this goal.

Infant Development and Family Involvement

Also critical to infant assessment is an understanding of how infant development affects and is affected by family functioning. This is especially salient during infancy, given that an individual's ecology is more limited to his or her immediate families during infancy than at any other time during the life span. A growing body of information attests to the relationship between family functioning and infant development (e.g., Belsky & Isabella, 1988; Teti & Ablard, 1989). Further, the ability of the family to cope with a developmental disorder may have important prognostic implications for the infant, as Ostfeld and Gibbs (this volume) note.

The interdependence of infant development and family functioning also makes clear the need for parents of at-risk infants to be involved in the assessment process. PL 94-142 mandates the right of parents of school-aged children to be so involved. With the passage of PL 99-457 and the creation of the Individualized Family Service Plan (IFSP), early intervention programs are broadening their scope and considering the needs of both family and child. It is now commonplace for interdisciplinary teams to involve parents of infants as important and essential members of the assessment team. Despite the fact that most parents lack the expertise of the various members of the assessment team, it is they who know their infant's and family's needs best and who are in the best position to intervene with their infants and monitor their progress.

CHARACTERISTICS AND FUNCTIONS OF INFANT ASSESSMENTS

Most infant assessments can be categorized into one of two major types: *norm referenced* and *criterion referenced*. Norm-referenced assessments refer to those that have undergone standardization on a carefully chosen reference group, one that, it is hoped, is large and demographically representative of the population to be tested, from which age norms are derived. Examples of norm-referenced assessments are the Bayley Scales of Infant Development (Bayley, 1969), the Battelle Developmental Inventory (Newborg, Stock, Wnek, Guidubaldi, & Svinick, 1984), and the Stanford-Binet Intelligence Scale (Terman & Merrill, 1973). Children's raw scores on these examinations are compared to the distribution of raw scores obtained for their same-age standardization group, and the intelligence or developmental quotients are derived based on that part of the standardization distribution on which the scores fall. Thus, norm-referenced developmental assessments allow a child to be compared to a same-age reference group on a particular construct, and the score reflects whether the child is average, below average, or above average with respect to that group.

By contrast, criterion-referenced assessments provide information about how a child performs on a particular population or series of items, without reference or comparison to some normative group. An example of a criterion-referenced assessment is the Uzgiris-Hunt Ordinal Scales of Psychological Development (Uzgiris & Hunt, 1975), which assess infant performance on a variety of Piagetian-based tasks (e.g., visual pursuit and the permanence of objects, means-ends behavior, vocal and gestural imitation). The child's performance presumably reflects her or his developmental substage with respect to sensorimotor intelligence, regardless of age or how the child compares to other children of similar age.

Typically, infant assessment is done to fulfill one of three initial goals: screening, diagnosis, or prescription. Screening assessments can be used to determine whether or not an infant is "at risk" for significant developmental deviation or lag relative to the general population. As Brooks-Gunn and Lewis (1983) noted, a successful screening procedure should be brief and easy to administer and score by professionals in pediatricians' offices, community health services, and outpatient and well-baby clinics, to ensure that it will indeed be used. In addition, a good screening test should minimize false negatives. Tests that are too cumbersome and/or require extensive training are unlikely to be used by already overburdened medical staff. We refer the interested reader to Gabel (1980) for a more in-depth treatment of infant screening procedures.

Diagnostic tests are typically used after it is established that an infant is "at risk" and may fulfill three purposes: 1) to confirm a developmental problem, 2) to describe an infant's level of functioning in one or more developmental domains, and 3) to identify the type of problem (e.g., mental retardation, autism, cerebral palsy). Diagnostic assessments typically are norm referenced and can be repeatedly administered to monitor the infant's progress. Some of the most frequently used diagnostic tests are norm-referenced infant intelligence tests, which can take a trained examiner anywhere from 30 minutes to 1 hour to complete (see Gibbs, this volume). Prescriptive assessments, by contrast, are done for the purpose of obtaining information that will facilitate the development of appropriate intervention strategies. These assessments are often criterion referenced rather than norm referenced, and from them a developmental progression of skills and an intervention program can be specified for a particular child (see Bagnato & Hofkosh, this volume).

It should be mentioned that diagnostic and prescriptive procedures are not mutually exclusive, and assessment of a given infant frequently involves a collection of procedures to address both diagnostic and prescriptive concerns.

OUTLINE OF BOOK

The present volume is divided into six sections. Section I, *Foundations,* presents a broad overview of the major issues confronting researchers and practitioners in their attempts to understand the processes and implications of infant assessment. In this first chapter, we have attempted to present the historical, conceptual, and definitional issues pertaining to infant assessment. In Chapter 2, Smith discusses methodological issues encountered in the creation and administration of infant assessments, with special consideration given to issues of validity, reliability, and the establishment of norms. An understanding of these somewhat technical issues is essential if early intervention specialists are to interpret correctly the results of any given assessment.

Section II, *Assessing Neuromotor Integrity,* introduces the reader to the assessment of the neurologically and motorically based aspects of infant development. Worobey and Brazelton (Chapter 3) begin with a presentation of the Brazelton Neonatal Behavioral Assessment Scale (NBAS) as an index of newborns' neuromotor functioning and interactive capacity. The use of the NBAS with atypical infants as an intervention vehicle with parents is also discussed. In Chapter 4, Chandler discusses methods of assessing infants' neuromotor status and screening for motor dysfunction. Alexander (Chapter 5) follows with a presentation of assessments of oral-motor and respiratory-phonatory functioning.

Section III, *Cognitive, Language, and Developmental Assessment,* reviews a variety of assessments, including conventional tests of infant mental ability and general developmental progress as well as the recently emerging curriculum-based and information processing methods of assessing infant development. In Chapter 6, Gibbs describes conventional norm-referenced tests of infant mental development and their use as diagnostic tools. Also addressed is the ability of these tests to predict later intelligence and how practitioners can use these assessments when predictive validity is poor. Dunst and his colleagues (Chapter 7) then present the assessment of sensorimotor competencies using criterion-referenced methods (i.e., the Uzgiris-Hunt Scales and a neo-Piagetian assessment called the Observation of Behavior in Socially and Ecologically Relevant and Valid Environments [OBSERVE]). Bond and her colleagues (Chapter 8) follow with a review of a variety of play assessments that offer useful alternative indices of infant cognitive level, including unobtrusive free play and structured procedures. In Chapter 9, Zelazo and Weiss discuss the new generation of information processing infant intelligence tests that focus on infant habituation and novelty preference, and explore how these new measures can be used in conjunction with traditional tests of infant mental ability. Roth (Chapter 10) reviews procedures for examining children's communication skills, with attention to both the structural and pragmatic aspects of language development. Bagnato and Hofkosh (Chapter 11) then follow with a discussion of curriculum-based assessments and their use in developing early intervention strategies within the interdisciplinary context. Chapter 12, by Robinson and Rosenberg, addresses issues in the assessment of children with multiple handicaps, highlighting their PARTICIPATE model of assessment that can be used to identify areas of skill deficit and to develop intervention strategies.

Section IV, *Assessing Social Behavior and Characteristics of the Social Environment,* focuses on the assessment of infant social behavior and the social environment. In Chapter

13, Teti and Nakagawa offer a theoretical discussion of the development of infant-parent attachment and the systems that have been used to assess it, with particular attention to the Ainsworth Strange Situation procedure. The applicability of the Strange Situation procedure and other systems to assess attachment in handicapped infants and their efficacy as clinical evaluation tools are discussed. In Chapter 14, Williamson and Zeitlin present a conceptualization of infant temperament and coping and their influence on the infant's adaptive functioning. In addition, they review temperament measures and their own newly developed measure of infant coping, the Early Coping Inventory. Farran and her colleagues (Chapter 15) review methods of assessing parent-child interaction and discuss the possible uses and misuses of these types of assessments. In Chapter 16, Ostfeld and Gibbs discuss the importance of viewing infant development within the context of the family system and review some of the means of conducting family assessment.

Section V, _The Assessment Process_, focuses more explicitly on the process rather than the content of assessment. In Chapter 17, Foley presents a historical overview of the multi-, inter-, and transdisciplinary team approaches to infant assessment and provides a detailed discussion of how the transdisciplinary approach might be implemented. Kjerland and Kovach (Chapter 18) follow with a discussion of the importance of involving parents in the assessment and intervention process and describe how the staff of the PROJECT DAKOTA were able to increase their responsiveness to parents and tailor their assessment efforts to the needs of the family. Finally, Murphy (Chapter 19) closes this section by addressing the issue of how professionals can effectively communicate assessment information to parents. This skill is paramount in that it affects parents' inclinations to use the assessor's recommendations and influences the quality of relationship that parents establish with professional staff.

In Section VI, _Conclusion_, Gibbs and Teti (Chapter 20) evaluate and integrate information presented in the volume and attempt to provide a global picture of the current status of infant assessment. In addition, they offer recommendations for the future directions of this emerging and exciting field.

Finally, the Appendix contains listings of the assessments discussed in this volume, along with information regarding whom to contact about training and administration of specific measures.

REFERENCES

Ainsworth, M.D.S., Blehar, M., Waters, E., & Wall, S. (1978). *Patterns of attachment: A psychological study of the strange situation.* Hillsdale, NJ: Erlbaum.

Ainsworth, M.D., & Wittig, B.A. (1969). Attachment and exploratory behavior of one year olds in a strange situation. In B.M. Foss (Ed.), *Determinants of infant behavior* (Vol. 4). London: Methuen.

Albee, G.W., & Joffe, J.M. (Eds.). (1977). *Primary prevention of psychopathology. Vol I: The issues.* Hanover, NH: University Press of New England.

Bates, E., Bretherton, I., Beeghly-Smith, M., & McNew, S. (1982). Social bases of language development: A reassessment. In H.W. Reese & L.P. Lipsitt (Eds.), *Advances in child development and behavior* (Vol. 16, pp. 7–75). New York: Academic Press.

Bayley, N. (1969). *Bayley scales of infant development.* New York: Psychological Corporation.

Belsky, Jr., & Isabella, R. (1988). Maternal, infant, and social-contextual determinants of attachment security. In J. Belsky & T. Nezworski (Eds.), *Clinical implications of attachment.* Hillsdale, NJ: Erlbaum.

Bornstein, M.H., & Sigman, M.D. (1986). Continuity in mental development from infancy. *Child Development, 57,* 251–274.

Bowlby, J. (1951). *Maternal care and mental health.* Geneva: World Health Organization.

Bowlby, J. (1969/1982). *Attachment and loss (Vol 1). Attachment.* New York: Basic Books.

Belsky, J. (1986). Infant day care: A cause for concern? *Zero to Three, 6*(5), 1–7.

Bricker, D.D. (1986). *Early education of at-risk and handicapped infants, toddlers, and preschool children*. Glenview, IL: Scott, Foresman, & Co.

Brooks, J., & Weinraub, M. (1976). A history of infant intelligence testing. In M. Lewis (Ed.), *The origins of intelligence* (pp. 19–57). Plenum Press.

Brooks-Gunn, J., & Lewis, M. (1983). Screening and diagnosing handicapped infants. *Topics in Early Childhood Special Education, 3*, 14–28.

Cairns, R. (1983). The emergence of developmental psychology. In W. Kessen (Ed.), *History, theory, and methods* (4th ed., Vol. 4). In P.H. Mussen (Gen. Ed.), *Handbook of child psychology* (pp. 41–102). New York: Wiley.

Carew, J.V. (1980). Experience and the development of intelligence in young children in home and in day care. *Monographs of the Society for Research in Child Development, 45* (6–7, Serial No. 187).

Clarke-Stewart, K.A. (1973). Interactions between mothers and their young children: Characteristics and consequences. *Monographs of the Society for Research in Child Development, 38* (6–7, Serial No. 153).

Cohen, S.E., & Beckwith, L. (1979). Preterm-infant interaction with the caregiver in the first year of life and competence at age two. *Child Development, 50*, 769–776.

Darwin, C. (1968). *On the origin of species*. New York: Penguin. (Original work published 1859.)

Erikson, E. (1963). *Childhood and society* (2nd ed.). New York: Norton.

Frank, L.K. (1943). Research in child psychology: History and prospect. In R. Barker, J. Kounin, & H. Wright (Eds.), *Child behavior and development* (pp. 1–15). New York: McGraw-Hill.

Freud, S. (1940). *An outline of psychoanalysis*. New York: Norton.

Gabel, S. (1980). Screening procedures. In S. Gabel & M.T. Erickson (Eds.), *Child development and developmental disabilities*. Boston: Little, Brown & Co.

Gallagher, J.J., & Vietze, P.M. (Eds.). (1986). *Families of handicapped persons: Research, programs, and policy issues*. Baltimore: Paul H. Brookes Publishing Co.

Hall, G.S. (1904). *Adolescence* (Vols. 1–2). New York: Appleton-Century-Crofts.

Haynes, U. (1976). *Staff development handbook: A resource for the transdisciplinary process*. New York: United Cerebral Palsy Association, Inc.

LaFreniere, P.J., & Sroufe, L.A. (1985). Profiles of peer competence in the preschool; Interrelations between measures, influence of social ecology, and relation to attachment history. *Developmental Psychology, 21*, 56–69.

Lamb, M.E. (Ed.). (1981). *The role of the father in child development* (2nd ed.). New York: Wiley.

Lamb, M.E., & Bornstein, M.H. (1987). *Development in infancy* (2nd ed.). New York: Random House.

Lamb, M.E., Thompson, R.A., Gardner, W., & Charnov, E.L. (1985). *Infant-mother attachment: The origins and developmental significance of individual differences in Strange Situation behavior*. Hillsdale, NJ: Lawrence Erlbaum Associates.

Main, M., & Weston, D.R. (1981). The quality of the toddler's relationship to mother and to father: Related to conflict behavior and the readiness to establish new relationships. *Child Development, 52*, 932–940.

Newborg, J., Stock, J.E., Wnek, L., Guidubaldi, J., & Svinick, J. (1984). *Battelle Developmental Inventory*. Allen, TX: DLM Teaching Resources.

Pastor, D.L. (1981). The quality of mother-infant attachment and its relationship to toddlers' initial sociability with peers. *Developmental Psychology, 17*, 326–335.

Phillips, D., McCartney, K., Scarr, S., & Howes, C. (1987). Selective review of infant day care research: A cause for concern! *Zero to Three, 7*(2), 18–21.

Piaget, J. (1926a). *Judgment and reasoning in the child* (trans. M. Warden). New York: Harcourt, Brace, & World, Inc.

Piaget, J. (1926b). *The language and thought of the child* (trans. M. Gabain). London: Routledge & Kegan Paul Ltd.

Piaget, J. (1952). *The origins of intelligence in children* (trans. M. Cook). New York: International Universities Press.

Rosenblith, J.F., & Sims-Knight, J.E. (1985). *In the beginning: Development in the first two years*. Monterey, CA: Brooks/Cole.

Sameroff, A.J. (1975). Early influences on development: Fact or fancy? *Merrill-Palmer Quarterly, 21*, 267–294.

Sears, R.R. (1975). *Your ancients revisited: A history of child development*. Chicago: University of Chicago Press.

Shonkoff, J.P., & Hauser-Cram, P. (1987). Early intervention for disabled infants and their families: A quantitative analyses. *Pediatrics, 80*, 650–658.

Stevenson, M.B., & Lamb, M.E. (1979). Effects of infant sociability and the caretaking environment on infant cognitive performance. *Child Development, 50*, 340–369.

Terman, L.M., & Merrill, M.A. (1973). *Stanford-Binet Intelligence Scale: Manual for the Third Revision, Form L-M*. Boston: Houghton Mifflin.

Teti, D.M., Gibbs, E.D., & Bond, L.A. (1989). Sibling interaction, birth spacing, and intellectual/linguistic development. In P.G. Zukow (Ed.), *Sibling interaction across cultures: Theoretical and methodological issues* (pp. 117–139). New York: Springer-Verlag.

Thomas, A., Chess, S., & Birch, H.G. (1968). *Temperament and behavior disorders in children*. New York: New York University Press.

Uzgiris, I.C., & Hunt, J.McV. (1975). *Assessment in infancy: Ordinal Scales of Psychological Development*. Urbana: University of Illinois Press.

White, K.R. (1985–86). Efficacy of early intervention. *Journal of Special Education, 19,* 401–416.

Zigler, E.F., & Finn-Stevenson, M. (1987). *Children: Development and social issues*. Lexington, MA: D.C. Heath.

Zukow, P.G. (Ed.) (1989). *Sibling interaction across cultures: Theoretical and methodological issues*. New York: Springer-Verlag.

2 Questions of Measurement in Early Childhood

Jeffrey K. Smith

The purpose of this chapter is to answer questions and explore issues of measurement in early childhood. Some of the issues concern measurement generally and would be just as applicable for high school students or adults; others are unique to the peculiarities of trying to measure infants and small children. The chapter is organized around a series of questions and is intended to provide a practical guide to early childhood professionals who need to use measurement in their work. The purpose of the chapter is to inform; the goal of the chapter is to demystify. The essential questions of measurement should not be solely the domain of measurement specialists. There is nothing about the basics of measurement that is so complicated that it cannot be understood by a practitioner.

In this chapter, terms such as "reliability," "validity," "standard error of measurement," "stanines," and "norm- and criterion-referenced testing" will be explained along with a general approach to engaging in measurement activities with some level of confidence. There is no need to take these claims on faith. Try a paragraph or two and see how it goes.

WHAT IS MEASUREMENT?

Measurement is the process of quantifying characteristics of individuals. On an informal level, we do this all the time. We speak of people as being "husky," or "withdrawn," or "gregarious," or "colicky." We might modify these attributions with adjectives such as "extremely," "somewhat," "slightly," "terribly," or "moderately." After a little consideration, it is not hard to see that there are implicit scales operating here. A person can be located on a scale from "extremely gregarious" to "terribly withdrawn" in terms of the amount of introversion/extroversion he or she displays. In psychology and education, we like to be a bit more systematic in the rules we generate for purposes of measurement, but our systems are not so different from the example given above.

In trying to define measurement, it is necessary to look at three related terms: 1) "test," 2) "assessment," and 3) "evaluation." Along with the term "measurement," they are often used interchangeably in the literature. Unfortunately, different writers use these terms differently. You might run into different usages, but what is generally agreed upon is the following. First, a *test* is an activity that involves providing a stimulus to a person and observing the response (e.g., the Peabody Picture Vocabulary Test). Usually the stimuli are test items and usually there are several of them that are grouped together to make an overall score. A test with many subscores is often called a "battery." On a test the examiner is usually looking for the best that a person can do. The individual responses are usually scored as right or wrong, or sometimes on a scale (1 to 5, 1 to 10, etc.). However, if we are measuring self-concept, the notion of the best a person can do doesn't seem appropriate. Here, we are more interested in a person's "typical" response as opposed to his or her "best" response. Also, we are more likely to collect the data through the use of an observation schedule or rating scale. In these settings, the use of the word "test" is too limiting. A better word is "measurement." A test, then, is a particular kind of measurement. Measurement is the general term for turning characteristics of individuals into amounts, usually numbers.

Assessment is the difficult term in the group. People are continually generating definitions for assessment, and what it means in any given application can only be determined by its context. More often than not, it is used as a broader, more holistic, child-centered synonym for measurement. People often use it in preference to measurement to indicate that the measures taken were sufficient to render a useful judgment. The phrase, "We've done an assessment on Johnny . . ." connotes accuracy and thoroughness. It is similar to someone saying, "Let me share this with you," when he or she means, "Let me do the talking for awhile." The definition I favor is that assessment is the attempt to match the child to his or her environment. This definition, however, does not have enough currency to justify its use in a chapter of this nature. Unless explicitly defined otherwise, consider assessment to be a synonym for measurement.

Evaluation is the broadest term in the group. It is often used in relationship to determining the quality of an educational program or set of curriculum materials. When used with respect to individuals, it means a broad set of measures taken on a child with an eye toward providing an overall view of the child's strengths and weaknesses.

This chapter focuses on *measurement*, and the discussion encompasses testing but does not delve into issues of program or curricular evaluation. Primarily, we want to understand the process of trying to quantify a characteristic of a young child. Roughly speaking, there are three steps in the measurement process:

1. The characteristic of individuals that the examiner wants to measure must be defined in such a way as to make measurement possible.
2. A system for observing the characteristic must be developed.
3. A set of rules for turning the observations into numbers must be devised.

This may seem like a neat explanation of a fairly simple process, but an example will show that this is not the case in practice. Let's consider the seemingly straightforward problem of measuring height in basketball players. Height is usually the first thing one wants to know about a basketball player. This is not because of a pressing need to order proper-sized uniforms, or because one wants to know if the players can help put the nets up on the rims. The truth is that taller basketball players are more likely to get rebounds, are more likely to block shots, are less likely to have their shots blocked, and are generally better basketball players than shorter persons. Now we need a definition of height that allows for its measurement. This seems straightforward: Height is how tall a person is. Let's move to the second step: What system for measuring height do we want? The standard system is as follows:

1. The person is standing flat-footed,
2. without shoes,
3. and is measured to the top of his or her head.

This is instructive for our purposes because these simple rules do not correspond to the needs expressed for knowing height in the first place. A person's head (that is, its elevation) is not a particularly critical consideration in basketball. All of the basketball activities described above involve the hands, not the head. Why not measure:

1. The height of an outstretched (upward) hand,
2. with the person standing on the balls of the feet,
3. in basketball shoes.

One might even argue that standing is not what is desired since most basketball activities take place when a person is in the air. Expanding our consideration of measuring height in this way would mean including jumping ability, which is an entirely different variable.

It can be seen here that the set of rules used for measuring a variable may yield observations that are not exactly what was desired. One can argue that height (to the top of the head) is a fairly good approximation of "rebounding, shot-blocking" height, but this example shows that a variable that is as easy to conceptualize as height can still move an examiner slightly off track in trying to set up the rules to simply *observe* the variable. Given the difficulty in this situation, one can imagine the problems in trying to set up rules for variables of interest to early childhood. Measurement of variables such as "slow to warm up" or "effectiveness in coping" could lead to severe derailments.

The final step in our simple system of measurement is to transform the observations into numbers. For height, this truly is simple: we merely use a measuring tape and measure from the ground to the top of the basketball player's head. This may require a chair for our measurement expert, but shouldn't require too much else (unless we're playing in the Olympics, in which case the measurement has to be in meters instead of feet and inches). Whatever our numbering system is, it has to be comprehensible. In order to be comprehensible, it has to be in a numbering system with which people are already comfortable (such as feet and inches, or IQ points), or it has to have a referent that people can comprehend (such as 43rd percentile or "very colicky"). Concepts such as 24 hours in a day and 7 days in a week have no intrinsic meaning; they are as socially derived as "attentiveness," but have wider acceptability and simpler rules for measurement.

WHY DO WE WANT TO MEASURE?

Of the questions posed in this chapter, this is the most important. In a sense, it can never be answered by a measurement specialist; it must be answered by the professional who is using a measure. The answer should always be some variant of, "I need to know . . . about this person." That is, measurement should always follow an information need. The person obtaining the measure should know just what it is he or she will do with the measure once it is obtained. Among the valid needs for information are the following:

1. Diagnosis of a problem
2. Placement into one of several programs
3. Design of an intervention plan
4. Knowledge of an individual's progress
5. Evaluation of an intervention plan
6. Evaluation of the efficacy of a program
7. The conduct of research

There are other needs, and many refinements of the needs listed above, but one should be wary of falling into the trap of gathering measurements out of habit. Children have better things to do with their childhood than be tested out of habit or institutional policy.

The reason we often engage in measurement, particularly formal measurement, rather than using "professional judgment" is that we have a better idea of what we are about when we use formal procedures. Later we will see that we need a healthy skepticism about formal methods, but first let us be skeptical about professional judgment.

Formal measurement began in Paris with the psychologist Alfred Binet, who was Director of the Laboratory of Physiological Psychology at the Sorbonne. Binet was commissioned by the city of Paris to develop a series of scales to determine which children would benefit most from placement into one of a number of special schools. His work, conducted with Theodore Simon, lead to the Binet-Simon Intelligence Scales (Binet, 1905; Binet & Simon, 1908). These scales eventually led to the Stanford-Binet Intelligence Scale (Terman & Merrill, 1937) which is the more familiar form. It should be noted that Binet developed the concept of conservation of length and number (Binet, 1890) as well as the general method of closely observing a small sample of children intensively (his own two daughters) as a research technique. Many of his ideas were adopted and developed by Jean Piaget, who worked in Binet's lab for Simon shortly after Binet's death in 1911 (Wolf, 1966).

For our purposes here, it is Binet's famous work in the development of intelligence scales that is of interest to us. The problem that the city of Paris faced was the improper placement of students into schools specially designed for students with learning difficulties. Placements were being made by medical doctors and the results were most unsatisfactory. What one doctor would label severe retardation another would call mild retardation. A system was needed that would produce consistent results regardless of where and when the measurement was given; this is known as "objective" measurement. Note that objective does not refer to a type of testing, such as multiple choice or even paper and pencil. A test is objective if the results do not depend on the circumstances of the administration and if the results mean the same thing for all individuals who get the same score. It is not difficult to see that this is desirable.

It is interesting to observe that Binet's clearly defined measurement need, the proper placement of students into differentiated treatment programs, is not often the rationale given today for giving IQ tests. Even though our measurement activities may become institutionalized, there should always be a solid rationale for the administration of any instrument. That administration should either directly benefit the individual being measured or be of substantial research or evaluation significance. This is not a technical issue. The answer to the question, "Why are we conducting this measurement?" should not rest on any technical discussion. It should generate a response of the nature, "Because we need to know . . . ," and what we need to know should be clear to anyone. A good way to be sure that we have an answer to that question is to be able to state what is going to be done with that information. If this cannot be stated, then the use of the measure should be reconsidered.

WHAT ARE THE CHARACTERISTICS OF A GOOD MEASUREMENT?

It is important to note at the beginning of this section that the question posed is not, "What is a good test?" or "What is a good instrument?" or even "What is a good measure?" A good measurement must have certain characteristics. There is an important distinction between an instrument and a particular application of that instrument. In order for an instrument to be useful, it must be used appropriately. If used for the wrong reasons, on the wrong individual, or in the wrong fashion, any instrument can be useless, and even harmful. Compare a test instrument with a musical instrument, a Stradivarius or Guarneri violin, for example. Used appropriately—by the right person in the right fashion on the right piece of music—it represents the pinnacle in musical achievement. Used on the wrong piece of music (consider a Sousa march, for example) and the effect would be greatly diminished. Used by the wrong person (consider this author) and it could do damage to the unsuspecting ear. The same holds true with an instrument developed to measure psychological characteristics. The user must consider each application anew. Is this the right age level? Are the problems of this child too severe (or too slight) to detect with this instrument? Can the paraprofessional get a good measure with this instrument, or does a professional have to administer it?

The topics we are about to discuss are the classic measurement topics of reliability, bias, validity, and the like. What is critical to remember is that the consideration of these issues must be reevaluated for every new application of a measure. Tests don't have validity, *uses* of tests have validity (Cronbach, 1971). The same holds true for their other characteristics. It is important not to lose sight of this, because when we read about test validity and reliability, this concept is often lost in the language. Almost all measurement specialists agree with the ideas presented here, but sometimes they slip into shorthand language that makes it seem as if once a test has been validated, it is valid for all time and all purposes.

Five desirable characteristics of tests will be presented here: validity, reliability, objectivity, freedom from bias, and efficiency. Other authors may use a slightly different breakdown, but these five represent a compromise between being overly simplistic and providing a laundry list of attributes.

Validity

If a measurement gives us the information we want, it can be said to be valid. Validity is the sine qua non of measurement; the remaining four items listed above are really special aspects of validity. What does it mean to say that a measurement should give us what we want? Let's consider the basketball players again. A 7-foot-tall player who has a very long neck and short arms may not have a basketball playing height as great as that of a 6-foot, 6-inch-tall player with a short neck and very long arms. That is, when they both hold their hands up, the 6-foot, 6-inch-tall player may be able to reach higher. The problem here is one of validity—we are not getting exactly what we want with our measurement "to the top of the head."

Moving into the realm of measuring infants, consider trying to get a measure of cognitive ability in a child with cerebral palsy. Given the level of motor task demands of the measure and the degree of impairment, we may end up with a measure of motor ability that we believe to be a measure of cognitive ability. As another example, when we ask parents about temperament, are we measuring the child or the parent? These are questions of the validity of the measures involved.

We have already stated that the validity of a measurement must be reconsidered for each application. A second concern in validity is that the validity of a measurement exists independently of the evidence that a researcher might gather about it. This is somewhat analogous to criminal guilt. People are guilty or not guilty of crimes independently of whether there is sufficient evidence to convict them. Also, the fact that there is some evidence does not mean that there is guilt. This analogy falls apart, however, when we consider degree of validity. With crimes, guilt is usually dichotomous—one either is or is not guilty. With validity, it is always a matter of degrees. The statement, "This measurement is valid," really means, "This measurement has a good amount of validity in this particular instance." Rarely does an individual believe that the score obtained is a perfect reflection of the trait under consideration. For the user of a particular measure, the issue boils down to, "Is this measure sufficiently valid for my needs?" When examining the validity evidence that exists for a measure, the question becomes, "Do I have enough evidence to justify my use of this instrument?" How much evidence is necessary will vary according to the situation and ultimately is a judgment call on the part of the user of the instrument. A good rule of thumb might be, "Would I want this instrument used in this way on me or my child?"

When measures are developed for purposes of publication, the publisher, or author, usually conducts some type of validity study or studies on the measure. The purpose of these is to establish that the measure is functioning in an appropriate fashion for the intended study population. Unlike reliability studies, there is no fixed format that these studies must take. They vary with the nature of the measure. The studies are usually classified into one of three categories: construct validity, criterion-related validity, or content validity.

Construct Validity

Construct validity refers to whether the trait (or construct) is behaving the way we think it should on the measure. Construct here does not refer to how the measure was constructed, but to whether the psychological construct (trait, variable, etc.) is being measured appropriately. There are basically two aspects to construct validity. First, does the construct exist in the fashion in which it is being hypothesized to exist? This may seem somewhat metaphysical, but consider the variable of IQ. When someone is given an IQ as a result of an IQ test, we are saying that there is such a thing as intelligence and it is: 1) unidimensional, 2) stable over a long period of time, and 3) predictive of a person's ability to do a number of cognitive tasks, including learning new material. If a researcher does not consider these statements to be true, he or she is questioning the construct validity of the measure. The researcher is saying that the construct does not exist in humans in the way it is being hypothesized to exist. If the researcher considers these statements to be true for adults, but not for 2-year-old children, then he or she is questioning the construct validity of the measure for a particular population. The point here is that the validity of a measure should be reconsidered with each new application.

The second aspect of construct validity is whether the measure captures the construct as it is hypothesized. It is one thing to say that a variable exists and behaves in a certain fashion, and quite another to say that a particular measure accurately represents that construct. When researchers conduct validity studies of the construct validity type, they usually begin by posing questions about how a construct should behave under certain circumstances, and then they run a study to see if the measure lives up to expectations. For example, if the variable of height behaves in the fashion we think it should, then:

1. Children should get taller as they get older.
2. Taller people should generally weigh more than shorter people.
3. Height should not be related to hair color.

These are all testable hypotheses and they all relate to how we think height should behave as a construct. Of course it is a fairly simple construct to think about. We will consider some more interesting examples once we have discussed criterion-related and content validity.

Criterion-Related Validity

Criterion-related validity evidence refers to the degree to which the characteristic in question correlates with other indicators of the characteristic. These indicators are called criterion measures and may be obtained from a sample of individuals at the same time the measure in question is administered, in which case we refer to the relationship as *concurrent* validity evidence, or they may be measured in the future, in which case we refer to the relationship as *predictive* validity evidence. For example, if we have a short-form indicator of temperament, we may want to correlate it with a well-established longer measure of temperament. We give both to a sample of individuals at the same time and correlate the results. This yields an estimate of the concurrent validity of the short form. Or we may have a measure that purports to predict success in school. Here we have to give the measure prior to school entry for a sample of preschoolers, and then measure school success several years later. The correlation between the measure and school success is an estimate of the predictive validity of the measure.

It may have occurred to you that in both of these cases the quality of our estimate depends in large part on the validity of the criterion measure. That is, if the long-form measure of temperament isn't particularly valid, what good does it do to correlate a short form to it? If the correlation is low, it may be because the short form is valid and the long form is not (or that neither are, or that the long form is valid and the short form is not). If the correlation is high, it could still be the case that although the two measures in fact measure the same thing, neither measures temperament. An issue for all estimates of criterion-related validity evidence is the validity of the criterion. This has to be established independently of the validity study. In the case of predicting school success, one might argue that a grade point average is a perfect criterion in that it is exactly what one wants to be able to predict.

Content Validity

Content validity evidence refers to the nature of the measure itself—the items on the test or the procedures used to gather the information that comprises the measure. Here we are interested in assessing the degree of relationship between the test items or ratings that produce the observations and the definition of the construct to be measured. The question addressed by content validity evidence is: Do the items on this instrument comprise a representative sample of the behavior one is interested in? Some people refer to this idea as "face validity." Although just looking to see if the items *look like* a measure of, say, temperament is not sufficient, that is the basic idea. For example, if we are measuring adaptiveness, have we given the child a thorough opportunity to display adaptiveness? Are the items appropriate to the age range? Turning one's eyes toward a light source may be a good indicator for a 5-month-old, but a weak one for a 24-month-old. There are three ways in which an instrument can err in attempting to produce desired results:

1. The items may not be directly related to the desired concept (e.g., using a sorting task as a measure of memory).
2. The items may not represent all aspects of the desired concept (e.g., omitting two-hand coordination tasks in a fine muscle measure).
3. The items may represent more than the desired concept (e.g., cutting along a line with scissors as a measure of body coordination).

Avoiding these three possibilities is in essence an attempt to get "the truth, the whole truth, and nothing but the truth."

In some settings, this is a fairly simple task. If we are interested in measuring knowledge of addition facts for single-digit numbers, the domain of possibilities is fairly limited and establishing content validity evidence should be straightforward. If we are measuring temperament in 3-year-olds, the idea of a representative sample of stimuli rapidly becomes more problematical. Content validity evidence is typically gathered by having a panel of experts in the area of the trait under consideration review the measure with something like the following set of questions in mind:

1. Is each item (stimulus) directly related to the construct being measured?
2. Do skills, behaviors, or attitudes other than those being measured impinge on any of the items?
3. Do the items as a set comprise a reasonable representation of the construct being measured?

An Example of Establishing Validity

It might be useful at this point to tie together some of the preceding discussion with a concrete example. Imagine that we were interested in developing a brief assessment of preverbal communication that would identify which infants were most likely to experience speech and language difficulties during the preschool years. Furthermore, let's say that we wanted an instrument that would only take 15 minutes to administer and that could be administered by a paraprofessional without specialized training in giving the instrument. In our example, assume the instrument has already been created and our task is to establish the validity of the measure. For ease of reference, we will call this instrument the communication abilities "screening device."

The first study to undertake would be a content validity study. Here we would gather a group of specialists in early childhood and communication disorders and have them examine the measure. They would be asked to comment on its thoroughness (given its brevity), its relevance to the trait under consideration, and whether each item or stimulus was being given in the proper fashion. The experts could interact as a group, or they might render their judgments independently of one another.

A second study might be a concurrent validity study (recall that this is a type of criterion-related validity). We might take a sample of infants and administer the screening device to all of them. Then we could have them undergo a more extensive measurement procedure using an established instrument whose validity was already known, such as the Sequenced Inventory of Communication Development. A correlation between these scores would be an indicator of the validity of the new screening device. We might also have these infants observed by infant specialists while interacting with their parents. These experts could rate them in terms of their likelihood to show speech and language difficulties later in school. A correlation between the screening device and the ratings would be another indicator of concurrent validity.

Since our measure is designed to predict future behavior, a predictive validity study is really the critical test. Here we would give the measure to a group of infants and then get a measure of the degree to which the group exhibits speech and language difficulties in school several years later. There are some interesting considerations in this study. First, since a fairly low proportion of students exhibit communication difficulties, we probably would not want to start with a random sample of infants. We would probably want about half of the study infants to have been identified as likely to have difficulties by the screening device and half to have been identified as unlikely to have difficulties. Then we would want to *not* intervene for *any* children in the study. This is obviously a moral problem. How can we identify children as likely to have problems and then not provide them with help? The problem is that if help is provided and is successful, then the children will not show problems in schools. As researchers, we don't know if the problems didn't show up because the intervention was successful or because the instrument misidentified the children in the first place. In situations such as this, the decision typically made is to forego the validity study in favor of the intervention.

A final type of validity study that should be mentioned because of the frequency with which it is done is the factor analytic study. Factor analytic studies are usually categorized under the heading of construct validity. Factor analysis is a statistical tool that takes a large number of variables (in our case the responses to the items on a test) and tries to reduce those variables into a smaller number of factors. For example, the items on an IQ test can usually be factored down into verbal, quantitative, and spatial ability. We might give the screening device to a (fairly large) sample and factor analyze the results. If we believe that the screening device measures only one underlying variable (speech and language disability), then we would want all variables to "load on one factor" (correlate with one underlying construct). If this occurred, it would be evidence that the instrument was working in the way we wanted. For some instruments (our IQ example) we may want more than one factor to come out. Cooley and Lohnes (1971) provide a good description of factor analysis for those who need to understand it. It should be pointed out, however, that of all the tricks in the statistician's bag, factor analysis comes the closest to alchemy. The probability of an expert being misled by a factor analysis is high; for a novice it's almost a lead-pipe cinch. Looking at factor analytic results is the numerical equivalent of looking at Rorschach ink blots; they are as revealing of the interpreter as of anything else.

Summary

To sum up our validity discussion, it is important to keep the following ideas in mind:

1. Measures don't have validity, measurements (of individuals) do.
2. Validity exists or does not independently of the evidence of that validity.
3. There are three general categories of validity evidence (content, criterion-related, and construct) and many types of studies within any given category.
4. The question to ask of any measure is, "What evidence is there that this measure will give me what I want?"

Reliability

A measurement that produces consistent results may be said to be reliable. Reliability is a special kind of validity. If a measurement does not produce consistent results from one administration to the next, how can it be valid? On the other hand, the fact that the results are consistent across administrations doesn't mean that we are measuring what we want; it just means that we are measuring *something* consistently. Consider taking a class of schoolchildren out to the playground and having them all throw a baseball as far as they can. Measure the distance each can throw. Now repeat the process a week later. Correlate the results. The correlation will be a measure of the reliability of the baseball throw measure. Now use those results to make determinations about who needs remedial academic work and who is going into the gifted and talented class. Here you have a case of very high reliability and zero validity. We have a consistent measurement, but it isn't what we want.

Many authors consider the reliability of a test to be an upper limit to its validity. That is, a test cannot be any more valid than it is reliable. This is probably correct, but it leads one to think of validity as a concept that can be captured in a single correlation coefficient, like a reliability coefficient. This is too limiting a conceptualization of validity. Perhaps a better conceptualization of the relationship between the two ideas would be to compare it to the relationship between old and antique. Old (reliable) is a necessary condition for antique (valid); if something is an antique (valid) it has to be old (reliable). On the other hand, lots of things are old (reliable) but they are not necessarily antique (valid).

There are three ways that measurement specialists look at the concept of reliability. The first way is primarily a commonsense approach. This is the concept of reliability as an index of the stability of the measurement: Does the score we receive on an individual stay stable over time? The second way of looking at reliability is as an index of differentiability. This is not a commonsense approach. Differentiability is the ability of a measure to reproduce in individuals score differences that are believed to exist in the population. If our yardsticks only measured whole yards, almost all adults would be 2 yards tall (rounded off). The measures would be highly stable, but they could not capture the height differential between Kareem Abdul Jabbar and Mary Lou Retton. Both would be 2 yards tall. This measure would be reliable from a stability perspective, but unreliable from a differentiability perspective. The third way reliability is conceptualized is as an index of the degree of agreement between two raters.

*Stability: Test-Retest
and Parallel Forms Reliability*

The first type of reliability to be considered is the stability indicators. There are basically two methods here: *test-retest* and *parallel forms*. They are both quite simple. In test-retest reliability, the measure is administered to a sample of individuals for whom the measure is intended on two occasions, usually a week or two apart. The results of these two administrations are correlated and the resultant correlation coefficient is the reliability estimate. The only problems with test-retest reliability estimates are: 1) they require two administrations of a test, and 2) if the test is reactive, the second administration is usually not a good measurement. For example, if we are interested in infants' responses to novel situations, test-retest reliability is of little use because the second time we administer the instrument the situation isn't novel anymore. We will begin to see a practice or learning effect. Similarly, older children remember answers from the first administration of the test. The problem of remembering answers can be solved by moving to the second type of stability index, parallel forms. Two tests are considered to be parallel if they have the same means, standard deviations, and reliabilities. Tests are not necessarily parallel if they have the same number of items and generally measure the same trait. In parallel forms reliability, half of the testees get form A during the first administration and form B during the second administration. The other half get B first, then A. Once this is done performance on A is correlated with performance on B and the correlation coefficient is the reliability estimate. The test-retest problem of remembering specific items may be solved, but other reactivity problems may well exist. With regard to the learning effect, if we change the situations in the retest in order to maintain novelty, the child may come to expect novelty in the test setting.

Generally speaking, if the problem of reactivity does not seem to be severe, stability indicators are very good measures of reliability, especially for young children. A problem with measuring young children is that they are so unstable themselves, both in terms of many of the traits that one might want to measure and in the variability they exhibit in terms of cooperating in a testing situation. A stability index of some sort is probably critical in determining reliability for most measures involving young children.

Internal Consistency: Split-Halves and Coefficient Alpha

Giving a test twice for purposes of estimating reliability is often quite difficult to accomplish. In an effort to address this difficulty, measurement specialists came up with the notion of considering the odd-numbered items on a test as one "form" of a test and the even-numbered items as a second "form." One could then correlate the two "forms" and have an estimate of the reliability of the test. This is the notion of a "split-half" reliability. There are just three problems with this otherwise brilliant piece of insight. First, what we would have is a measure not of the reliability of the test, but of the reliability of half of the test. This problem was solved by Spearman and Brown when they developed what is referred to as the Spearman-Brown Prophecy formula. A good description of the workings of the formula can be found in Anastasi (1982).

The second problem with split-halves is that there is no longer any notion of stability over time being measured here. With a split-half reliability, all of the information is gathered in one administration. This caused a rethinking of what reliability might be and led to the notion of differentiability or internal consistency. Differentiability is the ability of a measure to find the real differences that exist among people. Returning to our yardstick example, the problem with a height measure that could only measure how many yards tall people were is that it would not have good differentiability. Internal consistency is the degree to which all items on a test are measuring the same concept. Differentiability and internal consistency are different concepts, but they often go hand in hand. If we have good internal consistency, we usually also find good differentiability. The split-halves approach to reliability addresses this concept of reliability; if what you are interested in is a measure of the degree to which all items on the test are measuring the same concept and the degree to which the test as a whole is producing different results for different people, then a split-halves reliability will work fairly well. Internal consistency reliability is very important for conducting research (a measure wouldn't be useful if everyone got the same score, or nearly so). However, for clinical purposes, measures of internal consistency may not be as useful as measures of stability.

The third problem with split-halves is that odd and even items is not the only way to split a test in half. In fact, there are millions of ways to split a 30-item test in half. Each split could produce a slightly different estimate of the reliability, so the split that is chosen is important to the results. Kuder and Richardson (1937) invented a way to essentially take the average of all possible ways of splitting a test in half. Their approach is called Kuder-Richardson Formula 20 (often just "KR20"). KR20 only works for tests that have dichotomously scored items, that is, items that are scored right or wrong (or pass/fail). Cronbach (1951) developed the same idea for items that could be scored in any quantitative fashion (right/wrong, rating scales, judgments, etc.). He called his generalization of the KR20 formula "coefficient alpha." KR20 *is* coefficient alpha when the test is one that can be scored right/wrong. Descriptions of the formulas and how they work can be found in Anastasi (1982).

It should be emphasized that a critical problem with internal consistency measures of reliability is that they do not yield an estimate of stability over time. As mentioned, this problem may well be a serious one for measuring young children.

Interrater Reliability

Many measures, particularly those involving young children, use raters or judges to assess performance, ability, attitude, and the like. This can be done in a variety of ways. First, a simple overall rating may be generated by someone who knows the child well (a teacher or parent). This might be an index of distractibility or sociability. Second, a trained observer might be recording observations of particular behavior in a controlled setting, such as the number of times a child engages in the desired task, or the number of social bids a child makes to other children. Third, a judge may be making an assessment of a product of the child, such as a rating of the use of color in a painting, or the complexity of a drawing. All of these instances involve an additional step in the measurement process in that the measure is not taken directly from the child but is filtered through the perception of an adult. This allows for an additional source of unreliability to creep into the picture.

Reliability estimates involving raters can get very complex very quickly. If we want to know the reliability of using one rater for all children, we have a simple reliability setting. If we want to use two raters on each child, the situation is more complex. If we want to use two raters, but each child is only rated by one rater, still more complexity enters in. If we want to know how reliable any given parent or teacher is at rating a child, we have a very complex task in order to establish reliability. At its simplest level (the reliability of a given rater on all children), interrater reliability involves generating a set of scores from two raters on the same sample of subjects. The correlation between the two raters is the measure of interrater reliability. The interrater reliability by itself, however, is not the entire reliability picture in most instances. One would typically still need a stability estimate to see if the measure was stable over time. One could have a measure that was easy to rate reliably in any given instance, but that would produce very different results over even short time intervals. For example, it could be very easy for raters to decide whether a given child was being highly vocal or not at a given time, but that behavior couild change on a minute-to-minute basis. Here we would have good interrater reliability, but poor stability.

The Standard Error of Measurement

The standard error of measurement is a different way of thinking about the idea of reliability. It is an approach to reliability that can be extremely useful to the clinician. In order to examine the idea of standard error of measurement, we need an example with which all readers will be familiar. The best candidate for this is probably an IQ score. An individualized administration of an IQ measure typically will have a reliability (internal consistency) of about .90. The standard deviation of IQ scores is usually 15, and the mean is almost always 100. This doesn't occur by accident; the psychologists developing the measures have constructed them so that, whatever the performance is on the measure, it is transformed to have a mean of 100 and a standard deviation of 15. If the standard deviation is 15 and the reliability is .90, then the standard error of measurement will be about 5. In order to get a measure of the accuracy of a score, just add and subtract one or two standard errors of measurement to the score (one standard error in each direction yields a 67% confidence level; two standard errors of measurement yield a 96% confidence level). Thus if a child gets a score of 94, we are about 67% certain that his or her true IQ is between 89 and 99, and we are 96% certain that his or her IQ is between 84 and 104. If we had used a short form of an IQ measure with a reliability of only .64, the standard error of measurement would jump to 9. Thus a score of 94 would have a confidence range (96%) of 76 to 112. We can see that measures with reliabilities below .90 are often of questionable value in making decisions about individual children.

Other Desirable Test Characteristics

Objectivity

A measure that does not depend upon who is giving it and under what conditions it is given or scored can be said to be objective. If parents were the only input to placement decisions, far more children would be gifted than presently seems to be the case. If we moved to grandparents, we might have the entire population. If our measurement is colored by who is doing the observing, then it obviously cannot be valid. It also may not be reliable. This issue should not be confused with the fact that the person doing the observing must be capable of seeing what the measure is intended to find. Sometimes a highly trained professional is required, whereas other situations require only adults who know the child very well, such as parents. The point is that we must always remember the source of our information and the possibility that subjectivity is reducing the accuracy of the score.

Freedom from Bias

If the score a person receives is not influenced by characteristics extraneous to the measure, then the measure can be said to be free from bias. The best known examples of extraneous characteristics are race, sex, ethnicity, and language. In measuring young children, especially where the measurement calls for adult interpretation or even recording of behavior, many other possible extraneous characteristics can come into play. For example, children who are not well-dressed may be thought to be disruptive, withdrawn, or less intelligent while their well-dressed counterparts may be seen as vivacious, reflective, and more intelligent. Children who are highly verbal may be seen as more creative than quieter children. The number of possibilities is substantial. Although there are statistical approaches to studying these issues, the practitioner mostly needs to keep a watchful eye out for them.

Efficiency

Measurement ought to be as unobtrusive and efficient as possible. Testing doesn't typically become particularly obnoxious to individuals until they reach third or fourth grade. In my experience, children's attitudes toward testing seem to develop in rough parallel to their attitudes toward going to the dentist. This observation notwithstanding, there ought to be a certain, almost reverential respect toward the concept of childhood that should have an inhibitive effect on making children spend too much time in testing. We should test when we are fairly certain it is in the child's benefit (or for research or evaluation necessity), and when we do so, it ought to be an efficient process.

WHAT ARE NORMS, STANINES, AGE-EQUIVALENTS, AND ALL THOSE OTHER TERMS?

A score that stands alone is hard to understand. "Mary got a 34 on this measure" is not a statement that has any meaning unless we know what a 34 is relative to any other possible score. Sometimes meaning can come from a real-life understanding of the measure itself. "Mark is 6 feet tall" has meaning because we understand height. "Mary's IQ is 127" has meaning because we understand IQ (or think we do). However, on a new or unfamiliar measure we don't know what the scores mean unless we have some sort of *referent*. In measurement, we usually use one of two types of referent: *norm* or *criterion*. Norm-referenced tests are tests that use some sort of normative data to interpret the score. Statements such as "Joan is in the 34th percentile" or "Children need to be in the eighth stanine or above to get into the program" are norm-referenced statements. Criterion-referenced tests rely on some absolute standard for score interpretation. Statements such as "You need to get 80% on your unit test to move to the next chapter" or "The Apgar ratings were 6 and 8" are criterion referenced. Many measures developed for use with infants and young children give norm-referenced scores, so it is important to have some sense of what norms are.

Norms

A norm is a statement of how people typically behave in some setting. In measurement, norms are a baseline for comparing the performance of an individual to a set of peers. Norms are developed by collecting information on a large set of subjects who are members of the appropriate group. For example, we might want to norm a new measure of temperament. The first thing we have to do is to define the population we are interested in. This might be 12–36-month-old children. Further, we might want to have norms for children in 3-month intervals, that is, 12–14, 15–17, 18–20, 21–23, and so on. Also, we might want to have separate norms for boys and girls. We now actually have 24 norming studies to conduct instead of just one (12 age groups times 2 sexes). The task now becomes one of finding the data. Ideally, we would have a random sample from the overall population. This sample would have to be large enough to get a good measure of the extremes. For clinical purposes, the most important aspect of norms is a good indicator of the difference between low-normal and the point where intervention should occur. Unfortunately, in the general population there are few cases in that range. Thus, the sample has to be large. Furthermore, most parents aren't interested in having their children measured for the sake of norms development. Also, since children of this age typically are not in school, study cases must be acquired one at a time. The combination of these factors often leads to less than satisfactory norms.

Assuming we can overcome some of these problems, what do norms look like and what do they do? The easiest norms to think of are height and weight norms. They are simply an indicator of how tall and heavy a child is in relation to other children his or her age and sex. We use them to detect growth patterns that are sufficiently atypical to indicate that the child may need special attention. Test norms are no different than height and weight norms in theory. In practice, they are probably nowhere near as accurate. Every time a child goes to a doctor the height and weight norms get additional data, whereas most testing measures are usually normed once in their lifetimes (except for measures like the Stanford-Binet).

There are a variety of ways to communicate normed scores: 1) percentiles, 2) stanines, 3) age or grade equivalents, and 4) standardized scores.

Percentiles

Percentiles simply indicate what percentage of the individuals in the norm group scored below a given child. A child whose height is in the 83rd percentile is taller than 83% of the children that age and sex. Test norms don't usually involve sex, just age. It is important to point out that not all norms are national norms. On many measures, the norm group may be children from a dozen day care centers near the home base of the individual who developed the test. The technical material that comes with the test must be read in order to get information on the norm group.

Stanines

Stanines were developed by the army in order to be able to record a recruit's score on a test in a single column of a computer card. "Stanine" is an abbreviation of "standard nine." Stanines are single-digit scores running from 1 (low) to 9 (high). They are based on the statistical concepts of the mean and the standard deviation. The mean is the average score for a group of people and the standard deviation is a number that indicates how far the scores are spread out. Without going into a mathematical description of standard deviations, for IQ tests the standard deviation is 15; for SAT scores it is about 100. For stanines, the mean is 5 and the standard deviation 2. All scores are rounded off to whole numbers. Therefore, a stanine of 7 indicates that on the measure in question this child scored one standard deviation above the mean. This is equivalent to an IQ of 115 or an SAT score of roughly 600. A stanine of 2 is 1.5 standard deviations below the mean (IQ = 78, SAT = 350).

Age or Grade Equivalents

The idea of age or grade equivalents was probably started by Binet, who talked about children's mental age as compared to their chronological age. An age-equivalent score is a score obtained by the average child of the age given in the score. If a child's age-equivalent height is 2.7, it means he or she is as tall as an average child who is 2.7 years old. Grade equivalents work exactly the same way for school children. A grade-equivalent score of 4.5 means a child did as well on the test in question as one would predict the average child in the fifth month of fourth grade would do.

Age- and grade-equivalent scores have some technical problems that make them less than optimal to use in score reporting. They tend to mislead individuals. This occurs more often with grade equivalents. Even though this text does not concern grade-school children, this problem is sufficiently widespread to merit one paragraph here. If a fourth-grade student takes a fourth-grade reading test and gets a grade-equivalent score of 7.2, it does not necessarily mean he or she can read seventh-grade material. It means he or she reads fourth-grade material as well as an average seventh grader would. To be even more precise, it means he or she reads fourth-grade material as well as the testing company *thinks* a seventh grader would read it. (In developing norms, no one has seventh graders tested on fourth-grade material.) The problem with age and grade equivalencies is that they tend to get our thinking about children somewhat confused.

Standardized Scores

"Standardized score" is a catch-all term. There are many different types of standardized scores; IQ scores and SAT scores are the two most widely recognized. They can be developed in a variety of different ways. Basically, a standardized score is useful for statistical purposes. Testing companies use them to develop all of the other scores they give, and they are usually the best scores to use when conducting program evaluations. Other than that, unless an examiner already understands them (such as IQ scores), he or she should use percentiles or some other score. (I have received Tests of English as a Foreign Language [TOEFL] scores as part of applications for graduate study from international students for 12 years and still do not understand the standard score system they use.)

Overall, percentiles are probably the easiest scores to use. All scores give you basically the same information: how well this child did compared to the children in the norming group.

HOW SHOULD A CLINICIAN SELECT A MEASURE?

Selecting a measure to use is like buying a car, but is more important. There is a tendency to feel inadequate to the task and a fear that the measure selected won't really be what we want. The following are some ideas on how to get the information that is needed for any particular purpose.

Define Your Needs. Remember, you aren't really selecting a measure, you are meeting your information needs. What do you want to know about your children and why? Write out what you want. Hold a meeting and discuss it with your colleagues. A good definition of the information needs that are leading to the selection of a measure is critical.

Get Some Assistance. Call the nearest university that has infant specialists and speak with them. This is a new area in which new developments occur on a fairly regular basis. You may be surprised at how willing researchers are to help you with this problem.

Find Out What's Available. A university library will have reference material on what tests are available. Two widely known sources of information are *Tests In Print III*, (which is the testing equivalent of *Books In Print*), and *Mental Measurement Yearbook*, (the 10th edition will probably be out sometime before this chapter is published). *Mental Measurement Yearbook* provides descriptions and critical reviews of thousands of published tests, including dozens on infant behavior. Both are published by the Buros Institute of Mental Measurements at the University of Nebraska–Lincoln.

Evaluate What You Have. This is the most difficult step. First, gather all of the available material on the measure. This may well require a phone call to the publisher asking for technical information. Once you have the material, you need to ask yourself, "What information is presented here that will tell me if this measure will give me what I want?" You are likely to have reliability measures. You are more likely to get split-halves or KR20 than test-retest or parallel forms. Remember that for your purposes, stability measures (test-retest, parallel forms) are probably more useful. How reliable should the measure be? For making decisions about individual children, reliability should be above .90. A measure with a reliability of .83 may be better than no measure at all, but reliabilities below .80 will be of questionable value to you.

What about validity? Few measures will provide much in the way of validity information. This is unfortunate since validity is really the key. Also keep in mind that the validity of your use of the test may be different from the validity evidence reported in a technical manual. Finally, the fact that a measure has no validity evidence appropriate for your use does not mean that the use you have in mind is not valid; it just means there is no evidence that it *is* valid.

How can you get other information? There are several options here. First, read the review in *Mental Measurement Yearbook* or elsewhere. Professional journals in your field may contain reviews. A librarian can help to find information on the measure you are considering. Second, find someone else who is using the measure. Ask your colleagues from other institutions, or ask the publisher to provide you with other purchasers of the measure whom you can contact. Third, go to your university source for help in assessing the measure. Finally, read the items or tasks on the measure. Be your own content validity study. Get your colleagues to help. If the measure doesn't ask the questions or pose the tasks that you think belong on the measure, then maybe your idea of the concept being measured and the idea of the measure's authors are not the same. This should give you cause to reconsider.

Try It Out. Give your measure a pilot test before reaching a final decision. Maybe you can try out two or three candidates. Think of this activity as like buying a tool. If you don't like it in use, it isn't going to *be* of any use to you.

SUMMING UP, OR WHERE DO WE GO FROM HERE?

There is a great deal more that could be said about measurement, but that would make this a measurement *book* instead of a measurement chapter, so it is time for summation and final thoughts and recommendations. Instead of recapitulating the preceding pages, I will finish with a few good rules of thumb for engaging in measurement in a reasonable and satisfactory way.

Know What You're About Before You Begin. Ask yourself the following questions: "Is this test necessary? Why? What am I going to know from the results that I don't know now? How am I going to work differently with this child as a result of this test?"

Make the Results Make Sense. People go off on the strangest tangents on the basis of test results. Real, living children produce test results. The measures were designed to help you understand those children. If the results confuse more than clarify, something is wrong. You should rarely just ignore test results, but you should be extremely wary of doing things that don't seem right to you on the basis of a test. One side point here: It is easier for a score that seems low to be wrong than a score that seems high. That is, there are many ways for people with ability in what you are measuring to do poorly. It is less likely that a person without much ability will do very well.

Use Multiple Sources of Information. In some respects, all information is biased. In order to hope to get an accurate picture of an individual, you almost always need more than one source of information.

Find the Child. Again, remember that real children produce test results. Try to find a complete picture of a child in your test data and then fit that picture to what you can reasonably accomplish in your program. Weigh the pluses and minuses of the alternatives available to you. The fact that a child shows a deficiency in a given area does not necessarily mean that now is the time to work on it. There may be other needs of the child (or of the class) that are more important right now. Also remember that it may be more useful to build on strengths than to try to remediate weaknesses in some situations. The purpose of measurement is to augment your professional abilities and resources, not to supplant them.

REFERENCES

Anastasi, A. (1982). *Psychological testing* (5th ed.). New York: Macmillan.

Binet, A. (1890). La perception des longueurs et des nombres chez quelques petits enfants [Perception of length and numbers in several small infants]. *Revue Philospohique, 29,* 68–81.

Binet, A. (1905). A propos de la mesure de l'intelligence [On measuring intelligence]. *Annee Psychologique, 11,* 69–82.

Binet, A., & Simon, T. (1908). Le developpement de l'intelligence chez les enfants [The development of intelligence in infants]. *Annee Psychologique, 14,* 1–94.

Cooley, W.W., & Lohnes, P.R. (1971). *Multivariate data analysis.* New York: John Wiley & Sons.

Cronbach, L.J. (1951). Coefficient alpha and the internal structure of tests. *Psychometrika, 16,* 297–334.

Cronbach, L.J. (1971). Test validation. In R.L. Thorndike (Ed.), *Educational measurement* (2nd ed.). Washington, DC: American Council on Education.

Kuder, G.F., & Richardson, M.W. (1937). The theory of the estimation of test reliability. *Psychometrika, 2,* 151–160.

Terman, L.M., & Merrill, M.A. (1937). *Measuring intelligence.* Boston: Houghton Mifflin.

Wolf, T.H. (1966). Intuition and experiment: Alfred Binet's first efforts in child psychology. *Journal of the History of the Behavioral Sciences, 2*(3), 233–239.

II
ASSESSING NEUROMOTOR INTEGRITY

3 Newborn Assessment and Support for Parenting
The Neonatal Behavioral Assessment Scale

John Worobey and T. Berry Brazelton

Assessment techniques for the neonate may be grouped under one of three headings, that is, screening tests, neurological examinations, or behavioral assessments (St. Clair, 1978). Such a typology, while derived from the intended purpose behind their administration, is nevertheless somewhat arbitrary, inasmuch as all three of these techniques rely on newborn *behavior* to determine viability, maturity, or individuality (Francis, Self, & Horowitz, 1987). In the past 20 years, the increasing realization that *interactive* behavior, specifically that between caregiver and neonate, may better predict later infant functioning than a singular focus on the newborn—no matter how rigorous the evaluation—has led to the development and extensive use of the Neonatal Behavioral Assessment Scale (NBAS). An outgrowth of the collaborative efforts of pediatricians and psychologists, the NBAS (Brazelton, 1973, 1984) is currently the most widely used research device employed with newborn populations. Nearly 150 published reports to date have included the NBAS as an outcome measure, as an index of behavioral individuality, as a way of predicting the baby's effect on parents, and to offer support for parents in their new role (Brazelton, Nugent, & Lester, 1987).

Since its appearance some 15 years ago, the utility, validity, and reliability of the NBAS have been subjected to numerous reviews and evaluations (e.g., Als, Tronick, Lester, & Brazelton, 1979; Brazelton et al., 1987; Horowitz & Linn, 1982; Sameroff, 1978). Each of these efforts provide detailed information on the NBAS, describing the development of the scale, specifying the procedures for training, administration, and scoring, and documenting its research and clinical applications. In addition, the NBAS manual, in both its first (Brazelton, 1973) and its revised (Brazelton, 1984) editions, devotes considerable space to employing the scale in an appropriate manner.

For such reasons, then, the purpose of the present chapter is not to reiterate information that is widely available elsewhere, but instead to focus on current trends in the use of the NBAS with at-risk families and their newborns. Nevertheless, because the present volume is designed to serve as a comprehensive resource for professionals who may be quite skilled with some devices, yet understandably less familiar with others, we will begin with a description of the NBAS, including procedures for the administration and scoring of the scale. The reader should recognize, however, that the present chapter in no way serves as a substitute for the detailed information outlined in the second edition of the manual (Brazelton, 1984). Next, we will outline the use of the scale with

---

Work on this chapter by the first author was facilitated by an Academic Study leave from Rutgers University and a Fellowship in Child Study awarded him by Skidmore College.

at-risk families, focusing on work that describes the ability of the NBAS to identify behavioral compromises in the high-risk neonate that may have an impact upon subsequent development. Finally, we will describe recent work with the NBAS as an intervention device, and draw some conclusions from extant data on how to empower parents with the skills that may best promote optimal family development and attachment to the new infant.

CONCEPTUAL BASE OF THE NBAS

The original intent in developing the NBAS was to describe the integration and separate functioning of the interactive, motoric, state, and autonomic systems in the healthy, normal, full-term newborn (Als et al., 1979; Brazelton et al., 1987). Unlike other tests or devices, the NBAS was conceptualized as an interactive assessment, wherein a sensitive adult would draw out the organizational skills of the neonate by supporting the newborn's responsive capacities. The primary emphasis was on establishing the newborn's capacities and limits in contributing to the caregiving environment. With a single assessment performed a few days postpartum, a slice of the dynamic continuum of the neonate's adjustment to labor, delivery, and the extrauterine environment would be obtained. Since such an early assessment is admittedly capturing the newborn in the midst of a transition, through *repeated* assessments over the first month the newborn's coping and organizational capacities in interaction with a responsive environment can be better tracked. In this way, the neonate's contribution to its caregiving and perhaps to its own future functioning can be best predicted.

Central to the administration of the assessment is the newborn's state of consciousness, because the newborn's use of "states" is an expression of both internal organization and the ability to control reactions to external stimuli. Six levels of state are identified, and their observation is so critical to an understanding of the neonate that the initial state, predominant states, and state changes noted throughout the course of the actual assessment are all considered when evaluating and interpreting the newborn's behavioral assets (Brazelton, 1979).

Unlike most standardized assessment procedures, the infant's score is also based on *best*, rather than average, performance. The scoring of best performance is preferred in order to overcome any subtle environmental differences that might influence a particular newborn's responses, and to push the neonate to his or her limits, so to speak, which may be a better predictor of subsequent functioning than everyday behavior (Brazelton, 1984). A "modal" set of scoring guidelines does exist (Horowitz, Sullivan, & Linn, 1978; Lancioni, Horowitz, & Sullivan, 1980), and may be used *in addition to* the best score if the examiner has had a sufficient sample of behavior to describe the typical level of responding to certain of the items.

Being able to elicit best performance requires a flexible examiner. In contrast to most tests, in which the examiner's role is clear cut, detached, and controlled by the instructions, the NBAS requires an interactant who is both skilled and sensitive. One must be comfortable in handling babies, of course, but also in facilitating arousal and altering feedback to the infant, in adaptively moving from one series of items to another based on the infant's signals, and in speaking with information-hungry, yet oftentimes anxious, parents (Worobey & Brazelton, 1986). Therefore, the training of examiners to an acceptable level of reliability in the administration and scoring of the NBAS is of prime importance (Nugent & Sepkoski, 1984). Indeed, a number of training centers throughout the world now exist to certify examiners for research and clinical purposes (Brazelton, 1984).

CONTENT OF THE NBAS

As shown in Tables 1 and 2, the NBAS includes 28 behavioral items and 20 reflexive items, which encompass passive movements. In addition, nine supplemental items, currently under investigation, are described as appropri-

Table 1. Behavior items included in Neonatal Behavioral Assessment Scale

Standard Items

1. Response decrement to light
2. Response decrement to rattle
3. Response decrement to bell
4. Response decrement to tactile stimulation of foot (pinprick)
5. Orientation—inanimate visual (ball)
6. Orientation—inanimate auditory (rattle)
7. Orientation—inanimate visual and auditory (moving rattle)
8. Orientation—animate visual (face)
9. Orientation—animate auditory (voice)
10. Orientation—animate visual and auditory (face and voice)
11. Alertness
12. General tone
13. Motor maturity
14. Pull-to-sit
15. Cuddliness
16. Defensive movements (cloth on face)
17. Consolability with intervention
18. Peak of excitement
19. Rapidity of buildup
20. Irritability
21. Activity
22. Tremulousness
23. Amount of startle during exam
24. Lability of skin color
25. Lability of states
26. Self-quieting activity
27. Hand-to-mouth facility
28. Smiles

Supplementary Items

29. Quality of alert responsiveness
30. Cost of attention
31. Examiner persistence
32. General irritability
33. Robustness and endurance
34. Regulatory capacity
35. State regulation
36. Balance of motor tone
37. Reinforcement value of infant's behavior

Table 2. Reflex items included in Neonatal Behavioral Assessment Scale

1. Plantar grasp
2. Palmar grasp
3. Ankle clonus
4. Babinski reflex
5. Standing
6. Automatic walking
7. Placing
8. Incurvation
9. Crawling
10. Glabella reflex
11. Tonic deviation of head and eyes
12. Nystagmus
13. Tonic neck reflex
14. Moro reflex
15. Intensity of rooting
16. Intensity of sucking
17. Passive movement—right arm
18. Passive movement—left arm
19. Passive movement—right leg
20. Passive movement—left leg

ate for differentiating progress and individuality in infants, especially preterm and fragile ones. While the behavioral and neurological items make up the component parts of the assessment, it is the newborn's state of arousal that forms the requisite structure for administering the scale.

The NBAS provides for the observation of six states of arousal (Prechtl & Beintema, 1964). Two sleep states are included: deep sleep and light sleep. A three-level continuum of alertness is represented by the drowsy, alert, and active states. Finally, the criterion for a crying state is reached when active fussing persists for 15 or more seconds. An ideal examination will allow for movement through the entire spectrum of states, so that the neonate's capacity to handle stimulation while in each state may be assessed (Brazelton, 1984).

Following an assessment of the newborn's initial state, which ideally would be deep or light sleep, the discrete items that comprise the habituation cluster (Lester, Als, & Brazelton, 1982) may be presented. First, a flashlight is used to determine the newborn's response decrement to light after it has been repeatedly shined in the infant's closed eyes. Next, the response decrement to a rattle and a bell are scored, following the repeated presentations of these auditory stimuli. By this point in the procedures, many newborns will begin to rouse. To facilitate this state transition the baby may be uncovered, with reactions such as a rapidity of buildup in agitation or any lability of skin color being noted.

If the newborn remains in a quiet sleep state, the response decrement to tactile stimulation of the foot should next be determined, via a light pinprick. Again, the neonate's buildup to an upset state should be noted if it occurs here, as well as fussing being counted toward the eventual irritability score. With the infant still dressed, ankle clonus and the Babinski and plantar grasp reflexes should be elicited. Most newborns will have reached at least a drowsy state by now, although the accompanying undressing should assist if alertness has not yet been achieved. Assuming for our present purpose that true alertness has not yet been exhibited, nor has it been exceeded by crying, the newborn's passive movements of arms and legs should be gauged through manipulation, and an initial estimate of general tonus be made. The palmar grasp is then elicited. As before, any lability of state and skin color, or exhibition of spontaneous startles or tremulousness, should be noted.

The pull-to-sit maneuver can now be employed, with concomitant irritability and state changes observed. Following this procedure, the standing, automatic walking, and placing reflexes may be elicited. The newborn should then be picked up and held across the examiner's hand, to assess incurvation of the spine, general tone and motor maturity, and the crawling response to being placed back down in a prone position. After this sequence, the newborn may again be picked up, but this time held in an outward position while the examiner spins to determine tonic deviation of the head and eyes, and a nystagmus response. At this point, the newborn may be held more naturally to the shoulder and tucked in the examiner's arm, so as to assess cuddliness and to discretely elicit a glabella reflex via tapping the forehead. At the same time, rooting to the examiner's finger and its subsequent sucking can be assessed.

By now, a state of bright, sustained alertness is typically reached, and the infant is ready for the orientation cluster of items (Lester et al., 1982). Seated comfortably, the examiner attempts to elicit visual pursuit of a colored ball, and scores the newborn's orientation to this inanimate visual object. Immediately thereafter, a shaking rattle is held to either side of the infant in order to assess orientation to the inanimate auditory stimulus. Still shaking the rattle, it may next be brought across the newborn's visual field to determine orientation to an inanimate visual and auditory display. As has been repeatedly observed, the human face and voice are far more attractive to the neonate than even the most exciting rattle. Hence, attending to the examiner's face, voice, and back-and-forth movement is assessed after the inanimate stimuli have been presented. These items comprise orientation to the animate visual, auditory, and visual and auditory sequence.

The infant is then placed back on the table or in the bassinette, in a supine position, and the cloth is brought to the face to observe any defensive movements of the head, arms, and hands. The tonic neck reflex is next elicited, and the Moro reflex stands as the final item to be administered.

Because these last few items are relatively disturbing, and oftentimes bring the newborn to his or her peak of excitement, the opportunity usually presents itself to observe self-quieting behavior and what techniques, if any, are needed by the examiner to soothe the crying infant. If, after 15 seconds, the newborn cannot bring himself or herself down to a lower state of arousal, the examiner does of course console the baby, albeit in a prescribed, orderly, and additive manner (Worobey, Laub, & Schilmoeller, 1983). Consolability efforts are implemented sequentially from the distal stimulation inherent in using the face and voice, through restraining the infant's arms, up to simultaneously holding, rocking, and talking to the infant.

It is worth emphasizing that while the above procedures are being implemented, the examiner must simultaneously be making note of any smiles, startles, tremulousness, changes in skin color, and hand-mouth facility, as well as continuously monitoring activity level and states of arousal. Such considerations serve as a reminder of the difficulty in administering the examination, and why training and ultimately certification are so critical.

SCORING OF THE EXAMINATION

Detailed definitions for each point on every scale have been formulated, tested, and revised based on years of research with the instrument. However, unlike a traditional inventory, the examination does not lend itself to a total summary score. For one reason, the infant's organizational *processes* are of interest, rather than a viewing of the neonate as a finished product. Second, the clusters of behaviors that the examination taps provide more information than would a single numerical outcome.

To this end, a variety of approaches exist for summarizing the contents of the examination, with three methods utilized most frequently. They are the nonparametric approach (Adamson, Als, Tronick, & Brazelton, 1975), the factor-analytic approach (Kaye, 1978), and the conceptual-empirical clustering approach (Jacobson, Fein, Jacobson, & Schwartz, 1984; Lester et al., 1982). Although the Lester et al. (1982) clusters are proving to be the most fruitful from a research perspective, the a priori approach formulated by Adamson et al. (1975) may be best suited for obtaining a clinical sense of the newborn's organization, and sharing these impressions with parents (Worobey, 1987).

This a priori approach does not depend on interval scale coding, normality of distribution, or linear relationships, yet it includes all of the information in the NBAS and is quite useful for describing individual newborn performance. The items are grouped into four dimensions: *interactive processes, motoric processes,* organizational responses as related to *state control,* and organizational responses as related to physiological *responses to stress* (Als et al., 1979). Qualitative information is used from each item to produce a single score for each dimension to reflect optimal, normal, or inadequate performance (Adamson et al., 1975). While a conceptually meaningful profile may be constructed for each newborn, it remains for further research to determine if newborns labeled as inadequate indeed go on to develop abnormally (Brazelton et al., 1987). Again, the necessity of repeated assessments is obvious.

STUDIES WITH HIGH-RISK FAMILIES

Although the NBAS was developed in order to assess the healthy, full-term neonate, it has been used in an increasing number of investigations to examine the effects on newborn behavior of a wide variety of risk factors, ranging from prematurity to maternal substance abuse. Two recent reviews describe the use of the NBAS in assessing the status of high-risk infants and their families (Brazelton et al., 1987; Horowitz & Linn, 1984), so the present discussion will simply highlight, where possible, the consensus of findings relative to a particular risk factor.

Prematurity

Early efforts at assessing the behavior of the preterm neonate revealed that responsivity and attention were lower for low-birth-weight infants than for full-term infants (e.g., Lester, Emory, Hoffman, & Eitzman, 1976). In an intriguing comparative investigation, Field and her colleagues (Field et al., 1978) found postmature newborns (i.e., 42 weeks' gestation) to be as inferior in interactive and motoric processes as were the preterm newborns they studied. Recently, Tynan (1986) found poorer stability of state and interactive processes in his low-birth-weight sample.

Despite the face validity of such results, the use of the NBAS in its original form with preterm infants is deemed as inappropriate. Too much is expected of the fragile infant, when one considers that recovery must precede organization. This recognition has led to the development of nine additional descriptors that supplement the core of behavioral items. Drawn from the work of the Boston (Als, Lester, Tronick, & Brazelton, 1982) and Kansas (Horowitz et al., 1978) groups, these supplementary items attempt to summarize the quality of the newborn's responsiveness, the cost to him or her of responding, and the amount of input necessary from the examiner to organize his or her responses (Brazelton et al., 1987). As of this writing, the items are preliminary and optional, although future work may bear out their ability to elucidate the unique behavioral patterns of the premature infant (Brazelton, 1984).

Even with these qualifiers, the scale should not be used before the infant is 36 weeks of gestational age or until a fragile infant is off supports and in room air. Indeed, one might prefer to wait until the preterm infant is ready to be discharged home (Tronick, Scanlon, & Scanlon, 1985). At that time, and as discussed below, a demonstration to the parents of the infant's capabilities serves as a critical intervention. As before, the reader is urged to consult the manual for further descriptive and scoring information (Brazelton, 1984).

Smallness for Dates

A number of studies have looked at the performance of infants who, although born full term and apparently healthy, were underweight for their length at birth. Als, Tronick, Adamson, and Brazelton (1976), for example, found such infants to score lower than normal full-term infants in interactive processes, motoric processes, and reflexes. Other work with underweight infants has since replicated these findings, and extended the affected domains to reduced state control and inadequate responses to stress (Zeskind, 1981). Because fetal malnutrition is the likely culprit in underweight outcomes, the depressed NBAS scores across all behavioral clusters provide additional evidence for the importance of prenatal care and dietary practices during pregnancy (Lester, Garcia-Coll, Valcarcel, Hoffman, & Brazelton, 1986).

Jaundice (ictericia)

The behavioral organization of newborns with elevated bilirubin levels who receive phototherapy has been examined with the NBAS in two studies. While some small but significant differences in alertness and orientation have been found between jaundiced and control neonates, and favor the latter group (Nelson & Horowitz, 1982), the impact of jaundice and phototherapy may be interactive. That is, newborns with jaundice who received phototherapy have displayed diminished alertness, social responsivity, and consolability as late as 10 days after its termination, in comparison to their jaundiced peers who did not receive treatment (Telzrow, Snyder, Tronick, Als, & Brazelton, 1980).

Drugs and Alcohol

While the effects of obstetric medication may only emerge in combination with other perinatal variables (Lester et al., 1982; Woodson & DaCosta-Woodson, 1980), the effects of narcotics on the behavior of newborns can clearly be traced to addiction in their mothers. Increased irritability, reduced alertness, and depressed orientation supplement the real narcotic withdrawal the newborns of such mothers undergo (Kron, Finnegan, Kaplan, Litt, & Phoenix, 1975). Despite methadone treatment to end heroin addiction, affected newborns exhibit decreased orientation, rapid lability of states, more tremulousness, poorer motor maturity, and increased irritability (Chasnoff, Hatcher, & Burns, 1982; Soule, Standley, Copans, & Davis, 1974).

In a similar fashion, infants born to alcoholic mothers exhibit poorer habituation and lower arousal than do infants of nonalcoholic mothers (Streissguth, Barr, & Martin, 1983), even after adjusting for nutrition, caffeine use, and smoking. And smoking, by itself, during pregnancy seems to adversely affect habituation, orientation, and autonomic stability in the neonate (Picone, Allen, Olsen, & Ferris, 1982).

Maternal Diabetes

Yogman, Cole, Als, and Lester (1982) found that newborns of diabetic mothers, delivered by elective cesarean section, had poorer scores on the orientation, motoric, and autonomic stability clusters of the NBAS than did a control group of healthy newborns who were also delivered by cesarean. Because cesarean delivery, even when controlling for obstetric medication, does not appear to reduce NBAS performance (Field & Widmayer, 1980), the depressed performance of the Yogman et al. (1982) sample must be attributed to the diabetic status of the mothers.

Environmental Toxins

In a promising model for future research, Jacobson, Jacobson, Fein, Schwartz, and Dowler (1984) studied the effects of maternal exposure to environmental toxins on neonatal behavior. Maternal exposure to polychlorinated biphenyls (PCBs) was measured from umbilical cord blood, and indirectly through the mothers' reports of having ingested contaminated fish. The consumption of contaminated fish during pregnancy predicted worrisome performance on the NBAS, with range of state, reflexes, and autonomic stability all adversely affected by PCB exposure.

USE OF THE NBAS AS AN INTERVENTION DEVICE

Since its initial publication in 1973, a number of investigations have employed the NBAS as a vehicle for providing new parents with information about their normal newborns. By helping parents to gauge their newborn's readability, predictability, and responsivity (Goldberg, 1977), developmental researchers and health care professionals have documented the efficacy of NBAS-based interventions in facilitating parent-infant interaction (Brazelton et al., 1987; Worobey, 1985). Such educational interventions allow for the communication of NBAS information at one of three levels, in terms of parental involvement with the newborn (Worobey, 1987).

At the lower level, the newborn's performance on the NBAS assessment is shared with the caregiver by means of a verbal description following the administration of the examination. At the intermediate level, the caregiver observes the actual assessment, with the examiner attempting to draw out the neonate's best performance, addressing the observer as appropriate to highlight various procedures and newborn behaviors as they are demonstrated. At the highest level, the caregiver is actually guided through an NBAS-based interaction with the newborn, while the role of the examiner is more facilitative than directive (Worobey & Belsky, 1982). In watching parents with their newborns, the questions they volunteer as they experience such interactions can further magnify the effectiveness of the intervention. The NBAS thus serves as a departure point for the caregiver and infant, with the examiner sharing in the encounter between the competent newborn and the individual who is and will continue to be the most important force in his or her life (Worobey & Brazelton, 1986).

In the earliest studies the NBAS was discussed with or demonstrated for middle-income parents, with mild improvements resulting in their attitudes and behaviors. In the second wave of studies the NBAS has been employed with other than normative populations, and results indicate that premature newborns, adolescent mothers, and families at lower socioeconomic levels can improve their interactions, with subsequent improvements in infant development as well (Worobey, 1985). It has been shown that NBAS clusters, as component parts of more extensive interventions aimed at improving parental behavior, can be extremely effective with populations at risk (e.g., Rauh, Achenbach, Nurcombe, Howell, & Teti, 1988; Soule et al., 1974). However, the full-length NBAS has shown itself to be useful as a script for early contacts within at-risk families.

Premature Infants

With a sample of preterm newborns, Eyler (1979) compared the results of repeated NBAS demonstrations for mothers to results in an equivalent control group. While the demonstrations had no apparent effect on maternal attitudes or infant capabilities over the first month postpartum, the intervention did result in more visiting and calling by mothers, as well as more looking at and talking to the infants. Widmayer and Field (1980) employed the

NBAS, and an adaptation of the examination designed for maternal use, with mothers of healthy preterm infants. One month after the NBAS itself was administered to all the newborns in their sample, mothers of the preterm infants (who additionally completed the maternal questionnaire) were different from all other comparison groups. They interacted more, tended to gaze more, and used more physical activity in playing with their infants; in addition, the infants gazed back at their mothers more, vocalized more, and displayed more animate features than did those in the other preterm groups. As in work with low-risk samples (e.g., Myers & Worobey, 1986), the opportunity for these mothers to actively elicit responses from their preterm newborns may have been the critical feature of the intervention, because the mothers who were denied observing the examiner-administered NBAS, but who nevertheless completed the maternal questionnaire, seemed quite similar to the true experimental group.

Dolby, English, and Warren (1982) also used the questionnaire version of the NBAS in their investigation, and additionally shared a videotape of the examiner's NBAS assessment of the preterm infants with the still-hospitalized mothers. Mothers who watched the videotaped NBAS and completed the questionnaire were more responsive to their infants' needs, more affectionate, and more reciprocating in play interactions a full 6 months later. Although she did not follow her infants as long, Martin's (1985) results may be more impressive, because mothers who were guided in interaction with their preterm infants via the NBAS displayed more gaze behavior, vocalizations, and contingent responding, among other improvements, while their infants scored better in physical activity, facial expressions, and fussiness.

In a recent report by Rauh et al. (1988), the results of an early intervention program for low-birth-weight infants was described. Critical to their transactional intervention was the inclusion of NBAS demonstrations to emphasize the infant's potential for self-regulation and interaction, as well as the presence of homeostatic reflexes and motor behaviors. Maternal improvements in self-confidence, satisfaction, and perceptions of the infants' temperaments were impressive, yet the most striking results were evident in the infants themselves. While the control group of low-birth-weight infants was equivalent to the experimental low-birth-weight and full-term control groups through 12 months, their mental performance declined with age. In contrast, the experimental group kept pace with the full-term control infants at 3 years, and matched their mental performance at the 4-year assessment.

Although they may not qualify as premature, full-term but low-birth-weight infants (i.e., those below the 10th percentile for weight) have been found to be developmentally at risk, and to present parents with caregiving problems. Recently, Nugent, Hoffman, and Brazelton (1986) found that despite the absence of any improvement in orientation over the first 2 weeks postpartum for such babies, their interactive scores improved over the next 2 weeks if their mothers received the NBAS-based intervention, with a concomitant decrease in anxiety by the mothers.

Low Socioeconomic Status

The impact of lower socioeconomic status (SES) is sometimes confounded in reports of premature outcomes, by virtue of the correlation between at-risk pregnancies and low maternal or family income. The Widmayer and Field (1980) sample, described above, was comprised of low-income mothers of preterm infants who received and were helped with the NBAS interventions. Other work in using the NBAS as an intervention device has targeted low-SES families specifically, and has shown, at a minimum, an improvement in maternal visual regard as early as 2 hours after treatment (McLaughlin, Drake, Deni, & Constantini, 1983). A recent report of the effects of an NBAS demonstration study had greater success, with heightened mother-infant reciprocity 2 weeks after the intervention (Poley-Strobel & Beckman, 1987).

Adolescent Maternity

While her infant may be born full term and healthy, the teenage mother may be at risk for other reasons, not the least of which may be her strained relationship with her own mother in response to her pregnancy (Townsend & Worobey, 1987). To the degree that NBAS interventions may be effective with adolescent mothers, they should at least be considered (Clarke & Tesh, 1980). Indeed, the Widmayer and Field (1980) mothers of preterm infants, already described as low in SES, were teenagers as well. In another well-designed study of young but poor single mothers, Olsen, Olsen, Pernice, and Bloom (1980) assigned mothers to an NBAS demonstration group or one of two controls. All mothers were later observed in feeding their newborns, with the demonstration mothers being more sensitive to their infants' cues and more fostering of cognitive and emotional growth. On a questionnaire that was also completed, the demonstration group indicated a greater awareness of newborn capabilities and, again, infant cues. While outcome measures were limited to the day following treatment, the consistency across the blind observations and the maternal reports speaks well for the benefits of observing the NBAS.

CONCLUSION

The assessment of an infant is a multidimensional opportunity—for diagnosis, for prediction, and for entering and influencing the parent-infant system (Brazelton, 1983). The NBAS provides this opportunity at a time that is much earlier than was previously thought possible. Through the careful efforts of countless researchers and clinicians the NBAS has become a powerful tool for evaluating the status of the newborn. Despite the progress that has been made in refining the dimensions of the NBAS for assessing the full-term normal neonate, however, the ultimate usefulness of the NBAS in diagnosing, predicting, and intervening with high-risk infants must be documented through further research.

Some good work has given us a strong foundation. With premature infants, for example, we have learned much about their fragile status, their sensitive abilities, and how taxing yet valuable the NBAS examination may be in anticipating their further progress toward normal development. To evaluate such progress we need repeated assessments (Brazelton et al., 1987). Parents of a premature infant have a real opportunity to understand their baby's recovery processes through observing the infant on these repeated examinations. Their own recovery from the initial grief process can parallel the progress they witness in their infant (Brazelton & Nugent, 1987). However, we must learn more about the condition of the ill neonate, the underweight infant, and the newborn exposed to disease or poisoning through the mother's system, and, as with the preterm infant, repeated assessments are the only fair test of recovery.

With respect to intervention, we have learned that the effectiveness of an NBAS demonstration may depend upon the level at which the mother (and father) participate in the assessment. We have learned in our own work that parental participation may come from passive observation or active handling of the baby. It is enhanced by the observer's attempt to include the parent in understanding the baby's organizational efforts. In essence, the baby is used as a way to make the relationship. As the baby is brought from one state to another, as the newborn participates in habituation, orientation, and other behaviors, the examiner has an opportunity to engage the parent through an explanation of the neonatal processes that are involved.

By sharing this behavior and the examiner's understanding of its meaning, the parents have the opportunity to ask questions, to air their own concerns, and to model on the examiner's handling of the baby. We have found that the baby's behavior becomes a powerful bridge to a relationship with the parent, because all new parents are hungry for an understanding of their new job in relating to their infant. By sharing the baby's organized behavior, the professional is taken out of the teaching role, which is sometimes patronizing, and assumes a more powerful role of sharing the parents' concerns and eagerness to understand their baby.

We know that such interventions may also be more effective with some families than others, but we must learn more about their ability to assist the parent who is at risk in a number of spheres. We have come far in gauging the individual assets of the neonate, whether normal or high risk. We can identify the unique strengths of the mother, whether well adjusted or overwhelmed. We must work with each partner in the family system—the newborn, the mother, the father—so as to empower the parents of the fragile infant with the belief that they will make a difference (Worobey & Brazelton, 1986).

REFERENCES

Adamson, L., Als, H., Tronick, E., & Brazelton, T.B. (1975). *A-priori profiles for the Brazelton Neonatal Behavioral Assessment Scale*. Unpublished manuscript, Child Development Unit, Children's Hospital, Boston.

Als, H., Lester, B.M., Tronick, E., & Brazelton, T.B. (1982). Towards a research instrument for the assessment of preterm infants' behavior. In H.E. Fitzgerald, B.M. Lester, & M. Yogman (Eds.), *Theory and research in behavioral pediatrics* (pp. 35–63). New York: Plenum.

Als, H., Tronick, E., Adamson, L., & Brazelton, T.B. (1976). The behavior of the full-term yet underweight newborn. *Developmental Medicine and Child Neurology, 18,* 590.

Als, H., Tronick, E., Lester, B.M., & Brazelton, T.B. (1979). Specific neonatal measures: The Brazelton Neonatal Behavioral Assessment Scale. In J. Osofsky (Ed.), *Handbook of infant development* (pp. 185–215). New York: John Wiley.

Brazelton, T.B. (1973). *Neonatal Behavioral Assessment Scale*. Clinics in Developmental Medicine, No. 50. Philadelphia: J.B. Lippincott.

Brazelton, T.B. (1979). Behavioral competence of the newborn infant. *Seminars in Perinatology, 3,* 35–44.

Brazelton, T.B. (1983). Assessment techniques for enhancing infant development. In J.D. Call, E. Galenson, & R.L. Tyson (Eds.), *Frontiers of infant psychiatry* (pp. 347–361). New York: Basic Books.

Brazelton, T.B. (Ed.) (1984). *Neonatal Behavioral Assessment Scale* (2nd ed.). Clinics in Developmental Medicine, No. 88. Philadelphia: J.B. Lippincott.

Brazelton, T.B., & Nugent, J.K. (1987). Neonatal assessment as intervention. In H. Rauh & H.C. Steinhausen (Eds.), *Psychobiology and early development* (pp. 215–229). Amsterdam: North Holland.

Brazelton, T.B., Nugent, J.K., & Lester, B.M. (1987). Neonatal behavioral assessment scale. In J. Osofsky (Ed.), *Handbook of infant development* (2nd ed.) (pp. 780–817). New York: John Wiley.

Chasnoff, I.J., Hatcher, R., & Burns, W.J. (1982). Polydrug- and methadone-addicted newborns: A continuum of impairment? *Pediatrics, 70,* 210–213.

Clarke, B.A., & Tesh, E. (1980, April). *Promoting development in infants of teenage mothers*. Paper presented at the meetings of the Robert Wood Johnson Foundation, Nashville.

Dolby, R., English, B., & Warren, B. (1982, April). *Brazelton demonstrations for mothers and fathers: Impact on the developing parent-infant relationship*. Paper presented at the International Conference on Infant Studies, Austin.

Eyler, F.D. (1979, April). *Assessment and intervention with mothers and their premature newborns*. Paper presented at the Biennial Meetings of the Society for Research in Child Development, San Francisco.

Field, T., Hallock, N., Ting, G., Dempsey, J., Dabiri, C., & Shuman, H.H. (1978). A first-year follow-up of high-risk infants: Formulating a cumulative risk index. *Child Development, 49,* 119–131.

Field, T., & Widmayer, S.M. (1980). Developmental follow-up of infants delivered by Cesarean-section and general anesthesia. *Infant Behavior and Development, 3,* 253–264.

Francis, P.L., Self, P.A., & Horowitz, F.D. (1987). The behavioral assessment of the neonate: An overview. In J. Osofsky (Ed.), *Handbook of infant development* (2nd ed., pp. 723–779). New York: John Wiley.

Goldberg, S. (1977). Social competence in infancy: A model of parent-infant interaction. *Merrill-Palmer Quarterly, 23,* 163–178.

Horowitz, F.D., & Linn, P.L. (1982). The Neonatal Behavioral Assessment Scale: Assessing the behavioral repertoire of the newborn infant. In M. Wolraich & D.K. Routh (Eds.), *Advances in developmental and behavioral pediatrics* (pp. 223–256). Greenwich, CT: JAI.

Horowitz, F.D., & Linn, P.L. (1984). Use of the NBAS in research. In T.B. Brazelton (Ed.), *Neonatal Behavioral Assessment Scale* (2nd ed., pp. 97–104). Clinics in Developmental Medicine, No. 88. Philadelphia: J.B. Lippincott.

Horowitz, F.D., Sullivan, J.W., & Linn, P. (1978). Stability and instability in the newborn infant: The quest for elusive threads. In A.J. Sameroff (Ed.) Organization and stability of newborn behavior: A commentary on the Brazelton Neonatal Behavioral Assessment Scale (pp. 29–45). *Monographs of the Society for Research in Child Development, 43.*

Jacobson, J.L., Fein, G.G., Jacobson, S.W., & Schwartz, P.M. (1984). Factors and clusters for the Brazelton Scale: An investigation of the dimensions of neonatal behavior. *Developmental Psychology, 20,* 339–353.

Jacobson, J.L., Jacobson, S., Fein, G.G., Schwartz, P.M., & Dowler, J.K. (1984). Prenatal exposure to an environmental toxin: A test of the multiple effects model. *Developmental Psychology, 20,* 523–532.

Kaye, K. (1978). Discriminating among normal infants by multivariate analysis of Brazelton scores. In A.J. Sameroff (Ed.) Organization and stability of newborn behavior: A commentary on the Brazelton Neonatal Behavioral Assessment Scale (pp. 60–80). *Monographs of the Society for Research in Child Development, 43.*

Kron, R.E., Finnegan, L.P., Kaplan, B.L., Litt, M., & Phoenix, M.D. (1975). The assessment of behavioral change in infants undergoing narcotic withdrawal: Comparative data from clinical and objective methods. *Addictive Diseases, 2,* 257–275.

Lancioni, G.E., Horowitz, F.D., & Sullivan, J.W. (1980). The NBAS-K: I. A study of its stability and structure over the first month of life. *Infant Behavior and Development, 3,* 341–359.

Lester, B.M., Als, H., & Brazelton, T.B. (1982). Regional obstetric anesthesia and newborn behavior: A reanalysis toward synergistic effects. *Child Development, 53,* 687–692.

Lester, B.M., Emory, E.K., Hoffman, J., & Eitzman, D.V. (1976). A multivariate study of the effects of high-risk factors on performance on the Brazelton Neonatal Assessment Scale. *Child Development, 47,* 515–517.

Lester, B.M., Garcia-Coll, C., Valcarcel, M., Hoffman, J., & Brazelton, T.B. (1986). Effects of atypical patterns of fetal growth on newborn behavior. *Child Development, 57,* 11–19.

Martin, P.P. (1985, April). *Hospital-based intervention with mothers of preterms.* Paper presented at the Biennial Meetings of the Society for Research in Child Development, Toronto.

McLaughlin, F.J., Drake, D.I., Deni, R., & Constantini, F.D. (1983, April). *Sequential analysis of maternal behavior recorded after passive exposure to Brazelton Assessment procedures.* Paper presented at the Biennial Meetings of the Society for Research in Child Development, Detroit.

Myers, B.J., & Worobey, J. (1986, April). *Active vs. passive intervention strategies with low-risk families.* In J. Worobey (Chair), The NBAS as an intervention device: Issues of who, what, when, where and why. Symposium at the International Conference on Infant Studies, Los Angeles.

Nelson, C.A., & Horowitz, F.D. (1982). The short-term behavioral sequelae of neonatal jaundice treated with phototherapy. *Infant Behavior and Development, 5,* 289–299.

Nugent, J.K., Hoffman, J., & Brazelton, T.B. (1986, April). *An NBAS-based intervention with full term LBW infants.* In J. Worobey (Chair), The NBAS as an intervention device: Issues of who, what, when, where and why. Symposium at the International Conference on Infant Studies, Los Angeles.

Nugent, J.K., & Sepkoski, C. (1984). The training of NBAS examiners. In T.B. Brazelton (Ed.), *Neonatal Behavioral Assessment Scale* (2nd ed., pp. 78–84). Clinics in Developmental Medicine, No. 88. Philadelphia: J.B. Lippincott.

Olsen, R., Olsen, G., Pernice, J., & Bloom, K. (1980, April). *The use of the Brazelton Assessment as an intervention with high risk mothers.* Paper presented at the Ambulatory Pediatric Association Annual Meeting, San Francisco.

Picone, T.A., Allen, L.H., Olsen, P.N., & Ferris, M.E. (1982). Pregnancy outcome in North American women: Effects of diet, cigarette smoking, stress, and weight gain on placentas, and on neonatal physical and behavioral characteristics. *American Journal of Clinical Nutrition, 36,* 1214–1224.

Poley-Strobel, B.A., & Beckman, C.A. (1987). The effects of a teaching-modeling intervention on early mother-infant reciprocity. *Infant Behavior and Development, 10,* 467–476.

Prechtl, H.F., & Beintema, D. (1964). *The neurological examination of the full-term newborn infant.* Clinics in Developmental Medicine, No. 27. Oxford: Blackwell Scientific Publications Ltd.

Rauh, V.A., Achenbach, T., Nurcombe, B., Howell, C.T., & Teti, D.M. (1988). Minimizing adverse effects of low birthweight: Four-year results of an early intervention program. *Child Development, 59,* 544–553.

St. Clair, K.L. (1978). Neonatal assessment procedures: A historical review. *Child Development, 49,* 280–292.

Sameroff, A.J. (Ed.). (1978). Organization and stability of newborn behavior: A commentary on the Brazelton Neonatal Behavioral Assessment

Scale. *Monographs of the Society for Research in Child Development, 43*.

Soule, A.B., Standley, K., Copans, S.A., & Davis, M. (1974). Clinical uses of the Brazelton Scale. *Pediatrics, 54*, 583–586.

Streissguth, A.P., Barr, H.M., & Martin, D.C. (1983). Maternal alcohol use and neonatal habituation assessed with the Brazelton Scale. *Child Development, 54*, 1109–1118.

Telzrow, R.W., Snyder, M., Tronick, E., Als, H., & Brazelton, T.B. (1980). The behavior of jaundiced infants undergoing phototherapy. *Developmental Medicine and Child Neurology, 22*, 317–326.

Townsend, J.K., & Worobey, J. (1987). Mother and daughter perceptions of their relationship: The influence of adolescent pregnancy status. *Adolescence, 22*, 487–496.

Tronick, E., Scanlon, K.B., & Scanlon, J.W. (1985). A comparative analysis of the validity of several approaches to the scoring of the behavior of the preterm infant. *Infant Behavior and Development, 8*, 395–411.

Tynan, W.D. (1986). Behavioral stability predicts morbidity and mortality in infants from a neonatal intensive care unit. *Infant Behavior and Development, 9*, 71–79.

Widmayer, S.M., & Field, T. (1980). Effects of Brazelton demonstrations on early interactions of preterm infants and their teenage mothers. *Infant Behavior and Development, 3*, 79–89.

Woodson, R.H., & DaCosta-Woodson, E.M. (1980). Covariates of analgesia in a clinical sample and their effect on the relationship between analgesia and infant behavior. *Infant Behavior and Development, 3*, 78–89.

Worobey, J. (1985). A review of Brazelton-based interventions to enhance parent-infant interaction. *Journal of Reproductive and Infant Psychology, 3*, 64–73.

Worobey, J. (1987). Employing the Brazelton Scale to influence mothering: A closer look. *Parenting Studies, 1*, 105–108.

Worobey, J., & Belsky, J. (1982). Employing the Brazelton Scale to influence mothering: An experimental comparison of three strategies. *Developmental Psychology, 18*, 736–743.

Worobey, J., & Brazelton, T.B. (1986). Experimenting with the family in the newborn period: A commentary. *Child Development, 57*, 1298–1300.

Worobey, J., Laub, K.W., & Schilmoeller, G.L. (1983). Maternal and paternal responses to infant distress. *Merrill-Palmer Quarterly, 79*, 33–45.

Yogman, M., Cole, P., Als, H., & Lester, B.M. (1982). Behavior of newborns of diabetic mothers. *Infant Behavior and Development, 5*, 331–340.

Zeskind, P.S. (1981). Behavioral dimensions and cry sounds of infants of differential fetal growth. *Infant Behavior and Development, 4*, 297–306.

4 Neuromotor Assessment

Lynette S. Chandler

Developmental studies have been a part of the professional literature since the 1920s, beginning with the study of normal growth and development and leading to the present-day eclectic contribution by developmentalists in many professions (Kopp & Krakow, 1983). In the arena of motor development, the primary impetus for research has been the need to prevent, detect, and ameliorate handicapping conditions (Piper, 1987). A second impetus has been the increased demand for accountability regarding the outcome of treatment. This demand has grown since the United States government has taken more responsibility for children as mandated by Public Laws 94-142 and 99-457, and as professionals have come to realize that there is a finite source of monies for the care of children. This demand has generated a renewed interest in the scientific application of evaluation techniques.

This need for accountability has resulted in the development of new assessment instruments and a reevaluation of older instruments. Assessment instruments can be neurological, developmental, or neurodevelopmental in their focus. Towen (1976) stated that "the neurological assessment should try to relate findings to the quality of underlying neural mechanisms" (p. 4), whereas the developmental exam evaluates functional or adaptive ability. The combination of these two perspectives of movement in the form of the neurodevelopmental exam seems to yield the highest predictive validity, as noted below, but the relative contribution of each to detection and treatment is still unknown (Campbell & Wilhelm, 1985; Harris, Swanson, et al., 1984). The developmental and neurodevelopmental instruments describe the development of infants and children in the first year and a half of life, a time when sensorimotor development is proceeding rapidly. Neurodevelopmental exams will be the primary focus of this discussion on assessment, although two developmental assessments are also discussed.

Eight instruments, which together serve to evaluate the motor development of infants through the age span of the viable preterm infant to the 3-year-old child, will be discussed in this chapter. No one instrument serves the wide range of need for this age group. Instruments that evaluate the neurodevelopmental status of the infant have been designed to assess preterm infants (infants born at a gestational age of less than 38 weeks) as well as term infants. The Neurological Assessment of the Preterm and Full-Term Infant (Dubowitz & Dubowitz, 1981) and its sibling exam, the Neonatal Neurobehavioral Examiniation (Morgan, Koch, Lee, & Aldag, 1988), are two such tests. The Movement Assessment of Infants (MAI) (Chandler, Andrews, & Swanson, 1980) is used to assess infants throughout the first year of life through a combined neurological and developmental evaluation. The Chandler Movement Assessment of Infants–Screening Test (CMAI-ST) (Chandler, Andrews, & Swanson, 1983) is used to screen infants in the first year of life who otherwise have not been noted to be at risk. The CMAI-ST was developed from the longer parent test, the MAI, and retains the neurological and developmental components. The Milani-Comparetti Motor Development Screening Test as revised by Trembath (1977) is also a combined neurological and developmental test, but spans the first 2 years of life. A unique and valuable instrument that combines a neurological assessment with hand function up to 15 months is the Erhardt Developmental Prehension Assessment (Erhardt, 1982). The final two tests are used to assess developmental outcome and do not include a neurological component. The Bayley Scales of Infant Development by Bayley (1969) provide three scales for testing infants from the newborn period until 30 months of age; only the Psychomotor Developmental Index (PDI) of the Bayley will be discussed for its contribution to motor assessment (see Gibbs, this volume, for coverage of the Mental Development Index). Finally, the Peabody Developmental Motor Scales by Folio and Dubose (1983) is an instrument designed to assess the development of gross and fine motor volitional movement in children from the newborn period to 6.9 years of age.

Medical risk exams, such as the well-known Apgar (Apgar, 1953), and neurobehavioral exams, such as those written by Brazelton (1984) and Als (1986), form an important content area when evaluating motor behaviors. A description and discussion of the Neonatal Behavioral Assessment Scale is presented by Worobey and Brazelton in this volume. Professionals interested in a comprehensive review of some of the more recent trends in neurobehavioral assessment may wish to avail themselves of the review article by Gorski, Lewkowicz, and Huntington (1987).

SENSITIVITY AND SPECIFICITY OF MOTOR ASSESSMENTS

Before turning to a description and discussion of the instruments themselves, it is important to introduce some issues related to movement assessment. The goal of performing an early evaluation is to assist infants and their families through early diagnosis and intervention as necessary and as mandated by PL 99-457. This assumes that we are assessing the appropriate population of infants and assumes that examiners, using the instruments described below, can correctly detect disabled infants. Unfortunately, most neurodevelopmental and developmental assessments yield high numbers of infants with movement deficits who are not identified or infants who do not have movement deficits who are incorrectly identified. Therefore, the examiner should be aware of the sensitivity and the specificity of the assessments that he or she is using and should interpret results of the assessments with caution.

The sensitivity and specificity of a movement assessment instrument are measures of the validity of the instrument. The sensitivity of an instrument measures the ability of the instrument to accurately detect a movement dysfunction. The specificity of an instrument measures the ability of the instrument to accurately detect which infants do not have a movement dysfunction. Thus an instrument has to be sensitive to movement dysfunction and still be able to specify which infants are normal (see Table 1). Results of sensitivity and specificity studies for different neurological and developmental assessments are given in Table 2. What is missing from the table are the data as to the population of infants tested (term or preterm infants, healthy or fragile infants), the age at which the infants were tested (the older the infant at the time of testing the greater the general accuracy), and the level of the risk score set by the researchers. The table is simply illustrative of

Table 1. Formulas for the calculation of sensitivity and specificity[a]

Assessment results	Outcome	
	Disorder	Normal
Referral	Correct referral (A)	Overreferral (B)
Nonreferral	Underreferral (C)	Correct nonreferral (D)

[a]Sensitivity = [A/(A+C)] × 100
　　　　　　= percentage of correct identifications of infants with a disorder.
　Specificity = [D/(B+D)] × 100
　　　　　　= percentage of correct identifications of normal infants.

Table 2. Reported sensitivity and specificity scores for various assessment instruments.

Instrument	Source[a]	N	Sensitivity	Specificity
Ultrasound	1	111	78%	84%
Neurological exam (Dubowitz & Dubowitz, 1981)	1	111	67%	61%
Combined ultrasound/ neurological exam	1	111	100%	57%
Movement Assessment of Infants	2	66	83%	78%
Bayley Psychomotor Index	2	66	17%	97%

[a]1, Stewart, Hope, Hamilton, Costello, Baudin, Bradford, Amiel-Tison, and Reynolds (1988); 2, Swanson (1988).

the problem of sensitivity versus specificity. Generally, if examiners do not want to miss an infant with a movement deficit, they set a rigorous standard for passing. As a result, many infants who are normal are identified as having a movement deficit. Thus a high sensitivity score frequently yields a low specificity score or vice versa. It is still unclear whether the greater cost is to the handicapped infant who is assessed as normal or the normal infant who is thought to have a motor dysfunction. The former infant does not begin an early treatment program; the latter infant's parents worry needlessly about their child.

The reasons for the questionable sensitivity and specificity scores of neurological, neurodevelopmental, and developmental assessments are many; four factors are discussed here. First, *the greatest variability seems to lie within the infants themselves.* Infant assessments appear to be strongly influenced by behavioral state (Brazelton, 1984; Dubowitz, 1988; Prechtl, 1977), time of feedings, wellness, gestational age at birth, and many other extraneous factors. The Als (1986) synactive model would suggest that examiners need to assist the infants in the control of their autonomic nervous system (temperature, blood pressure, heart rate), motor system (tremors), and state (sleep to awake to agitated state) in order to allow for reliable testing of the infant's ability to attend to other tasks. Given the magnitude of the problems of premature infants and sick infants, this control is not always possible.

A second confounding factor is the *variation of normal movement* observed among infants. Data collected by Chandler (1988) indicate that variation among normal infants is extensive even from item to item; given an assessment with multiple items the possible combinations of normal are infinite. An example of this variation is crawling on all fours; 17% of the children studied by Chandler accomplished this milestone at 6 months, but it was not until 11 months of age that 100% of the children demonstrated crawling. The prerequisite skill of creeping forward on the stomach gives the examiner some indication that the skill is emerging. However, the range for skill development is from 5 months to 11 months, even among normal children (Fig. 1). Thus it is important to use an instrument that accounts for

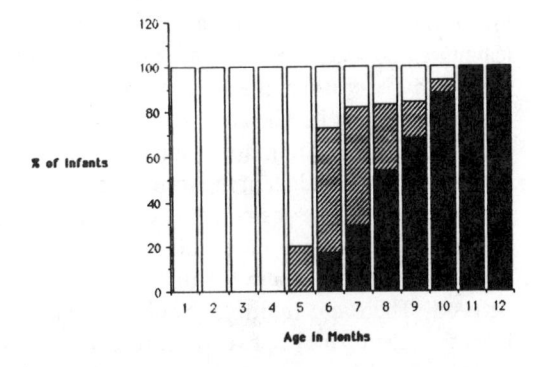

Figure 1. Percentage of infants crawling on all fours or creeping on stomach for each month of the first year of life. *Open,* no progression; *diagonal slashes,* creeping; *solid,* crawling.

the variation of normal movement, that is, an instrument that has established norms. Although many developmental assessments have norms for the first year of life, only the CMAI-ST combines neurological and developmental items with established norms for healthy term infants for the first year of life (Chandler, 1988). No instrument has been used to norm the development of the normal preterm infant before the age of 40 weeks' gestation, apparently because of the fragile nature of that population. The normal development of the preterm infant after that age has not been systematically documented. Swanson (1988) has established norms for preterm infants on the MAI at 4 and 8 months corrected age. She also has data on the term infant at those same ages.

The third confounding factor speaks to the *discrepancy between the environment of the researchers* who have authored assessment instruments *and the environment of the professionals* who are using the instruments. The efficient experimental design for the researcher who is trying to develop an evaluation instrument that is both sensitive to movement disorders and specific to normal movement would include testing of infants in an environment where a disproportionate number of infants would demonstrate a movement disorder. For example, if one assessed 1,000 4-month-old infants from the general population of infants, only 1 of the infants would have a neurological deficit. However, if one assessed 1,000 4-month-old infants from a population of infants leaving a neonatal intensive care unit, perhaps as many as 50 or 100 of the infants would have a neurological deficit. The cost of evaluating the instrument in a community environment is rarely within the budget of the researcher. With the exception of the instruments designed for the neonatal intensive care unit (NICU), this environment is not where the instruments will be used. There are multiple problems arising from the discrepancy between the research environment where an assessment is designed and the community environment where it will be used. It is possible, in fact probable, that the two populations of infants are distinct. Extensive useful data have been accumulated on the development of normal and abnormal movement in preterm infants, but the generalization of this information to term infants needs to be evaluated. It is also true that the average professional in the community does not have the time to spend on an extensive assessment of each full-term infant—time that is available to the researcher. The reality of the clinic situation is that professionals adapt the longer instruments to their use, thus bringing into question the validity of the assessment instrument. In addition, the intended use of the instrument may be distinct both from researcher to professional and from professional to professional. For example, the early evaluations of the medically unstable infant are correctly intended to give the physician information upon which to make critical and immediate decisions that will in turn affect the morbidity and mortality of the infant. The physician may look at the posture or the alertness of an infant to determine whether ultrasonography should be performed to rule out intracranial hemorrhage (Shankaran, Slovis, Bedard, & Poland, 1982). In the medically stable infant the physician, physical therapist, or occupational therapist may note the same behaviors as indicators of developmental status. The therapist would also be using the assessment information to design a protocol to enhance normal development. The population of infants to be assessed and the intended use of the information from the testing does have an impact upon the relative usefulness of the assessment instrument to the researcher versus the professional in the community.

The last factor confounding the accuracy of assessment may still lie with the *common problems of instrumentation, validity, and reliability* of the various instruments. In general, these problems seem to dominate the neurological and neurodevelopmental tests. Neurological exams are performed on fragile infants who cannot endure the more rigorous demands of research such as test-retest reliability. Also, the more medically oriented authors have not, until recently, been given the time from their critical medical responsibilities to document their vast knowledge of assessment. In addition, the body of knowledge needed for research, so common to some disciplines, has not had the priority in the education of medical professionals. These psychometric problems are documented within the discussion for each instrument.

ORGANIZATION FOR LEARNING MOVEMENT ASSESSMENTS

The eight instruments to be discussed below include those that predominantly assess developmental status, those that assess neurodevelopmental status, and those that assess neurological status. Some of these instruments are designed to evaluate movement of older children and typically include a large proportion of developmental items. Others are designed for infants and preterm infants and include a large proportion of neurological items. This is not surprising when one realizes that the major developmental milestones of movement (e.g., walking and the fine pincer grasp) have emerged for most children by 1–1.5 years. Thus, children between 1 and 3 years are generally evaluated on their increasingly sophisticated use of the components of movement, which have already been established. By contrast, children under 1 year of age and those infants born prematurely are generally evaluated on the development of the components of movement and the presence of abnormal patterns of movement. This diversity of focus requires increased professional expertise and sophistication. Instruments that focus largely on developmental milestones are easier to administer in that target children are generally older and their health status less fragile or, at least, more clearly defined. Neurological assessments are more often administered to younger children and infants, who are often medically fragile. Thus, having the medical skill required "to do no harm" to the infants and young children becomes a professional obligation not simply limited to the physician.

INSTRUMENTS FOR ASSESSING MOVEMENT DEVELOPMENT

Peabody Developmental Motor Scales (PDMS) (Folio & Fewell, 1983)

Purpose and Target Population

This instrument is designed to evaluate gross motor and fine motor development from birth to 6.9 years of age. The gross motor section is subdivided into the five skill areas of reflexes, balance, nonlocomotor, locomotor, and receipt and propulsion. The fine motor section is subdivided into the four areas of grasping, hand use, eye-hand coordination, and manual dexterity. This method of categorizing items into skill areas makes it possible for examiners to determine whether a given deficit is pervasive or confined to a particular skill. This division of sections into skill areas is helpful in interpreting test results and in planning intervention programs. Although the gross motor section does include a reflex skill area, the assessment is developmental rather than neurodevelopmental in substance. The authors designed the PDMS so that the information gained from the assessment would be used in program planning. To that end, the test kit includes a set of cards with programming suggestions.

Time to Administer

Each section of the PDMS, gross motor or fine motor, can be completed in less than 30 minutes; the entire test is completed in 45–60 minutes. The authors state that the two sections do not have to be administered in the same session, but suggest that the two sections be administered within 5 days of each other. The suggestion to administer the two sections separately is appropriate because children do tire when given both within the same hour. Although the PDMS is designed for use with an individual child, it can be set up for evaluation of groups of children. This latter format makes the PDMS a cost-effective evaluation instrument. The authors for example, report taking 1.75 hours to test 36 children on both scales.

Scoring and Interpretation

Each item of the PDMS is scored as a 0, 1, or 2, with 2 representing that the criteria have been met easily, 1 indicating that the criteria are not fully met, and 0 representing a failing response. The examiner determines a basal and a ceiling level. A raw score is then derived and converted to age-equivalent scores, developmental quotients, percentiles, and Z scores. These values greatly assist in the interpretation of the test, especially since the converted scores can be derived for each of the nine skill areas.

Training

The authors suggest that the test be administered at least three times as practice. An agreement reliability of 85% of the items should then be achieved by an experienced tester before he or she tests a child about whom there may be a concern. Since the test spans 6 years, it seems appropriate that that standard be set for any one age grouping.

Equipment

The test kit provides some of the required equipment. The remaining equipment is usually found in the standard setting for testing of motor development, although a tricycle, balance beam, and stopwatch could substantially add to the cost of administering this instrument.

Psychometric Qualities

The authors reported good interrater reliability of the PDMS with 36 children. The children spanned all ages appropriate for the test and were evenly distributed across those ages. A mean reliability coefficient of .97 was achieved for the gross motor scales and a mean reliability coefficient of .94 was achieved for the fine motor scales. Test-retest reliability studies were also reported, using 38 children from the norming sample tested twice in the span of one week. Again, the children spanned all ages appropriate for the test and were evenly distributed across those ages. A mean reliability coefficient of .95 was achieved for the gross motor scales and a mean reliability coefficient of .80 was achieved for the fine motor scales.

Evidence of concurrent validity was presented. The correlations between the Bayley Scales of Infant Development and the PDMS Fine Motor Scale were significant ($r = .78$ with the Mental Scale and $r = .36$ with the Psychomotor Scale). The PDMS Gross Motor Scale was significantly correlated with the Bayley Psychomotor Scale ($r = .37$) but not correlated with the Bayley Mental Scale ($r = .03$). The above data seem intuitively correct, because successful completion of fine motor items frequently requires stability (support) from gross motor skills and the Bayley Mental Scale has many items that are dependent on fine motor skills. Gross motor skills are not affected by the level of fine motor abilities. Sensitivity and specificity studies were not presented, although the above information would indicate that the percentages may be strong.

Norms were established for the PDMS on 617 children, relatively evenly distributed by age groups, regions of the United States, and sex. Races represented in the norming sample were white, black, and Hispanic, closely matching the percentages of those races in the July 1976 Census Bureau estimates.

Summary

The ease of use of this instrument makes the PDMS a viable tool to the professional just entering the field of movement assessment of developmentally delayed children. The professional who is new to intervention strategies for movement delays may find that the skill cards provide ideas for programming. The psychometric qualities of the instrument are fairly well documented. Limitations of the assessment relate to its use with neurologically impaired children. Connolly (1987) expressed concern that "the activity cards may be inappropriate" (p. 16) for the child with severe handicaps. A concern expressed by DeGangi

(1987) is that the scoring criteria do not allow for measures of the quality of the performance.

The Bayley Scales of Infant Development (BSID) (Bayley, 1969)

Purpose and Target Population

The BSID tests infants from the newborn period until 30 months of age. The three scales are the Mental Scale scored as the Mental Developmental Index (MDI), the Psychomotor Scale scored as the Psychomotor Developmental Index (PDI), and an Infant Behavior Record (IBR). The Mental Scale is a compilation of skills that require multiple abilities, such as perception, memory, problem solving, and verbal skills. Although it is not the intent of the Mental Scale to assess childrens' motor skills, it is true that a child with motor deficits will not do as well on those mental scale items that require dexterity or speed. The Motor Scale, which is described below, requires both fine and gross skills for successful completion. The IBR provides a comprehensive checklist of testing related behaviors. Professionals new to the field of testing would find that the IBR is a good introduction to children's test-taking skills. The three scales together provide the examiner with a comprehensive perspective of how the children are functioning at the time of testing. The scales provide data for referral for diagnostic evaluation on a child who is delayed and for referral for intervention. According to the author, the indexes "have limited value as predictors of later abilities" (p. 4) (see Gibbs, this volume, for a discussion of this issue).

The BSID is a developmental test; only the PDI will be discussed in this chapter. The use of the PDI as a motor assessment is not recommended since there are a paucity of test items for some months, sometimes limited to one or two, and the test does not have any neurological components. Conservatively, the results of the PDI should only be interpreted as a screening of motor behaviors. Therefore, a low PDI should presuade the examiner to refer the child for a movement evaluation. Items on the Bayley should not be used for programming.

Time to Administer

The author of the BSID suggested that most children can be tested on both the Mental Scale and the Motor Scale in 45 minutes. In unusual circumstances, some children may take 90 minutes, according to Bayley. The motor scale itself should take approximately one third of the time it takes for the entire Bayley, thus 15–30 minutes.

Scoring and Interpretation

An easy method for scoring has been devised for the BSID. Each item is simply scored pass or fail, depending on whether the child meets criteria for the item. In addition, there are several related items that are presented as one item, but scored differently based on the level of performance of the child. For example, a cube is presented and the type of prehension constitutes a passing or failing performance for three separate items. The situation codes allow the examiner to identify related items efficiently, whether one is using the score sheet or the manual. During testing the examiner determines a basal and a ceiling level; six consecutive items passed is the basal level and six consecutive items failed is the ceiling. A raw score is easily calculated following the exam and converted to a developmental index with a mean of 100 and a standard deviation of 16. It is also possible to convert the raw score to an age-equivalent score.

Training

There is no formal training program for learning to administer the BSID. Bayley does recommend that examiners should be selected for their ability to relate well with infants and their parents. Evaluators should also have some background in theory of measurement and interpretation of test results, according to the author. This advice is applicable for all tests but has particular relevance here when interpreting the results of the MDI. A process for training evaluators is described by the author that recommends first observation, then supervised presentation of the test, and finally practice with children at each month in the first year of life and every 3 months thereafter. Although not recommended in the manual, new examiners should probably reach a high standard of interobserver reliability before testing a child on their own.

Equipment

The test kit provides most of the equipment required to administer the BSID. Some of the remaining equipment includes a standard set of stairs, a standard walking board, and a stopwatch. The equipment represents a costly first investment.

Psychometric Qualities

The Bayley Scales of Infant Development are standardized. The history of that process is discussed in the manual. The 1969 BSID, discussed here, reports a sample of 1,262 children tested in approximately equal numbers throughout the ages of 2 to 30 months, with at least 83 children in each age group. The sample was well distributed for sex, race, and educational level of the head of the household according to the ratios reported in the 1960 United States Census. An attempt was also made to balance the children for urban-rural residence, but according to the author children from rural areas were not appropriately represented in the sample.

Reliability scores are reported on 8-month-old infants. Ninety infants were tested for tester-observer reliability (observer was behind a one-way mirror) and 28 infants were tested twice for test-retest reliability. Motor Scale agreement scores were reported for tester-observer reliability as 93.4% with a standard deviation of 3.2% and for test-retest reliability as 75.3% with a standard deviation of 14.5%.

Sensitivity and specificity are not reported in the manual but have been reported by researchers who were using the Bayley Motor Scale for concurrent validity. Campbell and Wilhelm (1985), in a study of 15 infants tested at 3 months of age, reported a sensitivity score to neurodevelopmental delays of 88.9% and a specificity score to normal infants of 66.7%. Harris (1987), in a study of 153 infants tested at 4 months of age, reported a sensitivity score to neurodevelopmental delays of 35.3% and a specificity score to normal infants of 94.4%.

Summary

The BSID was historically one of the first thorough developmental assessments designed for infants and young children. The BSID is not a neurological evaluation. The Motor Scale, given its simplicity and high reliability measures, is an appropriate first choice for the professional who is learning to assess movement. However, the Mental Scale should be given at the same time and the results of this test should be interpreted by examiners with considerable experience and ability. The psychometric qualities of the instrument are thorough. Caution is recommended in the use of the Motor Scale with neurologically impaired children. Researchers' reports vary on sensitivity and specificity scores for the PDI; that is, the instrument may not correctly identify the neurologically impaired infants.

Erhardt Developmental Prehension Assessment (EDPA) (Erhardt, 1982)

Purpose and Target Population

The EDPA is a comprehensive neurodevelopmental evaluation instrument of prehension. The author attempts to assess all behaviors in the domain of prehension. The EDPA is divided into three developmental prehension sequence clusters. The first cluster is positional-reflexive in content and is entitled Primarily Involuntary Arm-Hand Patterns. The second cluster is cognitively directed in content and is entitled Primarily Voluntary Movements. The third cluster is entitled Pre-Writing Skills. The EDPA is an evaluation of 17 distinct skill areas: 6 for cluster one, 9 for cluster two, and 2 for cluster three. Each of the 17 skill areas has a number of prerequisite motor behaviors or transitional skills. An example would best portray the extensive detail of this evaluation instrument. In cluster two, Primarily Voluntary Movements, one of the nine skill areas is entitled Grasp of the Pellet. The culmination of development for that skill area is the fine pincer grasp tested by the grasping of a pin at 12 months of age. The transitional skills would be pincer grasp at 10 months, inferior pincer grasp at 9 months, scissors grasp at 8 months, inferior scissors grasp at 7 months, raking at 6 months, and visually attending at 5 months. This extensive criterion-based format provides professionals with intervention strategies, and three chapters in the book in which the EDPA is published make that transition for the reader on three children with distinct neuromotor problems. This instrument documents the development of prehension, which in the child with normal development culminates at 15 months.

Time to Administer

The EDPA takes approximately 1 hour for administration and scoring.

Scoring and Interpretation

The system for scoring seems complex enough to cause difficulties for the professional who is new to the field of motor assessment. Each component of movement is scored on protocol sheets that provide pictures and criteria for components of movement patterns. Each component is scored on a 3-point scale indicating that the child has a normal pattern (+), an emerging pattern (+/ −), or an absent pattern (−). If the pattern is absent because a child is using a more mature pattern in its place, then a (+ +) is given. This latter addition to the otherwise straightforward scoring system requires professional judgment and, in the instance of testing reflex behaviors, may be inappropriately scored. When completing the 17 protocol sheets, the scores from the protocol sheets are then transferred to a score sheet. This is time consuming and redundant but allows one to test the child while looking at a picture of intended skill and then to see the entire summary on one sheet. An estimate of the developmental level for each of the three sections of the test, arm-hand patterns, voluntary movements, and prewriting skills, is made from the final score sheet.

Training

Training is not addressed except as it was designed for the study on interrater reliability. Training was provided in a workshop format for occupational therapists, using videotapes of children with neurological deficits.

Equipment

The equipment to be used for the EDPA is specific in the requirements of dimension. Three sizes of dowels, cubes, pellets, nesting boxes, and pill bottles are needed. A pencil and crayon and tote bucket are also necessary.

Psychometric Qualities

Percent agreement scores were used to determine interobserver reliability. Two clusters of eight raters each observed videotapes of two children tested on the EDPA; the children were different for each cluster. The raters' scores were compared to the scores of the author of the assessment. Interobserver reliability is reported by the author as 70.8 for one cluster of raters and 94.5 for the second cluster of raters. Test-retest reliability studies are not reported in the manual, although the author acknowledges the need for these studies. Validity studies also need to be done. Sensitivity and specificity have not been reported, but that was not the goal of the author. The EDPA reflects the interest of the author to remediate rather than identify hand dysfunction in a population of infants.

Summary

The EDPA provides a comprehensive format for assessing hand function and is the most thorough work available. It was designed from the perspective of a therapist who wanted a format for intervention. The strength of the EDPA lies in the design, which establishes goals for treatment. It is highly recommended for the professional who is learning the intricacies of hand function and who has a mentor to assist in the process of learning. The weakness of the EDPA lies in the inadequate documentation of psychometric qualities.

Milani-Comparetti Motor Development Screening Test (MC) (Milani-Comparetti & Gidoni, 1967)

Purpose and Target Population

The MC is intended to screen neurological and developmental behaviors of infants and young children, ages newborn to 2.5 years. It provides the tester with information about the infants' postural control, active movement, primitive reflexes, automatic reactions, parachute reactions, and tilting reactions. Thus the MC provides information on basic components of movement—those movements that appear to be preprogrammed by the central nervous system and that allow for the emergence of developmental milestones. The tool provides expected ages for the appearance of the various behaviors and, in the case of reflexes, the integration of the items. Although the designated ages are newborn to 2 years, children with movement disorders who are older than 2 can be tested for level of motor abilities. It is unlikely that the MC will be used to program a treatment format because of its design as a screening test.

Time to Administer

The test can be completed in 4–8 minutes.

Scoring and Interpretation

Four systems for scoring and interpretation of the MC have been presented by various researchers. The two original systems are described by Trembath (1978), with two additional scoring systems suggested by Ellison, Browning, Larson, and Denny (1983) and VanderLinden (1985). The revised system suggested by Trembath (1978) is recommended for its simplicity and for the information that it yields on the individual movement skills. Each response assessed is noted to be present or absent. If the behavior is normal for the child's age, the age is marked on the appropriate age line. If a behavior is delayed, the child's age is marked on the line that corresponds to the observed behavior. The interpretation of the pattern of delays is left to the tester. The lack of a summary score makes the interpretation of the test awkward.

Training

No training program is recommended by the authors of the manual. However, a thorough reading of the manual is recommended, as is the testing of a number of normal children in the selected age groups. Testing with a second examiner is suggested until a level of reliability is reached that meets the clinical standards of the center testing the infants. A trainee should achieve reliability on the individual items and on the interpretation of the pattern of passes and fails.

Equipment

There is not a test kit available for purchase. The only piece of equipment that may be at all difficult to provide is a tilt board, but since this does not have standardized dimensions one can use any surface that is easily tilted.

Psychometric Qualities

This test is criterion referenced and ages for motor milestones are given, although the test has not been normed. Observer and test-retest reliability have not been reported. A sensitivity of 44% and specificity of 78% were reported by VanderLinden (1985) in a study of 18 infants. The 15 high-risk children and 3 low-risk children in the study were assessed at 3 months on the MC and at 1 year on the Bayley Scales of Infant Development. Although not reported in a format that can be interpreted for sensitivity or specificity, a study on 999 children by Ellison et al. (1983) concluded that the MC, using their scoring system, can distinguish children with abnormal movement from children with transient abnormalities.

Summary

One of the strengths of the MC lies in the simplicity of learning the assessment, when using the manual written by Trembath (1978). The professional learning neurological assessment skills will find this an easy method for observing the neurological behaviors of infants. It should be noted that the MC was an innovative screening test at the time of its first publication. Limitations of the assessment include the awkwardness of scoring, the rigor with which the psychometric qualities have been tested, and the limited conclusions that can be drawn from the results of the testing.

Movement Assessment of Infants (MAI) (Chandler et al., 1980)

Purpose and Target Population

This neurodevelopmental instrument provides the examiner with a thorough appraisal of motor development in the first year of life, testing four distinct components of movement: tone, primitive reflexes, automatic reactions, and volitional movement. The MAI was designed to identify motor dysfunction in infants up through the first year of life. The authors caution that the MAI is used to assess infants' motor abilities, but does not provide a diagnosis for infants' movement disabilities. The items are criterion referenced and there are four or five (tone section only) possible levels of movement behavior for each item. In other words, each item describes a movement behavior and the movement behaviors that lead up to that movement. The MAI can be used to establish a baseline for treatment because each item is criterion referenced. In this way it can be used for children over 12 months of age who are functioning below that age in their motor abilities. The caution to be observed here is to consider the relative contribution of normal growth and development, environment, and other factors in the improvement noted in the infants.

Time to Administer

The evaluation averages 20–30 minutes to administer in the hands of a skilled practitioner, with an additional 10 minutes to score.

Scoring and Interpretation

Each item in the MAI is scored on a scale of 1 to 4 except the tone items, which are scored on a scale of 1 to 5. In the sections on primitive reflexes, automatic reactions, and volitional movement, the most mature response of the behavior (item) is scored as a 1. A score of 4 is then given when the behavior is not seen, as in the volitional movement and automatic reaction sections, or when the behavior is obligatory, as in the reflex section. Tone is scored quite differently. A 3 is given when the tone is normal, a 1 or 2 when low (atonic), and a 4 or 5 when high (spastic). The examiner observes a child's behavior and determines which descriptor, scored as 1 to 4 or 1 to 5, best matches the observed behavior. If the child is 4 or 8 months old the score is then matched against a set of risk scores that have been provided for each item. Children who are either 4 or 8 months old can be given a total risk score and risk scores for each of the four sections. Giving section risk scores allows the examiner to make some assumptions about the neurological nature of the deficit. For example, an infant with cerebral palsy should have high-risk scores in all four sections of the MAI. The infant with developmental delay may have normal scores in tone or risk scores for low tone, a normal profile for primitive reflexes, and delays in automatic reactions and volitional movement.

Training

Two training formats have been instituted by the authors. Weekend workshops are provided throughout the United States and Canada or interested professionals in the proximity of Seattle can sign up for a 1-day-a-week semester practicum at the site of the development of the test (the Child Developmental Center at the University of Washington). The authors suggest that the test can be learned through extensive reading of the manual, practice on many normal children, and achievement of a respectable interrater reliability with a second professional. A videotape is now available from the center to assist in this process.

Equipment

Equipment can be purchased in any toy store. A rattle, bell, ball, and red ring are needed. The most awkward additional piece of equipment needed is a surface for tilting the child in prone.

Psychometric Qualities

The authors of a study on the interrater reliability of the MAI with 53 infants reported a reliability coefficient of .72 for the total risk score on infants at 4 months of age. The age was corrected for prematurity on those infants who where not born at term (Harris, Haley, Tada, & Swanson, 1984). The same authors also reported a test-retest reliability coefficient of .76 on 29 of the infants.

Sensitivity and Specificity. Harris (1987), in a study of 153 infants tested at 4 months of age, reported a sensitivity score to neurodevelopmental delays of 73.5% and a specificity score to normal infants of 62.7%. Swanson (1988), in a study of 66 infants tested at 4 months of age, reported a sensitivity score to neurodevelopmental delays of 83.3% and a specificity score to normal infants of 78.2%. The same author, in a study of 73 infants tested at 8 months of age, reported a sensitivity score to neurodevelopmental delays of 96.1% and a specificity score to normal infants of 64.5% (Swanson, 1988).

Summary

The MAI has as its strength the extensive evaluation of movement and the ability to score that movement for clinical and research use. It is criterion referenced. The lack of risk scores for all but the 4- and 8-month ages is perhaps its greatest drawback. In addition, the MAI needs to be normed.

Chandler Movement Assessment of Infants–Screening Test (CMAI-ST) (Chandler et al., 1983).

Purpose and Target Population

This neurodevelopmental screening test evolved from the MAI and is similar in structure to its parent test. The four components of movement remain the same, that is, tone, primitive reflexes, automatic reactions, and volitional movement. The CMAI-ST has fewer items defining each component. The CMAI-ST is designed as a screening test and can be used in many settings and by professionals who do not have an expertise in movement assessment. The CMAI-ST contains only those items thought to be sensitive to movement deficits.

Time to Administer

The CMAI-ST takes no longer than 10 minutes to administer and score. However, this presumes that the examiner is not expected to take a history from the parent or establish a professional-to-parent trusting relationship. In other words, the child may be given the CMAI-ST in the context of a public health clinic, doctor's office, or day care center, for example.

Scoring and Interpretation

Each item in the CMAI-ST is scored on a scale of 1 to 3, including the section on muscle tone. The most mature form of the behavior (item) is scored as a 1. A score of 3 is then given when the behavior is not seen, as in the volitional movement and automatic reaction sections, or when the behavior is strong, as in the reflex section, or when the behavior is aberrant, as in the tone section (atonic or spastic). The examiner observes a child's behavior and determines which descriptor, scored as 1, 2, or 3, best matches the observed behavior. Since the screening test has been normed on term infants from 1.5 to 12.5 months of age, risk scores have been provided for each item for children of any age in that first year of life, except the newborn. A risk score is that least mature behavior that occurs in 10%–15% or fewer of the infant in any one age grouping. Total risk and section risk scores can be given and allow the examiner to make some assumptions about the neurological nature of the deficit. Infants can receive up to three risk scores and still be functioning within normal limits.

Training

The training takes place in a 4- or 6-hour workshop; the 6-hour workshop contains a 2-hour practicum. The examiner must then practice in a supervised situation until reliabilities are acceptable for the screening program. This level of reliability is generally reached by the third child in an age/function grouping. Three functional groups are recommended: children who cannot sit, children who can sit when placed in sitting but cannot get into sitting independently, and children who can get into sitting and crawl on all fours.

Equipment

A rattle, bell, ball, and red ring are needed.

Psychometric Qualities

Each of the items is criterion referenced and normed for the ages of 1.5–12.5. The norms were gathered at Madigan Army Medical Center and a Tacoma Public Health facility. A minimum of 20 infants were tested in each age group. The age group that constitutes the 2-month norms are those children who were 1 month 16 days to 2 months 15 days old at the time of testing. This same pattern was used up to and including the 12-month-old. The data on the final norms for the 8.5–12.5 age groups have not been analyzed as yet, but the authors have been relatively successful in having each age group evenly matched for the sex of the child. Also, every effort is being made to match the children to the 1980 Census for race and education of parents.

Test-retest reliabilities have been found by Chandler (1986) to range from 87.2 to 97.4 for 10 children. Interrater reliabilities on the second testing of those same 10 infants ranged from 81.1 to 94.9.

Summary

The CMAI-ST is a neurodevelopmental screening test that can be used by professionals who are not trained in movement. It focuses on movement behaviors in the first year of life. It is the only neurodevelopmental test in this grouping that presents norms. The psychometric qualities still need to be strengthened. The test is not yet published for general distribution.

Neurological Assessment of the Preterm and Full-Term Infant (NAPI&Fl) (Dubowitz & Dubowitz, 1981)

Purpose and Target Population

This evaluation tool, as described by the authors, was designed to be administered on newborn infants to assess the influence of the perinatal environment on the infants. Dubowitz and Dubowitz (1981) thought that there was a need for a neurological evaluation instrument to be used as part of a "routine clinical assessment of newborns" (p. 4), whether the infants were born preterm or term. The clinical/medical uses of this tool have been clearly established. When this evaluation is given repeatedly, changes in infants' behaviors can be documented at the time that they occur. The particular set of circumstances surrounding the onset of a change for the worse can be assessed to determine cause for pathological incidence. A better understanding of behaviors will lead to prevention and amelioration of pathology. The NAPI&Fl is particularly valuable for its safe use with sick infants in the neonatal intensive care unit.

The NAPI&Fl can also be used to assess an infant for probable long-term developmental outcome. Dubowitz et al. (1984) demonstrated that the instrument accurately predicted the developmental outcome of 82 of 101 infants who had been born prematurely. It is this latter function that makes the tool valuable to therapists and educators whose skills are needed for intervention purposes. If children can leave the intensive care units with an assessment that predicts 1-year outcomes, then those infants who are assessed as neurologically abnormal can be followed closely by parents and professionals to determine further the impact of the neurological deficit on development.

The NAPI&Fl was not designed for programming of follow-up care. The format of the items may suggest consultation plans to a therapist (e.g., positioning the infant during sleep, feeding, and other activities that consume a caregiver's and an infant's day). The format of the items may also suggest a treatment plan to the therapist (e.g., helping the infant develop from an extended posture to a more flexed posture through encouraging a balance between active flexion and extension). It is not the NAPI&Fl but rather extensive training in infant development that provides the background necessary for the consultation and treatment plans. It does seem unlikely, therefore, that the professional will devise a program of intervention from the NAPI&Fl, but rather will use the information to determine areas of concern for initial treatment plans and for further assessment when the infant is less fragile. It is important that professionals who work with infants understand the content of and process for administering the instrument so that they can appropriately interpret the findings. Other instruments will need to be used to program care for the infant.

An important precaution noted by Dubowitz et al. (1984) is that the plasticity of the brain may lead to a resolution of the infants' abnormalities, presumably without intervention. This should not dissuade the professional from assisting the parents with intervention, but should force the professional to be cautious in making predictions about the benefits of intervention.

Time to Administer

The evaluation takes 10–15 minutes to administer and score. However, the evaluation is to be given at at least two points in time and the interpretation of the evaluation lies in the relative change in the infant from the first to the second test.

Scoring and Interpretation

In order to achieve the predictive validity noted above by Dubowitz et al. (1984), infants are scored as normal, borderline, or abnormal depending on the tone, head control, or number of deviant signs on their exam. Even normal infants may score one deviant sign as long as their tone is thought to be normal for gestational age. Poor head control and two deviant signs indicates a borderline status for the infant. Three or more deviant signs, low trunk tone, or marked head lag are thought to be clearly abnormal indicators.

Training

Special training in neurological assessment is not needed, beyond one's knowledge of the infants in special care. This latter statement, however, demands knowledge of the NICU and fragile infants and usually implies training beyond one's training for entry into one of the fields of medicine (e.g., physician, nurse, therapist).

Equipment

Equipment needed is minimal. A small flashlight, rattle, and small cloth are all that are needed.

Psychometric Qualities

No definitive study has been made of the interrater reliability of the NAPI&Fl. An informal assessment of interrater reliability is noted in the manual, with the authors stating that there is high agreement between examiners. In the hands of a practiced clinician, however, the NAPI&Fl had high content validity. Data presented by Dubowitz and Dubowitz (1981) reported the relationship between five of the items on their test and the presence of intraventricular hemorrhage (IVH). A sensitivity score of 77% for 31 infants, a specificity of 95% for 37 infants, and an agreement of 87% can be derived from their data. This means that within the NICU a professional can note the changes in infants' behaviors and suggest further evaluation, in this case the need for a confirming ultrasound to determine the presence of an IVH. A study that looked at 1-year-old outcomes on the Griffiths Mental Developmental Scale as compared to term predictions of outcomes (Dubowitz et al., 1984) demonstrated that the NAPI&Fl has a sensitivity of 65% (abnormal infants correctly identified), a specificity of 91% (normal infants correctly identified), and an agreement of 81% (all infants correctly identified). These percentages are in keeping with those reported for other evaluation instruments, and do present the NAPI&Fl as an instrument with substantial predictive validity for neurological integrity and ultimate development at 1 year.

The instrument identifies infant behaviors

in the categories of habituation, movement and tone, reflexes, and neurobehavioral items. Each behavior is described on a continuum from no response to strong response (habituation, reflexes, neurobehavioral) or from immature to mature (movement and tone). Abnormal responses, thought never to appear in a normal sequence of behaviors, are also described.

Summary

The strength of the assessment is its versatility for use within the NICU with fragile infants. The text on the NAPI&Fl provides insight about the neurological status of infants in an NICU and suggests many viable and valuable research questions. Psychometric qualities have not been tested on this criterion-referenced test but there are indicators that the test will withstand psychometric verification of reliability and validity.

Neonatal Neurobehavioral Examination (NNE) (Morgan et al., 1988)

Purpose and Target Population

This is a neurodevelopmental evaluation instrument that was designed to establish the neurological status of neonates. Like the NAPI&Fl it is an assessment of movement and tone, reflexes, and neurobehavioral items of preterm and term infants. The tool does have a system for developing a score that should be useful in assessing a child's status over time. The scoring system for the NNE is clearly an advantage over the NAPI&Fl. However, the design, content, and uses of both instruments are the same or very similar.

Time to Administer

The test is administered and scored in 15 minutes.

Scoring and Interpretation

The infants are scored on a scale of 1, 2, 3, or A (abnormal). A 1 is the most immature score and represents behaviors of preterm infants under 32 weeks' gestation, whereas a 3 is the most mature score and represents behaviors of preterm infants over 36 weeks' gestation. An A is given to those behaviors that are not seen as normal at any age.

Training

Special training in neurological assessment is not needed, beyond one's knowledge of the infants in special care. As in the case of the NAPI&Fl this latter statement demands knowledge of the NICU and fragile infants and usually implies training beyond one's training for entry into one of the fields of medicine (e.g., physician, nurse, therapist).

Equipment

A small cloth is the only need.

Psychometric Qualities

Morgan et al. (1988) reported interobserver reliability on normal term 2-day-old infants ranging from 88% on items to 95% on sections of the instrument. The number of infants tested was reported as 54. The data reported by these same authors for 298 high-risk infants indicated that total scores and section scores on the NNE were significantly different between conceptual age groups but that "no clinically significant score differences were associated with severity of illness and gestational age at birth" (p. 1352).

Summary

This criterion-referenced assessment offers an advantage over the NAPI&Fl in that it offers a scoring system. If, as reported by the authors, illness had no impact on the behaviors of infants of similar conceptual age, then this may simply serve as a test of gestational age and have no implication for evaluation of the neurological status of the infants. This deserves continued research with preterm infants.

SUMMARY

The current status of neuromotor assessment and the instruments that have been designed to measure movement have been discussed in depth. Eight instruments are described for their contribution to neurological, developmental, or neurodevelopmental evaluation of movement. Knowledge of normal movement is rapidly accumulating for preterm infants and young children through the age of 3 years because of the efforts of professionals from the relatively diverse backgrounds of medicine, physical therapy, occupational therapy, psychology, and education. Assessment of infants' movement status may well prove to be one of the primary methods by which professionals will be able to document indicators for early intervention.

Professionals working in the arena of movement assessment are beginning to report the possible risks to preterm infants as a result of the stress of inappropriate pacing and timing of assessment (Sweeney, 1986). This information, coupled with the rapidly accumulating and somewhat disappointing data about the sensitivity and specificity of all of the instruments, should be a warning to professionals to test medically fragile infants with extreme caution. Test results must be interpreted with knowledge of infants' behavioral state, autonomic nervous system stability, and level of motor control. Variations of normal movement need to be acknowledged. Generalizability of assessments across populations needs to be assessed.

The arena of movement assessment is rapidly growing. Information generated to date appears to have influenced positively our ability to help the vulnerable infant. The excitement among professionals and the commitment of our government, as implied by PL 99-457, should result in a plethora of useful data.

REFERENCES

Als, H. (1986). A synactive model of neonatal behavioral organization: Framework for the assessment of neurobehavioral development in the premature infant and for support of infants and parents in the neonatal intensive care environment. In J.K. Sweeney (Ed.), *The high-risk neonate: Developmental therapy perspective* (pp. 3–53). New York: The Haworth Press.

Apgar, V. (1953). A proposal for a new method of evaluating the newborn infant. *Current Researches in Anesthesia and Analgesia, 32*(4), 260–267.

Bayley, N. (1969). *Bayley Scales of Infant Development: A manual.* New York: The Psychological Corporation.

Brazelton, T.B. (1984). *Neonatal Behavioral Assessment Scale* (2nd ed.). Philadelphia: J.B. Lippincott.

Campbell, S., & Wilhelm, I. (1985). Development from birth to 3 years of age of 15 children at high risk for central nervous dysfunction. *Physical Therapy, 65*(4), 463–469.

Chandler, L. (1986). Screening for movement dysfunction. In J.K. Sweeney (Ed.), *The high-risk neonate: Developmental therapy perspective* (pp. 171–189). New York: The Haworth Press.

Chandler, L. (1988). [Norms for the CMAI-ST]. Unpublished raw data.

Chandler, L., Andrews, M., & Swanson, M. (1980). *The Movement Assessment of Infants: A manual.* Rolling Bay, WA: Infant Movement Research.

Chandler, L., Andrews, M., & Swanson, M. (1983). *The Chandler Movement Assessment of Infants–Screening Test.* Unpublished manuscript.

Connolly, B.H. (1987). Tests and assessment. In B.H. Connolly & P.C. Montgomery (Eds.), *Therapeutic exercise in developmental disabilities* (pp. 9–19). Chattanooga, TN: Chattanooga Corporation.

DeGangi, G.A. (1987). Sensorimotor tests. In L. King-Thomas & B.J. Hacker (Eds.), *A therapist's guide to pediatric assessment* (pp. 143–225). Boston: Little, Brown.

Dubowitz, L. (1988). Neurologic assessment. In R.A. Ballard (Ed.), *Pediatric care of the ICN graduate* (pp. 59–110). Philadelphia: W.B. Saunders.

Dubowitz, L., & Dubowitz, V. (1981). The neurological examination of the full term newborn infant. In *Clinics in Developmental Medicine, No. 79.* Philadelphia: J.B. Lippincott.

Dubowitz, L., Dubowitz, V., Palmer, P., Miller, G., Fawer, C., & Levene, M. (1984). Correlation of neurologic assessment in the preterm newborn infant with outcome at 1 year. *Journal of Pediatrics, 105,* 452–456.

Ellison, P., Browning, C., Larson, B., & Denny, J. (1983). Development of a scoring system for the Milani-Comparetti and Gidoni method of assessing neurologic abnormality in infancy. *Physical Therapy, 63*(9), 1414–1423.

Erhardt, R.P. (1982). *Developmental hand dysfunction.* Laurel, MD: Ramsco.

Folio, R., & Dubose, R. (1983). *Peabody Develop-

mental Motor Scales. Hingham, MA: Teaching Resources Corporation.

Folio, M.R., & Fewell, R.R. (1983). *Peabody Developmental Motor Scales and Activity Cards: A manual*. Allen, TX: DLM Teaching Resources.

Gorski, P., Lewkowicz, D., & Huntington, L. (1987). Advances in neonatal and infant behavioral assessment: Toward a comprehensive evaluation of early patterns of development. *Developmental and Behavioral Pediatrics, 8*(1), 39–53.

Harris, S. (1987). Early detection of cerebral palsy: Sensitivity and specificity of two motor assessment tools. *Journal of Perinatology, 7*(1), 11–15.

Harris, S., Haley, S., Tada, W., & Swanson, M. (1984). Reliability of observational measures of the movement assessment of infants. *Physical Therapy, 64,* 471–475.

Harris, S., Swanson, M., Chandler, L.S., Andrews, M.S., Sells, C.J., Robinson, N.M., & Bennette, F.C. (1984). Predictive validity of the Movement Assessment of Infants. *Journal of Developmental and Behavioral Pediatrics, 5,* 336–342.

Kopp, C.B., & Krakow, J.B. (1983). The developmentalist and the study of biological risk: A view of the past with an eye toward the future. *Child Development, 54,* 1086–1108.

Milani-Comparetti, A., & Gidoni, E. (1967). Routine developmental examination in normal and retarded children. *Developmental Medicine and Child Neurology, 9,* 631–638.

Morgan, A.M., Koch, V., Lee, V., & Aldag, J. (1988). Neonatal Neurobehavioral Examination: A new instrument for quantitative analysis of neonatal neurological status. *Physical Therapy, 68*(9).

Piper, M.C. (1987). Issues and priorities in pediatric therapy research. In *Proceedings of the Symposium on Priorities for Physical Therapy in Maternal and Child Health* (pp. 1–9). Chapel Hill, University of North Carolina, Division of Physical Therapy.

Prechtl, H.F. (1977). The neurological examination of the full-term newborn infant. In *Clinics in Developmental Medicine, No. 63*. Philadelphia: J.B. Lippincott.

Shankaran, S., Slovis, T.L., Bedard, M.P., & Poland, R.L. (1982). Sonographic classification in intracranial hemorrhage: A prognostic indicator of mortality, morbidity, and short-term neurological outcome. *Journal of Pediatrics, 100,* 469.

Stewart, A., Hope, P.L., Hamilton, P., De-L Costello, A.M., Baudin, J., Bradford, B., Amiel-Tison, C., & Reynolds, E.D.R. (1988). Prediction in very preterm infants of satisfactory neurodevelopmental progress at 12 months. *Developmental Medicine and Child Neurology, 30,* 53–63.

Swanson, M. (1988). [Norms for the MAI at 4 and 8 months]. Unpublished raw data.

Sweeney, J.K. (1986). Physiologic adaption of neonates to neurological assessment. In J.K. Sweeney (Ed.), *The high-risk neonate: Developmental therapy perspective*. New York: The Haworth Press.

Towen, B. (1976). Neurological development in infancy. In *Clinics in Developmental Medicine, No. 59*. Philadelphia: J.B. Lippincott.

Trembath, J. (1977). *The Milani-Comparetti Motor Development Screening Test*. Omaha: Meyer Children's Rehabilitation Institute, University of Nebraska Medical Center.

VanderLinden, D. (1985). Ability of the Milani-Comparetti developmental examination to predict motor outcome. *Physical and Occupational Therapy in Pediatrics, 5*(1), 27–38.

5 Oral-Motor and Respiratory-Phonatory Assessment

Rona Alexander

The assessment of oral-motor and respiratory function during feeding, general movement, and sound production activities can provide some of the earliest clues to the existence of problems that may interfere with an infant's developmental process. Such an evaluation will need to analyze qualitatively these functional activities so as to differentiate problems that are structural in origin from those that reflect central or peripheral nervous system dysfunction. The recommendation of appropriate intervention strategies will depend on the gathering of information through a comprehensive diagnostic process.

COMPONENTS OF NORMAL DEVELOPMENT

It is essential for the professional providing a comprehensive clinical assessment to have an extensive foundation in the normal developmental process, including knowledge of anatomical and kinesiological characteristics as well as the sequence of components of development in the areas of oral-motor, respiratory-phonatory, general movement, and upper extremity function. Although a thorough review of these areas cannot be provided here, an overview of significant anatomical/kinesiological and developmental characteristics will be discussed. A glossary of general terms used in this discussion can be found in Table 1 (for further information see Alexander, 1983; Morris, 1982a, 1982b; Morris & Klein, 1987).

Birth through Four Months

The oral-motor and respiratory-phonatory functions of the full-term newborn are directly influenced by the infant's passive or physiological flexion, small oral mechanism, high-positioned rib cage with the upper ribs almost perpendicular to the spine, elevated and internally rotated shoulder girdle, short and high-positioned pharyngeal mechanism, and sucking pads located in the cheeks. The interaction between these anatomical and physiological factors and the newborn's neurological and sensorimotor activity is apparent in the infant's ability to take liquid in during breastfeeding or bottle drinking using negative pressure in the mouth. This negative pressure, characteristic of sucking activity, is produced by a total pattern of oral movements.

The newborn's belly breathing pattern is characterized by expansion of the belly and lower ribs (rib flaring) on inhalation. This pattern will modify somewhat when there is stress or effort involved in an activity, with less belly expansion and a collapse or retraction of the sternum and anterior portion of the ribs evident.

Sound is produced on exhalation and is generally short, soft, and nasal in quality. The infant must be actively moving his or her body in order to produce sounds.

Table 1. General terms related to the components of normal development

Abdominal muscles	Muscles of the abdominal wall, including the external and internal obliques, the transversus abdominus, the rectus abdominus, and the quadratus lumborum; primary roles in active antigravity trunk flexion and stabilizing the lower rib cage during respiration.
Abdominal-thoracic breathing	A respiratory pattern characterized by expansion of the thoracic and upper abdominal areas on inhalation; the rib cage elevates as it expands laterally and in the anterior-posterior dimension, while the diaphragm contracts and lowers, creating expansion vertically.
Abduction	Movement of the limbs outward from the midline of the body.
Adduction	Movement of the limbs inward toward the midline of the body.
Belly breathing	A respiratory pattern in which the diaphragm contracts and pushes against the abdominal wall, resulting in belly expansion and flaring of the lower ribs as air is taken in on inhalation.
Chewing	The process used to break up solid foods in preparation for swallowing.
Controlled lateral movements	Antigravity movements in a lateral plane or sideways; as the body's center of gravity is shifted to one side, lateral flexion of the body to the other side prevents falling.
Controlled, sustained bite	The easy, graded closure of the teeth through a solid food with an easy, graded release for chewing.
Extension	The straightening out of a bent part of the body; opposite of flexion.
External rotation	Turning of a limb outward away from the midline of the body.
Flexion	The bringing together of two body surfaces or bending of the trunk or limbs (e.g., bending the elbow, tucking the chin).
Hyperextension	Extension of a joint beyond that which is needed for straightening.
Internal rotation	Turning of a limb inward toward the midline of the body.
Laryngeal area	A valving system starting at the base of the tongue extending down to the top of the trachea designed to keep food from entering the airway; primarily consists structurally of the epiglottis, valleculae, pyriform sinuses, false vocal folds, true vocal folds, aryepiglottic folds, and the cuneiform, cricoid, thyroid, and arytenoid cartilages.
Munching	Early chewing activity composed of rhythmical up-down jaw movements with spreading, flattening, and some up-down tongue movements.
Oral cavity	Area consisting of the upper jaw (maxilla), lower jaw (mandible), teeth, lips, cheeks, tongue, floor of the mouth, hard and soft palates, uvula, and anterior and posterior faucial arches.
Pharyngeal area	Musculomembranous tube from the base of the skull extending downward to the top of the esophagus (cricopharyngeus muscle); formed primarily by the superior, medial, and inferior pharyngeal constrictor muscles; subdivided into nasopharynx, oropharynx, and laryngopharynx.
Prone	Lying on the stomach.
Rotation	Twisting of a body part around its longitudinal axis; in movement it reflects integration of antigravity extension, flexion, and lateral control (e.g., trunk rotation).
Sucking	A rhythmical method of obtaining liquid and food using small up-down jaw movements, up-down tongue movements, lip closure, and cheek activity that creates negative pressure in the oral cavity.
Sucking pads	Round, encapsulated fatty tissue deposits within the cheeks of the young infant.
Suckling	An early lick type of sucking pattern characterized by rhythmical forward-backward tongue movements, large rhythmical up-down and forward-backward jaw movements, and minimal cheek and lip activity.

Within the first month of life, the total pattern of oral movement noted in the newborn's negative-pressure sucking pattern modifies as the infant begins to develop antigravity head extension. Suckling becomes the true active oral-motor pattern in feeding, and is composed of large rhythmical, up-down and forward-backward jaw movements, large rhythmical forward-backward tongue movements, and minimal activity of the cheeks and lips. The tongue is thin and cupped in contour. The lips are forward in position due to stability provided by the sucking pads, although they do not reveal any active holding on the nipple. This suckling pattern will be seen during early sound production and environmental exploration as well as initially whenever a new feeding activity is introduced.

By 4 months of age, infants have developed a balance between antigravity extension and flexion, evident in their midline head orientation and neck elongation when they are lying prone on their tummies or supine on their backs. The spinal extension against gravity that they have been developing is beginning to be balanced by active use of abdominal musculature (i.e., the rectus abdominus). As the abdominals begin to pull the rib cage downward, decreasing the angle between ribs and spine, the shoulder girdle will begin to depress, providing a greater point of stability for both the upper rib cage and the pharyngeal/neck musculature.

These changes in body movement will affect the respiratory pattern, with deeper belly expansion evident. A greater variety of vowel and beginning consonant productions with increased duration, loudness, and pitch variation will become possible.

Although suckling continues to be the predominant pattern seen in bottle drinking and breastfeeding, the 4-month-old begins to use the center portions of the lips to actively hold onto the nipple. This early lip activity not only is a significant component of development for future lip function, but also provides an essential active point of stability for future changes in overall oral-motor function. If spoon feeding is introduced, a suckling pattern will be used.

Five through Six Months

Between 5 and 6 months, the infant is developing finer head control with neck elongation in prone and supine as the abdominals provide greater stability to the rib cage and shoulder girdle, controlled lateral movements in prone that are essential for the use of the arms in reaching, and greater use of the hips and abdominals for stability in sitting to allow for freer upper extremity and head movements. Increased abdominal musculature activity is providing an essential base of stability for the rib cage from below that will result in longer, more controlled exhalation for longer sound production duration. The infant's more stable, depressed shoulder girdle will provide a base from which finer pharyngeal and oral function can be used for expanded sound production, which continues to be directly influenced by the infant's body movements.

The 6-month-old is using a coordinated sucking pattern in bottle drinking and breastfeeding that is composed of small vertical movements of the jaw, up-down movements of the tongue within the oral cavity, inward activity of the cheeks, and active holding by the lips as they close around the nipple. The tongue is thin and cupped around the nipple. Suckling activity with some loss of liquid may be noted on nipple insertion or removal.

In spoon feeding, the infant can quiet the mouth as food is brought in, although movements of the tongue and jaw characteristic of suckling continue to be predominant. The 6-month-old begins to show upward and outward movement of the lower lip as it stabilizes under the spoon and downward movement of the upper lip.

Cup drinking is often introduced at 6 months, although little liquid intake is actually achieved. The infant uses a suckling pattern to handle the liquid. Some active lower lip elevation and protrusion under the cup rim may be noted.

Since the teething process generally begins at 5–6 months, infants may receive some hard solids at this time. Although the primary reason for the presentation of hard solids is to provide the infant with something that can be rubbed on the gums to help reduce swelling and pain, these solids also provide stimulation for the infant to begin handling a new texture using the suckling and sucking patterns he or she already has, as well as developing new patterns of movement, such as munching. In munching the jaw reveals small vertical movements and the tongue remains passive in the oral cavity, with occasional up-down movements. This new pattern of movement marks the beginning of the chewing process.

Seven through Twelve Months

With more consistent active use of the abdominal musculature (rectus abdominus and external obliques), greater bilateral shoulder girdle depression, greater dissociation of arm and leg movements, active trunk elongation, increased hip mobility, and a more active balance of spinal extension, flexion, lateral movements, and rotation within the trunk at 7–9 months, the young child has developed the essential movement components required for the further integration of more refined coordinated activity. Respiratory function and its coordination with oral and pharyngeal activity dramatically change as the external obliques stabilize the lower rib cage, providing the foundation from which the intercostals (muscles located between the ribs) will become active on inhalation; flaring of the lower ribs will gradually disappear; longer, more controlled exhalation will occur; and the process of developing and using a more adult-like abdominal-thoracic breathing pattern will begin.

Although sound can now be produced separately from body movements, long sequences of consonant-vowel syllables with a wide variety of intonation patterns will be produced most frequently during active play. The respiratory control required for the efficient and effective use of speech for communication is primarily developed by 13–15 months of age.

Coordinated movements of the jaw, cheeks, lips, and tongue that produced the negative-pressure sucking pattern noted at 6 months during bottle drinking and breastfeeding have become more fully integrated by 9 months of age. Wide-range suckling movements are no longer noted and no loss of liquid occurs.

During cup drinking, suckling continues to be used until the young child attempts to use the tongue and lower lip to provide a base of stability from which negative pressure can be achieved at 9–10 months. The tongue protrudes under the cup and the lower lip elevates and surrounds the tongue, compensating for excessive jaw instability. By 12–15 months, the child is biting on the cup rim while using the cheeks/lips and tongue more actively to control liquid flow. The internal coordination of the jaw musculature required for active jaw stability in cup drinking gradually develops and is generally evident by 24 months of age. With more successful cup drinking as a means for liquid intake at 12 months, the use of bottle drinking or breastfeeding can begin to be reduced.

By 7–8 months of age, lip protrusion and rounding occur as the spoon is brought to the mouth in spoon feeding. As the spoon enters the mouth, the lips move toward closure. The lower lip maintains an elevated and protruded position under the spoon for stability as the child uses upper lip activity and head flexion with neck elongation to remove the food. Up-down tongue and jaw movements as well as cheek and lip activity are used to move the food back for swallowing, although intermittent suckling movements will still be evident. By 12 months the child has developed a finely coordinated sequence of movement components for food removal that include controlled head flexion and extension, neck elongation, shoulder girdle depression, trunk elongation, controlled forward-backward hip mobility, graded depression and elevation of the jaw, active tongue stability, upward and forward-backward lower lip movements, and downward and forward-backward upper lip activity. Sucking with negative pressure is now used to move food back for swallowing.

Success at biting and chewing is influenced by the type of solid food the child is attempting to eat. Small, vertical phasic bite-release movements of the jaw for biting are used until approximately 8 months of age on a cracker or soft solid; this pattern may continue to be seen on a hard solid at 10–12 months. Biting through a soft solid modifies as the child closes and positions the jaw so that a piece can be broken off for chewing at 8 months and develops active use of a more controlled, sustained bite by approximately 10 months of age. This graded biting activity may not be evident on a hard solid until 12–13 months.

The chewing process modifies as the 7-month-old responds to solids placed on the biting surfaces of the side gums by horizontally shifting the tongue over to touch the food. In conjunction with these gross lateral tongue movements, the jaw will move in a lateral-diagonal plane. Food placed in the center of the mouth will be handled with suckling or sucking activity.

As the tongue more actively transfers food side-to-center and center-to-side at about 10 months, jaw activity modifies to include up-down, forward-backward, and circular-lateral-diagonal movements and the cheeks and lips begin to actively assist in keeping food on the biting surfaces for chewing. Tongue movements become more coordinated for side-to-side lateralization by 12–15 months, at which time greater circular-diagonal movements of the jaw will be noted. The development of well-integrated rotary jaw movement with controlled grinding and shearing activity continues over the next 2 years.

ORAL-MOTOR AND RESPIRATORY-PHONATORY DYSFUNCTION

Oral-motor and respiratory-phonatory dysfunction, as will be discussed here, relates specifically to those infants who have neuromotor involvement due to cerebral palsy, although infants with neuromotor involvement due to peripheral nervous system disorders, genetic disorders, severe seizure disorders, or traumatic injury may exhibit similar problems. In addition, oral-motor and respiratory-phonatory dysfunction may occur as a consequence of conditions not necessarily related to neuromotor involvement, such as craniofacial anomalies (e.g., cleft palate) and structural abnormalities of the gastrointestinal, respiratory, or cardiac systems. The oral-motor and respiratory-phonatory activity used by these infants, which results in functional problems during feeding, sound production, or general movement, may appear similar, but will require different intervention strategies because of the varied etiologies that exist.

Many infants with cerebral palsy who have early problems with feeding and respiration exhibit head-neck hyperextension and tongue retraction. (See Table 2 for a glossary of terms related to oral-motor dysfunction.) These infants use their head-neck hyperextension and tongue retraction to abnormally hold for stability on a low muscle tone base in order to open the mouth and lift and turn the head. As gravity pulls them into greater abnormal extension, the cheeks, lips, and jaw will also be pulled back into gravity, creating jaw thrusting with retraction and cheek-lip retraction.

During feeding, head-neck hyperextension and tongue retraction put the infant at risk for aspiration, choking, limited nutritional intake, and the loss of liquid or food through the nose. Since the retracted tongue is thick in contour, no active cupping of the tongue can be used to control the speed and direction of liquids and food, which are being moved quickly back in the oral cavity by gravity. This is true whether the food or liquid is presented by bottle, spoon, or cup.

As infants feed with head-neck hyperextension and tongue retraction, they often develop compensatory movements in an attempt to control their head and neck position as well as the flow of liquid or food. Shoulder elevation

Table 2. Terms related to oral-motor dysfunction

Cheek-lip retraction	The abnormal pulling back of the cheeks and lips for stabilization; the lips appear thin as they form a line across the mouth; initially seen in conjunction with abnormal head-neck hyperextension and tongue retraction.
Exaggerated jaw closure	Excessive closure of the jaw used to obtain external jaw stability during feeding; occurs as a compensation for excessive jaw instability; not due to problems in tolerating oral tactile stimulation.
Jaw thrusting with protrusion	Abnormally strong depression with forward pushing of the lower jaw; often seen with attempts to close an unstable jaw that opened using thrusting with retraction; occurs as a compensatory jaw movement.
Jaw thrusting with retraction	Abnormally strong depression with backward pulling of the lower jaw; initially seen in conjunction with abnormal head-neck hyperextension and tongue retraction.
Lip pursing	A purse-string positioning of the lips and cheeks; the cheeks and lip corners are retracted for abnormal stability while the central portions of the lips are semiprotruded and appear to be puckering.
Tongue retraction	Strong pulling back of the tongue body into the oral-pharyngeal space for abnormal stability; the tongue appears thick in contour; reinforces abnormal head-neck hyperextension.
Tongue retraction with anterior tongue elevation	Abnormal stabilization of the tongue back in the oral cavity with the anterior portion elevated, pushing up against the alveolar ridge or hard palate; the back of the tongue is lowered as a result of the anterior tongue elevation; occurs as a compensation for excessive tongue instability.
Tongue thrusting	Abnormally strong forward pushing of the tongue, which is bunched and thick in appearance; occurs as a compensatory tongue movement.

(abnormal lifting and holding up of the shoulder girdle) will be used to hold the head and neck in a more stable position while abnormal upper trunk flexion into gravity may assist in bringing the body forward. Tongue thrusting may develop in an attempt to modify the speed and direction of the liquid or food. In order to obtain a more closed mouth posture, the infant may attempt to use compensatory lip pursing. If jaw thrusting with retraction and excessive jaw instability exist, the infant may begin to use exaggerated jaw closure to hold the jaw in a more closed position on the nipple, spoon, or cup rim, which makes bringing the liquid or food into the mouth very difficult. Jaw thrusting with protrusion may develop as the infant pushes the jaw forward to help hold the head up in prone or to help achieve jaw closure during feeding activities.

When severe respiratory problems exist, greater head-neck hyperextension may be used in an attempt to increase air intake by biomechanically enlarging the pharyngeal area, although this generally results in greater tongue retraction, which may actually occlude the airway. Some infants will compensate for this excessive tongue retraction by pushing the anterior portion of the tongue up to hold it against the hard palate or alveolar ridge. By doing so, the posterior portion of the tongue is lowered, which can help to open the airway for breathing. However, tongue retraction with anterior tongue elevation will compromise the infant's functional use of the mouth for feeding or phonation.

Some infants develop tongue retraction and head-neck hyperextension as compensations for their primary shoulder girdle problem of abnormal humeral extension with adduction and internal rotation (i.e., arms are pulled back with elbows flexed and are held against the body). They use this shoulder girdle posture as a means of obtaining stability and upper trunk extension. Oral-motor function will be affected as head-neck hyperextension, tongue retraction, and humeral extension with adduction and internal rotation are used to hold up the head and upper body in prone and sitting. When gravity begins pulling the infant into greater extension while in supported sitting, additional compensatory activity will be developed as attempts are made to move the body forward through the abnormal contraction of the rectus abdominus musculature.

Humeral extension with adduction and internal rotation and the compensatory movements that may result will have a significant impact on respiratory function and its coordination with oral activity. Although the rib cage may appear to be angled downward, this modification in placement has occurred as a result of the abnormal pull from the rectus abdominus and the pull from gravity on the ribs when in a sitting position and not from the use of musculature that has developed through active movements against gravity. Therefore, air intake on inhalation will be limited and abdominal musculature activity necessary for sustained exhalation will be inadequate. Generally, a belly breathing pattern with limited belly expansion and excessive flaring of the ribs laterally will be predominant. Respiratory coordination with oral and laryngeal function is greatly restricted, limiting the amount, variety, loudness, and quality of the infant's overall sound production.

Although infants with cerebral palsy and significant oral-motor and respiratory-phonatory dysfunction often reveal primary problems in the head, neck, oral, and shoulder girdle areas, some may exhibit dysfunction that can be traced to primary problems at the hips (e.g., spastic diplegia). Oral-motor activity for feeding may be functional, but there may be qualitatively abnormal movements noted during feeding activities. The fine coordination of oral-motor activity required for smooth, efficient articulation may be limited. More significant problems related to speech production exist as a result of the lack of sufficient abdominal musculature activity required to support extended exhalation for long phrases or sentences (for further information see Alexander, 1983, 1987; Boehme, 1987; Morris, 1982b; Morris & Klein, 1987).

ASSESSMENT STRATEGIES

Formal Assessment Measures

Reference to feeding and sound production milestones is found in many general screening and assessment tools presently used to examine an infant's overall developmental progress. However, information obtained through a milestone concept cannot accurately measure specifics regarding fine oral-motor and respiratory-phonatory coordination. The qualitative analysis of the components of an infant's oral-motor and respiratory-phonatory function is required if mild incoordination is to be recognized early or if treatment strategies are to be appropriately directed toward the movements that are primary causes of the dysfunction.

There are no standardized assessment tools now commercially available to provide a qualitative analysis of early feeding and sound production function. However, a number of formalized assessment tools and medical procedures do exist that can be useful in obtaining information about the infant's function in these areas. The following section will briefly discuss the significance of three of these measures—the Pre-Speech Assessment Scale, videofluoroscopy of the swallowing process, and testing for gastroesophageal reflux.

The Pre-Speech Assessment Scale

The Pre-Speech Assessment Scale (PSAS) developed by Suzanne Evans Morris (1982a), although not a standardized measure, does provide a rating scale for the measurement of specific prespeech behaviors (i.e., oral-motor and respiratory-phonatory function) in children from birth through 2 years of age with suspected or diagnosed neurological impairment. The PSAS was published in 1982 after 10 years of development as part of the Comprehensive Training Program for Infant and Young Cerebral Palsied Children, which was a U.S. Department of Education Handicapped Children's Early Education Project conducted at the Curative Rehabilitation Center in Milwaukee, Wisconsin.

Twenty-seven different performance areas are examined over the six major categorical divisions of feeding behavior, sucking, swallowing, biting and chewing, respiration-phonation, and sound play (see Table 3). The primary source of information in each performance area comes from the evaluator's observations of the child through a variety of feeding and sound production activities. In addition, the PSAS provides a system for gathering information from the parent/caregiver through a questionnaire so that the most comprehensive picture possible of the child's prespeech behaviors can be obtained.

A double scoring system is used to allow for the differentiation between abnormal movements in each prespeech performance area. When a child's activity is not completely described by the behavioral descriptions provided for specific scores in a performance area, a clinical judgment scoring procedure is available to allow the evaluator to assign a score to the behavior observed. Scores are transferred to a specially designed graph that can be used for comparisons of components among performance areas on one evaluation or for the charting of progress and change between performance areas over several evaluations.

At the beginning of each testing category there is an introductory section that provides information on basic concepts related to the category being evaluated, the relationship of the prespeech behaviors within the category to communication function, movement characteristics relevant to the category, and definitions common to all performance areas within the category. Testing procedures and specific scoring information are provided for each performance area. Although an extensive amount of descriptive and procedural information is delineated, evaluators should have knowledge of the components of normal and abnormal oral-motor and respiratory-phonatory sound production development and experience in working with the neuromotor-involved pediatric population to most effectively use the PSAS and interpret its information for intervention programming.

Videofluoroscopy

When assessing an infant's feeding function, questions often arise regarding areas that may be compromising the child's health or overall nutritional intake as well as those pertaining to movements that are not easily visualized through clinical observation. Videofluoroscopy of the swallowing process (i.e., videoswallow study, oral-pharyngeal motility study, modified barium swallow study) can be

Table 3. Categories and performance areas of the Pre-Speech Assessment Scale (PSAS)

I. Feeding Behavior
  1. Length of time
  2. Amount of food
  3. Types of food
  4. Position for feeding
II. Sucking
  5. Liquids from bottle or breast
  6. Liquids from the cup
  7. Pureed foods from a spoon
III. Swallowing
  8. Liquids
  9. Semi-solids
  10. Solids
  11. Coordination of sucking, swallowing and breathing
  12. Control of drooling
IV. Biting and Chewing
  13. Jaw movement in biting
  14. Jaw movement in chewing
  15. Tongue movement in chewing
  16. Lip movement in chewing
V. Respiration-Phonation
  17. Ease of initiation of phonation
  18. Duration of phonation
  19. Loudness of phonation
  20. Pitch and intonation patterns
  21. Voice quality during non-speech phonation
  22. Voice quality during early speech phonation
VI. Sound Play
  23. Type of sound play
  24. Jaw movement during phonation
  25. Tongue movement during phonation
  26. Lip movement during phonation
  27. Velopharyngeal movement during phonation

From: Morris, S.E. (1982). *Pre-Speech Assessment Scale* (p. 1). Clifton, NJ: J.A. Preston.

used for the more accurate evaluation of the speed and pattern of movements of the structures of the oral and pharyngeal areas during specific feeding/swallowing tasks. If aspiration is suspected based upon an infant's history of frequent respiratory illness or pneumonia, frequent coughing or gagging during feeding, consistent wet, gurgly vocalizations, and increased respiratory distress during feeding, a videoswallow study should be conducted to better analyze if and when aspiration occurs and what aspects of the swallowing process contribute to its occurrence (Fee, Charney, & Robertson, 1988).

Although procedures for conducting a videoswallow study have not been definitively established for the pediatric population, those now using such studies have modified procedures developed for the evaluation of the adult population with suspected oral or pharyngeal swallowing dysfunction (Logemann, 1983, 1986). It is essential that a specially trained professional with knowledge in pediatric oral-pharyngeal function, most often a speech-language pathologist, be involved in the testing and the careful analysis of the videoswallow study in order to ensure the qualitative analysis of information obtained and the appropriate interpretation of that information. Information obtained from both clinical and videofluoroscopic evaluations not only provides important diagnostic data, but also establishes a strong foundation for the development of appropriate intervention strategies (Castell & Donner, 1987; Sorin, Somers, Austin, & Bester, 1988).

Radiography

An infant's feeding may further be complicated by gastroesophageal reflux (GER), which is the return flow of the contents of the stomach up into the esophagus and sometimes up into the pharyngeal area, most often as a result of incompetence of the sphincter connecting the esophagus and stomach (lower esophageal sphincter). Gastroesophageal reflux can be treated through changes in position and food textures, medications, or surgical intervention (Fee et al., 1988). When a history is presented that includes vomiting at periods during or after a meal, increased irritability after specific amounts of nutritional intake, extreme fussiness regarding the intake of certain types or textures of food, poor weight gain, or aspiration pneumonia, the existence of GER is highly probable.

In order to document GER, it will be necessary to have a battery of tests conducted, including barium sulfate radiography of the swallow and upper gastrointestinal tract with a GER scan or continuous intraesophageal pH probe monitoring. The infant's primary physician may choose to prescribe such testing or may refer the infant to a pediatric gastroenterologist for a complete examination. If GER persists the infant will become more resistant to feeding, limiting the possibility of improving oral-motor function during such activities as well as preventing increased nutritional intake for weight gain.

Informal Clinical Assessment

Although there is a paucity of standardized evaluation tools available, informal procedures do exist for the clinical assessment of the oral-motor and respiratory-phonatory function of young children. A comprehensive informal assessment should obtain information on: 1) the movements of the individual parts of the infant's oral mechanism as well as the quality and coordination of these oral movements during feeding, general movement, and sound production; 2) the influence of postural tone, movement, and sensory stimulation (e.g., tactile, auditory, taste) on oral-motor and respiratory-phonatory function; 3) the infant's respiratory function and its coordination with oral activity during feeding, general movement, and sound production; and 4) the infant's use of different modes of communication (e.g., facial expression, gestures, eye pointing, sound production) during general movements and feeding activities. Analysis of this information requires that the evaluator have knowledge of the components of normal and abnormal oral-motor and respiratory-phonatory development and function as well as experience in interpreting the information for appropriate recommendations in regard to the infant's need for intervention programming.

The evaluator will need to gather information through careful questioning of the parent or caregiver, observation of the infant with the caregiver during activities, and when possible, direct testing procedures. Since feeding is a very personal area for both the infant and parent, the evaluator must be sensitive to this throughout the evaluation process.

Parent Interview

Case history information specifically pertaining to respiratory illnesses and pneumonia, vomiting or spitting up during or after meals, past use of tube feeding, and past use of ventilation or other respiratory support systems should be obtained directly from the parents. Such information will be essential in determining the need for additional testing (e.g., videoswallow study, GER scan) prior to the development of intervention strategies related to modifying the infant's feeding activity.

Questions should be posed to obtain descriptive information on mealtime length, amount of nutritional intake, preferred food textures, feeding utensils, and positioning used for mealtime feeding. Additional information should be gathered by asking the parent to describe his or her child's oral movements during specific feeding activities (e.g., spoon feeding, cup drinking).

Special care must be taken to make sure that the caregiver is not required to make any qualitative judgments on his or her child's feeding activity. These decisions will be based on the adequacy of nutritional intake rather than on the quality of oral-motor function being used.

Observation

The evaluator must recognize that infants generally reveal a more accurate picture of their functional abilities during feeding and communication activities when interacting with the individual with whom they feel most comfortable and secure. Therefore, the most valuable information obtained during an assessment is often found through the observation of the infant and caregiver rather than through formal direct testing procedures.

Although observation of the infant's oral movements and respiratory coordination during feeding comprises a significant part of the assessment, function in these areas must also be analyzed during general movement and communication activities as well as in response to different sensory stimulation. Patterns of movements should be observed in regard to the effect of abnormal and compensatory activity of the head, neck, shoulder girdle, trunk, pelvis, and hips on oral-motor and respiratory-phonatory functioning. In addition, it is important to note the influence of oral and respiratory function on changes in postural tone and general movement during feeding, communication, and sound production activities.

Observations of the caregiver and infant during the feeding process should emphasize obtaining information that describes the position of the child for feeding and any changes that may occur in positioning during the mealtime; the utensils being used for feeding and any modifications that may have been made in them (e.g., enlarged nipple hole); how food and liquid are presented and how the infant responds to these presentations; the jaw, cheek, lip, and tongue movements used by the infant; and the infant's coordination of breathing with oral movements during feeding. It is also important to note the ways that the infant communicates and interacts with the caregiver as well as the ways in which the caregiver interprets and responds to the infant's interactions.

Direct Testing

After observing the infant and caregiver, direct testing by the evaluator may be appropriate to more specifically analyze previously observed movements or to facilitate changes in oral-motor and respiratory-phonatory function in order to more clearly define areas requiring intervention programming. Feeding activities that have not yet been attempted by the parent or were not successful in the past may be presented to better analyze the infant's ability to tolerate them (e.g., presenting liquid by cup to an infant over 6 months; placing a teething biscuit on the side gums of an infant over 5 months). Handling that stimulates greater active, antigravity movements and greater rib cage mobility may be provided in order to evaluate potential for changes in respiratory-phonatory coordination, sound production, and oral-motor activity. Of course, if direct testing is not possible, sufficient information should have been gathered through questions and observations to determine the appropriateness of intervention programming or the need for further evaluation procedures.

IMPLICATIONS FOR INTERVENTION PROGRAMMING

Once it is determined that oral-motor and respiratory-phonatory dysfunction exist, it is necessary to develop an intervention program that reflects both the need for direct treatment goals and strategies and the need for goals and strategies specifically related to daily carryover activities such as mealtime feeding. Direct treatment provided by a qualified speech-language pathologist emphasizes goals and strategies for the development of the functional movement components (e.g., active lip closure, up-down tongue movements, jaw grading) required for the use of the oral and respiratory-phonatory mechanisms for feeding, crying, sound/speech production, and communication (e.g., facial expression). Goals and strategies established for a carryover activity must not interfere with the primary purpose of the activity, which in the case of mealtime feeding is maximum nutritional intake.

In order to stimulate improved oral-motor function and respiratory-phonatory coordination during direct treatment, it is necessary to facilitate more active, antigravity movements of the head, neck, oral mechanism, shoulder girdle, spine, rib cage, pelvis, and hips by the infant through strategies based on handling procedures. In a carryover activity like mealtime feeding, proper body alignment through positioning will be essential in order to provide a foundation of central stability from which better oral movements and respiratory coordination can be established specifically for that activity. The generalization of new oral-motor and respiratory-phonatory function to a variety of activities requires their active stimulation through treatment and their incorporation into carryover tasks as they become a more consistent part of the infant's overall functional abilities.

The following case study is presented to better explain the balance necessary between direct treatment and carryover programming. Please note that this example is only discussing the child's needs in regard to oral-motor and respiratory-phonatory intervention and does not represent programming that may be required from a physical therapist, occupational therapist, special educator, or other trained professional.

A child 1 year and 6 months of age with a diagnosis of cerebral palsy, spastic quadriplegia, was evaluated by a speech-language pathologist. A videoswallow study was conducted, revealing no aspiration of liquids or semisolids; a slight delay in the triggering of a reflexive swallow, especially on liquids; and slow, restricted forward-backward movements of the tongue, which appeared thick in contour throughout all feeding activities. The informal clinical assessment found that the infant had head-neck hyperextension, tongue retraction, cheek-lip retraction, and jaw thrusting with retraction noted in bottle drinking and spoon feeding and when initiating sound production; no experience with cup drinking; limited experience with solids, although some horizontal tongue movements were noted in response to a hard solid (teething biscuit) placed on the side gums; a shallow, belly-breathing pattern when at rest; a belly-breathing pattern with retraction of the anterior rib cage during feeding, crying, and body movements; minimal production of sound except for a weak cry; and use of crying and abnormal movements into extension for communication, although quieting with eye contact was noted in response to the mother's voice.

Since significant oral-motor and respiratory-phonatory dysfunction was noted during the assessment, an intervention program was developed. Direct treatment with a qualified speech-language pathologist was initiated with goals to: 1) increase active forward-backward, up-down, and lateral tongue movements with reduced tongue retraction during general movement, feeding, and sound production activities; 2) increase active lip closure with reduced cheek-lip retraction during general movement, feeding, and sound production activities; 3) increase active grading of jaw movements with reduced jaw thrusting with retraction during general movement, feeding, and sound production activities; 4) increase coordination of respiratory function with oral movements during general movement, feeding, and sound production activities; 5) increase the length, loudness, and variety of sound productions; 6) increase the use of facial expression and other appropriate modes of communication; and 7) provide suggestions for mealtime carryover activities at home and in school programming.

Handling to stimulate active antigravity movements while inhibiting abnormal movements such as head-neck hyperextension and procedures to provide oral tactile sensory preparation were the foundation for all strategies used to achieve goals during direct treatment. Once deeper belly breathing with greater rib cage mobility was noted, procedures for stimulating sound production were incorporated with handling. Feeding activities, oral exploration activities, and sound play activities were introduced to stimulate more coordinated oral-motor activity (e.g., lip closure, up-down tongue movements, graded up-down jaw movements) as a greater foundation in active antigravity movements developed.

Initially several direct treatment sessions were used to develop strategies for improving nutritional intake during mealtime. Body alignment for feeding was analyzed and a special insert was fabricated to fit in a car seat that provided a stable positional base from which greater oral-motor activity could be used during mealtime feeding. Modifications in food texture, feeding utensils, and food presentation that appeared to improve oral activity as well as enhancing nutritional intake were incorporated into mealtime feeding. As greater, more consistent active movements of the tongue, cheeks, lips, and jaw were noted in direct treatment, procedures used at mealtime were modified to encourage use of these new movements without interfering with food intake. All procedures found useful for feeding were carefully discussed and reviewed with the child's parents and others who were involved in mealtime feeding in order to make sure that they were comfortable with using the procedures. If specific procedures appeared unrealistic for the caregivers to implement during mealtime, they were either modified or disregarded and other procedures were suggested.

It is essential to keep in mind that if questions exist subsequent to an assessment regarding the existence of aspiration or reflux, further testing will be necessary before intervention programming can focus on making major modifications in or through the feeding area. However, this should not rule out the implementation of programming directed toward improved oral-motor and respiratory-phonatory function, since such function develops and is used by the infant in a variety of different activities (e.g., general movements, early environment exploration, sound play). When dysfunction is recognized early through comprehensive evaluation, appropriate intervention programming can be established to improve the infant's overall oral-motor and respiratory-phonatory function.

REFERENCES

Alexander, R. (1983). Developing pre-speech and feeding abilities in children. In S. Shanks (Ed.), *Nursing and the management of pediatric communication disorders* (pp. 165–223). Waltham, MA: College-Hill Press/Little, Brown & Co.

Alexander, R. (1987). Prespeech and feeding development. In E. McDonald (Ed.), *Treating cerebral palsy: For clinicians by clinicians* (pp. 133–152). Austin, TX: PRO-ED.

Boehme, R. (1987). *Approach to treatment of the baby*. Milwaukee, WI: Boehme Workshops.

Castell, D., & Donner, M. (1987). Evaluation of dysphagia: A careful history is crucial. *Dysphagia*, 2(2), 65–71.

Fee, M., Charney, E., & Robertson, W. (1988). Nutritional assessment of the young child with cerebral palsy. *Infants and Young Children*, 1(1), 33–40.

Logemann, J. (1983). *Evaluation and treatment of swallowing disorders*. Waltham, MA: College-Hill Press/Little, Brown & Co.

Logemann, J. (1986). *Manual for the videofluorographic study of swallowing*. Waltham, MA: College-Hill Press/Little, Brown & Co.

Morris, S. (1982a). *Pre-speech assessment scale*. Clifton, NJ: J. A. Preston.

Morris, S. (1982b). *The normal acquisition of oral feeding skills: Implications for assessment and treatment*. Santa Barbara, CA: Therapeutic Media.

Morris, S., & Klein, M. (1987). *Pre-feeding skills*. Tucson, AZ: Therapy Skill Builders.

Sorin, R., Somers, S., Austin, W., & Bester, S. (1988). The influence of videofluoroscopy on the management of the dysphagic patient. *Dysphagia*, 2(3), 127–135.

III
COGNITIVE, LANGUAGE, AND DEVELOPMENTAL ASSESSMENT

6 Assessment of Infant Mental Ability
Conventional Tests and Issues of Prediction

Elizabeth D. Gibbs

A primary goal of most early intervention programs is to promote the infants' cognitive and behavioral development in order to minimize future delays or disabilities. Assessment of the infant can serve diagnostic and prescriptive purposes. The first purpose, diagnosis, is to identify infants who are developmentally delayed or at risk of becoming so. For this purpose, it is desirable to identify infants who require intervention rather than those whose delays are transitory and will resolve without intervention. The second purpose of assessment, prescription, is to obtain a thorough understanding of the infant's behavior, abilities, interactions, and environment so that an effective intervention plan can be developed.

Tests of infant mental development have been used extensively by infant assessors to identify infants at risk for mental retardation and to design interventions to enhance cognitive development. However, there is growing concern regarding the appropriateness of traditional tests of infant mental ability for clinical assessment and diagnosis (Lewis & McGurk, 1972). This concern stems from research findings that indicate that infant tests are poor predictors of later intelligence (McCall, 1979). Thus, an infant who scores poorly on an infant test may demonstrate average abilities during childhood or vice versa. Furthermore, recent research has revealed that information-processing assessments that measure an infant's attentional abilities in response to familiar and unfamiliar stimuli are better predictors of later intelligence than are conventional measures (Bornstein & Sigman, 1986). These findings demand that infant assessors take a careful look at the value and the limitations of conventional tests of infant mental development.

Accordingly, the goals of this chapter are: 1) to review several of the most commonly used standardized assessments for measuring mental development in infants and toddlers, 2) to examine the research on the ability of infant tests to predict later developmental status or intelligence, and 3) to discuss the implications of research findings for the clinical infant specialist.

STANDARDIZED ASSESSMENTS OF INFANT DEVELOPMENT

Tests of infant mental development began to emerge in the early 1900s following the publication of the Stanford-Binet Intelligence Scale for Children in 1916. The development of these infant tests was motivated by a desire both to measure intelligence earlier and to gain a better understanding of the normative process of early development. Gesell's approach favored the latter whereas Stutsman's Merrill-Palmer Scale of Mental Tests emphasized the former. Bayley's approach was more of a combination of both goals. While tests of intelligence in children were composed predominantly of verbal and conceptual problem-solving tasks, infant tests focused on the developing sensorimotor capabilities of the infant. For example, the development of the infant's ability to use and coordinate eyes, ears, hands, and voice is central to infant assessment. In addition, the infant's understanding of the basic properties of objects and persons (i.e., permanence, responsiveness) is assessed. Only in the second year of life do infant tests begin to resemble the early childhood tests of intelligence. As can be seen in later sections of this chapter, the changing nature of infants' mental development may affect the predictability of infant tests.

Before delving into the research on infant intelligence and the predictability of infant tests, let us become familiar with several tests of infant mental ability. Four tests of infant mental development will be described here in detail. The Revised Gesell Developmental Schedules and the Battelle Developmental Inventory are global developmental assessments that attempt to measure mental ability along with other aspects of development. The Merrill-Palmer Scale and the Bayley Scales of Infant Development have a much stronger or exclusive focus on measuring mental ability. They will be presented here roughly in order of when the original version was developed.

Revised Gesell Developmental Schedules

The original Gesell Developmental Schedules were based on the extensive, longitudinal observations of 107 middle-class infants conducted by Arnold Gesell and Catherine Amatruda during the early 1900s (Ball, 1977; Gesell, 1925). The creation of the Gesell Developmental Schedules was motivated by an interest in normative patterns of infant development rather than a desire to measure "intelligence" as early as possible. Nonetheless, an understanding of normative patterns of development provided the ability to identify infants whose development was atypical. Gesell endorsed a predominantly maturational view of development. In the most recent (1974) revision of *Developmental Diagnosis* by Hilda Knobloch and Benjamin Pasamanick, the maturational view is tempered and greater emphasis is given to the influence of environmental factors. A revision of the Developmental Schedules was undertaken by Hilda Knobloch and her colleagues in 1975 since there were indications that the rate of infant development had accelerated since the original schedules had been published (Knobloch, Stevens, & Malone, 1987). In fact, in the revised schedules adaptive behavior items were achieved about 10% earlier, language behavior items 12% earlier, gross motor behavior items 17% earlier, and personal-social behavior items 16% earlier than in the original sample (Campbell, Siegel, Parr, & Ramey, 1986). Acquisition of fine motor behaviors remained at approximately equivalent age levels.

The Gesell Developmental Schedules were designed to assess the developmental progress of infants between the ages of 4 weeks and 36 months. They were designed to assist in the early identification of developmental problems in infants and young children. The schedules assess development in five domains: Adaptive, Gross Motor, Fine Motor, Language, and Personal-Social behavior. Administration of the schedules involves direct testing and observation of the infant and takes approximately 45 minutes. A parent-completed questionnaire that parallels the test items can be given to augment the direct test administration. Based on the pattern of the child's performance on items at different age levels, the evaluator determines a maturity level or age-equivalent level for each domain. A Developmental Quotient (DQ) is then obtained for each domain by dividing the maturity level by the child's chronological age. The Adaptive domain assesses abilities that Knobloch et al. (1987) considered to be the "forerunner of later 'intelligence' " (p. 4). Items in the Adaptive domain assess abilities such as visual following, coordinated reaching and grasping, finding hidden objects, using tools to obtain objects, completing form boards, drawing, and building block towers. Knobloch et al. cautioned that the Adaptive DQ should not be rigidly interpreted as an accurate measure of a child's intellectual potential. Rather, a judgment of the child's potential must be based on an experienced clinician's integration of the assessment results and other clinical findings.

The revision of item age placements on the Revised Gesell Developmental Schedules was based upon the assessment of 927 normally developing infants recruited from the Albany, New York area. The recruited sample tended to be more highly educated than a representative sample of the Albany area. Based on this sample, items were placed in the age range where 50% of the standardization sample had achieved the behavior. Interrater reliabilities for individual items were determined using a sample of 48 cases and ranged from 88% to 97% agreement. No data are provided in the manual concerning test-retest reliability. Predictive validity of an earlier version of the scales was examined in a study by Knobloch and Pasamanick (1960). Using a sample of 500 premature infants and 492 full-term infants, they found that the Gesell Developmental Schedules DQ at 40 weeks correlated highly ($r = .87$) with the Stanford-Binet IQ at 3 years of age. This high degree of predictability is not typical of infant tests, as will be discussed later in this chapter. The high predictability found in the Knobloch and Pasamanick study may well relate to their use of a heterogeneous sample. Certainly, replication of this study with the revised schedules would provide important information about the reliability of the earlier findings.

In summary, the Revised Gesell Developmental Schedules provide a thorough assessment of the infant's developing abilities. The revised schedules are based on a fairly representative sample of American children and now provide accurate and up-to-date maturity levels. The manual provides useful information concerning integrating the administration of the schedules into a comprehensive medical and neurological evaluation of the infant.

Merrill-Palmer Scale of Mental Tests

The Merrill-Palmer Scale of Mental Tests (MPS) was developed by Rachel Stutsman and was first published in 1931. The scale was designed to measure the mental ability of children between 18 and 65 months of age. The scales are composed of 38 tests (93 items) most of which are nonverbal and performance-like tests (e.g., form boards, puzzles, block building, drawing, folding paper). The testing materials are in some cases outdated, depicting old-fashioned styles of dress and items (oil lamps) that may not be familiar to modern-day children. Only four of the tests are designed to measure verbal ability. It takes approximately 1 hour to administer the MPS. It is quite easy to maintain the child's cooperation since the tests are playful and enjoyable for young children. The MPS yields a total score that can be converted, using the tables provided, to a mental age score, standard deviation score, or percentile. The test does not provide scores for comparing the child's abilities on verbal versus performance tasks. Stutsman did not recommend converting scores to IQs on this test.

The scale was standardized prior to the 1931 publication using 631 children. Details concerning the demographic characteristics of the standardization sample are not provided in the manual. In addition, no data are presented concerning the reliability of the scale. Stott and Ball (1965) indicated that test-retest reliabilities were later reported to be between .72 and .96. Other researchers have found poorer test-retest reliabilities, with average correlations ranging from .50 to .60. Thus, the reliability of this scale is questionable. Studies concerning the MPS's validity have yielded mixed results. In their review of these studies, Stott and Ball (1965) reported concurrent validity with the Stanford-Binet ranging from .36 to .79. One study found that the MPS correlated more highly with the nonverbal portion of the Minnesota Preschool Scale (Goodenough & Maurer, 1942) than with the verbal portion. Some degree of predictive validity is suggested by a study reporting a correlation of .61 between performance on the MPS at 2–3 years and performance on the Stanford-Binet at 5+ years.

In summary, the Merrill-Palmer Scale is an outdated assessment of mental ability among young children that places greater emphasis on nonverbal than verbal abilities. Since the scale has not been renormed since its original publication in 1931, its derived scores are not likely to be appropriate for today's youngsters. Although its content has considerable appeal to young children, the dated material, the lack of recent norms, and the uncertain reliability all argue against using this assessment routinely.

Bayley Scales of Infant Development

The Bayley Scales of Infant Development (BSID) (Bayley, 1969) are the most widely used and most carefully standardized measure of infant development. The 1969 version is the culmination of a long development process that began with the Berkeley Growth Study, an early investigation into the nature of development in infants. Nancy Bayley published the first precursor of the BSID, named the California First Year Mental Scale, in 1933. The scale was revised and expanded for research purposes in 1960 and was again expanded, standardized, normed, and published in its current form in 1969.

The BSID was designed to assess the developmental status and progress of infants and toddlers between 2 and 30 months of age. Since research on previous versions of the scale (Bayley, 1949) revealed that infant mental ability was a poor predictor of later intelligence, the current manual clearly states that the assessment provides an indication of an infant's current developmental status but is not intended to predict later development. The BSID consists of three components: the Mental Scale, the Motor Scale, and the Infant Behavior Record. The Mental Scale consists of items that assess sensory discrimination, eye-hand coordination, object permanence, vocal ability, verbal knowledge, and elementary problem-solving. The Motor Scale assesses motor coordination, balance, and fine motor prehension abilities. The Infant Behavior Record (IBR) assesses a child's behavioral and temperamental characteristics, such as social responsiveness, general emotional tone, and goal directedness. The BSID takes approximately 45 minutes to administer and is typically interesting and enjoyable for the infant or young child. The 163 items on the Mental Scale and the 81 items on the Motor Scale are arranged in order of age placement (the age at which 50 of the children at that age in the norm group passed the item). Conveniently, the age ranges at which 5% and 95% of the children passed the item are indicated in brackets below the age placement. Total scores on the Mental and Motor Scales are converted to standard scores called the Mental Development Index (MDI) and the Psychomotor Development Index (PDI), respectively, each with a mean of 100 and a standard deviation of 16. Extrapolated indexes for children achieving standard scores below 50 have been published by Naglieri (1981). The IBR consists of rating scales for 24 different behavioral characteristics that are completed by the evaluator following the administration of the Mental and Motor Scales. No global scores are derived for the IBR. For purposes of interpretation, the child's rating on each characteristic can be compared to the distribution of scores for children of the same age in the standardization sample.

The BSID was standardized using a sample of 1,262 normally developing children approximately equally distributed between 2 and 30 months of age. This sample was selected from several regions throughout the United States using a stratified sample design. Thus, the characteristics of the standardization sample approximate those of the U.S. population. The manual reports that children from rural communities are somewhat underrepresented in the sample obtained. Recent research by Campbell and colleagues (1986) suggests that the BSID needs to be renormed since it appears to overestimate a child's mental age.

Reliability of the BSID was evaluated using a variety of methods. Split-half reliability correlations obtained were adequate for the Mental Scales (ranging from .81 to .93 [mean = .88]) and were somewhat lower on The Motor Scale (ranging from .69 to .92 [mean = .84]). The standard error of measurement is reasonably small and ranges from 4.2 to 6.9 points on the Mental Scale and from 4.6

to 9.0 points on the Motor Scale. To calculate interrater reliability, a second rater observed through a one-way mirror and scored the administration of the scales. Using a sample of 90 8-month-olds, averages of 89.4% and 93% agreement were obtained on the Mental and Motor Scales, respectively. Test-retest reliabilities were calculated on a small sample of 28 of the above-mentioned 8-month-olds and yielded 76.4% and 75.3% agreement on the Mental and Motor Scales, respectively. Taken as a whole, these results suggest that the scale can be reliably administered and scored and yields moderately consistent scores across closely spaced administrations for 8-month-olds. Test-retest and interrater reliabilities for children at other ages are not available but would be useful.

In the test manual, Bayley reports on one attempt to establish concurrent validity of the Mental Scale by comparing children's MDIs to their performance on the Stanford-Binet Intelligence Scale. Both assessments were administered to a sample of 350 children ages 18 to 30 months. Based on a subsample of 120 who had achieved a basal on the Stanford-Binet, a correlation between the two assessments of .57 was obtained. This correlation is quite high considering the restriction of scores that occurred as a result of floor and ceiling effects. The manual does not present any of the research concerning predictive validity of the BSID. Instead it clearly states that "the indexes derived from the Mental and Motor Scales have limited value as predictors of later ability since rates of development in the first year or two of life may be highly variable over the course of a few months" (Bayley, 1969, p. 4).

In summary, the Bayley Scales of Infant Development continue to be one of the best standardized and most widely used of the infant diagnostic assessments. The test can be administered in a reasonable amount of time and provides the evaluator with important and useful information about the child's abilities and behavioral style. Given their focus on mental and motor ability, the scales provide little information about adaptive abilities such as feeding, dressing, or toileting. In addition, adaptations for handicapped infants are not provided.

Battelle Developmental Inventory

The Battelle Developmental Inventory (BDI) (Newborg, Stock, Wnek, Guidubaldi, & Svinicki, 1984), first published in 1984, is a relative newcomer to the assessment arena. Like the Gesell Developmental Schedules, it is designed to assess a child's developmental status or progress across several domains. Like the Bayley Scales of Infant Development, it can provide a standardized score based on adequate norming samples. The BDI covers the birth to 8-year age range with a total of 341 items. It is administered through a combination of direct administration, interview, and observation. Specific instructions are provided for modifying the test for motorically, visually, and hearing-impaired children. Administration time for the full BDI is quite long, ranging from 45 minutes to 2 hours. The assessment yields scores for each of five domains: Personal-Social, Adaptive, Motor, Communication, and Cognition. In addition, each domain is divided into subdomains each of which receives a score. For example, the cognitive subdomains are perceptual discrimination, memory, academic and reasoning skills, and conceptual abilities. Using tables provided, the child's scores can be converted to percentile ranks and then to standard scores.

The BDI norming group of 800 children was obtained using a stratified quota sampling procedure. Thus, the distribution of race, sex, and other demographic characteristics of the norming group closely reflects the distribution of these characteristics in the U.S. population. For each age range, a minimum of 49 children were assessed. Various measures of reliability were examined and all suggest that the BDI is a reliable assessment instrument. The standard errors of measurement are all uniformly low across domains and subdomains. Test-retest reliabilities conducted on a sample of 183 children using a 4-week interval between tests yielded correlations between .84 and .99 for domain totals at different ages. Interrater reliability was obtained by having a second rater observe and score 148 children. Reliability correlations obtained ranged from .85 to .99 for domain totals at different ages. The correlations for both the test-retest and interrater reliabilities were more variable for subdomain scores, yet all these correlations were above .70.

Efforts to establish content and construct validity of the BDI are well documented in the manual. Concurrent validity of the BDI was examined by comparing the performance of 36 children on the BDI and on both the Vineland Social Maturity Scales (Doll, 1965) and the Developmental Activities Screening Inventory (Dubose & Langley, 1977). High correlations with both measures were obtained ($r = .94$ and .91, respectively). In a sample of 23 preschool children (ages not reported) the BDI correlated .43 with the Stanford-Binet. Interestingly, the domain that correlated most highly with IQ was Fine Motor ($r = .61$). Correlations of the Stanford-Binet with the other domains fell between .40 and .55. The correlation of the Cognitive domain with the Standord-Binet IQ was .50. Since the BDI measures a broad array of abilities, the moderate correlations with IQ are not surprising. Since all of these studies are based on small sample sizes and the ages of the children tested were not specified, further studies of the validity of the BDI are needed.

Thus, the Battelle Developmental Inventory is a well-standardized and comprehensive assessment of developmental abilities in infants and children. Its coverage of the entire preschool age range makes it a desireable measure for following children over the infant, toddler, and preschool years. Unfortunately, with the breadth of coverage, the assessment is, at times, lacking in an adequate number of items to provide a comprehensive view of the child. It is particularly useful for assessing handicapped children since it provides procedures for modifying the administration. Its major drawback is its lengthy administration time. This drawback can be partially overcome during team assessments by having team members be responsible for separate domains.

ISSUES OF PREDICTION

In order to use infant tests appropriately, it is important for clinicians to examine whether their assumptions about the nature of early development and the meaning of an infant's score on a standardized test are accurate.

Begin examining your own assumptions by asking yourself the following questions:

1. Do infants develop at a fairly steady, continuous pace?
2. Would you expect an infant who performed better than average on a mental ability test at 1 year of age to perform at a better than average level on the same test 1 year later?
3. Would you expect the more developmentally advanced infants to become smarter children or better school achievers?
4. Would you expect the more developmentally delayed infants to be slower or retarded or poorer school achievers?
5. Can we measure an infant's intelligence?

Most people, lay people and professionals alike, expect a certain degree of continuity in development, a degree of sameness that forms an individual's identity (as a bright person, a witty person, a solemn person, a slow learner). Many parents look for signs that they have a bright baby, a baby who will grow to be a bright child and, they hope, become an intelligent, successful, well-adjusted adult. Professionals also have expected stability in individual traits such as intelligence. An individual's underlying intelligence, as quantified by the IQ, is expected to remain stable over the life of the individual, barring unusual circumstances. In fact, studies of older children and adults seem to support this view. McCall (1979) reported correlations between yearly IQ tests in late childhood ranging between .80 and .90. However, the research on the stability and predictive validity of infant test scores presents a very different picture.

Stability of Infants' Performance on Mental Ability Assessments

To examine the stability of infants' performance on mental tests during the first 2 years of life, researchers have tested the same infants repeatedly and correlated the infants' scores from one age with their scores at other ages. The resulting correlations are thought to reflect the degree to which infants remain in the same rank order relative to one another (i.e., lower scoring children remain lower scoring and higher scoring children remain higher scoring).

McCall (1979) compiled the results of several different studies of infant development and found that there is remarkably little stability of infant mental ability as measured by infant tests. As can be seen in Table 1, tests that were done more closely together in time have the highest correlations, whereas tests done a full year or more apart have low correlations. This pattern of gradually decreasing correlations as the time interval between tests increases suggests that the developmental changes in infants' abilities relative to one another are occurring gradually (Honzik, 1976).

To help conceptualize what may be happening, consider the developmental course of five hypothetical infants presented in Figure 1. At the first testing they are rank ordered in numerical order with infant #1 performing the most poorly and infant #5 performing the best. If all infants developed at the same rate this rank ordering would remain the same over time. However, the research suggests that development is highly variable, with different children developing at different rates. In fact, an individual child's rate of development may well proceed as a series of growth spurts and plateaus (see infants #2 and #3 in Fig. 1) rather than in a simple linear fashion (see infants #1 and #4). Examining the new rank orderings at the second testing, we can see that they become increasingly different from the original ordering, as the empirical research suggests. Furthermore, if we consider infant #4 as the "average" child (the imaginary child depicted by the norms) and the shaded area as representing the "normal range," we will notice that infant #2 was significantly delayed at the first testing yet caught up by the last testing. Infant #5 was performing within the average range at the first testing and was delayed at the last testing. This pattern of variability is not unusual during infancy and makes accurate long-term prognoses difficult if not impossible to make for the vast majority of infants.

Prediction of Later Mental Ability from Performance on Infant Tests

Our ability to predict later mental development or intelligence in childhood from infant test scores is very poor, particularly among normally developing infants. McCall (1979) compiled the results of studies that had attempted to predict childhood IQ from infant test scores. As shown in Table 2, correlations between tests in the first year of life and later IQ are negligible. Only for tests conducted on infants 18 months or older do correlations increase to moderate levels. This rise in predictiveness may occur because the tests begin to measure symbolic and linguistic abilities, abilities similar to those tapped by IQ tests. Honzik (1976) suggested that this rise in predictiveness occurs somewhat earlier in girls than boys be-

Table 1. Median correlations across studies between infant test scores at various ages during the first 2 years of life

Age of later test (months)	Age of earlier test (months)			
	1–3	4–6	7–12	13–18
1–6	.52[a]			
7–12	.29	.40		
13–18	.08	.39	.46	
19–24	−.04	.32	.31	.47

Adapted from McCall (1979).

[a]Decimal entries indicate median correlations. Median *r* values were based on from 3 to 18 separate correlations obtained from between 3 and 10 different studies.

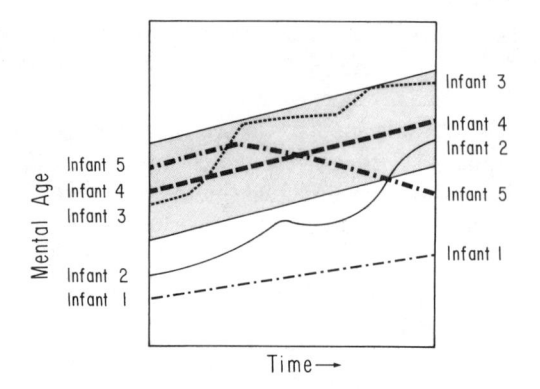

Figure 1. Chart of the hypothetical developmental course of several infants. *Shaded area* represents the "average range."

cause girls develop stable verbal skills earlier than boys. Despite the emergence of moderate correlations in late infancy, McCall (1981) warned clinicians that "prediction coefficients from infant to later IQ are sufficiently low to be conceptually uninteresting and clinically useless" (p. 141).

Between 18 months and 4 years of age, the ability of mental tests to predict later IQ increases gradually. By 5 years of age, correlations with IQ at 18 years of age can be as high as .80 to .90 (Kopp & McCall, 1982). Kopp and McCall (1982) pointed out that the high correlations obtained in group research studies may lead people to expect greater stability for individuals than actually exists. To illustrate their point, they reference the results of the Fels Longitudinal Study of children between 2.5 and 17 years of age. Over this age span, the average change in IQ was 28.5 points, with the IQs of one-seventh of the children shifting by more than 40 points and those for some children by as many as 74 points. All of these findings are certainly humbling to those who previously assumed that development was continuous and predictable.

Prediction of Later Development Among At-Risk and Low-Functioning Infants

The studies from which McCall derived data had all tested normally developing children and excluded abnormal infants. Interestingly, studies of children referred to developmental evaluation clinics and samples including low-functioning children reveal greater cross-age stability of functioning on infant test scores and better prediction of childhood functioning from infant functioning (Honzik, 1976; Kopp & McCall, 1982). For example, MacRae (1955) evaluated 40 infants being considered for adoption and found moderately high correlations ($r = .56$) between their scores on infant tests administered prior to 12 months and their WISC IQ scores at 5 years of age. In addition, using a five-category rating system (definitely superior, somewhat above average, average, somewhat below average, definitely deficient), he found that half of the children remained in the same classification while the other half of the children shifted by only one category. Only two children shifted more than two categories. In another study, Knobloch and Pasamanick (1960) found much higher predictive correlations between the Gesell Developmental Schedules administered at 40 weeks and the Stanford-Binet administered at 3 years among a group of abnormally developing

Table 2. Median correlations across studies between infant test scores and childhood IQ

Age of childhood test (years)	Age of infant test (months)				Marginals
	1–6	7–12	13–18	19–30	
8–18	.06	.25	.32	.49	.28
5–7	.09	.20	.34	.39	.25
3–4	.21	.32	.50	.59	.40
	.12	.26	.39	.49	

Adapted from McCall (1979).

[a]Decimal entries indicate median correlations. Median *r* values were based on from 3 to 34 separate correlations obtained from between 3 and 12 different studies. Marginal correlations are the average of median correlations in the row or column.

(physically or mentally) than among a group of normally developing premature infants ($r =$ .74 and .43, respectively). In their review of studies of at-risk and clinically referred infants, Kopp and McCall (1982) found that moderate-sized predictive correlations emerge for these infants by the end of their first year as compared to 18–24 months for normally developing infants. Again, they cautioned that individual clinical prediction cannot be made accurately on the basis of the infant test score alone.

The better predictability found in these studies may simply reflect their use of more heterogeneous samples of infants, which makes obtaining high correlations more feasible. Studies of normally developing infants may, in fact, underestimate the predictive validity of infant tests for all infants. It may also be that the more severely impaired infant has a reduced capacity for developmental growth and is therefore less likely to be drastically influenced by factors that might alter the course of development for a normally developing child. This does not mean that the development of a severely delayed child cannot be affected by environmental influences but rather that the range of possible outcomes is restricted compared to that of a nonimpaired child. This restriction of developmental outcomes makes prediction of future development somewhat better (but certainly not perfect) for lower functioning children.

Reasons Underlying the Poor Predictability of Infant Tests

Why is it that individual differences in infants' mental ability are so unstable over the first 2 years of life yet become increasingly stable thereafter? Why is our ability to predict an infant's later functioning so poor? Several different explanations have been proposed to account for the instability and poor predictability of early infant tests (see reviews by Brooks-Gunn & Lewis, 1983; Bornstein & Sigman, 1986; Honzik, 1976; Horowitz & Dunn, 1978, McCall, 1979, 1981, 1983; Thoman & Becker, 1979).

First of all, the nature of the developmental process itself may not be as continuous as we may have assumed. As pointed out by Thoman and Becker (1979), individuals may not all develop at the same rate. In fact, an individual may develop at different rates at different times (as illustrated by infants #2, #3, and #5 in Fig. 1, presented earlier). Further, a number of developmental theorists, most notably Jean Piaget, suggest that development is a discontinuous process involving qualitative changes in mental organization resulting in abrupt transitions between stages (as illustrated by infant #3 in Fig. 1). McCall (1983) supported this viewpoint with data revealing greater instability of individual differences when a greater number of stage transitions occur between the testings (independent of the number of months between testings).

A second possible explanation of our inability to predict later development from infant tests is that the nature of intelligence in infancy (and specifically what we measure) is distinctively different from intelligence in childhood. Specifically, infant development is primarily nonverbal and nonsymbolic, whereas later development is highly verbal and symbolic. Early items on infant tests focus on perceptual and fine motor abilities, whereas later items tap the child's verbal and conceptual abilities. The acquisition of symbolic and linguistic abilities typically occurs around 18 months of age, the period during which the infant tests gain greater predictive ability.

Third, the manner in which development is influenced by social and environmental factors may preclude good prediction from infancy to later ages. Many of the studies of infant development have found that the socioeconomic status (SES) of an infant's family is the best predictor of the infant's childhood intellectual functioning (Broman, Nichols, & Kennedy, 1975; Cohen & Parmelee, 1983). Interestingly, until 18–24 months SES is not related to measures of infant development. McCall (1983) described a way of thinking about early development that offers a possible explanation of these results. He proposed that under typical environmental circumstances, early development follows a fairly predictable course. During approximately the first 2 years of life "nature tightly controls the developmental function" (p. 122). During this period, infants have a strong "self-righting tendency" or ability to recover from environmental insults. Hence, most environmental effects cannot push a child too far off the typical path. After the first 18–24 months, the constraints placed on development are gradually relaxed and environmental influences can have more pronounced and lasting effects upon development. This conceptualization of development would explain why SES has little apparent effect on infant functioning yet becomes a significant factor in accounting for childhood functioning. It would also explain why early developmental delays are not necessarily predictive of later delays. In fact, many early interventionists have witnessed the remarkable self-righting or recovery that occurs among premature infants.

The strong relationship between SES and childhood functioning offers little information about exactly what is influencing development since SES presumably encompasses both genetic and environmental factors. Sameroff and Chandler's (1975) transactional model of development provides a useful model of how genetic and environmental factors interact to determine the child's developmental course. Essentially, this model depicts development as being the outcome of ongoing, minute-by-minute and day-by-day transactions between the infant-organism and its environment. The model also assumes that the human organism has a strong self-righting tendency. Abnormal or exceptional outcomes are the result of either "an insult to the organism's integrative mechanisms [which] prevents the functioning of its self-righting ability" (p. 283), or sustained environmental input (or lack thereof) that inhibits development, or some combination of the two.

Adherence to a transactional model of development has a number of implications. First, successful prediction of an infant's developmental outcome requires not only an assessment of current abilities but also assessments of the infant's environment and how the transactions between the two are proceeding. Second, even with an accurate assessment of the infant-environment transactions, successful prediction can only by theoretically possible if the reciprocal influences remain fairly constant and stable (e.g., the family financial situation remains stable, the family constellation remains unchanged, or supportive services remain in place). Since an individual's circumstances are seldom stable and unchanging, successful prediction of development becomes very difficult.

Cohen and Parmelee's (1983) research offered preliminary support for the transactional model and for the importance of responsive parent-infant interaction during infancy. These researchers studied 100 preterm infants from birth through age 5. They found that the quality of the caregiver-infant interaction in the first year of life was a better predictor of infant development at 9 and at 24 months than was the family's SES. For English-speaking families, caregiver-infant interaction at 2 years was also a better predictor of the child's IQ than SES.

Cohen and Parmelee's research also suggested that environmental factors play an important role in promoting or hindering an infant's development. They were able to document that shifts in the child's performance between 9 months and 5 years were related to the quality of caregiving received in the first 2 years of life. Children whose performance had improved had experienced more responsive, reciprocal, and autonomy-encouraging interactions with their caregiver during infancy.

These findings support a transactional model of development that predicts that ongoing and positive parent-child transactions should promote a child's development. In summary, the appeal of the transactional model is that an infant influences and is influenced by the environment in such a way that prediction of later development from a single measure of mental ability in infancy becomes extremely difficult. Yet, on the positive side, the possibilities for the child remain open and malleable rather than fixed and unchangeable.

IMPLICATIONS FOR THE CLINICAL INFANT SPECIALIST

Regardless of whether or not tests of mental ability predict later intelligence, these assessments can provide important and useful information for diagnosis and intervention, if used and interpreted appropriately. These assessments can provide a standard means of interacting with and observing the infant. The structured assessment provides an opportunity to observe the child's interaction with objects, fine motor abilities, interaction style, and tolerance of structured activities. In this setting, the clinician may detect motor or sensory impairments during the course of the assessment that might be less noticeable in unstructured interaction with the infant. There are, however, a number of important considerations to take into account when using assessments of mental or developmental ability such as those described in this chapter.

Tests of infant mental ability should be used as part of a comprehensive evaluation. The assessment of mental ability covers only one aspect of infant functioning and should always be performed in the context of a more comprehensive evaluation. Test scores should never be interpreted without additional knowledge of the child and family. Accurate interpretation of a child's functioning cannot be made without considering information about a child's medical status and history, motor ability, social history and environment, and the quality of his or her current relationships. The clinician's ability to integrate information from various disciplines is crucial to the assessment and diagnostic process. The specific tool used to assist in the assessment process, the test of mental or developmental ability, cannot and should not be used in isolation. It must be used by a skilled infant specialist who is knowledgeable of the nature of infant development and the properties of assessment instruments.

Conventional tests of infant mental ability are not "pure" measures of mental ability. In fact, tests of infant mental ability would be better conceptualized as integrated assessments of infant's functional development, reflecting not only their cognitive abilities but also their motor skills, their social-interactional style, their sensory intactness, and their experiential history. For assessing children with known physical or sensory handicaps, the evaluator should use assessments that are specifically normed for that population or use a process-oriented approach (see Rosenberg & Robinson, this volume).

The information-processing assessments that are being developed are perhaps as close as we can currently get to a "pure" measure of mental ability, although factors of temperament, sensory intactness, and experiential history may contaminate these measures as well. Once these measures become readily available, they could be used when it is important to isolate the child's level of cognitive functioning. However, the more integrative measures of infant development will still be needed to document the child's abilities, disabilities, and response style.

The purpose of the assessment will determine the assessment chosen. The assessment chosen by an evaluator should be related to the goals of the assessment. For diagnostic assessments, the more conventional standardized measures, such as the Bayley Scales of Infant Development, offer an efficient means of gathering information about the child's abilities and the extent to which the child's abilities deviate from the norm-referenced group. While the skilled clinician can make programmatic recommendations based on the results of conventional assessments of mental ability, the development of comprehensive intervention demands more in-depth assessment of the child's functional abilities, the child's environment, and the family's needs more generally. Conventional tests of infant mental ability can also be useful as part of research or program evaluation efforts in which the evaluator is interested in whether the intervention in use promotes general developmental growth as opposed to growth only on specifically targeted tasks.

Evaluators must search carefully for the reasons underlying developmental de-

lay. When an infant's performance falls outside the norms, it is the evaluator's responsibility to search for possible explanations for the infant's delay. Is the infant's hearing or vision abnormal? Are there cultural differences in expectations and experience that may account for the difference? Have the child's social experiences been appropriate or has the quality of the parent-child interaction been compromised? Does the child have a recognizable medical or genetic condition that is known to cause delays? Has the child been hospitalized repeatedly? This kind of hypothesis testing may lead to a diagnosis and provides the basis for arriving at recommendations.

Prognoses about future development should be made with caution. Clinicians are inevitably and understandably asked by parents to make predictions about children's future development. Given what we know about the nature of early development, predictions must be made with caution and with proper qualification. Use the opportunity to educate parents about how infants' development proceeds. Explain that better predictions can be made based on a series of assessments rather than on a one-time observation. Explain that assessments of functioning in the second, third, or fourth year of life will become progressively better predictors.

For children with mild developmental delays (between two and three standard deviations below the mean) of unknown or uncertain origin, the clinician should not make any firm predictions about an infant's later development based solely upon the results of an infant assessment. If the child has a specific diagnosis or condition (i.e., Down syndrome, Williams syndrome, hearing impairment), more extensive discussion of the range of later functioning is possible. However, for most children exhibiting mild developmental delays it is most appropriate to offer parents an optimistic view. For children with moderate to severe delays that are sustained into the second year of life, the clinician has the delicate task of preparing the parents for ongoing developmental problems while remaining optimistic about the child's ability to make developmental gains.

CONCLUSION

Many infant evaluators continue to use conventional tests of infant mental or developmental ability despite criticisms that these tests lack predictive validity, fail to assess pure mental ability, and are inappropriate for children with motor or sensory impairments. The ongoing use of these assessments relates to their ability to provide the clinician with useful information about the child's general functioning and their provision of a norm-based reference. However, their continued use may also relate to lack of alternative assessments that meet the diagnostician's need for norm-based assessments that are "motor free" and that offer adaptations for motor and sensory impairments. Over the next decade, clinicians, researchers, and test developers need to work together to gain a better understanding of infants whose development is delayed or atypical. Carefully designed observations of development among specific groups of children of different cultures or different handicapping conditions and the development of test norms for these groups would assist the infant specialist in making the best diagnoses and predictions. In the meantime, clinicians need to choose their assessments with care and interpret their findings with full knowledge of the assessments' limitations.

REFERENCES

Ball, R.S. (1977). The Gesell Developmental Schedules: Arnold Gesell (1880–1961). *Journal of Abnormal Child Psychology, 5,* 233–239.

Bayley, N. (1949). Consistancy and variability in the growth of intelligence from birth to eighteen months. *Journal of Genetic Psychology, 75,* 165–196.

Bayley, N. (1969). *Bayley Scales of Infant Development.* New York: The Psychological Corporation.

Bornstein, M.H., & Sigman, M.D. (1986). Continuity in mental development from infancy. *Child Development, 57*, 251–274.

Broman, S.H., Nichols, P.L., & Kennedy, W.A. (1975). *Preschool IQ: Prenatal and early developmental correlates*. New Jersey: Lawrence Erlbaum Associates.

Brooks-Gunn, J., & Lewis, M. (1983). Screening and diagnosing handicapped infants. *Topics in Early Childhood Special Education, 3*(1), 14–28.

Campbell, S.K., Siegel, E., Parr, C.A., & Ramey, C.T. (1986). Evidence for the need to renorm the Bayley Scales of Infant Development based on the performance of a population-based sample of 12-month-old infants. *Topics in Early Childhood Special Education, 6*, 83–96.

Cohen, S.E., & Parmelee, A.H. (1983). Prediction of five-year Stanford-Binet scores in preterm infants. *Child Development, 54*, 1241–1253.

Doll, E. (1965). *Vineland Social Maturity Scale*. Circle Pines, MN: American Guidance Service.

Dubose, R.F., & Langley, M.B. (1977). *Developmental Activities Screening Inventory*. Hingham, MA: Teaching Resources Corporation.

Gesell, A. (1925). *The mental growth of the preschool child*. New York: Macmillan.

Goodenough, F.L., & Maurer, K.M. (1942). *The mental growth of children from two to fourteen*. Minneapolis: University of Minnesota Press.

Honzik, M.P. (1976). Value and limitations of infant tests: An overview. In M. Lewis (Ed.), *Origins of intelligence* (pp. 59–95). New York: Plenum Press.

Horowitz, F.D., & Dunn, M. (1978). Infant intelligence testing. In F.D. Minifie & L.L. Lloyd (Eds.), *Communicative and cognitive abilities: Early behavioral assessment* (pp. 21–36). Baltimore: University Park Press.

Knobloch, H., & Pasamanick, B. (1960). An evaluation of the consistency and predictive value of the fourth-week Gesell developmental schedule. In G. Shagass & B. Pasamanick (Eds.), *Child Development and Child Psychiatry* (Psychiatric Research Report of the American Psychiatric Association), *13*, 10–31.

Knobloch, H., & Pasamanick, B. (1974). *Gesell and Amatruda's Developmental Diagnosis*, 3rd ed. New York: Harper & Row.

Knobloch, H. Stevens, F., & Malone, A. (1987). *Manual of developmental diagnosis*. Houston, TX: Developmental Evaluation Materials, Inc.

Kopp, C.B., & McCall, R.B. (1982). Predicting later mental performance for normal, at-risk, and handicapped infants. In P.B. Baltes & O.G. Brim (Eds.), *Life-span development and behavior* (Vol. 4, pp. 33–61). New York: Academic Press.

Lewis, M., & McGurk, H. (1972). Evaluation of infant intelligence. *Science, 178*, 1174–1177.

MacRae, J.M. (1955). Retests of children given mental tests as infants. *Journal of Genetic Psychology, 87*, 111.

McCall, R.B. (1979). The development of intellectual functioning in infancy and the prediction of later IQ. In J.D. Osofsky (Ed.), *Handbook of infant development*. New York: John Wiley.

McCall, R.B. (1981). Early predictors of later IQ: The search continues. *Intelligence, 5*, 141–147.

McCall, R.B. (1983). A conceptual approach to early mental development. In M. Lewis (Ed.), *Origins of intelligence* (pp. 107–133). New York: Plenum Press.

Naglieri, J.A. (1981). Extrapolated developmental indices for the Bayley Scales of Infant Development. *American Journal of Mental Deficiency, 85*, 548–550.

Newborg, J., Stock, J.R., Wnek, L., Guidubaldi, J., & Svinicki, J. (1984). *Battelle Developmental Inventory*. Allen, TX: DLM Teaching Resources.

Sameroff, A.J., & Chandler, M.J. (1975). Reproductive risk and the continuum of caretaking casualty. In F.D. Horowitz, M. Hetherington, S. Scarr-Salapatek, & G. Siegel (Eds.), *Review of child development research* (Vol. 4, pp. 187–244). Chicago: University of Chicago Press.

Stott, L.H., & Ball, R.S. (1965). Infant and preschool mental tests: Review and evaluation. *Monographs of the Society for Research in Child Development, 30* (Serial No. 101).

Thoman, E.B., & Becker, P.T. (1979). Issues in assessment and prediction for the infant born at risk. In T. Field (Ed.), *Infants born at risk*. Jamaica, NY: Spectrum.

7 Strategies for Assessing Infant Sensorimotor Interactive Competencies

Carl J. Dunst, Karen A. Holbert, and Linda L. Wilson

The time frame from birth to approximately 2 years of age is described as the sensorimotor period of development (McCall, 1979; Piaget, 1952; Uzgiris, 1983). The study of the sensorimotor capabilities of infants has its roots in Baldwin's (1895, 1897) psychobiological model of child development. It reached the forefront of psychology with Piaget's (1951, 1952, 1954) publication of his trilogy on infant intelligence, and has more recently been the focus of attention, most notably in the work of McCall (1979) and Uzgiris (1983).

The term sensorimotor development refers to qualitative changes in the psychological and psychosocial functioning of infants that occur as a result of organism-environment experiences and transactions (Dunst, 1984). Qualitative changes in sensorimotor functioning reflect the infant's capacity to acquire, store, and use information about the social and nonsocial world. This capacity is manifested in the various ways in which the child interacts with persons and things in the environment.

The sensorimotor period is generally considered to consist of a number of progressively more complex types of psychological and psychosocial competencies, where each level or stage in the progression represents specific capacities with respect to emerging competence and performance (Dunst, 1988). Although different theories of sensorimotor development specify different levels and stages of development, all are concerned with the changes in the ways in which infants learn and master different skills and capabilities. The importance of the sensorimotor period is evident from work reported in a number of books on the topic (e.g., Bornstein & Kessen, 1979; Lamb & Sherrod, 1981; Lewis, 1988; Uzgiris & Hunt, 1987).

Research on the development of both social and nonsocial sensorimotor capacities has generated a wide range of progressively more complex sequences of behavior attainments for quite varied developmental domains, including problem solving, object permanence, person permanence, spatial relationships, causality, vocal and gestural imitation, communication, emotional development, object play, social play, affective development, and social development (see Dunst, 1984; Uzgiris, 1983). These various models of sensorimotor development, and the research upon which they are based, have substantially added to our knowledge and understanding of the developing capacities of infants.

Piagetian and neo-Piagetian theory in par-

Appreciation is extended to Clara Hunt and Wilson Hamer for assistance in preparation of this chapter, and Lynne Austin, Linda Wortman-Lowe, and Pat Bartholomew for conducting the assessments of the children for the case examples.

ticular has served as the foundation for the development of both assessment (e.g., Chatelanat & Schoggen, 1980; Dunst, 1980; Robinson & Rosenberg, 1987; Uzgiris & Hunt, 1975) and intervention (e.g., Dunst, 1981; Dunst et al., 1987) procedures useful, respectively, for determining and promoting acquisition of a child's sensorimotor capabilities. The purpose of this chapter is to introduce the reader to two different assessment strategies for determining a child's capacities with respect to mastery of different sets and types of sensorimotor competencies. The first involves the use of sensorimotor assessment scales that determine a child's emerging capabilities in response to a priori validated eliciting situations (Dunst, 1980; Uzgiris & Hunt, 1975). The second involves the use of in vivo observation procedures for classifying a child's interactive competencies according to the levels and types of behavioral capabilities (Dunst & McWilliam, 1988). The descriptions of both approaches are designed to provide the reader and potential user of either strategy with the necessary background information to pursue further reading and training. The interested reader should consult Dunst (1980, 1981, 1982), Dunst and Gallagher (1983), Dunst and McWilliam (1988), Dunst et al. (1987), and Uzgiris and Hunt (1975, 1987) for more complete descriptions of the two different assessment procedures.

PIAGETIAN-BASED SENSORIMOTOR ASSESSMENT SCALES

In his now classic trilogy on infant development, Piaget (1951, 1952, 1954) described the emergence of sensorimotor intelligence in eight parallel areas of development: problem solving, object permanence, spatial relationships, causality, time, vocal imitation, gestural imitation, and play. According to Piaget, behaviors in each of these domains emerge through the same six-stage sequence, beginning at birth and culminating in the ability to use representational and symbolic behaviors by 2 years of age. Each stage in this sequence is characterized by response classes that define distinct levels of sensorimotor achievements.

Table 1 shows selected characteristics of the attainments in seven domains of sensorimotor intelligence.

The majority of sensorimotor infant scales developed over the past 15 years are based primarily upon Piaget's (1951, 1952, 1954) descriptions of the genesis of sensorimotor intelligence, and the assumptions and presuppositions upon which his theory is based (see Uzgiris & Hunt, 1975). Although Piaget never intended that his theory provide a framework for assessing the sensorimotor competencies of very young children, his descriptions of the genesis of sensorimotor intelligence have been found useful for this purpose. Casati and Lezine (1968), Escalona and Corman (1966), and Uzgiris and Hunt (1975), among others (see Uzgiris, 1983), have all used Piaget's theory as a framework for constructing ordinal scales of infant development.

Ordinal scales of infant development are based upon a number of assumptions regarding the acquisition of sensorimotor competencies, and the qualitative changes and transitions that occur during the sensorimotor period. First, it is assumed that there are distinct levels in the genesis of different sensorimotor capabilities (e.g., object permanence), and that each level represents progress toward mastery of the cognitive constructs. Second, it is assumed that there is a "hierarchical relationship between the achievements at different levels, so that in principle the achievements of the higher level do not incidentally follow, but are intrinsically derived from those at the preceding level and encompass them within the highest level" (Uzgiris & Hunt, 1975, p. 11). Ordinal scales are designed to assess progressively more complex levels and forms of particular types of sensorimotor capacities where lower level behaviors serve as the "foundation" for learning higher level capabilities.

The Uzgiris and Hunt Scales

The best constructed and known ordinal scales are those developed by Uzgiris and Hunt (1975). These scales measure emerging sensorimotor competencies in seven domains:

I—Visual Pursuit and the Permanence of Objects
II—Means for Obtaining Desired Environmental Events
IIIA—Development of Vocal Imitation
IIIB—Development of Gestural Imitation
IV—Development of Operational Causality
V—Construction of Object Relations in Space
VI—Development of Schemes for Relating to Objects (play)

The landmarks on each of these scales parallel the achievements of sensorimotor intelligence as described by Piaget (1951, 1952, 1954). However, rather than measure just six levels (i.e., stages) of development (see Table 1 above), these scales measure within-stage performances as well. The items on the different scales vary from 7 (causality) to 14 (object permanence).

The test items on these ordinal assessment scales consist of eliciting situations designed to evoke a possible range of critical actions and behaviors from the infant. *Critical actions* are those behaviors that "imply that an infant has attained a particular level of functioning in a given branch of development" (Uzgiris & Hunt, 1975, p. 49). For example, one eliciting situation on the gestural imitation scale involves modeling a midline gesture composed of familiar actions already performed by the infant (e.g., a pat-a-cake behavior). There are several possible critical actions that might be evoked in response to this eliciting situation:

Consistent performance of a particular action, but one different from the modeled behavior (e.g., an up-and-down banging motion)
A single attempt at imitating the gesture
Imitation through gradual approximation
Immediate and consistent imitation of the gesture

Based on the child's responses to this and other eliciting situations on the same scale, the child's level of development in that particular domain can be ascertained by noting the highest landmark achieved. This can be done because of the hierarchical nature of ordinal scales. Inasmuch as the items on ordinal scales are arranged according to level of difficulty, a child's level of development can be determined by noting at which point along a particular developmental continuum the child is functioning. This is the point at which the highest level achieved is followed by the failure to manifest critical actions at all subsequent levels of development.

Clinical Use of the Uzgiris and Hunt Scales

The use of the Uzgiris and Hunt scales for both assessment and intervention purposes has been described by Dunst (1980, 1981, 1982; Dunst & Gallagher, 1983). His approach to use of the scales for clinical purposes is designed to determine: 1) whether a child is showing delayed or nondelayed sensorimotor performance; 2) whether a child is showing normal or atypical patterns of sensorimotor development; 3) the extent to which deviations are present in a child's patterns of development; 4) the exact nature of the deviations, if any; and 5) what types of interventions are most appropriate for enhancing the child's acquisition of sensorimotor competencies. Achievement of these goals is facilitated by use of a set of record forms specifically developed for the clinical use of the scales. An example of one record form is shown in Figure 1.

Each record form includes eight sections: 1) the scale steps showing the sequence of attainments of the developmental landmarks; 2) the estimated developmental age (EDA) placements of the hierarchically arranged items; 3) the Piagetian stage placements of the scale landmarks; 4) the eliciting contexts used to evoke a possible range of behaviors from the child; 5) the critical action codes that identify the assessment items in the Uzgiris and Hunt (1975) book; 6) the critical behaviors that constitute the sequential developmental landmarks; 7) space for scoring the child's responses to the eliciting situations; and 8) space for recording observations and responses of particular interest to the examiner. The information gleaned from the administration of the scales provides a basis for both the quantitative description and

Table 1. Selected characteristics of the attainments of the sensorimotor period

Stages (age in months)	Purposeful problem solving	Object permanence	Spatial relationships	Causality	Vocal imitation	Gestural imitation	Play[a]
I Use of reflexes (0–1)	Shows only reflexive reactions in response to external stimuli	No active search for objects vanishing from sight	No signs of appreciation of spatial relationship between objects	No signs of understanding causal relationships	Vocal contagion: cries on hearing another infant cry	No signs of imitation of movements he/she performs	No signs of intentional play behavior
II Primary circular reactions (1–4)	First acquired adaptations, coordination of two behavioral schemes (e.g., hand-mouth coordination)	Attempts to maintain visual contact with objects moving outside the visual field	Reacts to external stimuli as representing independent spatial fields (e.g., visual, auditory) rather than as a spatial nexus	Shows signs of precausal understanding (e.g., places thumb in the mouth to suck on it)	Repeats sound just produced following adult imitation of the sound	Repeats movements just made following adult imitation of the action	Produces primary circular reactions repeatedly in an enjoyable manner
III Secondary circular reactions (4–8)	Procedures for making interesting sights last: repeats actions to maintain the reinforcing consequences produced by the action	Reinstates visual contact with objects by (a) anticipating the terminal position of a moving object, and (b) removing a cloth placed over his/her face. Retrieves a partially hidden object	Shows signs of understanding relationships between self and external events (e.g., follows trajectory of rapidly falling objects)	Uses "phenomenalistic procedures" (e.g., generalized excitement) as a causal action to have an adult repeat an interesting spectacle	Imitates sounds already in his/her repertoire	Imitates simple gestures already in his/her repertoire that are *visible* to self	Repetition of interesting actions applied to familiar objects
IV Coordination of secondary circular reactions (8–12)	Serializes two heretofore separate behaviors in goal-directed sequences	Secures objects *seen* hidden under, behind, etc. a single barrier	Rotates and examines objects with signs of appreciation of their three-dimensional attributes, size, shape, weight, etc.	Touches adult's hands to have that person instigate or continue an interesting game or action	Imitates novel sounds but only ones that are similar to those he/she already produces	Imitates (a) self-movements that are *invisible* (e.g., sticking out the tongue), and (b) novel movements comprised of	During problem solving sequences, he/she abandons the terminus in favor of playing with the means. Ritualization:

V Tertiary circular reactions (12–18)	Discovers "novel" means behavior needed to obtain a desired goal	Secures objects hidden through a series of *visible* displacements	Combines and relates objects in different spatial configurations (e.g., places blocks into a cup)	Hands an object to an adult to have that person repeat or instigate a desired action	Imitates novel sound patterns and words that he/she has not previously heard	Imitates novel movements that he/she cannot see self perform (i.e., *invisible* gestures) and that he/she has not previously performed	applies appropriate social actions to different objects Adaptive play: begins to use one object (e.g., doll, cup) as a substitute for another (e.g., adult-size cup) during play with objects
VI Representation and foresight (18–24)	"Invents" means behavior, via internal thought processes, needed to obtain a desired goal	Recreate sequences of displacements to secure objects: secures objects hidden through a sequence of *invisible* displacements	Manifests the ability to "represent" the nature of spatial relationships that exist between objects, and between objects and self	Shows capacity to (a) infer a cause, given only its effect, and (b) foresee an effect, given a cause	Imitates complex verbalizations. Reproduces previously heard sounds and words from memory; deferred imitation	Imitates complex motor movements. Reproduces previously observed actions from memory; deferred imitation	Symbolic play: uses one object as a "signifier" for another (e.g., a box for a doll bed). Symbolically enacts an event without having ordinarily used objects present

From Dunst, C.J. (1980). *A clinical and educational manual for use with the Uzgiris and Hunt Scales of Infant Psychological Development* (p. 2). Austin, TX: PRO-ED; reprinted by permission.

[a]The Schemes for Relating to Objects scale on the Uzgiris and Hunt assessment instrument parallels the achievements of the Play domain as explicated by Piaget (1945/1951).

II. **DEVELOPMENT OF MEANS FOR OBTAINING DESIRED ENVIRONMENTAL EVENTS** Child's Name _____ Date of Birth _____ Date of Test _____

SCALE STEP	AGE PLACEMENT (Months)	DEVELOP-MENTAL STAGE	ELICITING CONTEXT	CRITICAL ACTION CODE	CRITICAL BEHAVIORS	SCORING 1 2 3 4 5	OBSERVATIONS
E_0	2	I	Visual Awareness	—	Activity level increases or decreases on seeing a visually presented object		
1	2	II	Hand Watching	1b	Child engages in hand watching		
2	3	III	Secondary Circular Reaction	3c	Repeats arm movements to keep a toy activated		
3	4	III	Visually Directed Reaching	2b	Visually directed reaching—hand and object both in view		
4	5	III	Visual Directed Reaching	2c	Visually directed reaching—brings hand up to object		
E_9	5	III	Visually Directed Reaching	2d	Visually directed reaching—shapes hand in anticipation of securing object		
5	7	IV	Multiple Objects	4c	Drops one or both objects held in hands to obtain a third object		
E_{10}	8	IV	Barrier	—	Pushes obstruction (e.g., pillow or Plexiglas) out of the way to obtain an object		
6	8	IV	Support	6d 6c	Pulls support to obtain an object placed on it		
7	9	IV	Locomotion	5c	Uses some form of locomotion as a means to obtain an out-of-reach object		
8	10	V	Support	7c	Does not pull support with object held above it		
E_{11}	10	V	Support	—	Does not pull either of two supports with object placed between them		
9	11	V	String (horizontal)	8c 8d	Pulls string along a horizontal surface to obtain an object attached to it		
E_{12}	12	V	String (horizontal)	—	Pulls the correct one of two strings to obtain an object attached to one string		
10	13	V	String (vertical)	9e 9f	Uses string vertically— pulls object up from floor		
E_{13}	18	V	T-Stick	—	Uses T stick as a tool to obtain an out of reach object		
11	19	V	Stick	10d 10e	Uses a stick as a tool to obtain an out of reach object		
E_{14}	19	V	Matchbox	—	Opens and removes the contents of a small matchbox		
E_{15}	19	V	Necklace (container)	11d	Invents method to place the necklace into the container		
E_{16}	19	V	Solid Ring	12c	Solid ring - attempts to stack - avoids subsequently		
12	20	VI	Necklace (container)	11e	Shows foresight in placing the necklace into the container		
E_{17}	20	VI	Matchbox	—	Shows foresight in placing a chain into a matchbox		
13	24	VI	Solid Ring	12d	Shows foresight by not stacking the solid ring		
E_{18}	24	VI	Tube (clear)	—	Uses stick to push out a toy inserted in a clear tube		
E_{19}	26	VI	Tube (opaque)	—	Uses stick to push out a toy inserted in an opaque tube		

Figure 1. A clinical record form for assessing the sensorimotor capacities of infants using the Uzgiris and Hunt scales. (*NOTE*: The E [Experimental] items and rationale for this inclusion are described in Dunst [1980]). (From Dunst, C.J. [1980]. *A clinical and educational manual for use with the Uzgiris and Hunt scales of infant psychological development*. Austin, TX: PRO-ED; reprinted by permission.)

the qualitative characterization of a child's emerging patterns of sensorimotor performance.

Quantitative Descriptions

The description of a child's sensorimotor performance in quantitative terms is based upon the EDAs assigned to the landmarks on the Uzgiris and Hunt scales. Assignment of EDAs to the scale landmarks was based on the best empirical evidence available regarding the modal age at which infants generally acquire the achievements (see Dunst, 1980). Although the plasticity in the rate of development of sensorimotor intelligence has led Hunt (1977) to seriously question the usefulness of age placements of the scale items, Dunst (1980) has argued that knowledge of at least the approximate ages at which infants generally acquire the landmarks can be of value in the clinical use of the scales inasmuch as age continues to be the principal benchmark used to gauge developmental status. Additionally, the validity of the developmental age placements has been established in a number of studies (Dunst, 1980; Dunst & Rheingrover, 1986; Heffernan & Black, 1984; Sexton, Miller, Scott, & Rogers, 1988).

The EDAs can be used for several purposes. First, a child's performance in each of the different branches of development can be described in terms of the EDA itself. For example, if the highest item passed by a child on a particular scale is an 11-month item, it can be said that the child is functioning at approximately an 11-month level in that domain of development. Second, a child's range of performance can be ascertained using the EDAs from all the scales. For example, based on the administration of all seven Uzgiris and Hunt scales, the child's performance can be described as "ranging from an 8- to a 13-month level of development." Third, the child's overall or average level of performance can be described in terms of his or her sensorimotor age (average of the seven EDAs). For example, a child whose average EDA is 17 months can be said to have attained a sensorimotor age equivalent to that level of functioning. Fourth, the child's degree of advancement or delay in development can be described in terms of how many months ahead or behind the child is in any one developmental area relative to his or her chronological age. For example, a 16-month-old infant who is found to be functioning at a 10-month level in a particular domain of development can be said to be 6 months delayed in his or her performance in that area.

The description of a child's sensorimotor performance in quantitative terms is not unlike methods used in determining developmental status using psychometric infant tests, although the EDAs should not be construed as having normative value. These scores provide one and only one basis for determining a child's relative developmental standing using his or her chronological age as a reference point for determining advancements or delays in performance. As Lezak (1976) pointed out, a test score "represents one narrowly defined aspect of behavior (p. 118). In other words, quantitative scores, despite their communicative utility, provide little useful information concerning either a child's unique patterns of performance or the types of experiences best suited for enhancing the acquisition of sensorimotor competencies. Only the qualitative description and analysis of a child's sensorimotor performance can provide the type of information necessary to accomplish these goals.

Qualitative Characteristics

The description of the child's sensorimotor capabilities in qualitative terms represents the most important step in the clinical use of the Uzgiris and Hunt scales. Three types of data and information are used to ascertain the qualitative characteristics of a child's unique patterns of sensorimotor performance.

First, the child's development is described in terms of the highest behavior achieved in each branch of development for which an assessment is made. This provides concrete descriptive information regarding the child's specific capabilities in the separate branches of development. That is, knowledge of the *highest landmark achieved* provides information concerning the particular point along a developmental continuum at which a child is functioning. Thus, a child who attains a Stage IV level of development in, say, the means-ends domain, would have his or her performance described in terms of "in order to" relationships (e.g., the child is able to obtain an object out-of-reach by crawling toward it in order to secure the desired goal). Performances in the other sensorimotor areas would likewise be described in such specific terms.

Second, the child's development is described in terms of his or her *modal stage of performance*. Inasmuch as stages are intended to index the qualitative changes that occur in the development of particular competencies, knowledge of the child's developmental standing according to stage placements provides a basis for describing the child's capabilities in terms of the most typical cognitive operations the child is able to perform. For example, if a child was found to be functioning primarily in Stage III, we would know that he or she has mastered an understanding that simple, repetitious actions directed toward objects (e.g., batting at a mobile) and persons (e.g., smiling and vocalizing) have the effect of maintaining interesting consequences in the environment that the behaviors were intended to elicit (e.g., auditory feedback from a mobile and an adult producing an interesting facial gesture, respectively).

Third, the child's strengths and weaknesses, or *unique patterns of development,* can be ascertained by constructing a profile of abilities of his or her sensorimotor capabilities. A profile of abilities provides: 1) a graphic representation of a child's patterns of performance, 2) a means for discerning whether or not a child is showing normal or atypical patterns of development, 3) information on the extent to which deviations in a child's patterns of development are present, and 4) information on the nature of such atypical patterns, if any (see Figs. 2 and 3 below).

Case Examples

Four examples of assessment findings based on the administration of the Uzgiris and Hunt scales are briefly described next to illustrate the clinical use of Piagetian-based scales of sensorimotor development. The cases are presented in pairs—one normally developing and one developmentally disabled child—as a basis for comparing different patterns of development.

Andrew and Helen

"Andrew," a normally developing child, was 12 months old when assessed. "Helen," a child with Down syndrome, was 24 months old when administered the Uzgiris and Hunt scales. At the time of their assessments, both children were also administered the Griffiths (1954) Mental Development Scales. Andrew and Helen attained mental ages (MAs) of 14 and 15 months, respectively. Their Developmental Quotients (DQs) on the Griffiths scales were, respectively, 114 and 61.

Figure 2 presents Andrew's and Helen's profiles of abilities. The figure indicates that, with the exception of the means-ends abilities and vocal imitation scales, the children show different patterns of development. Andrew attained Stage V performance in two areas and Stage IV performance in five areas, whereas Helen attained Stage V performance in five areas and Stage IV performance in two areas. However, despite the differences in their patterns of performance, both children show normal variability in their development (see Dunst, 1980). It is particularly worth noting that although both children had nearly identical MAs, the nature of their sensorimotor competencies varied considerably. The usefulness of ordinal scales for clinical purposes is reflected in the fact that one can discern such variations in unique patterns of development among different infants.

Susan and Craig

"Susan," a normally developing child, was 13 months old when administered the Uzgiris and Hunt scales. "Craig," a child diagnosed as brain damaged with gross motor dysfunction attributed to a nonspecific neurological impairment, was 23 months old when

Uzgiris and Hunt Scales of Infant Psychological Development
PROFILE OF ABILITIES FORM

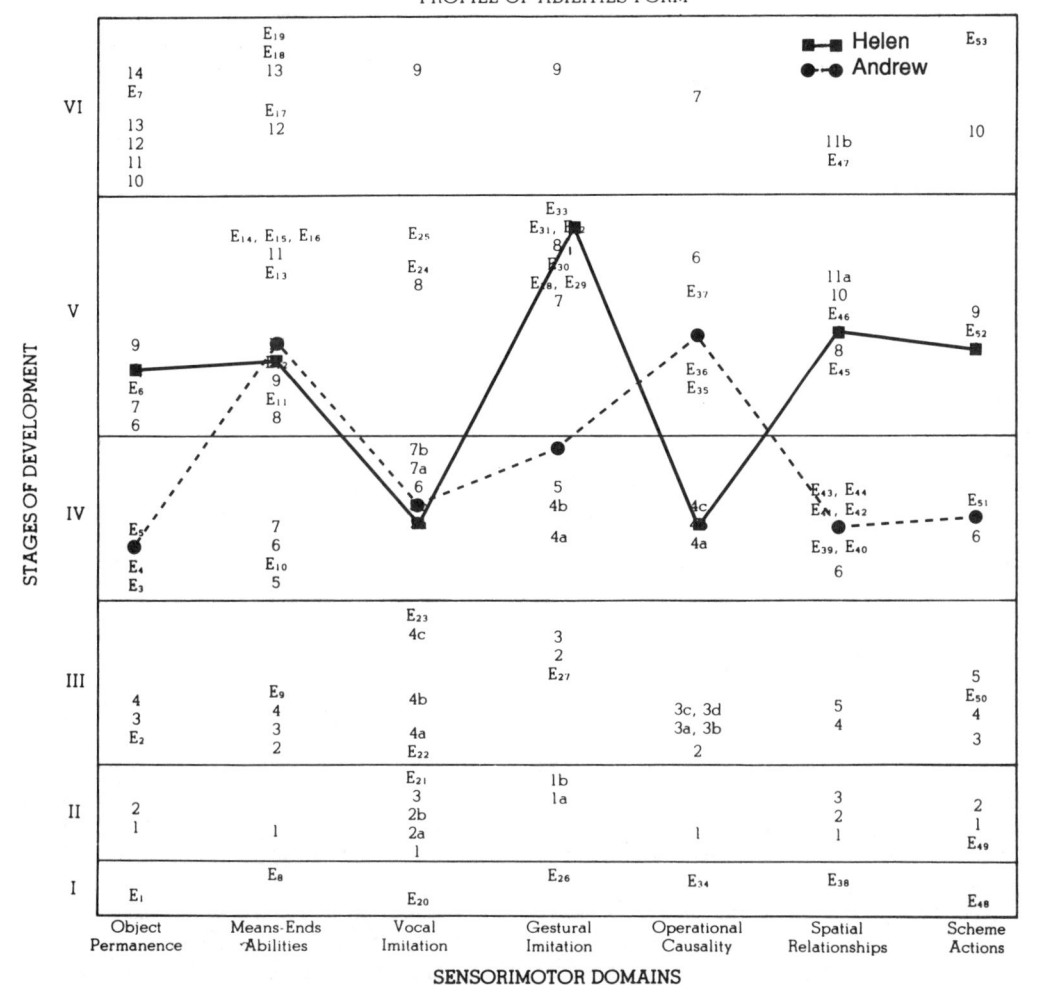

Figure 2. Profiles of abilities for a normally developing 12-month-old infant (Andrew) and a 24-month-old child (Helen) with Down syndrome. (*NOTE:* The horizontal placement of items within stages is according to the model ages at which the landmarks generally are mastered [see Dunst, 1980]). (From Dunst, C.J. [1982]. The clinical utility of Piagetian-based scales of infant development. *Infant Mental Health Journal, 3*, p. 272; reprinted by permission.)

tested. On the Griffiths scales, Susan and Craig attained MAs of 14 and 12 months and DQs of 109 and 52, respectively.

The profiles of abilities of both Susan and Craig are shown in Figure 3. Although both children's modal level of performance was Stage V, it is clear that Susan and Craig manifested quite divergent patterns of development. Whereas Susan's performance straddled just two stages, Craig's performance varied across four stages (Stages II–V). Inspection of Craig's profile of abilities shows that he manifested significant delays in both imitation domains. Such large disparities reflect an atypical pattern of development. Again it is noteworthy that the use of ordinal scales for clinical purposes permits the specification of such disparities, which are generally masked when only quantitative scores (MAs) are used for describing a child's developmental status.

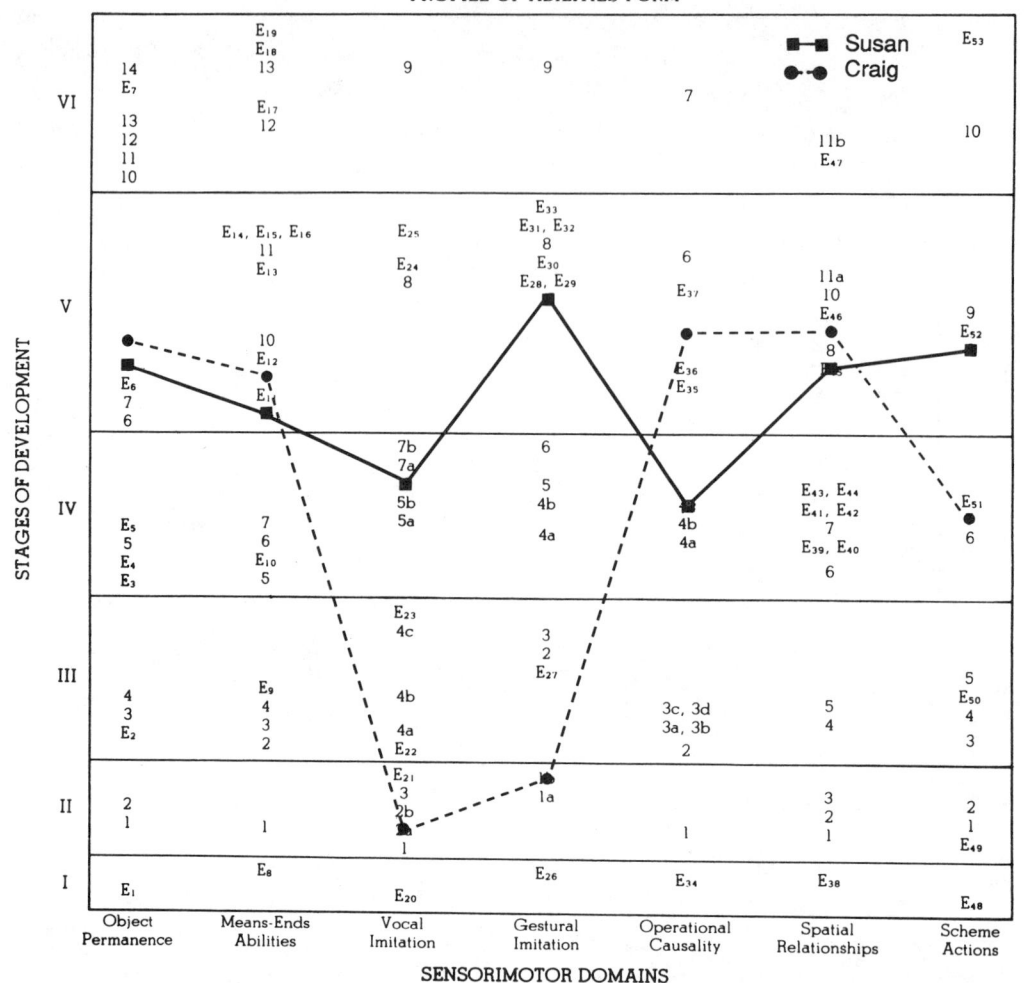

Figure 3. Profiles of abilities for a normally developing 13-month-old infant (Susan) and a 23-month-old child (Craig) diagnosed as brain damaged. (From Dunst, C.J. [1982]. The clinical utility of Piagetian-based scales of infant development. *Infant Mental Health Journal, 3,* p. 273; reprinted by permission.)

A NEO-PIAGETIAN OBSERVATION ASSESSMENT STRATEGY

In addition to discerning a child's emerging sensorimotor capabilities using infant assessment scales, a child's sensorimotor capacities and competencies can also be assessed using in vivo observation procedures. Dunst and McWilliam (1988) recently developed an assessment strategy called the OBSERVE (*Ob*servation of *B*ehavior in *S*ocially and *E*cologically *R*elevant and *V*alid *E*nvironments) specifically designed to capture the range of a child's interactive competencies used to initiate, control, and master different aspects of the social and nonsocial environment. The assessment strategy includes a neo-Piagetian developmental model that serves as a framework for classifying a child's competencies according to levels of performance, and a set of procedures for eliciting, evoking, and recording a child's interactive capabilities.

The major goal of the assessment process

is mapping the topography of both the levels and types of interactive competencies manifested by a child in different ecological settings and contexts. In contrast to traditional approaches to sensorimotor assessment that require the child to match his or her behavior to the response demands of specific test items, the OBSERVE is designed to identify those indicators of sensorimotor competence that meet the criteria of the five levels of cognition defined by our model of development (see below). Stated differently, the purpose of the assessment strategy is to discern the manner in which a particular child manifests interactive competencies at each level of performance. The focus is not on whether the child can produce certain preselected overt indicators of sensorimotor cognition, but rather on how the child demonstrates interactive competencies in everyday situations and interactions with people and things. That is, any behavior demonstrated by the child either spontaneously or in response to environmental changes can be "scored" and used as a basis for discerning his or her behavior topography. Thus, one child may be able to verbalize needs, another may use sign language to make needs known, and yet another may use a prosthetic device (e.g., symbol board) to convey needs; nonetheless, all three children would have manifested identical levels of interactive competencies using different types and forms of expression. To the extent that a child can manifest different types of interactive behaviors, regardless of the particular type and form, a child's topography of sensorimotor competencies can be determined.

A Developmental Model of Sensorimotor Interactive Competence

The model that serves as the foundation for assessing a child's sensorimotor capabilities focuses on the child's adaptive capacities as manifested in everyday situations. Table 2 outlines the five levels of interactive competencies, each of which describes mutually exclusive and progressively more complex sets of interactive behavior that reflect emerging conventionalization and a shift in balance of power toward the developing child. The term "conventionalized" refers to socially and culturally defined and recognized behavior that permits an infant to become a more competent and socially adaptive participant in different settings and contexts. "Balance of power" refers to the child's ability to exercise control over the social and nonsocial environment through increased use of conventionalized and social-adaptive competencies (Bronfenbrenner, 1979).

Attentional Interactions

Attentional interactions refer to the child's capacity to attend to and discriminate between stimuli (Cohen, DeLoache, & Strauss, 1979; McDonough, 1982; Miranda & Fantz, 1974). Operationally, attentional interactions are defined as behaviors that infants use to respond to and maintain stimulus inputs (e.g., orienting toward and maintaining attention to an adult's face). These behaviors provide a basis for ascertaining the infant's attention-getting and attention-holding capacities.

Attentional behaviors may be manifested in response to different stimulus events and demonstrated in numerous ways. These include, but are not restricted to, the following: *looking* at an object or person, *orienting* toward sounds, *tracking* an object moving across the child's visual field, *smiling* in response to seeing a familiar person, *laughing* in response to seeing an interesting event, *rooting* toward a nipple placed against the child's cheek, *grasping* an object placed in the child's hand, *cessation* of body movement upon hearing a familiar voice, and *crying* in response to a sudden noise. Collectively, attentional capabilities are behaviors that are *elicited by* environmental input rather than behaviors used by the child to evoke stimulus events.

Contingency Interactions

Contingency interactive behaviors refer to the infant's capacity to initiate and sustain interactions with the environment in a simple but efficacious manner. Piaget (1952) labeled these behaviors "secondary circular reactions," Watson (1972) "response-contingent" behavior, Uzgiris (1983) "simple unitary actions," and

Table 2. A developmental model of interactive competencies

Level	Interactive type	Definition	Function	Examples
I	Attentional Interactions	The capacity to attend to and discriminate between stimuli	Provides a basis for establishing selective attention to salient and consequently reinforcing features of the environment	1. Smiling upon seeing a familiar person 2. Anticipatory feeding response
II	Contingency Interactions	The use of simple, undifferentiated forms of behavior to initiate and sustain control over reinforcing consequences	Provides a basis for the infant to learn about his or her own capabilities as well as the propensities of social and nonsocial objects	1. Simple lap games (e.g., "so-big") 2. Swiping at a mobile
III	Differentiated Interactions	The coordination and regulation of behavior that reflects elaboration and progress toward conventionalization	Provides the infant with a set of behaviors that permit adaptations to environmental demands and expectations, especially social standards	1. Nonverbal gestures (point, give, etc.) 2. Independent cup drinking
IV	Encoded Interactions	The use of conventionalized forms of behavior that are context-bound and depend upon referents as a basis for evoking the behaviors	Provides the child with a set of "rule governed" behaviors that permit increased "balance of power" (independence) favoring the developing child	1. Verbal or nonverbal communication (e.g., sign language, communication board) 2. Helping "set" a table
V	Symbolic Interactions	The use of conventionalized forms (language, pretend play, sign language, drawings, etc.) to "capture, preserve, invent, and communicate information" (Wolf & Gardner, 1981)	Provides the child with a set of behaviors that permit recollections of previous occurrences, requests for future occurrences, and construction of novel forms of "rule governed" behavior	1. Communicating "want drink" in the absence of reference giving cues 2. Role taking (e.g., enacting part of a previously heard story)

From Dunst, C.J., & McWilliam, R.A. (1988). Cognitive assessment of multiply handicapped young children. In T.D. Wachs & R. Sheehan (Eds.), *Assessment of young developmentally disabled children* (p. 216). New York: Plenum Press; reprinted by permission.

learning theorists "operants." These types of interactions are *instrumental* in producing reinforcing consequences as a result of the infant's actions on the social and nonsocial environment.

Operationally, contingency interactions are defined as undifferentiated response-contingent behaviors that are used in a *repetitious manner* to maintain interesting feedback produced by the child's own actions (e.g., repeatedly producing a reinforcing consequence by swiping at a roly-poly). Contingency interactions lead to the infant's acquisition of three very important developmental capacities: contingency awareness, controllability, and predictability (Friedman & Vietze, 1972; Lamb,

1981; Watson, 1966, 1972). These capacities provide the infant a basis to learn about his or her own capabilities as well as the propensities of social and nonsocial objects.

Contingency interactive behaviors include, but are not limited to, the following: *batting* at a mobile to produce auditory feedback, *touching* an adult's mouth to get the person to repeat an interesting sound, *shaking* or *banging* a rattle to produce a sound, *vocalizing* to get someone's attention, *smiling* to get a person to repeat an interesting spectacle, and *rolling* over to reinstigate a social interaction (see Dunst, 1981, and Dunst & Lesko, 1988, for more complete compilations of infant response-contingent behavior). In contrast to the attention-getting and attention-holding behaviors characteristic of attentional interactions, contingency interactions represent a set of behaviors that allow a child to interact with the environment in a simple but nonetheless competent manner. Contingency behaviors are those that *elicit* as opposed to ones that are elicited by environmental stimuli.

Differentiated Interactions

Differentiated interactions refer to the infant's capacity to both *coordinate* and *regulate* (modify, adjust, etc.) behavior in a manner that reflects elaboration and progress toward conventionalization. Operationally, differentiated interactions are defined as non-rule-governed, socially defined behaviors that match or approximate social standards and expectations (cup drinking, walking, waving, extending the arms out to be picked up, etc.). The child's acquisition of differentiated behavior is affected in part by environmental demands and adaptations, but especially by adult expectations regarding the infant's use of conventionalized behavior. Differentiated conventionalized behaviors make the child "social," so to speak, and provide the child with a set of behavior competencies that permit greater control over social and nonsocial events using culturally expected models of interactions.

Differentiated behaviors include, but are not limited to, the following: *intermediaries* (strings, supports, "tools," etc.) used as means to secure desired objects, *imitating* novel sounds and gestures, *socially recognized* actions used in play with objects, *locomotion* (of any form) to obtain a desired object, use of a *cup or spoon* (as tools) to feed oneself, use of *nonverbal gestures* to communicate needs and desires, and attempts *to take off and put on* clothes. Taken together, these various behaviors reflect differentiated elaborations and adaptations as well as increased conventionalization in response to interactions with the environment.

Encoded Interactions

Encoded interactive behaviors refer to a child's capacity to use conventionalized forms of behavior (either culturally [e.g., verbal language] or arbitrarily [e.g., Rebus symbols] established) that are based upon a set of rules that govern their construction. Encoded behaviors equip the child with a range of competencies that he or she can use to both initiate and sustain interactions (e.g., signing "more play" to indicate a desire to continue a game) and adapt and respond to requests and demands (e.g., answering questions using a communication board). Operationally, encoded interactions are defined as conventionalized signals that reflect an underlying set of rules that govern their construction but that depend upon perceptually present stimuli in order to be manifested.

In contrast to Uzgiris (1983) and others (e.g., Siebert, Hogan, & Mundy, 1982), who equate encoded behaviors with representational behaviors (à la Piaget, 1951), we make a fundamental distinction between the two types of cognitive capacities. This distinction is consistent with evidence indicating that encoded behaviors are a transitional level of functioning between behaviors typifying differentiated actions and symbolic functioning (see especially McCune-Nicolich, 1981). In our model, encoded behaviors may take the form of signifiers for the signified, but their manifestation is apparently the result of reference-giving cues that evoke the behaviors. For example, Bloom (1970) described a situation in which a child used the words "mommy bounce" to request continuation of a game involving the mother bouncing the child up and down on a bed, a game that the mother had initiated. In this instance, the context-bound nature of the interaction plays a fundamental role in the child's use of the words.

Encoded interactions may be demonstrated in any of the following ways: verbal language, sign language, symbol systems, computerized voice-synthesized communication devices, pretend play, "following rules," and the like. In contrast to differentiated behaviors, which are often trial-and-error and non–rule governed, encoded behaviors are characterized by the preplanning of actions followed by deployment based upon culturally or arbitrarily established rules.

Symbolic Interactions

Symbolic interactions refer to the child's capacity to use words, images, figures, memory, drawings, numbers, and the like as signifiers for the objects, persons, events, and so forth that are symbolized. In contrast to encoded behaviors, which are manifested in response to the immediate demands of the environment in which the child is presently functioning, symbolic behaviors permit recollection of previous events or evocations of future events (e.g., saying "see doggie" to communicate an encounter that happened several days ago). Operationally, symbolic interactions are defined as rule-governed conventionalized behaviors that are used to describe, request, enact, and so on persons, objects, or events in the *absence* of reference-giving cues.

The major characteristics of symbolic behavior are: *decontextualization* (lessening of reliance on stimulus support for signifiers to be used to signify objects, persons, and events); *distancing* (capacity to use signifiers that are both physically different and increasingly distant from the referent in time and space); and *sign-signifier differentiation* (the use of socially recognized and defined signs as signifiers) (Bates, Benigni, Bretherton, Camaioni, & Volterra, 1979; McCune-Nicolich, 1981; Wolf & Gardner, 1981). Symbolic interactive competencies provide the child with a set of rule-governed behaviors that permit the child to interact with the social and nonsocial environment in an adaptive manner using almost entirely conventionalized behavior. In contrast to encoded behaviors, which are context-bound, symbolic interactions permit reflections on the past, requests for future events, and the construction of new forms of expression through combinations of different symbols and signs.

As discussed elsewhere (Dunst & McWilliam, 1988; Dunst et al., 1987), this developmental model of interactive competence has been found useful as an alternative framework for assessing and capturing the interactive capacities of both nonhandicapped and handicapped infants, but particularly multiply handicapped children, inasmuch as the model permits the use of a wide variety of behavior indicators for inferring mastery of different levels and types of competence. Indeed, the model was originally developed, and accompanying assessment procedures devised, in response to the failure of traditional infant assessment procedures, including Piagetian-based sensorimotor scales (Dunst, 1980; Uzgiris & Hunt, 1975), to capture the capabilities of handicapped infants. Quite often, infants were observed demonstrating interactive competencies in everyday interactions with their social and nonsocial environment despite the fact that they did not display equivalent forms of the behaviors when administered either or both psychometric and Piagetian-based assessment scales. The OBSERVE grew out of this oftentimes observed difference.

An Observation Assessment Strategy

The OBSERVE assessment strategy includes a record form for recording the ongoing interactions a child has with the social and nonsocial environment and a set of "eliciting" situations designed to evoke a range of adaptations to changes in the events experienced by the child. The assessment process itself entails the "mapping" of a child's interactive behavior across a variety of settings and contexts in order to discern the levels, types, and forms of interactive competencies of which the child is capable. Basically, any behavior manifested by the child, regardless of its type or form, is recorded as an interactive competency to the extent that it meets the criteria for assignment to a particular level of development according to our interactive competency model.

OBSERVE Record Form

The OBSERVE form (see Fig. 4 below) includes space for noting the particular interactive behaviors manifested by the child and space for noting the particular level of interactive competency to which the behavior is assigned. The form also includes space for recording a child's name, birth date, and age; assessment date; the context or setting in which the assessment was conducted; and the person recording the child's behavior capabilities.

As noted above, the developmental model used as a framework for mapping a child's topography of interactive competencies includes five mutually exclusive sets or levels of behavior capabilities. We have found it useful on both theoretical and practical grounds to consider the intermediate points between levels as transitional periods, so that behaviors that "fall in between" can be accurately classified and assigned to particular levels of functioning. For example, a child who is able to pick up a toy and bang it on a table surface but does not yet do so in any conventionalized way would be said to be in a transition phase between the contingency and differentiated interactive competency levels. The five major levels plus the four transition points generate a nine-level model that provides a broader based framework for capturing the levels and types of interactive competencies displayed by a child. This nine-level framework is a major feature of the OBSERVE record form.

The use of the OBSERVE for assessment purposes includes nothing more than a running account of behaviors demonstrated by the child in particular settings and contexts. A "set" of OBSERVE record forms are generated for each assessment setting. The findings from the combined set of record forms permit comparison between settings with regard to the child's topography of interactive competencies (see Table 3 below). A portion of a completed assessment is shown in Figure 4 for a 36-month-old handicapped child functioning at a 9-month developmental level according to the Griffiths (1954) scales. As can be seen, the results yield a picture of the child's response topography with respect to both level and type of behavior capabilities. The usefulness of the OBSERVE derives from its ability to help structure data collection and classification.

Methods for Eliciting Interactive Competencies

A child's topography of interactive competencies may be determined in a number of ways; however, it is most easily determined by observing the child's responsiveness to different environmental stimuli and events in different settings and contexts. Uzgiris and Hunt (1975), in their description of the use of ordinal scales of infant psychological development, make a distinction between eliciting situations and critical behaviors manifested in response to such situations, which also has been found useful in our own work. Eliciting situations are procedures that are designed to evoke a possible range of critical behaviors that represent different levels of cognitive functioning. Broadly conceived, any stimulus event to which a child is exposed represents an eliciting situation and the child's range of responses provides a basis for discerning cognitive competence. Thus, a child's sensorimotor capacities can be discerned by noting which stimulus events (eliciting situations) evoke different types and forms of behavior. Such an approach will yield valuable information regarding a child's topography of interactive competencies.

Eliciting situations may be conceptualized in a number of different ways. At their simplest level, they may be thought of as naturally occurring events (e.g., feeding) that take place on a routine basis in the child's life. The question posed at this level is, "What types and forms of interactive competencies are manifested during routine events?" At a second level, we may vary a typical routine (e.g., not responding to a communicative bid) and ask the question, "How does the child adapt to disconfirmation of an expectation?" We know, for example, that

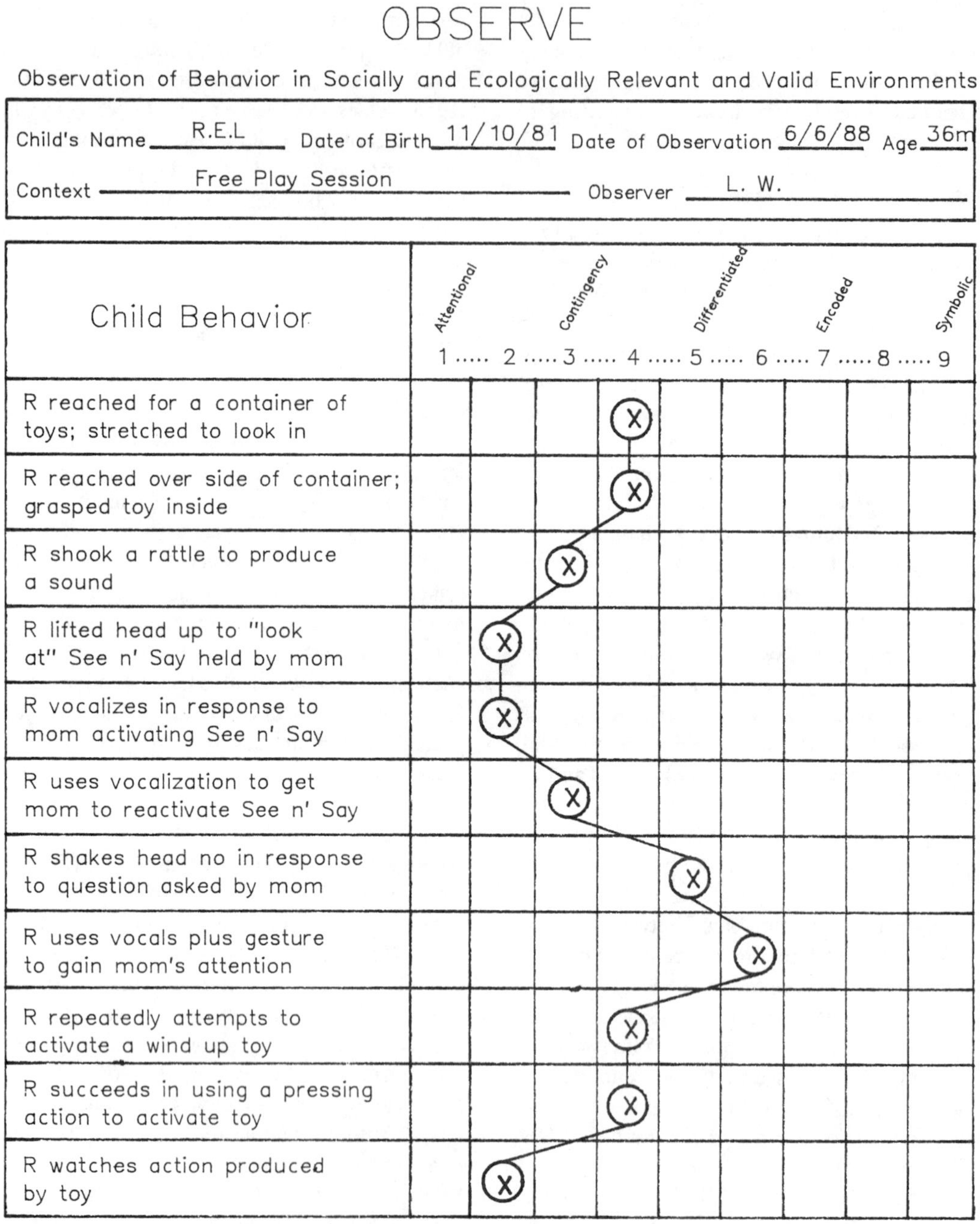

OBSERVE

Observation of Behavior in Socially and Ecologically Relevant and Valid Environments

Child's Name: R.E.L Date of Birth: 11/10/81 Date of Observation: 6/6/88 Age: 36m
Context: Free Play Session Observer: L. W.

Child Behavior	Attentional 1....2....3	Contingency 3....4	Differentiated 4....5....6	Encoded 6....7....8	Symbolic 8....9
R reached for a container of toys; stretched to look in			X (4)		
R reached over side of container; grasped toy inside			X (4)		
R shook a rattle to produce a sound		X (3)			
R lifted head up to "look at" See n' Say held by mom	X (2)				
R vocalizes in response to mom activating See n' Say	X (2)				
R uses vocalization to get mom to reactivate See n' Say		X (3)			
R shakes head no in response to question asked by mom			X (5)		
R uses vocals plus gesture to gain mom's attention				X (6)	
R repeatedly attempts to activate a wind up toy			X (4)		
R succeeds in using a pressing action to activate toy			X (4)		
R watches action produced by toy	X (2)				

Figure 4. Portions of assessment findings using the OBSERVE to map a child's topography of interactive competencies.

disconfirmations typically have the effect of evoking adaptations, and if the child has the capacity to manifest differentiated, encoded, or symbolic behaviors, the probability of the child producing these types of behaviors will be enhanced considerably. At a third level, we may introduce novelty into a routine (e.g., introducing new materials) and ask the question, "Do the types and forms of behavior reflect the child's capacity to master features of the demands posed by the novelty?" At a fourth level, we may vary the interpersonal context of the child's interactions with the environment (e.g., introducing a second adult or second child into a child-person play episode) and ask the question, "What types and forms of behavior are manifested as a function of variations in interpersonal context?" At a fifth level, we may change the physical context for the child (e.g., move the child from one setting to another) and ask the question, "Do the types and forms of behavior vary as a function of context, and in what manner?" By no means are these five types of eliciting situations mutually exclusive or exhaustive. The point that we want to make is that each and every stimulus event with which the child is confronted represents a potential eliciting situation, and the extent to which we capture a child's responses to these eliciting situations permits a determination of his or her sensorimotor interactive competencies.

Case Examples

Two sets of case examples are presented next to illustrate the utility of both our developmental model and the OBSERVE for assessment purposes. The first shows the additional information obtained from the OBSERVE compared to that found using traditional psychometric tests. The second presents portions of an assessment conducted with a child within a preschool classroom setting to illustrate how the OBSERVE can detect differences in the display of competence across different settings.

OBSERVE Versus
Traditional Assessment Procedures

The extent to which the OBSERVE produced similar or different findings compared to results obtained on traditional psychometric tests (Griffiths, 1954) was determined for four children with cerebral palsy, each differing in the severity of their developmental disability (DQs). Each child had obtained about an 8-month MA on the Griffiths (1954) scales. The frequency of occurrence of behaviors at each of the nine levels on the OBSERVE was determined for each child based upon a 15-minute free-play episode involving the children and their mothers. The frequency of occurrence of behavior on the Griffiths scales was determined by assigning all the scale items to one of the nine OBSERVE levels, counting the frequency of "passes" of items at each level, and adjusting the total score by the differences in the amount of time required to administer both assessment procedures (15 minutes vs. 30–40 minutes, on the average). The latter provided a basis for comparing the "relative" yield from the two assessment methods controlling for the amount of time needed to characterize a child's topography of interactive competencies.

The results are shown in Figure 5. Overall, the assessment findings generally showed that the OBSERVE yielded a larger proportion of behaviors at each level of development. For three of the children (A, B, and C), the findings showed that the OBSERVE detected emerging capacities at one level higher than that found on the Griffiths scales. Collectively, the data displayed in Figure 5 illustrate that the two different assessment approaches yield different "topographies" of behavior capabilities, and that the OBSERVE provided additional information not discernible from the Griffiths results.

Across-Setting Comparisons

Table 3 shows portions of an assessment conducted with "Jason," a 60-month-old, severely impaired, multiply handicapped cerebral palsied child, as part of his participation in a classroom program. At the time of the assessment, Jason was functioning at a 14-month level according to the Griffiths (1954) Mental Development Scales. Within our levels of interactive competence framework, this would place him approximately at the differentiated level of development. As Table 3 clearly shows, however, Jason was capable of much more sophisticated types and forms of interactive competencies when alternative indicators of sensorimotor functioning were used to map his topography of behavior. Specifically, he displayed a broad range of encoded interactive competencies, although as one can see, this varied as a function of the particular classroom

Table 3. Selected findings from using the OBSERVE for mapping Jason's Topography of Behavior[a]

| Levels of development | Context of assessment ||||||
	Circle time	Free play	Group time	Meals	Outside play	Bathroom
Attentional Interactions	1) Looks at caregiver when she's talking/singing 2) Orients toward different caregivers/children when they talk	1) Attends to caregiver's actions 2) Laughs at funny events 3) Tracks objects moving in and out of visual field	1) Smiles when talked to 2) Attends to other children 3) Looks with interest at toys placed on his travel chair tray	1) Watches other children at the table 2) Searches for sources of sounds	1) Orients toward voice when his name is called 2) Pays attention to sights and sounds on the playground	1) Tracks children/caregivers as they come and go
Contingency Interactions	1) Reaches for child to initiate interaction 2) Vocalizes to get adult's attention	1) Makes kite (suspended from ceiling) move using a string attached to the child's arm 2) Swipes at wind chimes to make them move 3) Rolls over to re-initiate social interaction	1) Smiles/laughs to get adult to continue activity 2) Picks up toys and "examines" them	1) Finger feeds self with some difficulty	1) Vocalizes to have an adult continue activity (e.g., swinging)	
Differentiated Interactions	1) Responds to "What do you want to sing now?" using arm movements to indicate which song he wants to hear (nonconventional gestures) 2) Imitates actions of other children/caregivers	1) Moves toward play activity in walker 2) Points to items on shelf	1) Chooses "favorite" activity among several options 2) Points to items he wants if out of reach	1) Uses head shake/facial expression to indicate yes/no 2) Reaches for/grasps spoon to help with feeding	1) Moves toward children (in walker) to engage in play episodes 2) Will imitate motor actions made by other children	1) Will indicate yes/no when asked if he has to go to the bathroom 2) "Raises arms" to be taken out of walker/chair

108

Differentiated Interactions (con't)	3) Engages in reciprocal turn taking during interactive episodes	3) Uses objects/toys to initiate play with caregiver 4) Demonstrates complex motor action with objects (rolls car) 5) "Talks" and holds pretend phone conversations	3) Associates sound with action (attempts car sounds) 4) Hands adult toys and objects to have them activated 5) Shows ability to feed doll using spoon and bottle	3) Uses spoon to eat with (although with considerable difficulty)	3) Plays cooperatively with other children (takes turns trying to throw ball)
Encoded Interactions		1) Engages in pretend play (makes hotdogs, puts them in the oven to cook) 2) Pretends to "drive car"—vocalizations in attempt to make a motor sound 3) Uses communication board to indicate desired activity 4) Engages in pretend eating/drinking in doll corner	1) Displays problem solving abilities in getting to objects/activities he wants 2) Will put dolls in appropriate situations when playing house, (e.g., baby in bed in bedroom, car in garage, stove in kitchen)	1) Uses symbol board to select food item he wants	1) Chooses from approximately 10 outside activities on communication board 2) Follows series of two related commands
Symbolic Interactions				1) Uses a symbol board to signal desire to go to the kitchen and eat	

From Dunst, C.J., & McWilliam, R.A. (1988). Cognitive assessment of multiply handicapped young children. In T.D. Wachs & R. Sheehan (Eds.), *Assessment of young developmentally disabled children* (pp. 220–223). New York: Plenum Press; reprinted by permission.

[a]Many of the behaviors that Jason displayed were approximations of those described because of his physical impairment. In all instances, however, he conveyed his understanding/capabilities using overt indicators that permitted one to infer a certain level of mastery and interactive capabilities.

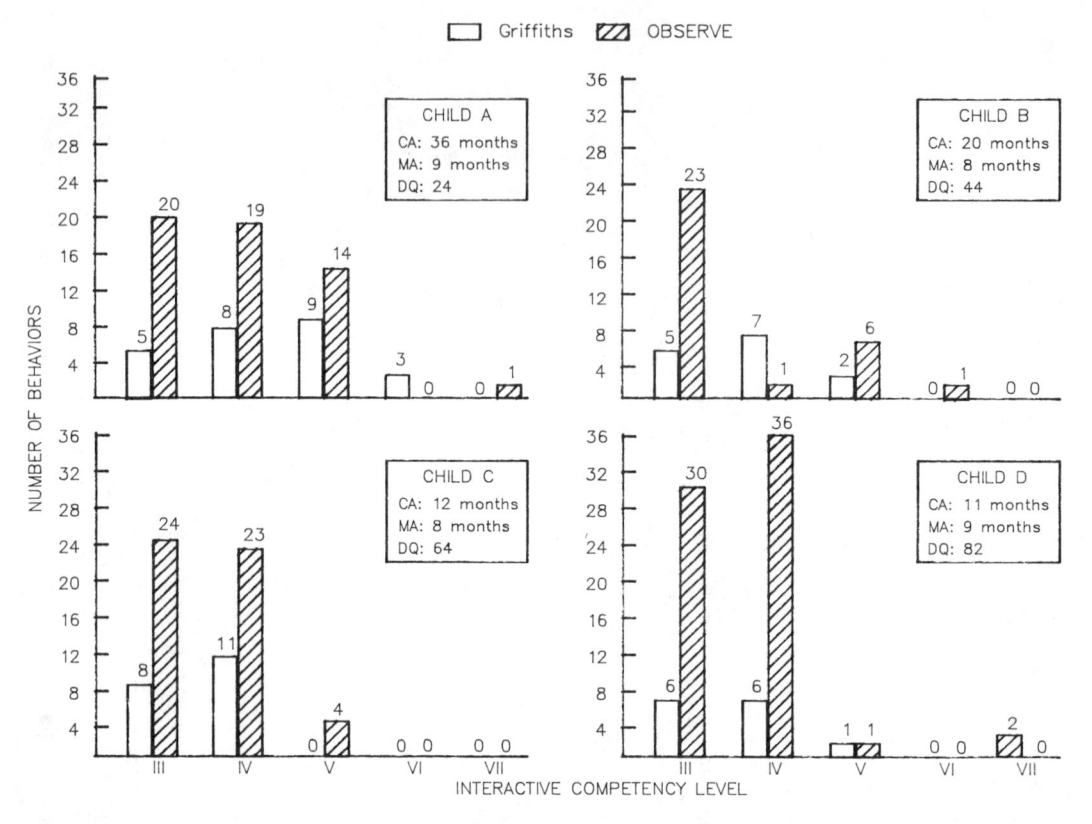

Figure 5. Comparison of the results of two differing approaches to assessing sensorimotor development of four children with cerebral palsy. (*NOTE:* The occurrence of behaviors at each level for the two assessment strategies has been adjusted based upon the different lengths of time required to administer each approach—see text.)

routine in which the assessment was conducted. Nonetheless, the "mapping" process illustrates the utility of this assessment approach for discerning the types and forms of interactive competencies displayed by a child. It also demonstrates the additional "yield" obtained using the OBSERVE compared to a more traditional method of cognitive assessment.

SUMMARY AND CONCLUSION

The purpose of this chapter was to describe two different approaches for assessing the sensorimotor interactive competencies of young children functioning developmentally between birth and approximately 2 years of age. The first illustrated the clinical use of the Uzgiris and Hunt (1975) scales for discerning a child's levels and unique pattern of sensorimotor functioning. The second illustrated the use of an observation procedure (Dunst & McWilliam, 1988) for mapping a child's topography of sensorimotor interactive competencies. A variety of case examples were used to show the strengths of both assessment strategies.

The assessment methods described in this chapter are designed to be used as part of early intervention practices for identifying and promoting a child's acquisition of sensorimotor competencies (Dunst, 1981; Dunst et al., 1987). More specifically, both assessment approaches are designed to establish a child's emerging sensorimotor capabilities as a basis for introducing learning activities that match a child's level of interest and functioning (Dunst, 1988), and that build upon, expand, and strengthen a child's social-adaptive capacities.

To the extent that either approach helps the early intervention practitioner to achieve these outcomes, the usefulness of the assessment methods will have been demonstrated.

REFERENCES

Baldwin, J.M. (1895). *Mental development in the child and the race: Methods and processes.* New York: Macmillan.

Baldwin, J.M. (1897). *Social and ethical interpretations in mental development.* New York: Macmillan.

Bates, E., Benigni, I., Bretherton, T., Camaioni, L., & Volterra, V. (1979). *The emergence of symbols.* New York: Academic Press.

Bloom, L. (1970). *Language development: Form and function of emerging grammars.* Cambridge, MA: MIT Press.

Bornstein, M., & Kessen, W. (Eds.). (1979). *Psychological development from infancy: Image to intention.* Hillsdale, NJ: Lawrence Erlbaum Associates.

Bronfenbrenner, U. (1979). *The ecology of human development.* Cambridge, MA: Harvard University Press.

Casati, L., & Lezine, I. (1968). *Les etapes de l'intelligence sensorimotrice.* Paris: Editions de Centre de Psychologie Applique.

Chatelanat, G., & Schoggen, M. (1980). Issues encountered in devising an observation system to assess spontaneous infant behavior—environment interactions. In J. Hogg & P. Mittler (Eds.), *Advances in mental handicap research* (pp. 230–251). New York: John Wiley & Sons.

Cohen, L., DeLoache, J., & Strauss, M. (1979). Infant visual perception. In J. Osofsky (Ed.), *Handbook of infant development* (pp. 393–438). New York: John Wiley & Sons.

Dunst, C.J. (1980). *A clinical and educational manual for use with the Uzgiris and Hunt Scales of Infant Psychological Development.* Austin, TX: PRO-ED.

Dunst, C.J. (1981). *Infant learning.* Allen, TX: Teaching Resources/DLM.

Dunst, C.J. (1982). The clinical utility of Piagetian-based scales of infant development. *Infant Mental Health Journal, 3,* 259–275.

Dunst, C.J. (1984). Toward a social-ecological perspective of sensorimotor development among the mentally retarded. In P. Brooks, R. Sperber, & C. McCauley (Eds.), *Learning and cognition in the mentally retarded* (pp. 359–387). Hillsdale, NJ: Lawrence Erlbaum Associates.

Dunst, C.J. (1988). *Development of young children: Implications for practice.* Paper presented at the North Carolina Symposium on Early Education for the Handicapped, Durham, NC.

Dunst, C.J., & Gallagher, J. (1983). Piagetian approaches to infant assessment. *Topics in Early Childhood Special Educations, 3*(1), 44–62.

Dunst, C.J., & Lesko, J. (1988). Promoting the active learning capabilities of young children with handicaps. *Early Childhood Intervention Monograph, 1,* Number 1. Morganton, NC: Family, Infant and Preschool Program, Western Carolina Center.

Dunst, C.J., Lesko, J.J., Holbert, K.A., Wilson, L.L., Sharpe, K.L., & Liles, R.F. (1987). A systemic approach to infant intervention. *Topics in Early Childhood Special Education, 7*(2), 19–37.

Dunst, C.J., & McWilliam, R.A. (1988). Cognitive assessment of multiply handicapped young children. In T.D. Wachs & R. Sheehan (Eds.), *Assessment of developmentally disabled children* (pp. 213–238). New York: Plenum Press.

Dunst, C.J., & Rheingrover, R.M. (1986). Concurrent validity of the Uzgiris and Hunt scales: Relationship to Bayley scale mental age. *Social and Behavioral Sciences Documents, 16,* 65.

Escalona, S., & Corman, H. (1966). *Albert Einstein scales of sensorimotor development.* Unpublished paper, Albert Einstein College of Medicine, Department of Psychiatry, New York, NY.

Friedman, S., & Vietze, P. (1972). The competent infant. *Peabody Journal of Education, 4,* 1–8.

Griffiths, R. (1954). *The abilities of babies.* London: University of London Press.

Heffernan, L., & Black, F. (1984). Use of the Uzgiris and Hunt scales with handicapped infants. *Journal of Psychoeducational Assessment, 2,* 159–168.

Hunt, J. McV. (1977, May). *Specificity in early development and experience.* Lecture presented at the Meyer Children's Rehabilitation Institute, University of Nebraska Medical Center, Omaha.

Lamb, M. (1981). The development of social expectations in the first year of life. In M. Lamb & L. Sherrod (Eds.), *Infant social cognition* (pp. 155–175). Hillsdale, NJ: Lawrence Erlbaum Associates.

Lamb, M., & Sherrod, S. (Eds.). (1981). *Infant social cognition.* Hillsdale, NJ: Lawrence Erlbaum Associates.

Lewis, M. (Ed.). (1988). *Origins of intelligence: Infancy and early childhood.* New York: Plenum Press.

Lezak, M. (1976). *Neuropsychological assessment.* New York: Oxford University Press.

McCall, R. (1979). Qualitative transitions in behavioral development in the first two years of life. In M. Bornstein & W. Kessen (Eds.), *Psychological development from infancy* (pp. 183–224). Hillsdale, NJ: Lawrence Erlbaum Associates.

McCune-Nicolich, L. (1981). Toward symbolic functioning: Structure of early pretend games and potential parallels with language. *Child Development, 52,* 785–792.

McDonough, S. (1982). Attention and memory in cerebral palsied infants. *Infant Behavior and Development, 5,* 347–353.

Miranda, S., & Fantz, R. (1974). Recognition memory in Down syndrome and normal infants. *Child Development, 45,* 657–660.

Piaget, J. (1951). *Plays, dreams and imitation in childhood* (C. Gattegno & F. Hodgson, Trans.). New York: W.W. Norton. (Original work published 1945)

Piaget, J. (1952). *The origins of intelligence in children* (M. Cook, Trans.). New York: International Universities Press.

Piaget, J. (1954). *The construction of reality in the child* (M. Cook, Trans.) New York: Basic Books.

Robinson, C., & Rosenberg, S. (1987). A strategy for assessing motorically-impaired infants. In I. Uzgiris & J. McV. Hunt (Eds.), *Infant performance and experience* (pp. 311–339). Urbana: University of Illinois Press.

Sexton, D., Miller, J., Scott, R., & Rogers, C. (1988). Concurrent validity data for the Uzgiris and Hunt scales and the Bayley mental scale. *Journal of the Division of Early Childhood, 12,* 368–375.

Siebert, J., Hogan, A., & Mundy, P. (1982). Assessing interactional competencies: The Early Social-Communication Scales. *Infant Mental Health Journal, 3,* 244–258.

Uzgiris, I. (1983). Organization and sensorimotor intelligence. In M. Lewis (Ed.), *Origins of intelligence* (2nd ed., pp. 135–189). New York: Plenum Press.

Uzgiris, I., & Hunt, J. McV. (1975). *Assessment in infancy*. Urbana: University of Illinois Press.

Uzgiris, I., & Hunt, J. McV. (Eds.). (1987). *Infant performance and experience*. Urbana: University of Illinois Press.

Watson, J.S. (1966). The development and generalization of contingency awareness in early infancy. *Merrill Palmer Quarterly, 12,* 123–136.

Watson, J.S. (1972). Smiling, cooing and the "Game." *Merrill Palmer Quarterly, 18,* 323–339.

Wolf, D., & Gardner, H. (1981). On the structure of early symbolization. In R. Schiefelbusch & D. Bricker (Eds.), *Early language acquisition and intervention* (pp. 287–327). Baltimore: University Park Press.

8 Play Assessment
Reflecting and Promoting Cognitive Competence

Lynne A. Bond, Gary L. Creasey, and Craig L. Abrams

Why observe play when your goal is to examine and promote the cognitive functioning of the child? For centuries, play was assumed to be an activity that occupied individuals' time when they were *not* thinking or problem solving. Yet the integral role of play in cognitive functioning has become appreciated increasingly over the past several decades. Infant play is closely related to infant competence, a construct integrating the highly interdependent processes of cognition and motivation (e.g., Ulvund, 1980). Play both promotes and reflects the competencies of the child.

On the one hand, play fosters the development of cognition and mastery motivation, and therefore can function as an effective and pleasurable intervention. Through play infants have opportunities to develop and experience effectiveness in their actions, increasing their competence motivation (e.g., White, 1959) and learning which behaviors are most appropriate for accomplishing desired ends. In this way, play promotes the acquisition, integration, and consolidation of concepts and skills (e.g., Bruner, 1973; Fein & Apfel, 1979; Weisler & McCall, 1976). Moreover, play "provides access to more avenues of information, . . . promotes creativity through the playful use of skills and concepts, . . . [and] through the use of cognitive operations, it promotes and maintains the effective functioning of the intellectual apparatus" (Athey, 1984, p. 14).

At the same time, play is a *reflection* of competence, providing an outlet for mastery motivation and the practice and synthesis of newly acquired skills (e.g., Piaget, 1962; Weisler & McCall, 1976). This is especially true during infancy, the period of sensorimotor intelligence, when much thought is externalized and, thus, reflected in the infant's actions. Not only is the sophistication of play significantly related to concurrent scores on traditional cognitive assessments such as the Wechsler Preschool and Primary Scale of Intelligence (WPPSI) IQ (Clune, Paolella, & Foley, 1979) and Bayley Mental Development Index (MDI; Bayley, 1969; Bond, Kelly, Teti, & Gibbs, 1983), but scores on traditional assessments at 12 months predict the sophistication of play at least 6 months later (e.g., Bond et al., 1983).

A number of researchers have described the regular and systematic changes in infant play and exploratory activity that not only accompany but appear to reflect maturation and cognitive development (e.g., Belsky & Most, 1981; Fein & Apfel, 1979; Fenson, Kagan, Kearsley, & Zelazo, 1976; Fenson & Ramsay, 1980; McCall, 1974; Nicolich, 1977). This work reveals a shift over the first two years of life from: 1) undifferentiated activity toward single objects (e.g., mouthing or banging one object at a time) to 2) behavior that is modified to fit the characteristics of individual objects (i.e., functional play) such as hitting a tambourine and gently patting a stuffed animal, and ultimately 3) functional play involving the interrelationships between objects (e.g., hammering a wooden peg into a peg board). Subsequently, 4) decontextualized and symbolic use of objects is displayed, first employing individual objects (e.g., pretending a bowl is a hat) and then involving multiple objects (pushing a stuffed animal on a plate while pretending that the animal is sledding).

To summarize, there are at least three major trends that emerge in play over the first 2.5 years of life that reflect early cognitive developmental transitions: 1) *decentration,* in which symbolic actions are freed from the child's own body, 2) *decontextualization,* in which pretend play becomes increasingly independent of environmental support, and 3) *integration,* leading to first sequentially and then hierarchically organized play (McCune-Nicolich & Fenson, 1984). Because play emerges in a systematic developmental sequence and maintains a reciprocally supporting relationship with cognition, we find it useful to use play behaviors both to assess developmental competence and to guide our intervention efforts.

This chapter examines various strategies for observing and analyzing infant and toddler *object* play as a vehicle for understanding and promoting the child's cognitive functioning. In general, the assessments we highlight were designed not as standardized assessments of cognitive level but rather to portray the child's physical and mental manipulation of the environment. The benefits of play assessments relative to more traditional cognitive measures depend upon one's specific goals as well as practical constraints (see discussion below), but their flexibility, adaptability, unobtrusive nature, and potential for framing instructional efforts make play assessments an attractive alternative for consideration. Moreover, as Belsky and Most (1981) suggested, analyses of individual differences in free-play behavior may provide a better prediction of future competence than traditional standardized assessments. Free play permits greater manifestation of individual differences in motivation that are both self-perpetuating and critical to infants' interactions with the environment (Yarrow & Pedersen, 1976). This motivational variation, revealed in free play but intentionally suppressed as much as possible in most standardized tests, may be a significant component of the stability of individual differences in functioning over time (Belsky & Most, 1981; Hrncir, Speller, & West, 1985).

Two general strategies for assessing infant play have emerged over the past several decades. One involves unobtrusive observation of the child's free play. The second involves explicit attempts to elicit an optimal level of cognitive performance through modeling and/or verbal instructions. First we will describe each of these strategies briefly; then we will elaborate upon specific assessments that fall into each of these categories.

STRATEGIES FOR ASSESSING INFANT PLAY

Unobtrusive Observation of Free Play

These free-play observations (e.g., Morgan, Harmon, & Bennett, 1976; Rubenstein & Howes, 1976) vary in the degree to which they employ naturalistic versus structured settings. In a very naturalistic approach, the child might be observed as he or she plays at home with his or her own toys, relatively unaware of being watched. In a more structured approach, the child might be presented with a particular set of objects, and/or observed in a specially arranged observation room. The naturalistic and structured settings each have distinct advantages. A structured or semistructured arrangement decreases the likelihood that differences observed in the play of one child versus another are a result of environmental context (e.g., number or quality of toys available) rather than developmental characteristics of the children. Moreover, a carefully designed prearranged environment may be especially beneficial in eliciting more sophisticated play from children who otherwise have limited access to highly stimulating objects or individuals. On the other hand, the use of more naturalistic settings allows one to observe the ways in which the child actually functions in his or her daily surroundings, a factor of considerable importance given the role of play in promoting further acquisition and integration of concepts and skills. In fact, among a middle/upper-middle–class population, Bond et al. (1983) found that infants' free play with their own toys was a significantly better predictor of Bayley MDI than sophistication of play with a standardized set of toys.

By observing child play across a variety of naturalistic settings, one can examine variations within and across individuals in the degree to which certain environmental contexts tend to, for example, stimulate, distract, motivate, or calm the child. For instance, there is evidence that the occurrence of more complex, symbolic/pretense behaviors diminishes during solitary object play (Rubenstein & Howes, 1976; Watson & Fischer, 1977). This type of information becomes particularly important when designing effective learning environments and interventions for individuals or groups of children. Naturalistic observations also have several practical advantages since they can be conducted at any time or place with few resources beyond the observer. One should not, however, assume that they require any less skill on the part of the observer. In fact, the lack of predictability that is introduced by naturalistic environments often presents extra challenges to obtaining reliable data.

Structured Elicitation

The second strategy for assessing infant play involves attempts to elicit an optimal level of cognitive performance by modeling and/or verbally describing a desired play behavior to the child. This method also allows the examiner to make inferences about a chlid's motivational level by observing the individual's persistence at and competence with a particular modeled task (e.g., Morgan et al., 1977) or by comparing the difference between the highest level of play obtained during free versus elicited play (e.g., Belsky, Garduque, & Hrncir, 1984; Vondra & Belsky, in press). As stated above, motivational variation among individuals may explain a significant portion of the stability of cognitive functioning across time

given the complex interrelationships between infant play, cognition, and motivation (e.g., Hrncir et al., 1985; Yarrow, Rubenstein, & Pedersen, 1975).

Both free-play and elicited-play strategies appear well suited for their respective goals, and each has its decided advantages and disadvantages whether used independently or in combination with one another. The methodological ease of observing naturalistic free play is a practical as well as ecological luxury, as is the fact that differences between the approachability and skills of individual examiners are minimized since no elicitation or modeling is introduced. Meanwhile, a multifaceted play assessment that involves several procedures, settings, and coding schemes is most likely to yield the most comprehensive understanding of a child's functioning.

SPECIFIC ASSESSMENT PROCEDURES

Infant Free-Play Assessments

Rubenstein and Howes Procedure

Rubenstein and Howes's procedure was first reported in their home-based study that compared toddler solitary free play with play in the company of a peer or mother (Rubenstein & Howes, 1976). Using a naturalistic procedure, the examiner attempts neither to elicit play nor to introduce novel toys to the toddler. Play is coded on a 5-point scale reflecting increasing levels of maturity:

Low Level Play
   1—Oral contact (e.g., mouthing a toy)
   2—Passive tactile contact (e.g., simply holding the object)
Active Play
   3—Active manipulation of a toy (e.g., banging a toy)
   4—Exploiting unique properties of an object (e.g., ringing a bell)
   5—Creative or imaginative play (e.g., pretending that a stick is a spoon).

Given the focus of this scale, it is probably most useful for observing the play of children who are approximately 8–30 months of age.

In a longitudinal study of children from 12 to 18 months of age, Bond et al. (1983) found that Rubenstein and Howes' play scores showed low but significant correlations with the Bayley MDI. Among 12-month-olds, a greater proportion of high-level play was associated with more sophisticated mental development ($r = .24$) while a greater proportion of active play was associated with lower mental development ($r = -.29$). This scale also revealed significant increases in active, high level, and overall mean play scores from 12 to 18 months of age (Bond et al., 1983).

The Rubenstein and Howes scale also has identified variations in toddler play that relate to the social environment. For example, solitary play appeared less sophisticated than play in the immediate presence of a familiar peer (Rubenstein & Howes, 1976), but more sophisticated than play in the presence of a preschool-age sibling (Bond, Gibbs, Teti, & Kelly, 1984); and children whose parents had positive attitudes toward childrearing exhibited more sophisticated levels of play than children whose parents had more restrictive views of childrearing (Howes & Stewart, 1987).

Kearsley Procedure

Kearsley's (1984) laboratory procedure consists of introducing the child (10 months to 5 years of age) to six sets of toys prearranged in a standardized fashion. As in most play assessments, the mother is present but is asked not to initiate contact with the child or to suggest playing with any specific toy. Kearsley recommends that the examiner leave the observation room once the mother and child are familiarized with the environment. A 10-minute observation is then conducted through a one-way mirror. A checklist is used to record, during each 10-second interval, the frequencies of four categories of play: 1) stereotypical (e.g., mouthing or banging a toy), 2) relational (use of two or more objects in a nonfunctional manner), 3) functional (use of a toy in an adult-determined fashion, and 4) functional/symbolic. Based upon these observations, the child is categorized into one of three general levels of play designed to capture the transitions of child play from simple functional to more complex levels such as functional/sequential and functional/symbolic play. The child's relative status within a play level can be further classified as to whether the child is in the early phase, the middle phase, or a later stage and likely to advance to a more sophisticated level in the near future.

Kearsley's assessment technique evolved from several cross-sectional studies designed to trace the systematic development of infant free play (Fenson et al., 1976; Ungerer, Zelazo, Kearsley, & O'Leary, 1981; Zelazo & Kearsley, 1980). In their study of 9.5–15.5-month-olds, Zelazo and Kearsley (1980) found a linear decrease in stereotypical play, a linear increase in functional play, and a curvilinear pattern in relational play (increasing from 9.5 to 11.5 months, and tending to decrease after 13.5 months). Using Kearsley's scale, Ungerer et al. (1981) documented age-related increases in symbolic play among 18–34-month-olds.

Belsky and Most Free-Play Procedure

The Belsky and Most (1981) procedure, like most other free-play assessments, was designed to capture and validate the developmental progression and complexities of infant play first outlined by Piaget (1952), and later refined and reformulated by several groups of investigators (e.g., Fenson & Ramsay, 1980; McCall, 1974; Nicolich, 1977). A 30-minute home-based free-play observation with a set of standardized toys is suggested, with both the mother and examiner remaining passive toward the child. The most competent play observed during each 10-second interval is recorded. Infant play is then classified into one of 12 forms that emerge in developmental sequence: 1) mouthing; 2) simple visually guided manipulation; 3) functional manipulation (that accommodates to the properties of the object); 4) relational (integrating two or more materials in a manner unintended by the manufacturer); 5) functional relational; 6) enactive naming (approximate pretense activity); 7) pretense behaviors directed toward the self; 8) pretense behaviors directed toward others; 9) substitution of objects or actions for one another in a creative fashion; 10) sequence of single pretense acts with minor variation; 11) sequence of related but distinct pretense acts; and 12) pretense play in which two objects are used to substitute for others in a single act (e.g., use a leaf as a blanket to cover the stick that represents the baby). The 12 levels can be examined individually or grouped into three global ratings: 1) low-level undifferentiated play (e.g., simple mouthing or object manipulation); 2) active transitional play (e.g., functional play); and 3) high-level decontextualized pretense play. It should be noted that Belsky and Most's procedure covers as wide a developmental range as any of the infant play assessments. At the same time it makes fine discriminations between levels of play sophistication, including increasingly complex forms of pretense play. Therefore this assessment is one of the most informative across a wide range of children (approximately 8–36 months).

Using a cross-sectional study, Belsky and Most (1981) demonstrated that their scale accurately described the developmental progression of infant/toddler play. Subsequently, longitudinal data based upon this assessment (Bond et al., 1983; Hrncir et al., 1985) have revealed that the sophistication of infants' spontaneous play at 12 months of age predicts the sophistication of their play 6 months later; moreover, the sophistication of 18-month-olds' play, as revealed by Belsky and Most's scale, corresponds to the children's MDI scores (r values = .35–.60). Bond et al. (1983) discovered that both of these sets of relationships were stronger when children were interacting with their own toys rather than with an unfamiliar set.

Morgan, Harmon, and Bennett Procedure

Morgan and his colleagues (Morgan et al., 1976) devised a free-play assessment for 8–24-month-olds. Although Morgan asserted that a laboratory setting is most desirable, the procedure may be used in other contexts, such as the home. Free play with a standardized set of toys is observed for about 40 minutes. The assessment is designed to distinguish exploratory play from cognitively mature play; thus the first 2 minutes of the session are coded for the former and minutes 8–22 are coded for the latter. The observer records the highest level of play observed during each 20-second interval (10- and 5-second intervals are suggested as options). Play is coded as representing one of six categories that are subsumed under three levels: *Passive Exploration*—1) simple looking at a toy, 2) simple contact or manipulation, and 3) mouthing; *Active Play*—4) active manual investigation of the toy; and *High-Level Play*—5) conventional or functional play, and 6) quasi-symbolic or pretense play. In addition, the observer records the specific toy that the child is manipulating in each instance, as well as mother-infant interactions within the play episodes.

Jennings, Harmon, Morgan, Gaiter, and Yarrow (1979) showed that 12-month-olds with more cognitively mature play also had higher scores on the Bayley MDI. Although they found that exploratory play was not related to MDI, Bond et al. (1983) found that the sophistication of children's play and exploratory play at both 12 and 18 months of age corresponded to Bayley MDI scores, particularly when infants were observed playing with their own toys rather than with an unfamiliar set.

Lowe and Costello Symbolic Play Test

In this assessment (Lowe & Costello, 1976), infants ages 12–36 months are presented four sets of standardized toys, one set at a time. Three toy sets consist of three dolls surrounded by functional objects (e.g., spoon, cup, bed, blanket, table, chair), and a fourth set consists of a truck, trailer, logs, and a miniature man. As in other assessments, mothers are present but are asked not to elicit or to engage the child with any particular toy. No time constraints are offered; however, the authors suggest that the child be allowed to play with a particular play set until the child's interest in the toys appears satiated. Each toy set has a separate coding scheme whereby the frequencies of specific play behaviors (ranging from simple relational play to pretend self to pretend other) are recorded and percentages of play behaviors/levels are subsequently tallied.

Examining a cross-section of 244 twelve-to thirty-six–month-olds, Lowe (1975) documented increasing sophistication and decentration in free play with age. While psychometric issues regarding the procedure itself (e.g., interrater reliability, number of coders) were not discussed, a subsequent investigation (Udwin & Yule, 1982) demonstrated strong interrater reliability across the various play behaviors.

McCune-Nicolich Procedure

Unlike the modal free-play assessment techniques, which tend to focus upon the sensorimotor period (e.g., Belsky & Most, 1981; Morgan et al., 1976; Rubenstein & Howes, 1976), McCune-Nicolich's (1983) procedure is designed primarily to assess the more complex, symbolic play of older toddlers (e.g., 15–36 months). The protocol employs a 30-minute observation of free play in the child's own home with a standardized set of 36 toys designed to elicit symbolic play. The mother and examiner are present but do not attempt to elicit play. McCune-Nicolich argues against the use of time sampling (e.g., coding only one behavior in each 10-second interval), asserting that a meaningful, codable play observation records the quality of infant play from the time a toy is contacted until the child's attention is no longer focused upon the object. Symbolic play levels can be categorized into simple presymbolic schemes (e.g., drinking out of an empty cup) or autosymbolic schemes (e.g., making drinking noises when drinking out of an empty cup) to more complex decentered symbolic games (feeding a doll), combinational symbolic games (feeding self and then doll), and internally directed symbolic games (pretending a stick is a horse and then feeding the stick).

This assessment has been used in a number of investigations. The pioneering work of Nicolich (1977) and the more recent efforts of Slade (1987a, 1987b) provided empirical evidence that Piaget's (1962) theorized stages of symbolic play unfold in a systematic, developmental progression. McCune-Nicolich's procedure is one of the few such play instruments whose psychometric properties have been explored beyond establishing simple interrater reliability. Administering this procedure twice to nineteen 12–24-month-olds over a 2-week period, Power, Chapieski, and McGrath (1985) found stable coefficients of both reproducibility (.96) and scalebility (.83).

Elicited/Structured-Play Procedures

Belsky et al. Executive Capacity Procedure

The procedure developed by Belsky et al. (1984) involves a 10-minute observation of infant free play (Belsky & Most, 1981) followed by a competence episode in which the examiner attempts to engage the child in more sophisticated play by a succession of verbal prompts and/or modeling. It is suggested that the prompting center around a toy that interested the child during the free-play episode. Thus, if the child played extensively with a doll, the examiner might verbally encourage him or her to feed the doll. If the child does not respond the examiner models the desired behavior, and if this fails the examiner combines modeling and verbal coaching. Both the free and elicited episodes are coded using the Belsky and Most (1981) assessment. Three different scores are then derived: 1) *performance* is defined as the highest level of free play, 2) *competence* refers to the highest level of elicited play, and 3) *executive capacity* is described as the difference between performance and competence. Belsky et al. (1984) asserted that highly motivated infants will be more likely to exhibit their full capacities during the free-play procedure, and that elicitation will do little in "boosting" performance. Thus, persistent, motivated infants will display little discrepancy between performance and competence.

It is theorized that individual differences in infant motivation are related not only to cognitive competence (as described earlier) but also to social competence (e.g., Belsky et al., 1984; Vondra & Belsky, in press). Belsky et al. (1984) examined the relationship between both free and elicited play levels and security of attachment among 12-, 15-, and 18-month-olds using the Strange Situation procedure (Ainsworth, Blehar, Waters, & Wall, 1978). As predicted, both free and elicited play increased in complexity with age. Although the sophistication of children's free and elicited play were not predictive of attachment classifications, securely attached 12–13-month-olds displayed smaller gaps between the sophistication of their free and elicited play than avoidant infants, who, in turn, showed smaller discrepancies than resistant infants. In addition, securely attached children more frequently explored the objects around them. These findings fit the theoretical perspective of exploration as classic attachment behavior (Ainsworth, 1973) and offer insights into the relationship between early social relationships and subsequent cognitive competence. Apparently, play not only reflects both social and cognitive competence, but may, at least in part, mediate the relationship between early social relations and later cognitive competence in that securely attached children will be more likely to explore the environment to their fullest capacity, thereby fostering their own cognitive development. These findings reinforce the use of play as a promotive intervention.

Meanwhile, the notion of executive competence as a window to cognitive competence has encountered subsequent conceptual difficulties when studied in a systematic, longitudinal fashion. Studying two cultures, Hrncir et al. (1985) found no evidence that 12- or 18-month executive competence corresponded to Bayley MDI scores, nor did a child's executive competence at 12 months predict his or her executive competence 6 months later ($r = .02$). However, greater "spontaneous mastery" (i.e., the sophistication of free play weighted by its frequency) at 12 months predicted more sophisticated mental development (Bayley MDI) 6 months later, suggesting that "the more proficient children are at mastering tasks on their own, the more inclined they might be to maximize their potentials in testing and learning environments (Yarrow et al., 1983)" (Hrncir et al., 1985, p. 231).

Yarrow et al. Mastery Motivation Tasks

Some intriguing examinations have employed the mastery motivation tasks developed by the late Leon Yarrow and his colleagues at the National Institute of Child Health and Human Development. (See Morgan & Harmon, 1984, for a comprehensive review of mastery motivation, the development of the assessment procedures, and subsequent research using the procedures.) These efforts are rooted theoretically in the work of Robert White (1959), who proposed that the rudiments of individual child competence revolve around an intrinsic motivation to affect the environment. Not only does mastery of the environment promote learning, but the feeling of mastery in itself is reinforcing. The research group's seminal work began with a recognition of individual differences in infant test-taking behavior during the Bayley (1969) exam (e.g., approach to and persistence on a particular test item), and subsequent identification of particular item clusters thought to tap cognitive/motivational functioning (e.g., goal-directedness, reaching and grasping, secondary circular reactions; Yarrow, Rubenstein, & Pedersen, 1975; Yarrow, Rubenstein, Pedersen, & Jankowski, 1972). The construct received further empirical support when it was reported that the cluster scores predicted Stanford-Binet scores for these children at 3.5 years of age, while the Bayley MDI did not (Yarrow, Klein, Lomonaco, & Morgan, 1975). Thus, it would be fair to say that *how* an infant plays with an object/task may be just as important as *what* the child does with it.

Several assessment protocols designed specifically to measure mastery motivation during infancy have been developed by this group (Harmon & Glicken, 1981; Morgan et al., 1977; Vietze et al., 1986). The basic paradigm for the procedures is the same in the sense that a number of tasks (e.g., a pegboard, activity center, three men in a tub) are modeled, one at a time; then the child is presented with the objects and observed in free play, unobtrusively, for a period of time (usually 3–5 minutes per task). Although the procedures differ in the types or number of tasks presented, the general coding scheme has been relatively consistent from study to study (Morgan & Harmon, 1984). Four general behaviors are coded from the episodes: 1) nontask behavior (e.g., bids to mother, inattention to object); 2) visual attention (e.g., looking at the object); 3) task-directed behavior (e.g., attempts to use an object in an appropriate way); and 4) success or solution of task/problem. Indices of motivation include both *persistence,* or amount of time in which the infant exhibits task-related behavior or solves a particular solution, and *latency of task,* or the amount of time before the child begins a task-related behavior. A measure of causality pleasure is often obtained (i.e., noting whether the infant displays positive affect following the completion of a difficult task). In addition, the tasks themselves can be grouped into three categories of complexity: 1) tasks that are primarily for *effect production* (activity center); 2) those that are for *practicing sensorimotor skills* (peg board); and 3) those primarily for *problem solving.*

Contrary to many of the assessment procedures described in this chapter, there has been an impressive amount of work establishing the validity and reliability of Yarrow et al.'s procedures, the construct of mastery motivation, and its indices (e.g., persistence). Interrater reliability has been consistently high across studies, suggesting the ease and clarity with which the tasks can be operationalized. The suggestion that there may be underlying motivational differences between specific groups of handicapped and nonhandicapped children has been validated by several studies that have examined: 1) *preterm infants,* who display higher levels of simple manipulation of objects and lower levels of task persistence and pleasure at mastery (Harmon, Morgan, & Glicken, 1984); 2) *children with Down syndrome,* who have longer latency thresholds (but resemble nonhandicapped children once they begin the task; MacTurk, Hunter, McCarthy, Vietze, & McQuiston, 1985; MacTurk, Vietze, McCarthy, McQuiston, & Yarrow, 1985); and 3) *physically handicapped children,* who demonstrate less preference for challenging tasks and less persistence (Jennings, Connors, & Stegman, 1988). Future research with these motivational assessment procedures should analyze the variability of individuals within these groups and identify those factors that contribute to or detract from the promotion of mastery motivation.

In terms of the construct of mastery, several studies have attempted to demonstrate age-related stability and change and/or its concurrent or predictive utility for cognitive competence. Yarrow et al. (1983) found a developmental progression in mastery behavior (from 6 to 12 months of age) from an emphasis on effect production to practicing sensorimotor skills to problem solving. A sequential analysis revealed that persistent, goal-directed behaviors are an antecedent to the infant's feelings of efficacy, further underscoring the importance of motivation as a rudiment of competence. Examining the predictive power of mastery behavior, Yarrow, Morgan, Jennings, Harmon, and Gaiter (1982) found that 12-month-olds' mastery scores corresponded to their Bayley MDI scores ($r = .60$). Infants' persistence and latency to task involvement also related to their MDI; greater persistence and briefer latencies before beginning the task were associated with higher MDI scores. Furthermore, Jennings, Yarrow, and Martin (1984) found that 12-month Bayley MDI and mastery scores each predicted cognitive ability (McCarthy Scales of Children's Abilities) but not mastery motivation at follow-up for 3.5-year-old girls. For boys, the opposite was true. Mastery and MDI each predicted motivational levels but not cognitive competence at 3.5 years of age. This finding supports the claim that cognitive functioning may be more consistent developmentally for girls than boys during early childhood (e.g., Bayley & Schaefer, 1964; Yarrow & Messer, 1983).

Watson and Fischer Elicitation Procedure

Watson and Fischer (1977) initially designed their play procedure to capture Piaget's (1962) notion of decentration (from self as agent to object as active agent) in pretend play. Their basic procedure involved a laboratory setting with specified toys arranged in a semicircle. There were four phases to the procedure:

1. A 3-minute familiarization phase in which the mother and examiner passively allow the toddler to explore the surroundings.

2. A modeling phase in which the mother holds the child in her lap while the examiner models a series of tasks involving pretend actions (e.g., eating, washing, sleeping) upon various agents (e.g., self, doll, a wooden block).
3. An 8-minute free play period in which the examiner leaves the room (mothers are asked to refrain from eliciting any particular infant behaviors).
4. A requested-imitation phase in which the examiner and mother attempt to encourage the infant to imitate the modeled behaviors.

The decision to employ modeling in this procedure grew from the belief that the low levels of pretense during solitary toddler free play are not representative of the toddler's actual abilities. Pretend behaviors are coded by action (e.g., eating, sleeping, washing) and by agent use. Four types of agent use are scored: 1) self as agent (e.g., feeding self); 2) passive other (e.g., lack of animation when interacting with an object, such as dragging the doll around the floor by its foot); 3) passive substitute (e.g., infant puts the block on a pillow); and 4) active agent (e.g., infant places the doll on the pillow).

Watson and Fischer (1977) and subsequent cross-sectional and longitudinal studies (Chapman, 1987; Corrigan, 1982, 1987) found marked developmental changes in agent use across the second year of life, with older children more likely to pretend and engage in more advanced agent use. These studies found modeling effective in eliciting pretense play in that pretense was minimal during the warm-up stage but well represented during the test phase. Of course, relatively undifferentiated exploration often occupies much of a toddler's time when he or she is first introduced to a set of novel toys.

Play Assessments under Development

Several assessments of considerable promise have not been detailed in this chapter because they are under development at the time of this writing or are in preliminary stages of psychometric scrutiny. The interested reader is urged to follow their development. They include: Jeffree and McConkey's (1976) scheme for recording children's imaginative play with dolls; Egan's (1986) miniature toys test for children between 18 months and 4.5 years; Westby's (1980) Symbolic Play Test; Gowen's (1981) procedure for assessing symbolic play; Largo and Howard's (1979) modeling procedure designed to elicit symbolic play; Fewell's 1986) Play Assessment Scale (PAS); and Bromwich's (1981) Play Assessment Checklist for Infants (PACFI). The assessments of Fewell (1986) and Bromwich (1981) deserve particular mention as examples of emerging procedures that have greater clinical focus. While both assessments are currently in "working draft" form, they provide clinicians and researchers rich frameworks in which to assess child functioning and style, and guide curriculum development.

Fewell's Play Assessment Scale

The PAS (Fewell, 1986) examines perceptual and conceptual skills or processes of 2–36-month-olds through observing the children's interactions with a series of toy sets designed to elicit a broad range of skills of progressive sophistication. Fewell incorporated two conditions in her procedure. The first focuses upon spontaneous play. The second employs verbal cues, then physical modeling, and then verbal and physical modeling, allowing the observer to examine the degree of assistance needed to elicit more sophisticated skills from the child. Fewell emphasized the importance of the observer recording the success of specific verbal and physical prompts since this "information is extremely valuable to teachers, parents or others developing appropriate play experiences for the child" (Fewell, 1986, p. 3).

Bromwich's Play Assessment Checklist for Infants

Bromwich's (1981) PACFI appears extremely promising for a variety of reasons. Designed as an observational aid for clinicians, educators, and daycare providers, it uses a well-chosen standardized toy set to tap cognitive functioning in spontaneous free-play settings among 9–30-month-olds. Moreover, the PACFI includes strategies for assessing temperamental characteristics of the child (e.g., approach to toys), social/linguistic behavior toward the parent (e.g., bids for attention), and cognitive/motivational behavior toward the play activity (e.g., attention span). The emphasis is very much upon the quality of the child's functioning, with the premise that "cognitive and affective development are inseparable in infancy" (1981, p. 2). This attention to individual play style as well as cognitive competence is particularly important for practitioners and parents as they strive to provide developmentally supportive environments.

THE PLAY OF HANDICAPPED CHILDREN: IMPLICATIONS FOR INTERVENTION AND ASSESSMENT

A number of investigators have identified differences between the play of nonhandicapped and various groups of handicapped children in early childhood (see Fewell & Kaminski, 1988; Quinn & Rubin, 1984; and Rogers, 1988, for reviews). These findings should not be surprising given the sensory, motoric, social, and intellectual characteristics associated with various handicaps. For example, children with limitations in manual dexterity would not be expected to physically manipulate their environments in the same manner as those without such limitations. At the same time, given the complex network of competencies that underlie children's play (e.g., sensory, motoric, social, and cognitive), one would not expect to be able to diagnose a particular handicap solely through observing a child's play. In fact, very little research has uncovered unique characteristics that actually *distinguish* the play of children with certain handicaps from others, autism being a possible exception (e.g., Sigman & Ungerer, 1984, and see review by Rogers, 1988). Rather, the value of play assessments vis-à-vis handicapped infants is that, as with nonhandicapped infants, their play both reflects and promotes cognitive (as well as sensory, motor, and social) competence.

It is well documented that the play of handicapped children follows the same basic developmental sequence as that of their nonhandicapped peers. For example, Gowen, Goldman, Johnson-Martin, and Hussey (1989) examined the play of children with a variety of handicaps (e.g., Down syndrome, cerebral palsy, severe developmental delay due to meningitis). While these children were less actively involved than nonhandicapped children who were matched for developmental age, they showed the same amount of objective exploration, mean level of play, and sequence of development. Similarly, Hill and McCune-Nicolich (1981) found a developmental progression of hierarchical stages of symbolic play in children with Down syndrome.

Much research has also demonstrated that the sophistication of the play of young handicapped children is related to their mental rather than chronological age (e.g., Gowen et al., in press; Hill & McCune-Nicolich, 1981; Hulme & Lunzer, 1966; Odom, 1981). It appears that early symbolic play emerges when a child's mental age is at least 20 months (Whittaker, 1980; Wing, Gould, Yeates, & Brierly, 1977). Symbolic development also appears to be related to affective/interpersonal development through the infancy and preschool years among children with Down syndrome (Hill & McCune-Nicolich, 1981; Motti, Cicchetti, & Sroufe, 1983), "attesting to the coherent cognitive development which children with Down Syndrome display over time" (Rogers, 1988, p. 164).

These findings help us not only to understand the development of children with a variety of handicaps, but also to validate our theoretical understanding of play in nonhandicapped children. The progression of play appears to be related to underlying developmental competencies rather than isolated age-related experiences.

Not only are play assessments appropriate for diagnosing and guiding the cognitive competencies of young handicapped children, but they have distinct advantages for doing so as well. Compared to many standardized assessments, free-play techniques often are more flexible in application and may be more sensitive to detecting individual variations in style, since they allow the child to demonstrate competencies in her or his *own* terms rather than within the constraints of a tester's structured paradigm. In addition, a careful analysis of play often pushes the examiner to look beyond the child's more obvious limitations, to detect abilities that are less apparent in handicapped individuals because of their physical, motoric, and/or verbal limitations. Furthermore, examining the patterns and variations in the development of play within and across handicapped groups might help us understand the ways in which particular handicaps influence development. This information, in turn, can also assist in guiding future treatment, and in preventive and promotive interventions.

At the same time, we must be cautious that we do not generalize from nonnormative characteristics of play to cognitive abilities when those characteristics may simply reflect more superficial qualities of the handicapping condition itself (e.g., difficulty in visual accommodation). Most importantly, because multiple factors can contribute to delays in the development of play behaviors, we cannot make simple direct connections between delays in play and cognition. More interesting, and often more conclusive for the diagnosis of cognitive competency, are those instances in which we discover play that is more sophisticated than that which we previously had observed or expected.

The assessment of play as an index of mastery motivation among handicapped individuals is critically important. The difficulties that certain types of behaviors present to children with specific handicaps may affect the children's interest in engaging in these actions. Motivation can be so important in multiplying and/or minimizing the effects of a handicap. Understanding distinctions between competence and performance is important to developing a complete appreciation of the child's abilities and inclinations. Thus the assessment of mastery motivation may be particularly informative in identifying the nature of the handicapped child's strengths and limitations.

While several groups of researchers (e.g., Jennings, Connors, Stegman, Sankaranarayan, & Mendelsohn, 1985; MacTurk, Hunter, McCarthy, Vietze, & McQuiston, 1985) documented lower mastery motivation among certain groups of handicapped children (e.g., those with Down syndrome) compared to nonhandicapped children, investigators have failed to examine individual variation in mastery motivation *within* specific special populations. Identifying these individual differences as well as their sources and repercussions is particularly important when designing or assigning intervention strategies.

SELECTING AND IMPLEMENTING PLAY ASSESSMENTS

The choice of one play assessment over another depends upon a variety of considerations beyond the psychometric qualities of the measures themselves. Each of the following issues should be considered when selecting among alternative assessments.

What are the characteristics of the population to be assessed? Consider the ages and general levels of skill of the targeted group. How broad a range of functioning do they span? As noted earlier, for example, the McCune-Nicolich (1983) scale is particularly useful for making fine discriminations among the symbolic skills of older toddlers; Belsky and Most's (1981) assessment distinguishes among the play behaviors of a wide age range and therefore is appropriate for tracking children's progression throughout their infant and toddler years or comparing a diverse group of children. Consider, as well, whether the target children have notable physical, behavioral, or social limitations that call for an assessment that focuses beyond verbal or manual skills, for example.

What are your general goals in conducting the assessment? Are you searching for a *quantitative* index to compare children over time or with one another, or an abbreviated technique for estimating some standardized intellectual measure such as IQ? For example, some assessments have been demonstrated to relate directly to IQ or Bayley MDI (e.g., Belsky & Most, 1981; Morgan et al., 1976). Are you searching for a more *qualitative* description of the child's style of cognitive functioning as a basis for examining how this style: 1) varies with environmental context, 2) compares with that of other children, 3) develops over time, and/or 4) responds to changes in the environment (e.g., in an effort to sensitize parents, caregivers, and educators and/or to inform future intervention efforts)? If so, a procedure such as the PACFI (Bromwich, 1981) may be most useful. Do you want to understand the child's level of performance or level of competence? Elicited play procedures generally provide more opportunity for examining a child's potential, but only some of these techniques allow the observer to obtain an index of motivational level (e.g., Belsky et al., 1984).

Is the goal of the assessment program evaluation, curriculum development, or both? For example, the simplicity of the Rubenstein and Howes (1976) procedure has advantages for documenting general individual progress over the course of a year (presenting reliable and systematic information); however, the same simplicity and lack of detail makes this assessment less effective in defining curriculum objectives.

Who will be using the assessment and what type of training and conceptual backgrounds will they have? Is the assessment to be used by specialists (e.g., medical personnel) in an attempt to obtain a more integrated view of the child than normally would be secured? Will it be used by parents to gain greater sensitivity to the skills of their own children? Will it be employed by educators and clinicians in an attempt to stand back and gain a more objective analysis of a child's functioning? Will the assessors have a working knowledge of child development theory and patterns of sensorimotor development or will it be important to rely upon quite explicit behavioral markers? These are important considerations since the assessments vary in the degree to which each requires the observer to make subjective judgments based upon an in-depth knowledge of early cognitive, sensory, motor, and emotional development.

What are the practical constraints upon the opportunities for implementation? Are there limitations in time, personnel, space, or location? Recall that while a number of the assessments can be used by observing the child in a variety of naturalistic and often impromptu settings, others require that the observer use particular props and/or observe the child in a specific context (e.g., a laboratory). Moreover the time and background required for both training and administration of the assessments varies with their complexity.

In summary, it is important to recognize that no single play assessment can be singled out as "best." The merits of each relate directly to its intended use.

In preparing for the implementation of an assessment, it is often important to write authors for a copy of an administration and scoring manual, even when the assessment has been published in a journal or book. A good administration manual addresses the subtleties of training procedures, contexts for implementation, the psychometric properties of the measure, and so on. In many ways, one must prepare for the use of a play assessment in much the way one would train for using many standardized assessments:

1. Practice with children who are at a variety of developmental levels so that you become familiar with coding a full range of activity.
2. Establish reliability with another observer so that you are assured that there is agreement regarding the ways in which specific behaviors should/could be defined (80% interrater reliability is a reasonable goal; talk through those instances in which there is disagreement until consensus is reached and you have refined the criteria for coding).
3. If possible, videotape play sessions so that you (and others) can code the same sequences several times as another check on reliability/consistency.
4. Try time-sampling procedures (e.g., code the child's most sophisticated behavior dur-

ing each 10-second interval, or code only what the child is doing at each 15-second marker) in order to examine the feasibility and representativeness of these procedures relative to continuous coding.
5. Try the coding scheme in informal clinical settings as well as more standardized environments in order to understand the sorts of information derived from each.

Once training is "completed," recheck reliability on an intermittent basis to counter the tendency to drift gradually away from the original coding criteria. Continue to experiment with the assessment in a variety of appropriate settings in an effort to determine the different sorts of information gained from each. Typically the most informative evaluations are those that implement multiple assessments in multiple settings. Therefore, continue to employ unstructured clinical observations in diverse contexts independently or in conjunction with gathering information in a more systematic fashion. Use the play scales either formally or informally at the same time you are observing parent-child, peer, or sibling interaction, or, for example, when watching a child wait for a parent conference to end. The play assessment can be integrated easily into a team assessment at multiple points in time. At the same time, be sensitive to the context in which you are observing the child and the ways in which that environment might affect the child's thinking and actions. Allow children to become familiar with the objects in a new environment in order to distinguish between exploration (of new objects) and play (once familiarity is established). These are distinct sets of behaviors.

CONCLUSION

Throughout this chapter we have noted the role of play assessments in guiding intervention activities, curriculum planning, and the identification of programmatic goals. The utility of these assessments as diagnostic tools is associated with their ability to identify (and distinguish between) the competencies and inclinations of individuals and groups of children. The systematic, hierarchical progression that emerges in the deployment of play provides us with a framework for tracing and guiding children's activities over time. Moreover, the sensitivity of play assessments to both qualitative and quantitative characteristics of behavior allows us to examine carefully the variations in individual behavior across contexts, as well as the variations between individuals and groups of individuals. Analyses such as these permit us to design interventions that are sensitive to intellectual, social, motoric, and linguistic characteristics and needs of individuals as well as groups (e.g., Rogers, 1988, described the ways in which distinct forms of sensorimotor play may fit the special curricular/developmental needs of children with varying handicaps).

The fact that play itself is so powerful in stimulating development allows us to employ play interventions in order to foster the development of a broad range of competencies (e.g., see Fewell & Kaminski, 1988, and Quinn & Rubin, 1984, for references to play interventions for handicapped children). This is a particularly attractive strategy because it is economical, practical, adaptive to multiple contexts, and engaging for the child. The tremendous satisfaction that is typically derived from play means that children not only will participate when placed in the intervention setting, but more importantly, they will be more likely to initiate play, that is, "implement the intervention" for themselves. Thus play is an excellent candidate for a self-sustaining intervention; and as we have learned through years of extensive program evaluation, it is the enduring influences that have the most enduring effects (Clarke & Clarke, 1976).

REFERENCES

Ainsworth, M.D.S. (1973). The development of infant-mother attachment. In B.M. Caldwell & H.N. Ricciuti (Eds.), *Review of child development research* (Vol. 3, pp. 1–94). Chicago: University of Chicago Press.

Ainsworth, M.D.S., Blehar, M.C., Waters, E., &

Wall, S. (1978). *Patterns of attachment: A psychological study of the strange situation.* Hillsdale, NJ: Lawrence Erlbaum Associates.

Athey, I. (1984). Contributions of play to development. In T.D. Yawkey & A.D. Pellegrini (Eds.), *Child's play: developmental and applied* (pp. 9–27). Hillsdale, NJ: Lawrence Erlbaum Associates.

Bayley, N. (1969) *Bayley scales of infant development.* New York: Psychological Corporation.

Bayley, N., & Schaefer, E.S. (1964). Correlations of maternal and child behaviors with the development of mental ability: Data from the Berkeley Growth Study. *Monographs of the Society for Research in Child Development, 29* (6, Serial No. 97).

Belsky, J., Garduque, L., & Hrncir, E. (1984). Assessing performance, competence, and executive capacity in infant play: Relations to home environment and security of attachment. *Developmental Psychology, 20,* 406–417.

Belsky, J., & Most, R.K. (1981). From exploration to play: A cross-sectional study of infant free play behavior. *Developmental Psychology, 17,* 630–639.

Bond, L.A., Gibbs, E.D., Teti, D.M., & Kelly, L.D. (1984, August). *Effects of siblings on infant interaction with objects.* Paper presented at the annual meetings of the American Psychological Association, Anaheim, CA.

Bond, L.A., Kelly, L.D., Teti, D.M., & Gibbs, E.D. (1983, April). *Longitudinal analyses of infant free play with familiar and unfamiliar toys.* Paper presented at the biennial meetings of the Society for Research in Child Development, Detroit.

Bromwich, R.M. (1981). *Play assessment checklist for infants.* (Available from author, Department of Educational Psychology, School of Education, California State University.)

Bruner, J.S. (1973). Organization of early skilled action. *Child Development, 44,* 1–11.

Chapman, M. (1987). A longitudinal study of cognitive representation in symbolic play, self-recognition, and object permanence during the second year. *International Journal of Behavioral Development, 10,* 151–170.

Clarke, A.M., & Clarke, A.D.B. (1976). *Early experience: Myth and evidence.* London: Open Books.

Clune, C., Paolella, J.M., & Foley, J.M. (1979). Free-play behavior of atypical children: An approach to assessment. *Journal of Autism and Developmental Disorders, 9,* 61–72.

Corrigan, R. (1982). The control of animate and inanimate components in pretend play and language. *Child Development, 53,* 1343–1353.

Corrigan, R. (1987). A developmental sequence of actor-object pretend play in young children. *Merrill-Palmer Quarterly, 33,* 87–106.

Egan, D.F. (1986). Developmental assessment: 18 months to 4½ years. The miniature toys test. *Child: Care, Health and Development, 12,* 167–181.

Fein, G.G., & Apfel, N. (1979). The development of play: Style, structure, and situations. *Genetic Psychology Monographs, 99,* 213–250.

Fenson, L., Kagan, J., Kearsley, R.B., & Zelazo, P. (1976). The developmental progression of manipulative play in the first two years. *Child Development, 47,* 232–236.

Fenson, L., & Ramsay, D.S. (1980). Decentration and integration of the child's play in the second year. *Child Development, 51,* 171–178.

Fewell, R. (1986). *Play assessment scale* (5th revision). Unpublished manuscript, University of Washington, Seattle.

Fewell, R.R., & Kaminski, R. (1988). Play skills development and instruction for young children with handicaps. In S.L. Odom & M.B. Karnes (Eds.), *Early intervention for infants and children with handicaps: An empirical base* (pp. 145–158). Baltimore: Paul H. Brookes Publishing Co.

Gowen, J.W. (1981). *Assessing the development of the symbolic function through play.* Unpublished manuscript, Frank Porter Graham Child Development Center, University of North Carolina, Chapel Hill.

Gowen, J.W., Goldman, B.D., Johnson-Martin, N., & Hussey, B. (1989). Object play and exploration of handicapped and nonhandicapped infants. *Journal of Applied Developmental Psychology, 10,* 53–72.

Harmon, R.J., & Glicken, A.D. (1981). *Mastery Motivation scoring manual for 12 month old infants.* Denver: University of Colorado School of Medicine, Infant Behavior Lab.

Harmon, R.J., Morgan, G.A., & Glicken, A.D. (1984). Continuities and discontinuities in affective and cognitive-motivational development. *International Journal of Child Abuse and Neglect, 8,* 157–167.

Hill, P.H., & McCune-Nicolich, L. (1981). Pretend play and patterns of cognition in Down's syndrome children. *Child Development, 52,* 611–617.

Howes, C., & Stewart, P. (1987). Child's play with adults, toys, and peers: An examination of family and child-care influences. *Developmental Psychology, 23,* 423–430.

Hrncir, E.J., Speller, G.M., & West, M. (1985). What are we testing? *Developmental Psychology, 21,* 226–232.

Hulme, I., & Lunzer, E.A. (1966). Play, language and reasoning in subnormal children. *Journal of Child Psychology and Psychiatry, 7,* 107–123.

Jeffree, D.M., & McConkey, R. (1976). An observational scheme for recording children's imaginative doll play. *Journal of Child Psychology and Psychiatry, 17,* 189–197.

Jennings, K.D., Connors, R.E., & Stegman, C.E. (1988). Does a physical handicap alter the development of mastery motivation during the preschool years? *Journal of the American Academy of Child and Adolescent Psychiatry, 27*, 312–317.

Jennings, K.D., Connors, R.E., Stegman, C.E., Sankaranarayan, P., & Mendelsohn, S. (1985). Mastery motivation in young preschoolers: Effect of a physical handicap and implications for educational programming. *Journal of the Division of Early Childhood, 9*, 162–169.

Jennings, K.D., Harmon, R.J., Morgan, G.A., Gaiter, J.L., & Yarrow, L.J. (1979). Exploratory play as an index of mastery motivation: Relationships to persistence, cognitive functioning, and environmental measures. *Developmental Psychology, 15*, 386–394.

Jennings, K.D., Yarrow, L.J., & Martin, P.P. (1984). Mastery motivation and cognitive development: A longitudinal study from infancy to 3½ years of age. *International Journal of Behavioral Development, 7*, 441–461.

Kearsley, R.B. (1984). *The systematic observation of children's play*. Unpublished scoring manual. (Available from author, Child Health Services, Manchester, NH.)

Largo, R.H., & Howard, J.A. (1979). Developmental progression in play behavior of children between nine and thirty months I: Spontaneous play and imitation. *Developmental Medicine and Child Neurology, 21*, 299–310.

Lowe, M. (1975). Trends in the development of representational play in infants from one to three years—an observational study. *Journal of Child Psychology and Psychiatry, 16*, 33–47.

Lowe, M., & Costello, A.J. (1976). *Manual for the Symbolic Play Test*. Windsor, England: NFR—Nelson Publishing Co.

MacTurk, R.H., Hunter, F.T., McCarthy, M.E., Vietze, P.M., & McQuiston, S. (1985). Social mastery motivation in Down syndrome and nondelayed infants. *Topics in Early Childhood/Special Education, 4*, 93–109.

MacTurk, R.H., Vietze, P.M., McCarthy, M.E., McQuiston, S., & Yarrow, L. (1985). The organization of exploratory behavior in Down syndrome and nondelayed infants. *Child Development, 56*, 573–581.

McCall, R.B. (1974). Exploratory manipulation and play in the human infant. *Monographs of the Society for Research in Child Development, 39*(2, Serial No. 155).

McCune-Nicolich, L. (1983). *A manual for analyzing free play*. New Brunswick, NJ: Department of Educational Psychology, Rutgers University.

McCune-Nicolich, L., & Fenson, L. (1984). Methodological issues in studying early pretend play. In T.D. Yawkey & A.D. Pellegrini (Eds.), *Child's play: developmental and applied*. Hillsdale, NJ: Lawrence Erlbaum Associates.

Morgan, G.A., & Harmon, R.A. (1984). Developmental transformations in mastery motivation: Measurement and validation. In R.N. Emde & R.J. Harmon (Eds.), *Continuities and discontinuities in development* (pp. 263–291). New York: Plenum Press.

Morgan, G.A., Harmon, R.J., & Bennett, C.A. (1976). A system for coding and scoring infants' spontaneous play with objects. JSAS *Catalog of Selected Documents in Psychology, 6*, 105 (Ms. No. 1355).

Morgan, G.A., Harmon, R.J., Gaiter, J.L., Jennings, K.D., Gist, N.F., & Yarrow, L. (1977). A method for assessing mastery motivation in one-year-old infants. JSAS *Catalog of Selected Documents in Psychology, 7*, 68 (Ms. No. 1517).

Motti, F., Cicchetti, D., Sroufe, L.A. (1983). From infant affect expression to symbolic play: The coherence of development in Down syndrome children. *Child Development, 54*, 1168–1175.

Nicolich, L.M. (1977). Beyond sensorimotor intelligence: Assessment of symbolic maturity through analysis of pretend play. *Merrill-Palmer Quarterly, 23*, 89–99.

Odom, S.L. (1981). The relationship of play to developmental level in mentally retarded preschool children. *Education and Training of the Mentally Retarded, 16*, 136–141.

Piaget, J. (1952). *The origins of intelligence in children*. New York: International Universities Press.

Piaget, J. (1962). *Play, dreams, and imitation in childhood*. New York: W.W. Norton.

Power, T.G., Chapieski, L., & McGrath, M.P. (1985). Assessment of individual differences in infant exploration and play. *Developmental Psychology, 21*, 974–981.

Quinn, J.M., & Rubin, K. (1984). The play of handicapped children. In T.D. Yawkey & A.D. Pellegrini (Eds.), *Child's play: developmental and applied*. Hillsdale, NJ: Lawrence Erlbaum Associates.

Rogers, S.J. (1988). Cognitive characteristics of handicapped children's play: A review. *Journal of the Division for Early Childhood, 12*, 161–168.

Rubenstein, J., & Howes, C. (1976). The effects of peers on toddler interaction with mothers and toys. *Child Development, 47*, 597–605.

Sigman, M., & Ungerer, J.A. (1984). Cognitive and language skills in autistic, mentally retarded, and normal children. *Developmental Psychology, 20*, 293–302.

Slade, A. (1987a). A longitudinal study of maternal involvement and symbolic play during the toddler period. *Child Development, 58*, 367–375.

Slade, A. (1987b). Quality of attachment and early symbolic play. *Developmental Psychology, 23*, 78–85.

Udwin, O., & Yule, W. (1982). Validational data on Lowe and Costello's symbolic play test. *Child: Care, Health and Development, 8*, 361–366.

Ulvund, S.E. (1980). Cognition and motivation in early infancy: An interactionist approach. *Human Development, 23,* 17–32.

Ungerer, J.A., Zelazo, P.R., Kearsley, R.B., & O'Leary, K.O. (1981). Developmental changes in the representation of objects in symbolic play from 18 to 34 months of age. *Child Development, 52,* 186–195.

Vietze, P.M., Pasnak, C.F., Tremblay, A., McCarthy, M.E., MacTurk, R.H., Klein, R.P., & Yarrow, L.J. (1986). Manual for assessing mastery motivation in 6- and 12-month old infants. *Psychological Documents, 15* (Ms. No. 2714).

Vondra, J., & Belsky, J. (in press). Infant play at one year: Characteristics and early antecedents. In J. Lockman & N. L. Hazen (Eds.), *Action in social context.* New York: Plenum Press.

Watson, M.W., & Fischer, K.W. (1977). A developmental sequence of agent use in late infancy. *Child Development, 48,* 828–836.

Weisler, A., & McCall, R. (1976). Exploration and play: Resume and redirection. *American Psychologist, 31,* 492–508.

Westby, C.E. (1980). Assessment of cognitive and language abilities through play. *Language, Speech and Hearing Services in Schools, 11,* 154–168.

White, R.W. (1959). Motivation reconsidered: The concept of competence. *Psychological Review, 66,* 297–333.

Whittaker, C.A. (1980). A note on developmental trends in the symbolic play of hospitalized profoundly retarded children. *Journal of Child Psychology and Psychiatry, 21,* 253–261.

Wing, L., Gould, J., Yeates, S.R., & Brierly, L.M. (1977). Symbolic play in severely mentally retarded and in autistic children. *Journal of Child Psychology and Psychiatry, 18,* 167–178.

Yarrow, L.J., Klein, R.P., Lomonaco, S., & Morgan, G.A. (1975). Cognitive and motivational development in early childhood. In B.Z. Friedlander, G.M. Sterrit, & G.E. Kirk (Eds.), *Exceptional infant 3: Assessment and intervention.* New York: Halstead Press.

Yarrow, L.J., McQuiston, S., MacTurk, R.H., McCarthy, M., Klein, R.P., & Vietze, P.M. (1983). Assessment of mastery motivation during the first year of life: contemporaneous and cross-age relationships. *Developmental Psychology, 19,* 159–171.

Yarrow, L.J., & Messer, D.J. (1983). Motivation and cognition during infancy. In M. Lewis (Ed.), *Origins of intelligence: Infancy and early childhood.* New York: Plenum Press.

Yarrow, L.J., Morgan, G.A., Jennings, K.D., Harmon, R.J., & Gaiter, J.L. (1982). Infants' persistence at tasks: Relationships to cognitive functioning and early experience. *Infant Behavior and Development, 5,* 131–141.

Yarrow, L.J., & Pedersen, F.A. (1976). The interplay between cognition and motivation in infancy. In M. Lewis (Ed.), *Origins of intelligence.* New York: Plenum Press.

Yarrow, L.J., Rubenstein, J.L., & Pedersen, F.A. (1975). *Infant and environment: Early cognitive and motivational development.* New York: Halstead Press.

Yarrow, L.J., Rubenstein, J.L., Pedersen, F.A., & Jankowski, J.J. (1972). Dimensions of early stimulation and their differential effects on infant development. *Merrill-Palmer Quarterly, 18,* 205–218.

Zelazo, P.R., & Kearsley, R.B. (1980). The emergence of functional play in infants: Evidence for a major cognitive transition. *Journal of Applied Developmental Psychology, 1,* 95–117.

9 Infant Information Processing
An Alternative Approach

Philip R. Zelazo and Michael J. Weiss

It has been acknowledged widely that conventional tests of infant-toddler development have low predictive validity (e.g., Bayley, 1970; Lewis & Brooks-Gunn, 1972; McCall, 1979; Stott & Ball, 1965). Indeed, under 18 months of age the predictive correlation to later development is virtually zero, although predictability is generally better for seriously delayed children, as Honzik (1976) pointed out. McCall (1979) summarized the stability-instability of individual differences in infant mental development, and concluded that "infant tests do not typically reveal highly stable individual differences within the first 18 months or from infancy to later IQ" (p. 715). Prior to 18 months of life, parental education and socioeconomic status are the best predictors of later childhood IQ; actually assessing an infant using a conventional test of mental development does not increase the validity of this prediction noticeably.

It has been shown that the most likely direction of error with conventional tests is toward identifying and labeling children as delayed when they may later prove to be intellectually normal (Hunt, 1976; McCall, 1982). In fact, conventional tests may be biased against those children for whom the need for assessment is greatest—children with developmental disabilities. Zelazo and Kearsley (1989) and Zelazo (1979, 1986) suggested that measures used in conventional tests to infer intellectual ability—indices of gross and fine motor development, receptive and productive language, and compliance during testing—are confounded with the handicapping conditions presented by children with developmental disabilities.

One category of conventional test items, neuromotor indices, are used so heavily during the first and second years of life that clinicians have equated delayed motor development with delayed mental development. Indeed, conventional tests of mental development rely extensively on gross and fine motor measures. For example, during the first year, motor facility is measured directly on the Bayley Mental Development Index (Bayley, 1969) with items such as "puts a cube in a cup on command" (9.4 months). During the second year, motor facility is measured indirectly with imitation items such as "pushes a car" (13.8 months). In theory imitation items reflect a mental process, but in practice they depend on facility with the upper extremities and therefore neuromotor difficulties can impair test performance.

This research was supported, in part, by grants from the Carnegie Corporation of New York and the National Institute of Child Health and Human Development (No. RO1-HD18029-01A1), the McGill–Montreal Children's Hospital Research Institute, and the Lisa Hoffman Schouela Fund to Philip R. Zelazo and from the Office of Special Education (No. GO7603979) to Philip R. Zelazo and Richard B. Kearsley. Philip Zelazo accepts full responsibility for the contents of this paper and thanks these agencies for their support.

We express appreciation to Jerome Kagan and Richard Kearsley for their significant contributions to this research.

The second category, receptive language items, measured during the second and third years, appears to be exclusively mental but, in practice, also requires facility with the upper extremities. For example, the item "point to or touch one's shoes" at 15.3 months on the Bayley Mental Scale reflects relatively sophisticated comprehension, but also requires both the ability to use one's arms and hands and a willingness to comply with the examiner's request. Productive language items require control of the vocal apparatus (also a motor skill to a large extent), particularly during the period when expressive language is acquired. Precisely because talking is itself a major developmental phenomenon, it is subject to sources of variability during acquisition that render it a poor indicator of central processing. Clinically, a delay with the onset of talking, like delayed walking, is a "red flag" that places the child at high risk for delayed mental development.

To complicate matters, children with seriously delayed expressive language are difficult to manage behaviorally (Caulfield, Fischel, DeBaryshe, & Whitehurst, in press; Zelazo, Kearsley, Stiles, & Randolph, 1985). Compliant behavior is a third implicit requirement of the conventional test format. The cooperation of the child at an age when noncompliance is a generalized characteristic confounds a child's unwillingness with inability. Compliance with the examiner's request cannot be guaranteed with children entering or in the middle of the "terrible twos." The noncompliant/resistant child who will not perform either will miss items or will be judged untestable, leaving doubt and concern about his or her mental ability. Doubt is tantamount to "delayed" because the observable behaviors are clearly delayed and/or abnormal in these clinical samples.

Thus, the major problem with inferring mental ability from conventional tests during the first 3 years of life is that the measures are confounded with the common disabilities. The harsh irony is that the children with neuromotor problems, productive language delays, and behavior problems—the vast majority of disabled children during the first 3 years of life—are the same children who require intellectual assessment. Unfortunately, difficulties in any one of these three problem areas will depress an estimate of a child's mental ability derived from a conventional test.

Alternative procedures to assess intellectual development among high-risk infants and toddlers can circumvent these limitations. What is desirable is a procedure that distinguishes central information processing (mental activity) from the confounding performance measures (expressive behaviors). Such a distinction provides greater precision in diagnosis and identifies children who have the potential to overcome their expressive delays. Response systems such as productive language and object use, which are themselves undergoing development, may be adversely influenced by behavioral difficulties that may mask intact mental ability. Fortunately, research on attentional ability in infancy indicates that these confounders can be bypassed, allowing a more direct probe of central processing ability and offering the potential to overcome some forms of developmental delay and mental retardation. By avoiding inaccurate diagnosis early in development, habilitation of expressive behaviors may occur before the task is insurmountable.

BRIEF BACKGROUND

Measures of attention allow for the dynamic assessment of a child's information-processing capacity. The data obtained to validate the information-processing procedure used in our laboratory imply that with repeated presentation of an event, an internal mental representation is created and recognition of this event is announced through a variety of behaviors. When new information is introduced, it is compared with the old information stored in memory and elicits renewed attention.

The measures of recognition are subtle and include indices such as visual attention, smiling, and heart rate changes, all of which are less susceptible to developmental aberrations than measures used in conventional tests. In contrast, traditional scales of mental development use a static format to assess previously stored information and rely on gross measures of expression that are vulnerable to fluctuations and disturbances in expressive development.

Recognition Memory and Infant Intelligence

Recognition memory is assessed using a visual preference procedure and is inferred when an infant displays a preference for a novel over a familiar stimulus when the two are presented together. The visual preference procedure consists of a Familiarization and a Novelty phase. During the Familiarization phase, two identical visual patterns are presented simultaneously. For example, an examiner may present two checkerboards each with 4-inch by 4-inch squares. During the Novelty phase, the familiar 4-inch by 4-inch stimulus is presented with a new pattern, such as a 2-inch by 2-inch checkerboard display. The lengths of visuaal fixation to each stimulus are recorded. Longer looking times at the 2-inch by 2-inch checkerboard squares would reveal a preference for the more complex pattern (i.e., the display with the smaller squares and a greater number of squares for a given area). A statistically demonstrated preference would establish that infants have the ability to discriminate between patterns. Recovery to novelty, the indication of recognition memory, is the duration of fixation to the novel target relative to the total amount of fixation during the test period. A higher level of fixation to the novel target implies that the infant recognizes the nonpreferred stimulus as familiar.

Almost from the beginning, research conducted by Fantz and Nevis (1967) and Fagan, Fantz, and Miranda (1971) attempted to establish infant recognition memory as a measure of intellectual ability. A variety of strategies were used. For example, Fantz and Nevis (1967) demonstrated that a novelty preference, indicating recognition memory, developed at an earlier age for the offspring of highly intelligent parents than for the offspring of parents with average intelligence. A similar result was reported by Miranda and Fantz (1974), who compared samples of normal and Down syndrome infants at 13, 24, and 36 weeks of age. Recognition memory was superior for normal relative to Down syndrome infants.

Research on recognition memory among handicapped and "at-risk" infants provides relatively strong concurrent validity. Children with characteristics known to be associated with later intellectual deficits tended to show relatively poor recognition memory when tested between 3 and 7 months of age. For example, prematurity is associated with a variety of handicaps, including cerebral palsy, mental retardation, and developmental difficulties (Caputo & Mandel, 1970). Fagan et al. (1971) and others (Caron & Caron, 1981; Cohen, 1981; Rose, Gottfried, & Bridger, 1979; Sigman & Parmelee, 1974) compared preterm and term infants on tests of recognition. With the exception of Fagan et al. (1971), this research consistently showed more advanced recognition memory for term than for preterm infants even when matched for conceptional age.

A study by Fagan and McGrath (1981) extended these validation efforts by generating modest predictive correlations. These researchers sought to determine whether infant visual recognition memory, based on longer visual fixation to novel as opposed to previously seen stimuli, could predict later intelligence using several standard verbal IQ measures. Predictive validity coefficients of .37 and .57 were obtained between 5–7-month infant recognition scores and verbal IQ at 5 and 7 years. Correlations between 4–5 months and 6.5–7.5 years are substantially above the median correlations for previous similar age comparisons of infant sensorimotor development and later intelligence (McCall, 1979). The correlations obtained by Fagan and McGrath did not vary by sex and could not be attributed to differences in parental education.

Fagan and Singer (1982) compared both recognition memory and Bayley Mental Development Index measures administered at 7 months of age to scores on the Stanford-Binet Intelligence Scale at 3 years in a sample of 19 infants with failure to thrive. Recognition memory predicted later intelligence with a moderately high validity coefficient of .51. Bayley scores yielded a substantially lower validity coefficient ($r = .23$). Correlations showing moderate predictive validity occur despite the relatively low split-half reliability resulting from the small sample of recognition tests and the moderately restricted ranges of intelligence (from 90 to 130) that were sampled in the Fagan studies. Thus, these data appear to show a clear association between recognition memory measures obtained between 4 and 7 months of age and conventional vocabulary tests of intelligence at 3 and 7 years of age. Together, these studies provide evidence of concurrent and predictive validity for infant recognition memory scores.

Habituation, Recovery, and Infant Intelligence

The habituation-recovery procedure also was adapted to study infant attention. In this procedure stimuli are usually presented in succession rather than simultaneously, and the duration of visual fixation to each presentation is recorded. Generally, one stimulus—a double arrow in a vertical orientation, for example—is repeated over trials until looking time decreases to a prescribed level. This decrement is called habituation and may be defined as a percentage reduction (e.g., 40%) from the visual fixation level on the first trial. Following habituation, one of two groups is shown a novel stimulus—the same arrow in an oblique orientation, for example—while the other continues to see the familiar stimulus. As in the visual preference procedure, renewed responding to the new stimulus relative to the familiar one is called recovery and not only indicates a capacity to discriminate the two stimuli, but reflects a preference for the new stimulus. Recovery of attention to the novel stimulus following habituation is similar to recovery to a novel stimulus in the visual preference procedure and similarly implies recognition memory for the familiar stimulus.

Lewis and Brooks-Gunn (1981) examined the relative predictability of different measures of cognitive functioning at 3 months for later intellectual ability using a habituation-recovery procedure. The Bayley Scales of Infant Development, the Corman and Escalona (1969) Scales of Sensorimotor Development, and a visual attention task were administered at 3 months and compared with the Bayley scales at 24 months. In the visual attention task, redundant slides were presented and followed by one novel slide. Each slide was shown for 30 seconds with a 30-second intertrial interval. Duration of visual fixation (total fixation divided by the number of fixations), habituation over trials, and degree of recovery to the novel stimulus were the principal dependent measures.

The results revealed that recovery to novel stimuli following habituation at 3 months predicted intellectual functioning on the Bayley scales at 24 months better than 3-month Bayley or object permanence scores. The Bayley Mental Development Index score at 24 months was positively related to response habituation (Sample 1, $r = .61$) and response recovery (Sample 1, $r = .52$; Sample 2, $r = .40$) at 3 months. None of the correlations for the Escalona-Corman and Bayley scores at 3 and 24 months were related. Moreover, those 3-month-old infants who were most likely to habituate to a redundant visual stimulus and recover to a novel one displayed the highest Bayley DQ scores at 24 months.

Lewis and Brooks-Gunn (1981) found that recovery predicted later intelligence in both samples, but the rate of habituation predicted later IQ for only the first sample. However, they argued that the high predictability for the first sample was accounted for by a high correlation between habituation and recovery. In the second sample only recognition memory predicted later intelligence. Similarly, Fagan and McGrath (1981) showed that recognition memory, but not habituation, at 4 and 7 months predicted intelligence at 4 and 7 years. Fagan and Singer (1982) reanalyzed the data reported by Fagan and McGrath (1981) to determine if rates of infant habituation predicted later IQ and found no association in their samples when tested between 6.5 and 7.5 years of age.

The finding that early recognition memory predicts later intelligence better than rate of habituation implies an important commonality between the habituation-recovery and visual preferences paradigms—the two procedures that have dominated the research on infant attention over the last two decades. In both cases, it is recovery of attention to the novel stimulus that yields predictability, implying that both procedures are assessing a common process. Not only are the findings from both procedures converging, but the habituation-recovery procedure has been extended to higher order information processing and the development of concepts.

McDonough and Cohen (1982) used the habituation-recovery procedure to investigate concept acquisition in infants with cerebral palsy. The paradigm was similar to the one used in the usual habituation studies except that different stimuli from the same abstract category (e.g., animals) were presented on each trial rather than repeated presentations of a single stimulus. They tested 24 children with cerebral palsy and 24 nonhandicapped infants matched for age, sex, and socioeconomic status in two age groups; 12–18 months and 19–24 months.

The results revealed that infants with cerebral palsy had longer latencies for initial orienting to the stimuli as a result of their motoric impairment. Moreover, infants with cerebral palsy looked less at the stimuli during familiarization and recovery trials than did nonhandicapped infants, although both groups habituated to the stimuli. The most important finding is that although both younger and older nonhandicapped infants displayed evidence of recognition memory, only the older (19–24-month-old) neuromotor-impaired infants did so. These results imply that, as a group, infants with cerebral palsy were delayed in their ability to acquire a simple basic-level concept relative to matched nonhandicapped controls. However, the information-processing procedures also discriminated among the younger children with cerebral palsy, since some of these children showed age-appropriate, whereas others showed delayed, ability to acquire a simple concept.

LIMITATIONS OF ATTENTION AS A MEASURE OF CENTRAL PROCESSING

Critiques by Clifton and Nelson (1976), McCall (1981), Reznick and Kagan (1982), and Sophian (1980) indicate that a number of basic issues must be resolved before the inference can be drawn that measures of memory and information processing are valid indices of central processing ability. An examination of these criticisms reveals at least four general observations: 1) there are many confounding variables in the research on the development of measures of attention; 2) no single paradigm meets all objections; 3) variability in the development of paradigms and measures should be encouraged, rather than discouraged, as occurs often in the scientific process; and 4) the research on memory formation and information processing has been guided principally by basic questions, not by the practical objective of developing a test of central processing ability as an alternative to conventional tests.

Both Sophian (1980) and Reznick and Kagan (1982) pointed out that measures of attention have different meanings at different ages. For example, a stationary stimulus of high contrast, such as a black stripe on a white field, is a primary elicitor of visual attention in a 3-day-old neonate. However, a dynamic causal sequence such as a toy car rolling down an incline and knocking over an object on impact is a principal elicitor of visual attention in 30-month-old toddlers. These authors argue that the recording of converging response measures such as heart rate changes and looking time can reduce this type of distortion in attentional elicitors caused by such developmental changes. Similarly, converging measures eliminate the confounding between specific attentional behaviors and memory. Moreover, they strengthen validity because they establish that response patterns are dictated by a central command that causes seemingly unrelated systems to behave in concert. Thus, multiple measures of central processing can reduce the confounding between a simple response system and central processing. A related solution to increase the probability that response measures reflect central processing is to elicit comparable responding to stimulation from two or more modalities, such as vision and audition (Zelazo, 1979).

To diminish potential confounders resulting from variations in the intensity or attractiveness of stimuli, complex sequences can be presented in several modalities, such as vision and audition. If similar reactions are elicited for two or more modalities, it is not likely that the physical characteristics such as the intensity or attractiveness of the stimulus are the primary determinants of attention because the stimulus characteristics are completely different for each modality. Rather, it is the child's mental representation of the event and the meaning attached to that mental representation that matters.

A procedure in which habituation is followed by several recovery sequences may increase the likelihood that infants will show recovery of interest and decrease the probability of lack of response caused by either disinteresting stimuli or a generalized habituation response. Moreover, as the work by Fagan and McGrath (1981) and Lewis and Brooks-Gunn (1981) indicates, information-processing approaches that emphasize recognition memory based on recovery of attention rather than rate of habituation are likely to be better predictors of later intelligence. Finally, Zelazo (1979) has argued that if an information-processing approach is to be clinically useful, it must span a larger age range than the 3–7-month range used by most earlier investigators.

THE DEVELOPMENT OF MENTAL REPRESENTATIONS

Many of the limitations of attentional measures as tests of mental ability are addressed in the Standard-Transformation-Return (STR) procedure (see Zelazo, 1979, 1986). The STR procedure is one of a variety of possible approaches to the creation of an information-processing test of mental ability. During the Standard phase, the child is given an opportunity to create an expectancy for a sequential event (called the standard). For example, in the car-doll sequence displayed in Figure 1, a toy car is released from its resting position at the top of a ramp, and allowed to roll down and tap over a brightly colored Styrofoam object upon contact. During the Transformation phase, the infant's ability to form a mental representation of the discrepancy itself (the transformed stimulus) is assessed. Thus, during the discrepant

Figure 1. Sequential car-doll stimulus.

variation of the car sequence, the car taps the object, but the object does not fall. During the Return phase, the infant's ability to recognize and assimilate the reappearance of the familiar standard following a transformed variation of the standard is measured. Thus, when the car rolls down the incline and hits the object, once again it falls over on impact.

There are six repetitions of the Standard in which the Styrofoam object falls when tapped by the car, three presentations of the Transformation in which the object does not fall when tapped, and three reappearances of the original event in which the object falls over on impact (Return). Generally, five sequential events—three auditory and two visual stimuli—are presented, requiring about 35 minutes.

The use of sequential stimuli like the car sequence, rather than static stimuli like the 4-inch by 4-inch checkerboard squares is one strategy for reducing the speed with which hypothesized mental representations are created by the infant. When visual stimuli are presented sequentially in the way that auditory stimuli occur normally, the speed with which a mental representation of the event occurs is decreased because the event itself takes time to unfold. Thus, sequential stimuli can allow for the gradual elicitation of reactions accompanying the process of creating mental representations and can permit an amplification of the process.

The child observes this sequence in a room resembling a puppet theater. The visual events are presented on a brightly lit stage in front of the child, who is seated on the mother's lap. The durations of the behavioral measures are coded on a button box by observers on each side of the stage. Surface leads attached to the infant's chest are used to produce an electrocardiogram that is converted to a beat-by-beat recording of heart rate using a cardiotachometer. The car sequence was constructed to produce signals indicating when the car was at the top, runway, or bottom segments of the ramp and whether the Styrofoam object was erect or down. Thus, the measures of the child's heart rate increases and decreases and of selected behaviors, including visual fixation, smiling, vocalizing, and pointing, are recorded on line and time locked with identifiable portions of the stimulus sequence during the Standard, Transformation, and Return portions of the event.

It is the speed with which young children process visual and auditory information that is measured in this procedure. Clusters of specified behaviors are used to draw inferences about children's capacities to process and respond to the standard sensory information, to retain that information in memory, and to retrieve it for comparison with the stimuli presented during the Transformation and Return Phases. The data from our research (Zelazo, 1972) indicate clearly that the process of creating mental representations—a cognitive phenomenon—has affective concomitants. For example, Hopkins, Zelazo, Jacobson, and Kagan (1976) and Zelazo, Hopkins, Jacobson, and Kagan (1974) showed that visual fixation, operant responding (in this case, pressing a bar to light the stimulus for 2 seconds), smiling, and vocalizing occurred in concert and were highest to stimuli that were moderately different from a standard stimulus. Similarly, Reznick and Kagan (1982) demonstrated that affective responses such as smiling and vocalizing also accompany attentional behaviors, such as visual fixation, during concept formation tasks. This synchrony of elicited responding for affective and cognitive behaviors implies the existence of a central command common to both domains and overcomes the major limitation of visual fixation as a sole measure of central processing (Clifton & Nelson, 1976).

It is the speed of processing of sequential visual and auditory events that is assessed in this procedure. A crucial development that has advanced the dynamic assessment of information processing is the use of clusters of behaviors to announce recognition and infer that a mental representation has been created. These clusters, which are highly reliable (Zelazo, 1986; Zelazo & Kearsley, 1982), are defined to include a high level of visual fixation to ensure that the child's reactions are stimulus related, a minimum cardiac deceleration that is equal to or greater than 6 beats (an empirically determined level that exceeds most chance variation in this context), and one or more of the following expressive behaviors: smiling, vocalizing, laughing, pointing, clapping, turning to mother, and appropriate speech. Only the positive expressive behaviors that occur with or following the cardiac deceleration during specified windows in the stimulus sequence define a cluster. For example, it is common to see a 22-month-old child point, smile, vocalize, and show a 15-beat cardiac deceleration while watching intently during the third presentation of the car sequence. The use of these clusters of elicited behaviors allows even a quadriplegic child to announce that he or she has "got it." The evidence implies that these elicited behaviors reflect the matching of an external event to a mental representation of that event, as was shown for the infant smile (Zelazo, 1972, 1979).

Infant responsiveness to the information-processing procedures reflects broad classifications of ability rather than month-by-month profiles. The summary of results presented here is drawn from both cross-sectional and longitudinal samples of nonhandicapped children collected in collaboration with Kagan and Kearsley (Kagan, Kearsley, & Zelazo, 1978). Moreover, the utility of these procedures has been explored with children displaying varying handicaps, including children with cerebral palsy and Down syndrome. The principal emphasis and experience has been with children who display developmental delays of unknown etiology at 22 and 32 months and cross-sectional samples of nonhandicapped children collected at 22, 27, and 32 months. It is from these samples that the following descriptive profiles of age-appropriate behavior were drawn.

Between about 3 and 10 months of age, infants display increased attention and responsiveness to both visual and auditory events. However, reactivity is generally disjointed and vocalization in particular declines measurably at about 9.5 months. The first appearance of integrated clusters of behaviors occurs at about 11.5 months in our samples. By the end of the first year, attention continues to increase and there is evidence of cardiac acceleration, implying mental effort (Kahneman, Tursky, Shapiro, & Crider, 1969; Zelazo, 1982), during the anticipatory phase of the car sequence (i.e., when the car is at the top of the ramp). In addition, clusters of behaviors, including vocalization, begin to occur late during the Standard and Return segments of the sequences (see Zelazo, Kagan, & Hartmann, 1975).

At about 22 months of age interest remains high, and clusters of behavior occur sooner in each sequence and are more uniform across the four principal sequences that are used. It is common for clusters to occur to the third or fourth presentation of the standard and to the first or second reappearance of the standard following the discrepancy, but not to the discrepancy itself. At about 32 months of age, the discrepant variations of the standards themselves elicit unambiguous clusters of behaviors that imply rapid formation of mental representations for the discrepant events. Generally, clusters of responses to the Standard and Return portions of the sequences are clear, quick, and uniform across the sequences.

First clusters of reactivity, implying the formation of a mental representation, occur sooner in the sequence as the child gets older. Moreover, the use of discrepant variations of the standards seem to distinguish nonhandicapped children at the older ages. These factors combined with the use of fixed numbers of trials imply that the procedures are measuring the speed with which information is processed and memories are formed over the first 3 years of life (Zelazo & Kearsley, 1982).

This procedure was designed to maximize attention and responsiveness in order to increase its potential as a clinically useful tool. A primary intention was to create a procedure that would permit the inference that infant attention is centrally mediated (i.e., occurs in the brain and not at a peripheral level) and that information processing follows a predictable pattern over the first 3 years. If these goals could be realized, the possibility for identifying both age-appropriate and delayed recognition memory reactions to visual and auditory sequences could form the basis for an alternative test of infant-toddler mental development.

This approach contains a number of distinct advantages over both conventional mental assessment procedures and the basic research on memory formation in infancy. First, it permits the use of both visual and auditory stimuli, extending its usefulness to two modalities that are primary avenues for future cognitive development. Moreover, the use of two modalities eliminates the confounding between behavioral responses and central processing. Second, sequential rather than static visual stimuli are used. Sequential visual stimuli such as the car sequence are analogous to auditory stimuli and represent large units of information that occur over time, as does a spoken phrase. Because of this deliberate similarity in presentation of stimuli infants often respond similarly to both visual and auditory events. Third, the procedures described here are appropriate for children between the ages of about 3 and 42 months. Because most of the basic research on infant recognition memory was conducted with babies between 3 and 7 months of age, clinical tests of infant intelligence derived from this work are restricted to this age range also. Fourth, because subtle elicited responses, rather than gross and fine motor behaviors, are measured, these procedures are less demanding and less likely to be confounded with a child's disability, resulting in a less biased estimate of a child's mental ability.

EMPIRICAL SUPPORT

Experimental Validation of the STR Procedure: Identification, Intervention, and Predicted Differential Outcome

The validity of the STR information-processing procedures was strongly supported by the results of a recently completed study of children with developmental delays of unknown etiology (Zelazo & Kearsley, 1989). The objective of this study was to identify children with intact processing ability from among a sample of children with delays on conventional tests who were followed prospectively for 26 months. The information-processing procedures were used to discriminate infants whose central processing ability appeared age appropriate from those who showed significant impairment. It was hypothesized that children with intact processing ability would show delays on an expressive level, whereas children with impaired processing ability would present centrally mediated delays. It was predicted that "intact processors" in this sample would display greater improvement in response to a treatment plan designed to facilitate the development of expressive ability, including expressive language and play.

Children enrolled in the study were either 22 or 32 months of age, had no evidence of congenital or acquired disorders associated with mental or motor retardation, and had delays on the Bayley Mental Development Index of at least 4 or 5 months, respectively. The information-processing procedures were used to sort children into intact or impaired processors. All children were given 10 months of parent-implemented treatment. Children were reevaluated at the end of active treatment (at 10 months) using either the Bayley Mental Development Index or the Stanford-Binet Intelligence Scale. Follow-up evaluations were obtained 6 and 18 months after the active treatment phase. Ethical considerations precluded the assignment of children to no-treatment control groups during this initial investigation.

The treatment plan was designed to stimulate productive language and age-appropriate object use and to eliminate maladaptive behaviors (Zelazo, Kearsley, & Ungerer, 1984). First, noncompliant, resistant, and maladaptive behaviors that seemed to arrest development in "intact processors" were identified. The principal objective of the treatment plan was to change children's resistant and noncompliant responses to parental requests to compliant reactions. Compliance was first encouraged to simple actions, followed by functional play and imitative verbal responses, including naming objects. Eventually, talking in response to parental questions became the focus of the plan. Training occurred during daily 12-minute sessions for at least 5–7 days per week. Parents were shown how to encourage generalization of newly acquired behaviors from the training sessions (such as talking) to their daily routines in the home. Of equal importance, they were taught how to discourage inappropriate and maladaptive behaviors that interfered with development (see Zelazo, Kearsley, & Ungerer, 1984, for details).

Mental age (MA) scores were compared at entry, the end of the 10-month treatment phase, and the end of the 6- and 18-month follow-up periods. It was predicted that children whose information-processing ability appeared age appropriate would improve more over testings than children with impaired processing ability. The predicted results were confirmed and supported the validity of the test of central processing, and also demonstrated the effectiveness of the parent-implemented treatment procedures. Delays were reduced from a mean of 8.0 to 0.4 months for the intact group by the 18-month follow-up test, whereas the magnitude of the delays for the impaired group increased from a mean of 15.1 to 28.8 months.

Of the 41 children in the prospective sample for whom complete data were available, 31 (75.6%) displayed intact information-processing ability, indicating that conventional testing was misleading. This finding deserves emphasis: *Three of every four children with delayed conventional test scores displayed intact information-processing ability in this sample*. Moreover, within the intact sample, 61% eliminated their delays and achieved Stanford-Binet Intelligence Scale scores that equaled or exceeded their chronological ages (CAs) by the 18-month follow-up evaluation. Seven of the intact children failed to show any reduction in the magnitude of their initial delays despite treatment. In contrast, one impaired child's delay was reduced by 5.75 months, whereas 90% had delays that increased by an average of 15.2 months despite treatment of comparable intensity. Follow-up evaluations 2 years later, although with some attrition to the sample, indicate that this pattern of results continued as children entered kindergarten and first grade.

In an effort to determine whether developmental delays of unknown etiology undergo spontaneous improvement, two retrospective control groups were recruited. A review of hospital records identified eight additional children at 37 and five at 49 months of age who had documented evidence of developmental delays of unknown etiology at 22 or 32 months, respectively. Children in the retrospective control groups received the same evaluation as those in the prospective treatment groups during the follow-up phase and did not receive active treatment in our program. However, many were enrolled in state and federally mandated early intervention programs.

Initial testings were examined for two prospective and two retrospective samples. Analyses revealed that the rates of mental development (MA/CA) were comparable for all four age groups (0.62, 0.65, 0.66, and 0.68 at 22, 32, 37, and 49 months, respectively), but that the magnitude of delays in mental age increased with age. Delays for the four age groups were 8.2, 11.1, 12.4, and 15.6 months, respectively, indicating that children in this sample did not undergo spontaneous improvement. On the contrary, children were more likely to display larger delays as they got older.

The information-processing procedures were used in this study to identify children whose mental ability was intact despite significant expressive delays. The elimination of those delays with treatment for a substantial number of children demonstrates their validity experimentally. Strong support also is provided for the treatment procedures because both accurate diagnosis and effective treatment were necessary to produce the results.

Neonatal Processing: Discriminant and Predictive Validity

A second major longitudinal project is underway to compare relative discriminant and predictive validities for traditional and information-processing measures over the first 2.5 years. An additional objective of this study is to demonstrate that neonates process auditory information and that information-processing ability can discriminate among newborns at normal, moderate, or high risk for subsequently delayed mental development.

The neonate's ability to turn toward sounds led to the development of a habituation-recovery procedure using rattle (Zelazo, Brody, & Chaika, 1984) and speech (Brody, Zelazo, & Chaika, 1984) sounds. This procedure capitalizes on the fact that if a neonate's back and legs are supported in the palm of one hand and the head in the palm of the other, he or she will actually turn the head up to a full 90° toward the sound. Newborns will "localize" a repeated word such as "tinder" even when the location of the sound is switched from side to side. Moreover, the localization response will habituate, or stop occurring, after about 20 trials. In fact, Zelazo, Weiss, Randolph, Swain, and Moore (1987) and Weiss, Zelazo, and Swain (1988) showed that if the stimulus is repeated after habituation is reached, neonates will actually turn away from the sound. This fact implies that neonates process the information because to turn away systematically, they must discriminate the word, compare it to a mental representation, recognize its familiarity, and execute a specific avoidant response. Swain and Zelazo (1987) showed partial retention of habituated head turning over 24 hours, a time course that vastly exceeds the duration implied for other interpretations and strongly implies long-term retention of the information. Comparable evidence for processing of visual stimuli was reported by Slater, Morrison, and Rose (1984). Thus, independent experimental data are consistent with the view that neonates create mental representations for events and process both visual and auditory information much like older infants, although at a slower rate.

Both discriminate and predictive validities for these auditory and visual information-processing procedures were assessed at 72 hours and 4 months. Forty-eight children at each of three levels of risk (normal, moderate, and high) for subsequently delayed mental ability were identified using prenatal and perinatal criteria (see Zelazo, Weiss, & Papageorgiou, 1987, for details).

The three risk samples, tested at 72 hours corrected for prematurity, using the head-turning procedure, differed during the recovery (Transformation) and dishabituation (Return) phases as predicted (Zelazo, Weiss, & Papageorgiou, 1987). Normal-risk neonates displayed the greatest recovery of head turning to the novel word and to the reappearance of the standard, as shown in Figure 2. Moderate-risk neonates displayed intermediate levels of recovery, and high-risk neonates appeared to be the slowest information processors. Comparable discriminations among groups were found using the visual fixation procedure (Weiss, Zelazo, Papageorgiou, & Laplante, 1988). Normal- and moderate-risk children displayed the greatest recovery of interest to the changed patterns following habituation, whereas high-risk infants displayed the least recovery.

Collectively, these data strongly support the hypothesis that newborn infants process visual and auditory information—a notion that has gained support only recently. Prior to about 1984, no procedures were available to convincingly demonstrate that newborn infants could create mental representations for events, and conclusions about infant information processing were limited to 3–7-month-olds.

Predictive correlations from 72 hours to 4 months are beginning to demonstrate continuity between these two ages and imply that neonates, like older infants, have the capacity

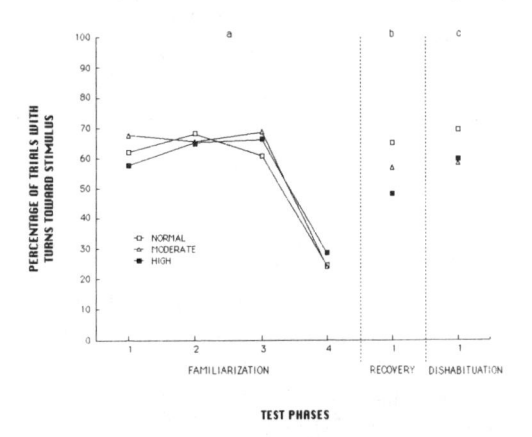

Figure 2. Orientation, habituation, recovery, and dishabituation of neonatal head turning for normal-, moderate-, and high-risk infants. (From Zelazo, P., Weiss, M., Papageorgiou, A., & Laplante, D. [1989]. Recovery and dishabituation of sound localization among normal, moderate and high risk newborns: Discriminant validity. *Infant Behavior and Development, 12*, p. 331).

to create mental representations. For example, the percentage of newborn head turning toward sound predicted attention to visual sequences in the STR procedure at 4 months (r values ranged from .51 to .62). Moreover, newborn looking to visual stimuli correlated positively with 4-month fixation to all phases of the visual sequences (r values ranged from .49 to .72). These data indicate that attention to visual and auditory stimuli discriminates among normal-, moderate-, and high-risk neonates and shows moderate to high predictability to visual and auditory attention at 4 months.

CONCLUSION

The information-processing approach articulated in the STR procedure assesses the child's ability to create mental representations for events and measures the rate at which these representations are formed and announced. This approach assesses a highly fluid process; the specific mental representations that are created are fleeting, unstable, and changing from moment to moment as new information is received.

Several lines of evidence lend support to the hypothesis that the information-processing procedures measure mental ability more accurately than conventional tests, particularly among disabled children. An increasing number of studies have found that infant information-processing indices predict intellectual functioning in later childhood better than conventional tests (e.g., Fagan & McGrath, 1981; Lewis & Brooks-Gunn, 1981). The ability of infant information-processing procedures to accurately discriminate between developmentally delayed children with intact central processing (who can benefit extensively from intervention) and those who have impaired central processing (who make limited progress with intervention) offers further supporting evidence (Zelazo & Kearsley, 1989). Finally, the documented relationship between neonates' risk status and their information-processing performance at 72 hours and at 4 months implies that these measures have better discriminant and predictive validity than conventional infant tests (Zelazo, Weiss, & Papageorgiou, 1987).

In particular, the STR procedure for assessing central processing ability may effectively pierce the circularity of a debilitating clinical/social syndrome that renders a permanent status to the label "developmental delay" (Zelazo, 1989). Our finding that developmentally delayed children do not spontaneously catch up was supported by research from the State University of New York at Stony Brook (Fischel, Whitehurst, Caulfield, & DeBarsyhe, 1989) and strongly questions the continuing use of this term. It has been widely held that developmental delays result from genetically slow timetables that are followed by spurts that produce a developmental catch-up. However, the data from Zelazo and Kearsley (1989) and Whitehurst et al. (1989) do not support this assumption. Thus, the term "developmental delay" may be misleading and perhaps should be reexamined. As the data from the Zelazo-Kearsley study indicate, contrary to the prevalent theory of spontaneous catch-up, it is extraordinarily difficult to overcome delays. Moreover, the effectiveness of the treatment procedures to facilitate expressive development implies a far stronger role for environmental influences in expressive language and early motor development than is generally acknowledged.

There are a variety of clinical advantages to the STR approach. First, this information-processing procedure is useful for children ranging in age from 3 to 36 months, and there is promise for analogous neonatal procedures indicated by the reasonable predictive validity reported above (Zelazo, Weiss, & Papageorgiou, 1987). Second, the STR procedure is relatively brief and easy to administer, allowing children with a wide range of disabilities to be assessed without unusual preparation or unacceptable dropout rates. Third, the STR procedure allows relative comparisons of central processing of visual and auditory information within the same child over time to validate the effects of treatment. For example, children with language delays show initially poor auditory processing that improves over successive testings (Zelazo & Kearsley, 1989) following treatment for expressive language delays (Zelazo, Kearsley, & Ungerer, 1984). These advantages inherent in the assessment of infant-toddler central processing enhance their value, particularly when used in conjunction with conventional tests, which serve as an anchor for normal development. Finally, our test of central processing described here allows for the identification of intact mental ability in the face of aberrant development. The treatment procedures that served as an independent variable in the experimental validation of the test of central processing (Zelazo, Kearsley, & Ungerer, 1984) offer an efficient vehicle to overcome those delays.

Our results indicate that the distinction between mental development (as monitored by the speed of information processing) and the development of expressive capabilities is not only valid, but desirable for early mental assessment. To fail to make this distinction is to inaccurately relegate the expressively delayed child to the status of mentally disabled; without this distinction it is possible to trap an intact mind in a "broken" body. As in the case of Christopher Nolan (1987), a quadriplegic Irish poet, it is possible to treat a neurologically impaired child as mentally defective. In his autobiography, Nolan confesses that students openly discussed his "lack of intelligence. . . . They bandied about the words weirdo, eejit, cripple, dummy and mental defective," (p. 29). In the case of the child with delays of unknown etiology, to fail to make the distinction between mental and expressive development may foster iatrogenic delays (Kearsley, 1979; Zelazo, 1982, 1986, 1989). Fortunately, when the information-processing assessment is coupled with effective procedures to stimulate expressive development, the circularity produced by delayed expressive development and fallible measures of mental ability can be broken.

REFERENCES

Bayley, N. (1969). *Bayley Scales of Infant Development*. New York: The Psychological Corporation.

Bayley, N. (1970). Development of mental abilities. In P.H. Mussen (Ed.), *Carmichael's manual of child psychology* (3rd ed., Vol. 1, pp. 1163–1209). New York: John Wiley & Sons.

Brody, L., Zelazo, P., & Chaika, H. (1984). Habituation-dishabituation to speech in the neonate. *Developmental Psychology*, 20, 114–119.

Caputo, D.V., & Mandel, W. (1970). Consequences of low birth-weight. *Developmental Psychology*, 3, 363–383.

Caron, A.J., & Caron, R.F. (1981). Processing of relational information as an index of infant risk. In S.L. Friedman & M. Sigman (Eds.), *Preterm birth and psychological development* (pp. 219–240). New York: Academic Press.

Caulfield, M.B., Fischel, J.E., DeBaryshe, B.D., & Whitehurst, G. (in press). Behavioral correlates of expressive language delay. *Journal of Abnormal Child Psychology*.

Clifton, R., & Nelson, M. (1976). Developmental study of habituation in infants: The importance of paradigm, response system and state. In T.J. Tighe & R.N. Leaton (Eds.), *Habituation: Perspectives from child development, animal behavior and neurophysiology* (pp. 159–205). Hillsdale, NJ: Lawrence Erlbaum Associates.

Cohen, L.B. (1981). Examination of habituation as a measure of aberrant infant development. In S. Friedman & M. Sigman (Eds.), *Preterm birth and psychological development* (pp. 241–253). New York: Academic Press.

Corman, H., & Escalona, S. (1969). Stages of sensorimotor development: A replication study. *Merrill-Palmer Quarterly*, 15, 351–361.

Fagan, J.F., Fantz, R.L., & Miranda, S.B. (1971, April). *Infants' attention to novel stimuli as a function of postnatal and conceptional age*. Paper presented at the Society for Research in Child Development, Minneapolis.

Fagan, J.F., & McGrath, S.N. (1981). Infant recognition memory and later intelligence. *Intelligence*, 5, 121–130.

Fagan, J.F., & Singer, L.T. (1982). Infant recognition memory as a measure of intelligence. In L.P. Lipsitt (Ed.), *Advances in infancy research* (Vol. 2). Norwood, NJ: Ablex.

Fantz, R.L., & Nevis, S. (1967). The predictive value of changes in visual preferences in early infancy. In J. Hellmuth (Ed.), *The exceptional infant* (Vol. 1, pp. 349–414). Seattle: Special Publications.

Fischel, J., Whitehurst, G., Caulfield, M., & DeBaryshe, B. (1989). Language growth in children with expressive language delay. *Pediatrics, 82*, 218–227.

Honzik, M. (1976). Value and limitations of infant tests: An overview. In M. Lewis (Ed.), *Origins of intelligence* (pp. 59–95). New York: Plenum Press.

Hopkins, J.R., Zelazo, P.R., Jacobson, S., & Kagan, J. (1976). Infant reactivity to stimulus-schema discrepancy. *Genetic Psychology Monographs, 93*, 27–62.

Hunt, J. McV. (1976). Environmental risk in fetal and neonatal life and measured infant intelligence. In M. Lewis (Ed.), *Origins of intelligence* (pp. 223–258). New York: Plenum Press.

Kagan, J., Kearsley, R., & Zelazo, P. (1978). *Infancy: Its place in human development*. Cambridge, MA: Harvard University Press.

Kahneman, D., Tursky, B., Shapiro, D., & Crider, A. (1969). Pupillary, heartrate and skin resistance changes during a mental task. *Journal of Experimental Psychology, 79*, 164–167.

Kearsley, R.B. (1979). Iatrogenic retardation: A syndrome of learned incompetence. In R.B. Kearsley & I. Sigel (Eds.), *Infants at risk: Assessment of cognitive functioning* (pp. 153–180). New York: Lawrence Erlbaum Associates.

Lewis, M., & Brooks-Gunn, J. (1972). Evaluation of infant intelligence. *Science, 178*, 1174.

Lewis, M., & Brooks-Gunn, J. (1981). Visual attention at three months as a predictor of cognitive functioning at two years of age. *Intelligence, 5*, 131–140.

McCall, R.B. (1979). The development of intellectual functioning in infancy and the prediction of later IQ. In J.D. Osofsky (Ed.), *Handbook of infant development* (pp. 707–741). New York: John Wiley & Sons.

McCall, R.B. (1981). Early predictors of later IQ: The search continues. *Intelligence, 5*, 141–147.

McCall, R.B. (1982). Issues in the early development of intelligence and its assessment. In M. Lewis & L. Taft (Eds.), *Developmental disabilities: Theory, assessment and intervention* (pp. 177–184). New York: S.P. Medical & Scientific Books.

McDonough, S., & Cohen, L. (1982, March). *Use of habituation to investigate concept acquisition in cerebral palsied infants*. Paper presented at the Third International Conference on Infant Studies, Austin, TX.

Miranda, S.B., & Fantz, R.L. (1974). Recognition memory in Down's syndrome and normal infants. *Child Development, 45*, 651–660.

Nolan, C. (1987). *Under the eye of the clock*. New York: St. Martin's Press.

Reznick, J.S., & Kagan, J. (1982). Category detection in infancy. In L. Lipsitt (Ed.), *Advances in Infancy Research* (Vol. 2). Norwood, NJ: Ablex.

Rose, S.A., Gottfried, A.W., & Bridger, W.H. (1979). Effects of haptic cues on visual recognition memory in fullterms and preterms. *Infant Behavior and Development, 2*, 55–67.

Sigman, M., & Parmelee, A.H. (1974). Visual preferences of four-month premature and fullterm infants. *Child Development, 45*, 959–965.

Slater, A., Morison, V., & Rose, D. (1984). Habituation in the newborn. *Infant Behavior and Development, 7*, 183–200.

Sophian, C. (1980). Habituation is not enough: Novelty preferences, search and memory in infancy. *Merrill-Palmer Quarterly, 26*, 239–256.

Stott, L.H., & Ball, R.S. (1965). Infant and preschool mental tests: Review and evaluation. *Monographs of the Society for Research in Child Development, 30* (Serial No. 101).

Swain, I.U., & Zelazo, P.R. (1987, April). *Newborn long-term retention of speech sounds*. Paper presented at the Society for Research in Child Development biennial meeting, Baltimore.

Weiss, M., Zelazo, P.R., Papageorgiou, A., & Laplante, D. (1988). *Relative habituation and recovery of attention to visual stimuli for normal, moderate and high risk neonates*. Manuscript in preparation.

Weiss, M.J., Zelazo, P.R., & Swain, I.U. (1988). Newborns' responses to auditory stimulus discrepancy. *Child Development, 59*, 1530–1541.

Whitehurst, G., Fischel, J., Caulfield, M., DeBaryshe, B., Falco, F., & Valdez-Menchaca, M. (1989). Assessment and treatment of early expressive language delay. In P. Zelazo & R. Barr (Eds.), *Challenges to Developmental Paradigms*. Hillsdale, NJ: Lawrence Erlbaum Associates.

Zelazo, P.R. (1972). Smiling and vocalizing: A cognitive emphasis. *Merrill-Palmer Quarterly, 18*, 349–365.

Zelazo, P.R. (1979). Reactivity to perceptual-cognitive events: Application for infant assessment. In R.B. Kearsley & I. Sigel (Eds.), *Infants at risk: Assessment of cognitive functioning*. Hillsdale, NJ: Lawrence Erlbaum Associates.

Zelazo, P.R. (1982). The year-old-infant: A period of major cognitive change. In T. Bever (Ed.), *Regressions in development: Basic phenomena and theoretical alternatives*. Hillsdale, NJ: Lawrence Erlbaum Associates.

Zelazo, P.R. (1986). Infant-toddler information processing and assessment. In B. Fitzgerald, B. Lester, & M. Yogman (Eds.), *Theory and research in behavioral pediatrics*. New York: Plenum Press.

Zelazo, P.R. (1989). Infant-toddler information processing and the development of expressive ability. In P.R. Zelazo & R. Barr (Eds.), *Challenges to developmental paradigms*. Hillsdale, NJ: Lawrence Erlbaum Associates.

Zelazo, P.R., Brody, L., & Chaika, H. (1984). Neonatal habituation and dishabituation of head turning to rattle sounds. *Infant Behavior and Development*, 7, 311–321.

Zelazo, P.R., Hopkins, J.R., Jacobson, S.N., & Kagan, J. (1974). Psychological reactivity to discrepant events: Support for the curvilinear hypothesis. *Cognition*, 2, 385–395.

Zelazo, P.R., Kagan, J., & Hartmann, R. (1975). Excitement and boredom as determinates of vocalization in infants. *Journal of Genetic Psychology*, 126, 107–117.

Zelazo, P.R., & Kearsley, R.B. (1982). Memory formation for visual sequences: Evidence for increased speed of processing with age. *Infant Behavior and Development*, 5, 263 (Abstract).

Zelazo, P.R., & Kearsley, R.B. (1989). *Validation of an information processing approach to infant-toddler intellectual assessment*. Manuscript submitted for publication.

Zelazo, P.R., Kearsley, R.B., Stiles, K., & Randolph, M. (1985, April). Parental facilitation of expressive language. In G. Whitehurst (Chair), *Early expressive language delay: Identification, correlates, and treatment*. Symposium conducted at the biennial meeting of the Society for Research in Child Development, Toronto.

Zelazo, P.R., Kearsley, R.B., & Ungerer, J. (1984). *Learning to speak: A manual for parents*. Hillsdale, NJ: Lawrence Erlbaum Associates.

Zelazo, P.R., Weiss, M.J., & Papageorgiou, A.N. (1987, April). *Dishabituation of sound localization among normal, moderate, and high risk newborns: A test of discriminant validity*. Poster presented at the Society for Research in Child Development biennial meeting, Baltimore.

Zelazo, P., Weiss, M., Papageorgiou, A., & Laplante, D. (1989). Recovery and dishabituation of sound localization among normal, moderate and high risk newborns: Discriminant validity. *Infant Behavior and Development*, 12, 321–340.

Zelazo, P.R., Weiss, M.J., Randolph, M., Swain, I.U., & Moore, D.S. (1987). The effects of delay on neonatal retention of habituated headturning. *Infant Behavior and Development*, 10, 417–434.

10   Early Language Assessment

Froma P. Roth

This chapter addresses the assessment of language in infants and young children during the developmental period from birth to 3 years. To adequately assess the integrity of an infant's linguistic system, it is necessary to examine two main aspects of language: pragmatic and structural. Pragmatic aspects involve the rules governing the use of language in a social context (Bates, 1976); structural aspects refer to the phonological, semantic, and syntactic rules of language. The assessment of both pragmatic and structural linguistic aspects is important for a number of reasons. First, to become a competent communicator, a child must master the pragmatic rules that underlie the way in which language is used for communication (Hymes, 1971), as well as the structural rules of language that specify linguistic form and content. These two aspects of language seem to develop independently at times. For example, there are children who demonstrate pragmatic deficits that are more severe than their problems with form and content or that exist in the presence of normal structural linguistic skills (e.g., Bernard-Opitz, 1982; Blank, Gessner, & Esposito, 1979). There also are children who manifest relatively intact pragmatic skills in the face of primary structural linguistic deficits (e.g., Curtiss, Prutting, & Lowell, 1979; Prizant & Duchan, 1981). The problems demonstrated by these children illustrate that structural linguistic knowledge alone does not guarantee appropriate language use and vice versa. Finally, this dual perspective is consistent with the two major objectives of assessment: 1) to determine the effectiveness of a child as a communicator, and 2) to provide recommendations regarding appropriate services and intervention strategies. To fulfill these objectives, language assessment must be viewed as a multifaceted process that involves gathering information about a child's language abilities in both structural and functional aspects of the linguistic system.

Given this background, the chapter begins with a brief discussion of general guidelines that underlie the language assessment process. Next, the area of structural language assessment is addressed. In the final and most extensive section, the assessment of pragmatic abilities is explored. Within each assessment section, information is provided regarding the relevant behavioral dimensions that warrant evaluation. In addition, specific assessment areas are identified and discussed. Finally, procedures and activities are described that can be used in the clinical evaluation of language behaviors.

GENERAL ASSESSMENT GUIDELINES

Regardless of the area of language assessment (structural or pragmatic), there are several general guidelines that require consideration. For the purposes of this chapter, relevant guidelines are discussed under the topics of data collection, data coding, and data interpretation.

Data Collection

Context

For many years, language skills have been assessed within an isolated setting with specific focus given to isolated components of the linguistic system. In other words, children have been expected to demonstrate their abilities in atypical situations in which language is not appropriately contextualized. To assess a child's language abilities, meaningful contexts are essential. The use of meaningful contexts is especially important in the assessment of young (and low-functioning) children; during the first years of life, the majority of pertinent diagnostic information is derived from documenting a child's routine auditory and visual behaviors. Furthermore, contrived assessment situations reduce the probability that the language behaviors demonstrated are typical of a child's everyday language performance. Therefore, familiar settings and motivating activities should be sought. Of course, the precise abilities to be assessed and the tasks used to measure a particular skill area will depend on a child's chronological or mental age and the child's sensory and motor capabilities.

Sampling Language Behaviors

It is important to be clear about the areas of language behaviors to be assessed. A complete assessment entails analysis of structural and pragmatic components of the linguistic systems, at the levels of both comprehension and production. Furthermore, the goal of data collection is to obtain a sample of behaviors that is representative of the full range of a child's capabilities. To accomplish this goal, an assessment battery should be comprised of a combination of naturalistic observations and structured elicitation procedures. Structured tasks can provide useful information and also compensate for the problems associated with naturalistic observation. First, analysis of naturalistic data is always limited by what a child produces. The mere absence of a particular linguistic behavior cannot necessarily be construed as an indication that such a skill is not part of the child's repertoire. Second, although a child may evidence a particular language behavior, it may not be demonstrated with sufficient frequency to assess it adequately. Thus, the use of structured tasks becomes an essential data collection supplement.

Data Coding Systems and Scales

This section relates primarily to the assessment of pragmatic language behaviors. Although a variety of taxonomies of pragmatic language behavior have been published, there is still no one approach that covers the full spectrum of communicative behaviors between birth and 3 years of age. Moreover, as Chapman (1981) and Dale (1980) have noted, the existing taxonomies typically have been used with only small numbers of children, and support for reliability and validity is either nonexistent or minimal. Despite these limitations, the systems available provide useful beginning guidelines for practitioners, especially when information from different sources is consolidated.

Data Interpretation

Because communicative competence is such a complex phenomenon, interpretation of language performance must involve an analysis of the interrelations between and among a variety of component skills. In other words, in addition to the assessment of individual skill areas, it is necessary to identify the relationships that exist across skill areas to obtain an accurate and integrated picture of a child's linguistic system in terms of areas of relative strength and weakness. Furthermore, it is important to examine *patterns* of performance rather than focusing merely on outcomes. That is, the language assessment process should accomplish more than documenting instances of correct versus incorrect performance. It should produce information about the way in which a child is approaching the language-learning process—for example, the strategies that a child is employing to understand incoming messages. This information can be obtained only by analyzing incorrect responses and identifying patterns that underlie those responses. Moreover, there is a need for the clinician to be aware of the quality of test reliability, test validity, and the norms of standardized tests that are administered to a child. Finally, diagnostic information must be interpreted within the context of a child's nonverbal cognitive level. It is this integration process that permits accurate decision making regarding the integrity of a child's linguistic system and permits the translation of diagnostic information into informed and appropriate recommendations.

STRUCTURAL LANGUAGE ABILITIES

In addition to informal observation, the assessment of structural language skills is accomplished through the use of standardized or norm-referenced tests and through criterion-referenced procedures.

Standardized Tests

Among the most commonly used standardized instruments for infants are the *Receptive-Expressive Emergent Language Scale* (REEL) (Bzoch & League, 1971) and the *Sequenced Inventory of Communication Development–Revised* (SICD-R) (Hedrick, Prather, & Tobin, 1984). These two measures also are typical of the available test retinue, and thus a brief review of each should provide the reader with a foundation for understanding assessment in this area.

Receptive-Expressive Emergent Language Scale

The REEL (Bzoch & League, 1971) was developed to evaluate the receptive and expressive language abilities of infants from birth to 36 months. There are 132 items on the REEL, which are distributed equally between the receptive and expressive language scales. The REEL utilizes an interview method of data collection in which a parent or other knowledgeable informant answers a series of both open-ended and specific questions about a child's language behaviors. Direct observation of the child by the examiner is recommended to clarify uncertain or ambiguous items. Each item receives a score of + (typical behavior), ± (emergent, partially exhibited), or − (not exhibited), from which a Receptive Language Age, an Expressive Language Age, and a Combined Language Age can be derived.

A major strength of the REEL is its breadth; it contains items that target a variety of phonological, semantic, syntactic, and pragmatic skills. Unfortunately, there are several problems with the technical adequacy of the REEL. Specifically, no sound rationale is provided for the selection of test items. The directions for administration and scoring are too general, leaving considerable room for subjectivity. The standardization sample was poorly defined and too small to allow generalization of the results. The reliability and validity support for the test is quite limited.

As a result of these problems, the REEL does not have the diagnostic capabilities envisioned by its authors. Its main utility would appear to be as a screening instrument to identify infants who may require further assessment.

Sequenced Inventory of Communication Development–Revised

The SICD-R (Hedrick et al., 1984) is a catalog of receptive and expressive communication milestones attained by normally developing children between 4 months and 4 years of age. Both the receptive and expressive items are assigned to age levels according to the subjects in the standardization sample. The receptive items are constructed to evaluate a child's awareness, discrimination, and comprehension of verbal and nonverbal auditory stimuli, including environmental sounds, object names, prepositions, plurals, colors, and directions. The expressive portion involves items that examine imitation, initiation, and responding behaviors. For children above 2 years of age, a spontaneous speech sample is also collected and analyzed for utterance length and structural complexity. Performance is evaluated on the basis of parental report and through direct observation of a child's motor, recognition, vocal, and verbal responses to test stimuli. Receptive and expressive profiles can be plotted, and Receptive and Expressive Communication

Ages can be obtained and compared with a child's chronological age and mental age.

To its credit, the SICD-R taps a broad array of prelinguistic and nonverbal social interaction abilities (e.g., turn taking, pat-a-cake) as well as verbal grammatical skills. In addition, test reliability and validity support is adequate. Perhaps the central concern with the SICD-R relates to the size and composition of the standardization sample. The number of children at each age level in the original sample was relatively small, and of restricted race, social class, and geographic representation. A subsequent study found that young black children's performance on the test was sufficiently different from that of white children that the use of separate norms was recommended. Thus, caution should be used in test interpretation and in the application of normative data to children who differ from the standardization group.

Utterance Length and Structural Complexity Measures

Measures also are available for assessing utterance length and complexity for children at the two-word stage and beyond. Most of these instruments are based on a spontaneous speech sample obtained from a child in a naturalistic setting. The most common index of utterance length is mean length of utterance (MLU) (Brown, 1973). MLU is the mean number of morphemes in an utterance, and provides information regarding the average length of a child's utterances. The structural complexity of utterances can be evaluated using Developmental Sentence Types (Lee, 1974) or Developmental Sentence Scoring (Lee, 1974), depending on the linguistic sophistication of the child. Both of these tests evaluate a child's grasp of a variety of morphological and syntactic structures.

Nonstandardized Tests

In addition to standardized tests, another approach to the assessment of emergent structural language abilities is the use of criterion-referenced measures. The selection of behaviors for inclusion on such tests and the age levels assigned to the behaviors are generally based on language milestone data reported in the child development literature.

Preschool Language Scale: Revised Edition (PLS)

One widely used criterion-referenced procedure is the PLS (Zimmerman, Steiner, & Pond, 1979). The PLS is an individually administered scale of receptive and expressive language abilities for children between 1.5 and 7 years of age. According to the authors, the PLS can be used both as a screening tool and a diagnostic instrument for identifying and describing maturational lags, and for planning intervention. It has two subscales, Auditory Comprehension and Verbal Ability, each comprised of 40 items divided among 10 age levels of 6- or 12-month intervals. The age levels are based on an estimate of average attainment age in normally developing children.

The Auditory Comprehension items for the 1.5–3-year age levels require picture pointing and object manipulation responses, and assess understanding of verbal concepts including body parts, object function, quantity (e.g., 1 versus more than 1), size (e.g., big versus little), spatial relations (e.g., *in, on,*), colors, and superordinate categories (e.g., animals, toys). Knowledge of morphological and syntactic forms is not addressed. The Verbal Ability items are designed to elicit verbal responses from a child and focus primarily on vocabulary development, memory span for digits and sentences, and speech articulation skills. Expressive syntactic skills are assessed only in a cursory manner with a few general items. Each passed item on a subscale (between 1.5 and 5 years) is awarded a credit of 1.5 months; the sum of the subscale credits constitutes an age score for receptive language and expressive language. The average of the two age scores yields an overall Language Age.

The PLS manual is explicit with regard to test administration and scoring. It is a relatively short test that is easily administered, and that provides useful information regarding certain aspects of receptive and expressive language development (namely, semantic aspects). However, there are a number of serious weaknesses associated with this test. First, it is not a comprehensive measure of language. For example, there are virtually no items that examine a child's comprehension or production of syntactic structures and morphological forms. Second, the PLS has not yet been standardized. Therefore, the age scores cannot be used as genuine norms, making it difficult to determine whether a child's language performance is within the average, below-average, or above-average range. Finally, the reliability and validity data for the revised edition (1979) were all established on the earlier version (1969) and thus cannot be considered representative of the 1979 edition. In short, the PLS may be best viewed as a screening instrument to highlight areas warranting further examination, or as a qualitative measure that yields descriptive information regarding a child's language performance.

Developmental Observation Scale

Another kind of criterion-referenced test that is frequently used in the evaluation of infants is a developmental observational scale that delineates prelinguistic and linguistic achievements exhibited by infants at different ages. A viable instrument for clinical use is the screening protocol developed by Miller (1983). Miller constructed a criterion-referenced scale to identify children who are at risk for communication disorders in the first 2 years of life. Guidelines are provided to aid the clinician in data interpretation and recommendations are made for follow-up evaluation of language or other developmental areas.

PRAGMATIC LANGUAGE ABILITIES

Pragmatics refers to the use of language for the purpose of communication. There are different levels at which communication skills can be analyzed, and any one message can be classified differently depending upon the level of analysis selected. The first level involves an examination of the *communicative intentions* that a speaker wishes to convey. For example, a message may be used to comment, request, greet, protest, or direct the behavior of others (Austin, 1962; Searle, 1969). At this level of analysis, the focus is on a single message that is encoded by a speaker and/or interpreted by a listener. The second level of analysis, *presupposition,* broadens this focus to encompass a speaker's message in relation to the specific information needs of a listener. Presupposition is information that is not necessarily explicit in a message but that must be shared by the communication partners if a message is to be understood (Bates, 1976; Rees, 1978). Implicit in the notion of presupposition is the ability to make appropriate inferences regarding shared knowledge and partner needs. The third area, *organization of conversational discourse,* has to do with maintaining a dialogue between and among partners over several conversational turns. This level further expands the analysis to focus on the dynamic and reciprocal nature of an ongoing social interaction (Roth & Spekman, 1984a).

To analyze communication behavior at any one of these levels, the context in which an interaction occurs must be considered (e.g., Bloom, 1970; Halliday, 1975; Keller-Cohen, 1978). The nature of the interaction is influenced, for example, by the channels available for communication and feedback, the physical environment itself, and the characteristics of the communication partners. Context is thus viewed as a variable that affects the type and form of communicative intentions conveyed, the information that must be presupposed, and the manner in which conversations are organized (Roth & Spekman, 1984a).

Communicative Intentions

The clinical assessment of communicative intentions involves gaining some idea of: 1) the types of intentions comprehended and expressed, 2) the linguistic forms of intentions comprehended and expressed, 3) the nonverbal and paralinguistic means for communicating intent, and 4) the social conventions that govern interpretation and selection of particular linguistic and nonverbal forms of intentions. Therefore, the evaluation of communicative intentions involves an analysis of both the range of intentions understood and expressed and the forms (verbal and/or nonverbal) in which they are coded (Roth & Spekman, 1984b).

Range of Intentions

There are many systems available for coding the range of communicative intentions. Selection of a particular coding system will depend on the linguistic sophistication of a child. For example, different systems have been proposed for preverbal children (e.g., Coggins & Carpenter, 1981; Dore, 1974; Halliday, 1975), those at the single-word stage of development (e.g., Dale, 1980; Dore, 1974; Halliday, 1975), and those beyond (e.g., Dore, 1977).

At approximately 9 months of age (during Stage 5 of sensorimotor cognitive development), the infant discovers intentional communication and begins to convey communicative meanings through gestures and vocalizations. Requests and statements are among the earliest and most general communicative intentions to emerge. Bates, Camaioni, and Volterra (1975) used the terms "protoimperative" and "protodeclarative," respectively, to refer to the nonverbal expression of these intentions. Protoimperatives represent the child's intentional use of the listener as an agent or tool in achieving some end (i.e., obtaining a desired object). Protodeclaratives are preverbal efforts to direct the adult's attention to some event or object in the world.

Bates et al. (1975), Escalona (1973), and Halliday (1975) have each identified a set of these early communicative behaviors. A comparison of their categories indicates that there is a core set of intentions communicated by preverbal children (see Table 1). Coggins and Carpenter (1981) developed the Communication Intention Inventory (CII), a criterion-referenced scoring system for evaluating eight intention categories selected from the work of Bates (1976), Dore (1975), Greenfield and Smith (1976), and Halliday (1975). In addition to coding each message for the type of intention, each message is analyzed also for its form (i.e., gestural, gestural-vocal, or verbal). Preverbal communicative intentions may be an important parameter to evaluate in light of

Table 1. Preverbal communicative intentions[a]

Intention	Descriptive example
1. Attention seeking	
a. to self	Child tugs on mother's jeans to secure attention.
b. to events, objects, or other people	Child points to airplane to draw mother's attention to it.
2. Requesting	
a. objects	Child points to toy animal that he or she wants.
b. action	Child hands book to adult to have story read.
c. information	Child points to usual location of cookie jar (which is not there) and simultaneously secures eye contact with mother to determine its whereabouts.
3. Greetings	Child waves 'hi' or 'bye.'
4. Transferring	Child gives mother the toy that he or she was playing with.
5. Protesting/rejecting	Child cries when mother takes away toy./Child pushes away a dish of oatmeal.
6. Responding/acknowledging	Child responds appropriately to simple directions./Child smiles when parent initiates a favorite game.
7. Informing	Child points to wheel on his or her toy truck to show mother that it is broken.

[a]Categories are derived, in part, from Bates, Camaioni, and Volterra (1975), Coggins and Carpenter (1981), Dore (1974), Escalona (1973), Greenfield and Smith (1976), and Halliday (1975).

Bates's (1976) suggestion that the amount of these early communicative acts that a child generates at this stage may be a prognostic indicator of how highly communicative the child will be at later stages of development.

To assess a child at the single-word stage of development, the work of Dale (1980), Dore (1974, 1975), and Halliday (1975) should be considered. These investigators have each outlined a system for classifying the communicative functions of one-word utterances. Table 2 presents a schema for coding these early linguistic intentions that is based on their proposals. For children beyond the single-word stage of language acquisition, the only available data are provided by Dore (1978a, 1978b) and Halliday (1975). Dore, for example, observed seven 3-year-old children in both play and structured school activities. He reported that his subjects' utterances fell into seven major categories of intentions: requests, responses, descriptions, statements, acknowledgments, conversational devices, and performatives. Dore's system is presented in a modified and condensed version appropriate for clinical use in Table 3.

Form of Intentions

The analysis of intention form may be approached in at least two ways. First, one can examine the sophistication with which an intention is coded by assessing whether a child uses gestural, paralinguistic, and/or linguistic means. A child who is at the single-word stage may encode certain intentions linguistically while relying on gestural means for conveying others. Failure to look at both forms may result in an inaccurate estimation of a child's communicative abilities. For example, a child's pattern may reflect a linguistic limitation rather than a restricted range of intentions. Second, the linguistic structures used to convey an intention can be analyzed. For a young language learner, a classification system of semantic intentions or relations can be employed (Bloom & Lahey, 1978; Brown, 1973). For a more syntactically advanced child, messages can be coded for sentence types (e.g., declarative, interroga-

Table 2. Communicative intentions expressed at the single-word level[a]

Intention	Definition
1. Naming	Common and proper nouns that label people, objects, events, and locations.
2. Commenting	Words that describe physical attributes of objects, events, and people, including size, shape, and location; observable movements and actions of objects and people; and words that refer to attributes that are not immediately observable, such as possession and usual location. These words are not contingent on prior utterances.

3. Requesting object
   a. present
   b. absent
	
	Words that solicit an object that is present in the environment.
	Words that solicit an absent object.

4. Requesting action	Words that solicit initiation or continuation of an action.
5. Requesting information	Words that solicit information about an object, action, person, or location. Rising intonation is also included.
6. Responding	Words that directly complement preceding utterances.
7. Protesting/rejecting	Words that express objection to ongoing or impending action or event.
8. Attention seeking	Words that solicit attention to the child or to aspects of the environment.
9. Greetings	Words that express salutations and other conventionalized rituals.

[a]Categories adapted from Dale (1980), Dore (1974), and Halliday (1975).

Table 3. Communicative intentions expressed at the multiword stage of language development[a]

Intention	Definition	Example
1. Requesting information	Utterances that solicit information, permission, confirmation, or repetition.	Where's Mary? Can I come?
2. Requesting action	Utterances that solicit action or cessation of action.	Give me the doll. Stop it. Don't do that.
3. Responding to requests	Utterances that supply solicited information or acknowledge preceding messages.	Okay. Mary is over there. No, you can't come. It's blue.
4. Stating or commenting	Utterances that state facts or rules; express beliefs, attitudes, or emotions; or describe environmental aspects.	This is a bird. You have to throw the dice, first. I don't like dogs. I'm happy today. My school is two blocks away. He can't do it.
5. Regulating conversational behavior	Utterances that monitor and regulate interpersonal contact.	Hey, Marvin! Yes, I see. Hi, bye, please Here you are. Know what I did?
6. Other performatives	Utterances that tease, warn, claim, exclaim, or convey humor.	You can't catch me. Watch out. It's my turn. The dog said, moo.

[a]Adapted from Dore (1977, 1978a).

tive, negative, passive, imperative, conjoined, embedded, and sentences with indirect object movement).

Assessment Methods

There are a variety of procedures and activities that are appropriate for use with preverbal and verbal children to assess the range and forms of communicative intentions expressed and comprehended. One procedure involves the application of an existing taxonomy (Coggins & Carpenter, 1981; Dale, 1980; Dore, 1974, 1977; Halliday, 1975) to a spontaneous speech communication sample obtained in a natural or guided-play situation.

One also can focus more directly on a particular communicative intent through the use of structured activities. These activities should be designed to provide facilitating contexts in which the communicative intention is obligatory or at least highly likely to occur (Spekman & Roth, 1984). For example, a facilitating context for requests for action is a situation in which someone wants or needs someone to perform, repeat, or cease some type of behavior or activity. Within this context, requests for actions can be elicited by providing a child with a series of interesting toys that cannot be opened by the child without adult assistance (e.g., placing a windup toy on the floor and letting it dance and run down; giving one part of a telephone to a child and putting the other portion on the shelf). Similarly, a facilitating context for requests for information is a situation in which someone wants or needs information. Using this context, appropriate elicitation activities would include introducing novel objects for which a child is likely to request a label or information regarding function, or introducing changes into familiar environments (e.g., hiding familiar toys), for which a child is likely to request explanatory information. Additional ways to stimulate request intentions include situations that require solutions, such as presenting the child with taped-together scissors, pencils with broken points, paints without brushes, or a puzzle with missing pieces.

With regard to the comprehension of intentions, there are no scales available that specifically address the understanding of various communicative intentions. However, some suggestions can be gleaned from empirical investigations. The clinician can issue those intentions that require some kind of overt response from the child (e.g., requests for action, requests for information) and observe the child's response. Structured tasks also can be devised. For example, Roth and Spekman (1984b) assessed preschool children's comprehension of directive forms by setting up familiar activities such as bathing a doll, dressing a mannequin, and pasting on parts of a snowman. A child's comprehension was assessed through compliance with a predetermined set of directive forms. Because a large proportion of adult-child interactions consist of directives issued by the parent, there are many opportunities for the clinician to assess a child's comprehension in naturalistic communicative contexts. Importantly, not all instances of noncompliance can be interpreted as instances of misunderstanding.

Presupposition

Developmental assessment in the area of presupposition focuses on the ability of children to take the perspective of their communicative partner, a skill commonly referred to as role taking. As noted above, speakers must infer information about their partners and the context in order to determine the appropriate context and form of a message; likewise, listeners must infer a speaker's intent rather than rely exclusively on a literal interpretation of what was said. It is understood that, within any interaction, there is some information that is "old" or taken for granted, and some that is "new." A speaker, as well as a listener, must differentiate between the two, between what may be presupposed and what must be asserted.

There is a scarcity of empirical data pertaining to the presuppositional development of children below 3 years of age. Moreover, there are no formalized coding systems available that address different aspects of role taking. It does appear, however, that one relevant dimension of presuppositional assessment in infancy and early childhood involves message informativeness.

Studies have shown that children, even at the one-word stage, tend to comment on those aspects of the environment that are maximally informative or communicative (Greenfield & Smith, 1976; Greenfield & Zukow, 1978; Skarakis & Greenfield, 1982; Snyder, 1978). To evaluate this aspect of a message, one can examine a young child's ability to encode the most informative or uncertain element in a situation. Using a task similar to Snyder's (1978), the clinician can engage a child in repetitive activities and then introduce a novel stimulus. Examples of such sequences include rolling a toy truck to a child several times and then rolling a ball; dropping numerous plastic rings into a bucket and then offering a stuffed animal; and hitting a drum with a stick several times and then offering a large wooden spoon. The child's responses can be analyzed according to the following questions: Did the child encode what is novel or merely comment on what is already given or known? Did the child code new information gesturally and/or linguistically? Were the messages informative, vague, or ambiguous? Bates (1976) hypothesized that the child's tendency to prefer new rather than old information probably has roots in infancy; for example, even during the fist few days of life, infants attend to novel stimuli more readily and intently than to old elements.

Organization of Conversational Discourse

The final level of analysis involves the assessment of a child's ability to function in, and contribute to, the ongoing stream of discourse or conversation. Of necessity, this involves a child functioning within both speaker and listener roles and the ability to alternately assume the responsibilities of each. Specifically, partners must address one another, agree upon a topic, take turns developing it, and make their contributions unambiguous and appropriate to the situation and partner. Speakers also must be adept at initiating, maintaining, terminating, and shifting topics and must be facile at repairing instances of potential communication breakdown and failure. The following variables represent the essential components of discourse assessment for infants and young children and may serve to guide a clinician's observations in this area.

Socialized Versus Nonsocialized Speech

Within a communication situation, children engage in a variety of verbal behaviors, only a portion of which can be considered conversational (Berninger & Garvey, 1981; Keenan, 1974). Speech that is addressed to the listener is considered social speech. It imposes some sort of obligation on the listener to respond and is typically characterized by being clearly produced and adapted to the listener, and by attempted repairs in instances of breakdown. Another kind of social verbal behavior, ritual verbal play, involves mutual engagement between the partners, turn alternation, and contingent responses. In this type of speech, the partners appear to be mutually engaged in word play, such as rhyming. Imitative sequences fall into this category. Other verbal behaviors are considered nonsocial in that they are not explicitly addressed to a listener and thus the partner is not obliged to respond. This category may include monologues, songs, rhymes, and individual sound play. Nonsocial speech behaviors may at times serve to initiate conversation, but the speaker does not attempt to repair when a reply is not received.

To assess a child's use of social speech, it is important to utilize situations that either require or at least facilitate interactions. Thus, social speech is more likely to occur when the partners are motivated, and interested in and familiar with the topic. Attention might be given to the nature of the toys used (e.g., building blocks, dress-up clothes, and dolls stimulate greater interaction than books, clay, or puzzles), as well as the communication partners (e.g., friend, familiar adults), situational context (e.g., mealtime, play), and topic. Situations that require a child to request information, assistance, or permission also are effective (Roth & Spekman, 1984b).

Attempts to quantify social versus nonsocial speech may involve determining the proportion of total utterances falling into each category. Currently, it is not possible to specify the proportional use of each type of speech that would be considered normal or atypical. All types occur naturally and normally, but use is determined, at least in part, by a child's age and other personal variables as well as the communicative context in which the utterance occurs.

Turn Taking and Talking Time

The origins of conversation appear to be in early infancy and can be seen in interactions between the infant and the caregiver. Observations of these interactions or "protoconversations" (Bateson, 1975) reveal the rudiments of reciprocal communication that conversation requires. Since it is believed that protoconversations form the basis for mature conversational development, they require attention in the assessment situation.

There is a large body of evidence that very early mother-infant interactions involve synchronous alternations of turns and temporally linked behaviors (Bruner, 1975, 1977; Kaye, 1977; Lewis & Freedle, 1973; Sander, 1977). For example, neonates respond to human speech by changing their movement patterns. This synchrony of movement to speech seems to be specific to human speech, whether live or recorded (Sander, 1975). Behavioral symmetry also is seen in the sucking-burst-pause patterns of newborns during breastfeeding (Kaye, 1977). When the baby pauses, the mother jiggles; when the mother stops jiggling, the infant sucks. The mother does not jiggle in the middle of a suck, and the infant does not resume sucking while the mother is jiggling. A final example of synchronization during the neonatal period involves the relationship between maternal and infant vocalizations. Lewis and Freedle (1973) found that the behavior that had the highest probability of occurrence within a 10-second period following a maternal vocalization to the infant was an infant vocalization followed by an infant smile. These exchanges show that caregiver-infant interactions are highly regulated and closely coordinated enterprises almost from birth.

In lieu of direct observation, perhaps the most practical assessment technique in this area is a set of questions addressed to the parent/caregiver regarding the presence/absence of these synchronous interaction patterns and the quality of the early social exchanges.

Turn-taking behavior also is seen in the highly ritualized and repetitive games played between mother and child. These gamelike exchanges become meaningful to the child well before the onset of verbal language. For these reasons, another aspect of preverbal communicative performance that warrants attention in the assessment situation is the child's ability to engage in social routines (e.g., peek-a-boo, I'm gonna get you). Many investigators (e.g., Bruner, 1977) believe that these routines represent the infant's entry into the communicative framework of conversational discourse; the routines facilitate turn-taking behavior and roles in dialogue, both of which are important building blocks to the organizational component of conversational exchanges. There also are researchers who posit that these early routinized social exchanges prepare the way for language development proper (e.g., Ferrier, 1978). Routines are ritualized forms of behavior that have a definite beginning, middle, and end, with clearly defined slots for appropriate action and vocalization. This constant structure makes parent-infant interactions successful because it permits a high degree of prediction of the order of events. Thus, each partner knows exactly what to expect from the other partner. The invariant structure also provides a stable context within which one partner can introduce variation.

In the assessment situation, the clinician can trace a developmental progression in the mastery of routines. Between 5 and 6 months of age, the infant shows enjoyment and pleasure (e.g., changes in facial expression and body posture) upon the caregiver's initiation of a routine. By 7 months, the infant anticipates the game when the adult says the word (before the production of any gestures). The 8–9-month-old demonstrates mastery of these early routines in that now he or she can both participate in and initiate the game.

At approximately 10–12 months of age, a slightly more sophisticated routine can be observed. This routine, the picture-book reading routine (Ninio & Brunner, 1978), may involve referential (verbal) language and consists of the following repetitive event sequence:

Adult: Look! [issues an attention-getting device]
Child: (touches, looks at, pats picture)
Adult: What are these? [query]
Child: (vocalization, smile, names picture) [response]
Adult: Yes, it is a horse. [feedback]

This routine may be desirable to simulate in the assessment situation because there is some evidence that this activity may serve a language teaching function—that of early labeling (e.g., Ninio & Brunner, 1978).

The assessment of turn taking in protoconversations also can be approached from a slightly different but related perspective. Bruner (1977) hypothesized that an important precursor to the initial acquisition of verbal communication involves joint attention and joint activity between the caregiver and infant. Bruner identified a four-stage developmental sequence in the acquisition of joint attention that can serve as a framework for assessment. At birth, the infant begins in the *demand mode,* during which he or she expresses discomfort that elicits an adult's response. By 3–4 months the baby enters the *request mode,* and his or her cry becomes shorter, more differentiated, and less insistent, and is now segmented with pauses in anticipation of an adult response. At this point, the adult can distinguish between different kinds of demand calling. Between 5 and 6 months of age the *exchange mode* emerges, during which the child requests and receives objects, and offers them back with the expectancy of exchange. By 8–9 months the exchange mode evolves into the *reciprocal mode,* wherein interactions are organized around a task with the partners assuming reciprocal and complementary roles. The task becomes the object of joint focus, and communication is expanded to include vocalizations that are slotted into these action dialogues. At this point the joint undertakings are regulated by both the infant and adult.

For a child at the two-word stage and beyond, the nature of the turn itself can be analyzed. Sacks, Schegloff, and Jefferson (1974) suggested each turn should consist of an acknowledgment of the preceding utterance, a primary contribution of the present speaker, and an indication of turn allocation. Thus, beyond the presence of turn taking, the manner in which turns are constructed and allocated also may be examined. For example, turn allocation techniques include asking questions, manipulating intonational contour, and pausing. Furthermore, an indication of whether a conversation is dominated by one of the participants or is more egalitarian in nature can be obtained by quantifying the number of times each partner talks and the proportion of total time that each child holds the conversational floor.

Conversational Initiation

Here one is interested in determining whether a child initiates conversational topics, initiation strategies, and the outcome (success or failure) of initiation attempts. Mueller (1972) identified several variables thought to be related to the success or failure of a message in preschool children: articulation clarity, grammatical completeness and form, social adaptation, use of attention-getting devices (e.g., "Hey," "Susan, . . ."), the degree to which content is relevant to ongoing activities and listener interests, eye contact, and physical proximity. Although securing a partner's attention was the best overall predictor of success in receiving a reply, the other variables all contributed to the outcome.

The topic initiation skills of children between 1 month and 2.5 years of age can be analyzed using the developmental sequence outlined by Foster (1986): 1) *self topics:* unintentional or deliberate messages conveyed by the neonate to the adult listener (e.g., warm forehead, hunger cry); 2) *environmental topics:* topics about things in the immediate environment (e.g., toys, bathing), which emerge at the end of the first year; and 3) *abstract topics:* topics about nonperceptible attributes of physical objects in the immediate environment (e.g., where objects come from, who they belong to) or about past or future events (e.g., going to the pool tomorrow), which appear by the middle of the second year. By 2.5 years, children typically demonstrate all three types of topic initiations.

With children between 2.5 and 3 years, simulated situations can be employed to examine a child's ability to initiate conversations in different contexts for different purposes. Seeking assistance with a broken toy and introducing enticing objects serve as good formats.

Conversational Maintenance

Maintenance of a topic or conversation is generally dependent upon the contingency of a response to a preceding message. Bloom, Rocissano, and Hood (1976) and Keenan (1975) have suggested that contingent utterances may be examined by differentiating between those that merely maintain the conversation (e.g., repetition or specific response to a question) and those that maintain the topic as well as add new information. Contingent responses of the first type serve to maintain the topic of conversation, but they may do so only minimally, with the conversational responsibility returning very quickly to the other partner. Simultaneous speech in the form of "yeah," "uh-huh," and "okay" while someone else is talking also serves to keep the conversation going but without transferring the conversational floor. Nonverbal devices such as head nods, facial expressions, and body postures also may serve this function.

Counter to Piaget's (1926) notion that preschool children are egocentric and therefore engage almost exclusively in collective monologues, it has been overwhelmingly demonstrated that young children do contribute to conversations with both adults and peers

(Bates, 1975; Camaioni, 1977; Garvey, 1975; Keenan, 1974; Keenan & Schieffelin, 1976; Mueller, 1972; Sachs, 1977; Shatz & Gelman, 1973). Bloom et al. (1976) and Keenan and Schieffelin (1976) have studied the number of turns over which young children can maintain a topic and have found it to be an extremely variable phenomenon. Their data suggest that adult-child conversations tend to be maintained over a larger number of turns when the child initiates the topic and when the conversational focus is an object present in the environment. Foster (1986) indicated that children initially are capable of extended sequences only within the context of social routines or predictable sequences such as dinnertime or bathtime. By 2.5 years they demonstrate the ability to sustain topics over several conversational turns.

To assess conversational maintenance, it is recommended that conversations be divided into units composed of nonverbal or verbal messages focused on the same topic. Although the establishment of specific criteria for determining topic continuity is difficult, one can look for a consistent and unifying theme (one or more related propositions) and contingent responses. Once such units have been identified, it is possible to examine the number of exchanges over which a topic is maintained. If a child has difficulty staying on topic, an analysis of off-topic remarks may indicate some pattern of error. For example, some children may consistently produce messages that are only tangentially related to the partner's topic, indicating possible problems in language comprehension. Others may produce comments without regard for the topic on the floor, or, conversely, may have difficulty switching to a new topic. Such behavior may indicate attentional problems of distractibility or perserveration. Of course, each hypothesis would need to be substantiated with additional evidence.

Other avenues also are available. Social routines such as peek-a-boo, give-and-take games, book-reading tasks, and greeting and farewell rituals can be extremely useful. These scaffolding dialogues permit evaluation of role ascription and turn-taking behaviors as well as the initiation and maintenance characteristics of discourse.

Conversational Repairs

In any conversation communication breakdown can occur. Breakdowns result in interruptions in the exchange of information and necessitate repair. Breakdowns that are not ultimately resolved result in communication failure. The assessment of conversational repairs entails an analysis of the repair strategies employed by children in their efforts to resolve communication breakdown. Since discourse is a dynamic process, repair strategies require analysis from two perspectives: 1) those used by the listener who has not received or understood the message, and 2) those utilized by the speaker, who may repair his or her message spontaneously or in response to listener confusion.

One classification system for assessing the repair strategies of young children involves an examination of the linguistic structure of the strategy used (Table 4). Based on the work of Clark and Andersen (1979) and Gallagher and Darnton (1978), it appears that the relative proportion of repair-type usage changes as a function of increased age and level of language development. Specifically, these investigators found that 2-year-old children at the two-word utterance stage predominately used phonological repairs (e.g., Where that *spoo* → Where that *spoon*?) to revise their utterances, whereas children at more advanced linguistic stages mainly used lexical repairs (e.g., *Cats* → *Big cats* scare me.) and syntactic repairs (e.g., *Is that* her → *That's* her doll?) when their messages met with listener confusion. The high proportion of phonological repair strategies seen at the two-word utterance stage is thought to reflect the primitive nature of the child's linguistic system. At this point, the child has few structural options available to revise utterances. When the child's linguistic system is more developed, other structural modifications become accessible and the frequency of phonological repairs decreases in favor of other strategies.

Repair strategies can be assessed by fabricating situations in which breakdowns are likely to occur. A clinician can mumble intentionally, fail to clearly establish a referent, re-

Table 4. Structural repair strategies

Repair strategy	Example
Phonological	Where's that *spoo*? → Where's that *spoon*?
Morphological	I see the *bit* → the *bat*.
	He *sleep* → He *sleeps* in a bed.
	She's → *He's* my daddy.
Lexical	*Cats* → *Big cats* scare me.
	I got *shoes* → *new shoes*.
Syntactic	*Is that* her → *That's* her doll?
	She has → These are *her* toys.

spond to a child's message with an unrelated response, or provide insufficient or ambiguous instructions for performing a task. Alternatively, indications can be given to a child that his or her own message is unclear by issuing different kinds of contingent queries. Nonverbal signals such as quizzical facial expressions can be used for the same purpose. These tasks facilitate assessment of a child's repair behaviors in both speaker and listener roles.

CONCLUSION

The intent of this chapter was to offer practitioners a framework for assessing language behaviors of infants and toddlers in a theoretically sound, concrete, and systematic fashion. While the procedures and activities presented in this chapter are described separately, it is clear that data for all areas of structural and functional analysis can be obtained through the same activities. A free-play situation serves as a good illustration. Based on a sample of a child's verbal and nonverbal behaviors, one can analyze communication patterns for utterance length and complexity, communicative intentions, presupposition, and conversational organization. By utilizing a comprehensive approach, the clinician is able to develop intervention goals that are tied directly to diagnostic findings.

REFERENCES

Austin, J.L. (1962). *How to do things with words.* New York: University Press.

Bates, E. (1975). Peer relations and the acquisition of language. In M. Lewis & L. Rosenblum (Eds.), *Friendship and peer relations.* New York: John Wiley & Sons.

Bates, E. (1976). Pragmatics and sociolinguistics in child language. In D.M. Morehead & A.E. Morehead (Eds.), *Normal and deficient child language.* Baltimore: University Park Press.

Bates, E., Camaioni, L., & Volterra, V. (1975). The acquisition of performatives prior to speech. *Merrill-Palmer Quarterly, 21,* 205–226.

Bateson, M.C. (1975). Mother-infant exchanges: the epigenesis of conversational interaction. In D. Aaronson & R.W. Rieber (Eds.), *Developmental psycholinguistics and communication disorders.* New York: New York Academy of Sciences.

Bernard-Opitz, V. (1982). Pragmatic analysis of the communicative behavior of an autistic child. *Journal of Speech and Hearing Disorders, 47,* 99–109.

Berninger, G., & Garvey, C. (1981). Questions and the allocation, construction, and timing of turns in child discourse. *Journal of Psycholinguistic Research, 10,* 375–402.

Blank, M., Gessner, M., & Esposito, A. (1979). Language without communication: A case study. *Journal of Child Language, 6,* 329–352.

Bloom, L. (1970). *Language development: Form and function in emerging grammar.* Cambridge, MA: MIT Press.

Bloom, L., & Lahey, M. (1978). *Language development and language disorders.* New York: John Wiley & Sons.

Bloom, L., Rocissano, L., & Hood, L. (1976). Adult-child discourse: Developmental interaction between information processing and linguistic interaction. *Cognitive Psychology, 8,* 521–552.

Brown, R.S. (1973). *A first language: The early stages.* Cambridge, MA: Harvard University Press.

Bruner, J. (1975). The ontogenesis of speech acts. *Journal of Child Language, 2,* 1–19.

Bruner, J. (1977). Early social interaction and language acquisition. In H.R. Schaffer (Ed.), *Studies in mother-infant interaction.* New York: Academic Press.

Bzoch, K., & League, R. (1971). *Assessing language skills in infancy: A handbook for the multidimensional analysis of emergent language.* Baltimore: University Park Press.

Camaioni, L. (1977). Child-adult and child-child conversations: An interactional approach. In E. Ochs & B.B. Schieffelin (Eds.), *Developmental pragmatics.* New York: Academic Press.

Chapman, R. (1981). Exploring children's communicative intents. In J. Miller (Ed.), *Assessing language production in children.* Baltimore: University Park Press.

Clark, E.V., & Andersen, E.S. (1979). Spontaneous repairs: Awareness in the process of acquiring language. *Papers and Reports on Child Language Development, 16,* 1–12.

Coggins, T.E., & Carpenter, R.L. (1981). The Communicative Intention Inventory: A system for coding children's early intentional communication. *Applied Psycholinguistics, 2,* 235–252.

Curtiss, S., Prutting, C.A., & Lowell, E.L. (1979). Pragmatic and semantic development in young children with impaired hearing. *Journal of Speech and Hearing Research, 22,* 534–552.

Dale, P.S. (1980). Is early pragmatic development measurable? *Journal of Child Language, 8,* 1–12.

Dore, J. (1974). A pragmatic description of early language development. *Journal of Psycholinguistic Research, 4,* 343–350.

Dore, J. (1975). Holophrases, speech acts, and language universals. *Journal of Child Language, 2,* 21–40.

Dore, J. (1977). "Oh them sheriff": A pragmatic analysis of children's responses to questions. In S. Ervin-Tripp & C. Mitchell-Kernan (Eds.), *Child discourse.* New York: Academic Press.

Dore, J. (1978a). Requestive systems in nursery school conversations: Analysis of talk in social context. In R.N. Campbell & P.T. Smith (Eds.), *Recent advances in the psychology of language development and mother-child interaction.* New York: Plenum Press.

Dore, J. (1978b). Variations in preschool children's conversational performances. In K. Nelson (Ed.), *Children's language* (Vol. 1). New York: Gardner Press.

Escalona, S. (1973). Basic modes of social interaction: Their emergence and patterning during the first two years of life. *Merrill-Palmer Quarterly, 19,* 205–232.

Ferrier, L.J. (1978). Some observations of error in context. In N. Waterson & C. Snow (Eds.), *The development of communication.* New York: John Wiley & Sons.

Foster, S.H. (1986). Learning discourse topic management in the preschool years. *Journal of Child Language, 13,* 231–250.

Gallagher, T.M., & Darnton, B.A. (1978). Conversational aspects of the speech of language-disordered children: Revision behaviors. *Journal of Speech and Hearing Disorders, 21,* 118–135.

Garvey, C. (1975). Requests and responses in children's speech. *Journal of Child Language, 2,* 41–64.

Greenfield, P.M., & Smith, J.H. (1976). *The structure of communication in early language development.* New York: Academic Press.

Greenfield, P., & Zukow, P. (1978). Why do children say what they say when they say it? *Papers and Reports in Child Language Development, 15,* 57–67.

Halliday, M.A.K. (1975). *Learning how to mean: Explorations in the development of language.* London: Edward Arnold.

Hedrick, D., Prather, E., & Tobin, A. (1984). *Sequenced Inventory of Communication Development.* Seattle, WA: University of Washington Press.

Hymes, D. (1971). Competence and performance in linguistic theory. In R. Huxley & E. Ingram (Eds.), *Language acquisition: Models and methods.* New York: Academic Press.

Kaye, R. (1977). Toward the origin of dialogue. In H.R. Schaffer (Ed.), *Studies in mother-infant interaction.* New York: Academic Press.

Keenan, E.O. (1974). Conversational competence in children. *Journal of Child Language, 1,* 163–184.

Keenan, E. (1975). Evolving discourse—the next step. *Papers and Reports on Child Language Development, 10,* 80–87.

Keenan, E., & Schieffelin, B. (1976). Topic as a discourse notion: A study of topic in the conversations of children and adults. In C. Li (Ed.), *Subject and topic.* New York: Academic Press.

Keller-Cohen, D. (1978). Context in child language. *Annual Review of Anthropology, 7,* 453–482.

Lee, L. (1974). *Northwestern Syntax Screening Test.* Evanston, IL: Northwestern University Press.

Lewis, M., & Freedle, R. (1973). Mother-infant dyad: The cradle of meaning. In P. Pliner, L. Krames, & T. Alloway (Eds.), *Communication and affect: Language and thought.* New York: Academic Press.

Miller, J.F. (1983). Identifying children with language disorders and describing their language performance. In J. Miller, D.E. Yoder, &

R. Schiefelbusch (Eds.), *Contemporary issues in language intervention*. Rockville, MD: ASHA.

Mueller, E. (1972). The maintenance of verbal exchange between young children. *Child Development, 43*, 930–938.

Ninio, A., & Bruner, J. (1978). The achievement of the antecedents of labelling. *Journal of Child Language, 5*, 1–15.

Piaget, J. (1926). *The language and thought of the child*. New York: Harcourt Brace.

Prizant, B., & Duchan, J. (1981). The functions of immediate echolalia in autistic children. *Journal of Speech and Hearing Disorders, 46*, 241–250.

Rees, N.S. (1978). Pragmatics of language: Applications to normal and disordered language development. In R.L. Schiefelbusch (Ed.), *Bases of language intervention*. Baltimore: University Park Press.

Roth, F.P., & Spekman, N.J. (1984a). Assessing the pragmatic abilities of children: Part 1. Organizational framework and assessment parameters. *Journal of Speech and Hearing Disorders, 49*, 2–11.

Roth, F.P., & Spekman, N.J. (1984b). Assessing the pragmatic abilities of children: Part 2. Guidelines, considerations, and specific evaluation procedures. *Journal of Speech and Hearing Disorders, 49*, 12–17.

Sachs, J. (1977). Talking about there and that. *Papers and Reports on Language Development, 3*, 47–53.

Sacks, H., Schegloff, E.A., & Jefferson, G. (1974). A simplest systematics for the organization of turn taking for conversation. *Language, 50*, 696–735.

Sander, L.W. (1975). Infant and caretaking environment: Investigation and conceptualization of adaptive behavior in a system of increasing complexity. In E.J. Anthony (Ed.), *Explorations in child psychiatry*. New York: Plenum Press.

Sander, L.W. (1977). The regulation of exchange in the infant-caretaker system and some aspects of the context-content relationship. In M. Lewis & L. Rosenbaum (Eds.), *Interaction, conversation, and the development of language*. New York: John Wiley & Sons.

Searle, J.R. (1969). *Speech acts: An essay in the philosophy of language*. London: Cambridge University Press.

Shatz, M., & Gelman, R. (1973). The development of communication skills: Modifications in the speech of young children as a function of the listener. *SRCD Monographs, 5*, 1–37.

Skarakis, E., & Greenfield, P.M. (1982). The role of new and old information in the verbal expression of language-disordered children. *Journal of Speech and Hearing Research, 25*, 462–476.

Snyder, L.S. (1978). Communicative and cognitive abilities and disabilities in the sensori-motor period. *Merrill-Palmer Quarterly, 24*, 161–180.

Spekman, N.J., & Roth, F.P. (1984). Intervention strategies for learning disabled children with oral communication disorders. *Learning Disability Quarterly, 7*, 7–18.

Zimmerman, I.L., Steiner, V.G., & Pond, R.E. (1979). *Preschool Language Scale*. Columbus, OH: Charles E. Merrill.

11

Curriculum-Based Developmental Assessment for Infants with Special Needs
Synchronizing the Pediatric Early Intervention Team

Stephen J. Bagnato and Dena Hofkosh

Assessment of the developmental competencies of at-risk and handicapped infants has relied upon norm-referenced measures for the purpose of developmental diagnosis. This conventional practice of inflexibly comparing the capabilities of special infants to those of nonhandicapped age peers to guide assignment to a clinical category is especially unproductive and misleading for children with sensory and neuromotor disabilities. The complex treatment needs of infants with neurodevelopmental disabilities demand *prescriptive* assessment strategies rather than only categorical diagnostic practices. Traditional norm-referenced scales are inadequate for either planning or monitoring the impact of comprehensive and individualized intervention programs.

To address the need for prescriptive assessment, the field of early intervention has promoted an interdisciplinary team approach and multimodal techniques for assessment, instruction, and therapy (Allen, Holm, & Schiefelbusch, 1978; Fewell, 1983; Odom & Karnes, 1988). *Curriculum-based developmental assessment* (CDA) has emerged as the structural framework for these team practices. CDA integrates the multisource appraisals within a pediatric team and generates developmental prescriptions that comprise the infant's and family's program of treatment. It is the only form of assessment that simultaneously addresses the organizational needs of interdisciplinary teams and the treatment needs of the infants that they serve (Neisworth & Bagnato, 1988). In contrast, traditional norm-based developmental assessment is designed solely to detect degree of developmental deficit by comparing the special or at-risk infant with normal expectancies while offering little guidance regarding intervention goals and strategies.

Within the past decade, service needs have been catalysts to alter our traditional practices of infant assessment. CDA has arisen as the most viable and effective alternative strategy for handicapped infants and their families. The primary advantage of CDA is the direct congruence between diagnosis and prescription or, more basically, testing and teaching. It links and synchronizes the three sequential purposes of intervention-focused appraisal: comprehensive prescriptive assessment → individualized program planning → progress evaluation. This chapter reviews and illustrates this CDA alternative by discussing definition, purpose, appropriate use, specific curricula, and clinical application. The major themes include the linkage between assessment and intervention and the coordination among pediatric medical and early intervention services that CDA facilitates so effectively. A case vignette is presented to illustrate the function and practical impact of CDA on interdisciplinary pediatric team efforts.

CURRICULUM-BASED DEVELOPMENTAL ASSESSMENT: A RATIONALE

Curriculum-based assessment is firmly grounded in the tradition of programmed instruction, precision teaching, and task analysis identified with special education and applied behavior analysis. Perhaps the greatest impetus to the development and refinement of CDA in early intervention has been federal funding of model preschool programs through the Handicapped Children's Early Education Programs (HCEEP). CDA technology emerged when programs needed finely graded sequences of developmental skills to structure the objectives that comprised each handicapped child's individualized education program (IEP) as mandated in PL 94-142. Most model preschool programs designed their own curricula for this purpose, and many have become commercially available through major publishers. The recently enacted PL 99-457 (Education of the Handicapped Act Amendments, 1986) will undoubtedly have the same impact on products and procedures to assess and serve exceptional infants and families based upon a transactional model.

Three provisions of the new law have particular implications for CDA design and use. The *individualized family service plan* (IFSP) serves as the conceptual structure that dictates assessment and intervention. Program planning must target reciprocally the developmental needs of the infant and the family's capabilities and needs to cope and to promote progress. Thus, assessment measures must be *multidimensional* so that they survey interrelated developmental, behavioral, and interactive competencies essential for enhancing coping, adaptive skills, and independence. Sensitive infant assessment will prescribe goals in such domains as cognitive, language, social, affective, neuromotor, physical, and self-care. Complementary family/caregiver competencies will include emotional responsivity, reading and responding to infant behavioral cues, choosing appropriate play activities, and structuring the environment. Curricula are being designed that dually target these critical interactive competencies so that they can be assessed, modeled, and evaluated. Finally, the new law mandates *interdisciplinary approaches* for service delivery. A pediatric team approach must integrate the work of medical and early intervention professionals with the parents as partners in intervention.

Simply, interdisciplinary, multidimensional, and intervention-focused services are mandated in the new law. CDA is the structural "bridge" that unifies and integrates the operation and focus of the early intervention team. It offers the framework and practical features that can synchronize child/family appraisal, comprehensive programming, and program/progress evaluation. CDA offers a common developmental base for medical and educational efforts.

Definition

"Curriculum-based assessment traces a child's achievement along a continuum of objectives, especially within a developmentally sequenced curriculum" (Neisworth & Bagnato, 1988). The hallmark of CDA is the direct synchrony between assessment, treatment, and progress evaluation. The foundation for CDA is the sequence or task analysis of developmental competencies that form the early intervention program's curriculum.

Purpose

Curriculum-based developmental assessment is unique in that it fulfills three primary purposes: 1) integrating interdisciplinary team assessments, 2) identifying treatment objectives, and 3) monitoring child progress and program impact.

Pediatric Team Integration

CDA offers the most effective vehicle to integrate the assessments and program decision making of each member of an interdisciplinary early intervention team. Of particular importance is the capability of CDA to synchronize pediatric medical and educational services.

Entry of a handicapped infant and family into the early intervention system often follows diagnostic evaluation and referral by a pediatrician. Unfortunately, further communication between medical and educational providers is often limited and cursory (Palfrey, Singer, Walker, & Butler, 1987). Although pediatricians have been exhorted in the literature to take an active role in early intervention efforts, few assume responsibility beyond diagnosis and referrals to appropriate community programs (Fischler & Tanser, 1984; Guralnick, Bennett, Heiser, & Richardson, 1987).

The pediatrician can offer assessment of functional areas of development such as feeding, sleep, activity level, and behavior; inform the programs of changes in medical status that affect developmental needs or endurance; evaluate the impact of the handicapping condition on siblings and the marital relationship; and contribute to an understanding of the family style of coping, other stressors present, and supports available to and utilized by the family. Developmental pediatricians have insight into infant characteristics and family dynamics, gained through long and intimate acquaintance with the family. These insights are crucial for program planning and progress evaluation.

Increasing numbers of disabled or at-risk infants entering the early intervention system have complex, multisystem medical conditions. Many are technology dependent, requiring tracheostomy, mechanical ventilation, or total parenteral nutrition. Many will have spent prolonged periods of time in an acute-care hospital following such procedures as organ transplantation. Such infants require ongoing, detailed, and specific input from the medical community. These needs require pediatricians and early interventionists to communicate with each other and with caregivers much more effectively (Bagnato & Feldman, 1989; Feldman & Bagnato, 1988). Educators convey evidence of the infant's progress to the referring pediatrician through the IEP/IFSP, a document that few physicians are trained to understand or value. Clearly, if physicians want to know what is happening in the intervention program to which they have referred an infant, they need to learn to read and contribute to the plan. If educators want to take advantage of the physician's intimate knowledge of the family and the implications of medical conditions they need to involve the physician actively in program planning and evaluation. Medical and educational providers must learn to speak the same language for the sake of parents and infants. CDA offers a concrete means to promote this "communication bridge." It enables the team to appraise the infant and family from varied points of view and to assimilate these observations in a common tool.

CDA structures the diagnostic and prescriptive efforts of several disciplines by concentrating the focus on uniform goals and objectives for each infant and caregiver(s). The team can then directly translate these goals into mutually agreeable service delivery options and strategies that each team member will emphasize in direct service and follow-up. For example, pediatricians in follow-up services can concentrate on observing improvements in the interaction patterns of parents and their cerebral palsied infants as well as pressing medical and physical health issues. Similarly, early educators can attend to the chronic health problems of impaired infants, including frequency of seizures and respiratory difficulties exacerbated by the infant/preschool program environment, as well as specific functional developmental goals. In addition, pediatricians will broaden the assessment sample by becoming effective assessors of social, affective, and communicative capabilities of infants.

By using a uniform curriculum of developmental objectives, the team not only fosters a holistic view of the infant and family, but also enables each team member to "cross-talk" in common terms with the others. Cross-talking enhances interdisciplinary communication and ultimately service delivery.

Comprehensive Treatment Objectives

Perhaps the most practical outcome of CDA is the selection of individualized intervention goals for infants and caregivers. Goal selection is possible because of the finely graded sequences or task analyses of developmental competencies that are becoming available for infants. The greater the differentiation of behaviors included in sequence, the more precise the assessment can be to accommodate the functional deficits of severely disabled infants and generate functional goals for instruction and therapy. These behaviors are operationally defined and include mastery criteria to document status and improvement.

Child Progress/Program Impact

The third major purpose and advantage of CDA is directly linked with goal selection: tracking child progress during and as a function of treatment. Developmental task analysis enables diagnosticians to determine ranges of fully acquired (+), absent (−), and emerging (±) capabilities that document an infant's current strengths and weaknesses. With task analyses surveying multiple developmental and behavioral domains (cognitive, affective, communication, neuromotor, self-regulation, social), early interventionists can offer comprehensive and sensitive appraisals of the infant's and caregiver's capabilities and needs. Unlike norm-based assessment, which relies upon *interindividual* comparisons, CDA tracks the learning of individual infants on specific curricular objectives. It emphasizes "self" or *intraindividual* comparisons in which an infant's postintervention capabilities are contrasted with previous skills. Thus, CDA provides a continuous record of treatment impact and a formative evaluation of child progress.

CDA integrates interdisciplinary team operation and focuses it upon purposeful and measurable goals that all specialties can target in treatment. The IFSP, including the infant's IEP, provides the structure of matched goals and strategies that unifies the team's clinical services. No other assessment form fulfills these crucial interrelated purposes.

Despite the unique theoretical and practical advantages of CDA, care must be exercised in the choice of a particular tool with: 1) well-established reliability and validity, 2) a firm and broad developmental base, 3) tasks that have functional purposes, and 4) good technical and/or field test support with disability groups (Bagnato & Murphy, 1989). Some CDA scales, like norm-referenced scales, measure the acquisition of isolated skills that have little functional purpose by themselves (e.g., inserting pegs in a pegboard). In using CDA scales, it is important to sample and prompt several interrelated competencies simultaneously so that the infant's behavior becomes adaptive for specific purposes and can more solidly generalize to new people, situations, and materials. For example, interventionists must strive to foster the development of functional adaptive behaviors for infants. In teaching the impaired infant to play purposefully with toys and people, this often means arranging a situation in which the infant must interact with an adult by simultaneously attending to a toy's movement, imitating an adult's action of pressing a switch on an action toy, smiling with surprise at the result of his or her own action on the toy, and gesturing to the adult to restart the toy in a turn-taking play routine. This scenario requires a more naturalistic give-and-take routine in which several curriculum competencies across developmental domains are modeled and taught together as operants, rather than teaching each behavior in isolation.

SELECTION CRITERIA FOR CDA INSTRUMENTS

Seven research-based assessment criteria should be considered when selecting CDA measures in order to link diagnosis and intervention (Bagnato, Neisworth, & Munson, 1989):

Developmental base indicates that the curriculum scale must reflect a developmental task or process base in its design, content, and structure.

Multidomain profile refers to the necessity for having broad coverage of several distinct, yet interrelated developmental and behavioral domains.

Multisource sample underscores the fact that data on infant status must be gained from several sources, including parents and team members.

Intervention links indicates that the scale must generate matched developmental goals and strategies that comprise the infant's program of therapy.

Adaptive options, through either structured or flexible procedures, should be available in the curriculum to accommodate the infant's sensory and response deficits.

Ecological emphasis refers to the CDA scale's capacity to appraise and describe characteristics of the caregiver-infant interaction or the physical aspects of the environment that influence infant behavior.

Technical support emphasizes that the use of the scale must be supported by research data in terms of reliability, validity, and treatment utility.

CLOSEUPS OF EARLY DEVELOPMENTAL CURRICULA

With the proliferation of curriculum-based measures, attempts have been made to categorize the available instruments into a *typology* of scales that dictates appropriate use (Bagnato, Neisworth, & Capone, 1986; Bailey, Jens, & Johnson, 1983; Neisworth & Bagnato, 1986, 1988). Two categories of curriculum-based scales are available and must be distinguished: curriculum referenced and curriculum imbedded. *Curriculum-referenced* scales are those that sample behaviors and "landmark" developmental tasks commonly emphasized in most infant/preschool curricula but are not integral to any one curriculum. The Brigance Diagnostic Inventory of Early Development (Brigance, 1978) is perhaps the best known and most widely used of these criterion-referenced measures (Johnson & Beauchamp, 1987). In contrast, *curriculum-imbedded* scales contain all the behaviors contained in the developmental curriculum's task analysis and, in fact, are essentially the curriculum objective themselves. Therapeutic and instructional strategies are then matched with these objectives to construct the curriculum package. In this instance, assessment and intervention (testing and teaching) focus upon similar activities.

This chapter will review only the curriculum-imbedded instruments for infants with special needs. Exemplary curricula and their scales will be concisely profiled under three headings or types: 1) normal developmental, 2) adaptive to handicap, and 3) ecological.

Normal Developmental Instruments

Normal developmental curricula contain activities that are linearly sequenced and/or hierarchically arranged according to the continuum of developmental milestones expected of nonhandicapped infants. *Developmental task curricula* represent the largest subgroup and are distinguished by the fact that they were designed by incorporating the same discrete behavioral tasks contained in traditional norm-based measures of infant development such as the Gesell Developmental Schedules (Knobloch & Pasamanick, 1974; Knobloch, Stevens, & Malone, 1980) and the Bayley Scales of Infant Development (Bayley, 1969). *Developmental process curricula* are more recently developed and are identified by their Piagetian base in content and structure. These curriculum scales survey qualitative changes in various cognitive developmental processes such as cause-effect and means-end problem solving. Many curricula are hybrids of these two subgroups.

Early Learning Accomplishment Profile (ELAP)

The ELAP (Glover, Preminger, & Sanford, 1978) was developed to assess and program for "developmentally young children," birth to 36 months of age. The ELAP provides a detailed task analysis for infants or severely handicapped children by surveying six domains of functioning: Gross Motor, Fine Motor, Cognitive, Language, Self-Help, and Social-Emotional. It is a normalized developmental task curriculum that has incorporated activities from several traditional sources. For example, the Social-Emotional domain of the system includes an array of important indicators of competence in interacting with adults, separating, smiling, developing a sense of self, and cooperative play. ELAP contains 410 tasks within its six domains. High concentrations of skills are apparent in the Cognitive (105), Gross Motor (86), and Fine Motor (73) areas.

The ELAP stands as a solid early example of developmental task curricula. Tasks are loosely sequenced in landmark fashion and are not to be viewed as a true task analysis in which each skill in the hierarchy is a prerequisite for each succeeding one. In the past decade, the ELAP has been extensively used in field settings, but few published data are available on its technical adequacy and effectiveness. Yet it is one of the most popular developmental curricula for early intervention programs.

Hawaii Early Learning Profile (HELP) Checklist

The HELP curriculum system (Furuno et al., 1979) is a multidimensional checklist of 685 normalized developmental task competencies that survey the birth to 36-month range in six functional domains: Cognitive, Language, Gross Motor, Fine Motor, Social-Emotional, and Self-Help. The system is composed of the HELP Chart, a visual display of the age placement and range of each skill; the HELP Activity Guide, a manual of activities and instructional procedures for parents and teachers for each skill in the curriculum; and the HELP Checklist, a sequential listing of the age placement and position of each curricular skill.

HELP is appropriate for both at-risk and developmentally disabled infants, although the skills may not be functional and sensitive enough for infants with severe deficits. The authors stress that some items are not essential in development, but are included because of their teachability; also, the items are not necessarily hierarchically sequenced or task analyzed. HELP has been extensively field tested since its introduction, but only one prominent research study has been conducted on its technical adequacy and effectiveness (Bagnato & Murphy, 1989).

Important practical features of the scale involve its density, scope, clarity, and interdisciplinary design. Each of the domains of the HELP was designed by the interdisciplinary specialist most expert in that area; for example, gross motor by a physical therapist and social-emotional by a developmental psychologist. HELP provides clear, practical, and easily implemented instructional strategies for both parents and professionals. The HELP curriculum scale is best employed by a program that involves a core intervention team of three specialists and the parents for its most effective and economical use.

Adaptive-to-Handicap Instruments

Curriculum-imbedded scales and intervention packages that include stimulus and response modifications of tasks for infants with various impairments are classified as adaptive-to-handicap (AH) instruments. AH measures are often designed specifically for various disabilities (e.g., visual impairment, autism, neuromotor handicaps, hearing impairment) and/or include or permit modifications of standard procedures to accommodate young children with these deficits. Common stimulus modifications include knobs on formboard shapes, microswitches on Jack-in-the-box toys, and enlarged and textured objects. Common alternative response modes involve response-contingent toys, eye localization, cloths instead of cups to uncover toys, and signing.

Developmental Programming for Infants and Young Children (DPIYC)

DPIYC is one of the most well-designed and practical adaptive systems for young handicapped children (Schafer & Moersch, 1981). The portion of the system that surveys the birth to 36-month age range is called the *Early Intervention Developmental Profile* (EIDP). DPIYC is used most effectively by an interdisciplinary team of three to six specialists to plan individualized programs in six distinct developmental domains: Cognitive, Language, Perceptual/Fine Motor, Social-Emotional, Gross Motor, and Self-Care. The developmental task analysis in each domain is organized hierarchically by age range (e.g., 6–8-month level) and skill area. For example, object constancy skills in searching for hidden objects are task analyzed over several functional ranges from 5 to 24 months of age. DPIYC combines developmental task and developmental process approaches by including Piagetian means-end, object constancy, and cause-effect tasks in the cognitive area, and recent child development research involving gestural imitation in the language area, primitive reflexes in the gross motor area, and attachment and smiling behaviors in the social-emotional area. Tasks from the EIDP are clustered so that intervention goals and activities from the Stimulation Guide can be determined to guide intervention. A prominent feature is the fact that developmental goals include structured and field-tested adaptations for infants with visual, hearing, and neuromotor impairments.

Finally, the system provides methods for determining the best level at which to start treatment (i.e., transitional ranges), assessing baseline status, and charting progress overtime. DPIYC has been used in early intervention research to document team congruence (Bagnato, 1984) and to analyze the efficacy of treatment for children with congenital and acquired brain insults (Bagnato & Mayes, 1986; Bagnato, Mayes, & Nichter, 1988; Bagnato & Neisworth, 1985).

Oregon Project Curriculum

Few practical packages exist for infants with visual impairments. A notable exception is the *Oregon Project Curriculum for Visually Impaired and Blind Preschool Children* (ORP) (Brown, Simmons, & Methvin, 1979). The ORP is an adaptive developmental curriculum covering the birth to 72-month age range, with particular emphasis on skills for infants under 36 months that emphasize tactile and auditory modes of experiencing and learning in order to circumvent the visual deficit and promote cognitive, language, and social development. The tasks are not necessarily arranged hierarchically but rather include critical prerequisite behaviors that a young blind child must acquire to function more independently, such as moving toward a sound cue. Intervention activities are provided for each critical skill. The entire curriculum includes 700 behaviors across Cognitive, Language, Self-Help, Socialization, Fine Motor, and Gross Motor domains. Status and progress are assessed and monitored by developmental ages as well as by a calculation of the percentage of critical skills or objectives attained within a particular time in order to create a "learning curve" for each infant.

The Carolina Infant Curriculum

One of the best and newest adaptive assessment/curriculum packages for infants is the *Carolina Curriculum for Handicapped Infants and Infants at Risk* (Johnson-Martin, Jens, & Attermeier, 1986). The Carolina is a Piagetian-based curriculum that appraises cognitive, affective, and sensorimotor competencies across the birth to 24-month age range. These competencies are organized into 24 domains, such as visually directed object manipulation, gestural communication, object permanence, and vocal imitation, and cross-referenced with the six traditional developmental domains included in most other curricula. Evaluation is conducted using an imbedded scale called the *Assessment Log and Developmental Progess Chart*. The curriculum includes adaptations for various impairments and provides a strategy by which early interventionists can select 8–10 teaching objectives at any one time. Long-term goals consist of activities that group skills across several interdependent domains. The Carolina is one of the most technically adequate and field tested of the available infant curricula.

Infant Learning

Few curricula match theory and practice as well as *Infant Learning: A Cognitive-Linguistic Intervention Strategy* (Dunst, 1981). Like the Carolina, Infant Learning is based on a Piagetian developmental model of infant cognitive, social, and adaptive skills. The objective is to focus on behaviors that allow the infant to become an active participant in his or her own development by teaching skills that are precursors for later independence. The assessment component that generates goals is the Infant Psychological Development Scale with Dunst's procedural and normative revisions. The system targets infants in the birth to 30-month age range in the following domains and subdomains: Means-End, Object Permanence, Spatial Relationships, Operational Causality, Vocal Imitation, Gestural Imitation, Schemes for Relating to Objects, and Communication. A matrix in the manual enables the early intervention team to construct activity packages for parents and professionals that simultaneously foster adaptive competencies in several areas but also across several situations—home, program, and other. This total model works to establish frequent "co-occurrences" or stimulus-response connections between the infant's behavior and its effect on people, objects, and events in the environment. This helps the team's treatment effects to generalize beyond the program to the community.

Evaluation and Programming System for Infants and Young Children (EPS)

Few available systems link assessment and intervention adequately. A prominent exception is the EPS, an experimental, linked assessment/intervention procedure (Bricker, Gentry, & Bailey, in press). While not yet commercially available, EPS has incorporated the recommendations from recent early intervention research to create an exemplary functional model. EPS is a *functional* system that emphasizes acquisition of purposeful social, adaptive, and cognitive behaviors whose age placements are deemphasized but whose positions in the developmental hierarchy are stressed as prerequisite competencies. Components are provided for both the team and the parents to independently appraise an infant's status and needs. The EPS manual discusses various procedures for adapting assessment tasks and scoring criteria for infants with visual, auditory, and neuromotor impairments. The EPS has a field-test and technical base (Bailey & Bricker, 1984, 1985; Bricker & Gumerlock, 1988). Its structure covers the birth to 36-month age range and focuses upon both developmental tasks and developmental processes. Most notably, the EPS makes provision for progress evaluations over time on a per-session, weekly, quarterly, and annual basis.

Ecological Instruments

Early intervention research and the legal mandates of PL 99-457 underscore the primacy of infant-caregiver interactions as the content for effective intervention with handicapped children. However, few adequately designed assessment/treatment packages are commercially available to guide the parent/family intervention efforts of interdisciplinary teams. Clearly, an ecological or family focus will be reflected in curriculum materials in the future.

Transactional Intervention Program

One of the few and most promising of these ecological systems is the Transactional Intervention Program (TIP) (Mahoney & Powell, 1986). The TIP emphasizes the match between caregiver and infant behavior to promote developmental progress. It stresses the quality of the interaction rather than specific prescriptions regarding activities. "The goal of the intervention is to increase the frequency of children's active engagement in interaction by enhancing the quality of caregiver's and teacher's interactions with them" (p. 4). The authors' research indicates that parents of handicapped infants typically dominate interactions and thus foster dependency and passivity, which blunts the development of adaptive competencies. The authors suggest that intervention activities that are overly prescriptive and directive force the parents into this mode of responding, which is not child centered. The TIP emphasizes assessments that focus on turn taking, signaling, following the infant's lead, and matching adult and infant behavior. A hierarchy of developmental objectives contained in the Developmental Profile provides a guide for assessment and intervention. The TIP program has been used successfully in preliminary field testing with organically impaired infants (e.g., those with Down syndrome, hydrocephalus, cerebral palsy, and spina bifida). The TIP represents the future in infant curriculum-based assessment. Ecological and interactive measures are discussed more fully in other chapters in this volume.

CHILD CASE VIGNETTE

Jeremy is a 15-month-old boy with cerebral palsy seen in an early intervention program semiweekly for physical, occupational, and speech therapy, and cognitive intervention. He is also seen frequently by his pediatrician for monitoring of weight gain, and there are frequent discussions with his parents on issues of behavior management, sleep, feeding, and general issues of well-child care.

Summary of Neonatal Course

Jeremy was the second of twins born prematurely at 26 weeks' gestation, weighing 840 grams (1.5 pounds). He was limp and required intubation and mechanical ventilation immediately in the delivery room. There were numerous complications during the neonatal period, including prolonged mechanical ventilation, jaundice requiring phototherapy, a heart defect requiring surgery, and multiple blood transfusions for anemia. In addition, he experienced a severe grade of intraventricular hemorrhage complicated by the development of hydrocephalus and a right porencephalic cyst.

Throughout the hospitalization, the pediatrician met with the family to discuss Jeremy's medical condition. As discharge approached, the focus of the discussions shifted from matters of survival to considerations of developmental, behavioral, and long-term functional outcome. Jeremy's parents were made aware that left-sided weakness was likely on the basis of the right porencephalic cyst and that cognitive development might be slow. The pediatrician was aware that the parents perceived Jeremy as vulnerable and that their interactions with him differed from those with his sister, whose neonatal course was free of complications of prematurity.

Because of these concerns, the pediatrician wanted to recommend an early intervention program that would not only provide therapy for Jeremy, but would be sensitive to the family and the interactional issues described. In addition, Jeremy's medical condition increased his vulnerability to illness and rendered him more fragile with respect to prolonged handling and even social interaction.

Initial Early Intervention Program Meeting

An appointment for initial evaluation at the early intervention program was scheduled for 1 month after discharge. The pediatrician joined the family and the agency early intervention team at the first program meeting. Attending that meeting were the social worker, psychologist, speech therapist, teacher, and physical therapist. The pediatrician discussed the medical issues that led to referral, the parents presented their goals for treatment, and the team discussed the approach for assessing Jeremy's current capabilities and needs.

On the basis of this preliminary planning meeting, the early intervention team formulated an assessment plan that would generate individualized goals to guide developmental and family programming. The following prescriptive CDA battery was selected based upon Jeremy's disabilities and needs:

1. Bayley Scales of Infant Development (BSID; Bayley, 1969)
   Norm based: Diagnoses degree of developmental deficit
2. Early Intervention Developmental Profile (EIDP; Schafer & Moersch, 1981)
   Curricular: Prescribes infant development goals
3. Evaluation and Programming System for Infants (EPS; Bricker, Gentry, & Bailey, in press)
   Curricular: Prescribes functional goals
4. Parent Behavior Progression (PBP; Bromwich, 1978)
   Curricular: Prescribes interaction goals

This interdisciplinary team assessment was conducted over a 3-day period and included the mother as a "partner" to assess status and needs. Team members shared roles in assessing competencies across areas; the pediatrician contributed descriptive and diagnostic data obtained during the office visits by documenting observations regarding the infant's affective and social patterns and the nature of the parent-child interaction and translating these into functional ratings on the EIDP and PBP curricula.

The BSID, with motor adaptations, was chosen as part of the diagnostic battery primarily to describe the extent of Jeremy's developmental dysfunctions compared to nonhandicapped peers. The team decided to use the EIDP as their primary curriculum-based instrument because it was designed to be used specifically by an interdisciplinary team and it includes field-tested adaptations to accommodate Jeremy's neuromotor deficits. Similarly, use of the EIDP was supplemented by the EPS system so that the team would target functional behaviors that require Jeremy to initiate and maintain social interactions with adults. Finally, the PBP was used to include goals that enhance the reciprocal interactions between Jeremy and his mother. This was judged important also given Mrs. R's feelings that Jeremy was fragile and vulnerable and their interactions were often stressful and unsatisfying.

Team Curriculum-Based Developmental Assessment

Figure 1 graphs the assessments of individual team members on the subscales of the EIDP from the Developmental Programming (DPIYC) curriculum. For example, the early educator and the pediatrician appraised Jeremy's social-emotional capabilities while the early educator and developmental school psychologist assessed competencies in the cognitive domain and Mrs. R assessed self-care competencies. Other team members appraised skills in the language and neuromotor areas. In summary, at this baseline assessment, the team determined that Jeremy demonstrated a range of functional capabilities that spanned competencies expected within the 5–10-month range. Strongest skills were observed in the social-emotional and cognitive areas; prominent deficits were apparent in the gross motor, perceptual/fine motor, self-care, and language domains. These deficits clearly reflect the impact of Jeremy's neuromotor and neurophysiological difficulties on developmental progress in other areas. Similarly, the team evaluated the character of the mother-infant interaction by using the PBP. In general, it was apparent that Jeremy's mother dominated interactions with him and allowed little opportunity for him to initiate behavior on his own. In addition, her interactions were not well paced, and neither partner seemed to enjoy face-to-face social play. In fact, the interaction was observed to be abrupt and anxious.

Interdisciplinary Curriculum Goal Planning

Based on this initial functional assessment, the team, including Jeremy's mother, selected curriculum goals that best matched Jeremy's current functional competencies and needs. This plan would structure the efforts of all team members in service delivery. Table 1, for example, offers a "snapshot" of Jeremy's performance on problem-solving and adaptive tasks that require him to find hidden objects and retrieve objects beyond reach or behind barriers. Transitional skills (±), those that are emerging in his repertoire of skills, were chosen as "curriculum entry points" by the team to promote cognitive skill development.

In greater detail, Table 2 profiles the intervention goals selected as an outcome of the team assessment that are most developmentally appropriate for Jeremy and his mother in seven major areas. Natural and structured learning situations will be created for Jeremy so that he and his mother can gain experience with clusters of these related skills in social play activities. For instance, proper positioning will be necessary so that Jeremy can remain upright in supported sitting and use his unimpaired right hand to play purposefully with toys. In

PHASE 2.0: Prescriptive Assessment

EARLY INTERVENTION PROGRESS PROFILE

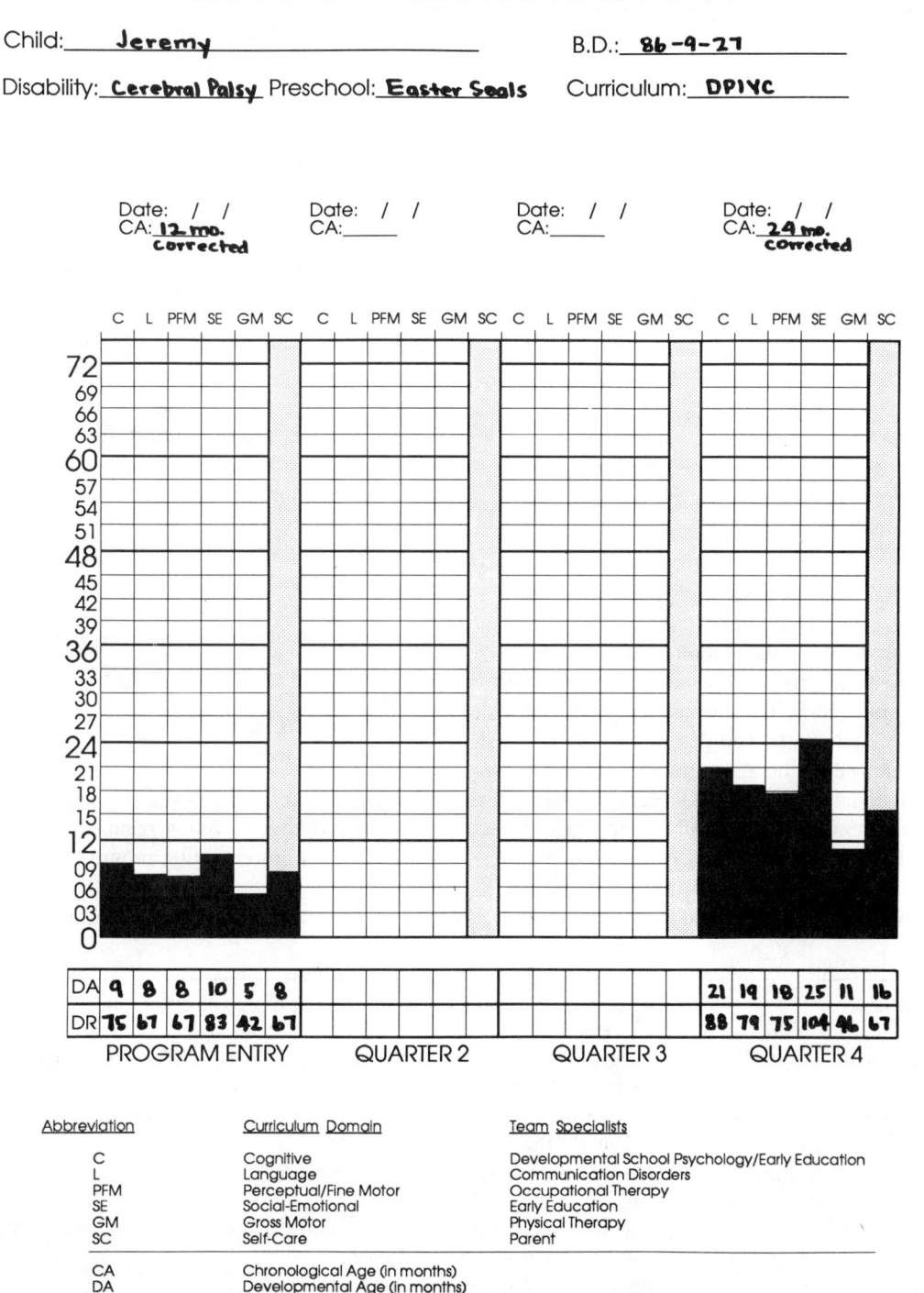

Child: **Jeremy**　　　　　　　　　　　　B.D.: **86-9-27**

Disability: **Cerebral Palsy** Preschool: **Easter Seals**　Curriculum: **DPIYC**

Date: / /　　　Date: / /　　　Date: / /　　　Date: / /
CA: **12 mo. Corrected**　CA: _____　CA: _____　CA: **24 mo. Corrected**

	C	L	PFM	SE	GM	SC
DA (Program Entry)	9	8	8	10	5	8
DR (Program Entry)	75	67	67	83	42	67
DA (Quarter 4)	21	19	18	25	11	16
DR (Quarter 4)	88	79	75	104	46	67

Abbreviation	Curriculum Domain	Team Specialists
C	Cognitive	Developmental School Psychology/Early Education
L	Language	Communication Disorders
PFM	Perceptual/Fine Motor	Occupational Therapy
SE	Social-Emotional	Early Education
GM	Gross Motor	Physical Therapy
SC	Self-Care	Parent
CA	Chronological Age (in months)	
DA	Developmental Age (in months)	
DR	Developmental Rate (Average = 100)	

Figure 1. Jeremy's team baseline and progress evaluations on the EIDP curriculum scale.

Table 1. Snapshot of Jeremy's curriculum-based assessment on the EIDP

Mastery level	Age range	Cognitive subskill task analysis
+	6– 8 mo	Attains partially hidden object
+	9–11 mo	Attains completely hidden object
+	9–11 mo	Pulls string to obtain toy
±	9–11 mo	Removes clear barrier to obtain toy
±	12–15 mo	Finds toy hidden under one of three covers
±	16–19 mo	Finds toy hidden under several covers
±	16–19 mo	Searches for toy hidden with one displacement
−	2–23 mo	Searches for toy hidden with three displacements
−	25–36 mo	Nests sequential cups

addition, the situation will be structured so that several social, language, play, and motor skills are integrated in interacting with toys and people.

Intervention Content, Settings, and Strategies

Table 3 offers a sample set of developmental learning activities generated from the team assessment results. Note that this plan emphasizes the facilitation of clusters of interrelated competencies that are adaptive and purposeful rather than isolated splinter skills. Also, integrated programming is stressed whereby each therapist promotes these skills in individual and combined therapy sessions with the parent-infant pair. Most important, these skills are integrated into naturalistic routines across typical settings and contexts (e.g., feeding, bedtime, preschool, bathing) so that Jeremy's learning can become generalized and under the stimulus control of different people, settings, and materials.

For example, during preschool an active Jack-in-the-box toy provides a motivating activity for reciprocal play routines, imitation, and reinforcement. Similarly, during bathing Jeremy's mother can foster the same behaviors using a squeezable soap bottle to encourage motor imitation and response-contingent behaviors.

Evaluation of Child Progress/Program Impact

Evaluation of the developmental and behavioral progress of young handicapped children within an intervention program is a cru-

Table 2. Curriculum-based team intervention goals for Jeremy from DPIYC, EPS, and PBP instruments

Developmental domains	Functional objectives
Cognitive	Retrieves toys beyond reach; searches for hidden objects; inspects novel toy features
Language	Imitates sounds of adult; looks toward named object or person; gestures or vocalizes for wants
Social-emotional	Participates in face-to-face play; initiates social games; smiles/laughs at funny events; separates from parent
Perceptual/fine motor	Activates switch toys with right arm/hand; opens covered boxes; relates objects purposefully
Gross motor	Maintains supported sitting; begins to reach in sitting; gets to hands and knees; gets to sitting from supine
Self-care	Feeds self with fingers; swallows with mouth closed; accepts textured foods
Parent-infant interaction	Mother interprets infant's mood and gestures; selects appropriate play activities; allows infant to initiate play; paces interaction with infant

Table 3. Sample integrated developmental learning activities across settings

Integrated goals	Adaptive strategies	Activities and settings — Preschool	Activities and settings — Bath time
Plays purposefully with action toys	Use beanbag chair or feeder seat for proper positioning	Reciprocal game with Jack-in-box toys: • Adult demonstrates • Prompts Jeremy • Jeremy initiates • Smile/clap as reward • Adult takes turn	Find rubber Kermit toy under washcloth
Imitates adult actions and sounds	Change play positions (e.g., prone on forearms with underarm roll support)		Jeremy reaches to touch bubbles from squeeze toy Jeremy imitates pat/squeeze of soap bottle
Smiles and claps when successful	Use movable, sound-producing, response-contingent toys with switches and levers	Cause-effect play with movable switch toy • Adult demonstrates • Jeremy presses microswitch • Repeat over 4 trials	
Sits with support and reaches	Arrange one-to-one setting initially with parent and therapist		
Increases endurance	Reduce distractions		

cial activity. Such "monitoring" provides ongoing evidence of the efficacy of a program's efforts and the appropriateness of the goals and strategies selected by the team; similarly, frequent and periodic evaluation allows the team to detect no-progress areas requiring changes in goals and methods. Progress during treatment is the only justifiable method for offering predictions regarding outcome (Bagnato, Neisworth, & Munson, 1989).

Figure 1 demonstrates that Jeremy improved during a 12-month period of treatment in important functional skills. An inspection of the specific goals attained and skills mastered is the best evidence of change; however, Jeremy's quantitative progress on the curriculum more globally shows that he now demonstrates a range of functional skills spanning the 11–25-month range. Notable changes are evident in cognitive and play skills, language capabilities, and continued strengths in social-emotional competencies. Also, despite his neuromotor impairments, Jeremy demonstrated progress in both perceptual/fine motor and gross motor domains. Despite his neuromotor impairments, through interdisciplinary treatment Jeremy demonstrates his best competencies in the cognitive and social areas. Skills in these areas are most comparable to those expected at 21 and 25 months of age, respectively. Gains in the cognitive area, particularly, are progressing at approximately 88% of the rate expected, which indicates functioning within the low-average range.

Based on this progress evaluation, the team will again meet and revise and update Jeremy's therapeutic plan based on his current capabilities and needs. Serial assessments will continue to determine progress and needs and serve as the basis for program revision.

SUMMARY

Special-needs infants require special assessment techniques. Curriculum-based developmental assessment is emerging as the preeminent strategy for infant appraisal. CDA links assessment, intervention, and progress evaluation as sequential components of the same process. Perhaps the most valuable organizational feature of CDA is its capability to coordinate interdisciplinary team collaboration in practical ways. CDA integrates the efforts of medical and early intervention professionals and parents within the same framework so that cross-talking is possible and decision making is easier and more organized. PL 99-457 will lead to creative advances in curriculum-based developmental assessment technology that will enhance services for at-risk and handicapped infants and families.

REFERENCES

Allen, K.E., Holm, V.A., & Schiefelbusch, R.L. (1978). *Early intervention: A team approach.* Baltimore: University Park Press.

Bagnato, S.J. (1984). Team congruence in developmental diagnosis and intervention: Comparing clinical judgment and child performance measures. *School Psychology Review, 13*(1), 7–16.

Bagnato, S.J., & Feldman, H. (1989). Closed head injury in infants and preschool children: Research and practice issues. *Infants and Young Children, 2*(1), 1–13.

Bagnato, S.J., & Mayes, S. (1986). Patterns of developmental and behavioral progress for young brain-injured children during interdisciplinary intervention. *Developmental Neuropsychology, 2,* 213–240.

Bagnato, S.J., Mayes, S., & Nichter, C. (1988). An interdisciplinary neurodevelopmental assessment model for brain injured infants and preschool children. *Journal of Head Trauma Rehabilitation, 2*(4), 44–55.

Bagnato, S.J., & Murphy, J.P. (1989). Validity of curriculum-based scales with young neurodevelopmentally disabled children: Implications for team assessment. *Early Education and Development, 1*(1), 50–63.

Bagnato, S.J., & Neisworth, J.T. (1985). Efficacy of interdisciplinary assessment and treatment for infants and preschoolers with congenital and acquired brain injury. *Analysis and Intervention in Developmental Disabilities, 5*(1/2), 118, 119.

Bagnato, S.J., Neisworth, J.T., & Capone, A. (1986). Curriculum-based assessment for the young exceptional child: Rationale and review. *Topics in Early Childhood Special Education, 6*(2), 97–110.

Bagnato, S.J., Neisworth, J.T., & Munson, S. (1989). *Linking developmental assessment and early intervention: Curriculum-based prescriptions* (2nd ed.). Rockville, MD: Aspen Publishers.

Bailey, E.J., & Bricker, D. (1984). The efficacy of early intervention for severely handicapped infants and young children. *Topics in Early Childhood Special Education, 4*(3), 30–51.

Bailey, E.J., & Bricker, D. (1985). Evaluation of a three-year early intervention demonstration project. *Topics in Early Childhood Special Education, 5*(2), 52–65.

Bailey, D.B., Jens, K.G., & Johnson, N. (1983). Curricula for handicapped infants. In S.G. Garwood & R. Fewell (Eds.), *Educating handicapped infants* (pp. 387–415). Rockville, MD: Aspen Publishers.

Bayley, N. (1969). *Bayley Scales of Infant Development.* New York: Psychological Corporation.

Bricker, D., Gentry, D., & Bailey, D. (in press). *Evaluation and programming system for infants and young children.* Eugene: University of Oregon, Center on Human Development.

Bricker, D., & Gumerlock, S. (1988). Application of a three-level evaluation plan for monitoring child progress and program effects. *The Journal of Special Education, 22*(1), 66–81.

Brigance, A. (1978). *The Brigance Diagnostic Inventory of Early Development.* N. Billerica, MS: Curriculum Associates.

Bromwich, R. (1978). *Working with infants and parents.* Austin, TX: PRO-ED.

Brown, D., Simmons, V., & Methvin, J. (1979). *The Oregon project for visually impaired and blind preschool children.* Medford, OR: Jackson County Education Service District.

Dunst, C.J. (1981). *Infant learning: A cognitive-linguistic intervention strategy.* Allen, TX: DLM/Teaching Resources.

Education of the Handicapped Act Amendments. (1986). Washington, DC: U.S. Government Printing Office.

Feldman, H., & Bagnato, S.J. (1988). *Developmental Support for Medically Handicapped Infants.* Washington, DC: HCEEP Field-Initiated Research Grant #HO24-f-80014-88.

Fewell, R.R. (1983). The team approach in infant education. In S.G. Garwood & R.R. Fewell (Eds.), *Educating handicapped infants* (pp. 232–254). Rockville, MD: Aspen Publishers.

Fischler, R.S., & Tanser, M. (1984). The primary physician's role in care for developmentally handicapped children. *Journal of Family Practice, 18,* 85–88.

Furuno, S., O'Reilly, K.A., Hosaka, C.M., Inatsuka, T.T., Allman, T.L., & Zeisloft, B. (1979). *Hawaii Early Learning Profile.* Palo Alto, CA: VORT Corporation.

Glover, M.E., Preminger, J.L., & Sanford, A.R. (1978). *Early Learning Accomplishment Profile.* Winston-Salem, NC: Kaplan School Supply.

Guralnick, M.J., Bennett, F.C., Heiser, K.E., & Richardson, H.B. (1987). Training future primary care pediatricians to serve handicapped children and their families. *Topics in Early Childhood Special Education, 6*(4), 1–11.

Johnson, L.J., & Beauchamp, K.D.F. (1987). Preschool assessment measures: What are teachers using? *Journal of the Division for Early Childhood, 12*(1), 70–76.

Johnson-Martin, N., Jens, K., & Attermeier, S. (1986). *The Carolina curriculum for handicapped infants and infants at risk.* Baltimore: Paul H. Brookes Publishing Co.

Knobloch, H., & Pasamanick, B. (1974). *Developmental diagnosis.* New York: Harper & Row.

Knobloch, H., Stevens, F., & Malone, A.F. (1980). *Manual of developmental diagnosis.* New York: Harper & Row.

Mahoney, G., & Powell, A. (1986). *Transactional intervention program.* Newington: University of Connecticut Health Center.

Neisworth, J.T., & Bagnato, S.J. (1986). Curriculum based developmental assessment: Congruence of testing and teaching. *School Psychology Reviews, 15*(2), 180–199.

Neisworth, J.T., & Bagnato, S.J. (1988). Assessment in early childhood special education: A typology of dependent measures. In S. Odom & M. Karnes (Eds.), *Early intervention for infants and children with handicaps: An empirical base* (pp. 23–49). Baltimore: Paul H. Brookes Publishing Co.

Odom, S.L., & Karnes, M.B. (1988). (Eds.). *Early intervention for infants and children with handicaps: An empirical base.* Baltimore: Paul H. Brookes Publishing Co.

Palfrey, J.S., Singer, J.D., Walker, D.R., & Butler, J.A. (1987). Early identification of children's special needs: A study in five metropolitan communities. *Journal of Pediatrics, 111,* 851–859.

Schafer, D.S., & Moersch, M.S. (1981). *Developmental programming for infants and young children.* Ann Arbor: University of Michigan Press.

12 Assessment of the Infant with Multiple Handicaps

Steven A. Rosenberg and Cordelia C. Robinson

This chapter considers issues involved in the assessment of infants who have multiple handicaps. The major issue that will be considered is the tenability of the assumptions that underlie the use of standardized assessment tools with infants who have physical or sensory handicaps. Given our concerns regarding the high probability of inappropriate classifications of children with multiple handicaps when they are assessed using standardized tools, a model for assessment involving an interdisciplinary team is described. The rationale and content of the Participate Decision Process that was developed for use with young children who have multiple or severe handicaps is described and illustrations of the use of this process are provided.

PURPOSES AND ASSUMPTIONS OF ASSESSMENT

These are several primary purposes for assessment, including: 1) identification or diagnosis of deviations from the typical pattern, 2) prediction of anticipated future rate of development, 3) analysis of patterns of strengths and weaknesses for the purpose of planning intervention, and 4) assessing progress in intervention. For children with multiple handicaps, we have argued elsewhere and continue to argue here that using traditional norm-referenced assessment tools is, at its most benign, gratuitous, and at its worst potentially injurious to the child, (Robinson, 1982; Robinson & Fieber, 1988; Robinson & Rosenberg, 1987). If classification of a child with physical or sensory handicaps as mentally retarded occurs as a function of administration of a standardized procedure, assumptions underlying the use of the tool have been violated (see Robinson & Fieber, 1988, for expanded discussion of the point). Also, there is the danger of intervention strategies being based upon an erroneous classification of a child as mentally retarded.

ASSESSMENT STRATEGIES

Clinicians have long recognized the inappropriateness of the use of norm-referenced assessment tools with individuals who have disabilities that exclude them from representation in the standardization sample (see Robinson & Fieber, 1988). The most frequently advocated strategy for assessment of such individuals is the use of a tool specifically designed to take a specific disability into account. Examples of such tools are the Hiskey-Nebraska Test of Learning Aptitude (Hiskey, 1966) for deaf persons and the adaptation of the Stanford-Binet Intelligence Scale for blind persons (Hayes, 1943). Adding to the utility of such instruments for blind or deaf persons is a growing body of literature on the development of deaf and blind children. This is literature that has gone beyond the classification of tasks that cannot be done as a consequence of a disability. Rather, the emphasis is on possible alternative developmental pathways and processes to end states that are potentially equivalent in function, if not in form, to the performance of the person who does not have the specific impairment (see Wachs & Sheehan, 1988, for a review of this literature).

When we looked for normed instruments and developmental literature to use as guidelines in the assessment of the infant or preschooler who is motorically impaired, we found much less guidance. What we found were advocates of a variety of assessment modification strategies (DuBose, Langley, & Stagg, 1977; Hauessermann, 1958; Jens & Johnson, 1982; Robinson, 1982; Robinson & Rosenberg, 1987; Simeonsson, 1977; Simeonsson, Huntington, & Parse, 1980). These "strategy" approaches involve a number of different techniques, generally relying on the assumption that underlying cognitive processes are tapped in the performance of the tasks (Haeussermann, 1958; Robinson & Robinson, 1978, 1983). Thus, rather than developing tests, a strategy or process approach involves efforts to modify tasks, materials, or responses in order to allow for responses that are logically feasible for the individual and that appear to reflect basic cognitive processes.

As an example of an assessment strategy, Simeonsson (1977) discussed assessment as a process distinct from testing, a process that can be used to evaluate strengths and deficits in order to provide a basis for intervention. Whether norm- or criterion-referenced tools are used, additional products of this assessment process include evaluation of the skills already mastered by the individual, response to interventions designed to teach specific skills or tasks, and the child's ability to perform given tasks in different settings and with different persons (Bourgeault, Harley, DuBose, & Langley, 1977; DuBose et al., 1977; Langley, 1978; Simeonsson et al., 1980).

DuBose et al. (1977) identified the assumptions made in a process-oriented approach to assessment. Those assumptions include:

1. A view of the child as an "active agent" who operates on his or her own development;
2. that the learning process used by the individual child can be measured and modified within the context of a process oriented assessment;
3. that the child's learning potential is best assessed by observing performance in a task where corrective feedback is provided, i.e., a learning task. (p. 3)

FRAMEWORK FOR THE PROCESS APPROACH

We believe that a process-oriented assessment strategy for the purpose of identifying strengths and weaknesses is the only meaningful approach to the assessment of young children with multiple disabilities. In addition, we believe that a developmental, conceptual framework is certainly helpful and, in our opinion, essential in approaching this task. This framework draws upon the writings of those who have interpreted Piaget's work on the sensorimotor period (Hunt, 1961; Uzgiris, 1976; Uzgiris & Hunt, 1975). Adding to those basic interpretations, we also draw guidance from the developmental literature for information regarding relationships among sensorimotor, communication, and social domains of development (Fisher, 1980; Golinkoff, 1981; Sroufe, 1979; Zelazo, 1979). We believe that information about normal developmental pathways contributes to interpretations of the performance of children with significant motor disabilities. In addition, this literature offers guidance regarding the impact that task modifications may have on expected performance and, therefore, facilitates the interpretation of that performance. Specifics of how we use the conceptual framework offered by the Uzgiris-Hunt Ordinal Scales (1975) are described elsewhere (Fieber, 1977, 1978; Robinson, 1982; Robinson & Fieber, 1988; Robinson & Robinson, 1978, 1983; Robinson & Rosenberg, 1987).

Interdisciplinary Team

The interdisciplinary team is an essential component to this prescriptive assessment and intervention approach with children with multiple handicaps. Because of the complexity of the problems displayed by infants with multiple handicaps, professionals from several disciplines are invariably involved in their educational programs. This team typically includes a physical therapist, an occupational therapist, a speech pathologist, and a special educator/psychologist who, in addition to having competencies in early intervention, is familiar with assessment and intervention approaches applied to sensory and physical disabilities.

Coordination of the efforts of these professionals is essential to the success of any efforts in assessment for prescriptive purposes. Successful coordination of activities and implementation of procedures depend upon all team members knowing how work with each child is being accomplished in order to ensure consistency among adults working with the pupil and the effective implementation of the program as planned. However, despite the desire of most parents and teachers to obtain input from all disciplines assessing and providing services for their child, it is often difficult to incorporate the multiple sets of goals, objectives, and intervention strategies presented by the various disciplines into a child's program. In many settings therapists have little interaction with each other and consequently have difficulty presenting complementary and cohesive plans to both parents and teachers.

Failures of coordination among staff produce delays and difficulties in implementation of interventions. Obstacles to coordinated team functioning have several sources. First, it can be difficult to obtain agreement from staff representing diverse disciplines. It is common for staff who do not share the same professional backgrounds to emphasize different objectives. For example, educational and physical therapy staff may differ on how much a child's trunk should be supported. Educators may wish to provide substantial support so the pupil will have optimal hand use in order to manipulate toys; therapists may want the child to have little trunk support so the child will have to practice trunk control. It is through collaboration within a team that diverse and even competing goals are reviewed and integrated. Systems for designing and implementing integrated intervention plans for children and families need to be developed. We suggest that the use of a problem-solving process by an interdisciplinary team will facilitate the design of integrated goals and strategies to be incorporated into school and home routines of daily living. The Participate Decision Process described by Rosenberg, Clark, Finkler, and Filer (1989), and which we will summarize here, provides such a framework for integrating goals and objectives.

PARTICIPATE DECISION PROCESS: A MODEL FOR PROCESS ASSESSMENT

Our work with infants, and preschoolers whose disabilities precluded active involvement in their educational program, has led to the development of the Participate Decision Process. The Participate Decision Process offers an approach that links assessment and intervention in a dynamic and cyclic process. The Participate Decision Process is drawn from the Project Participate Final Report (Rosenberg et al., 1989), and we will include here brief discussions of the developmental rationale for emphasizing active participation, the context of an interdisciplinary team, and the specific steps that are employed in application of the model.

Developmental Context

Children learn by acting on their environment. Numerous studies support the importance of active learning for the growth and development of young children (Bruner, 1975; Uzgiris & Hunt, 1975; White, 1959; Yarrow & Pedersen, 1976). Environments that offer few opportunities for active learning discourage development (e.g., MacPhee, Ramey, & Yeates, 1984). Children's development is impeded when motor or sensory disorders restrict their access to opportunities for active learning (Robinson & Fieber, 1988; Robinson & Rosenberg, 1987). Interestingly, although much has been written about the need to provide children opportunities for learning, far less has been written about the importance of helping children gain access to the opportunities their environments present. In part, this oversight has occurred because most children have no difficulty taking advantage of the opportunities offered by their environment. However, motor and sensory impairments have a significant impact on the extent to which young children can interact with the world around them. Areas of functioning that are often affected by motor disorders include mobility, communication, and hand skills. These children are at greater risk than others for participation-related problems because they have fewer opportunities to control events (either physical or social) in their environment than do nonhandicapped children.

For the physically impaired child, this lack of interaction with responsive toys and the lack of control over events in their lives can have several undesirable effects (Robinson, 1976; Robinson & Fieber, 1988; Robinson & Robinson, 1983). First, it seems likely that the inability to gain access to manipulable and responsive playthings can produce developmental delays in cognitive, communication, social, and self-help skills. Second, the motivation of such children to seek interesting activities may diminish. Indeed, children whose motor handicaps impede mastery of their environment display less persistence and curiosity than do their nonhandicapped peers (Jennings, Connors, Stegnan, Sankaranaryan, & Mendelsohn, 1985). We argue that this passivity is, in part, the result of their inability to control significant events in their lives (Seligman, 1975). The importance of learning to interact with and to exercise control over events is not limited to physical objects; children also learn through interaction with their parents and peers. However, children who have significant physical, sensory, and cognitive handicaps are less effective in acting on their social environment and are less able to engage in mutually satisfying interactions with their peers, parents, and teachers than are their nonhandicapped peers (Beckman-Bell, 1981; Jones, 1977; Kohl, Beckman, & Swenson-Pierce, 1984; Rosenberg & Robinson, 1988). Consequently, it is important to provide these children with assistance that allows them to be more active learners.

Assumptions

A basic assumption made in the development of the Participate Decision Process is that access to program activities is necessary for active child participation in educational activities, which, in turn, is necessary for achievement. We believe it is important to systematically provide home and classroom situations that provide children who have handicaps with opportunities to learn to control events and actively participate in their school activities in order to promote motivation and development of cognitive, communication, and social skills. Increasingly, a variety of compensatory strategies are being used to expand the ability of such children to communicate and act directly on their environment. The use of assistive devices to help people overcome the effects of handicaps has generated considerable interest in recent years as these devices have become more sophisticated and more easily used than ever before. Project Participate targeted a number of skill areas to which the Participate Decision Process was applied. These areas included communication, mobility, computer-assisted instruction, and play with preschool materials.

Interventions were applied within the framework of a process for planning and decision making. This decision process was derived from work done as part of Project Participate (Rosenberg, Buekelman, Clark, & Filer, 1987) and from work on participation done by Baumgart et al. (1982). The use of this decision process can assist educators' efforts to analyze the extent of a student's participation in classroom activities, identify factors potentially contributing to low levels of student participation, assist in the design of interventions that eliminate the barriers to active participation, and offer a model for evaluating the effectiveness of interventions designed to enhance child participation.

Thus, Project Participate's approach to assessment serves as a foundation for use of a problem-solving approach in the facilitation of child access and participation in program activities. This problem-solving orientation focuses on removing barriers to participation for activities in which learner involvement is low. Addressing specific activities in which participation is low helps focus efforts on identifying and eliminating barriers to involvement in those activities and increases the likelihood of successful outcomes. The Participate Decision Process can be contrasted with approaches that may focus on participation globally, seeking to maximize participation throughout the day. Instead, the approach used here encourages efforts to remediate specific deficits in participation. This focus on increasing participation in specific activities has the advantage of making efficient use of staff time and available assistive devices by calling for these where they are most needed. Moreover, the emphasis upon increasing participation in areas where increases are most needed focuses staff attention upon a limited number of problems until these are solved. Finally, this model focuses on the task of giving children access to the activities their school and home environments offer and does not specify a particular curriculum or integration model. As a consequence, the Participate Decision Process is compatible with a wide variety of curricula and integration models.

Decision Process Procedures

Although the selection of intervention strategies involves considerable clinical judgment, the Participate Decision Process illustrated in Figure 1 provides a useful guide to assessment and intervention when there are participation problems. The process used in this project begins with an assessment of the target child's baseline level of participation in each activity area (e.g., entry behaviors, self-help behaviors) included in the child's classroom curriculum or characteristic of the child's homelife. A measure of participation in daily activities was developed by the project (Rosenberg et al., 1989), but any curriculum-based assessment procedure would be appropriate.

Once participation deficits are observed, attention is turned to identifying the barriers that impede participation. Abilities affecting participation are organized by developmental capacities—motor, communication, cognitive/learning, sensory/perceptual, and social/personal. At this point in the decision process, the learner's skills and deficiencies in each area are noted, producing a fairly complete profile of the child's abilities. This knowledge of both strengths and weaknesses is needed for the next step in the decision process—the selection of intervention approaches. Steps in the process and strategies rather than specific measures are identified in the model procedures in order to ensure applicability across disability categories and classroom and curriculum models. The information needs are specified and staff use their own professional judgment as to how best to obtain the necessary information.

Intervention Strategies

Once the interdisciplinary team and primary intervention staff, which includes the parents, identify the abilities affecting participation through the clinical assessment process, efforts are directed to determining what interventions can be expected to overcome the effects of these barriers. Within application of this model, intervention strategies are identified during the interdisciplinary staffing and are implemented by primary intervention staff. In general, options that increase a child's level of both independence and competence are considered first. Strategies that require extensive dependence on others or on specialized equipment, or that circumvent opportunities to learn useful skills, are tried only when direct approaches to increased independence and competence are not feasible. For example, powered mobility would be offered when learners are unlikely to be functionally mobile using such simpler and more direct alternatives as walking with a walker.

Project Participate's decision process, depicted in Figure 1, specifies four intervention strategies for overcoming barriers to active participation: 1) increasing a specific skill,

PARTICIPATION DECISION PROCESS

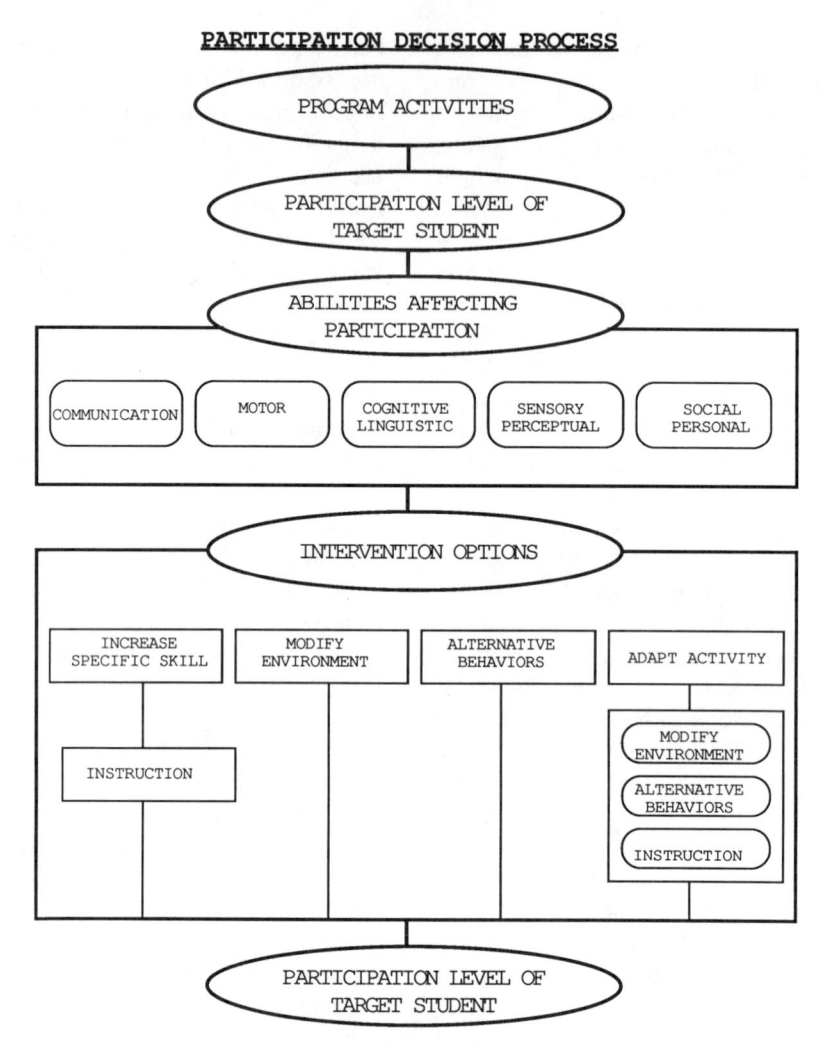

Figure 1. The Participate Decision Process. (From Rosenberg, S., Clark, M., Finkler, D., & Filer, J. [1989]. *Final report: Project Participate*. Omaha: Department of Psychology, University of Nebraska at Omaha.)

2) modifying the environment, 3) identifying an alternative behavior, and 4) adapting the activity. These strategies reflect the process approach to assessment outlined earlier. An intervention worksheet is then used as part of the staffing process to guide efforts to clarify the nature of the barriers to participation and identify intervention strategies.

Increasing Specific Skills

Directly addressing a specific skill is typically the first intervention strategy to consider. By teaching a child to perform those skills that are currently barriers to performance of the activity, the child will be able to be more independent and competent. This increased competence will then lead to increased independence in performing other types of activities as well. This option is contraindicated if the child simply cannot learn the skill because of presenting handicapping conditions. It is also possible that the skill may take an excessively long time to learn. In such a case, another intervention may be selected as either a permanent or a temporary alternative. For example, refined reach and grasp may not be a realistic short- or intermediate-term goal for some children with cerebral palsy. To delay working on spatial concepts until such a child is able to physically manipulate the materials typically used to facilitate such concepts would be inappropriate.

Environmental Modification

Environments may need to be modified to increase a child's performance of a skill. There are two reasons for deciding to modify the environment. First, the environment may be unsuitable for the activity in general. For example, if an activity is to be performed at a table and the child is seated too low to use his or her arms atop the table, a modification should be made of the seat and/or table. Second, the environment may be unsuitable because of unique characteristics of the child. For example, the child may have a visual problem that precludes focusing on an activity on a table. Presenting the activity on a vertical plane with the use of a typewriter stand may circumvent the visual problem. An environmental modification to increase social interaction might involve placing materials on the tray of a child's wheelchair. In so doing, children may be drawn to the child whose mobility is limited.

Alternative Behaviors

This option of use of alternative behaviors involves having the child use functionally equivalent responses within his or her repertoire to perform the activity. For example, a child may not be able to actively reach for an object but may be able to convey knowledge of the location of an object with a directed look. Alternative behaviors may be useful to the degree that they are functionally similar to the original target behaviors. They may be able to serve as long-term substitutes or short-term alternatives to be faded after the original target behavior is learned. While use of an alternative behavior may be functional, it may be unacceptable in certain contexts, such as where an alternative behavior would be unduly stigmatizing. For example, if a child's only means of self-locomotion is commando crawling and he or she is among all-ambulatory children, prothestic equipment for mobility should probably be considered as an alternative to crawling despite the greater independence of self-mobility. To crawl is probably more stigmatizing for anyone over 5 years of age than is a wheelchair or travel chair.

Adapting the Activity

Activities can be adapted in order to circumvent barriers that prevent a child's involvement in them. Unlike the other options, an adaptation of an activity involves changing the materials, the task, or the rules governing that activity. Often multiple adaptions are made to a single activity. Selection of one or several adaptations must be based on a review of the skills of the child and the requirements of the adapted response. Adaptation of an activity is indicated when the child's skill level is extremely discrepant from the skill requirements of the activity. Depending on the nature of the discrepancy, the adaptation may serve as a permanent solution or an interim solution to be used in tandem with one or more of the other options. After an adaptation has been selected, several questions must be considered: Does successful performance of the adapted activity require alternative behaviors? Does successful performance of this adaptation by the child require modification of the environment? What will the child need to be taught in order to use the adaptation? Adaptation of an activity is contraindicated when it will unduly stigmatize a child and when another alternative is available. It is also a questionable choice in situations in which it may reduce a child's motivation to perform without the adaptation.

Implementation of Interventions

Improvements in child participation are obtained as programs and learners achieve greater compatibility. Successful interventions to increase program-child compatibility and with it child participation are very demanding of professional staff. Primary-intervention staff need to have adequate knowledge and sufficient time to implement the intervention as well as prepare the materials required by the intervention. For example, some children who are unable to make choices verbally may be able to make a selection by pointing to photographs depicting the alternatives available to them. To implement this procedure, staff must know about the child's abilities to recognize photographic representations of choices and to indicate choices by pointing. Time and materials are also needed for the preparation of the photographs and to allow the staff member to familiarize the child with this system for indicating choices. Finally, staff need to know how to utilize these adaptations in environments that include groups of children, so that learners are integrated into such environments as active participants.

Project Participate used the decision process depicted in the context of classroom activities. An example of this process is given for a child with motor disabilities where one objective is to increase her opportunities for play with toys.

Promoting Play

Young children spend much of their time playing with toys that represent, in miniature, objects found in daily life. The ability to play with these materials is thought to aid in the development of skills in a number of domains: problem solving, receptive and expressive language, and fine motor and social skills. In addition to play with toys, young children also invest considerable energy learning to represent their world through drawing and by using blocks to create constructions. Opportunities to draw and build are essential to the development of a broad range of skills. These materials—implements for drawing and building—are made to be manipulated by hands. Consequently learners whose motor disorders impair their hand use have limited access to these materials. Compensatory strategies are required when children are unable to use these objects conventionally (Musselwhite, 1986). To play with objects and to draw in a normal fashion, children typically must be able to do the following: balance themselves without the use of their hands, voluntarily grasp and release an object, use their hands in a lead/assist fashion, interact with the environment in a constructive fashion, and coordinate eyes and hands in appropriate perceptual/motor fashion (Klein, 1982). The Participate Decision Process was used to generate the compensatory strategies outlined earlier to facilitate the ability of children to play with preschool materials. In Figure 2 an example of the use of the Intervention Strategy Worksheet with a specific child is provided. Once her cognitive level is assessed, in this case with reference to the Uzgiris-Hunt Scales of Infant Psychological Development, and combined with information regarding her use of her upper extremities, planning can proceed using the Intervention Strategy Worksheet.

To expand child access, playthings are often modified. Some modifications require changing the shape or size of the object to facilitate grasping and manipulation. For example, crayons are available in various sizes and shapes that facilitate grasping. Many times, however, access is increased by modifying the environment rather than the plaything itself. Environmental modifications that can increase access to activities involve changes in the learning environment. Stabilizing materials to prevent them from falling off or sliding out of reach is a common environmental modification (Schaefer, 1988). Specific modifications have included fixing the item's position (e.g., clamping an object to a work surface), restricting the movement of materials (e.g., damping movement with Dysam, which retards sliding), magnetizing materials so they tend to be held by a metal work surface, and placing a ridge around the periphery of a section of a work surface to restrict the area within which an object can move. Environmental modifications can also be used to expand the variety of playthings one child could obtain. For example, materials can be placed on a lazy Susan, enabling a child to reach more items than were previously accessible.

Evaluation of the Decision Process

The evaluation of the Participate Decision Process must begin by asking if the pupil outcomes based on its use are fruitful. Do pupils demonstrate increased participation in the curriculum as a consequence of staff interventions based on the model? Pupil intervention out-

Name:		Date:
Activity:	Center Activity	
Components of Activity:	Manipulation of objects/Fischer Price Toys/Doll House	
Purposes of Activity for this Child:	Imitation of familiar events	
Barrier(s) Identified:	Poor hand use	

Intervention Options	Relevant Child Characteristics	Priorities of Options
1. Increase specific skill. Specify potential instruction: a. Have occupational therapy continue to work on this b.	Child has poor hand use which interfers with her manipulation of small toys/objects when playing with Fischer Price Doll house. Child has an immature hand grasp.	Continue therapy
2. Compensatory skill. Specify potential compensation(s). a. Use raking motion to pick up objects b.	Child can maintain immature hand grasps.	Allow child to continue until hand splints are in place.
3. Environmental modification. Specify potential modification(s). a. Reduce height of table b. Use hand splints to put finger and thumb in opposition	Child's arms are raised too high for comfortable hand use.	Immediately
4. Activity adaptation. Specify potential adaptation(s). a. Attach magnets to toys and let child play with them on cookie sheet. b. Place velcro on toys and use velcro strap on child's hand.	Toys frequently roll out of child's reach and child cannot retrieve objects and must wait for someone to retrieve objects.	Immediately

Project Participate, University of Nebraska-Omaha, Psychology Department

Figure 2. A completed Participate Decision Process Intervention Strategy worksheet. (From Rosenberg, S., Clark, M., Finkler, D., & Filer, J. [1989]. *Final report: Project Participate.* Omaha: Department of Psychology, University of Nebraska at Omaha.)

comes were evaluated based on two different data sources, pupil files and ratings of videotapes of pupil performance in adapted and unadapted situations. All assessments and ratings were completed by project personnel and constitute internal evaluations. In each case, however, more than one staff member did the assessment and consensus was developed among raters without difficulty. The variety of data, while possibly subject to internal project bias, yields consistent results.

Nineteen videotaped paired instances of responses in adapted and unadapted task situations were assessed by project staff. They were asked to code each segment of tape for the amount of time the pupil spent interacting or participating with the curricular task/materials presented and to code the same tape segment for the amount of time on task using the materials functionally, or as intended. Thus, each tape segment was coded for time on task using both a loose definition in which any contact with the material was accepted and a second functional definition in which only appropriate behavior was coded. For example, with block play, tower building or a similar arrangement would be rated as functional and sliding blocks off a table rated as inappropriate or not functional. Most tape segments were about 2 minutes long. They varied from 47 seconds to 4 minutes 10 seconds, but most paired segments were of similar length. Functional time on task more than doubled under adapted intervention conditions and time on task using the loosest of definitions indicated that adapted conditions permitted greater task/material interaction as well (an increase of about 28%). Furthermore, 17 of the 19 pairs of tapes showed functional time on task to be greater in adapted than unadapted conditions. One pair of tapes had the same times and only one pair showed a reversal from what would be expected with successful interventions. Although the planning of interventions to increase curricular participation of these severely handicapped young pupils as a clinical process is not readily subject to observation in any standardized way, both written and videotaped case records documented the effectiveness of the great preponderance of interventions. This is direct evidence of the effectiveness of the interventions and indirect evidence of the utility of the Participate Decision Process.

CONCLUSIONS

In this chapter, we have argued for the use of a process approach to assessment as the one that will yield the most useful descriptive and programmatic information for children with significant motor impairment. We have based this argument on several points, including the problems in the use of traditional approaches to assessment, particularly the violation of underlying assumptions. In describing a process approach to assessment for use with motorically handicapped infants and preschoolers, we have advocated the use of a developmental-conceptual framework. The sources for this framework are Piagetian theory and current developmental research on infant and preschool-age children, research that reflects investigations of all domains of development and the integration of these domains.

Access to learning activities cannot be taken for granted when young children have motor and sensory disorders. These children are frequently unable to be active participants in their educational programs. To increase their participation, the effects of their motor and sensory disorders upon their ability to gain access to activities and materials must be mitigated. Successfully enhancing child participation is a difficult task that can be accomplished only through meticulous attention to optimizing child-program compatibility, in conjunction with careful planning and implementation by team members.

The Participate Decision Process offers a viable means by which young learners who have multiple disabilities can attain greater access to their educational environment and materials. It is our belief that educational personnel who have adequate time to work on participation problems and access to consultation from other team members can use these approaches to successfully increase the active involvement of these children in their educational programs.

An interdisciplinary approach is an important feature of the assessment strategies we describe. The effective use of these strategies requires a knowledge of content and developmental pathways in the motor, cognitive, language, and affective domains of development. This information must then be integrated across the domains of development, a process that we have found works best when an interdisciplinary team has ample opportunity to observe and assess a child, both in individual and in combined situations.

REFERENCES

Baumgart, D., Brown, L., Pumpian, I., Nisbet, J., Ford, A., Sweet, M., Messina, R., & Schroeder, J. (1982). Principle of partial participation and individualized adaptations in educational programs for severely handicapped students. *TASH Journal*, 7, 17–27.

Beckman-Bell, P. (1981). *Interactions between handicapped and non-handicapped preschoolers in an integrated setting*. Paper presented at the annual meeting of the Council for Exceptional Children, New York.

Bouregeault, S., Harley, R., DuBose, R., & Langley, M. (1977). Assessment and programming for blind children with severely handicapped conditions. *Journal of Visual Impairment and Blindness*, 71, 49–53.

Bruner, J. (1975). The ontogenesis of speech acts. *Journal of Child Language*, 2, 1–19.

DuBose, R., Langley, M., & Stagg, V. (1977). Assessing severely handicapped children. *Focus on Exceptional Children*, 9, 1–13.

Fieber, N. (1977). Cognitive skills. In N.G. Haring (Ed.), *Developing effective individualized education programs for severely handicapped children and youth*. Washington, DC: Department of Health, Education and Welfare, Office of Education, Bureau of Education for the Handicapped.

Fieber, N. (1978). *The deaf-blind/severely-profoundly handicapped*. Proceedings of Nebraska Statewide Conference, Cozad. Lincoln: Nebraska Department of Education.

Fisher, K.W. (1980). A theory of cognitive development: The control and construction of hierarchies of skills. *Psychological Review*, 87, 477–531.

Golinkoff, R.M. (1981). The influence of Piagetian theory on the study of the development of communication. In E.E. Sigel, D.M. Brodzinsky, & R.M. Golinkoff (Eds.), *New directions in Piagetian therapy and practice*. Hillsdale, NJ: Lawrence Erlbaum Associates.

Hauessermann, E. (1958). *Developmental potential of preschool children*. New York: Grune & Stratton.

Hayes, S. (1943). A second test scale for the mental measurement of the visually handicapped. *The New Outlook for the Blind*, 37, 37–41.

Hiskey, M. (1966). *Hiskey-Nebraska Test of Learning Aptitude*. Lincoln, NE: College Press.

Hunt, J. McV. (1961). *Intelligence and experience*. New York: Ronald Press.

Jennings, K., Connors, R., Stegnan, C., Sankaranaryan, P., & Mendolsohn, S. (1985). Mastery motivation in young preschoolers: Effect of a physical handicap and implications for educational programming. *Journal of the Division for Early Childhood*, 9, 162–169.

Jens, K.G., & Johnson, N.M. (1982). Affective development: A window to cognition in young handicapped children. *Topics in Early Childhood Special Education*, 2, 17–24.

Jones, O. (1977). Mother-child communication with prelinquistic Down's syndrome and normal infants. In H. Schaffer (Ed.), *Studies in mother-infant interactions: Proceedings of the Loch Lomand Symposium* (pp. 379–402). New York: John Wiley & Sons.

Klein, M. (1982). *Pre-writing skills: Skill starters for motor development*. Tucson, AZ: Communication Skill Builders.

Kohl, F., Beckman, P., & Swenson-Pierce, A. (1984). The effects of directed play on functional toy use and interactions of handicapped preschoolers. *Journal of the Division for Early Childhood*, 8, 114–118.

Langley, M. (1978). Psychoeducational assessment of the multiply handicapped blind child: Issues and methods. *Education of the Visually Handicapped*, 10, 95–115.

MacPhee, D., Ramey, C., & Yeates, K. (1984). Home environment and early cognitive development. In A. Gottfried (Ed.), *Home environment and early cognitive development: Longitudinal research*. Orlando, FL: Academic Press.

Musselwhite, C. (1986). *Adaptive play for special needs children*. San Diego: College-Hill Press.

Robinson, C. (1982). Questions regarding the effects of neuromotor problems on sensorimotor development. In D. Bricker (Ed.), *Intervention with at risk and handicapped infants: From research to application*. Baltimore: University Park Press.

Robinson, C., & Fieber, N. (1988). Cognitive assessment of motorically impaired infants and preschoolers. In T. Wachs & R. Sheehan (Eds.), *Assessment of young developmentally disabled children*. New York: Plenum Publishing Co.

Robinson, C., & Robinson, J. (1978). Sensorimotor functions and cognitive development. In M. Snell (Ed.), *Systematic instruction of the moderately and severely handicapped*. Columbus, OH: Charles E. Merrill.

Robinson, C., & Robinson, J. (1983). Sensorimotor functions and cognitive development. In M. Snell (Ed.), *Systematic instruction of the moderately and severely handicapped* (2nd ed.). Columbus, OH: Charles E. Merrill.

Robinson, C., & Rosenberg, S. (1987). A strategy for assessing infants with motor impairments. In I. Uzgiris & J. McV. Hunt (Eds.), *Infant performance and experience: New findings with the Ordinal Scales*. Chicago: University of Illinois Press.

Rosenberg, S., Buekelman, D., Clark, M., & Filer, J. (1987). *Increasing participation of preschoolers who have motor disorders*. Paper presented at the Consortium for Special Education 1987 Convention, Lincoln, NE.

Rosenberg, S., Clark, M., Finkler, D., & Filer, J. (1989). *Final report: Project Participate*. Omah: Department of Psychology, University of Nebraska at Omaha.

Rosenberg, S., & Robinson, C. (1988). Interactions of parents with their young handicapped children.

In S. Odom & M. Karnes (eds.), *Early intervention for infants and children with handicaps: An empirical base* (pp. 159–177). Baltimore: Paul H. Brookes Publishing Co.

Schaefer, C. (1988). Making toys accessible for children with cerebral palsy. *Teaching Exceptional Children, 20*, 26–28.

Seligman, M. (1975). *Helplessness: On depression, development and death*. San Francisco: W.H. Freeman.

Simeonsson, R. (1977). Infant assessment. In B. Caldwell, D. Stedman, & D. Goin (Eds.), *Infant Education: A guide for helping handicapped children in the first three years*. New York: Walker.

Simeonsson, R., Huntington, G., & Parse, S. (1980). Assessment of children with severe handicaps: Multiple problems-multivarate goals. *Journal for the Association for the Severely Handicapped, 5*, 55–72.

Sroufe, L.A. (1979). Socioemotional development. In J. Osofsky (Ed.), *Handbook for infant development*. New York: John Wiley & Sons.

Uzgiris, I. (1976). Organization of sensorimotor intelligence. In M. Lewis (Ed.), *Origins of intelligence: Infancy and early childhood*. New York: Plenum Press.

Uzgiris, I., & Hunt, J. (1975). *Assessment in infancy: Ordinal Scales of Psychological Development*. Urbana: University of Illinois Press.

Wachs, T., & Sheehan, R. (Eds.). (1988). *Assessment of young developmentally disabled children*. New York: Plenum Publishing Co.

White, R. W. (1959). Motivation reconsidered: The concept of competence. *Psychological Review, 66*, 297–333.

Yarrow, L., & Pedersen, F. (1976). Interplay between cognition and motivation in infancy. In M. Lewis (Ed.), *Origins of intelligence: Infancy and early childhood*. New York: Plenum Press.

Zelazo, P.R. (1979). Reactivity to perceptual-cognitive events: Application for infant assessment. In R.B. Kearsley & I.E. Sigel (Eds.), *Infants at risk: Assessment of cognitive functioning*. Hillsdale, NJ: Lawrence Erlbaum Associates.

IV
ASSESSING SOCIAL BEHAVIOR AND CHARACTERISTICS OF THE SOCIAL ENVIRONMENT

13. Assessing Attachment in Infancy
The Strange Situation and Alternate Systems

Douglas M. Teti and Miyuki Nakagawa

Interest in the correlates of socioemotional functioning is almost as old as psychology itself. For infants, this interest has sparked much theorizing about the developing infant-parent relationship, its centrality in shaping subsequent social relationships, and, ultimately, its role in personality development. Although psychoanalysts have differed in their conceptualizations of the infant-caregiver bond, they are unified in the view that the infant's first relationship with the caregiver provides the substrate for later social, emotional, and personality development. This is perhaps best exemplified by Freud's now-famous characterization of the infant-mother relationship as "unique, without parallel, established unalterably for a whole lifetime as the first and strongest love-object and as the prototype of all later love-relations—for both sexes" (Freud, 1940, p. 45). Thus, Freud in his later writings, and the ego psychology and object relations schools that followed him, viewed the infant's first attachment as a bona fide love relationship the quality of which had pervasive implications for later development (see reviews by Ainsworth, 1969, and Bowlby, 1969/1982, for more complete discussions of psychoanalytic notions of the child's tie to the parent).

Psychoanalytic theorists have contributed much by way of clinically rich, albeit retrospective, information regarding the nature and significance of early attachment. However, it was John Bowlby's (1969/1982) brilliant psychoanalytic-ethological synthesis, drawing similarities between early attachments in humans and those in other mammalian species and casting attachment within a control systems framework, that paved the way for the development of an important methodology for assessing the quality of infant-caregiver attachment. Mary Ainsworth, a colleague of Bowlby's and heavily influenced by his work, developed the *Strange Situation* procedure as a means of assessing an infant's relationship to the caregiver (Ainsworth & Bell, 1970; Ainsworth, Bell, & Stayton, 1971; Ainsworth, Blehar, Waters, & Wall, 1978; Ainsworth & Wittig, 1969). Over the last 15 years, this 22–24-minute, eight-episode structured laboratory procedure has unquestionably become the most well-known and accepted research metric for assessing infant-caregiver attachment, although, as we shall discuss, it is not uncontroversial.

In the present chapter, we discuss the theoretical framework that spawned the development of the Strange Situation procedure and follow with a detailed presentation of the assessment, its validity and stability, its use with special populations of infants, and its efficacy

---

The authors wish to express their appreciation to Kathleen M. Corns, Michael E. Lamb, Alicia Lieberman, Slobodan Petrovich, and Everett Waters for their helpful comments on earlier drafts of this chapter.

in identifying *individual* infants at risk for subsequent maladaptations. We turn finally to a brief presentation of some alternative systems for assessing attachment, with particular attention to the work of Everett Waters, Alicia Lieberman, and Stanley Greenspan.

THE FRAMEWORK: THE BOWLBY-AINSWORTH ATTACHMENT THEORY

An understanding of the Strange Situation procedure and its goals cannot be achieved without an appreciation of the attachment theory from which it was derived. In this section we provide the basic theoretical formulations of Bowlby and Ainsworth and refer the interested reader to Bowlby (1969/1982, 1973, 1980), Ainsworth et al. (1978), Sroufe and Waters (1977), and Lamb, Thompson, Gardner, and Charnov (1985) for further details.

The impact of Bowlby's *Attachment and Loss* trilogy (1969/1982, 1973, 1980) cannot be overestimated in terms of reorienting psychologists' views of how attachments develop and, even more importantly, providing a theory from which testable hypotheses could be derived regarding the development of early social relationships and their impact. Although Bowlby was and remains a psychoanalyst, he broke from traditional psychoanalytic thinking in several important ways. To begin, Bowlby (1969/1982) deemphasized traditional psychoanalytic notions that behavior was the result of the buildup and release of "psychical energy" and that the infant's attachment to the caregiver resulted from an association made between the caregiver and the provision of food. The latter premise, called the theory of "secondary drive," had the support of both psychoanalytic and learning theorists, which perhaps explains its uncontested popularity for some 30-40 years. By the 1960s, however, a plethora of evidence had accumulated from ethology and comparative psychology that cast serious doubt on secondary drive formulations of early attachment. The most famous of these studies was Harlow's (1958, 1961) now-classic observations of infant monkeys separated from their mothers at birth and reared with two "surrogate" mothers, one made of wire and from whose chest protruded a tube that provided food, and one made of terrycloth but with whom food was not associated in any way. When distressed, infant monkeys retreated to cling to the cloth surrogate, despite the fact that it played no role in feeding. Harlow's findings argued against the role of feeding in the development of infant attachments; rather, as Harlow and later Bowlby (1969/1982) proposed, they emphasized the infant's early "primary" need for physical contact and social interaction, preferably with an adult of the same species.

In responses to burgeoning empirical evidence, Bowlby (1969/1982) proposed that human infants are predisposed to form attachments to their caregivers by virtue of an *attachment behavioral system* that was the product of human evolutionary history. The attachment system, with its goal of maintaining proximity to the attachment figure, has clear survival value by functioning to protect the helpless infant from predators and other potential dangers. "Attachment" behaviors such as crying, vocalizing, and eye contact reliably elicit, under ordinary circumstances, the attention and approach of the caregiver, who in turn is also preadapted to respond to these signals by virtue of the evolutionary history of our species. The attachment system is thus a goal-directed system, which is particularly important prior to the onset of locomotion, when infants cannot initiate approach behaviors (i.e., crawling) themselves.

With the development of locomotion, the responsibility for proximity maintenance shifts gradually from parent to infant. Furthermore, Bowlby took note of the interplay between the development of the attachment behavioral system and the development of specific cognitive milestones such as person permanence, or the infant's emerging knowledge that the caregiver is an independent entity, which usually occurs around 8-10 months of age and is evidenced by the onset of stranger and separation anxiety. With this development, the attachment behavioral system shifts from a simpler, goal-directed system to a more complex "goal-corrected" one, in which the infant's efforts to maintain proximity to the caregiver (i.e., the "set goal" of proximity maintenance) wax and wane according to a variety of circumstances that are "exogenous" and/or "endogenous" to the infant. Exogenous factors include too great a separation from the caregiver, the approach of an unfamiliar person, and/or placement in unfamiliar surroundings, all of which the infant is preadapted to perceive as dangerous by virtue of the evolutionary history of our species. These occurrences in turn activate the attachment system to bring the infant under the protection of the attachment figure via such behaviors as crying, calling, following, and reaching. Endogenous factors that activate the attachment system include illness, fatigue, pain, hunger, and other internal states that require increased parental care. Thus, as infants near the end of their first year, the development of mobility, early person permanence, and intentional behavior bring about a goal-corrected attachment system characterized by the ability to vary the set goal of proximity maintenance according to particular exogenous and endogenous circumstances.

Bowlby saw the attachment system as only one of several organized, species-specific behavioral systems that guide behavior in infancy. Another, the exploratory system, operates in conjunction with, but antithetically to, the attachment system by orienting the infant away from the caregiver and toward the unfamiliar and novel. Infants quite naturally explore and manipulate their environment and will continue doing so in the absence of exogenous or endogenous circumstances that activate the attachment system and reorient the infant toward the caregiver. Indeed, the attachment and exploratory systems are in dynamic interplay, and this becomes especially evident by the end of the first year with the emergence of locomotion and person permanence. Novelty becomes both fascinating and frightening, and the attachment-exploration balance may tip in one direction or the other depending on environmental (e.g., the degree of novelty or unfamiliarity) and organismic (e.g., the onset of fatigue or illness) factors.

Finally, we wish to note Bowlby's notion that, concomitant with the development of a goal-corrected attachment-exploration balance, the infant's emergent cognitive and memory capacities late in the first year allow for the development of "working models" of the caregiver and the self. This premise, having a psychoanalytic tradition, holds that infants form a set of affectively laden cognitions vis-à-vis the caregiver and themselves, the content of which is shaped by the quality of care. Infants who have enjoyed a sensitive history of caregiving are presumed to develop an internal representation of that caregiver as warm, sensitive, and responsive, and ultimately of themselves as worthy of love and support. By contrast, infants whose caregivers have been insensitive, inconsistent, and/or rejecting develop an internal representation of the caregiver as unresponsive and of themselves as unworthy of love. As Bowlby (1973) and subsequent theorists (e.g., Ainsworth et al., 1978; Bretherton, 1985; Cassidy, 1986; Main, Kaplan, & Cassidy, 1985; Sroufe, 1983; Sroufe & Fleeson, 1986; Sroufe & Waters, 1977) have proposed, these inner representations or "internal working models" have a powerful organizational influence on behavior toward the caregiver and others, although, as the term "working" implies, they can also be further shaped by environmental circumstances. Indeed, in keeping with such psychodynamic theorists as E. Erikson (1963), Bowlby (1973) argued that the quality of the infant-caregiver relationship, and the content of the internal working models that ensue, have a direct impact on the child's ability to resolve subsequent psychosocial adaptations. Thus, infants who develop trusting relationships with sensitively responsive caregivers, touted by Erikson (1963) as the first crucial psychosocial adaptation of the life span, would be expected to negotiate subsequent adaptations (e.g., autonomy in toddlerhood) more successfully than infants who enter toddlerhood without this basic trust.

Bowlby thus extracted from psychoanalytic theory constructs that were more amenable to scientific investigation, deemphasized those that were untestable and/or patently unsupported by data, and drew from ethology and comparative psychology to construct a theory of early social relationships not only supported by extant data but that could be empirically evaluated. Gone or downplayed were the notions of psychical energy, secondary drive, oral gratification, and fixation; retained were the basic importance of the quality of the infant-caregiver relationship in shaping subsequent adaptations, and the notions of defenses as critical mental processes and of internal working models of self and other. Bowlby viewed infant attachment as a natural end product of human beings' evolutionary history, which endowed infants with a goal-corrected behavioral system that predisposes them to maintain proximity to the caregiver and whose specific expression is responsive to environmental variation and, thus, to learning.

Ainsworth's Contributions

Bowlby's theoretical notions were further elaborated upon by Mary Ainsworth, who was very much concerned with the empirical verifiability of Bowlby's theory and the identification and antecedents of healthy and unhealthy infant-parent attachments. In particular, Ainsworth related the quality of infant-parent attachment to disturbances in the attachment-exploration balance and to infants' ability or proclivity to use the attachment figure as a "secure base" to explore the world (Ainsworth, 1973, 1982; Ainsworth & Bell, 1970; Ainsworth, Bell, & Stayton, 1971, 1974; Ainsworth et al., 1978). In her view, the quality of the infant's secure base behavior is a more sensitive index of the quality or security of the infant's relationship with the caregiver than the degree of infant distress manifested during separations from the caregiver. Infants demonstrate secure base behavior by investigating new and unfamiliar territory fluidly and comfortably in the presence of the caregiver, with occasional, periodic checks on the caregiver's whereabouts and positive social interactive bids. When distressed, infants who use the caregiver as a secure base typically seek the proximity and comfort of the caregiver, soothe relatively quickly when picked up, and then ease back into an exploratory mode that, again, is characterized by periodic checks on the caregiver's whereabouts. Presumably, these infants derive sufficient security from the caregiver such that they can venture forth and explore the novel and unfamiliar in her or his presence. Although they may be perturbed during brief separations, they are able to reestablish that security upon reunion with the caregiver after actively seeking and receiving comfort. Other infants, by contrast, do not show an appropriate attachment-exploration balance, exploring new territory in the caregiver's presence in an almost compulsory fashion that is devoid of any checking back or social bidding. Still others react to a new environment with anger, petulance, and clinginess in the caregiver's presence, and are inconsolable despite the caregiver's attempts to comfort. Ainsworth and her colleagues thus elaborated on Bowlby's theory in emphasizing that the set goal of the attachment behavioral system was not the maintenance of proximity per se but "felt security," which interacted with environmental context to activate or terminate attachment behavior (see Sroufe & Waters, 1977, and Waters, 1981, for more detailed discussions of these issues). Further, she emphasized individual differences in the affective relationship that infants develop with their caregivers and how the security of this relationship influences the manner in which infants pattern their behavior vis-à-vis the caregiver. Indeed, attachment theory as modified by Ainsworth and her colleagues has today become the dominant social developmental position in accounting for the formation and significance of social relationships in infancy and early childhood.

THE AINSWORTH STRANGE SITUATION

Central to Ainsworth's research was her development of the Strange Situation procedure, an eight-episode, 22–24-minute structured laboratory observation involving the infant and attachment figure, typically the mother, as participants (Ainsworth et al., 1971, 1978; Ainsworth & Wittig, 1969). The intent of this procedure is to observe how the infant organizes his or her behavior vis-à-vis the caregiver and an unfamiliar person in an unfamiliar environment across episodes that vary in their ability to elicit infant distress and activate the attachment behavioral system. Particular attention is paid to the *patterning* of infant behavior during separations from and reunions with the caregiver and to the presence of an unfamiliar adult. The assumption is that separations from the caregiver and the approach of an unfamiliar person will elicit mild to moderate levels of fear and distress, which in turn will deactivate the tendency to explore the unfamiliar environment (the exploratory system) and activate the attachment system to reestablish the infant's "felt security." The Strange Situation procedure appears to be appropriate for normal infants from about 10 months of age, at which time the attachment behavioral system becomes goal corrected and infants demonstrate clear-cut attachments to consistent caregivers, to about 24 months of age, the point beyond which brief separations in unfamiliar environments are much less stressful to children.

Physical Setup

The physical setup of the Strange Situation procedure described here is that used by the first author, which approximates closely the setup described by Ainsworth et al. (1978). The present setup was constructed to maximize observers' ability to capture infants' facial expressions to caregivers and strangers during reunions. We refer the reader to Ainsworth et al. (1978) for a description of Ainsworth's original Johns Hopkins facilities. Although small variations may exist between our setup and that of Ainsworth et al. (1978), we do not believe they would lead to major differences in the quality of the infant-caregiver relationship and in the final assessment of attachment security.

The Strange Situation procedure requires a small, carpeted playroom with approximately a 9-foot by 9-foot square space for free play and additional space for two chairs, one for the caregiver and one for the stranger. Adjacent to the playroom is an observation room connected to the playroom by a one-way mirror to allow unobtrusive viewing of infant behavior and clear videotaping. Sound from the playroom is transmitted to the observation room from two microphones. Playroom toys should be chosen to cater to the play interests and exploratory behaviors of 10–24-month-old infants, including rattles, children's books, balls, crayons and drawing paper, shape sorters, a toy telephone, dolls, and other plastic figures. The toys are arranged in a 3–4-foot-diameter circle roughly in the center of the room. The caregiver's and stranger's chairs are placed on either end of the circle, about 3–4 feet from it and facing toward it such that observers from the observation room can get a profile view of the adults' faces.

Procedure

Table 1 presents the eight episodes and their content. At minimum, two observers are

Table 1. The Strange Situation procedure

Episode	Participants (length)
1	Infant, caregiver, and observer (3 minutes)
2	Infant and caregiver (3 minutes)
3	Infant, caregiver, and stranger (3 minutes)
4	Infant and stranger (3 minutes or less)
5	Infant and caregiver (3 minutes or more)
6	Infant alone (3 minutes or less)
7	Infant and stranger (3 minutes or less)
8	Infant and caregiver (3 minutes)

required to conduct the Strange Situation procedure. One observer, always an adult female, serves as the unfamiliar person. The other remains in the observation room to operate the video equipment or, if one chooses not to videotape, to rate infant behavior. Given the intricacies of infant behavior patterns across the eight episodes, however, we recommend videotaping the procedure to allow more careful scoring of the behavior from the videotapes. The observer designated to be the stranger remains out of sight of the infant until taping begins to maximize the stranger's unfamiliarity to the infant. A second observer ushers the caregiver and baby into the playroom. After the caregiver is seated comfortably and the baby is shown the toys, episode 1 begins as the observer describes to the caregiver the procedures to follow. We recommend that caregivers be given a brief copy of the Strange Situation activities to which they can refer if necessary.

In episode 2 the observer leaves the caregiver and baby alone for 3 minutes, and the caregiver's task is to attempt to interest the baby in the toys. While the baby explores, the caregiver is not to initiate play but is to respond to the baby's overtures as he or she normally does and to redirect the baby to the toys. Episode 3 (caregiver, baby, and stranger; 3 minutes), which begins with the stranger's entry into the playroom, is subdivided into three 1-minute sessions: During the first minute, the stranger briefly greets the mother, sits down, and remains silent. During the second minute, signaled by a light knock on the one-way mirror from the observation room, the stranger initiates a conversation with the caregiver. During the third minute, again signaled by a knock, the stranger initiates an interaction with the baby with the toys. The end of episode 3 is signaled by another knock, at which point the caregiver leaves the room while the baby is preoccupied by the stranger and the toys. Episode 4 (stranger and baby; 3 minutes or less) begins with the stranger reducing the amount of interaction with the baby. If the baby continues to play with the toys, the stranger sits down, responds to the baby's overtures, but does not initiate interaction so long as the baby is exploring. By contrast, if the baby reacts to the caregiver's absence with distress, the stranger attempts to comfort and soothe by offering a toy or, that failing, by picking up, patting, and talking to the baby if he or she will allow it. If the baby becomes very distressed and unresponsive to the stranger's efforts to calm, the episode is curtailed. Episode 5 (caregiver and baby; 3 minutes or more) begins with the caregiver speaking loudly enough behind the door so that the baby can hear, pausing for a few seconds, opening the door and entering, then pausing again to allow the baby to respond. The caregiver is instructed to comfort and soothe the baby if necessary and then to try to reinterest the baby in the toys, if the baby has not returned to them already. While the caregiver and baby are so engaged, the stranger exits and returns to the observation room. After 3 minutes, provided that the baby is again exploring the room, an observer knocks on the window to cue the caregiver to bid the baby goodbye and exit the room. If the baby still is not exploring by 3 minutes, the caregiver is given some extra time to settle the baby before leaving. The caregiver's exit initiates episode 6 (baby alone; 3 minutes or less), which runs its full course if the baby shows minimal to moderate distress and the ability to settle down and explore. On the other hand, the episode is shortened if the baby shows prolonged, intense distress. Episode 7 (stranger and baby; 3 minutes or less) begins with the stranger's entry into the playroom using the same basic sequence of vocalizations and pauses as the caregiver at the beginning of episode 5. If the baby is distressed, the stranger attempts to comfort and soothe and, if successful, attempts to reinterest the baby in the toys. Once the baby is engaged in play, or if the baby is so engaged when the stranger enters, the stranger sits down, responds to any overtures of the baby, but refrains from initiating. Episode 7 is shortened if the stranger does not manage to calm the baby. Episode 8 (caregiver and baby; 3 minutes) commences with the caregiver's entry into the playroom. The caregiver pauses by the open door to allow a spontaneous response from the baby. Then the caregiver enters fully, greets the baby, comforts and soothes if necessary, and then tries to reinterest the baby in the toys. Meanwhile, the stranger leaves the room. After 3 minutes, one of the observers enters the playroom to terminate the procedure.

Strange Situation Attachment Classifications

The power of Ainsworth's contributions lies not simply in the Strange Situation procedure but also in the attachment classifications she and her colleagues have derived from patterns of scores on the rating scales. This section presents an overview of the rating scales employed, the traditional attachment patterns that have been observed and some newly described patterns, and the logic behind their designation as "secure" or "insecure." This overview is not intended to provide a basis for training. Such training should be supervised by someone with extensive training in Strange Situation coding and who has proven to be reliable with other experts in the field.

Infant behavior along six dimensions is rated in episodes 2 through 8, using 7-point scales. The reader is referred to Ainsworth et al. (1978) for a detailed description of these rating scales and for behavioral exemplars for each scale point. These scales are:

Proximity- and contact-seeking behavior, assessing the vigor and quality with which the infant seeks the proximity of and contact with the caregiver or stranger.
Contact-maintaining behavior, measuring the degree to which the infant strives to maintain contact with the caregiver or stranger once contact has been achieved.
Resistant behavior, indexing the degree of resistant, angry, fussing, petulant behavior directed toward the caregiver or stranger.
Avoidant behavior, assessing the degree to which the infant avoids or snubs the caregiver or stranger.
Distance interaction, rating the amount of positive social interactive bids the baby directs to the caregiver or stranger.
Search behavior during separations, indexing the amount and intensity of searching for the caregiver during episodes 4, 6, and 7, when the baby is separated from the caregiver.

From these rating scales, Ainsworth and her colleagues (Ainsworth et al., 1971, 1978) identified three major patterns of attachment: secure (type B), with four subgroups; avoidant (type A), with two subgroups; and resistant (type C), with two subgroups. Infants manifesting secure attachment patterns typically greet the caregiver promptly on reunions and show some degree of proximity seeking, perhaps some contact maintenance, and low levels of avoidance and resistance. Typical of B-type infants is the ability to use the caregiver as a secure base to explore. If distressed, they tend to soothe quickly to the caregiver's ministrations during reunions, and their toy play is characterized by occasional checks on the caregiver's whereabouts. Thus, B-type infants display attachment patterns indicating an ability to derive security in ambiguous and/or threatening situations from the presence of the attachment figure.

The B pattern is contrasted with the A and C patterns, both of which are regarded as insecure patterns because A- and C-type babies do not appear to use the attachment figure as a secure base. A-type babies show conspicuous avoidance of the caregiver by showing either no greeting or a delayed greeting on reunions and by displaying other manifestations of avoidance, such as playing for long periods with their backs to the caregiver, avoiding eye contact, and/or ignoring the caregiver's social bids. Type C babies, by contrast, are noted for their repeated expressions of anger, crying, pouting, whining, and the like that are especially prevalent in infant-caregiver reunions. They are difficult to soothe by both the caregiver and stranger.

These A-B-C patterns seem fairly representative of those observed in infants of middle-class, relatively low-risk families. The majority of nonpathological U.S. samples have typically yielded about 20% A-type, 65% B-type, and 15% C-type babies (see Lamb, Thompson, Gardner, & Charnov, 1985, for a review). It should be noted, however, that classification of infants is sometimes problematic because of imprecise matching between the attachment pattern shown by a particular infant and the traditionally described patterns. Recently, there have been systematic attempts to expand the Ainsworth system to incorporate additional maladaptive attachment classifications, specifically the "D" classification, formally introduced by Main and Solomon (1986). As they note, the D category subsumes a variety of patterns, including "(a) disordering of expected temporal sequences (e.g., strong avoidance followed by strong proximity seeking), (b) simultaneous display of contradictory behavior patterns (e.g., approaching with head averted, gazing strongly away while in contact), (c) incomplete or undirected movements and expressions, including stereotypies (e.g., undirected expressions of fear or distress, stereotypic rocking), (d) direct indices of confusion and of apprehension (e.g., hand-to-mouth gestures immediately upon parent's entrance), and (e) behavioral stilling (e.g., cessation of movement in postures suggestive of confusion or depression—and dazed, disoriented expressions suggest the activation of competing, mutually inhibitory systems)" (Main & Solomon, 1986, p. 97). Thus, Main and Solomon (1986) argued that, whereas the A-B-C attachment patterns represent coherent, organized modes of attachment behavior vis-à-vis the caregiver, additional patterns exist that do not easily fit into the traditional A-B-C framework and that are collectively characterized by disorganization and/or disorientation. They note that, of the few middle-class samples studied, D-type babies typically have comprised between 10% and 13% of all classifications. Although the identification of the D classification is relatively recent, it has been used in several studies of high-risk samples (e.g., Egeland & Sroufe, 1981; see Spieker & Booth, 1988, for a review).

VALIDITY OF STRANGE SITUATION CLASSIFICATIONS

Much has been written on the usefulness of Strange Situation classifications in assessing the quality or security of the infant-caregiver relationship, and a number of very able reviews of this topic are now available (Ainsworth, 1982; Bretherton, 1985; Lamb, Thompson, Gardner, & Charnov, 1985; Lamb, Thompson, Gardner, Charnov, & Estes, 1984). This section will highlight the main points of this literature. To begin, it is important to note that the validity of Strange Situation classifications is based on predictions drawn from attachment theory. Thus, if the B pattern is indeed the most secure, then it should be predicted by caregiver responsiveness, sensitivity, and nurturance, qualities that would be expected to foster feelings of trust and security in the infant. Further, if security of attachment is indeed a developmental adaptation of major import for the infant, then successful achievement of that milestone should foster the ability to adapt successfully to subsequent adaptational milestones (e.g., the establishment of autonomy), a view held dear by a long tradition of psychodynamic theorists (e.g., Erikson, 1963) and most recently elaborated upon by Sroufe (1979, 1983).

Caregiver Antecedents of Strange Situation Classifications

There are now a variety of studies that lend general support to the hypothesis that early sensitive care leads to the secure, B attachment pattern. Ainsworth and her colleagues (Ainsworth et al., 1971, 1978; Blehar, Lieberman, & Ainsworth, 1977; Tracy & Ainsworth, 1981) reported that infants with sensitive, responsive mothers during the first year were more likely to display the secure, B-type attachment pattern at 51 weeks of age than were infants with unresponsive, insensitive mothers. Subsequent research has tended to support these findings (Bates, Maslin, & Frankel, 1985; Belsky, Rovine, & Taylor, 1984; Crockenberg, 1981; Egeland & Farber, 1984;

Erickson, Sroufe, & Egeland, 1985; Grossmann, Grossmann, Spangler, Suess, & Unzner, 1985; Miyake, Chen, & Campos, 1985; Smith & Pederson, 1983), although typically without the same strength of associations as those reported by Ainsworth's group (Goldsmith & Alansky, 1987).

The association between insensitive parenting and insecure attachments is especially evident in studies of attachment among maltreated (abused and/or neglected) infants (Crittenden, 1988; Egeland & Sroufe, 1981; Lamb, Gaensbauer, Malkin, & Schultz, 1985; Lyons-Ruth, Connell, Grunebaum, Botein, & Zoll, 1984; Lyons-Ruth, Connell, Zoll, & Stahl, 1985; Schneider-Rosen, Braunwald, Carlson, & Cicchetti, 1985; Schneider-Rosen & Cicchetti, 1984) and among infants of caregivers with psychopathology (Radke-Yarrow, Cummings, Kuczynski, & Chapman, 1985), which collectively report insecure attachments in at least two thirds (and frequently many more) of the infants in such samples. In particular, substantial associations have been reported between child abuse and avoidant attachments (Lamb, Gaensbauer, Malkin, & Schultz, 1985; Lyons-Ruth et al., 1987; Schneider-Rosen & Cicchetti, 1984; Schneider-Rosen et al., 1985). Main (1981; Main & Weston, 1982) has speculated that avoidance in stressful contexts like the Strange Situation procedure is a defensive behavior that functions to preserve behavioral organization in the face of intense conflict. She notes that, whereas avoidantly attached infants characteristically show a relative absence of hostile behavior toward the caregiver in the Strange Situation, they are much more likely to direct such behavior toward the caregiver in the home (e.g., angry crying, striking). This suggests that infants who avoid in the Strange Situation are angry, presumably in response to the anger and rejection displayed by the caregiver, but that this anger is expressed only in nonthreatening, stress-free contexts. By contrast, in stressful contexts that activate the attachment system, such infants avoid the caregiver as a response to a hypothetically irresolvable situation: On the one hand, the novelty of the laboratory environment and separation from the mother activate the attachment behavioral system and the desire to seek the proximity of the attachment figure. On the other hand, the mother's history of rejecting the infant makes proximity seeking difficult. Avoidance, then, hypothetically serves to deactivate the attachment system and resolve the infant's conflict. Although the infant remains angry, anger is suppressed because its expression may promote the caregiver's approach and thus intensify the conflict.

Importantly, however, the association between rejecting, hostile parenting and avoidant attachments is not straightforward. Elevations in the proportions of resistant attachments have also been found in samples of abused infants (Schneider-Rosen et al., 1985), and increases in the proportions of avoidant attachments have also been reported in infants with "psychologically unavailable" but not abusive caregivers (Egeland & Sroufe, 1981). Of course, psychological unavailability may be associated with hostility and rejection, regardless of the presence or absence of abuse. The fact remains, however, that whereas insensitive parenting has predicted insecure attachment patterns, differences between the specific antecedents of the A and C patterns are not yet clear. This has prompted some investigators to examine more closely the evolving interaction between parenting effectiveness and infant temperament in shaping Strange Situation attachment patterns (Thompson & Lamb, 1986; see Lamb, Thompson, Gardner, & Charnov, 1985, for a comprehensive review).

Some studies of high-risk infants are also noteworthy in finding elevated proportions of the D classification, suggesting that the traditional tripartite system may not adequately capture the full spectrum of attachment patterns in atypical rearing environments. For example, Crittenden's (1985) study of abused and neglected infants found 70% of abused infants and 18% of neglected infants to manifest high levels of avoidance *and* resistance, a pattern she labeled A/C and that qualifies as a variant of the "disorganized-disoriented" classification introduced by Main and Solomon (1986). Lyons-Ruth et al. (1987) reported similar attachment patterns in 40% of their abused infant group, and Radke-Yarrow et al. (1985) reported A/C attachment patterns in 29% of infants of bipolar depressive mothers and in 17% of infants of unipolar depressives. Even though the A/C pattern is only one variant of the D classification, these proportions are substantially higher than the 10%–13% of D babies that have been found in several low-risk samples (Main & Solomon, 1986). This suggests that investigations of high-risk samples should be especially sensitive to attachment patterns that depart from the traditional A-B-C classification system.

Contemporaneous and Predictive Correlates of Strange Situation Classifications

Additional research has been concerned with the relationships between Strange Situation classifications and areas of child functioning having theoretical links to attachment security, such as the emergence of autonomy and later psychological adjustment (Sroufe, 1979). Early security of attachment to caregivers would be expected to foster internal working models of the caregiver as responsive and caring and of the self as worthy of love, which in turn would expectably have a positive impact on the infant's ability to enter into and maintain relationships with the caregiver and with nonfamilial adults and peers.

To date, a wide variety of studies tend to support these hypotheses, although, as Lamb noted (Lamb, 1987; Lamb, Thompson et al., 1985; Lamb et al., 1984; Thompson & Lamb, 1986), support is strongest when environmental circumstances appear to be stable over time. Children classified as securely attached in infancy have later been found to be more socially competent with peers as toddlers (Pastor, 1981; Waters, Wippman, & Sroufe, 1979) and as preschoolers (LaFreniere & Sroufe, 1985; Sroufe, Schork, Motti, Lawroski, & LaFreniere, 1984; Waters et al., 1979) than have children with insecure infant attachments to mothers. Similar relationships, both contemporaneous and predictive, have been observed in studies of sociability with strange adults (Lutkenhaus, Grossmann, & Grossmann, 1985; Main, 1983; Main & Weston, 1981; Plunkett, Klein, & Meisels, 1988; Sagi, Lamb, & Gardner, 1986; Thompson & Lamb, 1983) and with older siblings (Teti & Ablard, in press). Other studies have reported that children with early secure attachments were more compliant and cooperative with maternal directives (Bates et al., 1985; Erickson & Crichton, 1981; Londerville & Main, 1981; Stayton, Hogan, & Ainsworth, 1971), more effective problem solvers with mothers (Matas, Arend, & Sroufe, 1978), more curious and ego resilient (Arend, Gove, & Sroufe, 1979), more competent in exploring a strange environment (Cassidy, 1986; Hazen & Durrett, 1982), more sophisticated in toy play (Belsky, Garduque, & Hrncir, 1984; Slade, 1987), and less dependent on adults (Sroufe, Fox, & Pancake, 1983) than were children whose early attachments were insecure. Finally, early insecure attachment has been associated with the development of subsequent behavior problems in later childhood, but only when other risk factors, such as low socioeconomic status and/or high life stress, were also present (Bates & Bayles, 1988; Bates et al., 1985; Erickson et al., 1985; Fagot & Kavanagh, 1988; Lewis, Feiring, McGuffog, & Jaskir, 1984).

Collectively, these studies support the predictive validity of Strange Situation classifications, or at least the B/"not-B" type distinction, especially when there is continuity in environmental circumstances and/or caregiving behavior over time (Lamb, Thompson et al., 1985). This latter point also applies to additional research examining the stability of Strange Situation classifications over a 6–7-month period (Egeland & Farber, 1984; Thompson, Lamb, & Estes, 1982; Vaughn, Egeland, Sroufe, & Waters, 1979; Waters, 1978). Specifically, stability in attachment classifications over this period appears to be associated with stable life circumstances; by contrast, instability appears to be associated with changing life circumstances.

THE USE OF THE STRANGE SITUATION PROCEDURE WITH HANDICAPPED INFANTS

The meaningful use of Strange Situation classifications requires the achievement of certain cognitive-affective milestones (i.e., early person permanence, stranger wariness, and separation protest) the development of which heralds the onset of goal-corrected attachment behavior. Thus, to a great extent, the Ainsworth system's use with handicapped infants depends on the impact of the handicap on cognitive-affective development. In addition, its applicability depends on the impact of the handicap on the infant's ability to detect the presence and absence of the caregiver and stranger and to engage in effortful proximity seeking and contact maintenance. If cognitive and affective development proceeds normally, and if the Strange Situation procedure and scoring criteria can be successfully adapted for individual handicaps, the formation of meaningful attachment classifications may be possible. We note, however, that such classifications will need to be validated by researchers in the same manner as those derived for normal infants.

Handicapped Infants without Intellectual Impairment

For infants with normal cognitive functioning, adaptation of the Strange Situation procedure should make use of those sensorimotor modalities that still function and that the infant can use to detect the presence and absence of the caregiver. Minimal adaptation may be required for deaf infants, who despite their handicap can see the approach of the stranger and the exits and entrances of the parent. A study by Meadow, Greenberg, and Erting (1983) supports this view in deriving clearcut attachment classifications among deaf children under the age of 3 years. To date, the Strange Situation procedure has not been used with blind infants; however, Fraiberg's (1975) seminal work indicates that blind infants of sufficient age display goal-corrected attachment behavior. Use of the Strange Situation with blind infants may be possible if the procedure makes use of these infants' tactile and auditory systems to signal the presence and departure of the caregiver and stranger. Blind infants might be given some time to explore the contents and dimensions of the playroom with the caregiver. In addition, caregivers and strangers might make use of tactile and auditory signals to communicate their exits, entrances, and general whereabouts to these infants. Of course, adaptations such as these would require extensive pilot research since it is expected that blind infants will differ from sighted infants in terms of the specific stimuli that affect the attachment-exploration balance. However, appropriate use of alternate sensory modalities may at a minimum allow blind infants to be broadly classified as secure, avoidant, or resistant, without regard to the subtle distinctions among the various subclassifications.

Other studies of children with neurological, orthopedic, respiratory, or facial handicaps again illustrate the general applicability, with appropriate modifications, of Strange Situation classifications in the absence of cognitive and affective impairment. For example, Wasserman, Lennon, Allen, and Shilansky (1987) observed similar patterns of Strange Situation behavior in a sample of infants with congenital facial/orthopedic malformations and a sample of normal infants. Using a modified Strange Situation procedure, Stahlecker and Cohen (1985) were able to classify 80% of a sample of infants with neurological impairments, which included cerebral palsy, spina bifida, hydrocephalus, and various degenerative neurological conditions. In addition, Fischer-Fay, Goldberg, Simmons, Morris, and Levison (1988) found no differences between the attachment patterns of a sample of normal infants and a sample of infants with cystic fibrosis. Finally, very promising efforts to adapt the Strange Situation procedure and scoring criteria to infants with varying degrees of motor impairments are now underway (Pianta, 1989; Sierra, 1989).

These studies suggest that Strange Situation classifications can be used with handicapped infants when the handicap does not involve cognitive delay. It should be noted, however, that none of these studies has examined antecedents and consequences of Strange Situation classifications, and thus the validity of Strange Situation classifications with such infants remains untested. Future research might well examine how well the correlates of Strange Situation classifications in samples of infants with sensorimotor handicaps compare with those established in samples of nonhandicapped infants.

Intellectually Handicapped Infants

When a handicap involves cognitive delay, the use of Strange Situation classifications becomes problematic. This is so not simply because of the delayed onset of object and person permanence but also because cognitive delay may be associated with subdued emotional expressiveness, as is found among infants with Down syndrome. Serafica and Cicchetti (1976) compared the Strange Situation behavior of a sample of 33-month-old infants with Down syndrome with a sample of nonhandicapped infants of the same age (mental age not matched), analyzing the children's behavioral/emotional responses in each episode. In contrast to nonhandicapped infants, infants with Down syndrome made very few attempts to search for or seek the proximity of their mothers by signaling, specifically crying. In addition, they engaged in less fine manipulatory activities with objects than did nonhandicapped infants, possibly because of a developmental lag in the acquisition of motor control and coordination. Importantly, the researchers noted that children with Down syndrome generally appeared to be less distressed by the Strange Situation procedure than nonhandicapped infants; however, children with Down syndrome did appear to be "attachment-like" in showing clear preferences for their mothers over strangers and greeting their mothers on reunions. In a subsequent study, Thompson, Cicchetti, Lamb, and Malkin (1985) compared 12.5- and 19-month-old nonhandicapped infants with 19-month-old children with Down syndrome, with the expectation that the cognitive functioning of the 12-month-old nonhandicapped children and the 19-month-old children with Down syndrome would be comparable. Still, they found children with Down syndrome to be emotionally subdued relative to nonhandicapped children at either age. Similar emotional unreactivity in 30–42-month-old children with Down syndrome in the Strange Situation was reported by Cicchetti and Serafica (1981), despite the clear expression of goal-corrected attachment behavior by this age.

None of the above-mentioned studies of infants with Down syndrome employed Strange Situation A-B-C classifications, clearly in response to the children's substantial cognitive delays and subdued emotional expressiveness. Indeed, as these studies indicate, such emotional flatness is evident even after infants with Down syndrome have developed a sense of person permanence. Cicchetti and Sroufe (1976) found a strong negative association between degree of developmental delay and affective expression among children with Down syndrome: The greater the cognitive delay the less children laughed at social stimuli. Other researchers have reported that children with Down syndrome seemed to have less intense physiological reactions to stressful events than do nonhandicapped infants (Cicchetti & Serafica, 1981; Thompson et al., 1985). These findings, along with more recent data (Vaughn, 1989), argue against the use of the Strange Situation procedure to assess *quality of attachment* among babies with Down syndrome.

The Strange Situation procedure may still be useful, however, in determining whether children with Down syndrome and other handicapped children show goal-corrected attachments to their caregivers regardless of quality. Along this line, Blacher (1987) used a modified Strange Situation to assess attachment in 100 severely mentally retarded children between 3 and 8 years of age. Although the tripartite classification was of little use with these children, Blacher nevertheless was able to determine whether the relationships the children established with their caregivers were "attachment-like." Specifically, she found that goal-corrected attachment behavior, regardless of quality, was least likely to be found among children with the most severe mental deficiencies.

Summary

In sum, extant research suggests that the Strange Situation procedure and its classifications might be used with populations of handicapped infants without substantial deviations in cognitive-affective development, provided that appropriate modifications are made in the procedure and scoring criteria. On the other hand, a variety of studies now call into question the applicability of Strange Situation classifications to infants and young children with intellectual handicaps, particularly those with Down syndrome. Additional research on this issue is clearly needed, given that it is still unclear whether the behavior of cognitively delayed children under more stressful circumstances would more closely resemble that of nonhandicapped infants in the Strange Situation procedure. Additional research might also address the applicability of the Strange Situation to samples of infants/toddlers with mild intellectual handicaps. At the least, it appears that the Strange Situation procedure might still be useful in assessing whether or not children with intellectual impairments display goal-corrected attachment behavior, regardless of quality.

USING THE STRANGE SITUATION WITH INDIVIDUAL INFANTS

To date, the Strange Situation procedure has been used primarily in research involving *samples* of infants, and very little information is available regarding its efficacy in identifying individual infants who might be at risk for subsequent maladaptation. Although the Strange Situation procedure has proven to be a powerful research tool and remains an important window into the infant-caregiver relationship, we recommend extreme caution in using it as an isolated assessment of individual infants. The present section discusses our rationale for this position and makes specific recommendations on how Strange Situation classifications might be integrated within an individual assessment framework.

As we noted earlier, the Strange Situation procedure presumably represents a mild to moderate stressor for most infants in U.S. samples. We would argue that although this may be true for most U.S. infants, it indeed may *not* be true for all infants in any given sample. It is conceivable that an infant with low-risk indicators in other areas of functioning and who appears to enjoy a satisfying relationship with a caregiver might yet be classified as "insecurely attached" because of transient environmental or constitutional influences whose relationship to Strange Situation behavior is still poorly understood. Indeed, although Strange Situation classifications may represent adequately the central tendencies of a *sample*, it may be too small a sampling of behavior to assess the quality of attachment at the level of the individual. We believe this concern is relevant regardless of whether the attachment is judged to be secure or insecure.

To illustrate, there is at present considerable controversy among social scientists regarding the "impact" of infant day care on the security of infant-parent attachment. On the one hand, some claim that infants who experience 20 or more hours of full-time out-of-home care per week are at risk for insecure attachments to their mothers (e.g., Belsky, 1986). Clarke-Stewart (1988; Clarke-Stewart & Fein, 1983) interpreted these data very differently, however, arguing that what is being called "avoidance" in the Strange Situation for these infants may actually be viewed as "independence." Infants placed in day care during the first year may become accustomed to repeated separations from and reunions with mothers and will thus manifest little distress during brief separations and perhaps a nonchalant response to mothers upon reunion. Thus, Clarke-Stewart raises an important concern about the Strange Situation. Specifically, how does the psychological experience of the Strange Situation vary across infants reared in different circumstances, and how does this relate to the validity of the Strange Situation as a marker of infant-parent attachment? It is noteworthy that this concern has been expressed independently by researchers examining attachment in other cultures, particularly by those who have found attachment distributions that differ from typical U.S. distributions (Grossmann et al., 1985; Lamb, Thompson et al., 1985; Miyake et al., 1985; Sagi et al., 1985). If at least some infants' "avoidant" behavior patterns actually reflect independence, then the conclusion that these infants are insecurely attached becomes problematic indeed, particularly if the Strange Situation is being used to assess *individual* risk.

Relatedly, it is important to note that the Strange Situation assesses attachment security by examining changes in the attachment-exploration balance as it relates to changes in "exogenous" factors, or factors external to the infant. Thus, infant behavior is observed in response to the approach of a stranger and to separations from and reunions with the attachment figure. However, exogenous factors represent only one set of variables to which, as Bowlby (1969/1982) theorized, the attachment-exploration balance is sensitive. "Endogenous" factors (e.g., fatigue, illness, hunger) comprise the other set, and how these endogenous factors might interact with exogenous factors to affect Strange Situation behavior is a virtual unknown. Is it possible, for example, that fatigue affects Strange Situation behavior by producing a stronger distress reaction than would be typical of a given infant and thereby potentiates the expression of irritability and anger, hallmarks of the resistant attachment category? To date, there are no answers to this question.

Finally, it is noteworthy that the negative impact of insensitive caregiving on Strange Situation classifications may increase over time. Thus, it is possible that infants at risk for abuse, neglect, or other forms of mistreatment may not display dysfunctional attachments at 10–12 months of age but will do so later in the second year. Egeland and Sroufe's (1981) data attest to this point in showing increases from 12 to 18 months in the proportion of insecure attachments among infants with psychologically unavailable mothers and infants with angry, hostile mothers. At 12 months, over half of these infants were classified as securely attached, suggesting that pathological environmental factors may take time to develop before affecting attachment security. The *sole use* of the Strange Situation as an assessment of individual risk status, especially at younger ages, could miss a substantial number of infants at risk for dysfunctional attachments and subsequent maladaptations.

In short, although the Ainsworth system has indeed proven to be viable in traditional research settings, we recommend that it be supplemented by additional observations of parent-infant interaction in any determination of the risk status of individual infants. Farran and her colleagues (this volume) discuss a variety of well-known parent-infant rating scales that can be employed in laboratory and in-home observations of parent-child interaction and that can be integrated with Strange Situation classifications to facilitate assessment. In addition, given that caregivers' behavior in a structured laboratory setting may be constrained and that Strange Situation classifications appear to have reliable in-home behavioral correlates, we recommend supplementing Strange Situation classifications whenever possible with observations of infant-caregiver interaction in the home. If the parent of an infant judged to be insecurely attached in the Strange Situation is insensitive, neglectful, hostile, abusive, or otherwise emotionally unavailable in the home, one's confidence in assigning this family to a high-risk category and in need of services improves. By contrast, if the caregiver in the home appears to be nurturant and sensitively attuned to the needs of the baby, and if the baby is equally positive and responsive in the home setting, additional information in the form of behavioral observations and parental reports is warranted. In general, we view the Strange Situation as contributing an important, albeit single, piece of information that must be integrated with other "windows" into the caregiver-infant relationship before any decision regarding individual risk status is made.

ALTERNATE SYSTEMS FOR ASSESSING ATTACHMENT

In this final section, we briefly present some alternate systems for assessing attachments in infancy. To begin, we note that there have been several attempts to evaluate Strange Situation behavior with alternate scoring systems (e.g., Connell, 1985; Cummings, Daniel, & El-Sheikh, 1986; Gardner, Lamb, Thompson, & Sagi, 1986), typically predicated on the inability of the tripartite classification system to capture the full range of reunion patterns observed (of course, this problem also motivated the formal creation of the "D" classification). These alternate systems, although interesting and methodologically elegant, are not as yet in widespread use and their discussion is beyond the scope of this chapter. We refer the interested reader to Lamb, Thompson et al. (1985) for a comprehensive review of these systems.

The Waters and Deane (1985) Attachment Q-Set

The Attachment Q-Set is a Q-sort measure that is theoretically consistent with the Strange Situation in emphasizing secure base behavior but differs in assessing such behavior in the home. The most recent version of the Q-Set is composed of 90 behavioral descriptors (e.g., "if held in mother's arms, child stops crying and quickly recovers after being frightened or upset"). Given that the Q-Set evaluates secure base behavior in the home, it is also useful beyond 24 months of age. Each descriptor is printed on a separate 3-inch by 5-inch index card. Trained observers familiar with the infant's home behavior vis-à-vis the caregiver, or the caregiver him- or herself, can complete the Q-Set by sorting each descriptor in terms of how like or unlike it is to the behavior of the target child during the last week. The sorting procedure ultimately yields nine piles of 10 cards each, with pile 9 being "very much like the child" and pile 1 being "very much unlike the child." Items in pile 9 are given a score of 9, items in pile 8 are given a score of 8, and so on.

The Attachment Q-set has been used exclusively in research settings to date. Evaluating a mother's or trained observer's "sort" of a given child's behavior requires an additional "criterion" sort, which is a set of averaged scores on the same items obtained from a variety of attachment experts in the field who were asked to complete the Q-Set for their hypothetical notions of the secure base behavior of the "most secure child." Reliability among these expert raters was quite high. A security score can be obtained by correlating, using Pearson's r, the mother/observer sort with the criterion sort, and the higher that correlation the more secure, hypothetically, is the particular child. If the correlation coefficient is to be used as a data point in statistical analyses, it should be transformed using the Fisher's r-to-z transformation procedure since correlation coefficients are not normally distributed. Thus, the Attachment Q-Set yields security scores that range along a continuum, which of course differs from the classification schemes traditionally used with the Strange Situation.

There are now a variety of investigations that attest to the validity of the Attachment Q-Set. Waters (1987) has demonstrated that securely and insecurely attached 1-year-old children so classified from the Strange Situation differed on a variety of in-home secure base behaviors tapped by the Q-Set. These differences were consistent with the predictions of attachment theory. Behaviors that were more descriptive of insecurely attached children included "expects adult to be unresponsive," "is demanding when initiating activities with mother," and "easily becomes angry with mother." In contrast, behaviors that were more descriptive of securely attached children included "easily comforted by mother," "does not become angry with toys," and "explores objects thoroughly." Similar reports of a close correspondence between infants' behavior in the Strange Situation and Q-Set data come from Bosso's (1985) and Vaughn's (1985) work with other American samples and from Valenzuela and Lara's (1987) study of malnourished and nutritionally healthy infants in Chile. Additional data are available indicating the utility of the Q-Set in predicting social competence in preschoolers, which is hailed by attachment theorists as a hallmark of secure attachment (Bosso, 1985; Denham, 1987; Teti & Ablard, in press).

The Attachment Q-Set is gaining popularity among researchers and appears to have potential for clinical use. Although there are no systematic criteria for distinguishing securely and insecurely attached infants, the criterion sort conveys important information about how attachment security can be conceptualized and defined in the infancy and preschool periods. Practitioners can develop clinical impressions of a given child from the scores of specific Q-Set items in relation to their scores on the criterion sort. Furthermore, practitioners may wish to delve more deeply into the family situation of a child who receives very low scores on the majority of items deemed by attachment experts to be characteristic of a securely attached child. As Waters (personal communication, 1988) suggests, either the full complement or a subset of Q-Set items can be used to obtain a profile of the secure base behavior of a particular child in the home, depending on one's specific question. In addition, the Q-Set might be used to enter into a dialogue with parents about their relationship with their child, and as a source of information that can be used to develop interventions tailored to a particular parent's needs. Thus, the Attachment Q-Set's versatility and ease of administration make it a potentially useful tool for both researchers and practitioners.

Clinical Assessment Systems of Lieberman and Greenspan

The classification systems outlined by Alicia Lieberman and Stanley Greenspan extend the Ainsworth system by providing specific behavioral critieria for assessing the quality of the infant-caregiver relationship from birth to 4 years of age. Unlike the Ainsworth scheme, these systems evaluate not only the quality of goal-corrected attachment behavior but also the early process of attachment formation under the assumption that early deviations from the norm can be reliably detected. Of course, early detection of disorders of attachment formation is of great importance from a preventive intervention perspective.

Lieberman and Pawl (1988) have drawn heavily from the Bowlby-Ainsworth theoretical perspective and from the psychoanalytic viewpoints of Selma Fraiberg in identifying three major categories of attachment disorders: 1) disorders of nonattachment; 2) disorders of anxious, ambivalent attachment; and 3) disorders of disrupted attachment. Disorders of nonattachment arise when infants have no opportunity to establish a relationship with a consistent caregiver, which in turn impedes their ability to enter into emotionally satisfying relationships later in life. Such children are also characterized by cognitive and linguistic delays, low frustration tolerance, and an inability to regulate aggressive impulses. Infants at risk for disorders of nonattachment are those who have experienced a series of short-term caregivers during the first year of life (as in the case of repeated placements in foster care) or perhaps those raised in a severely emotionally depriving home environment. Disorders of anxious, ambivalent attachment are conceptualized in terms of Ainsworth's secure base concept, with three distortions of secure base behavior identified: *recklessness and accident proneness,* characterized by the tendency to run off and explore strange territory with no apparent concern for the caregiver's whereabouts, and to become injured while doing so; *inhibition of exploration,* described by conspicuous and persistent withdrawal from social interaction with unfamiliar adults and from exploration of objects even while in the caregiver's presence; and *precocious competence in self-protection,* hallmarked by role reversal between caregiver and child in which the child becomes overprotective of the caregiver and acutely aware of the caregiver's particular needs. All three of these behavioral patterns reflect distortions in the attachment-exploration balance. Disorder of disrupted attachment are indicated by undue anxiety in reaction to a separation from the caregiver that compromises the ability to form trusting relationships.

Lieberman and Pawl's (1988) system clearly requires extensive training and repeated observations of the infant-caregiver relationship in a variety of settings. At present, it is used clinically by the Infant-Parent Program staff at the San Francisco General Hospital, a program that serves a variety of multirisk families referred by local hospitals and agencies of various types. Although information regarding interrater reliability is not yet available, we find this system potentially useful in that it augments Strange Situation classifications by identifying attachment disorders not predicated on the notion of secure base behavior per se. Indeed, the goal of the Strange Situation procedure and classifications is to evaluate the *security* of an already formed attachment, not to determine whether or not an attachment exists. In cases of disorders of nonattachment, Strange Situation behavior would be difficult to interpret.

Stanley Greenspan has contributed a developmental model of infant attachment that improves upon classifications of attachment disorders in the *Diagnostic and Statistical Manual of Mental Disorders (Third Edition)* in casting relational psychopathologies in terms of the normative developmental milestones expected of infants in different stages of growth (Greenspan & Lieberman, 1980, 1988; Greenspan & Lourie, 1981; Greenspan, Nover & Scheurer, 1987; Greenspan, Wieder, & Nover, 1985). Like that of Lieberman and Pawl (1988), Greenspan's system enables the assessment of disorders of attachment formation prior to as well as after the emergence of goal-corrected attachment behavior. Its developmental structuralist framework is decidely psychoanalytic and heavily influenced by Piaget. Greenspan has identified six developmental stages of attachment relationships, defining normative, healthy social functioning and mild, moderate, and severe deviations from these norms at each stage. In the first stage, *homeostasis* (0–3 months of age), the infant's self-regulatory capacities and orientation to the social environment are controlled by the maturing central nervous system and by the caregiver's capacity for contingent, appropriate responding to infant cues of distress, alertness, and withdrawal. Thus, even at this early age, the caregiver is given some responsibility for facilitating the infant's quality of orientation to the world, although it is acknowledged that the particular requirements of the caregiver may vary with individual differences in infants' nervous system functioning. Competent infant functioning during this stage is described by regular sleep-wake cycles, responsiveness to attempts by the caregiver to soothe, and regular periods of alertness that increase in frequency and duration as the infant matures. Deviations from this general norm include inordinate sleeping and lack of interest in social stimuli, or heightened excitement, distress, and reactivity to stimuli. Overlapping with the first stage is the stage of *attachment formation* (0-7 months of age), during which the infant normally develops clear preferences for specific adult caregivers. Competent functioning in this stage is characterized by the special interest and pleasure shown in interaction with attachment figures. By contrast, disordered functioning in indicated by varying degrees of gaze aversion to and withdrawal from the caregiver and perhaps other adults, or by an inability to become physically disengaged from the caregiver.

The third stage, which overlaps somewhat with stage 2, is called *somatopsychologic differentiation* (3–10 months), so called because of the development of a rudimentary self-other distinction and of intentionality in behavior. During this stage, normally functioning infants develop the ability to perceive cause-effect relationships between their behavior and an environmental consequence. They also become able to distinguish familiar caregivers from strangers and can engage in purposeful, reciprocal interaction with familiar adults, showing a wide range of affect. By contrast, disordered functioning in this stage is characterized by little responsivity to the caregiver or an unusually high demand for the caregiver's attention and very low tolerance for separation. In stage 4, *behavioral organization, initiative, and internalization* (9–18 months), infants' emerging cognitive and emotional capacities allow for the development of imitation, novel behavioral schemes, and increased diversity and breadth of emotional responsiveness. Competent functioning in this stage is described by the presence of organized behavioral schemes in response to interaction with, separation from, and reunion with the caregiver, by organized behavioral initiatives directed to objects and people, and by an increasing ability to respond positively to novelty. Disordered functioning, by contrast, is reflected by passivity, withdrawal, or negativism, and/or by disorganized behavioral schemes characterized by little novelty.

Stage 5, *representational capacity* (18–36 months), is so named for the child's developing capacity to use language and form mental representations of reality. These mental representations are akin to Bowlby's (1973) notions of "working models" and thus are expected to relate to the child's prior history with the caregiver. Children functioning competently in this stage can use words and symbolic actions to describe their emotional relationship with others. By contrast, children with disordered functioning in this stage may not use symbolic activity to represent attachment relationships, or may do so in a disorganized, fragmented fashion. Finally, in stage 6, *representational differentiation* (30–48 months), competent functioning is characterized by the ability to distinguish self from others and to discuss relationships on an affective level through the use of representational themes. Competently functioning children show high self-regard and have little problem switching back and forth from fantasy to reality. Children with disordered functioning manifest uneven self-regard and lack of impulse control, and use symbolic expression with objects but not with people. If symbolic play involves people, there is a clear blurring of the fantasy-reality distinction.

Greenspan and his colleagues (Greenspan & Lourie, 1981; Greenspan et al., 1985, 1987) have also established dimensions of maternal behavior that are associated with successful and unsuccessful infant adaptations in each of these stages. In addition, Greenspan, Lieberman, and Poisson (1981) have developed a coding scheme for recording infant and caregiver behaviors from videotapes (The Greenspan-Lieberman Observation System for Assessment of Caregiver-Infant Interaction during Semi-Structured Play; GLOS), for which Poisson (personal communication, 1988) reported interrater reliabilities ranging from 60% to 100% across all behavior categories based on 20 mother-infant dyads. Clearly, this developmental structuralist system requires extensive training and labor-intensive observations of infant-caregiver behavior. With such expertise, however, practitioners may find it of immediate relevance for assessment of and intervention with individual infants.

CONCLUSION

In this chapter we have discussed the Ainsworth Strange Situation as an assessment of infant-caregiver attachment in research and clinical settings and in samples of infants with various handicaps. We argue that Strange Situation classifications have been quite useful in research contexts but must be supplemented with additional observations of the infant-caregiver relationship in evaluating risk status at an individual level. Further, we argue that the efficacy of the Strange Situation procedure and classifications with handicapped infants depends upon the nature and severity of the handicap. Attachment classifications should not be used with handicaps involving substantial cognitive delay, although the Strange Situation procedure may be useful for establishing evidence that a goal-corrected attachment to the caregiver exists. Attachment classifications may be more meaningful with other handicaps, provided that the Strange Situation procedure and scoring criteria are appropriately adapted to the handicap in question.

Finally, we have briefly presented three additional systems for assessing attachment: the Waters and Deane Attachment Q-Set, and the clinical diagnostic systems of Lieberman and Greenspan. Like the Strange Situation, the Attachment Q-Set cannot be used to assess quality of attachment until late in the first year, when goal-corrected attachment behavior is well established. However, it augments the Strange Situation by enabling the evaluation of the quality of secure base behavior beyond the age of 24 months. To date, the Q-Set has been used most frequently in research settings, although it also holds promise for clinical use with nonhandicapped infants. Unlike the Strange Situation and Attachment Q-Set, the Lieberman and Greenspan systems have been primarily used as clinical tools for individual assessment and intervention with infants, particularly those from multirisk families. Both of these systems enable the practitioner to assess the health of infant social relationships before as well as after the emergence of goal-corrected attachment behavior. The requirements of these systems to obtain frequent and labor-intensive observations of individual families mitigates against their broad use in research settings. However, they may be of more immediate use to practitioners interested in individual assessment and intervention.

REFERENCES

Ainsworth, M.D.S. (1969). Object relations, dependency, and attachment: A theoretical review of the infant-mother relationship. *Child Development, 40*, 969–1025.

Ainsworth, M. (1973). The development of infant-mother attachment. In B. Caldwell & H. Riccuiti (Eds.), *Review of child development research* (Vol. 3). Chicago: University of Chicago Press.

Ainsworth, M.D.S. (1982). Attachment: Retrospect and prospect. In C.M. Parkes & J. Stevenson-Hinde (Eds.), *The place of attachment in human behavior* (pp. 3–30). New York: Basic Books.

Ainsworth, M.D.S., & Bell, S.M. (1970). Attachment, exploration, and separation: Illustrated by the behavior of one-year-olds in a strange situation. *Child Development, 41*, 49–67.

Ainsworth, M.D.S., Bell, S.M.V., & Stayton, D.J. (1971). Individual differences in Strange Situation behavior of one-year-olds. In H.R. Schaffer (Ed.), *The origins of human social relations* (pp. 17–57). London: Academic Press.

Ainsworth, M.D.S., Bell, S.M., & Stayton, D.J. (1974). Infant-mother attachment and social development: Socialization as a product of reciprocal responsiveness to signals. In M. Richards (Ed.), *The integration of the child into the social world*. Cambridge, England, Cambridge University Press.

Ainsworth, M.D.S., Blehar, M.C., Waters, E., & Wall, S. (1978). *Patterns of attachment: A psychological study of the strange situation*. Hillsdale, NJ: Lawrence Erlbaum Associates.

Ainsworth, M.D., & Wittig, B.A. (1969). Attachment and exploratory behavior of one year olds in a strange situation. In B.M. Foss (Ed.), *Determinants of infant behavior* (Vol. 4). London: Methuen.

Arend, R., Gove, F., & Sroufe, L.A. (1979). Continuity of individual adaptation from infancy to kindergarten: A predictive study of ego-resiliency and curiosity in preschoolers. *Child Development, 50*, 950–959.

Bates, J.E., & Bayles, K. (1988). Attachment and the development of behavior problems. In J. Belsky & T. Nezworski (Eds.), *Clinical implications of attachment* (pp. 253–299). Hillsdale, NJ: Lawrence Erlbaum Associates.

Bates, J.E., Maslin, C.A., & Frankel, K.A. (1985). Attachment security, mother-child interaction, and temperament as predictors of behavior problem ratings at age three years. In I. Bretherton & E. Waters (Eds.), *Growing points of attachment theory and research. Monographs of the Society for Research in Child Development, 50* (Serial No. 209, Nos. 1–2), 167–193.

Belsky, J. (1986). Infant day care: A cause for concern? *Zero to Three, 6*(5), 1–7.

Belsky, J., Garduque, L., & Hrncir, E. (1984). Assessing performance, competence, and executive capacity in infant play: Relations to home environment and security of attachment. *Developmental Psychology, 20*, 406–417.

Belsky, J., Rovine, M., & Taylor, D. (1984). The Pennsylvania Infant and Family Project, III: The origins of individual differences in infant mother attachment: Maternal and infant contributions. *Child Development, 55*, 718–728.

Blacher, J. (1987, April). *Attachment between severely impaired children and their mothers: Conceptual and methodological concerns*. Paper presented at the meeting of the Society for Research in Child Development, Baltimore.

Blehar, M.C., Lieberman, A.F., & Ainsworth, M.D.S. (1977). Early face-to-face interaction and its relation to later infant-mother attachment. *Child Development*, *48*, 182–194.

Bosso, R. (1985). Attachment quality and sibling relations: Responses of anxiously attached/avoidant and securely attached 18 to 32 month old firstborns toward their second-born siblings. *Dissertation Abstracts International*, *47*, 1293B.

Bowlby, J. (1969/1982). *Attachment and loss: Vol. 1. Attachment*. New York: Basic Books.

Bowlby, J. (1973). *Attachment and loss: Vol. 2. Separation*. New York: Basic Books.

Bowlby, J. (1980). *Attachment and loss: Vol. 3. Loss, sadness, and depression*. New York: Basic Books.

Bretherton, I. (1985). I. Attachment theory: Retrospect and prospect. In I. Bretherton & E. Waters (Eds.), *Growing points of attachment theory and research. Monographs of the Society for Research in Child Development*, *50* (Serial No. 209, Nos. 1–2), 3–35.

Cassidy, J. (1986). The ability to negotiate the environment: An aspect of infant competence as related to quality of attachment. *Child Development*, *57*, 331–337.

Cicchetti, D., & Serafica, F.C. (1981). Interplay among behavioral systems: Illustrations from the study of attachment, affiliation, and wariness in young children with Down's syndrome. *Developmental Psychology*, *17*, 36–49.

Cicchetti, D., & Sroufe, L.A. (1976). The relationship between affective and cognitive development in Down's syndrome infants. *Child Developmental*, *47*, 920–929.

Clarke-Stewart, K.A. (1988, April). *Is day care bad for babies?* In T. Field (Chair), *Infant daycare is not bad*. Symposium presented at the sixth meeting of the International Conference on Infant Studies, Washington, DC.

Clarke-Stewart, K.A., & Fein, G.G. (1983). Early childhood programs. In P.H. Mussen (Ed.), *Handbook of child psychology* (Vol. 2). New York: John Wiley & Sons.

Connell, J.P. (1985). A component process approach to the study of individual differences and developmental change in attachment system functioning. Contributing chapter to Lamb, M.E., Thompson, R.A., Gardner, W., & Charnov, R. *Infant-mother attachment: The origins and developmental significance of individual differences in Strange Situation Behavior*. Hillsdale, NJ: Lawrence Erlbaum Associates.

Crittenden, P.M. (1985). Maltreated infants: Vulnerability and resilience. *Journal of Child Psychology and Psychiatry*, *26*, 85–96.

Crittenden, P.M. (1988). Relationships at risk. In J. Belsky & T. Nezworski (Eds.), *Clinical implications of attachment* (pp. 136–174). Hillsdale, NJ: Lawrence Erlbaum Associates.

Crockenberg, S.B. (1981). Infant irritability, mother responsiveness, and social support influences on the security of infant-mother attachment. *Child Development*, *52*, 857–865.

Cummings, E.M., Daniel, D., & El-Sheikh, M. (1986). *An organizational scheme for the classification of attachments on a continuum of felt-security*. Paper presented at the meeting of the International Conference on Infant Studies, Los Angeles.

Denham, S.A. (1987, August). *Child competence and maternal emotion socialization correlates of attachment Q-sort variables*. Paper presented at the Meetings of the American Psychological Association, New York.

Egeland, B., & Farber, E.A. (1984). Infant-mother attachment: Factors related to its development and changes over time. *Child Development*, *55*, 753–771.

Egeland, B., & Sroufe, L.A. (1981). Developmental sequelae of maltreatment in infancy. In R. Rizley & D. Cicchetti (Eds.), *Developmental perspectives in child maltreatment* (pp. 77–92). San Francisco: Jossey-Bass.

Erikson, E. (1963). *Childhood and society* (2nd ed.). New York: W. W. Norton.

Erickson, M.F., & Crichton, L. (1981, April). *Antecedents of compliance in 2-year-olds from a high-risk sample*. Paper presented at the meeting of the Society for Research in Child Development, Boston.

Erickson, M.F., Sroufe, L.A., & Egeland, B. (1985). The relationship between quality of attachment and behavior problems in preschool in a high-risk sample. In I. Bretherton & E. Waters (Eds.), *Growing points of attachment theory and research. Monographs of the Society for Research in Child Development*, *50* (Serial No. 209, Nos. 1–2), 147–166.

Fagot, B.I., & Kavanagh, K. (1988, April). *The prediction of behavior problems from attachment classifications*. Paper presented at the meeting of the International Conference on Infant Studies, Washington, DC.

Fischer-Fay, A., Goldberg, S., Simmons, R., Morris, P., & Levison, H. (1988, April). *Chronic illness and infant-mother attachment*. Paper presented at the meeting of the International Conference on Infant Studies, Washington, DC.

Fraiberg, S. (1975). The development of human attachments in infants blind from birth. *Merrill-Palmer Quarterly*, *25*, 315–334.

Freud, S. (1940). *An outline of psychoanalysis*. New York: W.W. Norton.

Gardner, W. Lamb, M.E., Thompson, R.A., & Sagi, A. (1986). On individual differences in

Strange Situation behavior: Categorical and continuous measurement systems in a cross-cultural data set. *Infant Behavior and Development, 9,* 355–375.

Goldsmith, H.H., & Alansky, J.A. (1987). Maternal and infant temperamental predictors of attachment: A meta-analytic review. *Journal of Consulting and Clinical Psychology, 55,* 805–816.

Greenspan, S.I., & Lieberman, A.F. (1980). Infants, mothers, and their interaction: A quantitative clinical approach to developmental assessment. In S.I. Greenspan & G.H. Pollock (Eds.), *The course of life: Psychoanalytic contributions toward understanding personality development. Vol. 1: Infancy and early childhood* (pp. 271–312). (DHHS Publication No. ADM 80-786.) Washington, DC: U.S. Government Printing Office.

Greenspan, S.I., & Lieberman, A.F. (1988). A clinical approach to attachment. In J. Belsky & T. Nezworski (Eds.), *Clinical implications of attachment* (pp. 387–424). Hillsdale, NJ: Lawrence Erlbaum Associates.

Greenspan, S.I., Lieberman, A.F., & Poisson, S.S. (1981). *Greenspan-Lieberman observation system for assessment of caregiver-infant interaction during semi-structured play (GLOS).* Bethesda, MD: Mental Health Study Center, National Institute of Mental Health.

Greenspan, S.I., & Lourie, R.S. (1981). Developmental structuralist approach to the classification of adaptive and pathologic personality organizations: Infancy and early childhood. *American Journal of Psychiatry, 138,* 725–735.

Greenspan, S.I., Nover, R.A., & Scheuer, A.Q. (1987). A developmental diagnostic approach for infants, young children, and their families. In S.I. Greenspan, S. Wieder, R.A. Nover, A.F. Lieberman, R.S. Lourie, & M.E. Robinson (Eds.), *Infants in multirisk families* (pp. 431–498). Madison, CT: International Universities Press.

Greenspan, S.I., Wieder, S., & Nover, R.A. (1985). Diagnosis and preventive intervention of developmental and emotional disorders in infancy and early childhood: New perspectives. In M. Green (Ed.), *The psychosocial aspects of the family* (pp. 13–52). Lexington, MA: D.C. Health.

Grossmann, K., Grossmann, K.E., Spangler, G., Suess, G., & Unzner, L. (1985). Maternal sensitivity and newborns' orientation responses as related to quality of attachment in northern Germany. In I. Bretherton & E. Waters (Eds.), *Growing points of attachment* theory and research. *Monographs of the Society for Research in Child Development, 50,* (Serial No. 209, Nos. 1–2), 233–256.

Harlow, H.F. (1958). The nature of love. *American Psychologist, 13,* 673–685.

Harlow, H.F. (1961). The development of affectional patterns in infant monkeys. In B.M. Foss (Ed.), *Determinants of infant behavior* (Vol 1). London: Methuen.

Hazen, N.L., & Durrett, M.E. (1982). Relationship of security of attachment to exploration and cognitive mapping abilities in 2-year-olds. *Developmental Psychology, 18,* 751–759.

LaFreniere, P.J., & Sroufe, L.A. (1985). Profiles of peer competence in the preschool: Interrelations between measures, influence of social ecology, and relation to attachment history. *Developmental Psychology, 21,* 56–69.

Lamb, M.E. (1987). Predictive implications of individual differences in attachment. *Journal of Consulting and Clinical Psychology, 55,* 817–824.

Lamb, M.E., Gaensbauer, T.J., Malkin, C.M., & Schultz, L.A. (1985). The effects of child maltreatment on security of infant-adult attachment. *Infant Behavior and Development, 8,* 35–45.

Lamb, M.E., Hwang, C-P., Frodi, A.M., & Frodi, J. (1982). Security of mother- and father-infant attachment and its relation to sociability with strangers in traditional and nontraditional Swedish families. *Infant Behavior and Development, 5,* 355–367.

Lamb, M.E., Thompson, R.A., Gardner, W., & Charnov, E.L. (1985). *Infant-mother attachment: The origins and developmental significance of individual differences in Strange Situation behavior.* Hillsdale, Lawrence Erlbaum Associates.

Lamb, M.E., Thompson, R.A., Gardner, W.P., Charnov, E.L., & Estes, D. (1984). Security of infantile attachment as assessed in the "strange situation": Its study and biological interpretation. *The Behavioral and Brain Sciences, 7,* 127–171.

Lewis, M., Feiring, C., McGuffog, C., & Jaskir, J. (1984). Predicting psychopathology in six-year-olds from early social relations. *Child Development, 55,* 123–136.

Lieberman, A. F., & Pawl, J. H. (1988). Clinical applications of attachment theory. In J. Belsky & T. Nezworzski (Eds.), *Clinical implications of attachment* (pp. 327–351). Hillsdale, NJ: Lawrence Erlbaum Associates.

Londerville, S., & Main, M. (1981). Security of attachment, compliance, and maternal training methods in the second year of life. *Developmental Psychology, 17,* 289–299.

Lutkenhaus, P., Grossmann, K. E., & Grossmann, K. (1985). Infant-mother attachment at twelve months and style of interaction with a stranger at the age of three years. *Child Development, 56,* 1538–1542.

Lyons-Ruth, K., Connell, D., Grunebaum, H., Botein, S., & Zoll, D. (1984). Maternal family history, maternal caretaking and infant attachment in multiproblem families. *Preventive Psychiatry, 2,* 403–425.

Lyons-Ruth, K., Connell, D. B., Zoll, D., & Stahl, J. (1985, April). *Infants at social risk: Relationships among infant attachment behavior, infant development and maternal behavior at home in maltreated and non-maltreated infants.* Paper presented at the meeting of the Society for Research in Child Development, Toronto, Canada.

Lyons-Ruth, K., Connell, D. B., Zoll, D., & Stahl, J. (1987). Infants at social risk: Relations among infant maltreatment, maternal behavior, and infant attachment behavior. *Developmental Psychology, 23,* 223–232.

Main, M. (1981). Avoidance in the service of attachment: A working paper. In K. Immelmann, G. W. Barlow, L. Petrinovich, & M. Main (Eds.), *Behavioral development: The Bielefeld Interdisciplinary Project* (pp. 651–693). Cambridge, England: Cambridge University Press.

Main, M. (1983). Exploration, play, and cognitive functioning related to infant-mother attachment. *Infant Behavior and Development, 6,* 167–174.

Main, M., Kaplan, N., & Cassidy, J. (1985). Security in infancy, childhood, and adulthood: A move to the level of representation. In I. Bretherton & E. Waters (Eds.), Growing points of attachment theory and research. *Monographs of the Society for Research in Child Development, 50* (Serial No. 209, Nos. 1-2), 66–104.

Main, M., & Solomon, J. (1986). Discovery of an insecure-disorganized/disoriented attachment pattern. In T. B. Brazelton & M. W. Yogman (Eds.), *Affective development in infancy* (pp. 95–124). Norwood, NJ: Ablex.

Main, M., & Weston, D. R. (1981). The quality of the toddler's relationship to mother and to father: Related to conflict behavior and the readiness to establish new relationships. *Child Development, 52,* 932–940.

Main, M., & Weston, D. R. (1982). Avoidance of the attachment figure in infancy: Descriptions and interpretations. In C. M. Parkes & J. Stevenson-Hinde (Eds.), *The place of attachment in human behavior* (pp. 31–59). New York: Basic Books.

Matas, L., Arend, R. A., & Sroufe, L. A. (1978). Continuity of adaptation in the second year: The relationship between quality of attachment and later competence. *Child Development, 49,* 547–556.

Meadow, K. P., Greenberg, M. T., & Erting, C. (1983). Attachment behavior of deaf children with deaf parents. *Journal of the American Academy of Child Psychiatry, 22,* 23–28.

Miyake, K., Chen, S., & Campos, J. J. (1985). Infant temperament, mother's mode of interaction, and attachment in Japan: An interim report. In I. Bretherton & E. Waters (Eds.), Growing points of attachment theory and research. *Monographs of the Society for Research in Child Development, 50* (Serial No. 209, Nos. 1-2), 276–297.

Pastor, D. L. (1981). The quality of mother-infant attachment and its relationship to toddlers' initial sociability with peers. *Development Psychology, 17,* 326–335.

Pianta, R. C. (1989, April). Procedures for assessing and classifying attachment behavior of children with moderate to severe motor impairments. In R. Marvin (Chair), *Assessing attachment in special populations: Using the Ainsworth Strange Situation.* Symposium presented at the meetings of the Society for Research in Child Development, Kansas City, MO.

Plunkett, J. W., Klein, T., & Meisels, S. J. (1988). The relationship of preterm infant-mother attachment to stranger sociability at 3 years. *Infant Behavior and Development, 11,* 83–96.

Radke-Yarrow, M., Cummings, E. M., Kuczynski, L., & Chapman, M. (1985). Patterns of attachment in two- and three-year-olds in normal families and families with parental depression. *Child Development, 56,* 884–893.

Sagi, A., Lamb, M. E., & Gardner, W. (1986). Relations between Strange Situation behavior and stranger sociability among infants on Israeli kibbutzim. *Infant Behavior and Development, 9,* 271–282.

Sagi, A., Lamb, M.E., Lewkowicz, K.S., Shoham, R., Dvir, R., & Estes, D. (1985). Security of infant-mother, -father, and -metapelet attachments among kibbutz-reared Israeli children. In I. Bretherton & E. Waters (Eds.), Growing points of attachment theory and research. *Monographs of the Society for Research in Child Development, 50* (Serial No. 209, Nos. 1-2), 257–275.

Schneider-Rosen, K., Braunwald, K.G., Carlson, V., & Cicchetti, D. (1985). Current perspectives in attachment theory: Illustration from the study of maltreated infants. In I. Bretherton & E. Waters (Eds.), Growing points of attachment theory and research. *Monographs of the Society for Research in Child Development, 50* (Serial No. 209, Nos. 1-2), 194–210.

Schneider-Rosen, K., & Cicchetti, D. (1984). The relationship between affect and cognition in maltreated infants: Quality of attachment and the development of visual self-recognition. *Child Development, 55,* 648–658.

Serafica, F.C., & Cicchetti, D. (1976). Down's syndrome children in a strange situation: Attachment and exploration behaviors. *Merrill-Palmer Quarterly, 22,* 137–150.

Sierra, A.M. (1989, April). The assessment of attachment in infants with mild to moderate cerebral palsy. In R. Marvin (Chair), *Assessing attachment in special populations: Using the Ainsworth Strange Situation.* Symposium presented at the meetings of the Society for Research in Child Development, Kansas City, MO.

Slade, A. (1987). Quality of attachment and early

symbolic play. *Developmental Psychology, 23,* 78–85.

Smith, P.B., & Pederson, D.R. (1983). *Maternal sensitivity and patterns of infant-mother attachment.* Paper presented at the Meetings of the Society for Research in Child Development, Detroit.

Spieker, S.J., & Booth, C.L. (1988). Maternal antecedents of attachment quality. In J. Belsky & T. Nezworski (Eds.), *Clinical implications of attachment* (pp. 95–135). Hillsdale, NJ: Lawrence Erlbaum Associates.

Sroufe, L.A. (1979). The coherence of early development: Early care, attachment, and subsequent developmental issues. *American Psychologist, 34,* 834–841.

Sroufe, L.A. (1983). Individual patterns of adaptation from infancy to preschool. In M. Perlmutter (Ed.), *Development and policy concerning children with special needs. Minnesota symposium on child psychology* (Vol. 16). Hillsdale, NJ: Lawrence Erlbaum Associates.

Sroufe, L.A., & Fleeson, J. (1986). Attachment and the construction of relationships. In W. Hartup & Z. Rubin (Eds.), *The nature and development of relationships.* Hillsdale, NJ: Lawrence Erlbaum Associates.

Sroufe, L.A., Fox, N.E., & Pancake, V.R. (1983). Attachment and dependency in developmental perspective. *Child Development, 54,* 1615–1627.

Sroufe, L.A., Schork, E., Motti, E., Lawroski, N., & LaFreniere, P. (1984). The role of affect in emerging social competence. In C. Izard, J. Kagan, & R. Zajonc (Eds.), *Emotion, cognition and behavior* (pp. 289–319). New York: Cambridge University Press.

Sroufe, L.A., & Waters, E. (1977). Attachment as an organizational construct. *Child Development, 48,* 1184–1199.

Stahlecker, J.E., & Cohen, M.C. (1985). Application of the Strange Situation attachment paradigm to a neurologically impaired population. *Child Development, 56,* 502–507.

Stayton, D.J., Hogan, R., & Ainsworth, M.D.S. (1971). Infant obedience and maternal behavior: The origins of socialization reconsidered. *Child Development, 42,* 1057–1069.

Teti, D.M., & Ablard, K.A. (in press). Security of attachment and infant-sibling relationships: A laboratory study. *Child Development.*

Thompson, R.A., Cicchetti, D., Lamb, M.E., & Malkin, C. (1985). Emotional responses of Down's syndrome and normal infants in the Strange Situation: The organization of affective behavior in infants. *Developmental Psychology, 21,* 828–841.

Thompson, R.A., & Lamb, M.E. (1983). Security of attachment and stranger sociability in infancy. *Developmental Psychology. 19,* 184–191.

Thompson, R.A., & Lamb, M.E. (1986). Infant-mother attachment: New directions for theory and research. In P.B. Baltes, D.L. Featherman, & R.M. Lerner (Eds.), *Life-span development and behavior* (Vol. 7). Hillsdale, NJ: Lawrence Erlbaum Associates.

Thompson, R.A., Lamb, M.E., & Estes, D. (1982). Stability of infant-mother attachment and its relationship to changing life circumstances in an unselected middle-class sample. *Child Development, 53,* 144–148.

Tracy, R.L., & Ainsworth, M.D.S. (1981). Maternal affectionate behavior and infant-mother attachment patterns. *Child Development, 52,* 1341–1343.

Valenzuela, M., & Lara, V. (1987, April). Nutrition and attachment in an impoverished Chilean population: Use of the Attachment Q-Set in support of Strange Situation assessments. In B.E. Vaughn (Chair), *The Q-sort method in attachment research: Adaptations and advantages in diverse contexts.* Symposium conducted at the Meetings of the Society for Research in Child Development, Baltimore.

Vaughn, B.E. (1985, April). Relationships between the attachment behavior Q-set and Strange Situation classifications. In E. Waters (Chair), *Q-sort studies of child-parent attachment.* Symposium presented at the Meetings of the Society for Research in Child Development, Toronto, Canada.

Vaughn, B. (1989, April). Assessing attachment quality in a Down syndrome sample. In R. Marvin (Chair), *Assessing attachment in special populations: Using the Ainsworth Strange Situation.* Symposium presented at the meetings of the Society for Research in Child Development, Kansas City, MO.

Vaughn, B., Egeland, B., Sroufe, L.A., & Waters, E. (1979). Individual differences in infant-mother attachment at twelve and eighteen months: Stability and change in families under stress. *Child Development, 50,* 971–975.

Wasserman, G.A., Lennon, M.C., Allen, A., & Shilansky, M. (1987). Contributors to attachment in normal and physically handicapped infants. *Journal of the American Academy of Child and Adolescent Psychiatry, 26,* 9–15.

Waters, E. (1978). The reliability and stability of individual differences in infant-mother attachment. *Child Development, 49,* 483–494.

Waters, E. (1981). Traits, behavioral systems, and relationships: Three models of infant-adult attachment. In K. Immelmann, G.W. Barlow, L. Petrinovich, & M. Main (Eds.), *Behavioral development: The Bielefeld Interdisciplinary Project* (pp. 621–650). Cambridge, England: Cambridge University Press.

Waters, E. (1987, April). Validation of Strange Situation classifications via Q-Sort data on secure base behavior at home. In B.E. Vaughn (Chair),

The Q-sort method in attachment research: Adaptations and advantages in diverse contexts. Symposium conducted at the Meetings of the Society for Research in Child Development, Baltimore.

Waters, E., & Deane, K.E. (1985). Defining and assessing individual differences in attachment relationships: Q-methodology and the organization of behavior in infancy and early childhood. In I. Bretherton & E. Waters (Eds.), *Growing points of attachment theory and research. Monographs of the Society for Research in Child Development, 50*, (Serial No. 209, Nos. 1-2), 41–65.

Waters, E., Wippman, J., & Sroufe, L.A. (1979). Attachment, positive affect, and competence in the peer group: Two studies in construct validation. *Child Development, 50*, 821–829.

14 Assessment of Coping and Temperament
Contributions to Adaptive Functioning

G. Gordon Williamson and Shirley Zeitlin

Early intervention services for children with special needs have traditionally emphasized the acquisition of developmental skills. However, positive meaning is not generated by developmental skills per se but by their impact on the child's ability to cope with the challenges of daily living. There is increasing recognition of the importance of understanding the factors that influence the child's coping competence and therefore adaptive functioning. Knowledge of the infant's coping style and temperament assists the practitioner in designing an intervention plan that specifically enhances the infant's functional performance. This chapter provides an overview of coping and temperament followed by a discussion of assessment in each domain. It then addresses the status of children with developmental disabilities and implications for intervention.

THE COPING PROCESS

Coping is the process of making adaptations to meet personal needs and to respond to the demands of the environment (Williamson, Zeitlin, & Szczepanski, 1989). In this process, resources are used to maintain or enhance feelings of well-being. Through transactions with the environment, the child modifies previously acquired coping strategies and learns new ones. Coping effectiveness is influenced by the child's developmental skills and temperament, the environmental demands, the child's experience in managing the demands, and the environmental response to the child's coping efforts (Murphy & Moriarty, 1976).

Coping efforts are directed to managing stress, which is an inherent part of life even for infants. Stress is defined as a tension that is experienced when an event is perceived as being harmful, threatening, or challenging to one's personal feeling of well-being. It may be experienced cognitively, emotionally, or physically. Usually there is some combination of all three aspects (Lazarus & Folkman, 1984; Zeitlin, Williamson, & Rosenblatt, 1987).

The newborn copes with the stress of pain and discomfort by adjusting body postures, employing self-comforting behaviors, and crying. Stress is a component in the development of attachment and later separation, in the temporary disorganization experienced during transitional periods of reflex maturation, and in the learning process itself (Kagan, 1983; Lipsitt, 1983). Even the normal interaction between the infant and the caregiver can be a source of stress (Tronick, 1982). This stress can arise from such factors as the mistiming of emotional signals, unclear signals, misreading of signals, and overloading or underloading of stimulation. From the perspective of the authors, coping with stress is broadly defined and not restricted to the child managing negative, adversive circumstances. Indeed, a case can be made that a certain level of stress, different for each child, is generative and promotes learning (Zeitlin, 1981).

Various researchers have described the coping process (Antonovsky, 1979; Haan, 1977; Lazarus & Folkman, 1984). Drawing from their work, the authors developed a coping model that is designed to be clinically useful. It provides a structure for understanding and analyzing the adaptive functioning of children. Through assessing the child's stressors, coping resources, and coping efforts, an intervention plan can be created to foster adaptation. This transactional model views coping as a four-step, interrelated process (see Figure 1). Although presented from a cognitive-behavioral orientation, it is recognized that the mental processes in infants and toddlers are not so clearly delineated.

Determination of Meaning of an Event

The coping process is initiated by an event occurring externally in the environment or internally within the child (e.g., a physical sensation, thought, or feeling). In the first step of the model, the meaning of the event is determined as it is filtered through the child's emerging belief system. Based upon this interpretation, the event may be perceived as harmful, threatening, or challenging. In the young child emerging beliefs develop over time through experience and are rudimentary and global (e.g., an evolving sense of personal agency such as "When I cry, my needs will be met.").

Determination of an Action Plan

When an event is identified as a stressor, the next step is to decide upon a course of action. Decision-making skills are limited in young children. An action plan is determined by the personal meaning of the event (whether it generates a positive or negative emotion), the internal resources the child can draw upon, and the external resources that are available to support a coping effort. External resources are the human supports provided by caregivers, and the material and environmental supports.

Key internal resources are the young child's emerging beliefs, physical and psycho-

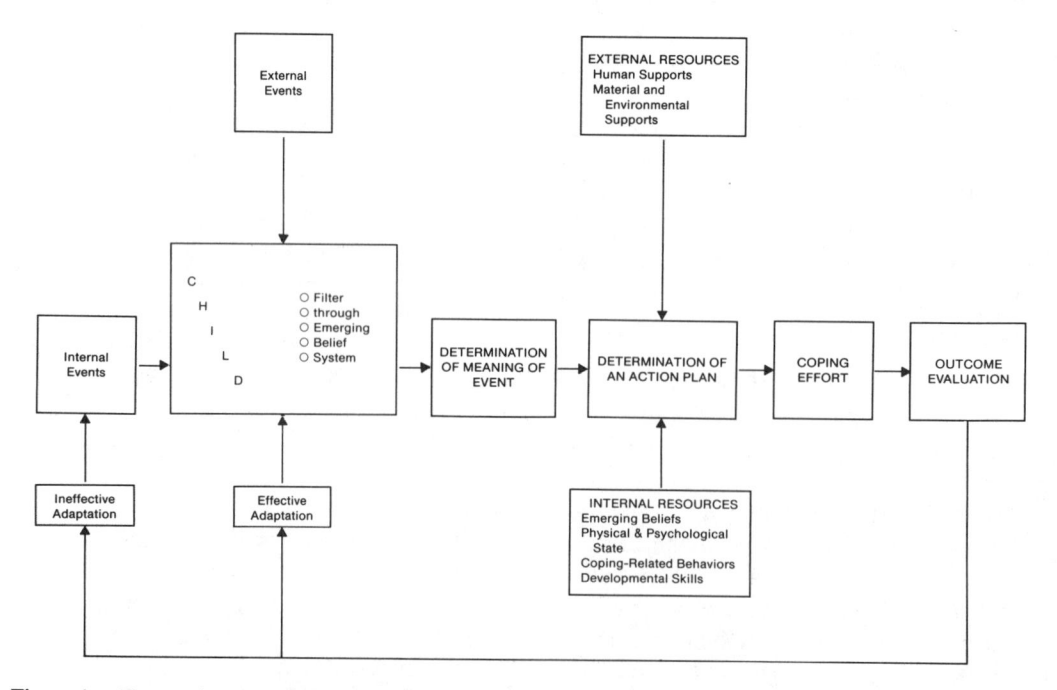

Figure 1. Transactional model of the coping process.

logical state, coping-related behaviors, and developmental skills. In this frame of reference coping-related behaviors reflect characteristics of the child that appear most related to adaptive functioning. They include task-oriented behaviors such as staying with an activity until it is completed, interactive behaviors such as reacting to social cues in the environment, and emotional behaviors such as being able to express a range of feelings. A further discussion of coping-related behaviors is presented later in the chapter. Within this model temperament is considered an influential factor in the expression of the more generic categories of physical and psychological state and coping-related behaviors.

Coping Effort

The third step in the process involves acting on the decision by making a coping effort that leads to some outcome. The coping effort can be action oriented to deal with the stressor, directed to managing the emotions associated with the stressor, or focused on modifying the related physical tension. The strategies applied in a specific situation often involve a combination of all three approaches. Many of the coping efforts of infants are targeted to eliciting the assistance of caregivers.

Evaluation of Outcome

The last step in the coping process involves evaluating the outcome of the coping effort. If the outcome is effective, the stress is reduced or alleviated and the cycle is completed. If the outcome is ineffective, the stress continues and may be viewed as an additional stressor, thereby generating another coping cycle.

Coping is a process that implies effort, not the success or failure of that effort. The effectiveness of those coping efforts is determined by the congruence or match between the child's actions and the situational demands (Lerner & East, 1984). This "goodness of fit" results when expectations and environmental demands are in accord with the child's resources. It does not imply an absence of stress and conflict, but rather the availability of resources to manage them. Poorness of fit can occur, even for a child with normally adequate resources, when environmental demands and expectations are excessive.

Thus coping effectiveness can range on a continuum from maladaptive to adaptive. There is growing evidence that adaptive coping enhances development and functional performance (Kennedy, 1984; Larson, 1984; Zeitlin, 1985). Effective coping appears to generate a sense of mastery that motivates the child to try new experiences when interacting with objects and people. Ineffective coping interferes with productive interaction and may foster over time additional stress and expectations of failure (Greenspan, 1988).

TEMPERAMENT

Temperament influences how a child copes and therefore how others respond to the child's coping efforts. Although temperament is defined in differing ways, most definitions reflect some variation of that originally postulated by Allport (1937):

Temperament refers to the characteristic phenomena of an individual's emotional nature, including his susceptibility to emotional stimulation, his customary strength and speed of response, the quality of his prevailing mood, and all the peculiarities of fluctuation and intensity of mood; these phenomena being regarded as dependent upon constitutional make-up, and therefore largely hereditary in origin. (p. 54)

There is general agreement that temperament is evidenced in behavioral tendencies rather than specific, discrete behaviors. Theorists emphasize its biological base and the relative continuity of these behavioral tendencies over time. It is recognized, however, that the expression of temperamental attributes is shaped and modified as a consequence of experience. The impact of temperament is most direct and evident in infancy, when idiosyncratic coping styles are developing.

A more comprehensive discussion of the current theories of temperament and how they differ is provided in the literature (Bates, 1987;

Goldsmith et al., 1987; Lamb & Bornstein, 1987). Theorists vary in their conceptual definitions and the set of dimensions that they consider temperamental in nature. For example, Buss and Plomin (1984) defined temperament as a set of early appearing, inherited personality traits (i.e., emotionality, activity, and sociability). Goldsmith and Campos (1986) considered temperament to reflect individual differences in primary emotions and arousal as expressed by the intensity and duration of behavioral responses. In the view of Rothbart and Derryberry (1981), temperament refers to constitutionally based differences in reactivity and self-regulation. By reactivity, they mean the biological sensitivity of the individual's response to changes in the environment. Self-regulation involves the attentional and behavioral patterns of approach and avoidance that are used to modulate this reactivity.

The work of Thomas and Chess (1977) deserves special note because of its influence on the study of temperament. They conceptualize temperament as the stylistic component of behavior—patterns in *how* actions are performed in contrast to the *why* (motivation) and *what* (content) of behavior. Their nine dimensions of temperament are: rhythmicity of biological functions, activity level, approach to or withdrawal from new stimuli, adaptability, sensory threshold, predominant quality of mood expression, distractibility, and persistence/attention span. In addition, they described three behavioral clusters that are designated as easy, difficult, and slow-to-warm-up temperament. The easy child is rhythmic, positive in initial approach, adaptive, mild in intensity, and positive in mood. The difficult child is irregular in rhythm, negative in approach (tends to withdraw), slow to adapt, intense, and negative in mood. The slow-to-warm-up child is low in activity, negative in approach, slow to adapt, mild in intensity, and negative in mood. Thomas and Chess emphasized that a substantial percentage of infants do not neatly fall into any of the three categories.

These dimensions and styles of temperament were derived from an investigation of a small number of children who initially participated in their New York Longitudinal Study (Thomas, Chess, & Birch, 1968). This seminal effort generated an array of research that examined their results. In general, their nine dimensions of temperament do not emerge in factor-analytic studies using scales designed to measure the dimensions (Hagekull, Lindhagen, & Bohlin, 1980; Lerner, Palermo, Spiro, & Nesselroade, 1982; Plomin & Rowe, 1977). There is some consensus in the field that the salient variables of temperament are fewer in number and are related to activity, reactivity, emotionality, and sociability (Goldsmith et al., 1987).

There is also a lack of agreement related to the concept of difficult temperament (Kagan, 1982; Plomin, 1982; Rothbart, 1982; Thomas, Chess, & Korn, 1982). In part this debate addresses the issue of whether difficultness is a social perception or an inherent characteristic of the child. Although Bates (1987) and Carey (1986) have varying definitions of difficult temperament, they both provide support for the validity and relevance of this construct.

The relation of temperament and coping is complex and not well understood. It appears, however, that temperament may influence coping in at least four ways (Campos, 1987; Lerner & East, 1984; Murphy & Moriarty, 1976). First, it may influence the child's exposure to potentially stressful situations. For example, an infant with a high activity level may vigorously explore the environment and therefore be confronted with a greater number of stressors. Second, temperament may determine the child's range of sensitivity to stress. An infant with strong sensory reactivity and arousal may have a low tolerance to environmental stimulation before becoming distressed. Third, temperament may influence the characteristic pattern of the child's coping efforts. For instance, it may modulate the latency, duration, and intensity of the infant's behavioral responses and emotional expression. Fourth, temperament may affect the availability of caregivers to assist the child's coping. Certain temperamental propensities may tend to evoke social support and shape parenting practices.

Werner and Smith (1982) monitored over an 18-year period the impact of a variety of biological and psychosocial risk factors, stressful life events, and protective factors on the development of an initial cohort of 698 infants. They found that certain temperamental characteristics played a role in influencing a child's resilience to stress and ability to cope. Activity level and social responsiveness were attributes that significantly differentiated resilient infants from those who later developed problems. The resilient children tended to have a positive socioemotional affect and an approach-oriented behavioral style. In contrast, nonresilient children tended to have a negative socioemotional affect and a withdrawal or ambivalent approach-withdrawal style.

ASSESSMENT OF TEMPERAMENT

The major approaches for assessing temperament are parent reports, observations of the child in the home, and laboratory procedures. Rothbart and Goldsmith (1985) have discussed the relative merits of each approach. For example, parent reports are based on a broad appreciation of the child and are economical to conduct but may be limited in objectivity. Home observations are performed in the child's naturalistic environment and are comparatively objective. However, observers usually collect a circumscribed amount of data in a small number of visits. Although laboratory investigation has the advantage of a precise, controlled format, the unfamiliar setting may restrict a representative sample of the child's behavior. A combination of assessment methods is generally recommended (Wilson & Matheny, 1983).

Parent questionnaires are the most frequently used measures of temperament. These instruments rely on the parent's perception of the child's temperament. It needs to be recognized that characteristics of the parents, such as their psychological and sociocultural status, may influence their rating of the questionnaire (Bates, Freeland, & Lounsbury, 1979; Sameroff, Seifer, & Elias, 1982). The importance of this rater bias depends in part on the purpose for conducting the assessment. From a clinical perspective, a primary interest *is* the parent's perception of the infant and its impact on interaction and caregiving (Carey, 1985; Chess & Thomas, 1986).

According to a review by Hubert, Wachs, Peters-Martin, and Gandour (1982), current temperament instruments vary greatly in their psychometric adequacy. They found generally high interrater reliability, moderate internal consistency and test-retest reliability, inconsistent stability data, and low interparent agreement coefficients. In addition, there were limited and inconsistent findings regarding concurrent and predictive validity as well as little convergence between instruments. They suggest that there is no single, psychometrically satisfactory measure of temperament.

Most of the infant temperament measures are designed for research purposes and not for direct clinical application. Two sample instruments are frequently employed in research studies. The Infant Behavior Questionnaire (Rothbart, 1981) is an 87-item tool that uses a 7-point parent rating scale based on the frequency of specific behaviors during the previous week. It assesses the dimensions of activity level, smiling and laughter, fear, distress to limitations (frustration), soothability, and duration of orienting. The Infant Characteristics Questionnaire (Bates et al., 1979) is a measure of temperamental difficultness. This instrument consists of 24 items scored on 7-point scales describing behavior. Its four dimensions are labeled fussy-difficult, unadaptable, dull, and unpredictable.

Two temperament instruments, based on the work of Chess and Thomas, were developed for use in clinical practice with young children: the Revised Infant Temperament Questionnaire (Carey & McDevitt, 1978) for children 4–8 months of age, and the Toddler Temperament Scale (Fullard, McDevitt, & Carey, 1978, 1984) for children 1–3 years of age. A discussion of these scales is warranted because of their popularity. Both instruments are similiar in construction and administration. Since the scale for toddlers covers a wider age range, it is described in some detail.

Toddler Temperament Scale

The Toddler Temperament Scale is used to assess the temperament of a child in order to contribute to an understanding of problems in behavior and to help the practitioner plan strategies of intervention that accommodate to the child's disposition. Results provide a basis for assisting parents to achieve a match between the child's behavioral style and child-rearing practices.

Description of the Instrument

The questionnaire has 97 behavioral items that assess the nine temperament dimensions described by Thomas and Chess. The instrument is rated by a parent or primary caregiver based upon current impressions and observations of the child. A 6-point rating scale is used indicating frequency of the behavior. For example, a rating of "1" indicates that the behavior is "almost never" observed. A rating of "6" suggests that the child exhibits the behavioral characteristic "almost always." A profile of the child is derived according to the nine temperament categories. Also, the child's temperament is classified as easy, difficult, slow-to-warm-up, or intermediate (i.e., no clearly defined behavioral style). Administration of the instrument takes 20–30 minutes, and scoring requires 10–25 minutes.

Items in the instrument address the child's behavioral pattern during daily activities. For example, the category of Rhythmicity considers whether the child gets sleepy at about the same time each evening, is consistent from day to day in the time of bowel movements, and is regular in appetite at the evening meal. Items in the category of Approach/Withdrawal include the child's reaction to seeing the doctor, having a new babysitter, or meeting another child for the first time. The Sensory Threshhold category examines such issues as the child's awareness of differences in the taste of familiar liquids, recognition of wet diapers, and reaction to a disliked food even when mixed with a preferred one. The Activity category includes how much the child moves when being dressed, whether the child fidgets during quiet activities, and how vigorously the child plays with toys in the house.

Technical Data

The Toddler Temperament Scale was standardized on 309 children in two pediatric practices (52% male). The majority of children were from white, middle-class families. Means and standard deviations are provided for children in the ranges of 12–23 months and 24–36 months. Hubert and her colleagues (1982) reported that the instrument has relatively high test-retest reliability, an acceptable level of internal consistency, and promising data related to its concurrent validity. As discussed previously, the nine dimensions of temperament do not appear to be conceptually independent and may be reduced to a fewer number of factors. Despite its relative psychometric limitations, the instrument continues to be used because its findings are helpful in planning intervention.

ASSESSMENT OF COPING

There is a dearth of available instruments designed to assess the coping of young children. A related tool in popular use is the Vineland Adaptive Behavior Scales (Sparrow, Balla, & Cicchetti, 1984). Although not a measure of coping per se, it is a standardized instrument that assesses the acquisition of developmental skills associated with a child's personal and social sufficiency. In response to the need for a clinically relevant instrument that is targeted to coping, the authors developed the Early Coping Inventory as a measure of adaptive functioning (Zeitlin, Williamson, & Szczepanski, 1988).

Early Coping Inventory

The Early Coping Inventory is used to determine the effectiveness of coping-related behaviors of children in the age range of 4–36 months. Coping-related behaviors are the repertoire of behaviors the child draws upon to manage the opportunities, challenges, and frustrations encountered in daily living. Each item in the instrument specifies a behavioral characteristic documented in the research literature or identified by expert clinical judgment as important to coping in young children. Since coping is an integrated process, items in the inventory tap a range of domains—temperament, sensory processing, motor control, psychological functions, and socioemotional factors. Coping is related to, but different from, any single contributing variable such as intelligence, language, temperament, or social competence (McNamee, 1982; Murphy & Moriarty, 1976).

The instrument does not assess coping efforts (i.e., skills or strategies used in a specific situation) but instead the broad behaviors, attributes, or competencies of the child that serve as a resource to support coping efforts. The specific actions by which a coping-related behavior is demonstrated vary. For example, "the ability to initiate action to communicate a need" is an item in the Early Coping Inventory that is representative of coping at all ages. However, the actual coping efforts used to implement this capacity are influenced by the child's developmental age: a 6-month-old infant may initiate actions to get needs met by crying or changing body posture; a 12-month-old infant may indicate a desire for an object by pointing; and a 2-year-old toddler may indicate needs or preferences by using words. Thus coping-related behaviors reflect the general capabilities of the child that influence the generation of purposeful, effortful responses to the multiple demands of functional living.

Description of the Instrument

The Early Coping Inventory consists of 48 items divided equally into three categories—Sensorimotor Organization, Reactive Behavior, and Self-Initiated Behavior (see Table 1). The three categories are not mutually exclusive but are used to group coping-related behaviors in order to foster systematic observation and description of the child. The instrument is primarily designed to be rated by professionals in their educational and therapeutic practice. The amount of time spent observing the child is determined by one's previous knowledge of the child and the amount and type of activity taking place during observation. For example, a child who is familiar to the rater may be rated from personal knowledge and prior experience, whereas planned and systematic observation is required for an unfamiliar child.

Sensorimotor organization refers to behaviors used to regulate psychophysiological functions and to integrate sensory and motor

Table 1. Sample items of the Early Coping Inventory

Sensorimotor Organization					
Child adapts to being moved by others during physical handling and caregiving.	1	2	3	4	5
Child organizes information from the different senses simultaneously for a response (e.g., combines looking, listening, and touching in exploring a toy).	1	2	3	4	5
Reactive Behavior					
Child accepts warmth and support from familiar persons.	1	2	3	4	5
Child responds to vocal or gestural direction.	1	2	3	4	5
Self-Initiated Behavior					
Child changes behavior when necessary to solve a problem or achieve a goal.	1	2	3	4	5
Child balances independent behavior with necessary dependence on adults.	1	2	3	4	5

Note: See page 222 for an explanation of the 5-point rating scale.

processes. Representative items in this category include the ability to demonstrate coordinated movement, to adapt to a range of intensity of touch, and to maintain visual attention to people and objects.

Reactive behaviors are actions used to respond to demands of the physical and social environments. Sample reactive behaviors include the ability to react to the feelings and moods of others, to adapt to changes in the environment, and to bounce back after stressful situations.

Self-initiated behaviors are autonomously generated, self-directed actions used to meet personal needs and to interact with objects and people. Whereas reactive behaviors are closely contingent upon environmental cues, self-initiated behaviors are more spontaneous and intrinsically motivated. They include the ability to demonstrate persistence during activities, to initiate interactions with others, and to apply previously acquired behaviors to new situations.

A 5-point rating scale measures the range of coping effectiveness. A rating of "1" indicates that the behavior is not effective. A rating of "2" implies that the behavior is minimally effective (i.e., inconsistent, rigidly repetitious, or generates negative outcomes over time). A rating of "3" suggests that the behavior is situationally effective. Behavior used in one type of situation is not generalized to other types of situations. A rating of "4" indicates that the behavior is effective more often than not (i.e., behavior is generalized to a variety of situations). The assignment of "5" to an item signifies that the behavior is consistently effective across situations.

In the qualitative rating scale, "effective" means the behavior is: 1) appropriate for the situations, 2) appropriate for the child's *developmental age,* and 3) successfully used by the child. Behaviors are not elicited in a test situation. Instead ratings are assigned following observations of the child in a variety of circumstances (e.g., in the presence and absence of caregivers, in familiar and novel settings, in one-to-one and small group situations). Varied observations of the child across situations are important for a representative assessment of coping-related behaviors.

The Early Coping Inventory yields three types of information. An Adaptive Behavior Index provides a global measure of the child's coping competence. It assists the practitioner in determining the extent of intervention that is required and encourages the setting of realistic expectations for outcome. A Coping Profile compares the child's level of effectiveness in the three behavioral categories (Sensorimotor Organization, Reactive Behavior, Self-Initiated Behavior). This presentation of the child's coping style helps to establish a primary focus for intervention. A listing of Most and Least Adaptive Coping Behaviors, identifying the child's specific coping-related strengths and vulnerabilities, guides the formulation of goals, objectives, and strategies for intervention. One can learn to use the Early Coping Inventory by reading its manual. Rating and scoring the instrument takes approximately 30 minutes in total.

Technical Data

Psychometric validation of the instrument is based on a series of studies that established its construct and content validity, interrater reliability, test-retest reliability, and item reliability. Interrater reliability coefficients of the three behavioral categories range from .80 to .94. Part of the technical data describes a large field study of 1,440 disabled and nondisabled infants and toddlers. The nondisabled group was further subdivided by family income above and below $10,000 a year. The coping ability of the disabled group was significantly less effective than the nondisabled group in all three categories of the instrument. In addition, the children from economically disadvantaged circumstances were less effective as a group than their peers with family income over $10,000.

CHILDREN WITH SPECIAL NEEDS

Research findings are mixed regarding the question of whether children with handicapping conditions are more prone to be temperamentally difficult. A study by Baron (1972) found that infants with Down syndrome had temperaments generally comparable to those of nondisabled infants, whereas other studies suggest that they are more difficult (Bridges & Cicchetti, 1982; Rothbart & Hanson, 1983). In an investigation of a varied group of toddlers with special needs (e.g., Down syndrome, cerebral palsy, epilepsy), there was no significant difference in their difficultness, but they were lower in activity and persistence (Heffernan, Black, & Poche, 1982). Greenberg and Field (1982) reported that nondisabled infants and those with Down syndrome had less difficult temperaments than those with cerebral palsy and sensory impairments.

Carlton (1988) studied the relationship of temperament and coping effectiveness of disabled and nondisabled young children using the Toddler Temperament Scale and the Early Coping Inventory. She found that there was no significant difference in the temperamental qualities of the two groups except for activity level. However, the handicapped group was significantly less effective in their coping-related behaviors involving sensorimotor organization and self-initiation. There were some correlations between dimensions of the two instruments. For example, in both groups higher threshhold levels of responsiveness tended to be related to more adaptive coping. Likewise, persistence was related in both groups to high effectiveness scores in self-initiated coping.

Other studies using the Early Coping Inventory have found similar results. Developmentally delayed and disabled children under 3 years of age are less effective as a group in their coping-related behaviors than their nondisabled peers (Williamson et al., 1989; Zeitlin et al., 1988). They appear particularly less competent in self-initiated behaviors. Comparable findings are documented with older disabled children (Lorch, 1981; Zeitlin, 1985). It is important to emphasize, however, that the presence of a handicapping condition does not imply that a particular child will have ineffective coping patterns. Rather, it suggests a higher degree of vulnerability to the stresses of daily living.

It appears that children with special needs frequently have fewer resources to support adaptive coping efforts. A handicapping condition may limit the acquisition of developmental skills, and thereby restrict the variety and sophistication of available coping strategies. Parents may be less accessible as a supportive external resource if they are experiencing psychological distress or exhaustion from the requirements of daily caregiving (Gallagher, Beckman, & Cross, 1983). Also, chronically ill or disabled children have to manage additional stressors such as treatment regimens, hospitalization, restrictions in activity, and disruptions in daily routines (Drotar, Crawford, & Ganofsky, 1984). Thus, they frequently face a greater number of stressors with a limited repertoire of coping resources.

IMPLICATIONS FOR INTERVENTION

Assessment of temperament contributes to an understanding of the infant's constitutional responsivity to the environment and self-regulation. For instance, temperament may influence the ability to cope with an unfamiliar situation by modulating the degree of sensitivity and susceptibility of the infant to new stimuli. It may also shape the temporal and intensive parameters of the child's coping efforts (e.g., the speed and strength of crying, reaching out, or crawling away). An appreciation of the child's temperamental attributes enables parents to modify their caregiving to encourage adaptive functioning. For example, flexible schedules may be useful for the arrhythmic infant and the older child who has low persistence and high distractibility (e.g., difficult to soothe when upset.) For the toddler who adapts slowly and tends to withdraw, advance warning of changes may provide time to adjust (Carey, 1986).

Although temperament is important, it is only one factor that influences the coping of a child (Kagan, 1984). Even an infant with a difficult temperament may cope adaptively if caring adults are responsive to the child's unique coping style. There is growing recognition that many children with special needs may be more successful in managing the challenges of daily living if they can be taught to cope more effectively. It appears that children with marginal coping styles continue to use ineffective strategies in order to avoid or gain control over stressful situations or because of a lack of alternative coping strategies (McNamee, 1982). The goal of intervention, therefore, is to establish a better match between environmental demands and expectations and the infant's coping resources. In this process the infant adapts previously learned coping strategies and acquires new ones.

There are three primary intervention options, based on the coping process, that foster this goodness of fit (Williamson & Zeitlin, in press): 1) parents and professionals can *change demands* to be congruent with the child's capabilities by establishing appropriate goals and grading stressors; 2) they can change the child's coping efforts by *enhancing developmental skills and other coping resources* through such practices as modeling, cueing, and structuring the environment for learning; and 3) they can *change their responses* to the child's efforts by responding contingently. It seems particularly critical that adults provide positive feedback to the infant's self-generated, purposeful behavior. Through a shared understanding of the child's temperament and coping style, parents and professionals are better able to facilitate adaptive outcomes for the child.

REFERENCES

Allport, G.W. (1937). *Personality: A psychosocial interpretation.* New York: Holt.

Antonovsky, A. (1979). *Health, stress, and coping.* San Francisco: Jossey-Bass.

Baron, J. (1972). Temperamental profile of children with Down's syndrome. *Developmental Medicine and Child Neurology, 14,* 640–643.

Bates, J.E. (1987). Temperament in infancy. In J.D. Osofsky (Ed.), *Handbook of infant development* (2nd ed.) (pp. 1101–1149). New York: John Wiley & Sons.

Bates, J.E., Freeland, C.A.B., & Lounsbury, M.L. (1979). Measurement of infant difficultness. *Child Development, 50,* 794–803.

Bridges, F.A., & Cicchetti, D. (1982). Mothers' ratings of the temperament characteristics of Down syndrome infants. *Developmental Psychology, 18,* 238–244.

Buss, A.H., & Plomin, R. (1984). *Temperament: Early developing personality traits.* Hillsdale, NJ: Lawrence Erlbaum Associates.

Campos, B.E. (1987). Coping with stress during childhood and adolescence. *Psychological Bulletin, 101,* 393–403.

Carey, W.B. (1985). Clinical use of temperament data in pediatrics. *Developmental and Behavioral Pediatrics, 6,* 137–142.

Carey, W.B. (1986). The difficult child. *Pediatrics in Review, 8,* 39–45.

Carey, W.B., & McDevitt, S.C. (1978). Revision of the Infant Temperament Questionnaire. *Pediatrics, 61,* 735–739.

Carlton, S.B. (1988). *The relationship between temperament and coping in handicapped and nonhandicapped infants and young children.* Unpublished doctoral dissertation, Rutgers, The State University of New Jersey, New Brunswick.

Chess, S., & Thomas, A. (1986). *Temperament in clinical practice.* New York: Guilford Press.

Drotar, D., Crawford, P., & Ganofsky, M.A. (1984). Prevention with chronically ill children. In M.C. Roberts & L. Peterson (Eds.), *Prevention of problems in children* (pp. 232–265). New York: John Wiley & Sons.

Fullard, W., McDevitt, S.C., & Carey, W.B. (1978). *The Toddler Temperament Scale.* Unpublished manuscript, Temple University, Department of Educational Psychology.

Fullard, W., McDevitt, S.C., & Carey, W.B. (1984). Assessing temperament in one- to three-year-old children. *Journal of Pediatric Psychology, 9,* 205–217.

Gallagher, J.J., Beckman, P., & Cross, A.H. (1983). Families of handicapped children: Sources of stress and its amelioration. *Exceptional Children, 50,* 10–19.

Goldsmith, H.H., Buss, A.H., Plomin, R., Rothbart, M.K., Thomas, A., Chess, S., Hinde, R.A., & McCall, R.B. (1987). Roundtable: What is temperament? Four approaches. *Child Development, 58,* 505–529.

Goldsmith, H.H., & Campos, J.J. (1986). Fundamental issues in the study of early temperament: The Denver twin temperament study. In M.E. Lamb, A.L. Brown, & B. Rogoff (Eds.), *Advances in developmental psychology* (Vol. 4, pp. 231–283). Hillsdale, NJ: Lawrence Erlbaum Associates.

Greenberg, R., & Field, T. (1982). Temperamental ratings of handicapped infants during classroom, mother, and teacher interaction. *Journal of Pediatric Psychology, 7,* 387–405.

Greenspan, S.I. (1988). Fostering emotional and social development in infants with disabilities. *Zero to Three, 9*(1), 8–18.

Haan, N. (1977). *Coping and defending: Processes of self-environment organization.* New York: Academic Press.

Hagekull, B., Lindhagen, K., & Bohlin, G. (1980). Behavioral dimensions in one-year-olds and dimensional stability in infancy. *International Journal of Behavioral Development, 3,* 351–364.

Heffernan, L., Black, F.W., & Poche, P. (1982). Temperament patterns in young neurologically impaired children. *Journal of Pediatric Psychology, 7,* 415–423.

Hubert, N.C., Wachs, T.D., Peters-Martin, P., & Gandour, M.J. (1982). The study of early temperament: Measurement and conceptual issues. *Child Development, 53,* 571–600.

Kagan, J. (1982). Comments on the construct of difficult temperament. *Merrill-Palmer Quarterly, 28,* 21–24.

Kagan, J. (1983). Stress and coping in early development. In N. Garmezy & M. Rutter (Eds.), *Stress, coping and development in children* (pp. 191–216). New York: McGraw-Hill.

Kagan, J. (1984). *The nature of the child.* New York: Basic Books.

Kennedy, B. (1984). *The relationship of coping behaviors and attribution of success to effort and school achievement of elementary school children.* Unpublished doctoral dissertation, State University of New York, Albany, NY.

Lamb, M.E., & Bornstein, M.H. (1987). *Development in infancy: An introduction* (2nd ed.). New York: Random House.

Larson, J.G. (1984). Relationship between coping behavior and achievement in kindergarten children. *Dissertation Abstracts International, 45,* 2389A. (University Microfilms No. 84-15514, 147)

Lazarus, R., & Folkman, S. (1984). *Stress, appraisal and coping.* New York: Springer-Verlag.

Lerner, R.M., & East, P.L. (1984). The role of temperament in stress, coping and socioemotional functioning in early development. *Infant Mental Health Journal, 5,* 148–159.

Lerner, R.M., Palermo, M., Spiro, A., & Nesselroade, J.R. (1982). Assessing the dimensions of temperamental individuality across the life span: The Dimensions of Temperament Survey (DOTS). *Child Development, 53,* 149–159.

Lipsitt, L. (1983). Stress in infancy: Toward understanding the origins of coping behavior. In N. Garmezy & M. Rutter (Eds.), *Stress, coping and development in children* (pp. 161–190). New York: McGraw-Hill.

Lorch, N. (1981). Coping behavior in preschool children with cerebral palsy. *Dissertation Abstracts International, 42,* 3431B. (University Microfilms No. 81-24310, 135)

McNamee, A.G. (1982). *Children and stress: Helping children cope.* Washington, DC: Association for Childhood Education International.

Murphy, L.B., & Moriarty, A.E. (1976). *Vulnerability, coping, and growth.* New Haven: Yale University Press.

Plomin, R. (1982). The difficult concept of temperament: A response to Thomas, Chess, and Korn. *Merrill-Palmer Quarterly, 28,* 25–33.

Plomin, R., & Rowe, D.C. (1977). A twin study of temperament in young children. *Journal of Psychology, 97,* 107–113.

Rothbart, M.K. (1981). Measurement of temperament in infancy. *Child Development, 52,* 569–578.

Rothbart, M.K. (1982). The concept of difficult temperament: A critical analysis. *Merrill-Palmer Quarterly, 28,* 35–40.

Rothbart, M.K., & Derryberry, D. (1981). Development of individual differences in temperament. In M.E. Lamb & A.L. Brown (Eds.), *Advances in Developmental Psychology* (Vol. 1, pp. 37–86). Hillsdale, NJ: Lawrence Erlbaum Associates.

Rothbart, M.K., & Goldsmith, H.H. (1985). Three approaches to the study of infant temperament. *Developmental Review, 5,* 237–260.

Rothbart, M.K., & Hanson, M.J. (1983). A caregiver report comparison of temperamental characteristics of Down syndrome and normal infants. *Developmental Psychology, 19,* 766–769.

Sameroff, A.J., Seifer, R., & Elias, P.K. (1982). Sociocultural variability in infant temperament ratings. *Child Development, 53,* 164–173.

Sparrow, S.S., Balla, D.A., & Cicchetti, D.V. (1984). *Vineland Adaptive Behavior Scales.* Circle Pines, MN: American Guidance Service.

Thomas, A., & Chess, S. (1977). *Temperament and development.* New York: Brunner/Mazel.

Thomas, A., Chess, S., & Birch, H. (1968). *Temperament and behavior disorders in children.* New York: New York University Press.

Thomas, A., Chess, S., & Korn, S.J. (1982). The reality of difficult temperament. *Merrill-Palmer Quarterly, 28,* 1–20.

Tronick, E. (1982). *Social interchange in infancy.* Baltimore: University Park Press.

Werner, E., & Smith, R. (1982). *Vulnerable but invincible: A longitudinal study of resilient children and youth.* New York: McGraw-Hill.

Williamson, G.G., & Zeitlin, S. (in press). *Coping in young children: Early intervention to enhance development and adaptive behavior.* Baltimore: Paul H. Brookes Publishing Co.

Williamson, G.G., Zeitlin, S., & Szczepanski, M.

(1989). Coping behavior: Implications for disabled infants and toddlers. *Infant Mental Health Journal, 10,* 3–13.

Wilson, R.S., & Matheny, A.P. (1983). Assessment of temperament in infant twins. *Developmental Psychology, 19.* 172–183.

Zeitlin, S. (1981). Coping, stress, and learning. *Journal of the Division for Early Childhood, 2,* 102–108.

Zeitlin, S. (1985). *Coping Inventory.* Bensenville, IL: Scholastic Testing Service.

Zeitlin, S., Williamson, G.G., & Szczepanski, M. (1988). *Early Coping Inventory.* Bensenville, IL: Scholastic Testing Service.

Zeitlin, S., Williamson, G.G., & Rosenblatt, W.P. (1987). The coping with stress model: A counseling approach for families with a handicapped child. *Journal of Counseling and Development, 65,* 443–446.

15 Measures of Parent-Child Interaction

Dale C. Farran, Kathryn A. Clark, and Adele R. Ray

ISSUES IN PARENT-CHILD INTERACTION MEASURES

Rationale for Examining Parent-Child Interactions

The passage of PL 99-457, with its emphasis on the development of an Individualized Family Service Plan that builds on family strengths and needs in determining intervention for handicapped infants and toddlers, has dramatically increased the need for and interest in measures of parenting. Even before the passage of this amendment to the Education for All Handicapped Children Act, professionals and practitioners were interested in describing more fully the parent side of the parent-child dyad. This interest stemmed from several sources: 1) a desire to understand parental behaviors in order to plan more effective and appropriate intervention plans, especially in programs that concentrated on the whole family; and 2) a sense that change for some infants was going to be very hard to effect, but that families were benefiting from the intervention provided, a benefit going unmeasured in the usual evaluations proposed.

Before a program adopts any parent-child behavioral assessment measure, important issues must be considered. Since the 1920s, developmental psychology has wrestled with the idea of vulnerabilty in young children. Both the dynamic and the behavioral perspectives assume that the child from infancy is influenced by the specific environment in which he or she is developing; this vulnerability has been thought to be more pronounced in the area of social development (the notion of immutable, innate intelligence was only seriously challenged with the publication of J. McVicker Hunt's *Intelligence and Experience* in 1961). It is not clear, however, how much difference early experiences make with regard to later functioning; for example, there are no longitudinal data that clearly link variations in early parent-child interactions with later social development. The best predictors of negative social outcomes (antisocial behavior, occupational and marital instability) appear to be a combination of predispositions in the infant (e.g., temperament) coupled with dramatic interruptive experiences or chronic stresses in the early years of life (Farran & Cooper, 1986). Thus, for infants in relatively normal circumstances, it may not be helpful to measure subtle, small differences in parenting interactions.

Parenting interactions for infants in unusual situations are likely to reflect the current environmental situation (poverty, high stress) and to interact with the environment to influence the baby's development. The interaction between parenting behaviors and the environment, however, has not been successfully described in ways practitioners could use in intervention programs. (What kinds of parenting behaviors are most successful in helping a developmentally delayed child cope with poverty? How can parents aid a chronically ill child in dealing with teachers and peers?) Too often, the modal parenting pattern exhibited by middle-class, stable families is presumed to be the normative one, applicable in situations that are far different in character and intensity. One benefit to using the types of scales reviewed in this chapter is the new information they may generate on the coping behaviors of parents.

Different disciplines will make different decisions about which parenting behaviors are most important to examine. Physical and occupational therapists will pay more attention to the physically therapeutic aspects of the parent's behavior. Nurses and other therapists have been more interested in feeding interactions. Even within a single discipline such as psychology, different theoretical perspectives have focused observations differently. For example, the dynamic perspective assumes that infants can experience complex emotions well before they have language sophisticated enough either to understand or to express the nuances of adult emotional states. Cognitive developmentalists are unlikely to concern themselves with using categories like "anxiety" or "avoidance" and more likely to focus on a behavior like "mutual play," whereas behaviorists examine behaviors in terms of a sequence including antecedents and consequences. Most practitioners have had little opportunity to determine their individual theoretical orientations and no chance to compare those orientations with others in the same agency who may be working with the same families. Choosing an instrument with a different theoretical perspective from one's own can make the "scores" less than interpretable.

Finally, another issue involves the larger context surrounding the parent-child dyad. This context can include the extended family; in some cultures the extended kin network is much more involved in child care than it is in the mainland United States. Within the kin network, there is likely to be more role diffusion. Mothers may not carry out the "playmate" role; that role may be left to the grandmother, a favorite aunt, an older sibling, or a cousin (Farran & Mistry, 1987). Assessing the parent's play behavior will tell the practitioner little about the amount or quality of play stimulation the child is receiving if that role is routinely handled by someone else.

Utility of Parent-Child Descriptions

Despite the problems outlined above, a description of parent-child interactions can often be a helpful supplement to the understanding of a family before an intervention plan is adopted. These descriptions should be thought of as another piece of the puzzle in fully understanding a particular family. They should be combined with information about the child, the kin network, and the larger social context surrounding the family. Only when all these aspects are understood can appropriate interventions be planned. Occasionally parent-child observations can provide the primary source for intervention planning; behaviors rated on a scale can be the target of the program and its success can be measured by gains on the parent-child interaction scale. This use of scale data is fairly rare, perhaps reserved for first-time, inexperienced, motivated parents or experienced, confident parents in a novel situation.

The most effective interventions are going to be those that build on a family's existing strengths. Unfortunately the tendency is to focus on the areas of a scale where a parent was not rated as high as other areas, leading to a deficit orientation. In most scales, it should be possible to find the areas where the parent scored well; those areas are the ones that should be singled out for praise and attention. If a scale will allow the observer to determine parent strengths, those can form the basis for a sound intervention plan that may be focused on aspects of the child's development unrelated to parenting per se. In fact, a treatment plan for the child is only truly individualized if, in addition to the target skills chosen for the child, the intervention strategies are based on the particular capabilities of the parent to carry them out.

Observational Setting

Choice of Setting

Assuming that you have decided to go ahead with a standard description of parenting behavior, the next decision is where to conduct the observations. With some scales (e.g., the Barnard Scales), the situation is predetermined by the use of the scale; these kinds of scales instruct the observer where and how to structure the observation. Others are more flexible. They can be used in naturalistic settings such as homes and clinics as well as in laboratory rooms where the coding is either done live through a one-way mirror or from videotapes.

More and more programs have the luxury of videotape facilities, which makes it easy to introduce a videotaped session of parent-child interaction into regular assessment visits. In some cases, videotapes of parent-child interaction sessions can be very productive and useful. When observing a videotape, one can watch and rewatch interactions, pausing as needed to reflect on various interactions or behaviors. From this type of objective viewing, along with the use of a parent-child interaction measure, the interventionist can gain insight into the dyad's style, such as typical antecedents and responses to various behaviors. This, in turn, can provide the basis for developing appropriate and tailored interventions. In fact, videotapes can be viewed jointly with families and used as a teaching tool. On the other hand, overzealous use of videotapes can be intrusive to families and a burden to staff. For example, some parents are extremely uncomfortable being videotaped and cannot act naturally during the taping. Videotapes can also seduce program planners into more complicated observational systems than they may actually need and certainly more than they can spare the time to learn and practice. Thus, the use of videotapes should be considered carefully and undertaken only when there are clearly defined and important uses for the information.

Length and Number of Sessions

There is considerable disagreement among the scales we studied over how long the session should be even for scales that were presumably looking at the same behaviors. Most scales suggest observing parent and child for around 20 minutes. Any shorter sessions probably will create problems in reliability and concerns about validity. The issues of length are most critical in the laboratory, where questions about validity can be legitimately raised—it may take mothers 5–10 minutes to acclimate to the laboratory observation room, and some groups of mothers may require more time, notably mothers who are very different from the assessor in ethnicity, religion, and/or social class.

There is also concern as to how often the sessions should be repeated. Few ongoing programs have the luxury of initially observing parents and children several times. It might be possible to improve the accuracy of the observations if the usual intake procedure for a family takes several days, either by having more than one staff member complete the rating scale or by having the same staff person complete one at the beginning and one at the end of the process, comparing perceptions across time.

Summary

The issues raised in this section should help focus discussion in any agency interested in adopting parent-child interaction measures as a part of its assessment and planning for families with handicapped children. The following section presents nine rating scales/observation procedures most likely to be the ones considered for practitioner use. We have arranged their descriptions alphabetically and have not endorsed any specific scale. Each of these could be appropriate for an agency or program depending on the specific focus and form of the services offered to parents. We believe that the first determinant of which scale to use should be a discussion among the clinical staff as to the purpose of using the scale, the information desired from it, and the theoretical orientation of the staff, utilizing issues raised at the beginning of this chapter as a guide for discussion. The second consideration must be the ease of training and availability of the scale.

SPECIFIC SCALES

Specific comparisons of the nine scales chosen are included in Table 1; references for

Table 1. Descriptive characteristics of nine parent-child interaction scales

Intended populations	Types of behaviors a. Parents b. Child c. Dyadic	Overall scale organization	Item level organization

Barnard Teaching Scale and Barnard Feeding Scale (NCAST) (1978 version)

| Mothers at medical risk during pregnancy, delivery, or postnatally; prematurity; failure to thrive; neglect and abuse. Infants 6–36 months. | a. 50 parent items in feeding and 50 parent behaviors in teaching covering such areas as sensitivity to cues, response to distress, social-emotional and cognitive growth fostering.
b. 26 child behaviors in feeding and 23 behaviors in teaching, covering such areas as clarity of cues and responsiveness to parent.
c. None. | Behaviors clustered by category (major types of behavior); parent and child items are listed separately; feeding and teaching are separate. | Binary scale for occurrence/nonoccurrence of 149 total behaviors. |

Greenspan-Lieberman Observation System for Assessment of Caregiver-Infant Interaction during Semi-Structured Play (GLOS)

| Poverty; adolescent mothers; drug abusing mothers; motorically impaired infants; psychiatrically ill mothers; normative. Infants ages 2–12 months (adaptations have been made for newborns and infants/toddlers). | a. 53 behaviors covering areas such as mother's relationship with her infant's body; pleasurable, neutral, or aversive tactile experiences; contingent responses to infant behaviors.
b. 43 child behaviors covering areas such as seeking or avoiding physical contact with caregiver and infant's responses to mother's behaviors.
c. None. | Behaviors are listed alphabetically by acronym. Parent and child behaviors grouped separately. | Behaviors are counted in 15-second intervals; combinations of behaviors indicate other behaviors. A shorter version uses a 5-page rating system; each of 80 behaviors is rated once in terms of percentage of occurrence in the session. |

Interpersonal Behavior Construct

| Cerebral palsy; mild to moderate mentally retarded; developmentally delayed. Children ages 2–10 years. | a. Measures of parental involvement and responsiveness to child.
b. Measures of child involvement and responsiveness to parent.
c. Contingency patterns of the joint occurrence of parent and child behaviors. | Twenty-three items grouped into eight clusters of major types of behavior. Same groupings used for both parent and child. | Three categories of behavior are coded for duration across 10-second time intervals; five categories of behavior are coded for frequency (once per 10-second interval). Contingencies are calculated by the cooccurrence of parent and child behaviors in the same 4-second interval. |

Observational session
  a. Length
  b. Structure
  c. Setting
	Training	Reliability
		  a. Interjudge
		  b. Stability
			Validity

a. Not specified b. Natural feeding situation for dyad; and structured session with two tasks for mother to teach, one at age level and one higher. c. Home, day care center, or clinic.	Two- to 3-day course conducted by certified Barnard trainers. Training utilizes four standard videotapes of feeding interaction. At least five field observations required, across ages birth to 12 months with normal infants. Training done in pairs.	a. During training, 65% agreement with one of four practice tapes; 85% agreement in three of five field home visits. Certificate awarded when these levels are achieved. Correlations of .70–.83 for two observers for feeding scale and .79–.83 for teaching scale. b. Comparisons across four-month span showed mother's behaviors more stable than child's (neither significant).	Moderate to high correlations between the Feeding Scale and the HOME concurrently and across time. Moderate correlations between the Teaching Scale and developmental outcomes as old as 36 months. Has been used to measure changes in interaction from intervention with premature infants (no effects shown).
a. 12 minutes. b. 3–5 minutes with mother-infant-observer, followed by 5–7 minutes with mother-infant alone in semistructured free play. Only the last portion is coded. c. Videotaped with time generator in laboratory playroom.	Three days' intensive training with designated experienced coder plus ½ day for each age group to be coded. Toddler version takes an additional 2 days. Written manual available (continually under revision).	a. Correlations of .80 between two observers except for .70 for the 2–3 affect codes. In practice, individual projects are having tapes coded by original, experienced coders for a fee. b. None specified.	Adolescent mothers compared to young adult mothers were less vocal with their 6-month-olds and more detached, more negative, and less vocal with their 24-month-olds. Some behaviors related to developmental outcomes at 6 and 24 months.
a. 30 minutes. b. Free play. c. Videotaped in laboratory or play room.	None specified. Written manual available.	a. 85% agreement between members of project staff; consensus coding with third observer to resolve differences. Ongoing reliability checks recommended. b. None established.	Parents of developmentally delayed infants show affect differences compared to normal; parents of severely handicapped infants show interactive differences compared to normal. Detects changes in interactions associated with behavioral coaching.

continued

Table 1. (*continued*)

Intended populations	Types of behaviors a. Parents b. Child c. Dyadic	Overall scale organization	Item level organization
Maternal Behavior Rating Scale			
Organically impaired, mentally retarded infants. Infants 12–36 months.	a. 18 interactive behaviors covering cognitive and social stimulation and response. b. 4 child behaviors indicating types of reaction to maternal stimulation. c. None.	Listing of 18 maternal behaviors with definitions. Yields 18 scores; not summarizable across behaviors.	Eighteen behaviors rated on a 1–5 scale; each point on the scale is behaviorally anchored. No child category definitions provided.
Parent Behavior Progression			
Handicapped and developmentally delayed; premature and low birth weight. Infants from birth to 36 months.	a. First three levels comprise affective behaviors believed to facilitate attachment. Last three levels consist of behaviors important for facilitating cognitive growth. b. Biological and social behaviors of infants provided in a supplement to PBP. c. None.	Seventeen behaviors clustered into six levels, creating a quasi-hierarchy of interactions from emotional to cognitive. Scores can be summarized across levels 1–3 and 4–6 separately for maximum total of 18 points.	Binary checklist for reported or observed behavior under each level.
Parent/Caregiver Involvement Scale			
Normative; families with handicapped child; poverty; adolescent mothers. Infants ages 3–36 months (application to older preschoolers underway).	a. 11 behaviors in major interactive modalities linked to cognitive and emotional growth (vocalizations, proximity, mutual play). b. None. c. Five general items rating overall interactive pattern.	Eleven behaviors rated along each of three dimensions: Amount, Quality, Developmental Appropriateness. Each dimension can be summarized across all 11 behaviors. (Checklist provided for rating from videotaped interactions.)	Behaviors rated on a 1–5 scale; odd-numbered points behaviorally anchored. Single rating and summary sheet accompanies manual.

Observational session
  a. Length
  b. Structure
  c. Setting
	Training	Reliability
		  a. Interjudge
		  b. Stability
			Validity

a. 20 minutes, code 10 minutes only. b. Free play with standard set of toys. c. Videotaped home observations.	Fifty hours. Written manual available.	a. Correlations of .76–.81 between two observers across all behaviors of exact agreement. Correlations within one point of .93–1.00. b. None specified.	Three factors derived from the scale accounted for 23% of the variance on Bayley MDI scores (concurrent). Two similar factors from shorter version.
a. 2–3 home visits of 1–1.5 hours each. b. Naturalistic observation. c. Home.	None specifically described; recommended for staff experienced in working with infants and parents.	a. Interrater agreement ranged from 33% to 100% across all behaviors. b. Correlations between consecutive ratings made at 4-month intervals ranged from .31 to .78.	HOME scores at 9 months correlated with PBP at 4, 8, and 12 months ($r = .47$, .69, and .75). HOME scores at 18 months correlated with PEP at 12 and 18 months ($r = .42$ and .60). Has distinguished parenting styles of mothers undergoing stress; has been related to infant developmental test scores.
a. 20 minutes of continuous interaction (younger infants observed for 10 minutes). b. Free play. Mothers instructed to play with infant as they would at home. c. Laboratory room with videotape OR live by observer in natural settings: home or waiting room.	Written manual with extensive descriptions; video training tape available with accompanying workbook and common interactive segments to rate.	a. Intraclass reliability correlations range from .77 to .87 in home observations and from .53 to .93 in laboratory observations. b. None specified.	Concurrent correlations related to infant temperament and maternal locus of control, maternal support, ambivalent diagnosis of physical status, and the provision of early intervention. Early version predicted positive changes in IQ scores from age 3 to 5 years.

continued

Table 1. (*continued*)

Intended populations	Types of behaviors a. Parents b. Child c. Dyadic	Overall scale organization	Item level organization

Parent-Child Early Relational Assessment

| Psychiatrically ill mothers; families at risk for early relational disturbances; normative. Children ages 12–48 months. (Manual indicates can be used with younger infants.) | a. Parental style, mood, affect, and expressed attitude toward child.
b. Child mood, affect, adaptive abilities, responses to parent's emotional state.
c. Affective quality of interaction and mutuality. | Six clusters of parent variables organizing 29 behaviors; four clusters of child behaviors organizing 28 behaviors; two clusters of dyadic variables organizing eight interactive behaviors. Ten items scored at a time; repeated viewings of videotaped interactions allow scoring entire scale. | Global rating instrument with 6-point Likert scale (6th point = not ratable). Each of five points are behaviorally anchored. Duration, frequency and intensity taken into account in each item. |

Parental Acceptance Scoring Manual

| Normative. Children from 18 months to 4 years in intact middle-class families. | a. Three types of parent behaviors: child's need for evaluation availability, and structure.
b. None.
c. None. | Behaviors organized under major headings in each of the three types of parental acceptance. Behaviors scored in terms of hierarchical levels derived from family exchange theory. | Thirteen major headings with 2–3 behaviors listed under each. Five levels scored, 3 points fully described. |

Response Class Matrix

| Developmentally and language delayed; physically abused; attention deficit disorder with hyperactivity; normative; divorcing families. Children ages 12 months (mental age) to 12 years. | a. Antecedents and consequences of social behaviors of parents with child.
b. Antecedents and consequences of social behaviors of child with parents.
c. Created by combining parent and child matrices. | Two coders simultaneously count behaviors of parent and child separately in 10-second intervals. | Record first scorable behavior unit per time interval. Decisions about whether behaviors are antecedents or consequences made while tallying behaviors. |

Observational session
  a. Length
  b. Structure
  c. Setting
	Training	Reliability
		  a. Interjudge
		  b. Stability
			Validity

a. 25 minutes. b. 5-minute free play warm-up followed by 5 minutes each of feeding, structured task, free play, and separation/reunion. May be followed by semistructured interview with parent and playback of segments of videotape. c. Videotaped in laboratory setting.	None specified. Written manual available.	a. (1980 scale version) Correlations of .83 for exact agreement between two raters and .98 for agreement within one point. b. None specified.	Significant differences between psychiatrically ill and well mothers on consistency and affective disturbance. No differences between mothers with different types of affective disorders.
a. 20 minutes. b. 5 minutes of free play followed by 5 minutes book reading with toys as distractors followed by 2 minute toy clean-up task followed by 2 minutes of easy problem-solving task and 2 minutes of difficult problem-solving task. c. Videotaped in laboratory setting.	20 hours of formal training followed by 40 hours of practice. Written manual available along with practice videotapes.	a. Correlations of .75–.80 between two observers. b. None specified.	Analyses in progress.
a. 10–30 minutes. b. Free play or assigned problem-solving task (command). c. Videotaped or live observation in clinic or laboratory.	Twenty to 25 hours required. Written manual available (revision in progress).	a. Correlations of .78–.96 between raters across all behavior categories. Agreement for matrix cells is 78%–87%. Ongoing reliability checks recommended. b. None specified.	Summary behavior scores differentiated various handicapped groups from normally developing children; differences found for mothers, fathers, siblings, and peers. Patterns related to stress, self-esteem, and perception of child and child's behavioral problems.

the information in Table 1 have not been included in the table for reasons of space. References are included either in the text or are provided at the end of the chapter; all summary information in Table 1 came from the references cited for each particular scale. This section presents the history and overall evaluation of each scale.

Barnard Teaching Scale and Barnard Feeding Scale

Development

The Barnard Teaching and Feeding Scales (also sometimes referred to as "NCAST" for Nursing Child Assessment Satellite Training) were developed through the Nursing Child Assessment Project (NCAP) at the University of Washington, Seattle, in the mid- to late 1970s (Nursing Child Assessment Satellite Training, 1978a, 1978b). The original goals of the NCAP were to identify the early factors that predict later child development outcomes, to find out which types of assessment should take place at which points of development for children and families, and to determine the permanence of high-risk characteristics.

NCAST depends on two structured situations, feeding and teaching. In both settings, parental and child behaviors are counted. Although items have somewhat different definitions, the same four general types of items are coded for parents in both settings (Sensitivity to Cues, Response to Child's Distress, Social-Emotional Growth Fostering, and Cognitive Growth Fostering). Two general categories of items are coded for children in each setting: Clarity of Cues and Responsiveness to Parent. NCAST materials are available only as part of a contracted training package and will not be sent as a response to an individual request. As reported in Table 1, NCAST requires much training to learn.

Validity Observations

The original, predominantly white sample contained healthy, middle-class women and their infants, half of whom were born with complications. Recently there has been wide usage of the scale by visiting nurses and medically oriented early intervention programs, both of which serve a more ethnically and economically diverse population than this original sample. There are no published data to show that the scale is suitable for a broader population than the original one. The scale is also being used as an outcome measure in intervention projects; the one published attempt to show changes in interaction as a function of intervention based on the scale found no effects (Barnard & Bee, 1983).

Evaluation

We have some concerns about the choice of feeding for an observation session. Feeding interactions have a strong biological overlay and thus may mask individual differences in parenting that might be important for predicting development within specific domains (e.g., cognitive). In Barnard's own work, the interactions observed during teaching were more predictive of later cognitive measures than the ones during feeding (Bee et al., 1982). At the same time, however, there may be very important reasons for observing mother-infant interactions during feeding. For example, if an infant suffers from a specific feeding disorder (e.g., an infant with failure to thrive), the use of the NCAST feeding scales may prove valuable in detecting elements of the feeding interaction in need of corrective intervention. Thus, the choice of whether to use one or both NCAST scales may depend on one's specific question.

Greenspan-Lieberman Observation System for Assessment of Caregiver-Infant Interaction during Semi-Structured Play

Development

The original version of the Greenspan-Lieberman Observation Scale (GLOS) was developed by the authors in the late 1970s through their work at the National Institute of Mental Health (NIMH). Their goal was to develop an instrument that defined observable and measurable indicator behaviors used clinically in observing and assessing mother-infant interaction. According to the authors (Greenspan & Lieberman, 1980), their observation system is based on three basic premises. The first premise is that the infant is capable of adaptive responses to the environment from birth. The second premise is that behavior becomes progressively more organized during the first 2 years. The third is that infants show individual differences from the time of birth and that these differences are related to the later development of coping skills, including precursors for a number of basic ego functions.

The complicated nature of the interactions observed demands that the GLOS be used with 10 minutes of videotaped interactions between mother and infant conducted in the laboratory; these tapes can be viewed repeatedly to obtain the GLOS scores. A large number of behaviors for both caregiver and infant are scored every 15 seconds and several behaviors can be simultaneously coded. Four versions of the GLOS now exist: the Newborn Scale (Hofheimer & Poisson, 1987) and the Infant GLOS, Toddler GLOS, and 3-year old version (all developed by Greenspan and Lieberman). According to Greenspan and Lieberman (1980), modification of the scales is planned before a final version is published. In addition, a shorter version of the GLOS has been developed using a 5-page rating system for 80 behaviors, each of which is rated once on a continuum of from 0% to 100% at the end of the 10-minute observation (S.S. Poisson, personal communication, 1988).

Validity Observations

Hofheimer and O'Grady (1986) used the Toddler Glos and other instruments to study the parenting behaviors of 66 low-socioeconomic-status (SES) adolescents and adults compared to 23 upper-middle-SES adults with infants 6 months old. This sample was reassessed when the children were 2 years old (because of attrition, sample size reduced to 48). A later study by Hofheimer, O'Grady, and Packer (1988) used the Toddler GLOS, SES, and risk factors to predict development at 4 years. Both studies found that differences in behaviors between groups of mothers were not significant when social risk factors were taken into account. A disadvantaged caregiving environment contributed significantly over time to the problematic development of infants of younger mothers regardless of other early social risk factors. The GLOS is currently being used to describe parenting interactions with motorically impaired infants and young children (Williamson, Greenspan, & Gilkerson, 1987), in clinical intervention with newborns (Hofheimer & Poisson, 1987), and with babies born to mothers addicted to cocaine and heroin (Fitzgerald, no date).

Evaluation

Greenspan, Lieberman, Poisson, Hofheimer, and their colleagues are a committed group of professionals who believe in the effectiveness of their scales as clinical tools. Although they acknowledge that the scales are complicated and contain many behaviors to be rated, they believe the information gained is useful for clinicians.

There are several characteristics, however, that may make the scales less useful than they might otherwise be. First, the alphabetical ordering of the behaviors in the scale makes learning and using the form difficult. In addition, it is unclear how a profile of developmental progress or status would be derived since both negative and positive behaviors exist side by side. A shortened version addresses this problem by requiring observers to plot behaviors across a 0%–100% range. However, interrater reliability and agreement among clinicians in a project would be difficult with this version.

In sum, the GLOS is a large, complicated tool that appears to need a good deal more work before it can easily be used in the field. In the hands of a skilled clinician, it might serve to focus the observations and the discussion of parenting. Whether or not it is too difficult for the average practitioner to use reliably remains a question.

Interpersonal Behavior Constructs

Development

The Interpersonal Behavior Construct (IBC) (Kogan et al., 1975) was developed at the University of Washington for the purpose of observing, analyzing, and delineating unique patterns and styles of mother-child interactions within a behavioral framework. The behavior of the child is viewed as being under the primary control of the immediate social environment; the social relationship between parent and child is viewed as bidirectional. Developed for clinical use, the IBC provides information regarding changes in parental and child interactive behaviors following a behaviorally focused, individualized intervention program.

The scale is designed around two types of observations, or what Kogan calls "constructs": those behaviors checked for duration, and those behaviors counted for frequency. The duration behaviors consist of attention, vocalization, and lead taking, and are scored when they last for 70% of a 40-second observational unit (Kogan et al., 1975; Kogan & Gordon, 1975b). (These behaviors were chosen because they were viewed as characterizing the primary interactive behaviors of the dyad.) The remaining behaviors are organized under the "frequency" construct and are scored if they occur at least once. This set of behaviors is viewed as contributing information about the quality of the interaction. In addition to noting the occurrence of the 23 frequency and duration behaviors, patterns of behavior are derived by contingency analysis methods (Kogan et al., 1975).

Validity Observations

The IBC has been used with young children with cerebral palsy, developmental delay, and mild to moderate retardation, and with young nonhandicapped children to examine the extent to which maternal and child behaviors can be modified as a result of intervention. Although it is the parent-child interaction that is being targeted for change, it is the mother's behavior that is directed. Using a "bug-in-the-ear" technique, Kogan and Gordon (1975a) found that a mother's interactive behaviors could be changed by providing instruction and guidance to parents during the observation.

Evaluation

Scoring of the IBC would be difficult without appropriate supporting machinery (e.g., videotape capability with date/time generator). The duration and frequency behaviors are scored differently, and depend on precise time notations to keep up with each. As a minor annoyance, the word "construct" is not used in the conventional way to refer to an underlying psychological process, making for some confusion in understanding the description of the scale's properties. The IBC appears to be sensitive to changes that occur following the kind of individualized, behavioral intervention employed by Kogan and her associates. Investigation of the IBC in a different kind of intervention program would provide information about its more general utility.

Maternal Behavior Rating Scale

Development

The Maternal Behavior Rating Scale (MBRS) was developed for the purpose of assessing the impact of early intervention services upon the quality of maternal interactive behavior; it is designed to be used with videotaped home observations of free-play interactions between mother and child (Mahoney, Finger, & Powell, 1985). The targeted populations are mother-child dyads in which the children are diagnosed with medical or physiological conditions associated with mental retardation, such as Down syndrome and hydrocephaly. The authors wanted to identify "patterns of maternal behavior that are related to different levels of children's development, rather than to determine whether there are differences in the manner that mothers interact with their children compared to mothers with nonretarded children" (Mahoney et al., 1985, p. 296). Although the authors do not expressly identify their theoretical perspective, it appears that they take a cognitive developmental viewpoint.

The MBRS rates 18 maternal behaviors on a 5-point Likert scale. Definitions for maternal behaviors and anchors for the five point ratings are provided in the scale manual (Mahoney, 1985). Four child behaviors are rated also, but the manual does not define these. A short form of the MBRS has been developed that consists of only seven items.

Validity Observations

Factor analyses of the 18-item long form and the 7-item short form both revealed two primary factors labeled Child Orientedness/Pleasure and Control (Mahoney et al., 1985; Mahoney, Powell, & Finger, 1986). Together these factors accounted for about 20% of the variance in the level of children's cognitive development. Findings from the original research with nonretarded children indicated that mothers' interactive styles tended to change as children grew older and that there was a relationship between maternal style and children's cognitive status (Mahoney et al., 1985).

Evaluation

As the authors themselves have pointed out, the primary problem in using the MBRS is in the amount of time it takes to use the scale and to achieve reliability (Mahoney et al., 1986). Since the results of the shortened form closely approximate those of the original form, it may provide a more convenient assessment of maternal interactive behavior. The drawback with the shortened form is the loss in reliability when the number of items is reduced. The authors recommend that the scale not be used for assessment purposes until the raters achieve at least 90% interrater agreement with an experienced observer and that the raters undergo continual monitoring so that shifts in rating criteria do not occur over time.

Intervention programs that focus on modifying mother-child interactions may find this scale appropriate. The MBRS appears to have items that will provide the clinician with insight as to how the dyad is currently functioning, despite its focus on maternal factors alone. The shortened form seems promising, but more research is needed before conclusions can be drawn.

Parent Behavior Progression

Development

The Parent Behavior Progression (PBP) was developed to be appropriate for an observational summary following two to three home visits with a mother and her premature or low-birth-weight baby, and is for the purpose of assessing maternal behaviors from which short-term goals may be formulated (Bromwich, 1981, 1983). Forms are completed following the home visits; either observed or reported behaviors are scored. Behaviors that are not checked as occurring may be targeted as goals for subsequent intervention.

The PBP was originally developed for use with parents of premature and low-birth-weight infants considered at risk for developmental problems (Bromwich, 1981). Parental behaviors are conceptualized as forming a six-level, quasi-hierarchical progression. Although this suggests that there is an increase in the skill level of parental behaviors, parents need not acquire behaviors at one level before they move on to another. Specific behaviors are described within each level that are checked as present or absent. The theoretical constructs Bromwich believes to be significant in the transactions between primary caregivers and their infants are those of bonding and attachment. The first three levels of the PBP establish an affective base that is believed to promote attachment. Levels 4–6 involve experiences that will optimize the infant's cognitive development.

There are two forms available. Form I is designed for parents whose infants range in age from birth to 9 months or for parents of older handicapped/delayed infants who are developmentally below the 9-month level. Form II is for parents whose infants range in age from 9 to 36 months.

Validity Observations

Bromwich and Parmelee (1979) investigated the relationship between the Bromwich

Behavior Progression Scale and other measures of parental competence, concluding that they had demonstrated construct validity for the scale. Bromwich (1983) cited a study by Silcock and Rogers (1981) for further evidence of construct validity; mothers with lowered scores on the Bromwich scale had experienced recent stress, such as marital and psychiatric problems. In addition, Sheehan (1981) found significant correlations between scores on the scale and the Bayley Scales of Infant Development both initially and 6 months later.

Allen, Affleck, McQueeney, and McGrade (1982) examined ratings on the scale over a 2-year period. Ratings were compared to measures obtained on the Home Observation for Measurement of the Environment (HOME). Families with improving or optimal PBP scores received higher HOME ratings.

Evaluation

Unfortunately the scoring of this scale is less well defined than one would wish. Bromwich and Parmelee (1979) noted that each section can receive a maximum rating of 9 points, and they mention a total maximum score of 18; it is unclear how this can be derived. Another difficulty arises in using the PBP as a tool for planning intervention and monitoring progress, because it is not a true hierarchy. Since behaviors at lower levels need not be acquired before behaviors at subsequent levels, it is not clear what the practitioner should do about lower level behaviors that did not and are not occurring when upper level behaviors are observed.

The PBP was designed at a time when the primary goals of early intervention were child directed. It served the purpose of sensitizing professionals to parental behaviors when little attention was given to this issue. Students and newcomers to the field of early intervention may find it helpful to use the PBP as a mechanism to increase their awareness of and sensitivity to parenting behaviors. It is to its credit that the PBP directs one's attention to recognizing and supporting the positive behaviors demonstrated by parents. This can be a helpful instrument clinically for those programs that share its philosophical orientation.

Parent/Caregiver Involvement Scale

Development

Development of the instrument that was to become the Parent/Caregiver Involvement Scale (P/CIS) was begun in 1979. The Jay-Farran Scale was first used in 1979 with a high-risk, impoverished sample; the goal was to compare the relative efficacy of a rating scale with that of frequency counts of maternal behavior in predicting growth in tested IQ in children from ages 3 to 5 years. Ratings of a series of maternal behaviors in videotaped free-play interaction in a laboratory setting proved to be significantly more predictive of the change in IQ between ages 3 and 5 years than strict counts of interactive behaviors (Jay & Farran, 1981). Since then the scale has been reconstructed to apply to interactions with children from 3 to 36 months sampled either in a laboratory or at home, live or videotaped; it has also been reconstructed to be equally appropriate for handicapped infants and their mothers (Farran, Kasari, Jay, & Comfort, 1986).

The scale is organized into 11 behaviors rated on three dimensions: Amount, Quality, and Developmental Appropriateness. Each of the behaviors is rated on a 5-point scale with odd-numbered points behaviorally anchored. In addition, there are five scale items included in a "General Impressions" section that allows the observer to reflect more global responses to the dyad.

Although unstated, the perspective inherent in the behaviors chosen and the particular emphasis taken in their definitions is a cognitive developmental one. For the most part, the behaviors rated are the ones presumed important for the child's cognitive growth and feelings of self-esteem. The presumption is that adults are important mediators of experience for the child, bridging between the child's immaturity/inexperience and interactions with objects and ideas in the world. The pace and sequence of the mediation should be smooth and seamless to allow optimal growth.

Validity Observations

The instrument has been applied to a socioeconomically high-risk sample and a handicapped sample, both followed longitudinally in a laboratory observation (Farran, Kasari, Yoder, Harber, Huntington, & Comfort-Smith, 1987); socioeconomic status proved more detrimental to high parental ratings than did the handicapped status of the child. A longitudinal sample of handicapped infants has been observed in their homes (Comfort & Farran, 1986; Farran et al., 1987; Simeonsson, Bailey, Huntington, & Comfort, 1986); ratings were found to be related to temperamental characteristics of the child as well as demographic and personality characteristics of the mothers (adolescent mothers were rated lower, as were mothers with less social support and an external locus of control). A sample of 3-month-olds whose mothers had undergone ultrasound diagnosis during pregnancy were found to differ only if there was a continuing ambiguous diagnosis for the child (Sparling, Seeds, & Farran, 1988). Maternal involvement with infants with cerebral palsy has also recently been investigated with the P/CIS (Blasco, Hrncir, & Blasco, 1988), as has a comparison of five parent-child interaction systems applied to a mixed sample of socioeconomically high-risk and handicapped infants (Summers, Huntington, Pope, & Saylor, 1988).

Evaluation

The P/CIS is a comprehensive description of caregiver interactions with normally developing and handicapped infants. However, because child behaviors are not rated, it does not address the contribution the child makes to those interactions. There is the suggestion that it is more related longitudinally to development in the infant than other similar systems (Summers et al., 1988). It has the advantage of having a video training tape to allow new users a standard format for achieving reliability. As with any global rating system, it is dependent on the observer's being able to adopt the same world view as the scale's developers. The developers strongly caution against using the P/CIS to measure change in parenting behavior; instead it is suggested that information derived from the scale be used in conjunction with that from the infant to plan a comprehensive support and intervention program.

Parent-Child Early Relational Assessment

Development

The first version of the Parent-Child Early Relational Assessment (PCERA) was developed between 1976 and 1981 for use in the Mothers' Project, an NIMH-funded clinical research and intervention project focused on psychotic mothers and their infants (Musick, Clark, & Cohlen, 1981). The PCERA was developed to capture the interrelationship between parent and child and the unique affective and behavioral characteristics of each. Ratings are based on 25 minutes of videotaped interactions in a series of structured conditions in the laboratory. The present revised version of the scale (Clark, 1985) was designed for use with the same target population and has been extended for use with families at risk for early relationship disturbances (failure to thrive, child maltreatment, families under severe stress).

The major premise behind both the intervention and the scale development is that maternal affect serves a regulatory or organizing function for the infant's social development, defining for the infant the boundaries for social interaction with the mother (Clark, 1986). Further, there is the assumption that the major task of early childhood is to maintain development in the child, with the mother bearing the primary responsibility for helping the child stay on course (Stott, Musick, Clark, & Cohler, 1983). Children of mentally ill mothers are thought by Stott et al. (1983) to be at multiple risk.

Validity Observations

The Mothers' Project used the scale to compare the behaviors of 65 psychiatrically ill mothers with those of 36 mentally healthy mothers who had preschool children. Half of the psychotic sample received intervention in a clinical setting, with the children in a therapeutic nursery school. A subsample of the same population consisted of 26 psychotic mothers with matched controls; comparison indicated that psychiatrically ill mothers were significantly different from healthy mothers on two factors of the scale: Affective Involvement and Consistency. No data have been reported on the sensitivity of the scale for measuring the effects of intervention.

More recently, Teti and his colleagues (Teti, Nakagawa, Das, Wirth, & Ablard, 1989) have demonstrated a number of statistically significant relationships between mother-infant interaction, as indexed by scales adapted from the PCERA, and infants' security of attachment to the mother, as indexed by the Ainsworth Strange Situation. Consistent with predictions from attachment theory, mothers of securely attached infants were found to be more sensitive, more effective in structuring their infant's play, less anxious, and less depressed and withdrawn with their babies than were mothers of insecurely attached infants during free-play observation. Securely attached infants displayed significantly less irritability, less avoidance and resistance, and less assertiveness and aggressivity than did insecurely attached infants. These findings suggest that the PCERA may be useful for capturing qualitative dimensions of mother-infant interaction that relate to infant socioemotional functioning.

Evaluation

This is a potentially useful training tool to sensitize clinical staff working with families at risk for early relational difficulties. The authors believe that in a hospital or clinic-based mental health setting with staff trained to work with severely disturbed families, this instrument could be used to focus clinical intervention efforts, evaluate program effectiveness, and contribute to program research and development. However, the latter goals do not appear to have been realized, at least in published reports. Effectiveness would require staff stability, careful training to criteria, and retraining as necessary. Training will be made more difficult because although items are clearly defined and well organized, behavioral anchors are not consistently well defined and demand both careful reading and sound clinical judgment.

Parental Acceptance Scoring Manual

Development

The Parental Acceptance Scoring Manual was developed through an ongoing research project at Boston College. The Family and Child Development Project began in May 1985 as a cross-sectional study of normal, middle-class, intact families. Mothers, fathers, and their young children are included. They are videotaped in a laboratory setting for 20 minutes, and the videotape is segmented into shorter structured interactions (e.g., book reading, toy clean-up). The project has been extended into a longitudinal study, in part to assess the predictive capability of the instrument. The manual was designed to examine the integration of a child's needs for evaluation, availability, and structure with the parents' needs and reality constraints (Rothbaum & Schneider-Rosen, 1988). The authors believe that parental acceptance is the single best predictor of their children's social competence.

Validity Observations

Reliability and validity studies are currently in progress, using the population of the Family and Child Development Project. The first of three studies evaluates 63 toddlers with their mothers and fathers to determine the relationship between parental acceptance and self-control. A second study evaluates a 2-year-old sample to assess the relationship between parental acceptance and the child's display of empathy toward the parent and competence in interactions with peers (Schneider-Rosen, 1987). A third study is a longitudinal follow-up of 4-year-old children who were evaluated at 18 or 24 months of age with their mothers and fathers, assessing stability of parental acceptance and the association between early acceptance and later child social competence. No data are yet published from any of these efforts.

Evaluation

The strength of this manual lies in its focus on parents and on its liberal use of examples of specific parent behaviors to help define criteria at Levels 1, 3, and 5. Early childhood educators, child development specialists, special educators, and early intervention staff in particular will find this manual understandable and useful even though this project was not designed for use with a typical early intervention population.

There are cautions, however. Reliability and validity studies are still in progress and are based on a middle-class, intact family sample. Behaviors are rated based on five 60-second observations. Such short segments may not yield useful (valid) information about typical parent or child behaviors. The authors list nine general issues about choosing the correct criteria and 14 issues regarding specific child needs or parent behaviors. This suggests that careful monitoring during training and frequent retraining will be needed. Finally, this is a complex instrument that asks observers to make judgments about child and parent behavior and situational contexts. For observers, a thorough grounding in child development and family dynamics is recommended.

Response Class Matrix

Development

The Response Class Matrix (RCM) is an observational procedure for examining dyadic family interactions (Mash & Terdal, 1973; Mash, Terdal, & Anderson, 1979). Interactions are recorded by using two matrices. One observer records the mother's response to specific antecedent behaviors of the child. A second observer simultaneously codes the child's response to specific behavioral antecedents of the mother. Using a time-sampling procedure with 10-second intervals, two observers record only the first scorable behavioral unit. After a 5-second pause in which the first behavior is marked, behaviors occurring within the next 10-second interval are scored. Thus, dyadic exchanges are sampled.

The scale is designed to give both researchers and clinicians a tool for identifying problem behaviors and a description of antecedent and consequent stimuli that contribute to the family system.

There are six categories of child behaviors and seven of maternal behaviors that are coded. The authors consider these to be exhaustive categories; operational definitions are provided in the manual (Mash, Terdal, & Anderson, 1979). The categories are consistent with a behavioral model in that they reflect features of maternal control, reward strategies, and responsivity to the child and features of child compliance, play, and responsivity to the mother. This recording of behavior provides an effective means by which to identify goals and monitor intervention/treatment procedures, including medication trials and behavioral therapy.

Validity Observations

Initially the RCM was developed for use with young developmentally delayed and handicapped children. It has also been utilized with hyperactive, language delayed, and physically abused children as well as with normal children from intact and separated families. There have been a relatively large number of studies using the RCM. The ages of children in these studies have ranged from 8 months to 12 years, with most focused on children between the ages of 4 and 9 years. Training parents in behavioral techniques has resulted in a decrease in mother's directiveness and questions while increasing interactions, and an increase in children's responsiveness to commands, questions, and interactions (Mash & Barkley, 1986). Hanzlik and Stevenson (1984; cited in Mash & Barkley, 1986) extended the findings of earlier research to younger children (with mean mental ages of 12 months) and to observations conducted in the home. More research is needed before conclusions can be drawn regarding the effectiveness of the RCM with this age group.

Evaluation

The observational code was simplified so that it can be reliably used with a minimal amount of training. Little time is required to summarize the data, so that immediate feedback to parents is possible. The coding permits examination of either mother or child responses to antecedent behaviors (Mash & Barkley, 1986).

One drawback to the clinician in the field of early intervention is the need to have two observers simultaneously coding interactions. Given that staff power is at a premium, for this reason alone the RCM may not be appropriate. In addition, programs without a behavioral focus may find it difficult and less than useful to adopt this theoretical perspective.

SUMMARY

Before discussing the positives and negatives of using one of these scales to measure parent-child interaction, it is essential that we comment on the difficulty we encountered in finding the information from which these summaries could be made. Almost every scale required direct, personal calls to the authors to obtain the information (all of whom, it must be stated, were extremely cooperative). Much of the data summarized here has not been published or exists in book chapters and scale manuals hard to track down through the usual means. It is unimaginable that a busy practitioner could devote even a small percentage of the time we took to locate a scale and supporting documents. This difficulty explains why so many duplicate scales continue to be developed; authors are simply unaware of other efforts.

We are concerned that so much of this information is unpublished. This means that the necessary validity and reliability data that would help practitioners determine scale utility have not undergone the scrutiny of peer review. Moreover, none of these scales has been brought out by a test publisher; thus none has the rigorous testing and sample selection that would have to take place if they were being offered in the marketplace. Most, in fact, are used by the authors that developed them and/or their students and are available by writing directly to the authors. Even the NCAST scale, the most widely "marketed" instrument of the ones surveyed, has had only two publications in refereed journals, both of which were concerned with a version of the scale different from the one currently being sold.

Despite those problems, there are reasons why practitioners may wish to go ahead with the selection and use of a measure of parent-child interaction. First, learning a scale is a useful experience for a staff, even one that has been together for a while. In learning a scale, the staff will be forced to discuss values, reveal biases, and then put biases aside as they go through a common training format. Staff members often proceed with intervention assuming other personnel share their same belief systems and are making the same recommendations to parents. Frequently this is not the case, and the adoption of a standard measure of parenting across all staff members can be the impetus for a useful, in-depth discussion.

Second, these scales can remove some of the intuitive base on which intervention with parents is often founded. With no other referent, staff rely on hearsay, their own past experiences, and other personal predilections in making judgments about parents and suggestions for altered behaviors.

Finally, their use can eventually result in a long-term investigation of different types of handicaps and whether they exert a main effect on parenting behaviors. Unless a large number of children with the same handicapping condition are observed with their parents using a common metric, questions about parenting needs of particular types of children will never be addressed. Presumably those answers should make intervention more focused and effective.

One of the major drawbacks to using any scale can also be a plus if suitable caution is used. Without caution, these more exact descriptions of parent-child interactions can lead to a deficit orientation, with a simple, straightforward, and unwarranted assumption that if a parent is rated low on a behavior, the interventionist's job is to "get the score up." We cannot state too emphatically how seldom this is the case. No parent-child measure can stand alone;

all observations must be combined with the total information available on the child, the family, medical status, future prognosis, the neighborhood, parent support systems, and available services before a plan for the child and family should be made. In planning, information from the scale that indicates parental strengths should be taken into account so that the intervention will have a greater likelihood of success. Thus, interaction ratings become part of the working store of information actively included in planning for the child but should not be used as the sole outcome variable by which the success of a program is measured.

REFERENCES

Introduction

Farran, D.C., & Cooper, D. (1986). Psychosocial risk: Which early experiences are important for whom? In D.C. Farran and J.D. McKinney (Eds.), *Risk in intellectual and psychosocial development* (pp. 187–226). New York: Academic Press.

Farran, D.C., & Mistry, J. (July, 1987). *Role diffusion in large social networks of part-Hawaiian preschool children*. Poster presented at the ninth biennial meeting of the International Society for the Study of Behavioral Development, Tokyo, Japan.

Hunt, J.McV. (1961). *Intelligence and experience*. New York: Ronald.

Barnard Teaching Scale and Barnard Feeding Scale (NCAST)

Barnard, K.E., & Bee, H.L. (1983). The impact of temporally patterned stimulation on the development of preterm infants. *Child Development, 54,* 1156–1167.

Bee, H.L., Barnard, K.E., Eyres, S.J., Gray, C.A., Hammond, M.A., Spietz, A.L., Snyder, C., & Clark, B. (1982). Prediction of IQ and language skill from prenatal status, child performance, family characteristics, and mother-infant interaction. *Child Development, 53,* 1134–1156.

Nursing Child Assessment Satellite Training (NCAST). (1978a). *Nursing Child Assessment Feeding Scale.* (Manual available during training with NCAST trainers. Contact Georgina Sumner, NCAST, WJ-10, University of Washington, Seattle, WA 98195)

Nursing Child Assessment Satellite Training (NCAST). (1978b). *Nursing Child Assessment Teaching Scale.* (Manual available during training with NCAST trainers. Contact Georgina Sumner, NCAST, WJ-10, University of Washington, Seattle, WA 98195)

Snyder, C., & Spietz, A.L. (1977, November–December). Characteristics of abuse: A report of five families. *Nurse Practitioner, 2*(8).

Greenspan-Lieberman Observation System for Assessment of Caregiver-Infant Interaction during Semi-Structured Play (GLOS)

Fitzgerald, E. (no date). [Doctoral dissertation in progress], New York University.

Fox, N., Stiften, C., Greenspan, S.I., & Poisson, S. (1985). *Vagal tone and its relation to cognitive and socio-emotional outcome in 24 month old children.* Paper presented at the Society for Research in Child Development, Toronto.

Greenspan, S., & Lieberman, A. (1980). Infants, mothers and their interactions: A quantitative clinical approach to developmental assessment. In *The course of life: Psychoanalytic contributions toward understanding personality development. Vol. 1: Infancy and early Childhood.* (pub. no. ADM 80-786). Washington, DC: U.S. Government Printing Office.

Greenspan, S., & Poisson, S. (1983). *Greenspan-Lieberman Observation System for Assessment of Caregiver-Infant Interaction during Semi-Structured Play (GLOS).* (Available from S. Poisson, Division of Maternal and Child Health, HRSA, DHHS, Rockville, MD 20850)

Hofheimer, J.A., & O'Grady, K.E. (1986, April). *Early interactions between adolescents and their infants as predictors of development at two years.* Paper presented at the International Conference on Infant Studies, Los Angeles.

Hofheimer, J.A., O'Grady, K.E., & Packer, A.B. (1988, April). *Infants born to adolescents: Predicting development at four years from early interaction and social risk.* Paper presented at the International Conference on Infant Studies, Washington, DC.

Hofheimer, J.A., & Poisson, S.S. (1987). Use of

quantitative profiles to describe clinical aspects of the caregiver-infant relationship. *Infant Mental Health Journal,* in press.

Nover, A., Shore, M.F., Timberlake, E.M., & Greenspan, S.I. (1984). The relationship of maternal perception and maternal behavior: A study of normal mothers and their infants. *American Journal of Orthopsychiatry, 54*(2), 210–223.

Williamson, G.G., Greenspan, S.I., & Gilkerson, L. (1987, December). *Facilitating motor control and emotional growth in infants and toddlers.* Paper presented at the National Center for Clinical Infant Programs 5th Biennial National Training Institute, Washington, DC.

Interpersonal Behavior Construct

Kogan, K., & Gordon, B. (1975a). A mother-instruction program: Documenting change in mother-child interactions. *Child Psychiatry and Human Development, 5,* 189–200.

Kogan, K., & Gordon, B. (1975b). Interpersonal behavior constructs: A revised approach to defining dyadic interaction styles. *Psychological Reports, 36,* 835–846.

Kogan, K. (1980). Interaction systems between preschool handicapped or developmentally delayed children and their parents. In T. Field, S. Goldberg, D. Stern, & A. Sostek (Eds.), *High-risk infants and children: Adult and peer interactions.* New York: Academic Press.

Kogan, K., Carey, K., Jarvis, M., Layden, T., Turner, P., & Van, D. (1975). *Interpersonal behavior constructs: A means for analyzing videotaped dyadic interaction.* (Available from Kate Kogan, Psychiatry and Behavioral Sciences, School of Medicine, University of Washington, Seattle, WA 98195)

Maternal Behavior Rating Scale

Mahoney, G. (1985). *Maternal Behavior Rating Scale Manual.* (Available from UCONN Health Center–Pediatric Dept., Farmington, CT 06032)

Mahoney, G., Finger, I., & Powell, A. (1985). Relationship of maternal behavioral style to the development of organically impaired mentally retarded infants. *American Journal of Mental Deficiency, 90,* 296–302.

Mahoney, G., Powell, A., & Finger, I. (1986). The Maternal Behavior Rating Scale. *Topics in Early Childhood Special Education, 6,* 44–56.

Parent Behavior Progression

Allen D., Affleck, G., McQueeny, M., & McGrade, B. (1982). Validation of the Parent Behavior Progression in early intervention programs. *Mental Retardation, 20,* 159–163.

Bromwich, R. (1981). *Working with parents and infants: An interactional approach.* Baltimore: University Park Press.

Bromwich, R. (1983). *Manual for the Parent Behavior Progression and Supplement.* (Available from Michael Moore, California State University, Northridge, CA 91330)

Bromwich, R., & Parmelee, A. (1979). An intervention program for preterm infants. In T. Field (Ed.), *Infants born at risk.* New York: Spectrum Publications.

Sheehan, R. (1981). Issues and documentation of early intervention with infants and parents. *Topics in Early Childhood Special Education, 3,* 67–76.

Parent/Caregiver Involvement Scale

Blasco, P., Hrncir, E.J., & Blasco, P.A. (1988). *The contribution of maternal involvement to the spontaneous mastery performance of infants with cerebral palsy.* Unpublished manuscript. (Available from Patricia Mulhearn Blasco, Frank Porter Graham Child Development Center, University of North Carolina at Chapel Hill, Chapel Hill, NC, 27514)

Comfort, M., & Farran, D. (1986, April). *Systematic assessment of maternal behavior during interactions with handicapped infants.* Poster presented at the Conference on Human Development, Nashville, TN.

Farran, D.C., Kasari, C., Jay, S., & Comfort, M. (1986). *Parent/Caregiver Involvement Scale.* (Available from Continuing Education, University of North Carolina at Greensboro, Greensboro, NC 27412)

Farran, D.C., Kasari, C., Yoder, P., Harber, L., Huntington, G., & Comfort-Smith, M. (1987). Rating mother-child interactions in handicapped and at-risk infants. In D. Tamir (Ed.), *Stimulation and intervention in infant development.* London: Freund Publishing House, Ltd.

Jay, S., & Farran, D.C. (1981). The relative efficacy of predicting IQ from mother-child interactions using ratings versus behavioral counts. *Journal of Applied Developmental Psychology, 2,* 165–177.

Kasari, C., Farran, D., & Harber, L. (1984, March). *Variability of infant social-communicative behavior in caregiver-infant interactions.* Paper presented at the 1984 Gatlinburg Conference on Research in Mental Retardation/Developmental Disabilities.

Simeonsson, R.J., Bailey, D.B., Huntington, G., & Comfort, M. (1986). Testing the concept of goodness of fit in early intervention. *Journal of Infant Mental Health, 7,* 81–94.

Sparling, J., Seeds, J., & Farran, D.C. (1988). The relationship of obstetrical ultrasound to parent and infant behavior. *Obstetrics & Gynocology, 72*, 902–907.

Summers, M., Huntington, L., Pope, J., & Saylor, C. (1988, March). *Coding interactions between handicapped infants and their mothers: Preliminary comparison of five systems.* Paper presented at the 34th annual meeting of the Southeastern Psychological Association, New Orleans.

Parent-Child Early Relational Assessment

Clark, R. (1985). *The Parent-Child Early Relational Assessment.* (Available from Roseanne Clark, Ph.D., Department of Psychiatry, University of Wisconsin Medical School, 600 Highland Avenue, Madison, WI 53792)

Clark, R. (1986, April). *Maternal affective disturbances and child competence.* Paper presented at the International Conference on Infant Studies, Los Angeles, California.

Musick, J.S., Clark, R., & Cohlen, B. (1981). The Mother's Project: A program for mentally ill mothers of young children. In *Infants: Their social environments* (pp. 111–127). Washington, DC: National Association for the Education of Young Children.

Stott, F.M., Musick, J.S., Clark, R., & Cohler, B. (1983). Developmental patterns in the infants and young children of mentally ill mothers. *Infant Mental Health Journal, 4*(3), 217–235.

Teti, D.M., Nakagawa, M., Das, R., Wirth, O., & Ablard, K.E., (1989, April). *Behavioral correlates of child-mother attachment and attachment concordance among infants and older siblings.* Paper presented at the biennial meeting of the Society for Research in Child Development, Kansas City, MO.

Parental Acceptance Scoring Manual

Rothbaum, F., & Schneider-Rosen, K. (1988). *Parental Acceptance Scoring Manual: A system for assessing interactions between parents and their young children.* (Available from Karen Schneider-Rosen, Ph.D., Boston College, Chestnut Hill, MA 02167)

Schneider-Rosen, K. (1987). *The classification of parent-child relationships beyond infancy.* (Available from Karen Schneider-Rosen, Ph.D., Boston College, Chestnut Hill, MA 02167)

Response Class Matrix

Mash, E., & Barkley, R. (1986). Assessment of family interaction with the Response Class Matrix. In R. Prinz (Ed.), *Assessment of children and families* (Vol. 2, pp. 29–67). Greenwich, CT: JAI Press.

Mash, E., & Terdal, L. (1973). The response-class matrix: A procedure for recording parent-child interaction. *Journal of Consulting and Clinical Psychology, 40*, 163–169.

Mash, E., Terdal, L., & Anderson, K. (1979). *The response-class matrix: A procedure for recording parent-child interactions.* (Available from Eric J. Mash, Department of Psychology, University of Calgary, Calgary, Alberta, Canada)

16 Use of Family Assessment in Early Intervention

Barbara M. Ostfeld and Elizabeth D. Gibbs

Living with a handicapped child and with the uncertainty of that child's future affects the emotional system and coping abilities of the entire family. (Murphy, 1982, p. 73)

Family functioning . . . [is] . . . a better predictor of child adjustment than [is] presence of illness. (B.L. Lewis & Khaw, 1982, p. 636)

There is a need to identify why some families succumb to the stressors . . . and others [do] not (Petersen, 1984, p. 338)

The role of the family in maintaining the well-being of its members has long been recognized (Glasser & Glasser, 1970; Hill, 1958). For the families of handicapped or chronically ill children, the association between family functioning and outcome is particularly vital (Beckman, 1984; Blacher, 1984; Bristol, 1987; McKinney & Peterson, 1987), since adaptive family functioning can enhance compliance with treatment (Newbrough, Simpkins, & Maurer, 1985) and reduce vulnerability to adjustment reactions and affective disorders sometimes triggered by the stress of illness (Ostfeld, 1988). For example, in addressing the family's effect upon the child with Tourette syndrome, a potentially debilitating neurological disorder, Cohen, Detlor, Shaywitz, and Leckman (1982) noted, "the adaptation of the patients reflects the capacity of the families to remain intact and supportive" (p. 39). In addition, family functioning also affects the child's development. For example, Sameroff and Chandler (1975) found that the individual differences in the development of high-risk infants could not be accounted for by early physical risk factors alone. Rather, environmental factors, including caregiver characteristics, were found to be important influences on the child's developmental outcome. Others have found that parent-child interaction can be a better predictor of development than are traditional developmental assessments (Bee et al., 1982). Thus, an individual's outcome is determined not only by what the disease or disability does to the individual but also by what the family does in dealing with the disease or disability (Holland, 1988). In short, families contribute to individualized outcomes (Bailey et al., 1986).

The appreciation of the contribution of the family to the development of the handicapped infant is reflected in recent federal legislation governing early intervention programs (Winton & Bailey, 1988). Whereas PL 94-142 served the child through the development of an individualized education program of teaching prescriptives and defined the role of the parent as the child's advocate in ensuring that the plan was implemented, the recently enacted PL 99-457 emphasizes the contribution of the family system itself to outcome and calls for the development of an individualized family service plan (IFSP) to assist each family in developing its ability to cope adaptively with the impact of handicap. That the IFSP is to be "individualized" calls attention to the variance in coping, because there are differences between families and within any given family over time in their perception of whether they are in crisis, in the quality of their emotional and tangible resources, and in the specific needs presented to programs (Featherstone, 1980; Lipsky, 1985; Weber & Parker, 1981). Just as one would not consider putting all infants through an identical intervention program, so too should a uniform parenting program or family service program be avoided (Kaiser & Hayden, 1984). Social support, for example, has consistently been found to contribute to family adjustment (Crnic, Greenberg, Ragozin, Robinson, & Basham, 1983; Dunst, Jenkins, & Trivette, 1984; McKinney & Peterson, 1987). Hence, one might be tempted to recommend the provision of a social support system as the first step in any intervention program for families of at-risk infants. However, professional intent and consumer perception are quite different things. If a family is satisfied with its support system, an intervention may be intrusive. Humenick, commenting in Brandt (1984), noted, "If one perceived no discrepancy [between] what is needed and what is received, then one feels adequately supported, regardless of actual level of support" (p. 240). As Brandt (1984) has noted, "Support is not support unless you want or need it" (p. 240). Thus, in order to individualize service and develop strategies for promoting the well-being of the family as a whole, early intervention professionals must learn to identify and evaluate the needs and strengths of families in areas that contribute to their ability to function adequately.

The goal of this chapter is to assist the early interventionist in the development of family assessment skills. We begin with a conceptual overview of the family as a system and follow with a selective review of the research documenting the reciprocal influence between family members and the influence of the handicapped child on the family. We then consider the determinants of family coping. Following is a sampling of methods and tools that can assist the interventionist in performing a family assessment. Finally, we consider the benefits and caveats of family assessment within the context of early intervention programs.

THE FAMILY AS A SYSTEM

In the course of living, individual family members and the family as a whole are faced with numerous daily demands, challenges, and tasks. The family's adaptation or coping ability can be conceptualized as the outcome of the degree of perceived stress these tasks create, moderated by the family's internal and external coping resources (Crnic, Freidrich, & Greenberg, 1983; Hill, 1958). If the demands exceed the family's coping resources, a crisis in family functioning can result. LeMasters (1957) noted that the changes demanded of the family by the birth of even a healthy baby increase stress and have the potential to precipitate a crisis. Certainly, the birth of a handicapped baby increases this potential (Wilton & Renaut, 1986). Most minor crises are resolved with relative ease, with the family seeking out additional resources or altering their patterns of functioning. Failure to resolve a crisis can be costly. The initial problem may soon be complicated by the emergence of secondary problems. For example, a family unable to soothe a colicky newborn may soon find that the baby's frantic crying has compromised the marital relationship as well as the parents' abilities to care for the older children in the home. The secondary problems intensify the initial crisis. Distracted by fatigue and by arguments, the parents will most likely find that their ability to read their baby's cues and their stamina for soothing him or her for long periods have been further compromised. As a result, the baby's problems may increase.

In the example, we see one of the basic characteristics of family life. The lives of the members are interdependent. The actions of one individual reverberate through the entire family system (Ackerman, 1958) and affect all members. Acknowledging the importance of the family in understanding the development of the individual, be it the developing child or the developing parent, Belsky (1981) noted that, "parenting affects and is affected by the infant who both influences and is influenced by the marital relationship which in turn both affects and is affected by parenting" (p. 7). In the family in our example, changes in characteristics of individual members (i.e., maturation), interpersonal relationships (i.e., role flexibility leading to better division of labor between parents), or the larger system in which the family operates (i.e., support from grandparents in the form of babysitting) may eventually alter the family's perception of its ability to meet the demands upon it. As adaptive functioning is restored, stress is reduced.

Thus, we encounter one additional facet of family life: that transactions are never static. In order to predict if and how an individual will cope with a problem, one must understand the system in which the individual operates and the variables that influence it (Jessop, Riessman, & Stein, 1988). Both developmental and health care literature (e.g., Anderson & Auslander, 1980; Mink & Nihara, 1986) now reflects this perspective that individual and interpersonal characteristics and the larger system in which the family functions (i.e., community, culture, personal history) determine, over time, the individual differences between family systems in their ability to adjust to new demands and thus resolve rather than exacerbate crises. With respect to the handicapped infant as well as the normally developing one, it would be counterproductive to treat the infant without appreciating that he or she is a member of a powerful system, the family, which is influenced by and which, in turn, shapes the infant's development.

The Reciprocal Influence between Family Members: Research Findings

The brief literature review that follows provides some examples of what has been gained by the focus upon the child within the context of the family. The research findings demonstrate that knowledge of the interaction among variables in the families of well or handicapped infants refines the ability to predict outcome. The interested reader is referred to Belsky (1981), Belsky, Lerner, and Spanier (1984), and Belsky, Robins, and Gamble (1984) for a more extensive review of the literature.

As Belsky (1981) noted, the effect of the parent upon the child's development has been a popular area of study that has yielded consistent findings, namely, responsive parenting results in enhanced intellectual, social, and emotional development in the child (Beckwith, Cohen, Kopp, Parmalee, & Marcy, 1976; Bell & Ainsworth, 1972; Clarke-Stewart, 1973; Crockenberg, 1981; M. Lewis & Goldberg, 1969). For example, in the now classic study of maternal responsiveness to infant crying, Bell and Ainsworth (1972) found that infants whose mothers responded more quickly to their crying were more linguistically advanced as young toddlers. Similarly, M. Lewis and Goldberg (1969) found that infants whose mothers had been more responsive to their crying demonstrated better performance on measures of information-processing ability.

Conversely, Lerner and Busch-Rossnagel (1981) have defined the infant not simply as a product of parental care, but also as a creator of his or her own development. S. Goldberg (1977) also found the infant to be a competent contributor to his or her environment. Just as the mother's responses influenced the baby, so too was she shaped by the baby's characteristics, such as his or her readability, predictability, and responsiveness (S. Goldberg, 1977; M. Lewis & Rosenbloom, 1974). A salient example of the child's influence on the caregiver is provided by Buss (1981) from a study of the effect of a child's activity level on parental behavior. Buss found that parents of active children were more likely than parents of quiescent children to respond with physical intrusion and to engage in power struggles.

Knowledge of how the child affects the parent can be refined even further, because there are individual differences in parental capacity to compensate for child characteristics. Specifically, the concept of *goodness of fit* (Thomas & Chess, 1977) provides a model for understanding how the same characteristics can have different effects upon different parents. For example, in a family that values high activity, an active child would be appreciated. However, in a family in which a parent has more sedentary habits, such a child may be more easily frustrated and more frequently reprimanded. With respect to infant difficultness, often a precursor of high activity, Bates, Freeland, and Lounsbury (1979) found that a mother's interpretation of infant difficultness was influenced in part by whether she was a new or an experienced parent and whether she was introverted or extraverted. Thus, it is not the behavior, per se, but the behavior in relation to relevant parental characteristics that determines the outcome.

With the consideration of both parents, family dynamics emerge. Belsky (1981) stated that, "inclusion of the father in the study of infancy . . . does more than create an additional parent-infant relationship. It transforms the mother-infant dyad into a family system comprised of marital and parent-infant relationships" (p. 5). There is also interaction between these relationships. For example, W.A. Goldberg and Easterbrooks (1984) confirmed the significance of the quality of the marital relationship as a contributor to both parent behavior and toddler functioning. Good marital quality was associated with increased sensitivity in parenting. Children in families with better marital relationships exhibited better progress. In another study (Pedersen, 1982), poor spousal support was associated with difficulty in feeding the infant.

In their delineation of a contextual theory of competent parenting and emergent child competence, Belsky, Robins, and Gamble (1984) expanded upon the factors that contribute to family functioning. Briefly, the competent parent, sensitive to and involved with his or her child, derives this ability through the interaction among personal resources (i.e., personal history) and subsystems of support (i.e., community) as well as child characteristics. Because there are multiple determinants to parenting competence, it is possible to compensate for areas of vulnerability.

The Family of the Handicapped Infant

The birth of a handicapped infant places unexpected stresses and demands upon the family system and places the family as a whole and individual members therein at increased risk for ineffective coping. Reviews of research on the impact of a child's disability on the family (Blacher, 1984; Crnic, Friedrich, & Greenberg, 1983; Murphy, 1982) make numerous references to maladaptive outcome. For example, parents of retarded children were found to be more likely to experience depression and emotional difficulties. Parents of older retarded children (although not those of younger children) reported less satisfaction with the marital relationship as compared to parents without retarded children. Furthermore, families of disabled children were found to experience more psychosocial problems, such as financial problems and restricted geographic mobility. Increased incidence of neglect and abuse of handicapped children has also been cited (Frodi, 1981).

Despite the frequent reports of maladaptive effects of the presence of a handicapped child in the family, Crnic, Friedrich, and Greenberg (1983) pointed out that these findings may reflect the bias of researchers toward focusing upon problems. When research has focused on variables that can ameliorate adverse effects, fewer negative outcomes are reported (Petersen, 1984).

More recently, social scientists have recognized that a handicapped child can also have a positive effect on the family system and have acknowledged that families can and do adapt successfully to a handicapped child (Lipsky, 1985; Petersen, 1984; Quine & Pahl, 1987). With respect to siblings of children with chronic illness, researchers have traditionally focused on the adverse effects of prolonged stress (Breslau, Weitzman, & Messinger, 1981). However, Tritt and Esses (1988) demonstrated that the type and degree of problems identified were not as bleak as previous studies had indicated, and went on to conclude that future studies "would benefit from a shift of perspective from preoccupation with universal negative effects to a less biased focus which includes siblings who cope well" (p. 218). Such a perspective enabled Grossman (1972) to note the positive effects of a handicap upon siblings.

DETERMINANTS OF FAMILY COPING

Models of Coping

Family dynamics can contribute to the resolution of stress despite illness, or to the production of stress despite health. In order to identify variables within the family system that contribute to its capacity to constructively resolve a crisis or, conversely, reduce its risk for maladaptive adjustment, it is helpful to review models of family coping. The ABCX coping model outlined by Hill (1958) defines vulnerability to crisis (X) as a function of characteristics of the event (A) itself interacting with the family's resources (B) and with the family's subjective interpretation of the threat (C) (Aadalen, 1980; Kazak, 1987). This model has been expanded by McCubbin (McCubbin, 1979; McCubbin & Patterson, 1981, 1983) to include assessments of strategies used for coping with a potential crisis (i.e., seeking services; doing things as a family) additional life stresses, social and psychological resources, and a delineation of possible outcomes. The coping model outlined by Zeitlin and Williamson (1988) also elaborates upon Hill's basic parameters. As depicted in their model (see Fig. 1), demands or tasks are evaluated by the family system and a plan of action for coping is determined. The family's subjective evaluation of the demand (Is it routine? stressful? intolerable?) and its action plan will be influenced by both its external and internal resources. External resources include resources to meet basic needs such as food, shelter, and clothing as well as social support resources, such as family, friends, and social institutions. Internal resources, when viewed from a family systems perspective, would include the family's beliefs and values, psychological states, and coping-related behavior. Also, they would include the important resource of family functioning, a multidimensional variable.

One example of a model that delineates the complex variables of family functioning is the Process Model of Family Functioning (Steinhauer, Santa-Barbara, & Skinner, 1984). The model identifies dimensions of family interaction that influence its task accomplishment or coping: Role Performance, Communication and Affective Expression, Affective Involvement, and Control. *Role Performance* refers to the assignment of different roles to family members so that tasks may be accomplished efficiently. Optimum assignment of roles reduces role conflict and creates role satisfaction. *Communication* refers to the quality of

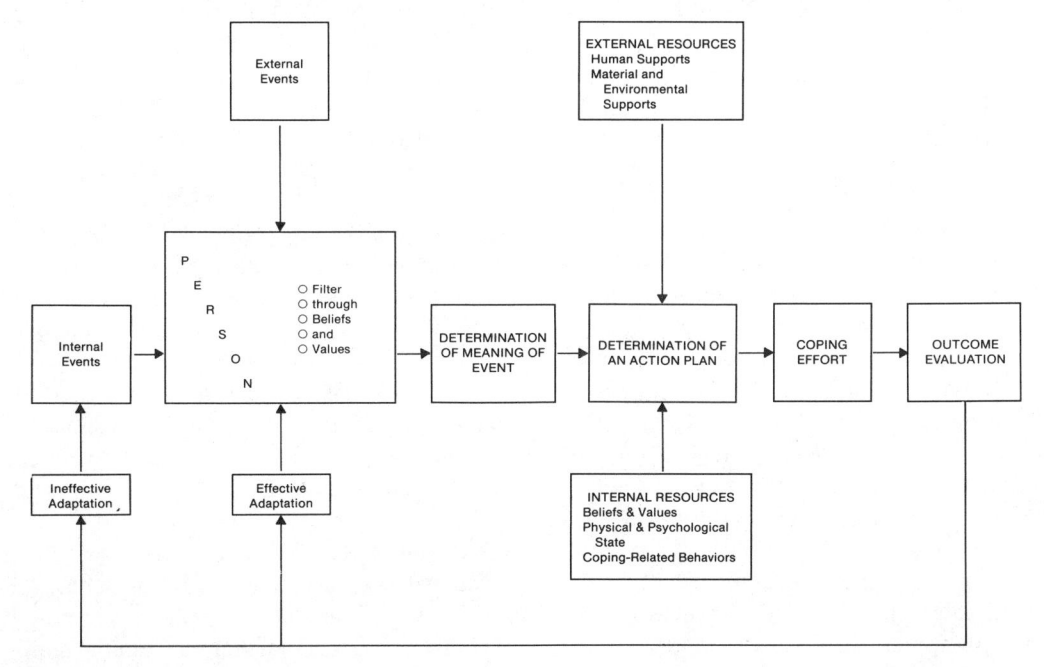

Figure 1. The coping process. (From Zeitlin, S.A., & Williamson G.G. [1988]. Developing family resources for adaptive coping. *Early Childhood, 12,* p. 139; reprinted with permission of the Division for Early Childhood of the Council for Exceptional Children.)

information exchange between family members and their ability to achieve mutual understanding. Both the clarity of the messages themselves (clear and direct versus ambiguous, indirect, or paradoxical) and the receptiveness of the receiver of the message (open and available versus closed and unavailable) must be considered. *Affective Expression,* a component of communication, addresses the exchange of feelings, including their content and intensity. *Affective Involvement* addresses the degree and quality of caring and concern that individual family members have for each other. Types of affective involvement range from uninvolved to narcissistic to empathetic to enmeshed. *Control* refers to the manner in which individuals influence each other in order to maintain family functioning and to adapt to changes. In this model, Steinhauer et al. identified four different types of control styles that differ on the dimensions of predictability (the degree of consistency in behavior) and constructiveness (the type of control technique used, education/nurturant versus shaming). Finally, the model recognizes the considerable influence of Values and Norms (family, subgroup, and societal) on all aspects of family functioning. The synthesis of these dimensions yields each family's unique functioning style.

Application of the Coping Models: Research Findings

Research findings reinforce the importance of the role of the variables cited in the coping models as predictors of adjustment. *Characteristics of the event* itself that have been associated with increased stress include ambiguity in the diagnosis and prognosis (Bernheimer, Young, & Winton, 1983; McCubbin, Cauble, & Patterson, 1982). Conversely, knowledge about the infant's condition is a significant contributor to adjustment (Weber & Parker, 1981). The physical challenge of caregiving demands (Beckman-Bell, 1981) also elevates stress levels. Jessop et al. (1988) reported a relationship between the child's functional limitations as perceived by the mother and the mother's own mental health status.

In terms of *internal resources,* a family's *belief system* and *subjective perceptions* modify their interpretation of crisis. Their reactions are affected by such factors as: 1) the subjective perception of the severity of the handicap (Klein & Simmons, 1979; Lazarus 1981); 2) the subjective perception of self-blame or guilt (Bristol & Schopler, 1984); 3) the symbolic meaning ascribed to the event; and 4) the belief in their ability to improve their infant's health (Affleck, Tennen, & Gershman, 1985; Wasserman, 1984). Specific examples of how parents' subjective beliefs influence outcome are found in the research literature. McKinney and Peterson (1987) found that a mother's perception of the child's behavior and temperament as measured by the Parenting Stress Index (Abidin, 1986) was a better predictor of her affect and sense of competence than was the diagnosis per se. McCubbin and Patterson (1981) found that parental belief in the value of the intervention program contributed to their ability to cope.

The *psychological state* of the parent, an internal resource, can be affected by the grief reaction experienced by parents mourning the loss of the child (Taylor, 1982). Following the birth of a handicapped baby, parents perceive themselves more negatively (Waisbren, 1980). They may experience symptoms of depression (Cummings, Bayley, & Rie, 1966) which, in turn, can adversely affect their children (Sameroff, Seifer, & Zax, 1982). In a study of healthy infants, Bettes (1988) demonstrated how elevated levels of maternal depression interfered with maternal behavior. In face-to-face interactions, depressed mothers failed to modify their behavior in response to their infant's behavior. Compared with the nondepressed group, these mothers were slower to respond to their infant's vocalization, more variable in their speech patterns, and less apt to exaggerate their intonations. A laboratory paradigm by Emde and Sorce (1983) suggests how adult emotional affect and child development may be associated. In their study, toddlers were presented with a novel, and thus threatening, stimulus while in the presence of their parents. Although all parents were physically accessible, only some were actively observing their children. The remaining parents were "distracted" with a reading task. Even at this early age, the toddlers were able to distinguish between those mothers who were "emotionally available" and those who were "distracted," and were less likely to engage in cognitively beneficial exploratory behavior in the presence of the "distracted" mother.

Specific characteristics of the family members can affect the internal resource of *interaction styles* and alter the courtship between parent and infant. A high-risk infant's capacity to perceive and respond to the environment may be diminished (Als, 1981; Ostfeld, Hegyi, & Hiatt, 1987). Parents may demonstrate a compensatory increase in activity (DiVitto & Goldberg, 1979) or, in other cases, decrease their involvement (Minde, Whitelaw, Brown, & Fitzhardinge, 1983). Initial alterations in behavior may persist. For example, in a study by Minde et al. (1983), mothers of seriously ill premature infants continued to demonstrate lower levels of interaction with their infants even after they had improved. Specifically, they smiled at and touched their infants less than did mothers whose infants had an easier postnatal course. As noted above, the persistence of an interaction style characteristic of depression can affect the infant's development.

With respect to family dynamics, Kazak (1987) noted that illness alone does not automatically predispose the family to interact dysfunctionally. However, where family dysfunction exists, it can predict the quality of the child's adjustment more accurately than does the illness itself (B.L. Lewis & Khaw, 1982). Conversely, good functioning facilitates adjustment. Using the Family Environment Scales to assess family functioning (Moos & Moos, 1981), Bristol (1984) found that such characteristics as cohesion, expressiveness, and active recreational orientation were associated with successful adjustment to autism.

With respect to *external resources, social support* improves the family's ability to cope (Dunst et al., 1984; Feiring, Fox, Jaskir, & Lewis, 1987; Jessop et al. 1988; Levitt, Weber, & Clark, 1986; Pugh & Russell, 1977). Most beneficial to coping is intimate or spousal support (Bristol, 1987; Freidrich, 1979). However, peer support from individuals going through similar events is also known to facilitate adjustment (Minde et al., 1980; Wasserman, 1984). Observing successful coping strategies increases the capacity of the observer to do the same thing (Meichenbaum, 1977). In addition, Leet and Dunst (1985) and Feiring et al. (1987) noted that effective support can also come in material form (goods), and Joyce, Singer, and Isralowitz (1983) found that access to respite care could contribute to improving family relationships.

Other *life stressors* may compound the problems facing the family of a handicapped infant (Jessop et al., 1988). The presence of other family illnesses, marital separation or divorce, economic hardships, or other difficulties may define the availability of the external resources, the vulnerability of the internal resources (Petersen, 1984), or the stability of the interactions.

METHODS AND TOOLS FOR FAMILY ASSESSMENT

The adaptation of a family to a developmentally disabled child is clearly a complex process, one that is influenced by a variety of factors. In order to gain an understanding of any particular family and identify what types of intervention may be helpful, the early intervention professional must view the family as a system and assess the different factors influencing it. Family assessment can be accomplished using a variety of methods, including interview, observation, and self-report inventories (Holman, 1983). Skinner (1987) noted that each modality contributes to the formation of an accurate picture of family functioning. In addition, the assessment can focus on one or more of the variables predictive of coping, such as material support, emotional support, parent-child interaction style, marital functioning, or parental beliefs. The method and the content area of the assessment should be chosen to fulfill the program's goals. The family is best served when the assessment is undertaken for a clear purpose and is part of a comprehensive service delivery model.

One example of a comprehensive assessment and intervention model is the Family Focused Intervention program (Bailey et al., 1986), which is intended to: 1) enhance the ability to cope with the handicapped infant's needs, 2) enhance family understanding of developmental needs, 3) facilitate mutually satisfying and appropriate interaction; and 4) protect family dignity through full involvement. To that end, staff work closely with the family to assess needs, generate hypotheses, provide feedback and clarify needs, formulate a plan, implement it, and evaluate it. In this model, self-report instruments and observations would be useful in the first and last steps, while structured interviews would be helpful for feedback and clarification.

A general strategy to undertake when selecting and evaluating an assessment method is to conduct a literature search to ascertain the latest data on reliabilty and validity and target populations for methods of interest. Works in progress do not usually provide data on predictive validity, making it difficult to understand the long-term implications of particular findings. As original study populations are followed prospectively, this information will become available and should be pursued. The reader should also note that in some instances, it is recommended that the task of interpreting the findings and making appropriate recommendations is best directed to a mental health practitioner with clinical experience in the counseling of families coping with the problems addressed in this text.

Interview Methods

One commonly used method of family assessment is the clinical interview or face-to-face discussion with family members, which can be used either to gather data or to refine information gathered through other means. Nondirected interviews permit the structure and direction to be established by the interviewee. However, while these may elicit rich clinical information and provide an excellent opportunity for building rapport, their lack of uniformity makes data gathering and goal setting difficult. Another type is the structured interview with specific questions or goals and either a limited choice of "forced responses" or an opportunity for individual responses. Such interviews can be especially useful for families who are uncomfortable with a questionnaire. They can also be used in conjunction with questionnaires to elaborate on selected responses, verify conclusions, and resolve ambiguities. Winton and Bailey (1988) have developed the Family Focused Interview, a structured interview that is designed to set families at ease, confirm and extend the information generated by the basic assessment, identify any additional needs or competence, resolve discrepancies between staff and family in the interpretation of needs, and determine priorities in meeting the needs. The procedure is designed to function with the Family Focused Intervention model cited above.

Adele Holman (1983), in her book entitled *Family Assessment: Tools for Understanding and Intervention,* discusses the use of several family system–focused interview tools. The Ecomap developed by Ann Hartland is a useful way of depicting the family's relationship with a variety of external resources, such as the immediate family, extended family, health care system, work, and church. The genogram provides a graphic depiction of the family tree, including significant life events, occupations of family members, and places of residences. In addition, an understanding of the family interaction patterns and functioning can emerge as a description of relationships between different family members is obtained. McGoldrick and Gerson's (1985) book provides an excellent resource on the use of the genogram in family assessment. Both of these techniques can provide a structured means of collecting family information during an interview.

Observational Methods

Observational methods, like interviews, can be structured or unstructured. Individuals who work directly with families gain a great deal of information through informal observations. However, it is also useful to perform structured observations when specific information is needed for developing interventions or evaluating a family's progress. An increasing number of observational measures of parent-child interaction are being developed (Farren, Clark, & Ray, this volume). These kinds of measures can assist in identifying aspects of the parent or infant interaction styles that can benefit from interventions designed to promote the quality of the dyadic interaction. The availability of videotaping enhances the observer's ability to review and code the behavior in the manner required by a particular measure.

One classic observation tool to assess the quality of the home environment is Caldwell's (1972) HOME Inventory, used by trained home visitors to provide a formal measure of aspects of the home such as Emotional and Verbal Responsivity of the Mother, Organization of the Physical and Temporal Environment, and Stimulation through Toys, Games and Reading Materials. More recently, the developers of the Family Assessment Measure (Skinner et al., 1983), a self-report instrument, have prepared a structured observational tool for assessing family functioning as well as a structured interview to complement the original self-report instrument. These tools are currently being evaluated.

Self-Report Questionnaire Measures

Self-report questionnaires offer an efficient, standardized way of gathering a great deal of information. Discussed below are well-known published instruments as well as promising "works in progress." All meet the following criteria: 1) they measure concepts addressed in this chapter; 2) they have been developed for or adapted to populations relevant to the reader; 3) their developers, in most instances, continue to refine or study the instrument and track its use in research; 4) they are cited in relevant research; and 5) adequate data on reliability and validity are available.

The presentation of selected self-report measures that follows will be clustered according to the aspects of family coping that are targeted: measures of stress, external resources, and internal resources and comprehensive measures of family coping.

Measures of Stress

The *Functional Status Measure* (Stein & Jessop, 1982) evaluates the mother's perception of the degree to which her child's illness interferes with normal functioning in the areas of communication, mobility, mood, energy, sleep, eating, and toileting. The measure refers to leisure-, work- and rest-associated activities in the home, the neighborhood, and school. The instrument is modified with appropriate items for four age groups, including infancy (birth to 8 months). In a study of chronic childhood illness, the more functionally limited the mother perceived the child to be, the more psychologically distressed was the mother (Jessop et al.,1988). In contrast to the mother's assessment, the medical provider's assessment of the burden entailed by the illness was *not* predictive of parental coping.

In order to gain a well-rounded view of the family, it is important to understand what life stress the family is dealing with and to gain information about how stressful the family perceives these events to be. The classic measure of life stress, the Social Readjustment Rating Scale developed by Holmes and Raye (1967), asked individuals to indicate which stressful life experiences (death of a spouse, change of job, vacation, etc.) they had experienced in the last year. Developed more recently, the 57-item Life Experiences Survey (LES) (Sarason, Johnson, & Siegel, 1978) addressed the limitations of earlier instruments that provided predetermined stressfulness scores for each life event or change regardless of the family's individual evaluation of the stress and viewed all change (positive or negative) as having a negative impact. On the LES, individuals not only indicate whether an event has occurred but also rate the desirability of events that have occurred.

Brandt (1984), citing the wide use of the LES, applied it to measure the effect of negative life events on mothers with developmentally delayed children. Negative life events had a significant and negative impact on mothers' satisfaction with support systems.

Measures of External Resources: Social Support and Resource Needs

Measures of social support generally try to identify what sources of support a family has available or uses. However, it is important to consider the parent's perception of both the availability and adequacy of different types of support. For an extensive review of social support measures, the reader is referred to Dunst, Trivette, and Deal (1988). Several of the more relevant and comprehensive measures of social support are described briefly below.

Levitt et al. (1986) adapted Kahn and Antonucci's (1984) model to create the Social Network Questionnaire for use with mothers with infants and young children. The tool consists of a network diagram measuring closeness of relationships, an assessment of the kinds of emotional and child care support functions provided by the individuals noted in the network, a measure of satisfaction with the network, a measure of satisfaction with spousal and parental support, and indices of well-being as measured by affect and life satisfaction. This instrument bears following because of its thoroughness, the clear definition of each construct, and its alliance with the comprehensive work of Kahn and Antonucci.

Dunst and his colleagues (1988) have developed a number of social support questionnaires that may be useful to early interventionists. The Family Support Scale (Dunst et al., 1984) consists of 18 identified potential sources of support and space to add other sources. The parent indicates whether a source of support is available and the degree to which it is helpful. In their assessment of the instrument, the authors noted that the extent of social support was related to measures of personal and family well-being and predicted frequency of parent-child interactions and child progress. The Family Resource Scale (Leet & Dunst, 1985) expands upon the concept of support by tapping basic resources such as money, time, and transportation.

Bailey and Simeonsson (1988, in press) have also developed an assessment of family needs for external resources or assistance, the Family Needs Survey. Like the instruments of Dunst and his colleagues, it is designed for use in early intervention programs. The family is asked to indicate their desire for help in a variety of areas such as, "I need to have more friends that I can talk to," or "I need more information about how to teach my child."

Measures of Internal Resources

Psychological Adjustment of Parents to Child's Handicap. Eden (1983) developed an instrument to assess thoughts and feelings parents experience in the course of adjusting to the diagnosis of a handicap. The three categories of emotional reaction are: 1) shock, guilt, despair; 2) refusal-denial; and 3) adjustment-recovery-acceptance. These categories are not presented as stages (Eden-Piercy, Blacher, & Eyman, 1986), but as types of reactions. Thus, the author avoids Allen and Affleck's (1985) criticism of models that have a preconceived notion of the course and duration of grief reactions and that attempt to "cure" families who deviate from this course. The instrument confronts some of the most painful feelings experienced by parents of handicapped children. While more research on psychometric properties is needed, it may ultimately assess a family's readiness to take on different aspects of an intervention program's agenda. Currently, this work in progress has been found to have therapeutic value. Eden (1983) pointed out anecdotally that completing the instrument enabled participants in her study to address and clarify their emotions and contributed to the productivity of the parent group.

Family Interaction or Functioning Style Although a number of questionnaires exist for evaluating family interaction or functioning style, they should be administered and interpreted by a mental health professional who is knowledgeable in the family systems theory associated with the measure. For the interested mental health professional, Skinner (1987) presents a review of the theoretical and psychometric properties of three of the more thoroughly studied and widely used self-report assessments of family functioning: the Family Environment Scale (Moos & Moos, 1981), the Family Adaptability and Cohesion Evaluation Scale III (Olson, Portner, & Lavee, 1985), and the Family Assessment Measure (Skinner, Steinhauer, & Santa-Barbara, 1983).

Although designed for use with the general population, all three instruments have been applied to families of disabled children in order to identify the impact of illness or disability on the family and to identify mediators of coping. For example, using the Family Environment Scale, Schafer, Glasgow, McCaul, and Dreher (1983) assessed family characteristics that affect compliance with a diabetic treatment protocol. The study found that family conflict was inversely associated with adherence to the treatment. Bristol (1987) found that successful adaptation to a handicap was associated with cohesion, expressiveness, and active-recreational orientation, parameters measured by the Family Environment Scale.

Comprehensive Measures of Family Coping

A number of instruments exist that offer a comprehensive assessment of family coping rather than an evaluation of only a single component such as internal or external resources.

The Chronicity Impact and Coping Instrument. The Chronicity Impact and Coping Instrument: Parent Questionnaire (CICI:PQ) (Hymovich, 1984) was one of the first instruments specifically developed to evaluate the effects of a child's chronic illness upon the family and the variety and effectiveness of resources and strategies used by the family to cope with the effects, as well as the continuing needs of the family. Designed to help nurses identify family needs, it is of value to all professionals charged with the development and implementation of individualized service plans (Hymovich & Baker, 1985). With its practical bent and attention to the diverse variables that contribute to adaptive coping, it is unique among family assessment measures. As a result of a comprehensive psychometric analysis of the CICI:PQ (Hymovich, 1988a), there has been revision of the original instrument, which is now called the Parent Perception Inventory (PPI). Preliminary information on normative data, reading level, and reliability are available for the revision (Hymovich, 1988b).

The PPI takes approximately 40 minutes for a parent to complete and consists of the following six scales: Concerns, Beliefs and Feelings, Coping, General Information, Spouse Concerns and Coping, and Siblings. The section dealing with Concerns allows the parent to indicate which concerns they have had (i.e., wondering what my child's future is likely to be, getting out of the house by myself), and another section allows them to indicate in what areas they want General Information (i.e., physical care of my child, managing child's behavior). In the section on Beliefs and Feelings, parents describe their subjective perceptions on such issues as locus of control (i.e., "There isn't much that I can do about my child's condition," or "It is usually better to talk about one's feelings with others") and their own emotional reactions and feelings. In the Coping section, parents rate the frequency with which they employ various coping strategies (i.e., crying, getting away for a while, exercising, praying) and indicate the helpfulness of each. The parents' use of family and community supports is detailed, although the adequacy of these supports is not directly addressed. The section on Spouse Concerns and Coping asks the parent completing the questionnaire to note his or her perception of the spouse's concerns and methods of coping. Finally, sibling reactions (i.e., jealousy, helps with child's therapy) are noted and areas of need related to the sibling (i.e., help managing child's behavior, helping child understand the other child's condition) are identified.

The PPI is a comprehensive instrument that is in step with current theories regarding family coping and adaptation. It is based closely on Hymovich's original instrument, for which criterion validity had been established (Hymovich & Baker, 1985). Hymovich remains actively involved in the development of the instrument, which includes tracking its use in research. Further validation and the expansion of the normative base are therefore reasonably assured.

The Parenting Stress Index. According to Abidin (1986), situational factors as well as various parent and child characteristics contribute to the development of stress, which, at high levels, is associated with maladaptive parenting and the emergence of emotional and behavioral problems in the child. The Parenting Stress Index (PSI) was developed to identify the sources and levels of stress perceived by the parent in relation to the child. It has been extensively used with families coping with physically, behaviorally, and developmentally disabled infants and children. Although parents of handicapped children do not necessarily experience a debilitating level of stress (Kazak, Reber, & Snitzer, 1988), for those who do, the instrument can assist in specifying the source of stress (McKinney & Peterson, 1987).

Given the level of interpretation required, the PSI should be administered and interpreted by a trained mental health professional. The 120 questions, available in English or Spanish, are divided into a Child Domain, Parent Domain, and Life Stress Index. The child domain consists of the following subscales: the child's adaptability to new situations, the acceptability of the child to the parent, the demands placed on the parent by the child, the child's mood, the child's distractability/hyperactivity, and the degree to which the child reinforces the parent. The subscales of the parent domain are: depression, attachment to the child, degree to which the parent feels restricted by the parenting role, sense of competence, social isolation, relationship with spouse, and health. Interpretation of the profiles on both domains provides a basis of developing specific intervention strategies.

Considerable effort has gone into the development of the PSI. Since its formal presentation in 1979, Abidin has continued to investigate the psychometric properties of the scale and has tracked relevant research and clinical applications. The interested reader is referred to Abidin (1986) for details of the instrument's measurement properties.

In general, studies of construct, discriminant, and predictive validity indicate that the instrument is suitable for identifying families at risk for maladaptive emotional and behavioral coping responses. For example, in a study on child abuse (Mash, Johnston, & Kovitz, 1983), the child character ratings made by abusive mothers were found to be higher (more problematic) than those made by nonabusive mothers about their children. This difference in rating was obtained even though there were no significant differences in the observed behavior of the children in both groups. The study also determined that stress levels were correlated with the quality of the parent's behavior toward her child. In a study cited earlier (McKinney & Peterson, 1987) maternal perception as measured by the PSI was a greater predictor of coping than was the child's diagnosis.

The Questionnaire on Resources and Stress. The Questionnaire on Resources and Stress (QRS) was developed by Holroyd (1974) to measure both the positive and negative impact of a handicapped or chronically ill person upon the family. It consists of 285 items that fall into three categories: parental problems, family functioning problems, and problems the parents perceive in the child or perceive that the child will face (Friedrich, Greenberg, & Crnic, 1983). A factor analysis on a population diagnosed with chronic medical or developmental disorders (Holroyd, 1974) resulted in the following factors: dependency and management, cognitive impairment, limits on family opportunity, life span care, family disharmony, lack of personal reward, terminal illness stress, physical limitations, financial stress, preference for institutional care, and personal burden for respondent. In a series of studies (Holroyd & Guthrie, 1979; Holroyd & McArthur, 1976; Wilton & Renaut, 1986) the instrument discriminated between stress patterns of parents of moderately, mildly, and nonhandicapped children.

Holroyd (1982) developed a short form of her instrument (QRS-SF), as have Friedrich et al. (1983) and Salisbury (1986). In the Friedrich et al. (1983) version, 52 items of the QRS were found to be most reliable. These items yielded four factors: parent and family problems, pessimism, child characteristics, and physical incapacity. In a study of concurrent validity, the first factor was positively correlated with a measure of depression and negatively correlated with a social desirability scale, which, the authors suggest, "supports the interesting theoretical relationship between denial or minimization and the coping process in families of handicapped children" (p. 45). The second factor, pessimism, was correlated with a depression scale. The third and fourth factors were correlated with measures of child problems.

Salisbury (1986) noted that since neither her 48-item version nor the Friedrich et al. (1983) version retain a social support factor, this important variable should be assessed independently of these scales. Salisbury also noted that the QRS is so broad in its focus on age and handicap that many items would not be applicable to infants.

The QRS in all its forms is an example of a work in progress that will most likely continue to be refined in response to further study and continued interest in its broad concepts.

The Inventory of Parent Experiences. The Inventory of Parent Experiences (IPE) consists of a group of assessment instruments developed or adapted for use in a series of studies conducted with mothers and infants at the University of Washington (i.e., Crnic, Greenberg, Ragozin, Robinson, & Basham, 1983; Crnic, Greenberg, Robinson, & Ragozin, 1984). This research tool has been extremely useful in generating valuable findings on populations of interest to the reader and bears following. Internal consistency measures are reported (Ragozin, Basham, Crnic, Greenberg, & Robinson, 1982) and a temporary manual is available.

The first component of the IPE is a Satisfaction with Parenting Scale, which is made up of two subscales: role satisfaction and pleasure with infant. The latter subscale assesses "the mother's degree of pleasure in childcare chores, doubts about maternal competency, irritation with her baby, regrets about having the baby, and overall feelings towards the baby" (Ragozin et al., 1982, p. 629). The second component, the Social Support Measure, was adapted from a scale by Henderson (Henderson, Byrne, & Duncan-Jones, 1981). It measures levels of social support ranging from intimate to community. The items are scored not only for availability of a particular source of support, but also for satisfaction with it. The last component consists of a single item that asks the mother to evaluate her satisfaction with her current life situation. In many projects conducted by the developers (i.e., Crnic, Greenberg, Ragozin, Robinson, & Basham, 1983) an adaptation of the Life Experiences Survey (Sarason et al., 1978) is added to the inventory.

Using the IPE and a measure of life stress, Crnic, Greenberg, Ragozin, Robinson, and Basham (1983) assessed the effect of social support and stress on the interactions of mothers and premature or term infants. Perhaps because the premature infants were essentially healthy, with no gross neurological or physical anomalies, no differences in behavior or satisfaction were found between groups. However, for pooled data, both stress levels and degree of social support, particularly intimate support, predicted maternal attitudes at 1 month and mother-infant interaction at 4 months.

Caveats Regarding Family Assessment Methods

Each assessment modality has specific limitations that should be noted and considered by interventionists. Unstructured interviews are inefficient for gathering large amounts of basic data and therefore pose a problem for programs faced with limited clinical resources. In addition, the lack of a standardization presents a challenge for programs attempting to conduct research or assess the effects of an intervention. Finally, clinically inexperienced staff members may have difficulty with interpretation of unstructured findings. These limitations can be overcome by the selection of more structured assessment techniques for gathering information, while the unstructured interview can be reserved for building rapport or clarification of concerns. Observational methods can provide the clinician with an actual view of family functioning and interaction. However, families who are "observed" as part of an evaluation may find it difficult to behave naturally. It may be easier for parents to cope with this approach once rapport has been established.

Self-report instruments contain questions that some parents may believe go beyond the mandate of a program. Individuals put off by what they perceive as an intrusive item or by the prospect of being "diagnosed" may distort data or decline to participate. This problem can be alleviated by empowering parents to be prudent consumers of the instrument. A general statement of purpose should be provided for each type of instrument. Parents can be instructed to omit questions to which they object. Parents need to have access to a staff member should reading or comprehension problems arise or should emotional concerns come up as they fill out the tool. Debriefing following a structured assessment is an especially helpful way of humanizing the process. Sometimes this step enables the parent to give responses to critical items that are more detailed than the tool was capable of encoding.

There are a number of caveats that apply to all assessments, regardless of modality. The assessment process provide programs with means of evaluating needs and strengths of families. The instruments are not intended to be used for the purpose of diagnosing emotional disorders. If there is a concern about the behavior of a family member, the family should be encouraged to meet with a mental health consultant who can identify those individuals whose grief or stress may have exacerbated a major depression, panic attack, or personality disorder, and who can make appropriate recommendations and referrals. Whether reactive or endogenous, the diagnosis and treatment of a mental health problem is beyond the scope of a program's mandate.

To be a good test evaluator, it is vital to appreciate the practical implications of theoretical differences among tests with seemingly similar goals. Theoretical orientation often determines the questions developed for an assessment tool. As a result, instruments that purport to measure the same parameter may operationally define it differently and therefore ask unrelated questions. A family functioning theory that associates well-being with "quality of communication" will develop questions tapping this construct. Another model may label "locus of control" as the key to good family dynamics, and will derive questions from this basis. Although each model may yield a family functioning test, it would not be inconceivable for a family to score poorly on one test and well on another. If both are perceived to measure the same issue, family functioning, the results would be contradictory. If the specific construct is recognized as the essence of what is being measured, however, then the contrasting results can be accommodated as simply two aspects of the complex variable called family functioning. Awareness of theoretical constructs is particularly important when the questionnaires contain broadly worded items such as "I get along with my family," rather than specific items such as "My spouse helps me feed our child." In the latter case, the evaluator usually appreciates what is being addressed by its clarity. Therefore, the interpretation and recommendations remain closely connected to the behavior discussed in the question. However, global questions and ambigiously broad titles given to a test may stimulate the evaluator to form generalizations about a family that go beyond the findings to conclude that there is an overall poor family relationship. So perceived, families would feel unfairly judged.

Individual differences need to be recognized and respected. An example of a behavior that traditionally has been viewed with concern by service providers is so-called "diagnosis shopping." Yet, for some parents this information-gathering activity may serve as an important step in coming to terms with a handicapping condition through the reduction of ambiguity, a recognized stressor (Quine & Pahl, 1987). For many infants, a diagnosis of developmental delay is derived on a "rule out" basis. Specific genetic, toxic, and traumatic causes are eliminated until one is left with a thorough description of symptoms that have no known etiology and, therefore, no clear prognosis. The uncertainty may be compounded by small variations in explanations offered by the different professionals the parents encounter in the course of obtaining a diagnosis. Attuned to any discrepancy, parents may continue to pursue information until they have achieved a level of understanding that enables them to feel more in control of the crisis. Occasionally, parents engaged in this process encounter a specialist who helps them achieve a breakthrough in diagnosis and treatment, resulting in a powerful reminder that a parent is the ultimate child advocate and a consistently valuable member of the team.

In summary, we can boil this commentary down to three guidelines: 1) know what a test purports to measure; 2) avoid interpretations that go beyond the data; and 3) recognize and respect individual differences between families.

CONCLUSIONS

The increasing recognition that family members have a profound and ongoing effect on each other has led to the recommendation that early intervention services be family focused. In order to promote optimum functioning of the disabled child, it is essential that early intervention professionals recognize the strengths and needs of the larger family system and develop interventions that promote the well-being of the family as a whole. In this chapter, we have introduced the reader to family system concepts and to a variety of assessment methods and tools that can assist early intervention professionals in developing a better understanding of the unique aspects of every family. Some of these assessments can be used easily by professionals of any discipline. However, many are better interpreted by professionals with mental health and family systems training, such as social workers and psychologists. As early intervention programs increase their attention to family issues, consultation from mental health professionals becomes increasingly important. In addition, personnel preparation programs for infant specialists will need to offer more family systems training and training programs for mental health professionals will need to offer a focus on families with infants and young children.

Finally, although the increased emphasis on families promises more comprehensive and effective services to families, for some families the family focus will feel intrusive. Early intervention professionals will need to be sensitive to differences between families in their need or willingness to share family information. Ultimately, families should have a choice of how family focused they want services to be.

REFERENCES

Aadalen, S. (1980). Coping with sudden infant death syndrome: Intervention strategies and a case study. *Family Relations, 29,* 584–590.

Abidin, R.R. (1986). *Parenting Stress Index* (2nd ed.). Charlottesville, VA: Pediatric Psychology Press.

Ackerman, N.W. (1958). *The psychodynamics of family life.* New York: Basic Books.

Affleck, G., Tennen, H., & Gershman, K. (1985). Cognitive adaptations to high-risk infants: The search for mastery, meaning and protection from future harm. *American Journal of Mental Deficiency, 89,* 653–656.

Allen, D.A., & Affleck, G. (1985). Are we stereotyping parents? A postscript to Blacher. *Mental Retardation, 23,* 200–202.

Als, H. (1981). *Infant individuality: Assessing patterns of very early development.* New York: Basic Books.

Anderson, B.J., & Auslander, W.F. (1980). Research on diabetes management and the family: A critique. *Diabetes Care, 3,* 696–702.

Bailey, D.B., & Simeonsson, R.J. (1988). *Family assessment in early intervention.* Columbus, OH: Merrill Publishing Co.

Bailey, D.B., & Simeonsson, R.J. (in press). Assessing the needs of families with handicapped infants. *Journal of Special Education.*

Bailey, D.B., Simeonsson, R.J., Winton, P., Huntington, G., Comfort, M., Isbel, P., O'Donnell, K., & Helm, J. (1986). Family-focused intervention: A functional model for planning, implementing and evaluating individual family services in early intervention. *Journal of the Division for Early Childhood, 10,* 156–171.

Bates, J.E., Freeland, C.A., & Lounsbury, M.L. (1979). Measurement of infant difficultness. *Child Development, 50,* 794–803.

Beckman, P.J. (1984). A transactional view of stress in families of handicapped children. In M. Lewis (Ed.), *Beyond the dyad.* New York: Plenum Press.

Beckman-Bell, P. (1981). Child-related stress in families of handicapped children. *Topics in Early Childhood Special Education, 1,* 45–53.

Beckwith, L., Cohen, S.E., Kopp, C.B., Parmalee, A.H., & Marcy, T.G. (1976). Caregiver-infant interaction and early cognitive development in preterm infants. *Child Development, 47,* 579–587.

Bee, H.L., Barnard, K.E., Eyres, S.J., Gray, C.A., Hammond, M.A., Spietz, A.L., Snyder, C., & Clark, B. (1982). Prediction of IQ and language skill from perinatal status, child performance, family characteristics and mother-infant interaction. *Child Development, 53,* 1134–1156.

Bell, S.M., & Ainsworth, M.D.S. (1972). Infant crying and maternal responsiveness. *Child Development, 43,* 1171–1190.

Belsky, J. (1981). Early human experience: A family perspective. *Developmental Psychology, 17,* 3–23.

Belsky, J., Lerner, R.M., & Spanier, G.B. (1984). *The child in the family.* New York: Random House.

Belsky, J., Robins, E., & Gamble, W. (1984). The determinants of parental competence: Toward a contextual theory. In M. Lewis (Ed.), *Beyond the dyad.* New York: Plenum Press.

Bernheimer, L., Young, M., & Winton, P. (1983). Stress over time: Parents with young handicapped children. *Developmental and Behavioral Pediatrics, 4,* 177–181.

Bettes, B.A. (1988). Maternal depression and motherese: Temporal and intonational features. *Child Development, 59,* 1089–1096.

Blacher, J. (1984). A dynamic perspective on the impact of a severely handicapped child on the family. In J. Blacher (Ed.), *Severely handicapped young children and their families: Research in review.* Orlando, FL: Academic Press.

Brandt, P.A. (1984). Social support and negative life events of mothers with developmentally delayed children. *Birth Defects, 20,* 205–244.

Breslau, N., Weitzman, M., & Messinger, K. (1981). Psychological functioning of siblings of disabled children. *Pediatrics, 67,* 344–353.

Bristol, M.M. (1984). Family resources and successful adjustment to autistic children. In E. Schopler & G. Mesibov (Eds.), *Autism in adolescents and adults.* New York: Plenum Press.

Bristol, M.M. (1987). Mothers of children with autism or communication disorders: Successful adaptation and the double ABCX model. *Journal of Autism & Developmental Disorders, 17,* 469–486.

Bristol, M.M., & Schopler, E. (1984). A developmental perspective on stress and coping in families of autistic children. In J. Blacher (Ed.), *Severely handicapped young children and their families: Research in review.* Orlando, FL: Academic Press.

Buss, D.M. (1981). Predicting parent-child interactions from children's activity level. *Developmental Psychology, 17,* 59–65.

Caldwell, B. (1972). *HOME Inventory.* Little Rock: University of Arkansas.

Clarke-Stewart, K.A. (1973). Interactions between mothers and their young children: Characteristics and consequences. *Monographs of the Society for Research in Child Development, 38*(153).

Cohen, D.J., Detlor, J., Shaywitz, B.A., & Leckman, J.F. (1982). Interaction of biological and psychological factors in the natural history of Tourette syndrome: A paradigm for childhood neuropsychiatric disorder. In A.J. Friedhoff & T.N. Chase (Eds.), *Advances in neurology: Gilles de la Tourette syndrome.* New York: Raven Press.

Crnic, K.A., Friedrich, W.N., & Greenberg, M.T. (1983). Adaptation of families with mentally retarded children: A model of stress, coping and family ecology. *American Journal of Mental Deficiency, 88,* 125–138.

Crnic, K.A., Greenberg, M.T., Ragozin, A.S., Robinson, N.M., & Basham, R.B. (1983). Effects of stress and social support on mothers and premature and full-term infants. *Child Development, 54,* 209–217.

Crnic, K.A., Greenberg, M.T., Robinson, N.M., & Ragozin, A.S. (1984). Maternal stress and social support: Effects on the mother-infant relationship from birth to eighteen months. *American Journal of Orthopsychiatry, 54,* 224–235.

Crockenberg, S.B. (1981). Infant irritability, mother responsiveness, and social support influences on the security of infant-mother attachment. *Child Development, 52,* 857–865.

Cummings, S.T., Bayley, H., & Rie, H. (1966). Effects of the child's deficiency on the mother: A study of mothers of mentally retarded, chronically ill, and neurotic children. *American Journal of Orthopsychiatry, 36,* 595–608.

DiVitto, B., & Goldberg, S. (1979). The effects of newborn medical status on early parent-infant interaction. In T.M. Field, A.M. Sistek, S. Goldberg, & H.H. Shuman (Eds.), *Infants born at risk.* New York: Spectrum Publications.

Dunst, C.J., Jenkins, V., & Trivette, C.M. (1984). The Family Support Scale: Reliability and validity. *Journal of Individual, Family and Community Wellness, 4,* 45–52.

Dunst, C.J., Trivette, C., & Deal, A. (1988). *Enabling and empowering families.* Cambridge, MA: Brookline Books.

Eden, G.V.S. (1983). *An instrument to assess parental adjustment to a handicapped child.* Unpublished master's thesis, University of California, Riverside.

Eden-Piercy, G.V.S., Blacher, J.B., & Eyman, R.K. (1986). Exploring parents' reactions to their young child with severe handicaps. *Mental Retardation, 24,* 285–291.

Emde, R.N., & Sorce, J.F. (1983). The rewards of infancy: Emotional availability and maternal referencing. In J.D. Call, E. Galenson, & R.L. Tyson (Eds.), *Frontiers of infant psychiatry.* New York: Basic Books.

Featherstone, H. (1980). *A difference in the family: Life with a disabled child.* New York: Basic Books.

Feiring, C., Fox, N.A., Jaskir, J., & Lewis, M. (1987). The relation between social support, infant risk status and mother-infant interaction. *Developmental Psychology, 23,* 400–405.

Friedrich, W. (1979). Predictors of the coping behavior of mothers of handicapped children. *Journal of Counseling and Clinical Psychology, 47,* 1140–1141.

Friedrich, W.N., Greenberg, M.T., & Crnic, K. (1983). A Short-Form of the Questionnaire on Resources and Stress. *American Journal of Mental Deficiency, 88,* 41–48.

Frodi, A.M. (1981). Contribution of infant characteristics to child abuse. *American Journal of Mental Deficiency, 85,* 341–349.

Glasser, P.H., & Glasser, L.N. (Eds.). (1970). *Families in crisis.* New York: Harper & Row.

Goldberg, S. (1977). Social competence in infancy: A model of parent-infant interaction. *Merrill-Palmer Quarterly, 23,* 163–177.

Goldberg, W.A., & Easterbrooks, M.A. (1984). Role of marital quality in toddler development. *Developmental Psychology, 20,* 504–513.

Grossman, F.K. (1972). *Brothers and sisters of retarded children.* New York: Syracuse University Press.

Henderson, S., Byrne, D., & Duncan-Jones, P. (1981). *Neuroses in the social environment.* New York: Academic Press.

Hill, R. (1958). Social stresses on the family. *Social Casework, 37,* 139–150.

Holland, J. (1988, April). *Emotional aspects of cancer.* Paper presented at Women at Risk: A professional education program sponsored by Fair Oaks Hospital and Pennsylvania Hospital, Atlantic City, NJ.

Holman, A. (1983). *Family assessment: Tools for understanding and intervention.* Beverly Hills, CA: Sage Publications.

Holmes, T.H., & Raye, R.H. (1967). The Social Readjustment Rating Scale. *Journal of Psychosomatic Research, 11,* 213–218.

Holroyd, J. (1974). The Questionnaire on Resources and Stress: An instrument to measure family response to a handicapped member. *Journal of Community Psychology, 2,* 92–94.

Holroyd, J. (1982). *Manual for the Questionnaire on Resources and Stress.* Los Angeles: UCLA Neuropsychiatric Institute.

Holroyd, J., & Guthrie, D. (1979). Stress in families of children with neuromuscular disease. *Journal of Clinical Psychology, 35,* 734–739.

Holroyd, J., & McArthur, D. (1976). Mental retardation and stress on the parents: A contrast between Down's syndrome and childhood autism. *American Journal of Mental Deficiency, 80,* 431–436.

Hymovich, D.P. (1984). Development of the Chronicity Impact and Coping Instrument: Parent Questionnaire (CICI:PQ). *Nursing Research, 33,* 218–222.

Hymovich, D.P. (1988a). *Psychometric properties of the Chronicity Impact and Coping Instrument (CICI:PQ) Coping Scale.* Unpublished manuscript, University of Pennsylvania, Philadelphia.

Hymovich, D.P. (1988b). *Parent Perception Inventory.* King of Prussia, PA: D. Hymovich.

Hymovich, D.P., & Baker, C. (1985). The needs, concerns and coping of parents of children with cystic fibrosis. *Family Relations, 34,* 91–97.

Jessop, D.J., Riessman, C.K., & Stein, R.E.K. (1988). Chronic childhood illness and maternal mental health. *Developmental and Behavioral Pediatrics, 9,* 147–156.

Joyce, K., Singer, M., & Isralowitz, R. (1983). Impact of respite care on parent's perceptions of quality of life. *Mental Retardation, 21,* 153–156.

Kahn, R.L., & Antonucci, T.C. (1984). *Social supports of the elderly: Family, friends, professionals* (Report No. AG01632). Bethesda, MD: National Institute on Aging.

Kaiser, C.E., & Hayden, A.H. (1984). Clinical research and policy issues in parenting severely handicapped infants. In J. Blacher (Ed.), *Severely handicapped young children and their families: Research in review.* Orlando, FL: Academic Press.

Kazak, A.E. (1987). Families with disabled children: stress and social networks in three samples. *Journal of Abnormal Child Psychology, 15,* 137–146.

Kazak, A., Reber, M., & Snitzer, L. (1988). Childhood chronic disease and family functioning: A study of phenylketonuria. *Pediatrics, 81,* 224–230.

Klein, S.D., & Simmons, R.G. (1979). Chronic disease and childhood development: Kidney disease and transplantation. In R.G. Simmons (Ed.), *Research in community and mental health* (Vol. 1). Greenwich, CT: JAI Press.

Lazarus, R.S. (1981). The costs and benefits of denial. In J. Spinella & P. Deasy-Spinella (Eds.),

Living with childhood cancer. St. Louis: C.V. Mosby.
Leet, H.E., & Dunst, C.J. (1985). *Family Resource Scale: Reliability and Validity.* Morganton, NC: Family, Infant and Preschool Program.
LeMasters, E. (1957). Parenthood as crisis. *Marriage and Family Living, 19,* 352–355.
Lerner, R., & Busch-Rossnagel, N. (1981). Individuals as producers of their development: Conceptual and empirical bases. In R.M. Lerner & N. Rossnagel (Eds.), *Individuals as producers of their own development: A lifespan perspective.* New York: Academic Press.
Levitt, M.J., Weber, R.A., & Clark, M.C. (1986). Social network relationships as sources of maternal support and well being. *Developmental Psychology, 22,* 310–316.
Lewis, B.L., & Khaw, K. (1982). Family functioning as a mediating variable affecting psychosocial adjustment of children with cystic fibrosis. *Journal of Pediatrics, 101,* 636–640.
Lewis, M., & Goldberg, S. (1969). Perceptual-cognitive development in infancy: A generalized expectancy model as a function of the mother-infant interaction. *Merrill-Palmer Quarterly, 15,* 81–100.
Lewis, M., & Rosenbloom, L. (Eds.). (1974). *The effect of the infant on its caregiver.* New York: John Wiley & Sons.
Lipsky, D.K. (1985). A parental perspective on stress and coping. *American Journal of Orthopsychiatry, 55,* 614–617.
Mash, E.J., Johnston, C., & Kovitz, K. (1983). A comparison of the mother-child interactions of physically abused and non-abused children during play and task situations. *Journal of Clinical Child Psychology, 12,* 337–346.
McCubbin, H. (1979). Integrating coping behavior in family stress theory. *Journal of Marriage and the Family, 42,* 237–244.
McCubbin, H.I., Cauble, A.E., & Patterson, J.M. (1982). *Family stress, coping, and social support.* Springfield, IL: Charles C Thomas.
McCubbin, H.I., & Patterson, J.M. (1981). *Systematic assessment of family stress, resources, and coping.* St. Paul: Family Stress Project, University of Minnesota.
McCubbin, H.I., & Patterson, J.M. (1983). The family stress process: The double ABCX model of adjustment and adaptation. In H.I. McCubbin, M.B. Sussman, & J.M. Patterson (Eds.), *Social structure and the family: Advances and developments in family stress theory and research.* New York: Haworth.
McGoldrick, M., & Gerson, R. (1985). *Genograms in family assessment.* New York: William Norton & Company.
McKinney, B., & Peterson, R.A. (1987). Predictors of stress in parents of developmentally disabled children. *Journal of Pediatric Psychology, 12,* 133–149.
Meichenbaum, D. (1977). *Cognitive-behavior modification: An integrative approach.* New York: Plenum Press.
Minde, K., Shosenberg, N., Marton, P., Thompson, J., Ripley, J., & Burns, S. (1980). Self-help groups in a premature nursery: A controlled evaluation. *Journal of Pediatrics, 96,* 933–940.
Minde, K., Whitelaw, A., Brown, J., & Fitzhardinge, P. (1983). Effect of neonatal complications in premature infants on early parent-infant interactions. *Developmental Medicine and Child Neurology, 25,* 763–777.
Mink, I.T., & Nihara, K. (1986). Family life-styles and child behaviors: A study of direction of effects. *Developmental Psychology, 22,* 610–616.
Moos, R., & Moos, B. (1981). *Family Environment Scale Manual.* Palo Alto, CA: Consulting Psychologists Press.
Murphy, M.A. (1982). The family with a handicapped child: A review of the literature. *Journal of Developmental and Behavioral Pediatrics, 3,* 73–82.
Newbrough, J.R., Simpkins, C.G., & Maurer, H. (1985). A family development approach to studying factors in the management and control of childhood diabetes. *Diabetes Care, 8,* 83–92.
Olson, D.H., Portner, J., & Lavee, Y. (1985). *FACES III.* St. Paul: Family Social Science, University of Minnesota.
Ostfeld, B.M. (1988). Psychological interventions in Gilles de la Tourette syndrome. *Psychiatric Annals, 18,* 411–420.
Ostfeld, B.M., Hegyi, T., & Hiatt, I.M. (1987). Altering the intensive care nursery: A caveat. *Children's Environments Quarterly, 4,* 46–48.
Pedersen, F. (1982). Mother, father and infant as an interactive system. In J. Belsky (Ed.), *In the beginning: Readings on infancy.* New York: Columbia University Press.
Petersen, P. (1984). Effects of moderator variables in reducing stress outcome in mothers of children with handicaps. *Journal of Psychosomatic Research, 28,* 337–344.
Pugh, G., & Russell, P. (1977). *Shared care: Support services for families with handicapped children.* London: National Children's Bureau.
Quine, L., & Pahl, J. (1987). First diagnosis of severe handicap: A study of parental reactions. *Developmental Medicine and Child Neurology, 29,* 232–242.
Ragozin, A.S., Basham, R.B., Crnic, K.A., Greenberg, M.T., & Robinson, N.M. (1982). Effects of maternal age on parenting role. *Developmental Psychology, 18,* 627–634.
Salisbury, C.L. (1986). Adaptation of the Questionnaire on Resources and Stress–Short Form.

American Journal of Mental Deficiency, 90, 456–459.

Sameroff, A.J., & Chandler, M.J. (1975). Reproductive risk and the continuum of caretaking casualty. In F.D. Horowitz (Ed.), *Review of child development research* (Vol. 4). Chicago: University of Chicago Press.

Sameroff, A.J., Seifer, R., & Zax, M. (1982). Early development of children at risk for emotional disorder. *Monographs of the Society for Research in Child Development, 47*(199).

Sarason, I.G., Johnson, J.H., & Siegel, J.M. (1978). Assessing the impact of life changes: Development of the Life Experiences Survey. *Journal of Consulting and Clinical Psychology, 46,* 932–946.

Schafer, L.C., Glasgow, R.E., McCaul, K.D., & Dreher, M. (1983). Adherence to IDDM regimens: Relationship to psychosocial variables and metabolic control. *Diabetes Care, 6,* 493–498.

Skinner, H.A. (1987). Self-report instruments for family assessment. In T. Jacob (Ed.), *Family interaction and psychopathology.* New York: Plenum Press.

Skinner, H.A., Steinhauer, P.D., & Santa-Barbara, J. (1983). The Family Assessment Measure. *Canadian Journal of Community Mental Health, 2,* 91–105.

Stein, R.K., & Jessop, D.J. (1982). A noncategorical approach to chronic childhood illness. *Public Health Report, 97,* 354–362.

Steinhauer, P.D., Santa-Barbara, J., & Skinner, H.A. (1984). The process model of family functioning. *Canadian Journal of Psychiatry, 29,* 77–88.

Taylor, D.C. (1982). Counseling the parents of handicapped children. *British Medical Journal, 284,* 1027–1028.

Thomas, A., & Chess, S. (1977). *Temperament and development.* New York: Brunner/Mazel.

Tritt, S.G., & Esses, L.M. (1988). Psychosocial adaptation of siblings of children with chronic medical illnesses. *American Journal of Orthopsychiatry, 58,* 211–220.

Waisbren, S.E. (1980). Parents' reaction after the birth of a developmentally disabled child. *American Journal of Mental Deficiency, 84,* 345–351.

Wasserman, A.L. (1984). A prospective study of the impact of home monitoring on the family. *Pediatrics, 74,* 323–329.

Weber, G., & Parker, T. (1981). A study of family and professional views of the factors affecting family adaptation to a disabled child. In N. Stinnert, J. DeFrain, K. King, P. Knaub, & G. Rowe (Eds.), *Family strengths 3: Roots of well-being.* Lincoln: University of Nebraska Press.

Wilton, K., & Renaut, J. (1986). Stress levels in families with intellectually handicapped preschool children and families with nonhandicapped preschool children. *Journal of Mental Deficiency Research, 30,* 163–169.

Winton, P.J., & Bailey, D.B. (1988). The family focused interview: A collaborative mechanism for family assessment and goal setting. *Journal of the Division for Early Childhood, 12,* 195–206.

Zeitlin, S.A., & Williamson, G.G. (1988). Developing family resources for adaptive coping. *Early Childhood, 12,* 137–146.

V
THE ASSESSMENT PROCESS

17 Portrait of the Arena Evaluation
Assessment in the Transdisciplinary Approach

Gilbert M. Foley

Although the terms "multidisciplinary," "interdisciplinary," and "transdisciplinary" are still used interchangeably, they are not synonymous (Giangreco, 1986). They represent different ways of thinking and behaving. This paper presents a comparison of the various models of team organization and service delivery in infant assessment with an emphasis on the transdisciplinary approach and particularly the arena evaluation.

Team organization refers to the professional composition of the assessment association as well as the formal and informal patterns of role assignment, status, authority, and social interaction among team members. Service delivery refers to the conceptual and operational style in which the team as a collective effort provides its expertise to the client.

In this chapter each model is described in terms of its historical evolution, theoretical frame of reference, concept of symptom causality, organizational configuration, and operational style.

UNIDISCIPLINARY APPROACH

During the middle of the 19th century, a major conceptual revolution occurred in the explanation of disease and aberrant behavior. The prevailing moral model, which ascribed symptom causality to external factors or internal flaws in moral fiber, gave way to a biological or medical model that suggested more natural explanations (Griesinger, 1867). An expanding knowledge of the nature of infectious disease and the anatomy and physiology of the brain gave impetus to this theoretical shift.

In its most fundamental form this biological model posited that a given symptom complex could be understood in a one-to-one relationship with an infectious agent or organic disease process. The natural history of syphilis, which in the tertiary stage sometimes results in neurological and behavioral symptoms, served as a prototype for the biological model of mental "illness."

This early biological frame of reference translated into a unidisciplinary approach to service delivery. It held that one discipline possessed the body of knowledge and skill necessary to diagnose and treat mental health problems. Because organic processes were inferred to be causal, medicine stood central in this conceptual framework. The medical model persisted in developmental disabilities through the 1960s, when many institutions for mentally retarded persons still mandated that superintendents be trained as physicians and the institutions be referred to as hospitals. The medical model persists in latent form expressed as efforts to reduce complex and heterogeneous problems to single-word labels. It is as if the diagnostic nosology stands metaphorically for unitary disease processes.

Service delivery in the unidisciplinary approach is individual, with the physician-patient relationship at its heart. A single discipline assumes primary responsibility for the diagnosis and treatment of the patient. The unity of the model is undoubtedly its strength, as expressed in the general practitioner model with emphasis on treatment of the whole patient. While many aspects of this model remain valid, its singularity of conceptual framework and unidimensional service delivery approach are not consonant with the vastly expanded pool of knowledge and the complex, multidimensional needs of developmentally disabled persons.

MULTIDISCIPLINARY APPROACH

Three important factors in the early 20th century contributed to the rise of the multidisciplinary approach: psychoanalysis, Henry Ford's assembly line, and World War I.

With the publication of the *Interpretation of Dreams* in 1900, Freud (1953) set a conceptual revolution in motion. Psychoanalysis offered the first viable psychological explanation for problems in adjustment and development. It explains human behavior in terms of the dynamic interplay of the individual's drives counterpointed against the demands of civilization within the structural and topographical model of the mind. In the broadest and simplest sense, psychoanalysis can be thought of as a psychosocial frame of reference.

Initially Freud transformed the infectious disease construct into a psychological model to explain hysterical symptoms. He postulated that repressed memories of early psychological trauma (the infectious agent) produced the symptoms (disease). Recovery of the repressed content and catharsis of the troubling and unacceptable memories through abreaction were thought to be curative. However, because this model and method did not yield long-lasting results, he abandoned the formulation for the concept of overdetermination or multiple causation of symptomatology. Broadly this might be thought of as an additive causal model implying that the symptoms or syndrome are a function of the summation and transformation of multiple factors.

Psychoanalysis also emphasized differentiation of function in its efforts to define the structural qualities of the mind and adaptive capacities of the ego. In essence, then, psychoanalysis provided a theoretical rationale for a multidisciplinary approach in the concepts of multiplicity of causation and differentiation of function.

These same ideas were simultaneously being applied in the industrial world by Henry Ford. His assembly line was built on the concepts of task analysis, division of labor, and specialization and may well have served as an operational prototype for the multidisciplinary approach.

The gruesome reality of World War I taxed the existing health delivery system to the limits and served as a reality trigger for an operational shift. Fueled with the concepts of multiple causality, differentiation of function, division of labor, and specialization, new disciplines evolved to meet the demand and treat specific symptoms of dysfunction. This differentiation of medical practice through the rise of the so-called allied health professions represented the breaking up of the unidisciplinary approach and, with it, a conceptual holism and unity of treatment. Out of it rose the multidisciplinary team approach—a division of labor by specialization (Ackerly, 1947).

The multidisciplinary approach, as it was originally conceptualized, represents a parallel model of service delivery. In this model, professionals tend to work next to each other but with minimal exchange of information or interaction among disciplines. The patient may be assessed individually by several disciplines, but only at the discretion and prescription of the "gatekeeper" head of the team. In medical settings, this is typically the physician; in educational settings, the psychologist. Assessments tend to be discipline specific and individual.

Separate reports are generated and submitted to the head of the team, who synthesizes the information and literally prescribes a treatment regimen. Each professional intervenes with the patient separately, following discipline-specific roles, and works independently of other disciplines. Plans may or may not reflect a group consensus. The family is peripheral and intervention is patient centered.

INTERDISCIPLINARY APPROACH

Three important factors in the early to mid-20th century contributed to the development of the interdisciplinary approach: an expanded theoretical horizon that included behaviorism, the rise of empiricism, and the tragedy of World War II.

Behaviorism emphasized the role of environment and learning in the causal hypotheses of human behavior and therapeutic efforts (Watson, 1924). These concepts, when considered in concert with intrapsychic factors, resulted in a new theoretical complexity (Dollard & Miller, 1950). Broadly speaking, I refer to this as a psychoeducational frame of reference.

As a theory of causality, this model represents an interactive approach that ascribes symptom formation to the interplay and transformation of multiple factors. Symptoms are understood as more than the sum of their parts. Sophisticated statistical methods such as multivariate analysis were later developed to measure empirically the relative influence of specific factors on a given effect.

Interactional theory spawned a greater attention to the interdependence of cognitive, psychodynamic, and biological systems in the genesis of dysfunction and implementation of treatment. Such thinking demanded an increased cooperation among specialists so that a tighter unity of conceptualization and intervention could be realized.

War again proved catalytic in effecting an operational progression in team organization. The existing medical delivery system was taxed to the limit in World War II by the gruesome magnitude of casualties—both physical and psychiatric. A more systematic and cooperative effort among disciplines was needed. This gave rise to the interdisciplinary approach, which extends beyond the multidisciplinary notion of "working next to" toward an ideal of cooperative cohesion among team members (Hutt, Menninger, & O'Keefe, 1947).

In this model, the client is assessed individually by several disciplines as standard procedure. Each professional functions in his or her discipline-specific and prescribed role. Following the assessment phase, the examining professionals meet (staffing) to exchange impressions of causal hypotheses, diagnostic classification, and treatment in a way that strives to reflect a group consensus.

In a manner, each clinician comes to the meeting with a puzzle piece gleaned from individual assessment, and efforts are made to assemble a configuration that makes sense out of the patient's problem. Because each piece is forged from separate samples of behavior, using different methods rising from varying theoretical assumptions, identification of unifying themes is often difficult. Clinicians frequently remain wedded to individual causal hypotheses and, lacking a common vision, language, or blueprint, the team not infrequently falls into the "tower of Babel syndrome." The process aims at cooperation among disciplines but frequently ends up in fragmentation.

Intervention is implemented in discipline-specific fashion with periodic staff meetings to share progress notes and update plans. In educational settings the child is placed in a classroom with "pull out" for specific therapeutic interventions. Often the teacher or parent has little training to provide continuity of intervention and, as a result, there may be reduced generalization of treatment effect as the child moves from one setting to the other. Sometimes there is even a counterproductive, canceling-out effect.

Group discussion and planning is encouraged but division of labor prevails. The family is parallel to the process. Variations on the interdisciplinary model tend to predominate in special education services and many early intervention programs. The model was widely popularized and disseminated in pediatrics and psychiatry through the child guidance movement in the 1940s and 1950s.

TRANSDISCIPLINARY APPROACH

History and Theory

Three main factors in the 1960s and early 1970s opened the way to the development of the transdisciplinary approach. They were the rise of the early intervention movement, a burst of infant research, and holistic concepts of health care.

During the 1960s the postwar myths of constancy and bliss in suburban arcadia began to wane in the tide of a waxing women's movement. The family structure was changing; women began working out of the home again and the need for child care became urgent. As services to typical young children became prevalent, the needs of young handicapped children were recognized and gave rise to the early childhood special education movement. This campaign became an organized political reality with the establishment of the Handicapped Children's Early Education Program in 1968.

During the 1960s major shifts in child development theory occurred as a result of the work of Hunt (1961), Bloom (1964), and Brunner (1960), which emphasized the role of early stimulation and the developmental plasticity of the child. The idea of early intervention through stimulation was embraced, and a burst of infant research followed. It revealed the heretofore untapped treasury of competencies possessed by the infant and validated the efficacy of early experience as an enricher of development.

Concurrent with the infant intervention and research movements was a growing interest in holistic health care. This represented an effort toward integration of the disparate, specialized health care system and grew out of the human potential movement of the 1960s. This synergistic and organismic theory focused on the whole person as more than the sum of his or her parts, resulting in a renaissance of the primary provider concept and an interest in natural and spiritual healing.

As infant intervention programs began to appear, they adopted the prevailing multidisciplinary and interdisciplinary approaches. However, deficits in these models were not surprising since they had been developed for adults. Nevertheless, the pattern of extending adult models downward to meet the needs of children persisted.

The national Collaborative Infant Project recognized the weaknesses of these models and applied the transdisciplinary approach to early intervention (Conner, Williamson, & Siepp, 1978; Haynes, 1983). Thus a new stage in the evolution of team functioning and service delivery was born. Originally described by Dorothy Hutchinson (1978), the transdisciplinary approach is a "deliberate pooling and exchange of information, knowledge and skill, crossing and re-crossing traditional disciplinary boundaries by various team members" (United Cerebral Palsy Association, 1976, p. 1).

The matrix presented in Table 1 is a descriptive scheme comparing and contrasting the essential components of each approach. Figure 1A–D consists of visual schemes comparing the various models of team organization

Table 1. The transdisciplinary approach: a differential definition

Frame of reference	Causal theory	Professional organization	Service delivery style
Biological/medical	Linear cause-effect	Unidisciplinary	Individual
Psychosocial	Additive	Multidisciplinary	Parallel
Psychoeducational	Interactional	Interdisciplinary	Cooperative
Biopsychosocial	Transactional	Transdisciplinary	Integrative

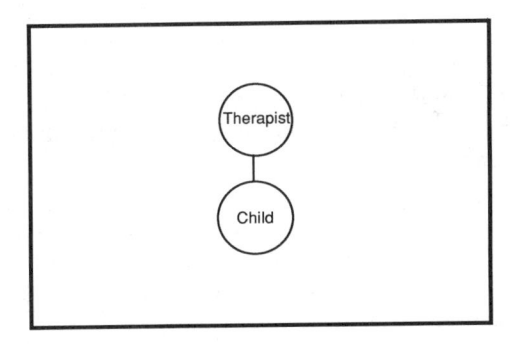

Figure 1A. Unidisciplinary teaming and service delivery approach. A single discipline assumes primary responsibility for the diagnosis and treatment of the child. The therapist-client relationship stands central in the delivery of service. The service delivery model is individual.

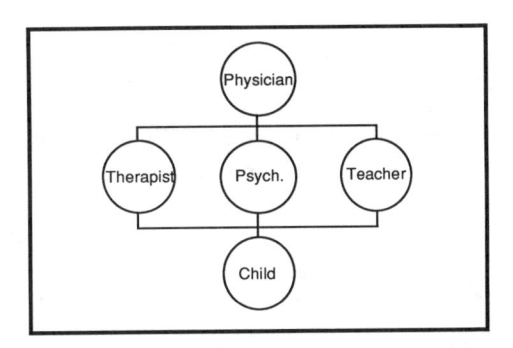

Figure 1B. Multidisciplinary teaming and service delivery approach. The child is assessed individually by several disciplines at the discretion of the "gatekeeper." Often a team leader such as a physician or psychologist synthesizes the information and literally prescribes treatment. Each professional intervenes with the child separately, following discipline-specific roles, and works independently of other disciplines. Plans may or may not reflect a group consensus. The service delivery model is parallel.

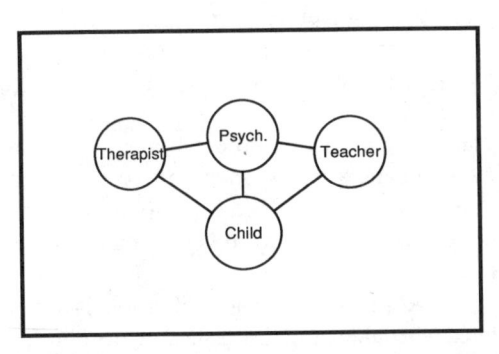

Figure 1C. Interdisciplinary teaming and service delivery approach. The child is assessed individually by members of several disciplines, each functioning in his or her discipline-prescribed and -defined role. A staffing follows; views are exchanged based on discipline-specific methodology. Diagnostic inferences and treatment plans strive to reflect a group consensus. Intervention, however, is implemented in a discipline-specific fashion. In educational settings this typically involves a classroom "pull-out" model. Staffing occurs with regularity and information is exchanged and processed. Group decision making and planning is encouraged, but division of labor by discipline prevails. The service delivery model is cooperative.

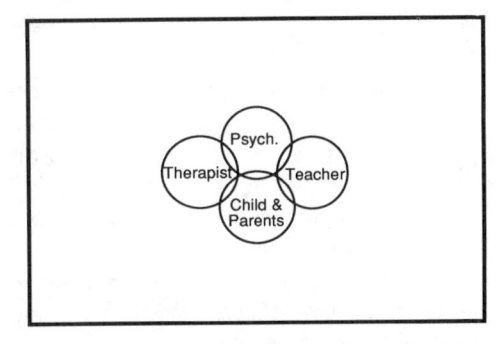

Figure 1D. Transdisciplinary teaming and service delivery approach. The child is assessed simultaneously by multiple professionals representing varying disciplines. The family is an integral part of the process. The assessment is more longitudinal, naturalistic, process oriented, and family centered than traditional discipline-specific assessments. A common sample of behavior is elicited from which professionals draw inferences. A staffing follows with the goal of formulating an integrated report and consensually validated cross-disciplinary individualized education program. A primary provider and a parent implement a comprehensive program with training in specific strategies and exchanges of information crossing disciplines through role release among professionals. The service delivery model is integrative.

and verbal abstracts comparing service delivery approaches.

The theoretical underpinnings of the transdisciplinary approach are to be found in the essential unity of development, the central role of the family, the critical position of human relationships in development, and the need to reduce multiple handling of infants. The transdisciplinary approach can be characterized as a developmental, biopsychosocial model in that it acknowledges the interrelatedness of developmental zones in the progressive change of the organism over time. My experience with the model also suggests that it stands as an applied form of transactional theory (Sameroff & Chandler, 1975).

I have extrapolated the following transactional principles that define a theory of symptom formation or causality and provide a theoretical rationale for the operational structure of the transdisciplinary approach.

Multiple factors converge to produce any given symptom complex. The development of any symptom is the result of a complex series of interrelated bidirectional forces with all elements in the system affecting and being affected by each other in linear and nonlinear ways.

The child must be understood as a whole person in an environmental context. Familial and social factors cross over to affect development and are often the most critical factors in tipping a child over the line from functional to handicapped.

The developmental domino theory or concept of crossing-over effects. Because of the unity of development in infancy there are intimate crossing-over effects among the zones of development that promote or prevent optimal progress.

The concept of cumulative adversity (McCrae, 1986). This implies that a developmental disability is a result of the accumulation of multiple misfortunes set in motion over time, rather than the result of some single unitary event.

Operational Principles

Service delivery in the transdisciplinary approach is characterized by three operational principles that distinguish it in practice from the previously discussed models. These are: role expansion, arena evaluation, and role release.

Role expansion refers to the educational, conceptual, and administrative adjustments that must occur to support transdisciplinary practice. Arena evaluation refers to the simultaneous assessment of the child by multiple professionals of differing disciplines. Role release is intervention focused and refers to the process of transferring specific skills, strategies, and techniques across disciplines to achieve integrated therapy.

Role Expansion

Role expansion has theoretical, educational, and administrative implications. As education, role expansion implies an ongoing formal and informal instructional process through which team members elaborate their theoretical knowledge across disciplinary boundaries. This occurs operationally as team members train one another in the theoretical and conceptual aspects of their respective disciplines. This process aims to preserve individuality within a matrix of shared knowledge and skill and serves as a foundation for transdisciplinary practice. Out of this process emerges a common vocabulary, expanded theoretical constructs, and an amplified capacity for the team to generate multiple hypotheses and integrated interventions.

The process of role expansion is facilitated when there is a designated team of professionals who have the opportunity to work together consistently over time. It is also promoted by an organizational chart that designates the team and its cross-disciplinary members in a circular, collegial relationship rather than a staff-line relationship organized by discipline. Such a model promotes identification and cohesion within teams, rather than identification and competition between disciplines. By expanding the organizational unit to include the team there is a redistribution of authority in the system, with increased influence, autonomy, and synergy accruing to the team. Each team must then have latitude within designated parameters to individuate itself through a process. Supervision in this team model is divided between administrative and clinical content. Each team may have a generic administrative supervisor or chair. Clinical teaching across disciplines should occur as a formal and informal process within the team. Clinical supervision is offered when professionals of like disciplines meet with a senior practitioner. Role expansion spawns a conceptual common ground from which the team can operationalize the transdisciplinary approach through a process along relatively individual lines.

Arena Evaluation

Arena evaluation is the simultaneous assessment of the child by multiple professionals of differing disciplines. Rather than each professional looking at the child through his or her individual window, the team designs a picture window so that a common sample of behavior can be collected. This allows for a more holistic view of the child with the aim of achieving a more integrated understanding of function, dysfunction, and the contributions of development across domains.

Its rationale rests in the developmental unity of the human infant. The relatively undifferentiated state of the infant renders discrete assessment by domain questionable. Such approaches tend to impose upon the infant a hypothetical differentiation that does not exist developmentally and yield an assessment more focused on the artifacts of development than development itself. The arena evaluation is a method that aims to be more consonant with the developmental status of the infant by creating a new unity among professionals. The method strives to preserve the expertise of interdisciplinary specialization within the conceptual holism of the unidisciplinary approach—complexity in unity.

Role Release

Role release is the process of transferring specific skills, strategies, and techniques across disciplines with the aim of achieving comprehensive and integrated intervention through a primary provider (and parents) and reducing multiple individual therapies. This does not preclude the possibility that some infants will nevertheless require individual therapy as well.

During this intervention stage the concept of primary elicitor is transformed into the role of primary provider (and parents) who delivers the comprehensive program to the degree possible. This means that one interventionist will need to implement movement experiences, learning opportunities, language encounters, and the like. When primary providers operate outside their specific disciplines they will need to be taught specific strategies. In this process the role-releasing professional retains responsibility for the specific strategies implemented by the role-receiving professional (Haynes, 1983). The role-release process must be taken seriously and entails the following:

Selection of a primary provider of intervention. The choice of person and discipline of the primary provider may be based on his or her experience, training, and the goodness of fit with child and family in terms of the presenting problem and emotional factors. In educational settings the teacher typically serves as the primary provider with the other specialists serving in the consultative role-release capacity.

Descriptions of specific strategies to be role-released.

Completion of consultation/training sessions by the role-releasing professionals to instruct the role-receiving professional.

Provision of ongoing follow-up consultation between role-releasing and role-receiving professionals.

Role release is a challenging concept that can create considerable anxiety among professionals. In establishing role-release parameters, the releasing professional might differentiate between essence and form, and prevail in areas of concept and judgment, while releasing only operations or procedures to fellow team members. The range of releasable strategies depends primarily upon the clinical discretion of the releasing professional, but should be tempered by the team process and consensus. All role release, of course, must be governed by one first-order principle—to do no harm.

Role release works best in cohesive teams

with shared trust where there is ample time for ongoing consultation. When successful, the benefits of role-release are cumulative. It promotes a more naturalistic intervention where strategies are woven into the fabric of daily life and implemented by parents. Treatment continuity and generalization are enhanced through role release, and the skill of team members is vastly amplified.

The Arena Evaluation in Focus: Content and Process

Team Members

Because the transdisciplinary approach is based on a biopsychosocial model, a full range of disciplinary expertise is desirable. The number and types of professionals, of course, may be limited by the constraints of availability and fiscal reality. However, as few as two professionals of different disciplines can function in an arena format. At a minimum, I believe it is essential that there be professional representation from the biological, psychoeducational, and psychosocial zones of development. The biological zone is typically represented by physicians (a developmental pediatrician is desirable), nurses (a pediatric nurse practitioner is desirable), and physical and occupational therapists. Speech and language clinicians cross the biological/psychoeducational zones. Early childhood special educators typically represent the psychoeducational zone. Psychologists cross the psychoeducational/psychosocial zones (those who have had psychodiagnostic as well as psychotherapeutic experience and supervision in working with young at-risk children and their families, regardless of subspecialty—clinical, counseling, school, or applied developmental—are desirable). The psychosocial zone is also represented by social workers and counselors.

The professionals outlined in these categories are not all-inclusive. The beauty of the transdisciplinary approach is that professionals are not rigidly fixed in prescribed discipline-specific roles. A speech and language clinician with expertise and experience in oral-motor-prespeech and feeding may play such a role on the team, while an occupational therapist with expertise in psychosocial dysfunction may play a more "psychological" role. The team can "reslice" the traditional "role pie" in a divergent way, consistent with the training and expertise of the individual members.

The question often arises as to who is best suited to work on a transdisciplinary team. This is a complex query that cannot be answered exhaustively in this work. I have found the following attributes to be important:

A feeling of confidence and positive identity about oneself as a professional.

An ability to share and derive feelings of self-worth and accomplishment from cooperative effort.

A knowledge that one's professional identity is derived as much from what one knows as from what one does. This is the notion that ideas and judgment are as important as techniques and procedures, thus allowing one to share a method without compromising one's professional essence.

The Concept of the Primary Elicitor

The arena evaluation should not look like serial test administration with a lineup of evaluators waiting a turn at bat. One of the purposes of arena evaluation is to reduce multiple handling of the infant. As a result the primary elicitor concept evolved. This implies that one person on the team interacts with the child and elicits the primary sample of structured behavior. The selection of that person may rest with the needs of a particular infant and the professional goodness of fit with a specific team member, or emerge spontaneously from the infant as "natural selection" in the course of interacting with various team members during the warm-up segment. This methodology does not preclude other team members from entering the arena as needed. A physical therapist may have to "lay on hands" to assess tone or facilitate a transitional posture because clinical judgment is a function of motor memory and intuition—and cannot be captured in observation alone.

Because of the primary elicitor concept,

each member of the team must therefore learn to administer the instrument or series of instruments that form the structured or more formal spine of the evaluation sample. This may mean learning to administer instruments outside one's discipline through role release. Since so many instruments draw from a common item pool (e.g., block building, bead stringing, picture vocabulary), learning test administration across disciplines has not proven unduly challenging.

The critical skill in assessment, however, rests not in test administration but in the insightful and intuitive nuances of interpretation. This aspect of testing and evaluation is shared over time, but ultimately remains with the clinician of the test-specific discipline. The preservation of interpretation with the test-specific specialists rests in the concept of clinical judgment, which evolves over time from seeing many cases and includes the development of clinical norms and refinement of intuitive sensibilities. This cannot be quickly taught or released in the way a technique or procedure might be. Thus the "idea" is retained by each specialist and the "operation" released across team members. Over time, however, there is a growing syntality among team members, and each person increasingly becomes a transdisciplinarian in his or her own right, possessing both operational and conceptual skills across disciplines.

Role of Parents

One aim of the transdisciplinary approach is to involve parents more centrally in the process of their child's assessment and intervention. The arena evaluation is often the first real introduction parents have to early intervention. Ideally parents will have been prepared for the arena assessment in advance by the family worker. This should include knowledge of the disciplines represented: their names and backgrounds, roles, functions, and methods. Parents' anxiety, resistances, and questions must be "worked through" sensitively with the clinician in advance of the arena. The worker serves as a continuous "red thread" through the process and a transitional person between the parents and team. The worker accompanies the family to the evaluation and serves as narrator.

In this model parents have the opportunity to observe the same sample of behavior from which inferences are drawn as the clinicians. This differs from some multi- or interdisciplinary approaches that more closely approximate what I refer to as the "supreme court" model. In this system the child may be evaluated in isolation and parents wait in a blind for a decision to be handed down from a bench of experts.

In the transdisciplinary approach parents may be prepared to present a portrait of their own child to the team if they are comfortable. Parents are available to refuel and support their child as well as guide the team to relate more effectively to their child. They may assist in eliciting optimal performance from their child. They help the team to know if their child's behavior has been representative and if the sample seems valid. Parents observe, comment, and respond to questions. Parents may qualify observations and relate variations of behavior observed at home. Parents add enormously to the reliability and validity of the evaluation, for ultimately they know their child best.

The relationship of the team to the parents is a professional one, characterized by respect, warmth, and empathy. Professional distance, however, is necessary so that objective decisions and challenging inferences can be made if necessary and matters of transference can be managed in a way that promotes growth and insight.

Because no evaluation is ever neutral, it is essential that all team members learn supportive skills so that the parents leave with the feeling that they have participated in a positive experience.

Space, Materials, Duration, Style, and Population

The arena evaluation should take place in a child-centered space that is flexible. The level of stimulation should be able to be modified to the needs of the child. Toys should be able to be concealed or exhibited as needed. Intermediate architecture in the form of screens or movable partitions should be available to create more enclosure or openness, depending on the child or sequence of assessment.

The anxious or overactive toddler may do better in an enclosed space, with few toys and neutral hues. The low-toned or depressed child may respond to greater openness, brighter hues, and a more complex environment.

For the toddler there should be ample space for active play, private play, and interaction—both structured and intimate. The space must also be sufficiently ample to allow clinicians to observe at the periphery if necessary. The scale of furniture and objects should be appropriate to the child, but adult furniture must be available to accommodate parents and observing clinicians.

An observation area with a one-way mirror window and sound transmission is very important. With distractible, disorganized toddlers the clinicians may want to be in the observation room. Sometimes children perform better with parents out of the space. The observation room affords needed flexibility.

The arena space should be equipped with infant toys, including rings, rattles, cubes, cups, action toys, and other accountrements of daily life with a baby. Standard playroom materials for the junior and senior toddler will include projective objects such as puppets and doll house, plastic materials such as clay and crayons, and objects with the potential to evoke an array of affective responses, including aggressive toys such as guns, nurturing toys such as dolls, and worry toys such as the doctor kit. These toys should be held in reserve and brought into the arena at appropriate times lest the space be overstimulating and too provocative. Task-centered cognitive and language materials are often a part of test kits. Motor materials, including mats, balls, ramps, and rolls, form an integral part of the room. Adaptive seating and other materials will need to be available as well.

The arena evaluation typically encompasses a period of 1–2.5 hours. This includes the brief staffing following the assessment, but not the extended staffing. For the toddler it typically consists of a series of modules, each addressing a different activity theme. For the infant it is less differentiated. Children may be seen over several shorter periods or a clinician may decide that a more standard individual session is necessary to supplement the arena. The team may also see a child in the home when appropriate. These are joint decisions between team and parents.

The arena evaluation is designed to reveal a developmental slice of life. It strives to be more naturalistic, organic, and longitudinal in style than typical assessments and might be comparable to a cross-section of the infant's daily life or nursery school experience in the case of the toddler. The sample of behavior is typically more continuous and complex than that obtained in standard individual assessments and is often richer in nuance and quality. The evaluation strives to sample a variety of states, affects, conditions, tasks, communicative modes, and action schemes. Therefore it is neither all play based nor all task centered. It is multimodal and aims to elicit play, interaction, reflection, task-centered effort, activity of daily life, spontaneity, stress, coping, relaxation, refueling, and the array of experience one would consider to be a part of a child's natural life.

The arena evaluation is best suited to children from birth through age 6. Beyond that age development becomes too complex. As the developmental zones become increasingly differentiated, more in-depth, domain-specific samples of behavior become necessary. The instrumentation is too lengthy for an arena evaluation to be conducted in a reasonable time frame.

The arena method is superior for infants who can be held in their mother's arms in an enclosed safe space. The overactive, distractible, expansive toddler can be a challenge in this model, but the range of tasks, the flexibility of environment, and the introduction of a changing cast of characters often allows the team to use the child's exuberance to his or her best advantage rather than working against his or her style. The flattened, low-tone child often comes delightfully alive, and the typically exhibitionistic, Oedipal-aged child often revels in the available audience who sensitively uses his stage-specific penchant for pageantry to promote success, but not exploit.

Selection of Assessment Domains and Instruments

The selection of an appropriate assessment instrument for the arena evaluation poses a challenging problem. My experience is that no single transdisciplinary test exists. Nevertheless, the collection of a structured sample of behavior is an essential part of any arena evaluation. This not only allows for psychometric precision and drawing comparisons, but also facilitates clinical judgment since the infants are seen within a consistently structured, contextual frame.

The choice of an assessment instrument should rest with the team and evolve out of a process. Initially each clinician should identify the essential information he or she wishes to learn from the evaluation and broadly operationalize the sample of behavior that would allow him or her to formulate such inferences. The team then constructs a general outline of the categories of assessment. Table 2 is an example of such an outline, but does not purport

Table 2. Outline of assessment (observations to be made in arena evaluation)

Behavior and style
  Appearance
  Temperament
  State regulation
  Rhythmicity
  Reactivity
  Attention
  Frustration tolerance
  Level of organization
  Kinetics
Object Interaction/Cognition
  Schema use
  Symbolic object use
  Discrimination
  Object classification
  Reality testing
  Learning style
    Sensory assimilation
    Imitation
    Trial and error
    Planned problem solving
  Learning modalities
Social/Emotional
  Contact/cueing style
  Reaction to strangers
  Predominant affect/mood
  Affective range
  Attachment/separation behavior
  Individuation/autonomy
  Coping strategies
  Defensive strategies
  Play style
    Solitary
    Observer
    Parallel
    Associative
  Adaptability
  Social appropriateness

Communication
  Mode of communication
  Frequency/duration
  Echolalia
  Speech
    Respiration
    Voice
    Vocalization
    Intonation
    Word approximation
    Intelligibility
    Articulation
    Rate
    Fluency
  Receptive language
    Receptive vocabulary
    Comprehension—direction/questions
    Comprehension—connected discourse
  Expressive language
    Spontaneity
    Vocabulary/retrieval
    Knowledge level
    Length & quality of connected discourse
  Pragmatics
    Communicative intent
    Turn taking
    Topic maintenance/expansion
    Felicity
  Syntax
    Grammatical form
    Overgeneralization

Sensorimotor
  Sensory
    Tactile responsivity/sensitivity
    Auditory/visual perception
    Vestibular/proprioceptive responsivity
    Body image
  Gross motor
    Primitive reflexes
    Postural tone
    Symmetry
    Components of movement
      Head control
      Trunk control
      Proximal joint control
      Weight shifting
      Dynamic equilibrium
      Rotation
      Antigravitational control
      Transitional postures
      Bilateral integration
      Locomotion
      Motor planning
  Fine motor
    Prehension
    Tool use
    Visual-motor accuracy
  Oral motor
    Infantile reflexes
    Sucking/drinking/chewing
    Tongue/jaw control
    Oral motor planning
Self-help
  Feeding
  Dressing
  Toileting
  Activities of daily living

to be exhaustive. The team will then review a sample of instruments from across disciplines. Because there is considerable duplication of items, the team should strive to identify a single arena instrument. Ideally this instrument will contain the broadest item pool and sample the most representative range of behaviors covering the most categories in the general outline within the constraints of time.

This instrument might then serve as the spine or core of the structured portion of the arena evaluation. This can be either a standardized or criterion-referenced instrument, depending on the assessment questions that must be answered by the team, local agencies, and state standards. I have found the Bayley Scales of Infant Development (Bayley, 1969); The Cattell Infant Intelligence Scale (Cattell, 1960); the Stanford-Binet Form LM (Terman & Merrill, 1973), which forms a continuous measure with the Cattell; Developmental Programming for Infants and Young Children (Rogers & D'Eugenio, 1981); the Infant/Toddler Developmental Assessment (IDA) (Provence, Palmeri, Erikson, & Epperson, 1985); or the Cognitive Observation Guide (Foley & Appel, 1987) to be acceptable core instruments.

Because most single instruments cannot sample the breadth of behavior or clinical nuance required by the whole team, a process of test elaboration occurs formally or informally as the team works together over time. This elaboration may take the form of appending items from other tests when this can be done with psychometric integrity, or adding clinical items. The flexibility of criterion-referenced tests accommodates this "embroidery" more easily than standardized measures. An example of clinical elaboration follows.

Most instruments have block items. After the block items have been administered in uniform fashion, the primary elicitor may ask the child to retrieve a block handed from above so that the physical therapist and the other role-expanded clinicians can observe head stability when the elbows are lifted off the supporting surface. The primary elicitor may ask the child to replace the cubes into the strategically placed box so that midline crossing can be observed. This allows the occupational therapist and team to observe bilateral integration. These additional clinical adaptations, which may be informal or written to form a protocol, become a kind of penumbra surrounding the items that form the core or spine of the structured evaluation.

Adjunctive instruments, such as the Attachment-Separation-Individuation Scale (Foley & Hobin, 1981), which can be scored from naturalistic observation in the arena, or others that can be scored from the generic sample of elicited behavior, provide multiple psychometric outcomes.

Process and Sequence

There is no script for an arena evaluation. In many ways it is like a jazz improvisation or impromptu choreography. The placement of team members, movement in and out of the arena, and even variations on instrumentation must often be made in situ according to the needs of the child or family. As teams work together over time they learn variations on themes and gain the flexibility that makes the model effective.

When evaluating young infants the process and sequence strive to approximate a slice of daily life. The infant is typically held and handled by the mother. She may even administer structured tasks with guidance. The occupational and physical therapist will also typically need to handle the baby to assess tone, reflexes, and postural status. It is useful to observe feeding, play, task-centered activity, state changes, diapering, spontaneous movement, handling, social interaction, vocalization, attachment behavior, stress, and coping style. Typically the team sits with the mother on a mat placed on the floor. The assessment sequence should be naturalistic and organic, with experiences melding together in response to the readiness and lead of the child. The space should be enclosed and create the ambiance of a holding environment.

When evaluating junior and senior toddlers the following more structured sequence might be followed.

Greeting and Warm-up. This initial period provides time for the family and team to visit and get acquainted. The family worker serves as liaison and, if the family is comfortable and has been prepared, they may present their child's history. The child is offered an opportunity to explore the area with guidance, and interact with the various team members. If spontaneous rapport occurs between the child and a specific team member, that clinician may serve as the primary elicitor. This prelude gives the team an opportunity to observe the child's coping strategies, style, and predominant mood, as well as reactions to novelty and anxiety. Based on clinical experience, the team formulates preliminary strategies regarding the space, sequence, style of interaction, instrumentation, and location of the team.

The Formal Task-Centered Segment. While the child is fresh and alert the formal testing occurs. The instrument chosen to be the spine of the assessment is administered by the primary elicitor. It may be scored by a colleague. Attention is given to proper positioning. The other clinicians may be scoring discipline-specific instruments from the generic sample of elicited behavior, or making clinical notes and comments. In either case attention to the transaction of function and dysfunction across zones is of primary importance. This segment is usually planned for 15–25 minutes in duration, depending on the attentional capacity of the child. Breaks are offered as necessary. Parents are available to facilitate coping and success.

Snack Breaks and Refueling. Following the hard work of the formal interlude comes an opportunity for both nourishment and emotional refueling. The child has snacks with his or her parents. These usually consist of a drink, finger food, and a snack requiring use of utensils. This is a splendid opportunity to observe self-help skills, oral motor functions, spontaneous language, and social interaction.

Separation and Reunion. Following snacks the primary elicitor takes the child for a bathroom break or short excursion about the office. This provides the team with an opportunity to observe separation behavior from family and spontaneous movement. Upon return to home base attention is paid to reunion behavior of child and parents. This activity provides a good opportunity to note the levels of separation anxiety, coping strategies, and style of reunion, such as avoidance, ambivalence, or engulfment.

"Story Time" or Teaching Samples. Once the child is reorganized and focused, the next segment is used to round out the sample of behavior or collect additional material as may be needed. The age and developmental status of the child will of course determine which course of action is most appropriate. A "story time" format for the senior toddler provides an opportunity to expand the language sample. Structured techniques may be a part of the content. A brief teaching sequence may also be completed to sample the child's responses to novel stimuli, capacity to assimilate and accommodate to new information, and ability to transfer and generalize learning to new toys and situations. Sometimes the technique of "backing down" is used in this segment. Key items that may have been failed on the more formal assessment are reintroduced and incrementally simplified to determine the child's actual functional level. This provides useful baseline data for intervention.

Free Play. This segment allows the team to observe spontaneous movement and interaction with toys. It provides the observers with an opportunity to better understand the style of the child. Toy selection, rituals, and play themes provide projective insights as well. The physical and occupational therapist may enter the arena at this time to "lay on hands" and facilitate directed movements.

Closing and Physical Exam. The primary elicitor and parents help the child to wind down. This may include some ritual play and contact comfort. If a physical exam is to be completed, it is done at this time.

Brief Staffing and Feedback. The team retires to formulate impressions briefly while the family worker collects the parents' comments about the encounter. Team and parents come together to share information and feelings. While this is not a complete or formal feedback session, it provides some closure so that parents do not depart with undue ambiguity and anxiety.

Formal Staffing and Interpretation. The team needs time to analyze data and reflect before a more definitive formulation can be articulated. Usually an interlude of at least a week transpires before the team reconvenes for a formal staffing. At this time they review data and impressions as well as organize a composite report and preliminary intervention plan. Parents may or may not be present, depending on their desires and needs. If they are present the family worker who has served as a "red thread" through the process can be an important transitional person between team and parents. If parents are not present, a formal feedback session or sessions are planned. The composition of that interpretive interview team becomes a matter of parent desire and need, as well as clinical judgment. Feedback is viewed as an ongoing organic process and will occur over time as child and family interact with team members in a therapeutic role.

Outcomes of Arena Evaluation

The outcomes of the arena evaluation can be categorized in terms of content and products. The following represent the content outcomes of arena evaluation. Of course the team may not always achieve these ends in each case, but they do represent an ideal to approximate.

A historical and contextual portrait. This is a descriptive review of the medical and social background as well as a portrait of the child's family and evironment.

Qualitative descriptions of the child's functioning across zones. This descriptive portrait answers the "in what manner" questions and may be far more important than the traditional psychometric outcomes, such as developmental age.

Quantitative assessments of levels of function. This psychometric portrait answers the "how much" questions and compares the child to himself or herself or to others if standardized measures were employed. This may include developmental or mental ages/levels.

Identification of dysfunctional developmental juncture points. This invoves the identification of critical areas where a deficit in one zone of development appears to be exerting an inhibiting influence on another zone. For example, low tone may interfere with an infant's ability to form differentiated facial expressions. This may render the infant more difficult to "read" and in turn leave the mother feeling confused, thus negatively coloring their interaction. In effect a motor problem crosses over to contribute to a psychosocial problem.

Construction of a developmental formulation. This constitutes a hypothetical developmental map of the natural history of the problems and the cumulative, progressive course of the dysfunction. It attempts to identify causal links that in turn provide a guide to intervention.

Diagnosis. A formal diagnosis may or may not be realized as an outcome of arena assessment. When a consensus can be reached it may be useful.

The product outcomes of the arena evaluation are as follows:

An integrated cross-disciplinary report. Ideally this document is an interwoven narrative where discipline-specific information is subsumed into the whole. This is difficult to achieve. More frequently each clinician contributes a segment that is discipline focused, with attention to transactions across zones. An integrated summary is composed at the staffing.

A comprehensive cross-disciplinary intervention plan formulated as a team effort. This plan is constructed in situ at the staffing by the team and serves as a comprehensive blueprint to intervention. It is cross-referenced by discipline and area so that primary providers of intervention will have available, in one integrated format, positioning, learning experiences, language encounters, materials, and so forth.

Conclusion

The transdisciplinary approach has many assets. It reduces multiple handling of the child and promotes a more integrated model of service delivery. Parents relate to a primary person rather than to a whole team, and case management is streamlined. Professional skills are enhanced with cumulative benefits for both staff and clients. The methodology provides a vehicle for providing comprehensive service in remote areas where discipline-specific interventions would be difficult to obtain (Margrum & Tigges, 1982). The arena evaluation offers a more holistic look at the infant in a manner more consonant with the inherent unity of development and the central role of the family.

On the challenging side, the model places considerable responsibility on team members for the implementation of strategies outside their disciplines. Ample time is required for role-release training, and resistances may arise as to the transfer of skills from both a professional and a legal perspective (Bray, Coleman, & Gotts, 1981).

Unfortunately, in recent years some sites have used transdisciplinary theory to rationalize a reduction in services and the elimination of specialist positions. Such ends were never intended as outcomes of the transdisciplinary approach in spirit or operation.

Empirical research of the model has been scant and is much needed. John Kiss (1983) conducted a cost-effectiveness study in arena evaluation and found it to be at a minimum 40% more cost-efficient than the interdisciplinary process for like services. Annette Lynch (1980) compared the outcomes of interdisciplinary and transdisciplinary assessments using the problem-oriented record. She found that the arena evaluation yielded significantly more problems of more meaningful quality when rated by clinicians than the interdisciplinary assessment. The approach has been vastly underinvestigated and remains a fertile topic for research.

The transdisciplinary approach is the only team model developed specifically with the developmentally young in mind. It represents the foremost step on the continuum of team evolution and remains a viable and clinically effective approach. It is hoped that the approach will be expanded, refined, and applied more widely under the new law, PL 99-457. The essence of the model rests in its exquisite ability to preserve complexity in a new frame of unity. Una Haynes frequently said that no single discipline holds the key to unlocking the complexity of the children we treat. Only through cooperative efforts to forge a master key will the mystery of the children we treat be unlocked, their growth promoted, and their families liberated.

REFERENCES

Ackerly, S. (1947). The clinic team. *American Journal of Orthopsychiatry, 17,* 191–195.

Bayley, N. (1969). *Manual for the Bayley Scales of Infant Development.* New York: Psychological Corporation.

Bloom, B.S. (1964). *Stability and changes in human characteristics.* New York: John Wiley & Sons.

Bray, N.M., Coleman, J.M., & Gotts, E.A. (1981). The transdisciplinary team: Challenges to effective functioning. *Teacher Education and Special Education, 4,* 44–49.

Brunner, J. (1960). *The process of education.* New York: Vintage.

Cattell, P. (1960). *The measurement of intelligence of infants and young children.* New York: Psychological Corporation.

Connor, F., Williamson, G., & Siepp, J.M. (Eds.). (1978). *Program guide for infants and toddlers with neuromotor and other developmental disabilities.* New York: Teachers College Press.

Dollard, J., & Miller, N. (1950). *Personality and psychotherapy.* New York: McGraw-Hill.

Foley, G.M., & Appel, M.H. (1987). *The Cognitive Observation Guide.* Reading, PA: The Family Centered Resource Project, Albright College.

Foley, G.M., & Hobin, M. (1981) *The Attachment-Separation-Individuation Scale.* Reading, PA: The Family Centered Resource Project, Albright College.

Freud, S. (1953). The interpretation of dreams. In J. Strachey (Ed. and Trans.), *The standard edition of the complete psychological works of Sigmund Freud* (Vols. 4 & 5). London: Hogarth Press. (Original work published 1900)

Giangreco, M.F. (1986). Delivery of therapeutic service in special education programs for learners with severe handicaps. *Physical and Occupational Therapy in Pediatrics, 6*(2), 5–15.

Griesinger, W. (1867). *Mental pathology and therapeutics* (C.L. Robertson & J. Rutherford, Trans.). London: New Sydenham Society. (Original work published 1845)

Haynes, U. (1983). *Holistic health care for children with developmental disabilities*. Baltimore: University Park Press.

Hunt, J.McV. (1961). *Intelligence and experience*. New York: Roland Press Co.

Hutchinson, D.J. (1978). The transdisciplinary approach. In J.B. Curry & K.K. Peppe (Eds.), *Mental retardation: Nursing approaches to care*. St. Louis: C.V. Mosby Company.

Hutt, M.L., Menninger, W.C., & O'Keefe, D.E. (1947). The neuropsychiatric team in the United States Army. *Mental Health, 31,* 103–119.

Kiss, J. (1983). *Transdisciplinary cost-effectiveness study*. Unpublished manuscript.

Lynch, A. (1980). *Evaluation of the function and impact of a multidisciplinary rehabilitation team upon the health and education of children enrolled in special education*. Reading, PA: Berks County Intermediate Unit.

Margrum, W.M., & Tigges, K.N. (1982). A transdisciplinary mobile intervention program for rural areas. *American Journal of Occupational Therapy, 36,* 90–94.

McCrae, M.Q. (1986). *Medical perspectives on brain damage and development*. Reading, PA: The Family-Centered Resource Project, Albright College.

Provence, S., Palmeri, S., Erikson, J., & Epperson, S. (1985). *Connecticut Infant/Toddler Developmental Assessment*. Unpublished manuscript, Connecticut Department of Health.

Rogers, S., & D'Eugenio, D.B. (1981). *Developmental programming for infants and young children: Assessment and application*. Ann Arbor: The University of Michigan Press.

Sameroff, A.J., & Chandler, M.J. (1975). Reproductive risk and the continuum of caretaking causality. In F.D. Horowitz, M. Hetherington, S. Scan-Salupatek, & G. Siegel (Eds.), *Review of child development research* (Vol. 4, pp. 187–244). Chicago: University of Chicago Press.

Terman, L.M., & Merrill, M.A. (1973). *Stanford-Binet Intelligence Scale*. Boston: Houghton Mifflin Co.

United Cerebral Palsy Association. (1976). *Staff development handbook: A resource for the transdisciplinary process*. New York: United Cerebral Palsy Association.

Watson, J.B. (1924). *Behaviorism*. New York: People's Publishing Co.

18 Family-Staff Collaboration for Tailored Infant Assessment

Linda Kjerland and JoAnne Kovach

Infants belong intimately to their families. Entering into the lives of families as an outsider is a delicate matter. To do so when childbirth has brought unexpected outcomes requires a great deal of self-awareness and understanding of what is valued and nonintrusive for families. That understanding can only be achieved by careful, thoughtful collaboration with each family. Such collaboration will result in tailored assessments and services that better meet the needs of family members as well as staff.

Tailored assessments of necessity, then, take place in a relaxed, collegial atmosphere with staff highly responsive to family priorities, style, and concerns. They occur at a time and location and in a manner that is comfortable and productive for families. Insights for parents and interventionists come from the free interchange of ideas and concerns throughout the entire process, from preparation for assessment to interpretation of findings.

The following scenario illustrates how a tailored, responsive assessment helps staff more effectively serve families.

Grandparents of a baby, premature and recently discharged from a neonatal intensive care unit, were very upset with the baby's parents for enrolling the infant in an early intervention program. They felt it would unduly label and hinder the baby. The parents encouraged them to come over for the assessment. When they arrived they saw the parents and one staff member sitting on the floor (while other staff observed) exploring the baby's awareness of sounds. "I'll show you he can hear!" said the grandfather as he proceeded to make clicking sounds from each of the kitchen doorways. Each time the baby looked to the sound as the grandfather predicted and all cheered. Skeptical grandparents became contributors to this assessment; they saw intervention not as inhibiting and labeling but as attention to the child's abilities and style, games, and interactions as well as support to understand challenging behaviors.

The arrival of PL 99-457's Individualized Family Service Plan has created tensions and anxieties for early intervention professionals. "What does it mean for assessment?" "How is it done?" Perhaps this era will be an opportunity to rethink some of the bad habits that evolved with PL 94-142, where responsibility has been confused with control. Often, individualized education program (IEP) assessments have been done at a time and place and in a manner chosen by professionals who then define for parents the child's status and problems. With that momentum, staff often proceed to define the plan of action for the parents. Staff are to give, parents are to receive.

Turnbull and Summers (1985) compared this unfortunate state of affairs to pre-Copernican thinking that placed the earth at the center of the universe. When Copernicus correctly placed the sun at the center, he set the direction for far more productive and logical thinking for astronomy. Similarly, special educators need a revolution that leaves behind an image of staff at the center who are drawing in "parent involvement." Instead, the task is to place families at the center and negotiate appropriate "staff involvement" with families.

Wright, Granger, and Sameroff (1984) provided a succinct description of this concept: "The role of the family is not an educational extension of the intervention program. Rather, the opposite is true, the intervention program should be an extension of the family (p. 86). If program staff are to respectfully intervene in ways complimentary to family efforts, they must learn to collaborate, to tailor their efforts in ways deemed responsive and helpful by families. For many staff, this approach is far removed from their preservice training.

Becoming family centered will require changes in philosophy and practices. This chapter will summarize the undertaking of Dakota, Inc., a private, nonprofit agency in Minnesota, as it evolved to collaborative family-centered practices. Dakota served 300 families in a 600-square-mile area via 12 transdisciplinary teams based in six different communities. The efforts required to change from staff control to staff-parent collaboration took several years and were aided by a U.S. Department of Education Handicapped Children's Early Education Program demonstration grant from 1983 to 1986, entitled Project Dakota. An example of family-staff collaboration is included in this chapter, as well as highlights of the program evaluation.

ELEMENTS IN TRANSFORMATION OF SERVICES FROM STAFF CONTROL TO STAFF-PARENT COLLABORATION

There were four major elements in Dakota's transformation of services: articulating a mission, reframing and mentoring, defining staff practices, and evaluating process and outcomes.

Articulating a Mission

A mission statement is essential if energy, resources, and problem solving are to proceed in a common direction. Dakota, Inc. wrestled with how to portray the child and the family in the mission. Who was the client? After much debate the agency defined the child as the client because child status determines eligibility; staff were given responsibility for helping and working alongside families. Hence, the mission statement was rewritten from "Promote optimal child development . . ." to "Assist the family and community to promote optimal development of the child and reduce the negative effects of delay or disability."

To further define the mission, Project Dakota articulated five goals:

1. Focus on child and family needs considered essential by parents.
2. Ensure direct and meaningful collaboration with families throughout the intervention process.
3. Promote the acquisition of knowledge, skill, and confidence by parents so that they can describe their child's strengths and needs and identify and carry out goals and strategies for their child.
4. Support the transmission of these strategies by staff and parents to other caregivers and settings.
5. Increase the child's ability to function in less restrictive environments by drawing upon natural settings and resources for intervention.

To resolve conflicts and debates on interpretation of these goals, Project Dakota defined service principles:

Families govern their investment of time and energy; there is no "hidden agenda" to increase or alter it. The goal is to have their current commitment fit their current energy, schedules, and priorities.

Intervention strategies can be a natural part of the daily routine and fit comfortably into the interactions and styles of family members.

Families should be offered ongoing information and assistance in using community resources so they may make informed decisions about what is available and whether it may play a role in their efforts.

Settings used by nondelayed peers should be used in preference to specialized or segregated settings.

Staff resources should supplement, not supplant, family and community resources.

Consultation and assistance should be available in the settings where the skills will be used or practiced.

Reframing and Mentoring

Once the mission, goals, and service principles were articulated, the next task was to understand and integrate them into the work day. Supervisors and team members committed time and energy to analyze experiences and interpret them in light of the mission and goals. An example of the commitment to turn from past practices and follow the new mission is evident in the situation in which a young mother was consistently not home when the staff member arrived for scheduled home visits. Analysis of the plan revealed an agenda set by the staff, not the parent. After guidance from fellow staff, this interventionist called the mother and told her she wanted to start over, this time building from the mother's agenda. From then on their efforts flourished. The mother later revealed that she had felt as though she was being treated like a child and resented everyone telling her what she needed and should do about it.

Another interventionist wondered why a team assessment had failed to generate any discussion from the mother. In recalling the afternoon, she realized that when the grandmother (who lived upstairs from the parent) poked her head in the doorway, it was the interventionist and not the parent who said she was welcome to participate. This parent felt betrayed because her authority to set limits had been ignored. The lesson learned was that staff should be accessible to extended family and friends but only through the parents' choice.

Staff in-service time was devoted to topics that elaborated upon and validated the mission and goals. These topics included family systems, adult learning styles, methods of consultation, transdisciplinary team work, research on family support, and functional programming. The work of Rose Bromwich (1978) on home-based intervention was analyzed and debated by staff. Her guidelines for intervention were then adopted:

Enable parents to remain in control.
Avoid the authority-layman gap.
Build on parents' strengths.
Respect parents' goals for the infant.
Involve parents in planning.
Respect individual styles of parent-infant interaction.
Use more than reinforcement, i.e., provide additional information on the why and how.
Give parents an 'out'; the option of rejecting any suggestion.
Share how it feels, i.e., the frustration staff may feel when interacting with an infant . . . (pp. 20–24)

Defining Staff Practices

The third effort undertaken was to establish specific practices to ensure that committing to a mission led to appropriate outcomes. Some staff were quite unconvinced of the value of a more tailored, responsive approach. Expectations needed to be set so that they would have sufficient experience in these alternative practices in order to directly judge their benefits. Toward this end a detailed service sequence was written with specific tasks and standards for each step in the assessment process.

Imposing practices prior to commitment to beliefs is supported by Thomas Guskey (1986). Beliefs, says Guskey, derive from having seen, over time, the outcomes of a set of practices. Therefore, to change a system it is not sufficient to tackle beliefs alone. Practices must be altered in ways that can be seen and felt by staff and thus build the base for new beliefs and commitment. The following example illustrates the impact of direct experience on learning:

A recent occupational therapy graduate was skeptical about families as the primary sources of intervention goals; she had been trained to be *the* source. After participating in her first parent-staff collaborative assessment and assessment interpretation, she was awed to find that her own list of goals was not only covered first by the family, but covered in more functional terms. That did more to convince her than all the philosophical arguments posed during new staff orientation.

Evaluating Process and Outcomes

The fourth element in helping Dakota achieve responsive assessment and services was program evaluation. Its purpose was to provide objective feedback to staff on how they were doing, what could be improved, and the results of efforts to do better.

Caldwell (1977, p. 158) suggested that staff "look at ourselves as closely as we look at children." The program evaluation for Project Dakota was therefore designed to capture the actual work of the team in action. Tools were created to help staff monitor their participation for measures of responsiveness and collaboration with families. These tools and results from that use will be described below.

The special education literature contains only a few reports of parent participation in program planning. Goldstein, Strickland, Turnbull, and Curry (1980) found parents accounted for less than 25% of total IEP conference contributions. McKinney and Hocutt (1982) reported that approximately one third of parents believed they had helped write the IEP. Brinckerhoff and Vincent (1986) developed a model that trained parents to increase participation and compared their experimental group with an untrained group. The experimental parent group made 41% of the contributions and 56% of the decisions compared to the control group's 23% participation rate and 28% decision rate.

Project Dakota chose instead to place responsibility on staff for the degree of parent contribution to the individualized plan. Staff developed an instituted collaborative practices for assessment and planning with families. Examining contributions of 21 families to the postassessment discussion on the child's abilities and interests indicated parent contributions of 64%. On the section on concerns and needs, parents' contributions were 68%. During planning parents were the source of 83% of goals and 40% of the strategies to achieve the goals. Collaboration led to diffusion of programming to other family members and community providers; 92% of strategies were utilized in the home, 19% in center, and 43% in community settings.

PROJECT DAKOTA PRACTICES FOR ASSESSMENT AND INTERVENTION PLANNING

The assessment practices of Project Dakota will be described in detail below. To help portray this method, examples of one family's experience will be shared.

Family's Assessment Focus and Preassessment Planning

Families are interviewed by a member of the Dakota Team upon referral. This team member, called a "facilitator," will conduct the assessment, lead the discussion that follows, and later serve as primary implementor along with the parents for this transdisciplinary team. Initial contacts have two purposes: to introduce the family to the agency's philosophy and resources, and to allow the family to introduce their child and their concerns and preferences. To assist in this step, family members are sent a *Family's Assessment Focus,* a questionnaire that is reviewed on an initial visit. The questions included in this questionnaire are shown in Table 1. This tool asks parents, prior to assessment, to identify their concerns so that they can be addressed during assessment. Then, using a structured interview entitled *Preassessment Planning: The Setting* (see Table 2), the parents state preferences for setting and time of day, and offer tips for interacting with their infant, including how they and the staff member can best work together to interact with the child. Differences in preference between parents range from one parent who wishes to observe and coach her 3-year-old to another who wishes to hold his infant and let his more experienced hands show staff how the child responds.

The following describes this step with parents of a 16-month-old with Down syndrome served by Project Dakota. It is their fourth assessment (assessments occurred every 4 months).

Mother and Dad had each filled out the Family's Assessment Focus. Their differing but complimentary observations and concerns were discussed by the facilitator and the mother in a home visit during which they planned the assessment.

Table 1. The Family's Assessment Focus (Project Dakota)

1. My child's name is _____ and I would describe her/him in this way:

2. Our relationship or time together is:

3. A typical day with my child includes:

4. My child enjoys or is interested in:

5. My child needs help with or avoids:

6. The most challenging aspect of raising my child is:

7. Recent progress or changes I have seen in my child at home:

8. Questions I have about my child:

9. My child does best when:

10. My child communicates by:

11. My child is really interested in:

12. I would like my child to learn or get better at:

13. I would like help with:

Mark's mother stated that she felt he needed to improve use of his fingers. She shares Dad's concern that he is now biting everything and everyone. She wants to know if they should discipline him and understands that emerging teeth may be causing the biting. The father's primary concern is Mark's gross motor development. The mother asks for information comparing his skills to other children his age but ex-

Table 2. Preassessment Planning: The Setting (Project Dakota)

1. Questions or concerns others have (e.g., babysitter, clinic, preschool) about my child:

2. Other places you can observe my child:

   Place: Place:
   Contact person: Contact person:
   What to observe: What to observe:

3. I want others to see what my child does when:

4. I prefer the assessment take place:
   _____ at home   _____ at another location   _____ at the center

5. A time when my child is alert and when working parents can be present is:
   _____ morning   _____ afternoon   _____ early evening

6. People who I would like to be there other than parents and early intervention staff:

7. My child's favorite toys or activities to help her/him become focused, motivated, and comfortable:

8. During the assessment, I prefer to:

   _____ a. Sit beside my child
   _____ b. Help with activities to explore her/his abilities
   _____ c. Offer comfort and support to my child
   _____ d. Exchange ideas with the facilitator
   _____ e. Carry out activities to explore my child's abilities
   _____ f. Permit facilitator to handle and carry out activities
   _____ g. Other:

---

presses confidence in his motor skills. Most of all she would love to have him learn to give her a hug.

To further describe the child, both the mother and father noted some beginning imitation games; he now claps and pounds after they do. His interest in looking at pictures is increasing, although he is not pointing at familiar objects or pictures.

The parents desire an early evening assessment in their home so that Mark's father can be present. It is a time when Mark is usually quite lively. Mark's mother suggests that they use two beach balls he loves to play with plus peek-a-boo games. They chose to participate in demonstrating his progress and some test items. The parents agree to include yearly standardized norm-referenced testing as part of this assessment.

To incorporate family planning into the comprehensive assessment, the facilitator returns to the center and reports the family's specifications. The facilitator also reviews other records about the child, his or her observations and impressions, and, if this is not the initial assessment, his or her progress notes. Staff from other disciplines draw upon their expertise and test batteries for activities that will elicit behaviors from the child. If the facilitator is unsure of how to elicit a particular behavior (e.g., trunk rotation), a staff member from the appropriate discipline demonstrates what it is, what to look for, and examples of how to elicit it.

Because Mom noted that Mark currently loved to play with two beach balls, activities were designed to capitalize on this interest to look at movement patterns and imitation. The facilitator related her observations of increased trunk rotation; Mark was now pulling up to stand, but he is not yet able to get down. The occupational therapist suggested positions and activities to cover during the assessment. The facilitator was concerned about the child's range of verbal and gestural imitation. The speech clinician suggested imitation and turn-taking games. A list of all the activities and test items was cooperatively drawn up, which the facilitator will use during assessment.

Assessment

Collaborative assessment requires detailed knowledge of test items, sequences, and standardized procedures. It also relies upon trust and confidence among team members because of the extensive role release. Fortunately, each assessment supports such staff development because members watch and learn from each other and see the interplay of all developmental areas.

During the assessment only the facilitator and/or parents directly interact with the child; other team members record observations of performance. The assessment begins with a review of its purpose and the procedures chosen by parents and staff. The pace throughout is relaxed and playful; activities are presented and removed smoothly, tapping into spontaneous play of the child. Standardized tests are used when required.

On the floor Mark and his mother are entertaining one another with a game of "peek-a-boo." This prompts the father to tell about a turn-taking game in which Mark and his siblings exchange caps; it was clearly a source of enjoyment to all. Mark crawls across the floor to pull up to a window, has a snack in the high chair, and pulls on kitchen drawers; throughout the hour specific test materials and activities have been administered.

The facilitator occasionally introduces developmental terminology for skills also described in functional terms. The occupational therapist and speech clinician quietly observe, take notes, and score standardized test protocols.

The teacher presents a standard test item from the "cause-and-effect" sequence; the item is not passed but his father tells of Mark's newest game: pulling on the window shade, which causes it to snap up. A discussion of cause and effect follows, including other daily activities in which Mark had begun to experience cause-and-effect and means-ends relationships.

Postassessment Discussion

Project Dakota diverges from two traditional methods used to organize and interpret assessment data: 1) compartmentalizing findings by developmental areas with a focus on performance deficits, and 2) reporting assessment findings to parents only after staff themselves have discussed the findings and reached consensus. Immediately following the assessment, parents and staff collectively describe the child—that is, what did they all see and learn about the child?

The facilitator begins by asking parents to critique the assessment: "Was your child/infant's behavior typical? How did you feel about it? What could we do differently next time?" Next, the facilitator asks the parents to list the child's strengths—including areas of progress, favorite activities, interests, and motivators. Staff supplement or expand this listing for a comprehensive view of the child. This format is repeated for the listing of problems, concerns, delays, difficulties, activities the child avoids, and frustrations experienced by the child or by the family and staff in interactions with the child. Any differences of opinion can be addressed by reviewing what all saw the child do and by deciding to do further assessment.

During this discussion all contributions are recorded on a large sheet of paper so that the team can refer to them throughout the planning process. They are simultaneously recorded on the Post-Assessment Discussion form shown in Figure 1. There are two reasons for this recording strategy. First, it slows the process so descriptors can be thought through, clarified, and elaborated upon rather than lost in a rush of words. Second, recording each members' contributions in their words reinforces the value of each contributor and is later used for program evaluation purposes. A simple coding method of initials is used to record who made each contribution. A staff member, early in the training process, confessed, "When you see a lot of your own initials it reminds you to slow down, listen, give time and space for parents to speak. They are the ones who have the most at stake."

The father's critique was that Mark was a little tired and didn't do a few of the things he can often do; these are listed. He began by stating that Mark will now stick up for himself and wrestles with his sister, he understands "come here," and he knows that getting a coat means going somewhere. Mom shared that he bumps you to get attention, pulls to stand better, and is trying side-stepping. The speech clinician said he turns to his name, and uses two gestures. The occupational therapist added that he is pulling to stand more easily and is shifting weight from one side to another.

In the list of concerns the occupational therapist explains that Mark's poor use of his thumb makes his pincer grasp inefficient. Also, two new concerns have surfaced: separation and forming words. The latter is supported by many language precursors on the "strengths" lists.

Multiple opportunities to think about, observe, and discuss their child expands parents (and staff's) understanding of the full range and interrelationships of developmental needs and abilities.

The last two steps in the postassessment discussion are drawing conclusions and setting priorities. Staff ask parents, "What seems most important? What stands out about your child now? What comes to mind when you look over these strengths and needs?" The purpose of drawing a conclusion is to synthesize the child's strengths and needs from the perspective of parents.

The entire postassessment discussion typically takes about 30 minutes. A more extensive developmental report is later written by the facilitator, drawing upon the observations and editing of each staff. Parents will edit this report, during a home visit, prior to writing the plan.

When staff have effectively acted as consultants with parents throughout the assessment and postassessment, a considerable amount of information will have been exchanged so that both have gained greater insight into and understanding of the child.

Setting Goals and Strategies

Next, major goal areas or priorities are identified. Parents are asked, "What do you want your child to get help with in the next few months?"

Mark's father succinctly summed up the family's primary feelings and goals: Mark is doing very well but the key is to keep him motivated. The mother also wants him to be able to hug her, communicate more, and handle separating from her more easily.

Within a week, the facilitator and parents meet to detail the goals and strategies. Strategies are actions by adults and children to help the child reach the goals. Parents are the principle source of goals; staff may suggest others but only with parents' agreement. Vincent (1983) cautions staff about side-tracking critical needs and issues raised by the family. Family priorities in this process are paramount.

After identifying each goal, parents and staff together describe the current behaviors of the child, as well as behaviors of adults interacting with the child. Next, the team generates ideas on *how* change can be made and *who* can help with that change. They are recorded on the individual program plan "Goals and Strategies" form (see Fig. 2). In behavioral terms this process examines context and the contingencies of the behavior.

Generally, only a small number of goals are chosen because the assessment process is

INDIVIDUAL PROGRAM PLAN
POST-ASSESSMENT DISCUSSION

DAKOTA, INC.
680 O'Neill Road
Eagan, MN. 55121

DAKOTA
Assisting the community
and people challenged by disabilities
to live and work together.

Name Mark	Date 11-14-83	Facilitator Catherine	Participants (Gay and Frank (parents), OT, Tchr, S/L therapist
Who	1. Strengths, Interests, Motivators, Progress, Abilities of Child; Family Activities and Interests	Who	2. Concerns, Problems, Delays, Frustrations, Needs of Child; Family Concerns about Child
Frank	imitates pounding on highchair and mouth actions also "da da da"	Gay	want him to be able to hug me
Gay	pulls up to stand better	Frank	want his biting us
Gay	pulls up and stands on his little step, falls down to get off	Frank	more steps - want to see it in the next month or two
Gay	opens and closes everything	Gay	his problems separating from me
Gay	claps	Gay	want more communicating 'lib by by'
Frank	plays ball - chases and pushes toys along	Frank	trying to say a word - not doing it yet
Gay	just starting to cruise		
T	family members are his motivators		
Gay	front door and window - looking out are motivators		
Gay	turns to see voices		
S/L	turns to, recognizes his name		
Gay	sticks up for his rights, wrestles with 2yrold cousin		
Gay	sits and plays for a long time		
S/L	understands 'come here'		
Gay	knows foods mean to go		
Frank	bumps into you, toilet you know hwords to go		

Who	3. Conclusions/Priorities/Questions:
Frank	pleased with his progress
Frank	need to keep looking for motivators to keep him going

4. Current Contact With Non-Delayed Peers		Who	5. Major Goal Areas
Sees cousins and neighbors 1-2 hrs a week		Gay	communicating more with us
		Frank	getting closer to walking

EI-107 (Rev. 9/85) WHITE - Office YELLOW - Parent/Guardian PHOTOCOPIES - Center & Facilitator

Figure 1. Sample Postassessment Discussion form.

INDIVIDUAL PROGRAM PLAN
GOALS AND STRATEGIES

DAKOTA
Assisting the community and people challenged by disabilities to live and work together

DAKOTA, INC.
680 O'Neill Road
Eagan, MN. 55121

Name	Date	Age	Facilitator
Mark	11-26-88	11 mos	Teni

Participants: Gay and Frank (parents) and Teni

The Individual Program Plan promotes optimal development and reduces the negative effects of delay or disability by responding to parent's priorities & using natural settings & resources.

Dakota, Inc. promotes learning in settings typically used by non-delayed children.

Group Setting(s)	No. of Times/Wk.	Individual Setting(s)	No. of Times/Wk.
- parent-child play group at EI center	1x mo.	home visit	2x mo
- toddler play group in community	1x wk		

GOAL: Mark will use social gestures — huggins and waving by loy

What Child/Adults Do Now	Reasons To Change/Adapt	Strategies, "How To"	Who	Status	Who Teach/Learn	Where
holds arms up to be held	want to have more ways to communicate with others	- hug Mark as onward - help him move his arms into a hug when he's being held or standing and held at waist lev. - family will wave to him when leaving and raise his arm for him — also notice when he just begins to do on own	Gay		Gay, Frank → brother and sister	home
crawls over to be picked up			Gay			
will play pat a cake and repeat back when he starts a sound (mouth) game					whole family	home

GOAL: Mark will cruise and take steps on own

What Child/Adults Do Now	Reasons To Change/Adapt	Strategies, "How To"	Who	Status	Who Teach/Learn	Where
- pulls up to stand	introduce more shifting of weight off any foot onto another so can raise one foot at a time	- pitch him up from crib but at a few feet from where he is so will try to walk there - put toys on couch just out of reach to one side	Gay		Gay	home
- can stand indefinitely						
- will let go and lean and get to stand from squat C twice without holding on			Gay		whole family and at Grandma's	home Grandma's
- goes up and down holding with one hand						

My priorities for my child are included in this Individual Program Plan.

Parent/Guardian Signature(s): ~~~~~~

WHITE – Office YELLOW – Parent/Guardian PHOTOCOPIES – Center & Facilitator

EI-181 (Rev. 9/85)

Figure 2. Sample Goals and Strategies form.

repeated every 4 months. These goals and strategies are reviewed and revised at least monthly in consultation with parents.

SUMMARY AND CONCLUSIONS

Interventionists must be careful not to inadvertently add stress to families already challenged, nor harm emerging and intimate parent-infant relationships. Rather than speculating on what will be supportive, nonintrusive, meaningful, and useful, staff need to carefully and methodically seek guidance and feedback from families themselves. Programs, therefore, must stringently examine their practices and particularly their approach to assessment, because this will set the tone for all interventions that follow. Similarly, program in-service and program evaluation efforts must support staff by addressing the intricacies of staff interactions with families.

Project Dakota devised practices that focus on needs identified by parents and that enhance their knowledge, skill, and confidence to identify the child's strengths and needs and design and carry out interventions. Key elements of Dakota's collaborative assessment were: preassessment planning with parents to tailor the what, how, where, and when of assessment; joint interpretation of observations, findings, and conclusions immediately after transdisciplinary assessment; and the design of intervention goals and strategies based on family priorities, preferences, and everyday settings and activities. The essence of collaboration was captured in the words of Sharyl Horbal, a parent who significantly influenced the staff of Project Dakota:

You have to believe the parent . . . the program has to do that. It's a moral obligation—not just a written down rule. If you're working like you should be— I'm the conductor putting it all together, I'm the one to say stop, and go and that's too much of this or that . . . [then] we'll harmonize really well. (Horbal, 1985)

REFERENCES

Brinckerhoff, J.L., & Vincent, L.J. (1986). Increasing parental decision-making at the individualized education program meeting. *Journal of the Division for Early Childhood, 11*(1), 46–58.

Bromwich, R. (1978). *Working with parents and infants.* Baltimore: University Park Press.

Caldwell, B.M. (1977). Evaluation of program effectiveness. In B.M. Caldwell & D.J. Stedman (Eds.), *Infant education: A guide for helping handicapped children in the first three years.* New York: Walker.

Goldstein, S., Strickland, B., Turnbull, A.P., & Curry, L. (1980). An observation analysis of the IEP conference. *Exceptional Children, 46*(4), 278–286.

Guskey, T. (1986, May). Staff development and the process of teacher change. *Educational Researcher,* pp. 5–12.

Horbal, S. (1985). Taped interview. *In Three families: Experiences and expectations for early intervention.* Eagan, MN: Project Dakota.

Kovach, J. (1987). *Final report for Project Dakota 1983–1986.* Eagan, MN: Dakota, Inc.

McKinney, J.D., & Hocutt, A.M. (1982). Public school involvement of parents of learning disabled children and average achievers. *Exceptional Education Quarterly, 3*(2), 64–73.

Turnbull, A.P., & Summers, J.A. (1985, April). *From parent involvement to family support: Evolution to revolution.* Paper presented at Down Syndrome State-of-the-Art Conference, Boston, MA.

Vincent, L. (1983, December). *Active decision making by parents.* Paper presented at the Conference of the Division for Early Childhood, Washington, D.C.

Wright, J.S., Granger, R.D., & Sameroff, A.J. (1984). Parental acceptance and developmental handicap. In J. Blachard (Ed.), *Severely handicapped young children and their families.* Orlando, FL: Academic Press.

19 Communicating Assessment Findings to Parents
Toward More Effective Informing

Ann Murphy

There is increased emphasis on training professionals in state-of-the-art techniques of assessing young children with developmental delays. Appropriate assessment has particular practical relevance because it can open up for the child at risk an array of interventions that may favorably alter the child's developmental progress. Unfortunately, an often-neglected aspect is formal training in how to transmit this information to the people who can utilize it on behalf of the child, particularly the parents. Typically, parents are not only the decision makers as to what services the child will receive but also the primary agents of many intervention services.

The purpose of this chapter is to describe the dynamics involved in communicating diagnostic findings to parents and to identify factors that can contribute to a more effective informing conference. Among other things, the professional should: 1) have an understanding of his or her own feelings and how they influence his or her behavior, 2) get to know the parents, 3) be aware of the discrepancies between his or her perspective and that of the parents regarding the implications of the child's symptoms, 4) be accepting of different coping strategies used by different families, and 5) plan the informing conference with the objective of engaging the parents in an active dialogue regarding the information. Informing should be parent centered and include a mix of what the parent should know as well as information the parent has requested. Following a discussion of the importance of the informing interview and the different styles of informing that occur, each of the above issues is considered in turn.

THE IMPORTANCE OF THE INFORMING CONFERENCE

The diagnostic conference is a time of crisis, a possible turning point in the parents' relationship with their child and with professionals. Most parents can recall in exquisite detail the circumstances in which they first heard that their child had a disability. Processing and integrating the information accurately is extremely difficult. The information being shared is often of high potential impact on the future options for the child. It may well imply that the child will not be able to achieve expected developmental and social milestones, such as self-help skills, communication, social relationships with peers, and normal school entrance and progress. Often parents recall being told information that can only be a distorted recollection of what was actually said. This is not surprising if one considers that this is a complex encounter between persons who have

---

The work of this program is supported by Maternal and Child Health Services Grant #928 and Administration for Developmental Disabilities Grant # 03 DD 135, U.S. Department of Health and Human Services.

widely different perspectives, different bodies of information, different time frames, and different levels of emotional investment in the child under discussion. It is not an uncommon coping mechanism to displace negative feeling onto the bearer of bad news rather than dealing directly with the information. Not infrequently parents will report being alienated and may break off the relationship with the individual professional or agency who made the original diagnosis. They may describe them as insensitive, as perfunctory in their assessment, or as focusing on the child's limitations, excluding any room for hope. This failed outcome of an informing conference can be the result of a situation where there was little opportunity for the meaningful dialogue that is necessary to work through misconceptions and achieve a balanced picture of the situation (Murphy & Pounds, 1972).

What the professional says about his or her assessment to the parents of a newborn with a birth defect is likely to have a very powerful impact, but one that differs from one family to another (Rapoport, 1965). The parents may feel very helpless and uncertain about whether to bond to a child who seems so different than they planned for. The professional may be endowed by the parents with wisdom he or she does not actually possess. They may press him or her to give specific guidance about the stresses the family will experience if they accept the child as a family member. The parents may incorporate the professional's implied or stated values about the child and act accordingly. A more constructive approach is to help the parents develop their own resolution of the issues that confront them. A first step is to support the parents in getting to know the child as a person as well as providing them factual information about the disability (Murphy, 1982).

STYLES OF INFORMING

In the past professionals sometimes believed it was appropriate to assume an authoritative role in informing parents. They would elucidate all possible developmental outcomes suggested by the assessment along with a prescription for how parents should adapt to the child. In earlier years this was often the precipitating reason for early institutionalization of children with birth defects such as Down syndrome (Aldrich, 1947). Other commonly quoted prescriptions were "take him home and love him" or "treat her like any other child." The ostensible reason for such professional pronouncements was to offer the parent something positive to mitigate their feelings of disappointment and loss. Such a strategy probably also served to provide the professionals with the illusion that they had something to offer in a situation in which they felt powerless.

Gradually a body of knowledge has been developed about attachment between parents and child and the implications of a defect in the child for the parental bond (Drotar, Baskewicz, Irwin, Kennell, & Klaus, 1975; Solnit & Stark, 1961). Also, society and the professional community now have a more positive orientation toward children with disabilities and their potential to be helped. The present trend is to defer diagnostic labels and focus on the immediate behaviors of the child in order to build a developmental profile and to establish short-term goals. There is often little emphasis placed on the longer range implications of the diagnostic information for future functioning of the individual. Nonspecific terms such as "developmental delay" and "special needs" are commonly used. This philosophy certainly corrects the overly negative and judgmental behavior of professionals in the past and acknowledges the individual differences among children in developmental progress as well as the potential positive influences of intervention. However, to maintain this posture in a situation in which it is clear that the child has a substantial handicap amounts to withholding information from the parents, who have a right to know. A realistic balance should be established.

An important factor in considering how much to share with parents is the reliability and validity of the clinical assessments that have been done. How predictive are they of the future course of the child's development? How substantial is the child's delay or deviance? What is the realistic probability that the child, with help, will overcome these problems? It is usually assumed that actual data should be shared, but there is less certainty about whether a diagnostic label should be given or what predictions should be made about future developmental progress. If the child is very young, has not received any special services, and the parent is newly aware of a problem, it is perhaps enough to confirm the presence of a delay, make a plan for intervention, and follow up to document progress. If the child has a substantial delay that is unlikely to resolve, it is the responsibility of the professional to inform the parents that the child may have some degree of continuing disability, even with treatment.

Some professionals believe it is best to avoid labels that have high impact, such as "mental retardation." However, if it is an accurate label, it should be introduced into the discussion. The parents will probably hear it from someone else and will think that the professional betrayed them by not telling the truth. Also labels have value in that they make it easier for the parents, when ready, to conceptualize and communicate about the disability. Parents who have been experiencing considerable difficulty in providing nurturance to a child with unusual behavior will sometimes welcome a label to put into perspective what has been a confusing and frustrating experience in parenting.

It is best to avoid making exact predictions about the particular child's future. Attempting to make long-term prognoses is hazardous even when parents push for this kind of information. A person's functioning is at least in part influenced by factors such as motivation, family support, and available opportunities. Achievements such as "ability to hold a job" or "caring for oneself" are open to widely different interpretations. Usually it is enough to say that the child may require special help in the forseeable future, the specifics of which can be determined by monitoring his or her developmental progress.

It is important to stress the child's assets as well as his or her limitations. Otherwise the parent will think the child is being devalued as a person. The fact that the child will progress and learn is also vital to convey because many parents take away the image of arrested development. If the parents reject findings that confirm a handicap there is little point in pressing the issue. If the parents have reasonable expectations of the child, are open to intervention services focusing on the symptoms, and are willing to return for follow-up, it is not necessary to come to an agreement about what the outcomes will be. Many parents who deny their child is delayed will, in practice, adapt their behavior to the actual developmental level of the child. Some parents need more time to work with the child before they can come to terms with the fact that a cure may not be possible.

FACTORS CONTRIBUTING TO AN EFFECTIVE INFORMING CONFERENCE

Getting in Touch with Feelings

It is well accepted that for parents to hear that their child is handicapped is a high-stress experience (Moses, 1983). There is less acknowledgment that giving negative information to families is a stressful situation for the professional as well. Trainees in professions often are more in touch with their uncomfortable feelings about assuming this role and can be quite articulate. More experienced professionals have developed coping mechanisms and may be less aware of their underlying personal feelings. Many beginners describe an identification with the parents' hopes and wishes and believe that, by giving test data that confirm a disability, they are inflicting pain, almost as if they are the cause of the problem. Others may identify with the needs of the child and the potential value of resources available to help. They may be impatient with parents who do not assign a high priority to following through on recommended services. They may be distressed by parents' expressions of negative feelings about their child and see themselves as better caregivers and advocates for the child. Other professionals might find it difficult to understand parents' devotion and commitment to a child with little apparent potential. They find it hard to view the situation from the parents' perspective. Some professionals are threatened by parents who do not readily accept findings and question their reliability and validity. As a result, a plan for communication can develop into a battle for control.

Such feelings and reactions on the part of professionals are not necessarily inappropriate to the situation. However, a professional who has little awareness of his or her own feelings and how they can influence his or her communication style relinquishes the ability to control his or her role in the informing session. Self-awareness should be cultivated during the initial training period as an important continuing component of professional development. Professionals should review their interactions with families according to the following criteria:

What were my feelings in this situation?
What was the source of my feelings?
How did they influence my behavior?

Often working as a member of a clinical team can enhance opportunities for feedback and support to a professional in stressful situations.

Getting to Know the Parents

Learning about the parents' perspective should be an important and explicit goal during the assessment process. Recognizing the importance of this information and bringing it into the discussion can result in increased sensitivity on the part of the professional to the parents' issues as well as the parents' feeling that their questions and concerns are valued and understood (Garrett, 1982). This is a beginning point for the working relationship between professional and parent and the establishment of common goals. The following content areas should be addressed:

1. Whose concerns prompted the evaluation? The parents, one or both? A local agency, physician, or members of the extended family? How did the parents feel about coming?
2. What do the parents see as problems? What words do they spontaneously use to label the behaviors that concern them?
3. What previous efforts have they made to get information about the child's symptoms? Other evaluations? Reading? Talking with other parents? What is their evaluation of what they learned?
4. What types of information are they seeking —a diagnosis, a cause, prognosis, treatment options, implications for the short-range or long-range future? If there is concern with cause, are there references to self-blame or a tendency to assign responsibility to other persons or events? What is their expectation from treatment? Do they emphasize treatments that professionals can offer or do they refer to activities they might undertake on behalf of the child? Have they already had experience with the service system, and how do they evaluate their contacts?
5. Who is in the family? Is it planned that both parents will participate in the evaluation at some point? If not, why not? Do both parents work? Do they have other responsibilities that make keeping appointments or undertaking home treatments difficult?

Recognizing Differences in the Perspective of Parents and Professionals

The different perspectives and background experiences with handicapping conditions of professionals and parents must be considered in preparing for an informing conference. The work experience of the professional involves multiple contacts with a large number of children at risk or with known handicaps over an extended period of time. Professionals have developed feelings of confidence and comfort in dealing with disabilities. They are aware of individual differences and value the positive results that can be accomplished through intervention. They are less influenced by stereotypes about handicapped people and not personally affected by the negative judgments of the general public. Sometimes they have had personal experiences with a family member who is handicapped, which may enhance their sensitivity.

In the course of an evaluation the professional may use a number of different types of well-established diagnostic tools such as physical examination, laboratory tests, standardized developmental assessment instruments, and clinical observation. This expertise allows him or her to draw inferences about the present developmental status of the child and the extent to which the child is at risk for a permanent disability. It may also be possible to generate information about possible causes. The purpose of some of the assessment tools or procedures used, what kind of information they can provide, and what their limitations are may not be apparent to parents. Often parents overvalue physical examinations, particularly neurological exams and laboratory work such as electroencephalograms and X rays, and are under the impression that these examinations can yield information about a child's functioning that, in fact, they cannot. On the other hand, they may devalue clinical observations and behavioral assessment tools as being unable to provide valid data. Time taken to explain the design of the evaluation and what each examination may provide in the way of data is important preparation for the informing session. Parents may also need to be told why certain examinations, which they were expecting, were not included. This allows the parent to learn something of how professionals think, how they problem solve, and how they arrive at their conclusions. It helps to demystify what may seem like an arbitrary or magical process.

Professionals also have a special vocabulary and are desensitized to words that have high impact for the parent. Cerebral palsy conjures up an image of severe physical impairment. Mild retardation is a serious handicap to parents who thought their child had normal intelligence. Some labels have been changed and may be meaningless to the uninformed, such as pervasive developmental disorder. Often different professionals define these terms and diagnostic labels differently. Professionals are also comfortable in using agencies and special services for disabled children that may be very alien to a parent who is newly encountering them.

Accepting Different Coping Patterns in Parents

Most professionals are knowledgeable about the theories regarding the typical adjustment phases of parents who learn they have a handicapped child. Professionals have learned to value the support services currently available and are invested in having parents use them. However, they are often impatient with the pace and style of individual parents who are negotiating this major adjustment. They forget that the theories only provide a general orientation to important aspects but do not reflect the unique experience of the individual parent. There are important personal and cultural differences that influence adaptation. Although talking about feelings is an important outlet for many people, some need to withdraw into themselves or from active contact with professionals as part of the healing process. Many parents need an opportunity for personal assimilation of this new way of thinking about their child before they begin to use a system that serves handicapped children. They also need time to make a personal transition before they can identify with other parents whose children have similar problems.

Some parents want to obtain a second opinion from another professional before accepting a diagnosis as fact. Others may want to pursue a therapeutic program, such as diet or exercise, that may have little scientific credibility. Professionals often feel uncomfortable with these plans and see the parent as postponing therapeutic actions that they believe would be more beneficial. Although there is no requirement that the parents' plan be endorsed, the professional can identify with the parents' right to ascertain how their child's needs can best be met. If the professional can allow the parent to explore various options, the relationship with the family has a better chance of being maintained. It is important that the parents be advised of the services potentially available to them and the professional's assessment of their importance. However, the professional must respect the parents' right to decide what services are most useful to them.

The Informing Conference

Every effort should be made to have both parents present at the informing conference. All too often the professional communicates only with the mother, which results in the mother having the burden of informing the father. This is a time when parents can support each other and it demonstrates that caring for a child with special needs is the responsibility of both parents. Sometimes a friend or a member of the extended family will accompany the parents. It is important to establish whether the parents see these people as sources of support and want to include them in the informing session.

The number of staff people attending the conference should be based on the expertise required to provide accurate information and the learning style of the parents. If the parents have demonstrated difficulty in relating to professional people, they may be overwhelmed by a panel of professionals. On the other hand, if they are eager for specifics, having access to the personnel who actually performed the evaluations may enhance their understanding of the content. Sufficient time should be alotted so that the significant issues can be addressed and the parents have the undivided attention of the professionals.

To be effective in communicating with parents the professional must realize that assimilating new information that requires modification of significant concepts and attitudes is not a passive process. All too often professionals move into a review of data without linking this information to the parents' existing beliefs and concerns. Frequently the professional will lose sight of the parents' specific questions and concepts that emerged in the process of taking the history. Learning is also an active process. Every effort should be made to facilitate a dialogue whereby the parents give clues as to how they are processing the information (Selig, 1983). What is their understanding of what is being said? What reservations do they have? What is synchronous with their perceptions? Do they think the professional got a good picture of the child's behavior?

Professionals should be sensitive to factors that can interfere with communication (Murphy & Pedulla, 1973). The setting in which the professional works may condition the parents' expectations and responses to what is said. A hospital has a different impact than a school. A large institution may arouse different feelings than a small office. Some parents may view the professional as an authority and have difficulty in challenging information that is being presented. They may fear that raising questions indicates ignorance or would not be welcomed by the professional. In such cases, the professional may be able to draw out the parents' concerns with statements like, "You must have some questions" or "You have been able to observe your child in many situations that I have not. How does this compare with your observations?" Sometimes it is difficult for parents to verbalize lack of interest or enthusiasm for recommendations that involve increased commitment of their time for fear of disapproval. Again, a professional may elicit a response from the parents by comments like "Some people find this difficult to do" or "How does this fit with other demands on your time?"

Technical vocabulary can pose barriers in communication. Common terms should be used because the parents may likely hear them from others. However, it is important to be concrete and provide supporting examples to demonstrate the meanings of words. Certain words have high impact and are associated with commonly accepted stereotypes. These words still should be used so that the parents can understand what is discussed. However, it is best to preface such words with a behavioral description drawn from the particular child so that the parents can develop a more accurate and positive association with the term. For example, a professional using the term "mental retardation" might introduce it in this way:

John is now 2 years of age. His responses in all aspects of development are more characteristic of a

1-year-old child. He has shown progress but his rate of development is slower than that of the average child. This is a substantial delay and it is unlikely that he can completely catch up with his age group. He is at risk for mental retardation. This term is commonly used to describe this degree of delay.

In informing parents about a child with an emotional disturbance, the professional might say:

Susan's difficulty in maintaining eye contact and lack of responsiveness is not a willful behavior or form of stubbornness. This is a reflection of her difficulty in relating to people. She needs special help in learning how to interact and communicate with people and develop socially appropriate behavior. This will take considerable time, effort, and patience from all the adults who work with or care for Susan.

The professional's feelings about giving information that has a negative impact may cause him or her to consider postponing giving the family the full facts. Although the parents may have some ambivalence about what they may be told, the fact that they have brought the child for the evaluation indicates that on some level they want to know what is wrong. Keeping them in suspense about the seriousness of the problem can be painful. They cannot begin to cope with the reality of the situation until it is presented to them honestly and directly. Professionals sometimes rationalize their own discomfort about presenting negative information by deciding that "the timing is wrong," "the parents are not ready," or "we need to await another procedure or to see what progress is made." It is important to evaluate what is to be gained by waiting. Another coping mechanism of professionals is to disguise the real meaning of the findings by such statements as "You can never tell what the year can bring." If the information being given is negative or differs from the parents' expectations, they should be allowed time to respond. A common tendency is to continue elaborating on the information or to try to mitigate its impact by offering reassurance. The professional should not defend his or her statements in anticipation of the parents' objection. It cuts them off and makes them feel it is wrong to object.

An important task of the informing conference is assisting parents with their feelings.

Finding out that their child has a handicap can arouse overwhelming feelings of loss and anxiety. The parents have to cope with having lost the healthy child they had hoped for or thought they had. Their fears about what the future will hold in caring for a handicapped child can be tremendous. Also, parents perceive their child as an extension of themselves and learning that the child has difficulties can arouse questions about their own adequacy as persons. Parents need to protect themselves against being overwhelmed by these feelings. They may have difficulty verbalizing these feelings and should not be pressed to do so. The parents defenses may be a major force interfering with the professional's attempts to communicate diagnostic information. Parents need these coping mechanisms, especially at first, and will be able to give them up only over time with support and opportunities to gradually assimilate the bad news. Some denial may last for years. The professional's job in the first informing conference is to present the findings clearly, and gently substantiate them. Acceptance by the parents cannot be forced, but parents should be given clear, direct, understandable replies to their questions.

The following are common ways parents may indicate their need to protect themselves from the full impact of the diagnostic information:

Parent: "It was not a good day for him."
Professional: "Children do have off days when they do not perform as well as is possible on a good day in a familiar setting. However, he is really too far behind for us to expect that his difficulties are only due to having a bad day."
Parent: "If only he could talk . . ."
Professional: "This is part of it, but his lack of speech reflects a more general problem. He has equal difficulty with many other types of tasks, such as use of his hands and exploring his environment."
Parent: "She is not familiar with these activities/toys/test materials."
Professional: "Experience plays a role, but we see many children who have not used these things before, but with some instruction they are able to use the test materials."

Many professionals are uncomfortable when parents express feelings. If parents cry the professional may feel helpless. A common reaction is to find a way to withdraw from the situation. This can be done by looking away or leaving the room to get coffee or tissues, allegedly as a source of comfort for the parent. This is used as something to offer to make amends. Actually such behavior may have the result of making the parent feel more isolated and anxious about his or her loss of control. It is better to remain seated and silent for a short time, looking at but not staring at the person. Then a supportive comment can be helpful: "I can understand why you would feel sad. It helps to express one's feelings."

In handling parents' anger it is important to determine its source. Anger can relate to a specific occurrence or it can be a way of handling sadness or guilt. Sometimes people attack when they feel threatened. Often professionals are afraid to explore the cause of the anger for fear the feelings might be directed at them. It is better to avoid making assumptions about the potential cause and simply ask the parents what is upsetting them.

It is best to limit the conference to an hour. To extend it much beyond that is of questionable benefit. If the family demonstrates a need for repeated clarification of the content or requests advice for a number of specific situations, it may represent their effort to cope with feelings of helplessness and sadness about the diagnosis. It is best to ask them to come back another time: "I can see you have many questions about what we have said. It is hard to take in all of this in one session. I think we should meet again to discuss this." Some families may say little and seem eager to leave, which may be a way of keeping their feelings under control. "You may have questions about this when you return home. Feel free to call me. Let us set up another time to meet after you have had a chance to think about it."

It is often helpful to recap briefly the findings and recommendations at the end of the conference. Both parents and professionals should be clear about their roles in making contacts with community agencies, when reports will be completed, and to whom they will be sent. The distribution of responsibilities will vary according to what needs to be done and how much responsibility the parents are able to assume. Some parents are anxious to take a very active role. Others may be too immobilized or ambivalent about what is said to take the initiative. A written report of the conference discussion can be useful to the parents in assimilating information.

CONCLUSION

The importance of the informing conference in enabling parents to understand the special needs of their child as well as the positive role professional people can play in their lives cannot be overstated. Valuable information and resources can go unutilized if the parents are unable to assimilate the content. The principal responsibility for presenting the findings in a form that can be meaningful to parents lies with professional people.

Acquiring effective informing skills should not be left to chance but should be taught as part of preparation for professional practice. Even well-trained and seasoned professionals should occasionally step back, reflect on their informing style, and consider how they might become even more empathetic and effective informers.

REFERENCES

Aldrich, C. (1947). Preventive medicine and mongolism. *American Journal of Mental Deficiency, 52,* 127–129.

Drotar, D., Baskewicz, A., Irwin, N., Kennell, J., & Klaus, M. (1975). The adaptation of parents to the birth of an infant with a malformation: A hypothetical model. *Pediatrics, 56,* 710–716.

Garrett, A. (1982). *Interviewing; its principles and methods.* (Revised by M. Mangold & E. Zaki. New York: Family Service Association of America.

Moses, K. (1983). The impact of initial diagnosis: Mobilizing family resources. In J. Mulick & S. Pueschel (Eds.), *Parent-professional partnerships in developmental disability services* (pp. 11–34). Cambridge, MA: The Ware Press.

Murphy, A. (1982). Positive and supportive counselling with families of infants with Down syndrome. In S. Pueschel & J. Rynders (Eds.), *Down syndrome: Advances in biomedicine and the behavioral sciences* (pp. 305–330). Cambridge, MA: The Ware Press.

Murphy, A., & Pedulla, B. (1973). *Communicating diagnostic findings to families*. Unpublished manuscript, Developmental Evaluation Clinic, The Children's Hospital, Boston, MA.

Murphy, A., & Pounds, L. (1972). Repeat evaluations of retarded children. *American Journal of Orthopsychiatry, 42*(1), 103–109.

Rapoport, L. (1965). Working with families in crisis. In *Crisis intervention: Selected readings* (pp. 22–31). New York: Family Service Association of America.

Selig, A. (1983). Common myths of family feedback conferences. *Developmental and Behavioral Pediatrics, 4*(1), 67–69.

Solnit, A.J., & Stark, M.H. (1961). Mourning and the birth of a defective child. *Psychoanalytic Study of the Child, 16,* 523–537.

VI
CONCLUSION

20 Issues and Future Directions in Infant and Family Assessment

Elizabeth D. Gibbs and Douglas M. Teti

The collection of chapters in this volume was chosen to provide the reader with a broad, interdisciplinary view of the current domains of infant assessment and state-of-the-art information on assessment methods and procedures. In an ever-changing, dynamic field, this volume reflects the status of infant assessment activities in the mid to late 1980s.

The state of infant assessment varies from one domain to another. Each domain has its own history and evolution. Although many issues are germane to all areas, some issues seem more salient in one domain than another.

For example, cognitive assessment has a relatively long history, with roots going back to the intelligence testing movement of the early 1900s. Given this history, many standardized cognitive assessments have been developed along with much data on validity. As a result, the issue of poor predictability of infant assessments is a salient one in the cognitive domain. In addition, the validity of these assessments has been questioned when used with motorically impaired, sensorially impaired, or multiply handicapped children. Only recently has more emphasis been placed on process-oriented assessments, which focus on the qualitative aspects of a child's learning (Dunst, Holbert, & Wilson, this volume; Rosenberg & Robinson, this volume). In addition, cognitive development became the first programmatic focus of many early intervention programs (e.g., Ramey, Bryant, Sparling, & Wasik, 1985). As a result, the issue of translating assessment results into useful interventions became salient and led to the development of curriculum-based assessments (Bagnato & Hofkosh, this volume). Finally, the abundance of different cognitive assessment tools has made choosing the most appropriate assessment a difficult task.

By contrast, neuromotor assessment has developed along a different course, generally emerging from the medical setting in response to the need to identify and treat motor disabilities (Chandler, this volume). The focus has been on hands-on clinical assessment of qualitative aspects of movement rather than on standardized assessment. Only recently have standardized procedures been developed and normative and validity information gathered. Thus, there remains a need to develop and validate more standardized tools and gather information regarding the range of normal variation in achieving neuromotor milestones. Additional validity issues arise where variability in motor development is wide and early motor dysfunction is often transient and resolves spontaneously.

The assessment of social development is a newly emerging area, developing out of the recognized inadequacy of cognitive and motor measures to describe the whole child and to predict the child's developmental course. As a result, there is now a felt need to broaden the scope of assessment to include the socioemo-

311

tional development of the infant and characteristics of the family environment. Given the recency of these developments, much of the information about socioemotional and family assessment has been gleaned from research projects. Thus, there is a need to bridge research and practice in order to develop clinically useful assessment tools. Again, in this domain the appropriateness of many assessments with multiply handicapped children is of concern. For example, current methods of assessing the security of attachment may not be valid for children with motor impairments or other handicapping conditions (Teti & Nakagawa, this volume). Finally, as programs begin to assess family interactions and needs, the importance of recognizing and respecting the individual differences between families becomes paramount.

In the remaining sections of this chapter, we discuss several of the major issues confronting infant assessors in more depth and consider what is needed to advance the field.

THE POOR PREDICTIVE VALIDITY OF INFANT TESTS

A major challenge in the field of infant assessment is accurately identifying children whose delays or differences are of long-term significance and making accurate long-term prognoses. The poor predictability of most forms of infant assessment make it difficult for the assessor to know whether to take a "wait-and-see" or a "let's intervene early" approach when they notice developmental delays. The former approach, which has been characteristic of pediatricians, has the disadvantage of underreferring children and delaying potentially beneficial services. The later approach, more characteristic of educators, has the disadvantage of overreferring and inappropriately labeling children whose differences are within the range of normal variation and perhaps inadvertently diminishing parental expectations for the child.

A variety of reasons underlie the poor predictability of infant assessments. Infants are notoriously difficult to assess. They move quickly from one state to another (i.e., quiet alert to crying to sleep) and are difficult to catch in a prolonged state of alertness, which is optimum for most assessments. Most cognitive tests place demands on the child to cooperate and rely heavily on the use of motor skills to demonstrate cognitive ability.

In addition, it is now recognized that infant developmental outcome is the result of ongoing transactions between the infant and the environment (Sameroff, 1975). Thus, individual measures of development will tend to have limited predictability. Multiple measures of both the infant and his or her environment must be considered in order to obtain a more accurate prediction of developmental outcome. Thus, assessment must extend beyond measurement of infant cognitive and motor functioning and consider the contribution of infant's temperament and social development, the parent's interactional style, and the fit between the infant and family.

Finally, an additional difficulty in providing accurate identification and prognosis is the limited availability of good normative information on infant assessments. When normative information is poor or missing, it is easy for assessors to overidentify children whose differences are truly transient and within the wide range of normal variation.

THE NEED TO DEVELOP ALTERNATE ASSESSMENT METHODS

In response to these issues, alternate assessment methods and procedures are emerging that may improve both the accuracy of identifying significant developmental differences and our intervention approaches. In response to the difficulty of maintaining the infant in an alert state and in soliciting cooperation, many of the newer assessment strategies rely on naturalistic observations. For example, the observation of infant play is becoming a more popular means of assessing the child's cognitive abilities (Bond, Creasey, & Abrams, this volume). Observation of play allows the assessor to see the child's typical response patterns. In addition, the infant can be observed in different settings and with different play partners in order to assess the child's motivation and abilities in different situations. This can provide invaluable information for the development of effective interventions. In support of observing children in naturally occurring situations, Bond, Kelly, Teti, and Gibbs (1983) found that observation of infants' play with their own toys was more predictive of infant cognitive ability than infants' play with unfamiliar toys of the examiner.

Infant information-processing tests are being developed that minimize the need for cooperation and motor skill (Zelazo & Weiss, this volume). These assessment procedures are proving to be better predictors of later cognitive ability than the conventional cognitive tests (Bornstein & Sigman, 1986). However, continued refinement of these methods is needed so that they become clinically useful and accessible.

Methods of assessing motorically and sensorially impaired children have been slow to develop despite the numbers of these children in early intervention programs. Some assessments (i.e., Battelle Developmental Inventory, Carolina Curriculum) specify alternate methods of administering items to impaired children. In addition, the use of a process-oriented approach (Rosenberg & Robinson, this volume) is promising in that it allows the assessor to individualize the assessment to the specific capabilities and handicaps of each child. Further development of assessments adapted to specific handicaps is clearly an area of need.

Until we have assessments that have good predictive validity, we must take care to provide families with accurate interpretations of the results of infant assessments. All infant assessors need to be sensitive to the dangers of diagnosing a problem when a potentially transient developmental difference is observed (Chamberlin, 1987). This need to identify problems only when they are unlikely to resolve spontaneously must be balanced with the need to identify problems as early as possible so that early intervention can minimize the child's disability and prevent secondary disabilities. The current service structure that requires that children be identified as having a problem before being eligible for services creates this often unresolvable dilemma for infant assessors. Given the movement in the field of special education toward maintaining individuals in the mainstream of society, the development of parent-child or family support programs for all parents and young children would offer an opportunity to provide early preventive care and support to infants with developmental differences and could be the context for providing early intervention services within a nonstigmatized, community environment. On the surface, this type of preventive approach may be more costly, but it may ultimately offer the most cost-effective approach to promoting optimal development in *all* children.

THE NEED TO BROADEN THE SCOPE OF INFANT ASSESSMENT

Over the past decade or two, the focus of infant assessment has broadened from a predominant focus on infant cognitive and motor development to include new emphases on infant socioemotional status and the family context of infant development. Program evaluators have become aware of the need to base their evaluation of the effectiveness of early intervention on more than IQ scores (Shonkoff & Hauser-Cram, 1988; White, 1986). Early intervention programs have recognized the need to understand not only infants' cognitive or motor functioning but also other aspects of the infants' being, such as their temperament, their attachments to others, and their coping style (see Teti & Nakagawa, this volume; Williamson & Zeitlin, this volume). In addition, there is growing awareness that we must assess the infant in the context of his or her familial and sociocultural system (Ostfeld & Gibbs, this volume). In fact, PL 99-457 explicitly requires that family needs, as they relate to the infant, be addressed in the Individualized Family Service Plan.

For the practitioner, the assessment of parent-child interaction and aspects of family life that have an impact on the child provide important means for developing effective interventions (see Farran, Clark, & Ray, this volume;

Ostfeld & Gibbs, this volume). For example, observational methods of assessing parent-child interaction can provide the assessor with critical information relevant to the prognosis of the child. Research suggests that when the dyadic interaction between a parent and a child is dysfunctional, the probability of the child's delay resolving naturally is diminished and the need for intervention is increased (Cohen & Parmelee, 1983). Parent-child interaction assessments allow the assessor to identify aspects of both the parents and child's behaviors that promote or hinder good reciprocal interaction and can develop an intervention around these specific behaviors.

Although the important influence of the family's internal and external resources on the child and family outcome is now widely recognized, assessing family strengths and needs is an area that early intervention programs have only begun to address. The role of early intervention programs in supporting family needs has now been sanctioned by recent legislation (PL 99-457). However, family assessment methods remain quite research oriented and intrusive. Increased involvement of family-oriented professionals (e.g., social workers and psychologists) in early intervention programs is needed to foster the development of appropriate family assessment and intervention approaches within early intervention. Ideally, programs will hire these professionals as full participants in the early intervention program planning, assessment, intervention, and evaluation.

THE NEED FOR INTERDISCIPLINARY COLLABORATION

The broadening scope of infant assessment and intervention has resulted in the need to involve multiple disciplines in the assessment process. This can be seen clearly in the wide range of disciplines covered by contributors to this book: developmental, clinical, and educational psychology; statistics and methodology; pediatrics; physical therapy; speech pathology; education; occupational therapy; and social work. The involvement of multiple disciplines has resulted in the evolution of different modes of team functioning (see Foley, this volume). The title of the book, *Interdisciplinary Assessment of Infants,* reflects our view that the infant assessment field as a whole has achieved a reasonable level of interdisciplinary team functioning. Professionals now recognize the need for input from multiple disciplines and in many cases meet as a team with other professionals to integrate their assessment findings. However, the more synthesized level of transdisciplinary team functioning has not been widely achieved.

Transdisciplinary team functioning is a highly desireable goal for early intervention programs (Foley, this volume). Having only one team member working directly with a family is not only cost-effective but also avoids overwhelming families with multiple service providers. However, transdisciplinary team functioning is a goal that requires that staff not only be well trained in their own discipline, but also that they be given adequate opportunity and training time to acquire the breadth of knowledge and experience needed to take on the role of other disciplines under consultation (Haynes, 1976). This level of expertise can only be achieved by an experienced staff person within a very supportive environment.

The goal of transdisciplinary team functioning is a lofty one under most circumstances since individuals in most disciplines acquire very little information concerning infancy during their formal training. For example, most clinical child psychologists are trained to work with school-age children or, if lucky, preschoolers. They lack the skills required to assess or intervene with infants and their families. This lack of training in the area of infancy occurs in many other disciplines as well. Over the next decade, efforts must be made to include information on infancy into the curriculum of all relevent disciplines.

THE NEED TO WORK WITH FAMILIES

Involvement of family members on the assessment team has become an important component of the assessment process. Not only do family members have the most intimate contact with and knowledge of the child, but they also are usually the primary person implementing the suggested interventions. Project Dakota has developed procedures to assist early intervention program staff in becoming responsive to parents' needs (Kjerland & Kovack, this volume). Other programs across the country are beginning to rethink their assessment procedures so that parents become active participants rather than passive observers/recipients of the assessment and intervention process. Worobey and Brazelton (this volume), for example, highlight the benefit of involving the parent in the neonatal assessment and thereby using the assessment as an educational intervention in and of itself. The increased involvement of family members in the design of the assessment and intervention process is essential if programs hope to meet families' needs.

An additional issue that becomes paramount when we begin to address family needs is that differences exist between families in their style of interaction, in their grieving/coping process, and in their desire for various services, among other things. It is critical that intervention programs recognize and respect the unique needs of families. This respect for differences must begin in the assessment process, where differences in the child's or parents' behavior must be interpreted in as nonjudgmental a fashion as possible. Cultural differences must be acknowledged. The adaptive function of apparently dysfunctional behavior must be sought out. Flexibility in the assessment and program formats must be built in in order to accommodate to the needs of different families.

THE NEED TO BRIDGE RESEARCH AND PRACTICE

As one attempts to learn and use different assessment methods, one may be frustrated by the fact that assessments are frequently developed by researchers for the purpose of studying infant development. These assessments are often cumbersome for the practitioner to integrate into his or her practice. Early intervention programs may lack the technology (i.e., regular or split-screen videos, visual habituation computer) required to use the assessment or may not have the time to complete the procedure (microanalyses of videotape, 1-hour assessment on one isolated developmental area). The assessments developed by the researchers may feel intrusive or inappropriate to use in a clinical context (i.e., long questionnaires about family interactions, videotapes of parent-child interaction).

These problems do not mean that practitioners should stop looking to basic researchers for information and ideas. In fact, much of our current knowledge of infant capabilities has been derived from the work of basic researchers. Rather, we need more efforts to translate research methods and findings into clinically useful methods. Over the next decade, it is hoped that many of the methods that seem overly research oriented will become translated into more useful tools. This movement is already evident in the assessment of play and parent-child interaction (see Bond, Creasey, & Abrams, this volume; Farran et al., this volume).

In the meantime, the practitioner should not completely ignore all assessments that are too cumbersome or research oriented to use on a regular basis. Learning some of these assessments can provide new ways of observing and conceptualizing infant behavior or interaction that can enhance informal observation skills and possibly lead to the development of a clinically useful form of a particular assessment.

At the other extreme, there are many areas of development for which there are few or no formal assessment methods. For example, oral motor assessment is generally achieved by knowledge of oral motor development and careful clinical observation of the child. While the development of more structured assessment methods and clearer norms concerning different milestones will be helpful for the practitioner, the use of informal clinical skills should not be underrated. In fact, in all areas of infant assessment, as Smith (this volume) aptly points out, the "purpose of measurement is to augment . . . professional abilities and resources, not to supplant them" (p. 30). This becomes abundantly clear when one assesses infant cognitive ability using a standardized test. Interpretation of the DQ or IQ involves a consideration of numerous factors beyond the actual score: Was the child attentive? Tired? Did a motor or sensory impairment interfere with the child's performance? Thus, structured assessments provide important means of focusing our assessment, of comparing children to norms, and of ensuring coverage of particular facets of behavior and development. However, they have not superceded the need for a well-trained and thoughtful clinician as the interpretor of the assessment results.

Thus, the field of infant assessment will require an ongoing interface between research and practice. Attempts to bridge the fields, such as the translation of research measures into clinically useful assessment tools or applied research on the characteristics of clinical tools or interventions, should be encouraged.

CHOOSING ASSESSMENTS

Given the wealth of assessments presented in this volume, the practitioner may well wonder how to choose the most appropriate assessment methods. Since most people have a limited amount of time set aside for formal assessment, the choice of assessments becomes an important issue. Measurement issues related to choosing an assessment are discussed in Smith's chapter (this volume). While measurement issues may seem dry and perplexing to many people-oriented clinicians and interventionists, these issues provide the basis for accurate interpretation of assessment information. For example, without a clear understanding of norms, an infant assessor would find it difficult to accurately interpret the results of a norm-referenced test, particularly when it is used with an infant from a minority culture not represented in the norming sample.

Given a working knowledge of measurement issues and the information regarding the development and validation of particular assessments of interest, it is still difficult to select assessments. Hubert and Wallander (1988) have presented a decision-making model that may be useful to clinicians as they attempt to select the most appropriate assessments. In brief, the elements of the model include specifying the assessment objectives or purposes, evaluating the importance of various measurement characteristics for the designated purpose, specifying and accommodating to the limitations of the child, and finally selecting the best instrument from available instruments based on these decisions.

The initial step involves specifying the purpose of the assessment. For example, an early intervention program may decide to focus its assessment efforts toward both developing an intervention plan and evaluating the effectiveness of its program. There are a number of broad purposes of assessment presented throughout this volume: screening for problems, diagnosis, prescription or development of an intervention plan or method, program evaluation, and research. Each of these purposes demands somewhat different characteristics from the assessment tool.

With the assessment purpose in mind, the staff then consider the importance of different measurement characteristics, including reliability, cost of error, normative reference, and range of coverage. Instruments with high levels of reliability and good normative reference are important for the diagnostician since the potential for harm (cost of error) if a misdiagnosis is made is high. In addition, because reliability is important, a single score is preferred. On the other hand, for the interventionist, the issues of reliability and need for normative reference are less crucial. Rather, it is important to assess a broad range of functional skills that would be appropriate and meaningful targets for intervention.

The third step involves taking the individual child's characteristics (i.e., age, developmental level) and handicaps (i.e., motorically impaired, hearing impaired) into account. Based on the first three steps, the pool of available assessments is narrowed to those meeting the desired criteria. In the final step, the best instrument or set of instruments are selected from this pool.

CHOOSING AN ASSESSMENT FORMAT

Aspects of the assessment situation other than the specific tools used also deserve consideration: for example, the setting where the assessment will occur, the composition of the team, coordination of the team members, and the timeline of the assessment. Assessment procedures vary widely. However, many infant assessments occur in diagnostic clinics or intervention program centers and involve structured interdisciplinary or transdisciplinary sessions that last from one to several hours. Based on these brief assessments, diagnoses are made and intervention plans are determined. The brevity of evaluations is efficient and cost effective. However, the validity of such short and at times unnatural observations has come into question (Fuchs, 1987). For the early intervention professionals who have ongoing contact with the family, there is the possibility of gathering assessment information in multiple settings and over multiple days. As Bond et al. (this volume) emphasize, observing a child's behavior in different settings and with different people can provide invaluable information upon which to develop intervention strategies. An extended period of assessment might well improve the quality of the assessment and the meaningfulness of the intervention plans. Karp, Herzog, and Weinberg (1985) have developed an extended method for assessing emotionally disturbed preschoolers through the use of a diagnostic nursery. More extended models of assessment like this one need to be considered. Just as intervention programs need to vary to accommodate the different needs of families, so too must different assessment strategies and methods be used to accommodate the different needs of programs and families. There is no one right assessment protocol for all families and situations.

CONCLUSIONS

The field of infant assessment and early intervention has grown dramatically over the past decade, broadening from a focus on the child's cognitive and motor abilities to a focus on the whole child in the context of his or her family and social environment. This expansion has brought professionals together in an effort to develop useful methods of assessing the strengths and needs of infants and their families. The importance of these developments to infants and their families has received national prominence with the passage of PL 99-457. However, the fields of infant assessment and early intervention are themselves in their infancy. Given that both infant research and intervention activities have only become prominent in the last 20 years, much work remains to bee done. Much of the information on infant capabilities has yet to be translated from the research to the clinical domain, and areas of concern to interventionists have yet to be researched. In the realm of professional training, there are relatively few programs in any discipline that offer comprehensive and interdisciplinary training in infancy. Thus, there is a shortage of adequately trained personnel to staff early intervention programs, to conduct applied research, and to develop new and better infant assessment methods (Burke, McLaughlin, & Valdivieso, 1988; Meisels, Harbin, Modigliani, & Olson, 1988).

The next decade must focus on integrating the research and clinical arenas and developing interdisciplinary training programs for infant researchers and clinicians alike. Initial efforts to establish such programs are exemplified by the development of Infant Specialist personnel preparation programs funded by the Office of Special Education of the U.S. Department of Education, and by an increasing number of graduate programs in applied developmental psychology. Most of these programs offer training in applied research and intervention approaches with infants. Newly emerging pediatric physical therapy programs are also providing a focus on infant and early childhood development and intervention. Clearly, the development of such applied and interdisciplinary research and clinical training programs should foster the advancement of this new and exciting field.

REFERENCES

Bond, L.A., Kelly, L.D., Teti, D.M., & Gibbs, E.D. (1983, April). *Longitudinal analyses of infant free play with familiar and unfamiliar toys.* Paper presented at the biennial meetings of the Society for Research in Child Development, Detroit.

Bornstein, M.H., & Sigman, M.D. (1986). Continuity in mental development in infancy. *Child Development, 57,* 251–274.

Burke, P.J., McLaughlin, M.J., & Valdivieso, C.H. (1988). Preparing professionals to educate handicapped infants and young children: Some policy considerations. *Topics in Early Childhood Special Education, 8,* 73–80.

Chamberlin, R.W. (1987). Developmental assessment and early intervention programs for young children: Lessons learned from longitudinal research. *Pediatrics in Review, 8,* 237–247.

Cohen, S.E., & Parmelee, A.H. (1983). Prediction of five-year Stanford Binet scores in preterm infants. *Child Development, 54,* 1241–1253.

Fuchs, D. (1987). Examiner familiarity effects on test performance: Implications for training and practice. *Topics in Early Childhood Special Education, 7,* 90–104.

Haynes, U. (1976). *Staff development handbook: A resource for the transdisciplinary process.* New York: United Cerebral Palsy Association.

Hubert, N.C., & Wallander, J.L. (1988). Instrument selection. In T.D. Wachs & R. Sheehan (Eds.), *Assessment of young developmentally disabled children.* New York: Plenum Press.

Karp, N.A., Herzog, E.P., & Weinberg, A.M. (1985). The diagnostic nursery. A new approach to evaluating preschoolers. *Journal of Child Clinical Psychology, 14,* 202–208.

Meisels, S.J., Harbin, G., Modigliani, K., & Olson, K. (1988). Formulating optimal state early childhood intervention policies. *Exceptional Children, 55,* 159–165.

Ramey, C.T., Bryant, D., Sparling, J.J., & Wasik, B.H. (1985). Educational interventions to enhance intellectual development: Comprehensive day care versus family education. In S. Harel & N.J. Anastasiow (Eds.), *The at-risk infant: Psycho/socio/medical aspects* (pp. 75–85). Baltimore: Paul H. Brookes Publishing Co.

Sameroff, A.J. (1975). Early influences on development: Fact or fancy. *Merrill-Palmer Quarterly, 21,* 267–294.

Shonkoff, J.P., & Hauser-Cram, P. (1988). Early intervention for disabled infants and their families: A quantitative analysis. *Pediatrics, 80,* 650–658.

White, K.R. (1986). Efficacy of early intervention. *The Journal of Special Education, 19,* 401–416.

VII
APPENDIX

BIBLIOGRAPHY OF ASSESSMENTS

CHAPTER 3: NEWBORN ASSESSMENT AND SUPPORT FOR PARENTING

Neonatal Behavioral Assessment Scale

Author(s):	T. Berry Brazelton
Published by:	J. B. Lippincott
Date:	1973, 1984
Available from:	Manual: J.B. Lippincott
	East Washington Square
	Philadelphia, PA 19105
	215/238-4200 or 800/638-3030
	Test kit: March of Dimes Birth Defects Foundation
	Materials and Supplies Division
	1275 Mamaroneck Avenue
	White Plains, NY 10605
	914/428-7100

CHAPTER 4: NEUROMOTOR ASSESSMENT

Bayley Scales of Infant Development

Author(s):	Nancy Bayley
Published by:	The Psychological Corporation, New York, NY
Date:	1969
Available from:	The Psychological Corporation
	P.O. Box 9954
	San Antonio, TX 78204-9954
	800/233-5682

The Chandler Movement Assessment of Infants—Screening Test

Author(s):	Lynette Chandler, Mary Andrews, and Marcia Swanson
Published by:	Infant Movement Research
Date:	1983
Available from:	Infant Movement Research
	P.O. Box 4631
	Rolling Bay, WA 98061
	206/454-8973

Erhardt Developmental Prehension Assessment

Author(s):	Rhoda Priest Erdhardt
Published by:	RAMSCO Publishing Company
Date:	1982
Available from:	RAMSCO Publishing Company
	P.O. Box N
	Laurel, MD 20707
	301/953-3699

The Milani-Comparetti Motor Development Screening Test

Author(s):	Jack Trembath
Published by:	Meyer Children's Rehabilitation Institute
Date:	1977
Available from:	University of Nebraska Medical Center Omaha, NB 68131 402/559-7467

The Movement Assessment of Infants

Author(s):	Lynette Chandler, Mary Andrews, and Marcia Swanson
Published by:	Infant Movement Research
Date:	1981
Available from:	Infant Movement Research P.O. Box 4631 Rolling Bay, WA 98061 206/454-8973

Neonatal Neurobehavioral Examination

Author(s):	Andrew M. Morgan, Vera Koch, Vicki Lee, and Jean Aldag
Published by:	American Physical Therapy Association, Inc.
Date:	1988
Available from:	Andrew M. Morgan P.O. Box 1649 The University of Illinois College of Medicine at Peoria Peoria, IL 61656 309/655-3863

The Neurological Assessment of the Preterm and Full-Term Infant

Author(s):	Lilly and Victor Dubowitz
Published by:	The Lavenham Press, LTD, London, England
Date:	1981
Available from:	J. B. Lippincott Company East Washington Square Philadelphia, PA 19105 800/242-7737

Peabody Developmental Motor Scales

Author(s):	M. Rhonda Folio and Rebecca R. Fewell
Published by:	DLM Teaching Resources
Date:	1983
Available from:	DLM Teaching Resources One DLM Park Allen, TX 75002 800/527-4747

CHAPTER 5: ORAL-MOTOR AND RESPIRATORY-PHONATORY ASSESSMENT

Pre-Speech Assessment Scale

Author(s):	Suzanne Evans Morris
Published by:	J. A. Preston Corporation
Date:	1982

Available from: J. A. Preston Corporation
60 Page Road
Clifton, NJ 07012
201/777-2700 or
800/631-7277

CHAPTER 6: ASSESSMENT OF INFANT MENTAL ABILITY

Battelle Developmental Inventory

Author(s):   J. Newborg, J. R. Stock, L. Wnek, J. Guidubaldi, and J. Svinicki
Published by: DLM Teaching Resources
Date: 1984
Available from: DLM Teaching Resources
One DLM Park
Allen, TX 75002
214/727-3346

Bayley Scales of Infant Development

Author(s):   Nancy Bayley
Published by: The Psychological Corporation, New York, NY
Date: 1969
Available from: The Psychological Corporation
P.O. Box 9954
San Antonio, TX 78204-9954
800/233-5682

Gesell Developmental Schedules–Revised

Author(s):   H. Knobloch, F. Stevens, and A. Malone
Published by: Developmental Evaluation Materials, Inc.
Date: 1987
Available from: Developmental Evaluation Materials, Inc.
P.O. Box 272391
Houston, TX 77277-2391
713/541-9063

Merrill-Palmer Scale of Mental Tests

Author(s):   R. Stutsman
Published by: Western Psychological Services
Date: 1931
Available from: Western Psychological Services
12031 Wilshire Boulevard
Los Angeles, CA 90025
213/478-2061 or 800/222-2670

CHAPTER 7: STRATEGIES FOR ASSESSING SENSORIMOTOR COMPETENCIES

OBSERVE (Observation of Behavior in Socially and Ecologically Relevant and Valid Environments)

Author(s):   C. J. Dunst and R. A. McWilliam
Published by: Plenum Press, New York, NY (in chapter in T.D. Wachs and R. Sheehan [Eds.], *Assessment of developmentally delayed children*)
Date: 1988

Available from: Family, Infant and Preschool Program
300 Enola Rd.
Morganton, NC 28655
704/433-2825

Scales of Infant Psychological Development

Author(s): I. Uzgiris and J. McV. Hunt
Published by: University of Illinois Press
Date: 1975
Available from: In book: Uzgiris, I., & Hunt, J. McV. (1975). *Assessment in infancy.* Urbana, IL: University of Illinois Press.

CHAPTER 8: PLAY ASSESSMENTS

Belsky and Most Free Play Procedure

Author(s): Jay Belsky and Robert K. Most
Published by: *Developmental Psychology, 17,* 630–639
Date: 1981
Available from: J. Belsky: 814/863-0267

Belsky et al.'s Executive Capacity Procedure

Author(s): Jay Belsky, L. Garduque, and Elizabeth Hrncir
Published by: *Developmental Psychology, 20,* 406–417
Date: 1984
Available from: J. Belsky: 814/863-0267

Egan Miniature Toys Test

Author(s): D. F. Egan and E. R. Brown
Published by: *Child: Care, Health and Development, 12,* 167–181
Date: 1986
Available from: D. F. Egan
9 Kensington Court Place
Kensington, London W85BJ
England

Gowen's Symbolic Play Procedure

Author(s): Jean W. Gowen
Published by: Frank Porter Graham Child Development Center, Chapel Hill, NC
Date: 1981
Available from: Dr. Jean Gowen
University of North Carolina
Chapel Hill, NC 27514
704/433-2661

Jeffree and McConkey Procedure

Author(s): Dorothy M. Jeffree and Roy McConkey
Published by: *Journal of Child Psychology and Psychiatry, 17,* 189–197
Date: 1976
Available from: Dorothy Jeffree
Hester Adrian Research Center

University of Manchester
Manchester M13 9PL
England

Largo and Howard Modeling Procedure

Author(s): Remo H. Largo and J. A. Howard
Published by: *Developmental Medicine and Child Neurology, 21,* 299–310
Date: 1979
Available from: R.H. Largo, M.D.
Kinderspital Zurich
Growth and Development Center
Steinwiesstrasse 75
CH-8032 Zurich, Switzerland
Largo (Zurich): 01-2597111

McCune-Nicolich Procedure

Author(s): Lorraine McCune-Nicolich
Published by: Unpublished
Date: 1983
Available from: Dr. Lorraine McCune
Department of Educational Psychology
Rutgers University
New Brunswick, NJ 08903
201/932-7180

Morgan, Harmon, and Bennett Procedure

Author(s): G. A. Morgan, R. J. Harmon, and C. A. Bennett
Published by: JSAS *Catalog of Selected Documents in Psychology, 6,* 105. (Ms. No. 1355).
Date: 1976
Available from: Gordon Morgan
Department of Human Development
Colorado State University
Fort Collins, CO 80523
Morgan: 303/491-5811
Harmon: 303/394-5505

Play Assessment Checklist for Infants

Author(s): Rose M. Bromwich
Published by: Unpublished
Date: 1981
Available from: Dr. Rose Bromwich
Department of Educational Psychology and Counseling
School of Education
California State University–Northridge
Northridge, CA 91330
818/885-1200

Play Assessment Scale

Author(s): Rebecca Fewell
Published by: Unpublished
Date: 1986

Available from: Dr. Rebecca Fewell
University of Washington
Seattle, WA 98195
206/543-4011

Rubenstein and Howes Procedure

Author(s): Judith Rubenstein and Carollee Howes
Published by: Child Development, 47, 597–605
Date: 1976
Available from: J. Rubenstein: 617/244-7132

Symbolic Play Test

Author(s): Marianne Lowe and Anthony J. Costello
Published by: Nelson Publishing Co., Windsor, England
Date: 1976
Available from: M. Lowe
Department of Psychological Medicine
Hospital for Sick Children
Great Ormond Street
London W.C.1
England

The Systematic Observation of Children's Play

Author(s): Richard B. Kearsley
Published by: Unpublished
Date: 1984
Available from: Dr. Richard Kearsley
Child Health Services
Manchester, NH
617/659-4906

Watson and Fischer Elicitation Procedure

Author(s): Malcolm W. Watson and Kurt W. Fischer
Published by: Child Development, 48, 828–836
Date: 1977
Available from: Malcolm Watson
Department of Psychology
Brandeis University
Waltham, MA 02254
617/736-3249

Westby's Symbolic Play Test

Author(s): Carol E. Westby
Published by: Language, Speech and Hearing Service in Schools, 11, 154–168
Date: 1980
Available from: Carol Westby
Dept. of Communication Disorders
University of New Mexico
2600 Marble Northwest
Albuquerque, NM 87131
502/277-2918

Yarrow et al.'s Mastery Motivation Tasks

Author(s): Leon J. Yarrow, George A. Morgan, Robert J. Harmon, and Peter Vietze
Published by: JSAS Catalog of Selected Documents in Psychology, 7, 68 (Ms. No. 1517)/ *Psychological Documents, 15* (Ms. No. 2714).
Date: 1977/1986
Available from: Gordon Morgan
Department of Human Development
Colorado State University
Fort Collins, CO 80523
Morgan: 303/491-5811
Harmon: 303/394-5505

CHAPTER 10: EARLY LANGUAGE ASSESSMENT

Communicative Intention Scale

Author(s): T. E. Coggins
Published by: University of Washington Press
Date: 1987
Available from: Communication Skill Builders
3830 East Bellevue
P.O. Box 42050
Tucson, AZ 85733
602/323-7500

Developmental and Criterion-Referenced Scale for Identification of Communication Deficits in the First Two Years

Author(s): J. F. Miller
Published by: University of Wisconsin–Madison
Date: 1983
Available from: Dr. Jon Miller
University of Wisconsin
Madison, WI 53706

Developmental Sentence Analysis

Author(s): L. Lee
Published by: Northwestern University Press
Date: 1974
Available from: Dr. L. Lee
Northwestern University
Evanston, IL 60201

Preschool Language Scale: Revised Edition

Author(s): I. L. Zimmerman, V. G. Steiner, and R. E. Pond
Published by: Charles E. Merrill Publishing Company
Date: 1979
Available from: Charles E. Merrill Publishing Company
Columbus, Ohio 43216

Receptive-Expressive Emergent Language Scale

Author(s):	K. Bzoch and R. League
Published by:	PRO-ED, Inc.
Date:	1978
Available from:	PRO-ED, Inc. 8700 Shoal Creek Boulevard Austin, TX 78758 512/451-3246 (FAX 8542)

Sequenced Inventory of Communication Development

Author(s):	D. L. Hedrick, E. M. Prather, and A. R. Tobin
Published by:	University of Washington Press
Date:	1975
Available from:	University of Washington Press Seattle, WA 98195

CHAPTER 11: CURRICULUM-BASED DEVELOPMENTAL ASSESSMENT

Carolina Curriculum for Handicapped Infants and Infants At Risk

Author(s):	Nancy Johnson-Martin, Kenneth G. Jens, and Susan M. Attermeier
Published by:	Paul H. Brookes Publishing Company
Date:	1986
Available from:	Paul H. Brookes Publishing Company P.O. Box 10624 Baltimore, MD 21285-0624 301/337-9580

Developmental Programming for Infants and Young Children—Stimulation Activities

Author(s):	Sara Brown and Carol M. Donovan
Published by:	The University of Michigan Press
Date:	1985
Available from:	The University of Michigan Press P.O. Box 1104 Ann Arbor, MI 48106 313/764-4392

Early Learning Accomplishment Profile

Author(s):	M. E. Glover, J. L. Preminger, and A. R. Sanford
Published by:	Kaplan School Supply
Date:	1978
Available from:	Kaplan School Supply P.O. Box 609 Lewisville, NC 27023-0610 800/334-2014 (NC: 800/642-0610)

Evaluation and Programming System For Infants and Young Children

Author(s):	D. Bricker, E. J. Bailey, S. Gumerlock, M. Buhl, and K. Slentz
Published by:	Center on Human Development, Eugene, OR
Date:	1986

Available from: Dr. D. Bricker
University of Oregon, Clinical Service Building
College of Education
Eugene, OR 97403
503/686-3568

Hawaii Early Learning Profile: Activity Guide

Author(s): Setsu Furuno, Katherine A. O'Reilly, Carol M. Hosaka, Takayo T. Inatsuka, Toney L. Allman, and Barbara Zeisloft
Published by: VORT Corporation
Date: 1985
Available from: VORT Corporation
P.O. Box 60880
Palo Alto, CA 94306
412/322-8282

Infant Learning: A Cognitive-Linguistic Intervention Strategy

Author(s): C. J. Dunst
Published by: DLM Teaching Resources
Date: 1981
Available from: DLM Teaching Resources
Box 4000
One DLM Park
Allen, TX 75002
800/527-4747

Oregon Project Curriculum for Visually Impaired and Blind Preschool Children

Author(s): D. Brown, V. Simmons, and J. Methvin
Published by: Jackson County Education Service District
Date: 1979
Available from: Jackson County Education Service District
101 North Grape Street
Medford, OR 97501
503/776-8580

Transactional Intervention Program

Author(s): G. Mahoney and A. Powell
Published by: Unpublished
Date: 1988
Available from: Dr. Gerald Mahoney
Pediatric Research and Training Center
Division of Child and Family Studies
University of Connecticut Health Center—Pediatric Department
The Exchange
Farmington, CT 06032

CHAPTER 13: ASSESSING ATTACHMENT IN INFANCY

Greenspan-Lieberman Observation System for Assessment of Caregiver-Infant Interaction during Semi-Structured Play (GLOS)

Author(s):	Stanley Greenspan, Alicia Lieberman, and Susan Poisson
Published by:	Unpublished
Date:	1983
Available from:	Sue Poisson Regional Center for Infants and Young Children 11710 Hunters Lane Rockville, MD 20852

Strange Situation

Author(s):	M. D. S. Ainsworth, M. C. Blehar, E. Waters, and S. Wall
Published by:	Lawrence Erlbaum Associates, Hillsdale, NJ (in Ainsworth, M.D.S., Blehar, M. C., Waters, E., & Wall, S. *Patterns of attachment: A psychological study of the strange situation*)
Date:	1978
Training from:	L. Alan Sroufe Institute of Child Development University of Minnesota Minneapolis, MN 55455

Waters and Deane Attachment Q-Set

Author(s):	E. Waters and K. E. Deane
Published by:	Latest version unpublished; earlier version is in *Monographs of the Society for Research in Child Development*, 50 (Serial No. 209, Nos. 1–2), 41–65
Date:	1985
Available from:	Everett Waters Department of Psychology State University of New York at Stony Brook Stony Brook, NY 11794 516/632-7845

CHAPTER 14: ASSESSMENT OF COPING AND TEMPERAMENT

Early Coping Inventory

Author(s):	Shirley Zeitlin and G. Gordon Williamson
Published by:	Scholastic Testing Service
Date:	1988
Available from:	Scholastic Testing Service 480 Meyer Road P.O. Box 1056 Bensenville, IL 60106-8056 312/766-7150

Infant Behavior Questionnaire

Author(s):	Mary Klevjord Rothbart
Published by:	Unpublished
Date:	1981

Available from: Mary Klevjord Rothbart, Ph.D.
Department of Psychology
University of Oregon
Eugene, OR 97403

Infant Characteristics Questionnaire

Author(s): John E. Bates
Published by: Unpublished
Date: 1979
Available from: John E. Bates, Ph.D.
Department of Psychology
Indiana University
Bloomington, IN 47405

Revised Infant Temperament Questionnaire

Author(s): William B. Carey and Sean C. McDevitt
Published by: Unpublished
Date: 1978
Available from: William B. Carey, M.D.
319 West Front Street
Media, PA 19063
215/566-6641

Toddler Temperament Scale

Author(s): W. Fullard, S. C. McDevitt, and W. B. Carey
Published by: Unpublished
Date: 1978
Available from: William Fullard, Ph.D.
Department of Educational Psychology
Temple University
Philadelphia, PA 19122
215/787-6022

Vineland Adaptive Behavior Scales

Author(s): Sara S. Sparrow, David A. Balla, and Domenic V. Cicchetti
Published by: American Guidance Service, Inc.
Date: 1984
Available from: American Guidance Service
P.O. Box 99
Publisher's Building
Circle Pines, MN 55014-1796
612/786-4343

CHAPTER 15: MEASURES OF PARENT-CHILD INTERACTION

Barnard Teaching Scale and B Feeding Scale

Author(s): Kathryn Barnard
Published by: Unpublished
Date: 1978
Available from: Georgina Summer
NCAST, WJ10

University of Washington
Seattle, WA 98195

Greenspan-Lieberman Observation System for Assessment of Caregiver-Infant Interaction during Semi-Structured Play (GLOS)

Author(s):	Stanley Greenspan, Alicia Lieberman, and Susan Poisson
Published by:	Unpublished
Date:	1983
Available from:	Sue Poisson Regional Center for Infants and Young Children 11710 Hunters Lane Rockville, MD 20852

Interpersonal Behavioral Construct

Author(s):	Kate Kogan, K. Carey, M. Jarvis, T. Layden, P. Turner, and D. Van
Published by:	Unpublished
Date:	1975
Available from:	Dr. Kate Kogan Psychiatry and Behavioral Sciences School of Medicine University of Washington Seattle, WA 98105

Maternal Behavior Rating Scale Subscales

Author(s):	Gerald Mahoney
Published by:	Unpublished
Date:	1985
Available from:	Dr. Gerald Mahoney Pediatric Research and Training Center Division of Child and Family Studies University of Connecticut Health Center–Pediatric Department The Exchange Farmington, CT 06032

Parent Behavior Progression

Author(s):	Rose Bromwich
Published by:	PRO-ED (in Bromwich, R. *Working with parents and infants*)
Date:	1981; 1983
Available from:	Book: PRO-ED 5341 Industrial Boulevard Austin, TX 78735 *Manual and 1983 Supplement:* Micheal J. Moore, Director Department of Educational Psychology and Counseling California State University–Northridge Northridge, CA 91330 512/892-3142

Parent/Caregiver Involvement Scale

Author(s):	Dale Farran, Connie Kasari, Marilee Comfort, and Susan Jay
Published by:	Unpublished
Date:	1986 (initial version, 1979)

Available from: Continuing Education
University of North Carolina–Greensboro
Greensboro, NC 27412
919/334-5451

Parent-Child Early Relational Assessment

Author(s):	Roseanne Clark
Published by:	Unpublished
Date:	1985
Available from:	Roseanne Clark, Ph.D. Department of Psychiatry University of Wisconsin Medical School 600 Highland Avenue Madison, WI 53792 608/263-6067

Parental Acceptance Scoring Manual

Author(s):	Fred Rothbaum and Karen Schneider-Rosen
Published by:	Unpublished
Date:	1988
Available from:	Karen Schneider-Rosen, Ph.D. Boston College Chestnut Hill, MA 02167

Response Class Matrix

Author(s):	E. Mash, L. Terdal, and K. Anderson
Published by:	Unpublished
Date:	1979
Available from:	Dr. Eric J. Mash Department of Psychology University of Calgary Calgary, Alberta Canada

CHAPTER 16: USE OF FAMILY ASSESSMENT IN EARLY INTERVENTION

Adaptation of the Questionnaire on Resources and Stress—Short Form

Author(s):	C. L. Salisbury
Published by:	Item numbers on long form are cited in *American Journal of Mental Deficiency, 90,* 456–459
Date:	1986
Available from:	Long form available from Jean Holroyd (see Questionnaire on Resources and Stress)

Assessment of Parental Adjustment to a Severely Handicapped Child

Author(s):	G. V. S. Eden
Published by:	Unpublished Masters Thesis; entire schedule can be found in Eden-Piercy, G. V. S., Blacher, J. B., & Eyman, R. K. (1986). Exploring parent's reactions to their young child with severe handicaps. *Mental Retardation, 24,* 285–291
Date:	1983
Available from:	G. V. S. Eden Department of Education

University of California, Riverside
Riverside, CA 92521

Family Adaptability and Cohesion Evaluation Scale

Author(s): D. H. Olson, J. Portner, and Y. Lavee
Published by: Unpublished
Date: 1985
Available from: David H. Olson
Family Social Science
University of Minnesota
290 McNeal Hall
1985 Buford Avenue
St. Paul, MN 55108

Family Assessment Measure

Author(s): H. A. Skinner, P. D. Steinhauer, and J. Santa-Barbara
Published by: FAM Project
Date: 1984
Available from: FAM Project
Addiction Research Foundation
33 Russell Street
Toronto, Ontario M5S 2S1
Canada
416/595-6000, ext. 7698

Family Environment Scale

Author(s): R. H. Moos and B. S. Moos
Published by: Consulting Psychologists Press
Date: 1981
Available from: Consulting Psychologists Press
577 College Avenue
Palo Alto, CA 94306

Family Focused Interview

Author(s): P. J. Winton and D. B. Bailey
Published by: *Journal of the Division of Early Childhood, 12,* 195–206
Date: 1988
Available from: Outlined in article cited above

Family Needs Survey

Author(s): D. B. Bailey and R. J. Simeonsson
Published by: *Journal of Special Education, 22,* 117–127
Date: 1988
Available from: Donald B. Bailey
Frank Porter Graham Child Development Center
University of North Carolina at Chapel Hill
Chapel Hill, NC 27514

Family Resource Scale

Author(s): H. E. Leet and C. J. Dunst
Published by: Brookline Books (In Dunst, C., Trivette, C., & Deal, A. [1988]. *Enabling and empowering families*)

Date: 1988
Available from: Family, Infant & Preschool Program
Western Carolina Center
300 Enola Road
Morganton, NC 28655
704/433-2674

Family Support Scale

Author(s): C. J. Dunst, V. Jenkins, and C. M. Trivette
Published by: Brookline Books (In Dunst, C., Trivette, C., & Deal, A. [1988]. *Enabling and empowering families*)
Date: 1988
Available from: Family, Infant and Preschool Program
Western Carolina Center
300 Enola Road
Morganton, NC 28655
704/433-2674

Functional Status Measure

Author(s): R. K. Stein & D. J. Jessop
Published by: *Public Health Report, 97,* 354–362
Date: 1982
Available from: R. K. Stein
Department of Pediatrics
Albert Einstein College of Medicine
1300 Morris Park Avenue
Bronx, NY 10461

HOME Inventory

Author(s): B. Caldwell
Published by: University of Arkansas
Date: 1972
Available from: Betty Caldwell
Center for Child Development and Education
University of Arkansas at Little Rock
Little Rock, AR 72204

Infant Study Questionnaire (Adapted Social Network Questionnaire)

Author(s): M. J. Levitt, R. A. Weber, and M. C. Clark
Published by: Unpublished
Date: 1986
Available from: Mary Levitt
Psychology Department
Florida International University
North Miami Campus
North Miami, FL 33181

Inventory of Parent Experiences

Author(s): K. A. Crnic, A. S. Ragozin, M. T. Greenberg, and N. M. Robinson
Published by: Unpublished; temporary manual available
Available from: Patricia Vadasy, Editor
Experimental Education Unit WJ-10

University of Washington
Seattle, WA 98195
206/543-4011

The Life Experiences Survey

Author(s):   I. G. Sarason, J. H. Johnson, and J. M. Siegel
Published by: *Journal of Consulting and Clinical Psychology, 46,* 932–946
Date: 1978
Available from:

Parent Perception Inventory

Author(s):   Debra P. Hymovich
Published by: Unpublished
Date: 1988
Available from: Debra P. Hymovitch
929 Longview Road
King of Prussia, PA 19406

Parenting Stress Index

Author(s):   R. R. Abidin
Published by: Pediatric Psychology Press
Date: 1983, 1986
Available from: Pediatric Psychology Press
320 Terrell Road West
Charlottesville, VA 22901

Questionnaire on Resources and Stress—Long Form

Author(s):   J. Holroyd
Published by: Unpublished
Date: 1974
Available from: Jean Holroyd
University of California School of Medicine
Neuropsychiatric Institute
Center for Health Science
760 Westwood Place
Los Angeles, CA 90024

Questionnaire on Resources and Stress—Short Form

Author(s):   W. N. Friedrich, M. T. Greenberg, and K. A. Crnic
Published by: *American Journal of Mental Deficiency, 88,* 41–48
Date: 1983
Available from: Long form available from Jean Holroyd (see Questionnaire on Resources and Stress)

Index

Abdominal muscles, 64
Abdominal-thoracic breathing, 64
Abduction, 64
Accident proneness, attachment and, 206
Activities, adaptation of, for infant with multiple handicaps, 183
Adapted Social Network Questionnaire, 335
Adaptive Developmental Quotient, 78–79
Adaptive functioning, coping and temperament in, 215–224
 see also Coping; Temperament
Adaptive-to-handicap instruments, for curriculum-based developmental assessment, 166–168
Addiction, maternal, Neonatal Behavioral Assessment Scale and, 38
Adduction, 64
Adolescent maternity, Neonatal Behavioral Assessment Scale and, 41
Affective expression, family functioning and, 254
Affective involvement, family functioning and, 254
Age, neuromotor assessment and, 49
Age equivalents, 27–28
Ainsworth, Mary, 192, 194
 see also Bowlby-Ainsworth attachment theory; Strange Situation procedure
Alcohol, Neonatal Behavioral Assessment Scale and, 38
Anger, of parents, 306
Anxious, ambivalent attachment, disorders of, 206–207
Arena evaluation, 277, 278–285
 assessment domains and instruments for, 281–282
 duration of, 280
 materials for, 280
 outcomes of, 284
 parents' role in, 279
 population for, 280–281
 primary elicitor in, 278–279
 process and sequence of, 282–284
 space for, 279–280
 style of, 280
 team members in, 278
 see also Transdisciplinary approach
Arousal states, neonatal, 35
Assessment
 definition of, 16
 see also Infant assessment(s); Measurement; specific type, e.g., Play assessment(s)
Assessment Log and Developmental Progress Chart, 167

Assessment of Parental Adjustment to a Severely Handicapped Child, 333
At-risk infants, curriculum-based developmental assessment for, 161–174
 see also Curriculum-based developmental assessment (CDA)
Attachment assessment, 191–209
 clinical systems of Lieberman and Greenspan in, 206–208
 instruments for, resources for, 329–330
 Strange Situation procedure in, 5, 195–205
 see also Strange Situation procedure
 Waters and Deane Attachment Q-Set in, 205–206
 see also Parent-child interaction
Attachment formation, 207
Attachment-Separation-Individuation Scale, 282
Attachment theory, Bowlby-Ainsworth, 192–194
Attention, as measure of central processing, limitations of, 133–134
Attentional interactions, 101, 102, 108
Avoidant behavior, 197

Barium swallow study, modified, 70–71
Barnard Teaching Scale and Barnard Feeding Scale, 230–231, 236, 331
Battelle Developmental Inventory, 9, 81–82, 323
Bayley Scales of Infant Development (BSID), 9, 282, 321, 323
 Mental Scale of, 80–81
 Psychomotor Developmental Index of, 46, 51–52
Behavior(s)
 alternative, for infant with multiple handicaps, 183
 classification of, in Strange Situation procedure, 197–198
 patterning of, in Strange Situation procedure, 195
 reactive, coping and, 221, 222
 self-initiated, coping and, 221, 222
 temperament and, see Temperament
Behavioral assessment, neonatal, 33–42
 see also Neonatal Behavioral Assessment Scale (NBAS)
Behavioral organization, 208
Behaviorism, interdisciplinary approach and, 273
Belief system, of family, 254
Belly breathing, 63, 64
Belsky and Most Free Play Procedure, 116–117, 324

Belsky et al. Executive Capacity Procedure, 118–119, 324
Bias, freedom from, measurement and, 26
Binet, Alfred, 4, 17–18
Binet-Simon test, 4
Biological model, unidisciplinary approach and, 271–272
Bite, controlled, sustained, 64, 67
Blindness, Oregon Project Curriculum and, 167, 329
Bowlby, John, 191
Bowlby-Ainsworth attachment theory, 192–194
Breathing pattern
 abdominal-thoracic, 64
 belly, 63, 64
 of newborn, 63, 64
Bromwich's Play Assessment Checklist for Infants (PACFI), 121–122, 325
BSID, see Bayley Scales of Infant Development

Carolina Curriculum for Handicapped Infants and Infants at Risk, 167, 328
Cattell Infant Intelligence Scale, 282
Causality, 94–95
 interdisciplinary approach and, 273
Cerebral palsy, oral-motor and respiratory-phonatory dysfunction in, 67–69
Chandler Movement Assessment of Infants–Screening Test (CMAI-ST), 45, 56–57, 321
Cheek-lip retraction, 68
Chewing, 64, 67
Child development, see Development
Child Study Movement, 4–5
Chronicity Impact and Coping Instrument: Parent Questionnaire (CICI:PQ), 259
Civil Rights Movement, 6
Closing, in arena evaluation, 283
CMAI-ST (Chandler Movement Assessment of Infants–Screening Test), 45, 56–57, 321
Coefficient alpha, 24
Cognitive development, 77, 311
 see also Information processing; Mental ability assessments; Play assessment(s); Sensorimotor interactive competencies
Cognitive Observation Guide, 282
Collaboration, see Family-staff collaboration; Interdisciplinary approach; Transdisciplinary approach
Collaborative Infant Project, 274
Communication
 of assessment findings, 299–306
  see also Informing conference
 family functioning and, 254
  see also Language assessment; Respiratory-phonatory assessment
Communicative Intention Scale, 327
Communicative intentions, 149–153
 assessment of, 152–153
 form of, 151–152
 range of, 150–151
Comprehensive Training Program for Infant and Young Cerebral Palsied Children, 69
Concurrent validity, 20
Construct validity, 19–20
Contact-maintaining behavior, 197
Contact-seeking behavior, 197
Content validity, 20–21
Context
 language skills and, 145–146
 parent-child interaction and, 228
 transdisciplinary approach and, 276
Contingency interactions, 101–103, 108
Control, family functioning and, 254
Conversational discourse, organization of, 153–158
 conversational maintenance and, 156–157
 conversational repairs and, 157–158
 initiation and, 156
 socialized versus nonsocialized speech and, 154
 turn taking and talking time and, 154–156
Coping
 assessment of, 220–222
  instruments for, 330
  intervention implications of, 223–224
 family, 250, 252–255
  comprehensive measures of, 259–261
 handicaps and, 223
 parental patterns of, 303–304
 process of, 215–217, 253
 temperament and, 218–219
  see also Temperament
Criterion-referenced assessment, 9
 of structural language abilities, 148–149
Criterion-referenced validity, 20
Critical actions, 93
Crossing-over effects, 276
Cumulative adversity concept, 276
Cup drinking, 65, 66
Curriculum-based developmental assessment (CDA), 161–174
 case example of, 169–173
 definition of, 162
 instruments used in
  adaptive-to-handicap, 166–168
  categories of, 165
  ecological, 168–169
  normal developmental, 165–166
  resources for, 328–329
  selection criteria for, 164–165
 purpose of, 162–164
 rationale for, 162–164
Curriculum-imbedded scales, 165
Curriculum-referenced scales, 165

Dakota, Inc., see Project Dakota
Darwin, Charles, 4
Day care, 7
Decentration, 114

Decontextualization, 104, 114
Development
  cognitive, 77
    see also Information processing; Mental ability assessments; Play assessment(s); Sensorimotor interactive competencies
  family involvement and, 8–9
  motor, see Neuromotor assessment
  sensorimotor, 92, 94–95
    see also Sensorimotor interactive competencies
  as transactional process, 6
Developmental and Criterion-Referenced Scale for Identification of Communication Deficits in the First Two Years, 327
Developmental assessment, curriculum-based, see Curriculum-based developmental assessment
Developmental continuity, 7–8
Developmental domino theory, 276
Developmental observation scale, for language assessment, 149
Developmental process curricula, 165
Developmental Programming for Infants and Young Children (DPIYC), 166–167, 282, 328
Developmental Quotient (DQ), 78–79
Developmental Sentence Analysis, 148, 327
Developmental task curricula, 165
Diabetes, maternal, Neonatal Behavioral Assessment Scale and, 38–39
"Diagnosis shopping," 262–263
Diagnostic assessments, 9
Diagnostic conference, see Informing conference
Differentiability, split-halves and, 24
Differentiated interactions, 102, 103, 108–109
Direct testing, in oral-motor assessment, 72–73
Discourse, see Conversational discourse
Disrupted attachment, disorders of, 207
Distance interaction, 197
Distancing, 104
Down syndrome
  mastery motivation tasks and, 120
  Strange Situation procedure and, 202–203
  temperament and, 222–223
DPIYC (Developmental Programming for Infants and Young Children), 166–167, 282, 328
DQ (Developmental Quotient), 78–79
Drinking, from cup, 65, 66
Drugs, Neonatal Behavioral Assessment Scale and, 38

Early and Periodic Screening, Diagnostic, and Treatment Program, 6
Early Coping Inventory, 220–222, 330
Early intervention, 161–174
  family assessment in, 249–263
    see also Family assessment
  see also Curriculum-based developmental assessment (CDA); Intervention
Early Intervention Developmental Profile (EIDP), 166–167
Early language assessment, see Language assessment
Early Learning Accomplishment Profile (ELAP), 165–166, 328
Ecological instruments, for curriculum-based developmental assessment, 168–169
Ecomap, 256
EDA (estimated developmental age), Uzgiris and Hunt scales and, 93, 97
EDPA (Erhardt Developmental Prehension Assessment), 46, 52–53, 321
Education for All Handicapped Children Act (PL 94-142), 6–7
Efficiency of measurement, 26
Egan Miniature Toys Test, 324
EIDP (Early Intervention Developmental Profile), 166–167
ELAP (Early Learning Accomplishment Profile), 165–166, 328
Elicitation, structured, in play assessment, 115, 118–121, 326
Emotions, informing conference and, 300–301, 305–306
Empiricism, interdisciplinary approach and, 273
Encoded interactions, 102, 103–104, 109
Environmental modification, for infant with multiple handicaps, 183
Environmental toxins, Neonatal Behavioral Assessment Scale and, 39
EPS (Evaluation and Programming System for Infants and Young Children), 168, 328–329
Erhardt Developmental Prehension Assessment (EDPA), 46, 52–53, 321
Estimated developmental age (EDA), Uzgiris and Hunt scales and, 93, 97
Evaluation, definition of, 16
Evaluation and Programming System for Infants and Young Children (EPS), 168, 328–329
Executive Capacity Procedure, 118–119, 324
Exploration, inhibition of, attachment and, 206
Extension, oral-motor assessment and, 64
External resources of family, 255, 258
External rotation, 64

Factor analytic studies, 22
Family(ies)
  of handicapped infant, 252
  high-risk, Neonatal Behavioral Assessment Scale and, 37–39
  involvement of
    importance of, 314–315
    infant development and, 8–9
  resources of
    external, 255, 258
    internal, 254–255, 258–259
    Questionnaire on Resources and Stress and,

Family(ies)—*continued*
    260–261, 333, 336
    scope of infant assessment and, 313–314
    as system, 250–252
    see also Parent *entries*
Family Adaptability and Cohesion Evaluation Scale III, 259, 334
Family assessment, 249–263
    determinants of coping in, 252–255
    methods and tools for, 255–263
        caveats regarding, 261–263
        interviews, 256
        observations, 256–257
        resources for, 333–336
        self-report questionnaires, 257–261
Family Assessment Measure, 259, 334
Family coping, 250, 252–255
    comprehensive measures of, 259–261
Family Environment Scale, 259, 334
Family Focused Intervention Model, 256
Family Focused Interview, 334
Family functioning style, 258–259
Family interaction style, 258–259
Family members, reciprocal influence between, 251–252
Family Needs Survey, 334
Family Resource Scale, 334–335
Family-staff collaboration, 287–297
    assessment practices for, 290–293
    intervention planning in, 294–297
    postassessment discussion in, 293–294
    transformation from staff control to, 288–290
Family Support Scale, 335
Family's Assessment Focus, 290–293
Feedback, in arena evaluation, 283
Feeding, oral-motor function during, *see* Oral-motor assessment
Feelings, informing conference and, 300–301, 305–306
Fewell's Play Assessment Scale (PAS), 121, 325–326
Flexion, 64
Free play
    in arena evaluation, 283
    specific assessment procedures for, 115–118, 324–327
    unobtrusive observation of, 114–115
Freud, Sigmund
    on infant-mother relationship, 191
    and multidisciplinary approach, 272
    psychodynamic theory of, 5
Functional Status Measure, 257, 335

Gastroesophageal reflux, 71
Genogram, 256
Gesell Developmental Schedules, 78, 323
Gestural imitation, 94–95
GLOS, *see* Greenspan-Lieberman Observation System for Assessment of Caregiver-Infant Interaction during Semi-Structured Play
Goal setting, family-staff collaboration and, 294–297
Gowen's Symbolic Play Procedure, 324
Grade equivalents, 27–28
Greenspan-Lieberman clinical assessment system, in attachment assessment, 206–208
Greenspan-Lieberman Observation System for Assessment of Caregiver-Infant Interaction during Semi-Structured Play (GLOS), 208, 230–231, 236–237, 330, 332
Greeting, in arena evaluation, 282–283

Habituation cluster, 35
Habituation-recovery procedure, 132–133
Hall, G. Stanley, 4
Handicapped children
    play of, 122–123
        mastery motivation tasks and, 120
    sociopolitical movements affecting, 6–7
    temperament of, 222–223
Handicapped Children's Early Education Assistance Act (PL 90-538), 6
Handicapped Children's Early Education Programs (HCEEP), 162
Handicapped infants
    curriculum-based developmental assessment for, 161–174
        see also Curriculum-based developmental assessment (CDA)
    family of, 252
    with multiple handicaps, 177–186
        see also Multiply handicapped infants
    Strange Situation procedure and, 201–203
Handicaps, parents' psychological adjustment to, 258
Hawaii Early Learning Profile (HELP) Checklist, 166, 329
HCEEP (Handicapped Children's Early Education Programs), 162
Head-neck hyperextension, 67–69
Head Start programs, 6
HELP (Hawaii Early Learning Profile) Checklist, 166, 329
High-risk families, Neonatal Behavioral Assessment Scale and, 37–39
HOME Inventory, 257, 335
Home observations
    in family assessment, 257, 335
    in temperament assessment, 219
Homeostasis stage of attachment relationships, 207
Hyperextension, 64
    head-neck, 67–69

IBC (Interpersonal Behavior Construct), 230–231, 238, 332
IBR (Infant Behavior Record), 46, 51, 80
IDA (Infant/Toddler Developmental Assessment), 282

Index

IEP (individualized education program), 162
IFSP, *see* Individualized family service plan
Imitation
   gestural, 94-95
   vocal, 94-95
Individualized education program (IEP), 162, 287
Individualized family service plan (IFSP), 162, 227, 249-250, 287
   see also Family assessment
Industrial prototype of multidisciplinary approach, 272
Infant assessment(s), 3-4
   characteristics and functions of, 9-10
   format for, selection of, 317
   historical antecedents of, 4-5
   issues and future directions in, 311-317
      need for alternative methods, 312-313
      need to bridge research and practice, 315-316
      need for broadened scope, 313-314
      need for interdisciplinary collaboration, 314
      need to work with families, 314-315
   modern era of, 5-7
   poor predictive validity of, 312
   selection of, 316
   special considerations in, 7-9
   see also specific type, e.g., Neuromotor assessment
Infant Behavior Questionnaire, 219, 330
Infant Behavior Record (IBR), 46, 51, 80
Infant Characteristics Questionnaire, 219, 330
Infant development, *see* Development
Infant Learning: A Cognitive-Linguistic Intervention Strategy, 167-168, 328-329
Infant-parent interaction, *see* Parent-child interaction
Infant Psychological Developmental Scale, 168
Infant Study Questionnaire, 335
Infant/Toddler Developmental Assessment (IDA), 282
Information processing, 129-141
   attention as measure of, limitations of, 133-134
   habituation-recovery procedure and, 132-133
   mental representations and, 134-137
   recognition memory and, 131-132
   Standard-Transformation-Return procedure and, 134-137
      empirical support for, 137-140
Informing conference, 299-306
   effective, 304-306
      accepting different coping patterns in, 303-304
      getting to know parents in, 302
      getting in touch with feelings in, 301-302
      recognizing differing perspectives in, 302-303
   importance of, 299-300
   styles of informing and, 300-301
Initiative
   attachment and, 208

conversational discourse and, 156
Integration
   in development of play, 114
   of pediatric team, curriculum-based developmental assessment and, 162-163
Intellectually handicapped infants, Strange Situation procedure and, 202-203
Intelligence
   Binet-Simon test of, 4
   habituation-recovery procedure and, 132-133
   predictability of, 7-8
   recognition memory and, 131-132
   Stanford-Binet scale of, 5, 9
   see also Information processing; Mental ability assessments
Intelligence quotient (IQ), 5
Interaction(s)
   attentional, 101, 102, 108
   contingency, 101-103, 108
   differentiated, 102, 103, 108-109
   encoded, 102, 103-104, 109
   parent-child, *see* Parent-child interaction
   styles of, family coping and, 255
   symbolic, 102, 104, 109
Interactional theory, interdisciplinary approach and, 273
Interactive competencies, *see* Sensorimotor interactive competencies
Interdisciplinary approach, 273-274, 275
   need for, 8, 314
   process approach and, 178-179
   see also Transdisciplinary approach
Internal consistency, reliability and, 24
Internal resources of family, 254-255, 258-259
Internal rotation, 64
Internalization, 208
Interpersonal Behavior Construct (IBC), 230-231, 238, 332
Interpretation, in arena evaluation, 283-284
Interrater reliability, 24-25
Intervention
   Neonatal Behavioral Assessment Scale and, 39-41
   oral-motor and respiratory-phonatory assessment and, 73-74
   Participate Decision Process and, 181-184
   see also Early intervention
Intervention planning, family-staff collaboration and, 294-297
Interviews, in family assessment, 256
Inventory of Parent Experiences (IPE), 261, 335
IQ (intelligence quotient), 5

Jaundice, Neonatal Behavioral Assessment Scale and, 38
Jaw closure, exaggerated, 68
Jaw thrusting, 68
Jeffree and McConkey Procedure, 324-325

Kearsley procedure, for infant free-play assessments, 116
Kuder-Richardson Formula 20 (KR20), 24

Labeling, in informing conference, 301, 304–305
Language assessment, 145–158
  general guidelines for, 145–147
  instruments for, resources for, 327
  of pragmatic language abilities, 149–158
    communicative intentions, 149–153
    organization of conversational discourse, 153–158
    presupposition, 153
  of structural language abilities, 147–149
    nonstandardized tests for, 148–149
    standardized tests for, 147–148
Largo and Howard Modeling Procedure, 325
Laryngeal area, 64
Lateral movements, controlled, 64
Lieberman, Alicia, *see* Greenspan-Lieberman *entries*
Life Experiences Survey (LES), 257–258, 336
Lip pursing, 68
Low socioeconomic status, Neonatal Behavioral Assessment Scale and, 40
Lowe and Costello Symbolic Play Test, 117–118

MAI (Movement Assessment of Infants), 45, 55–56, 322
Mastery Motivation Tasks, 119–120, 327
Materials, for arena evaluation, 280
Maternal Behavior Rating Scale (MBRS), 232–233, 238–239, 332
MC (Milani-Comparetti Motor Development Screening Test), 45–46, 54–55, 322
McCune-Nicolich procedure, for infant free-play assessments, 118, 325
Mean length of utterance (MLU), 148
Measurement, 15–30
  age equivalents in, 27–28
  definition of, 15–17
  good, characteristics of, 18–26
  grade equivalents in, 27–28
  need for, 17–18
  norms in, 26–27
  objectivity of, 25–26
  percentiles in, 27
  reliability of, 22–25
  rules of thumb for, 29–30
  selection of measure, 28–29, 316
  standard error of, 25
  standardized scores in, 28
  stanines in, 27
  validity of, 19–22
Medical model, unidisciplinary approach and, 271–272
Memory, recognition, and infant intelligence, 131–132
Mental ability assessments, 77–88
  implications of, for clinical infant specialist, 87–88
  prediction issues in, 82–86
  standardized, 77–82
    Battelle Developmental Inventory, 81–82
    Bayley Scales of Infant Development, 80–81
    Merrill-Palmer Scale of Mental Tests, 79–80
    resources for, 323
    Revised Gesell Developmental Schedules, 78–79
  see also Information processing; Intelligence
Mental representations, development of, 134–137
Mentoring, family-staff collaboration and, 289
Merrill-Palmer Scale of Mental Tests (MPS), 79–80, 323
Milani-Comparetti Motor Development Screening Test (MC), 45–46, 54–55, 322
Mission statement, family-staff collaboration and, 288–289
MLU (mean length of utterance), 148
Morgan, Harmon, and Bennett procedure, for infant free-play assessments, 117, 325
Mother(s)
  addiction in, Neonatal Behavioral Assessment Scale and, 38
  adolescent, Neonatal Behavioral Assessment Scale and, 41
  diabetic, Neonatal Behavioral Assessment Scale and, 38–39
  see also Parent *entries*
Motor development, *see* Neuromotor assessment; Oral-motor assessment
Movement Assessment of Infants (MAI), 45, 55–56, 322
MPS (Merrill-Palmer Scale of Mental Tests), 79–80
Multidisciplinary approach, 272–273, 275
Multiply handicapped infants, 177–186
  assessment of
    assumptions in, 177
    purposes of, 177
    strategies for, 177–178
  process approach to, 178–186
  see also Participate Decision Process
Multiword stage of language development, communicative intentions expressed at, 152
Munching, 64, 66
Muscles, abdominal, 64

NAPI&FI (Neurological Assessment of the Preterm and Full-Term Infant), 45, 57–59, 322
Narcotics, Neonatal Behavioral Assessment Scale and, 38
NBAS, *see* Neonatal Behavioral Assessment Scale
NCAP (Nursing Child Assessment Project), 236
NCAST (Nursing Child Assessment Satellite Training), 230–231, 236
Neonatal Behavioral Assessment Scale (NBAS),

33–42, 321
  behavior items in, 35
  conceptual base of, 34
  content of, 34–36
  high-risk families and, 37–39
  as intervention device, 39–41
  reflex items in, 35
  scoring of, 37
Neonatal information processing, measures of, discriminant and predictive validity of, 138–140
Neonatal Neurobehavioral Examination (NNE), 45, 59, 322
Neurological Assessment of the Preterm and Full-Term Infant (NAPI&FI), 45, 57–59, 322
Neurological impairments, Strange Situation procedure and, 201
Neuromotor assessment, 45–60, 311
  age and, 49
  environmental discrepancies and, 48
  instruments for, 45–46, 49–59
    Bayley Scales of Infant Development, 51–52
    Chandler Movement Assessment of Infants–Screening Test, 56–57
    Erhardt Developmental Prehension Assessment, 52–53
    Milani-Comparetti Motor Development Screening Test, 54–55
    Movement Assessment of Infants, 55–56
    Neonatal Neurobehavioral Examination, 59
    Neurological Assessment of the Preterm and Full-Term Infant, 57–59
    Peabody Developmental Motor Scales, 49–51
    problems with, 48–49
    resources for, 321–322
  sensitivity and specificity of, 46–49
  variability within infants and, 47
  variation of normal movement and, 47–48
  see also Oral-motor assessment
NNE (Neonatal Neurobehavioral Examination), 45, 59, 322
Nonattachment, disorders of, 206
Normative approach, 4
Norm-referenced assessment, 9
  of structural language abilities, 147–148
Norms, 26–27
Nursing Child Assessment Project (NCAP), 236
Nursing Child Assessment Satellite Training (NCAST), 230–231, 236

Object permanence, 94–95
Objectivity, measurement and, 25–26
Observation(s)
  in family assessment, 256–257
  in home
    family assessment and, 257, 335
    temperament assessment and, 219
  in oral-motor assessment, 72
  setting for, parent-child interaction and, 228–229
  unobtrusive, of free play, 114–115
Observation area, for arena evaluation, 279–280
OBSERVE strategy, 100–110, 323–324
  case examples of, 107–110
  developmental model of sensorimotor interactive competence and, 101–104
  methods for eliciting interactive competencies in, 105–107
  record form for, 105, 106
  traditional assessment procedures versus, 107
Oral cavity, 64
Oral-motor assessment, 63–74
  dysfunction and, 67–69
    intervention programming and, 73–74
  normal development and, 63–67
  resources for, 322–323
  strategies for, 69–73
Ordinal Scales of Psychological Development, see Uzgiris-Hunt Ordinal Scales of Psychological Development
Oregon Project Curriculum for Visually Impaired and Blind Preschool Children, 167, 329
Outcome evaluation, family-staff collaboration and, 290

PACFI (Play Assessment Checklist for Infants), 121–122, 325
Parallel forms, 23–24
Parent(s)
  communication of assessment findings to, 299–306
    see also Informing conference
  coping patterns in, 303–304
  feelings of, assistance with, 305–306
  interviews with, oral-motor assessment and, 72
  learning about, in informing conference, 302
  professionals and, differing perspectives of, 302–303
  psychological adjustment of, to child's handicap, 258
  role of, in arena evaluation, 279
  see also Family entries; Mother(s)
Parent Behavior Progression (PBP), 232–233, 239–240, 332
Parent/Caregiver Involvement Scale (P/CIS), 232–233, 240–241, 332–333
Parent-Child Early Relational Assessment (PCERA), 234–235, 241–242, 333
Parent-child interaction, 227–245
  examination of, rationale for, 227–228
  measures of
    Barnard Teaching Scale and Barnard Feeding Scale, 230–231, 236
    drawbacks of, 244–245
    Greenspan-Lieberman Observation System, 230–231, 236–237
    Interpersonal Behavior Construct, 230–231, 238

Parent-child interaction—*continued*
  issues in, 227–229
    Maternal Behavior Rating Scale, 232–233, 238–239
    NCAST, 230–231, 236
    Parent Behavior Progression, 232–233, 239–240
    Parent/Caregiver Involvement Scale, 232–233, 240–241
    Parent-Child Early Relational Assessment, 234–235, 241–242
    Parental Acceptance Scoring Manual, 234–235, 242–243
    resources for, 331–333
    Response Class Matrix, 234–235, 243–244
    usefulness of, 244
  observation of, setting for, 228–229
  origins of conversation in, 154–155
  see also Attachment *entries*
Parent Perception Inventory (PPI), 259, 336
Parent questionnaires
  in family assessment, 257–261
  in temperament assessment, 219–220
Parental Acceptance Scoring Manual, 234–235, 242–243, 333
Parenting Stress Index (PSI), 260, 336
Participate Decision Process, 179–186
  assumptions of, 180–181
  developmental context of, 179–180
  evaluation of, 184–186
  intervention strategies and, 181–183
    implementation of, 183–184
  procedures in, 181
PAS (Play Assessment Scale), 121, 325–326
PBP (Parent Behavior Progression), 232–233, 239–240, 332
PCERA (Parent-Child Early Relational Assessment), 234–235, 241–242, 333
P/CIS (Parent/Caregiver Involvement Scale), 232–233, 240–241, 332–333
Peabody Developmental Motor Scales (PDMS), 46, 49–51, 322
Pediatric team, *see* Team approach
Percentiles, 27
Personality, *see* Temperament
Pharyngeal area, 64
Physical examination, in arena evaluation, 283
Physically handicapped children
  mastery motivation tasks and, 120
  see also Handicapped children; Handicapped infants
Piagetian theory, 5
  sensorimotor assessment scales based on, 92–93, 96–100
  sensorimotor development and, 92, 94–95
PL 90-248, 6
PL 90-538 (Handicapped Children's Early Education Assistance Act), 6
PL 94-142 (Education for All Handicapped Children Act), 6–7
PL 99-457, 6–7, 227, 249
Play
  development of, 94–95
    cognitive development and, 113–114
  free
    in arena evaluation, 283
    specific assessment procedures for, 115–118, 324–326
    unobtrusive observation of, 114–115
  promotion of, multiple handicaps and, 184
Play assessment(s), 113–125
  under development, 121–122
  handicapped children and, 122–123
  selection and implementation of, 123–125
  specific procedures for, 115–122
    elicited/structured-play procedures, 118–121
    infant free-play assessments, 115–118
  resources for, 324–326
  strategies for, 114–115
Play Assessment Checklist for Infants (PACFI), 121–122, 325
Play Assessment Scale (PAS), 121, 325–326
PLS (Preschool Language Scale: Revised Edition), 148–149, 327
PPI (Parent Perception Inventory), 259, 336
Pragmatic language abilities, 149–158
  communicative intentions, 149–153
    assessment of, 152–153
    form of, 151–152
    range of, 150–151
  organization of conversational discourse, 153–158
    conversational maintenance and, 156–157
    conversational repairs and, 157–158
    initiation and, 156
    socialized versus nonsocialized speech and, 154
    turn taking and talking time and, 154–156
  presupposition, 153
Preassessment Planning: The Setting, 290–293
Predictive validity, 20, 312
  mental ability assessments and, 82–86, 129–130, 138–140
Prematurity
  mastery motivation tasks and, 120
  Neonatal Behavioral Assessment Scale and, 37–38, 39–40, 41
Preschool Language Scale: Revised Edition (PLS), 148–149, 327
Prescriptive assessments, 9–10
Pre-Speech Assessment Scale (PSAS), 69–70, 322–323
Presupposition, 153
Pretend play, Watson and Fischer procedure and, 120–121, 326
Preverbal communicative intentions, 150
Primary elicitor, 278–279
Primary prevention, 6

Problem solving, development of, 94-95
Process assessment, of infants with multiple handicaps, 178-186
    see also Participate Decision Process
Process evaluation, family-staff collaboration and, 290
Process Model of Family Functioning, 253-254
Professionals
    family collaboration with, see Family-staff collaboration
    parents and, differing perspectives of, 302-303
    team approach and, see Team approach
Program evaluation, family-staff collaboration and, 290
Project Dakota, 288-297, 315
    assessment in, 293
    Family's Assessment Focus in, 290-293
    intervention planning in, 294-297
    postassessment discussion in, 293-294
    Preassessment Planning in, 290-293
    transformation of services in, from staff control to staff-parent collaboration, 288-290
Project Participate, 180-184
    see also Participate Decision Process
Prone position, 64
Proximity-seeking behavior, 197
PSAS (Pre-Speech Assessment Scale), 69-70, 322-323
PSI (Parenting Stress Index), 260, 336
Psychoanalysis, and multidisciplinary approach, 272
Psychodynamic theory, 5
Psychological state, of parent, 254-255

Q-Set, in attachment assessment, 205-206, 330
Questionnaire on Resources and Stress (QRS), 260-261, 333, 336
Questionnaires
    in family assessment, 257-261
        caveats regarding, 262
        comprehensive measures of family coping, 259-261
        Family's Assessment Focus, 290-293
        measures of external resources, 258
        measures of internal resources, 258-259
        measures of stress, 257-258
    in temperament assessment, 219-220

Radiography, in oral-motor assessment, 71
RCM (Response Class Matrix), 234-235, 243-244, 333
Reactive behavior, coping and, 221, 222
Receptive-Expressive Emergent Language Scale (REEL), 147, 328
Recklessness, attachment and, 206
Recognition memory, and infant intelligence, 131-132
REEL (Receptive-Expressive Emergent Language Scale), 147, 328

Reframing, family-staff collaboration and, 289
Refueling, in arena evaluation, 283
Reliability of measurement, 22-25
    neuromotor assessment and, 48-49
Representational capacity, attachment and, 208
Representational differentiation, 208
Research, practice and, 315-316
Resistant behavior, 197
Resources
    for assessment instruments, 321-336
        see also specific instrument or type of assessment
    family
        external, 255, 258
        internal, 254-255, 258-259
        Questionnaire on Resources and Stress and, 260-261
Respiratory-phonatory assessment, 63-74
    dysfunction and, 67-69
    intervention programming and, 73-74
    normal development and, 63-67
    resources for, 322-323
    strategies for, 69-73
Response Class Matrix (RCM), 234-235, 243-244, 333
Revised Gesell Developmental Schedules, 78-79, 323
Revised Infant Temperament Questionnaire, 219-220, 331
Role expansion, transdisciplinary approach and, 276-277
Role performance, family functioning and, 253-254
Role release, transdisciplinary approach and, 277-278
Rotation, oral-motor assessment and, 64
Rubenstein and Howes procedure, for infant free-play assessments, 115-116, 326

Scales of Infant Psychological Development, see Uzgiris-Hunt Ordinal Scales of Psychological Development
Screening assessments, 9
Search behavior, during separations, 197
Self-initiated behavior, coping and, 221, 222
Self-protection, precocious competence in, attachment and, 206-207
Self-report questionnaires, in family assessment, 257-261
    caveats regarding, 262
Sensorimotor development, attainments of, 94-95
Sensorimotor interactive competencies, 91-111
    instruments assessing, resources for, 323-324
    neo-Piagetian observation assessment of, 100-110
        case examples of, 107-110
        developmental model and, 101-104
        strategy for, 104-107
    Piagetian-based assessment of, 92-100

Sensorimotor interactive competencies—*continued*
  case examples of, 98–100
  Uzgiris and Hunt scales in, 92–93, 96–98
Sensorimotor organization, coping and, 221–222
Separation(s)
  reunion and, in arena evaluation, 283
  search behavior during, 197
Sequenced Inventory of Communication Development–Revised (SICD-R), 147–148, 328
Service delivery, 271
  in interdisciplinary approach, 275
  in multidisciplinary approach, 275
  in transdisciplinary approach, 275
  in unidisciplinary approach, 272, 275
SES (socioeconomic status), Neonatal Behavioral Assessment Scale and, 40
SICD-R (Sequenced Inventory of Communication Development—Revised), 147–148, 328
Sign-signifier differentiation, 104
Simon, Theodore, 4
Single-word stage of language development, communicative intentions expressed at, 151
Smallness for dates, Neonatal Behavioral Assessment Scale and, 38
Smoking, maternal, Neonatal Behavioral Assessment Scale and, 38
Snack breaks, in arena evaluation, 283
Social support, family coping and, 255, 258
Socialized speech, nonsocialized speech versus, 154
Socioeconomic status, low, Neonatal Behavioral Assessment Scale and, 40
Socioemotional functioning
  assessment of, 311–312
  attachment and, 191
    see also Attachment assessment
  coping process and, 215–217
  parent-child interaction and, *see* Parent-child interaction
  temperament and, *see* Temperament
Sociopolitical movements, 6–7
Solid foods, 66
Somatopsychologic differentiation, 207–208
Sound production, *see* Respiratory-phonatory assessment; Speech
Space, for arena evaluation, 279–280
Spatial relationships, 94–95
Spearman-Brown Prophecy formula, 24
Speech, socialized versus nonsocialized, 154
Split-halves, reliability and, 24
Spoon feeding, 65, 66
Stability indicators, reliability and, 23–24
  mental ability assessments and, 82–83
Staff
  family collaboration with, *see* Family-staff collaboration
  parents and, differing perspectives of, 302–303
  team approach and, *see* Team approach
Standard error of measurement, 25

Standard-Transformation-Return (STR) procedure, 134–137
  advantages of, 140–141
  empirical support for, 137–140
Standardized scores, 28
Stanford-Binet Form LM, 282
Stanford-Binet Intelligence Scale, 5, 9
Stanines, 27
"Story Time," in arena evaluation, 283
Strange Situation procedure, 5, 191–192, 195–205, 329
  attachment classifications in, 197–198
    caregiver antecedents of, 198–200
    contemporaneous and predictive correlates of, 200
    validity of, 198–200
  episodes in, 195–197
  with handicapped infants, 201–203
  with individual infants, 203–205
  physical setup of, 195
  theoretical framework for, 192–194
STR procedure, *see* Standard-Transformation-Return procedure
Stress
  coping and, *see* Coping
  measures of, in family assessment, 257–258
Structural complexity of utterances, 148
Structural language abilities
  nonstandardized tests of, 148–149
  standardized tests of, 147–148
Structured elicitation, in play assessment, 115, 118–121
Subjective perceptions, of family, 254
Sucking, 64, 65
Sucking pads, 64
Suckling, 64, 65
Support systems, family coping and, 255, 258
Swallowing dysfunction, 71
Symbolic interactions, 102, 104, 109
Symbolic Play Test, 326
Symptom complex, multiple factors in, 276
Systematic Observation of Children's Play, 326

Tailored infant assessment, family-staff collaboration for, *see* Family-staff collaboration
Task-centered segment, formal, in arena evaluation, 283
Teaching samples, in arena evaluation, 283
Team approach
  curriculum-based developmental assessment and, 162–163
  importance of, 314
  interdisciplinary, 273–274
  process assessment and, 178–179
  team organization and, 271
  transdisciplinary, 274–285
    see also Transdisciplinary approach
Technical vocabulary, in informing conference, 303, 304–305

Teenage maternity, Neonatal Behavioral Assessment Scale and, 41
Temperament, 6, 217–220
   assessment of, 219–220
      instruments for, 330–331
      intervention implications of, 223
   handicaps and, 222–223
   see also Coping
Test-retest reliability, 23–24
Tests, definition of, 15–16
TIP (Transactional Intervention Program), 168–169, 329
Toddler Temperament Scale, 219–220, 331
Tongue elevation, anterior, tongue retraction with, 68
Tongue retraction, 67–69
Tongue thrusting, 68
Topic initiation skills, 156
Toxins, environmental, Neonatal Behavioral Assessment Scale and, 39
Toys, for arena evaluation, 280
Transactional Intervention Program (TIP), 168–169, 329
Transactional model of coping process, 216–217
Transdisciplinary approach, 274–285
   arena evaluation in, 277, 278–285
      see also Arena evaluation
   history of, 274
   operational principles of, 276–278
   theory of, 274–276
Turn taking, conversational discourse and, 154–156

Unidisciplinary approach, 271–272, 275
Utterance length, 148

Uzgiris-Hunt Ordinal Scales of Psychological Development, 5, 9, 92–93, 324
   clinical use of, 93, 96–98
   qualitative descriptions in, 97–98
   quantitative descriptions in, 97
   record forms for, 93, 96

Validity of measurement, 19–22
   neuromotor assessment and, 48
   predictive, see Predictive validity
   sensitivity and specificity and, 46
   Strange Situation classifications and, 198–200
Videofluoroscopy, in oral-motor assessment, 70–71
Videotapes, in observation of parent-child interaction, 229
Vineland Adaptive Behavior Scales, 220, 331
Visual impairment, Oregon Project Curriculum and, 167, 329
Vocabulary, in informing conference, 303, 304–305
Vocal imitation, 94–95

Warm-up, in arena evaluation, 282–283
Waters and Deane Attachment Q-Set, 205–206, 330
Watson and Fischer Elicitation Procedure, 120–121, 326
Westby's Symbolic Play Test, 326
Women's Liberation Movement, 7
World War I, multidisciplinary approach and, 272
World War II, interdisciplinary approach and, 273

Yarrow et al. Mastery Motivation Tasks, 119–120, 327